W9-CHS-420

Handbook for Reading Social Studies

One of the most important things you will do in your study of Social Studies this year is read this textbook. In order to understand important facts and ideas in any subject area—Social Studies, or Science, or even Mathematics—it is necessary to read in a certain way. This Reading Handbook will show you a few strategies for effectively reading social studies.

Main Idea and Supporting Details

As you read, remember to look for the **main idea** and **supporting details**. The main idea is what a paragraph or section is mostly about. The details support or expand the main idea. Keeping track of the main idea and supporting details will help you remember what you read.

- The first sentence of a paragraph often—but not always—contains the main idea.

- Use the titles and subheads in your book as a guide in identifying the main idea.

- Make an outline of the main ideas and supporting details of a lesson to help you review.

To Identify the Main Idea
Ask yourself:

• What is this paragraph or section mostly about?

To Identify the Supporting Details
Ask yourself:

• What words give more information about the main idea?

In your book you will read about the Maya farmers of ancient Mexico. Read this paragraph to find the main idea and supporting details.

> Maya farmers grew a plentiful supply of food for a large population. They used their knowledge of the environment to get the most out of their land. In hilly areas farmers built terraces to make level surfaces for planting. In swampy areas they built raised islands by piling up soil above the water. Farmers also moved their fields from place to place to help keep the soil from wearing out.
>
> *from page 62*

Main Idea:
Maya farmers used their knowledge to grow a plentiful supply of food.

Supporting Details:
built terraces on hills; built islands in swamps

TRY IT!

Read this paragraph. Copy and complete the main idea and supporting details chart.

The arrival of the horse on the Great Plains changed the lives of the Native Americans of the Plains in many ways. It made buffalo hunting easier and helped the Lakota become a powerful people. It also made them much more dependent on the buffalo than they had ever been before.

from page 101

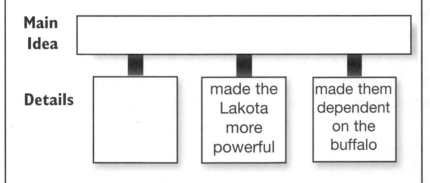

Main Idea

Details

| | made the Lakota more powerful | made them dependent on the buffalo |

• What steps did you take to find the main idea and details?

Practice Activities

1 **READ** Read the fourth paragraph under "Contact Brings Change" on page 143. What is the main idea of this paragraph?

2 **WRITE** Write about an event that changed your life. State the main idea and supporting details.

Keep in Mind...

For more help in reading social studies, try these strategies:

☑ **Reread**
Review each sentence carefully. Make sure you understand what each sentence means before you read further.

☑ **Look up unknown words**
Use a dictionary or the glossary in your book to find the meaning of any words or terms you do not know.

☑ **Form a mental picture**
As you read, think about what your reading would look like.

Context Clues

As you read a sentence or paragraph in your book, you may find a word or term that you do not know. One way to find the meaning of a new word is to look for **context clues**. Context clues are the words and sentences around the unfamiliar term. Using context clues helps you become a better reader.

- Have you heard this word before? How was it used?

- Write down the context clues you used to find the meaning of the new word.

- Use the new word in a sentence of your own to help you remember it.

To Use Context Clues

Ask yourself:

- What word is unfamiliar to me?

- What might the word mean?

- What other words, phrases, and sentences help me figure out the meaning of the new word?

- What information do these other words, phrases, and sentences provide?

In your book you will read about the California gold rush. Read this paragraph and use context clues to help identify the meaning of the word *gleam*.

Word:
gleam

Clue:
morning sun caught the gleam

One January morning in 1848, a carpenter named James Marshall stood beside the American River in California. The morning sun caught the gleam of something shiny in the water. "I reached my hand down and picked it up," remembered Marshall. "It made my heart thump, for I was certain it was gold."

from page 432

Clue:
it was gold

Clue:
something shiny

TRY IT!

Read the paragraph below about planters and enslaved people. Copy and complete the chart below to list context clues for the term *rebellion*.

One thing the planters feared most was rebellion. When they got the chance, some captives were willing to die for their freedom. In many rebellions enslaved people organized raids, burned houses, and killed people. In the Stono Rebellion of 1739, a captive named Cato led a rebellion in which 30 colonists of South Carolina were killed. To stop the rebellions the planters strengthened the slave codes.

from page 240

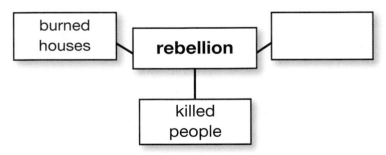

- What steps did you take to find the meaning of *rebellion*?

Practice Activities

1 **READ** Read the second paragraph under "Paul Revere" on page 301. Use context clues to find the meaning of the word *patrol*.

2 **WRITE** Write a sentence using context clues for the word *bicycle*.

Keep in Mind...

For more help in reading social studies, try these strategies:

☑ **Reread**
Review each sentence carefully. Make sure you understand what each sentence means before you read further.

☑ **Form the big picture**
As you read, think about the topic and the most important information in each paragraph or section.

☑ **Make predictions**
As you read, think about what might happen next in your reading.

Sequencing

As you read, look for the order in which things happen. **Sequencing** events is listing them in the order in which they happen. Sequencing events helps you understand and remember what you read.

- Look for dates—years, months, or centuries—that tell when events happened.

- Look for words like *first, next, then, followed, finally, last, before,* and *later* to identify the order of events.

- Use chapter time lines to help you remember the sequence of events.

To Use Sequencing

Ask yourself:

- Which event happened first?

- Which event happened next?

- Which order of events makes sense?

Read the following paragraph describing a buffalo hunt. Pay attention to the sequence of events.

Standing Bear, an 11-year-old boy, is at a buffalo hunt with his father and other men from their camp. First the hunters ride straight into the buffalo herd to create confusion. Then they go after a single buffalo using a lance, bow and arrow, or rifle. Standing Bear admires the great courage and skill it takes to do this. He is only here to help, but someday he will kill his own buffalo. His father cuts out the liver of a buffalo that has just been killed. He and Standing Bear eat some of it now. They save the rest for Standing Bear's mother and sister.

from page 98

Third Event:
The father cuts out the buffalo's liver.

First Event:
The hunters ride into the herd.

Second Event:
They go after one buffalo.

Last Event:
They eat some now. The rest is saved for others.

TRY IT!

Read these paragraphs from your book. Copy and complete the chart below to record the events in the proper sequence.

> Most people in slavery said the day "never really ended" on the plantation. After working in the fields or in the big house, slaves had to do their own chores. They fed animals, cut firewood, and tended their own gardens. Then they went to their cabins to make supper.
>
> After supper, enslaved people finally got to rest. They were tired, but they made time to talk, tell stories, and sing songs with their family members.
>
> *from page 238*

Slaves worked in the fields or big house.

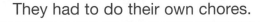

They had to do their own chores.

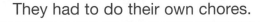

They went to their cabins to make supper.

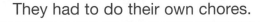

• How did you find the sequence of events?

Practice Activities

1 **READ** Read the section titled "Tenochtitlán Falls" on page 151 of your book. On a sheet of paper, list the key events in the correct sequence.

2 **WRITE** Write about how you clean up your room. Include words such as *first*, *then*, *next*, and *finally*.

Keep in Mind...

For more help in reading social studies, try these strategies:

☑ **Look up unknown words**
Use a dictionary or the glossary in your book to find the meanings of any words you do not know.

☑ **Reread**
Review each sentence carefully. Make sure you understand what each sentence is about before you read further.

☑ **Summarize**
In your own words, briefly describe what your reading is about. Look for topic sentences that contain the main ideas.

Make Predictions

As you read a paragraph or section in your book, think about what might come next. What you think will happen is your **prediction**. A prediction does not have a correct or incorrect answer. Making predictions helps you to carefully consider what you are reading.

- Think about other things you know that will help you make an "educated guess."

- Test your prediction: read further to see if you were correct.

- Revise your prediction: read further to see if more information changes your prediction.

To Make a Prediction

Ask yourself:

- What happened in this section?

- What background knowledge do I already know about the events in the text?

- What similar situations do I know of?

- What do I think might happen next?

Read this paragraph about Columbus's trip to America to see how a prediction might be made. Do you agree or disagree with this prediction?

On August 3, 1492, Columbus left Spain with three ships and sailed west into the unknown. Week after week dragged by with no sight of land. His men began to grumble, afraid they would never see home again. To calm their fears Columbus kept two records, or ship's logs. In the first he recorded the actual distance sailed each day. In the second he recorded a shorter distance. He showed his crew the second log so they would not know how far they really were from Spain.

from pages 140–141

Background Knowledge:
Columbus finally did reach land in 1492.

Text Information:
Two ship's logs; Columbus showed his crew the second log.

Prediction:
His crew may find out and complain.

TRY IT!

Read the following paragraph about President Jackson and the Native Americans. Copy and complete the prediction chart below.

One of the issues facing President Jackson was the conflict over land between white settlers and the Native Americans in the Southeast. Tensions increased in 1830 when gold was discovered on Cherokee lands in Georgia.

Jackson strongly believed that the Native Americans were a threat to the growth and expansion of the United States. To end the fighting, Jackson wanted the Native Americans to move to lands west of the Mississippi.

from page 397

Text Information

Background Information

Native Americans were given land in the West to move out of the Southeast.

My Prediction

Jackson would take steps to move Native Americans west.

• On what did you base your prediction?

Practice Activities

1 **READ** Read the second paragraph under "Eisenhower Becomes President" on page 610. What do you predict will happen? Test your prediction by reading the section "The Iron Curtain is Lifted" on page 635.

2 **WRITE** Write a paragraph about a recent event and predict its outcome.

Keep in Mind...

For more help in reading social studies, try these strategies:

☑ **Sequencing**
As you read, think about the order in which things happened.

☑ **Form the big picture**
As you read, find the most important information about the topic in the paragraph or section.

☑ **Relate to personal experience**
Think about how what you are reading relates to your own life.

Compare and Contrast

This book often **compares** and **contrasts** people or events. To compare things is to see how they are alike. To contrast things is to see how they are different. Comparing and contrasting helps you understand the relationships between things.

To Compare

Ask yourself:

- What are the things being compared?
- How are they alike?

To Contrast

Ask yourself:

- What are the things being contrasted?
- How are they different?

In your book you will read about the Erie Canal, built to connect New York City to the Great Lakes. A canal is a waterway built by people. Read this paragraph to compare and contrast shipping before and after the construction of the Erie Canal.

- To compare, look for clue words such as *like, similar, in common, same,* and *resemble.*

- To contrast, look for clue words such as *before, after, different from, unlike,* and *by contrast.*

The Erie Canal was an immediate success. Before, shipping goods over land between Buffalo on Lake Erie and New York City took 20 days and cost $100 a ton. The Erie Canal brought the price down to $10 a ton and cut travel time to eight days.

from page 413

Contrast:
shipping cost
Before: $100 a ton
After: $10 a ton

Compare:
Goods were shipped between Buffalo and New York before and after the canal was built.

Contrast:
shipping method
Before: land
After: water

Contrast:
shipping time
Before: 20 days
After: 8 days

TRY IT!

Read the following paragraph about women in the workplace. Copy and complete the Venn diagram below comparing and contrasting women of World War I with women of the 1920s.

> Although women had won the right to vote, they made little progress in the workplace during the 1920s. During World War I with most men serving as soldiers, many women went to work in factories and other businesses. After the war, however, many women returned to their homes. By 1920 fewer women worked outside the home than had done so a decade earlier. Most women worked at home as homemakers.
>
> *from page 589*

WWI Women | Women worked. | **1920s Women** Women worked as homemakers.

• What steps did you take to compare and contrast?

Practice Activities

1 **READ** Read the first paragraph under "Political Parties" on page 362. What two things are being contrasted?

2 **WRITE** Compare and contrast two movies.

Keep in Mind...

For more help in reading social studies, try these strategies:

☑ **Look up unknown words**
Use a dictionary or the glossary in your book to find the meaning of any unfamiliar words.

☑ **Form the big picture**
As you read, think about the most important information of the paragraph or section.

☑ **Summarize**
In your own words, briefly describe what your reading is about.

Summarize

After you read a paragraph or section of this book, you can **summarize** what you have read. In a **summary**, you briefly tell in your own words about the most important information in the section. Summarizing is a good way to help you understand what you read.

To Summarize

Ask yourself:

• What is this paragraph about?

• What information is most important?

• How can I say this in my own words?

In your book you will read about the geography of the Northwest Coast and its rich waters. Read this paragraph and sample summary.

TiP!

■ Look for titles, headings, and key words that identify important information.

■ Keep your summary brief, and organize the information in a clear way.

■ Don't include information and facts that are not the most important.

The salmon run was and still is an important event in the lives of the Native Americans of the Northwest Coast. The salmon run is the yearly return of salmon to lay eggs in the freshwater rivers where they were born. From early spring to late summer, millions of salmon swam from the Pacific Ocean to rivers, such as the Columbia.

from page 83

Summary:
During the salmon run, salmon swim inland from the oceans to lay their eggs.

Important information is underlined

TRY IT!

Read the following paragraph about conflicts in the western United States. Copy and complete the diagram below to organize a summary.

> The Native Americans of the Plains had clashed with settlers and soldiers many times during the middle 1800s. This period of conflict is often called the Plains Wars. The Native Americans usually lost these battles. Although the Native Americans of the Plains were skilled warriors known for their excellent horsemanship, they were no match for either the weapons or the growing numbers of new settlers that they faced.
>
> *from page 532*

Important Ideas

Native Americans clashed with settlers in the 1800s.

Plains Wars

Summary

The Native Americans usually lost the battles in the Plains Wars of the 1800s. Although skilled fighters, they could not match the weapons or people.

• How did you choose what to include in your summary?

Keep in Mind...

For more help in reading social studies, try these strategies:

☑ **Reread**
Review each sentence. Make sure you understand what each sentence means before you read further.

☑ **Form the big picture**
As you read, think about the topic and the main ideas of the paragraph or section.

☑ **Make an outline**
As you read, write an outline of the topic and the main ideas of the reading.

Practice Activities

1 READ Read the first paragraph under "A Revolution on Four Wheels" on page 586 of your book. Summarize changes caused by automobiles.

2 WRITE Write a summary of your favorite movie.

Use Visuals

One way to learn from your reading is to use **visuals**. Visuals are the graphs, charts, pictures, and maps in your book. Visuals provide useful information in a clear, easy-to-study form.

- Read the caption and labels for the information they provide.

- Look for objects in the picture that might give additional information.

- When looking at graphs, maps, or charts, be sure to read the legend or key to find the meanings of special symbols.

To Use Visuals

Look closely at the visual. Ask yourself:

- What does the graph, chart, picture, or map show?

- How does it help me to understand what I have read?

- How does it add to the information I have read?

- What information does the visual's caption or labels provide?

In your book you will read about a highly populated area in the United States called Boswash which runs from Boston, Massachusetts, to Washington, D.C. Study the pictures below showing a lighthouse and the northeastern part of the United States viewed from outer space.

The light that beams from this lighthouse (right) in the Northeast and the other lights from Boswash's large cities (far right) can be seen at night from outer space.

from pages 34–35

Caption:
Lights from Boswash can be seen from space.

The lighthouse is much larger than the people standing near it.

One picture shows the northeastern U.S. from outer space.

Visual:
The rectangle shows Boswash's large cities.

TRY IT!

Study the pictures below of people during World War II. Copy the chart. Think about the information shown in the pictures and complete the chart.

Both men and women built war planes (above) in the United States. "Rosie the Riveter" (right) represented the contribution of women.

from page 600

Caption:

Visual:
Planes have propellers; they don't look as modern as today's planes.

photos of women working on planes and "Rosie the Riveter"

Visual:
"Rosie the Riveter" character presents women as strong and able.

• What steps did you take to use the visuals?

Keep in Mind...

For more help in reading social studies, try these strategies:

☑ **Use Visuals**
Photographs and drawings of people and places will help you understand the reading.

☑ **Study the charts and graphs**
Charts and graphs provide information in an easy-to-understand form.

☑ **Study the unit and chapter openers**
The first page of a unit or chapter often summarizes what you will read about. It also may contain useful maps and pictures.

Practice Activities

1 **READ** Read page 91 in your book. Make a list of the ways the photos add to the information on the page.

2 **WRITE** Copy the chart above. Use information from the visual on pages 304 and 305 to complete the chart.

United States

ADVENTURES IN TIME AND PLACE

James A. Banks

Barry K. Beyer

Gloria Contreras

Jean Craven

Gloria Ladson-Billings

Mary A. McFarland

Walter C. Parker

NATIONAL
GEOGRAPHIC
SOCIETY

THIS STATUE OF THE AMERICAN
BALD EAGLE IS PERCHED OUTSIDE
A SILVERSMITH'S SHOP IN
NEWBURYPORT, MASSACHUSETTS.
THE BALD EAGLE HAS BEEN THE
NATIONAL BIRD OF THE UNITED
STATES SINCE 1782.

THE
PRINCETON
REVIEW

McGraw-Hill
School Division

New York   Farmington

PROGRAM AUTHORS

Dr. James A. Banks
Professor of Education and
  Director of the Center for
  Multicultural Education
University of Washington
Seattle, Washington

Dr. Barry K. Beyer
Professor Emeritus, Graduate
  School of Education
George Mason University
Fairfax, Virginia

Dr. Gloria Contreras
Professor of Education
University of North Texas
Denton, Texas

Jean Craven
District Coordinator of
  Curriculum Development
Albuquerque Public Schools
Albuquerque, New Mexico

Dr. Gloria Ladson-Billings
Professor of Education
University of Wisconsin
Madison, Wisconsin

Dr. Mary A. McFarland
Instructional Coordinator of
  Social Studies, K–12, and
  Director of Staff Development
Parkway School District
Chesterfield, Missouri

Dr. Walter C. Parker
Professor and Program Chair for
  Social Studies Education
University of Washington
Seattle, Washington

NATIONAL
GEOGRAPHIC
SOCIETY
Washington, D.C.

PROGRAM CONSULTANTS

Daniel Berman
Asian Studies Specialist
Coordinator of Social Studies
Bedford Central Schools
Bedford, New York

Dr. Khalid Y. Blankinship
Affiliated Scholar, Council on Islamic
  Education
Fountain Valley, California
Assistant Professor of Religion
Temple University
Philadelphia, Pennsylvania

Dr. John Bodnar
Professor of History
Indiana University
Bloomington, Indiana

Dr. Roberto R. Calderón
Department of Ethnic Studies
University of California at Riverside
Riverside, California

Dr. Sheilah Clarke-Ekong
Asst. Professor, Department of
  Anthropology and Research Associate,
  Center for International Studies
University of Missouri, St. Louis
St. Louis, Missouri

Dr. John L. Esposito
Professor of Religion and International
  Affairs
Georgetown University
Washington, D.C.

Dr. Darlene Clark Hine
John A. Hannah Professor of History
Michigan State University
East Lansing, Michigan

Paulla Dove Jennings
Project Director
The Rhode Island Indian Council, Inc.
Providence, Rhode Island

Dr. Henrietta Mann
Professor of Native American Studies
University of Montana, Missoula
Missoula, Montana

Dr. Gary Manson
Professor, Department of Geography
Michigan State University
East Lansing, Michigan

Dr. Juan Mora-Torrés
Professor of Latin American History
University of Texas at San Antonio
San Antonio, Texas

Dr. Valerie Ooka Pang
Professor, School of Teacher Education
San Diego State University
San Diego, California

Dr. Joseph R. Rosenbloom
Professor, Classics Department
Washington University
St. Louis, Missouri

Dr. Joseph B. Rubin
Director of Reading
Fort Worth Independent School District
Fort Worth, Texas

Dr. Robert M. Seltzer
Professor of Jewish History
Hunter College of The City University
  of New York
New York, New York

Dr. Peter N. Stearns
Dean, College of Humanities and
  Social Studies
Carnegie Mellon University
Pittsburgh, Pennsylvania

CONSULTING AUTHORS

Dr. James Flood
Professor of Teacher Education,
  Reading and Language Development
San Diego State University
San Diego, California

Dr. Diane Lapp
Professor of Teacher Education,
  Reading and Language Development
San Diego State University
San Diego, California

GRADE-LEVEL CONSULTANTS

Susan Kirk-Davalt
Fifth Grade Teacher
Crowfoot Elementary School
Lebanon, Oregon

Fred Popp
Fifth Grade Teacher
Blairsville Elementary School
Blairsville, Pennsylvania

Marci Thompson
Fifth Grade Teacher
Elm Dale School
Greenfield, Wisconsin

Diana Vallejo
Fifth Grade Bilingual Teacher
Linder Elementary School
Austin, Texas

Nancy Watson
Fifth Grade Teacher
Weeks Elementary School
Kansas City, Missouri

CONTRIBUTING WRITERS

Susan Banfield
Milford, Connecticut

Gaynor Ellis
New York, New York

Dan Greenberg
New Rochelle, New York

Pat Longoria
Bedford, Texas

Linda Scher
Raleigh, North Carolina

CONSULTANTS FOR TEST PREPARATION

THE
PRINCETON
REVIEW
The Princeton Review is not affiliated
with Princeton University or ETS.

Acknowledgments

The publisher gratefully acknowledges permission to reprint the following copyrighted materials:

From **Battle Cry of Freedom: The Civil War Era** by James M. McPherson. Copyright © 1988 by Oxford University Press, Inc. Reprinted by permission.
From **America Explored** by Adrian Johnson. Copyright © 1974 The Viking Press, Inc. Used by permission of Viking Penguin, a division of Penguin Books USA, Inc.
From **The Afro-American in United States** by B. Dasilva, M. Finkelstein, A. Loshin. Copyright © 1969. Globe Fearon.

(continued on page R102)

McGraw-Hill School Division
A Division of The McGraw·Hill Companies

Copyright © 2001, 2000, 1999 McGraw-Hill School Division, a Division of the Educational and Professional Publishing Group of The McGraw-Hill Companies, Inc.

All rights reserved. No part of this book may be reproduced or transmitted in any form or by any means, electronic or mechanical, including photocopying, recording, or by any information storage and retrieval system, without permission in writing from the publisher.

McGraw-Hill School Division
Two Penn Plaza
New York, New York 10121

Printed in the United States of America

ISBN 0-02-149137-2

2 3 4 5 6 7 8 9 027/046 04 03 02 01 00

CONTENTS

UNIT ONE   Americans and Our Environment
2

UNIT FOUR   *Colonization and Conflict*

198

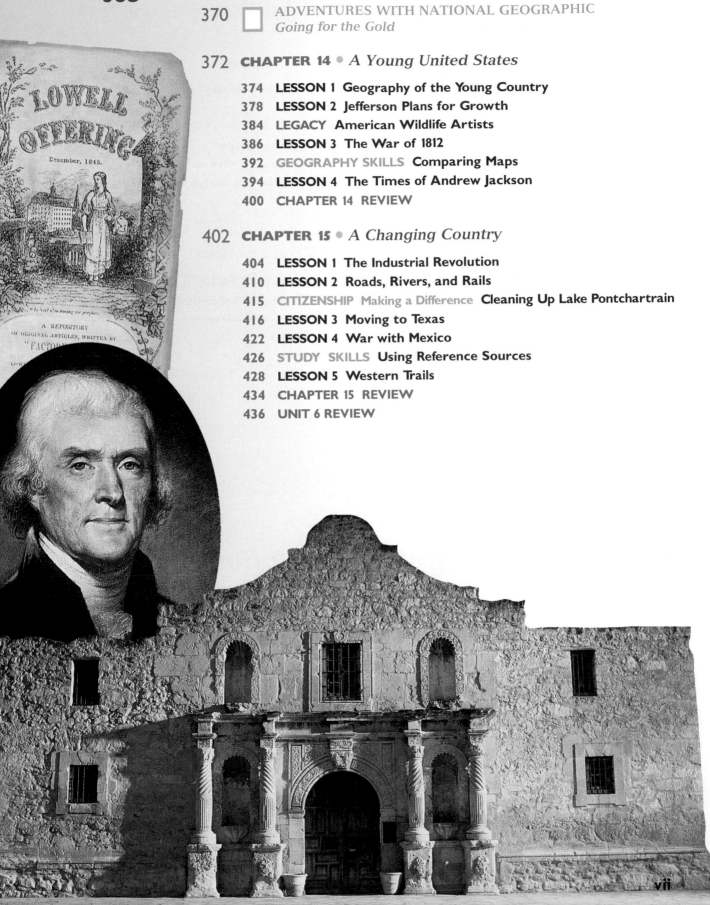

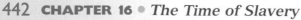

UNIT NINE

572

Hopes for Peace and Prosperity

SPECIAL SECTION

648

Canada and Latin America

REFERENCE SECTION

STANDARDIZED TEST SUPPORT

FEATURES

CHARTS, GRAPHS, & DIAGRAMS

TIME LINES

MAPS

YOUR TEXTBOOK
at a glance

Your textbook is called *United States: Adventures in Time and Place*. It has 21 chapters and a special section. Each chapter has three or more lessons. There are also many special features for you to study and enjoy.

NATIONAL GEOGRAPHIC

Five Themes of Geography

Region
What are some things that help make the West a special region?

Human/Environment Interactions
How have people changed this landscape in Alaska?

▲ Special pages right after these two pages and before each unit bring you ideas and **Adventures** in geography with **National Geographic**.

LESSON 4

1640 1670 1700 1760

The Colonial Way of Life

Read Aloud
"No gains without pains." Do you recognize this saying? Thousands of people in the 1700s read the writings of Benjamin Franklin in his newspaper, the *Pennsylvania Gazette*. Franklin is still known today for the many witty sayings he wrote. The one above is often used today by people to describe what they think about exercising.

Focus Activity

READ TO LEARN

What were some of Benjamin Franklin's contributions to Philadelphia?

VOCABULARY
- frontier
- almanac
- backcountry

PEOPLE
- Benjamin Franklin

PLACES
- Philadelphia
- Shenandoah Valley

THE BIG PICTURE

Benjamin Franklin grew up at a time when the English colonies were changing rapidly. Before 1700 eight out of ten colonists were English or had English parents. Then in the 1700s people from Germany, Ireland, France, Scotland, and Africa arrived in the colonies in large numbers. By 1750 these groups of newcomers had made their mark on every one of the 13 colonies. South Carolina had more Africans than Europeans. New York was a mixture of Dutch, Swedish, French, English, Jewish, and many other groups of people.

In almost every colony, people settled first along the coastline. As these areas became crowded, the frontier began to move westward. *Frontier* was a word used by colonists to describe land on the edge of European settlement. As colonists moved to the frontier, they took over more and more of the Native Americans' lands.

At the same time, colonial cities were growing larger. By 1775 Philadelphia had become the largest city in the 13 colonies. Benjamin Franklin was one of the people who helped it grow.

244

---

h Carolina Secedes
hen Lincoln won the election, peo- waited anxiously to see whether any es would carry out their threat of eeding from the Union. Lincoln called k of leaving the Union "humbug." In ecember 1860, however, the state of outh Carolina voted to secede.
By March 1861, Mississippi, Florida, Alabama, Georgia, Louisiana, Texas, and South Carolina had formed a new country, the Confederate States of America. They draft and named a preside Jefferson Davis, a L or from Mississippi had fought in the M Union was now split

WHY IT
By the late 1850s divi North and South bec they could no longer promise. For many S course of action left t secede. To newly elec coln, the answer was was illegal and woul The conflict between South was about to b

xiv

DID YOU KNOW?
Why was Lincoln called "Honest Abe"?
As an adult, Lincoln opened a store. When the store failed, he owed a lot of money. It took several years, but he repaid every penny. For this reason, he became known as "Honest Abe."
ILLINOIS

[oppose] the abuses of power . . . of men in authority."
The jury agreed with Hamilton and found Zenger not guilty. Zenger's victory helped establish an important right, freedom of speech. This right meant that colonists could speak or print the truth without fear of being put in jail.

African Americans Speak Out
Enslaved African Americans took special note of the growing calls for freedom. Alone and in groups, they had long fought to be free from slavery.
One African American who wrote of liberty was Phillis Wheatley. Born in what is now the country of Senegal in West Africa, she was kidnapped at the age of eight. Wheatley was then sold as a slave to John Wheatley in Boston. Mr. and Mrs. Wheatley taught young Phillis to read and write English. In 1773 she published a book of poetry while she was still enslaved. Wheatley urged the colonists to free their slaves. "In every human . . . God has implanted a principle, which we call love of freedom," she wrote. "The same principle lives in us."

WHY IT MATTERS
Since their earliest beginnings the 13 ticed some form of self- ing of Eng-

Links to LANGUAGE ARTS
The Power of Poetry
Why are Phillis Wheatley's poems remembered today?
People who are not free to do or say what they want sometimes write down their feelings to make them known. Phillis Wheatley was enslaved, and she could not vote. She used poetry to express her opinions about slavery. Find a poem or a poet you think has a home or in your library that you think a message. Share the poems aloud in class and talk about their meanings.

Reviewing Facts and Ideas

MAIN IDEAS
- The early colonial assemblies helped to establish self-government in the 13 colonies.
- Assemblies such as the House of Burgesses made laws to print money, collect taxes, build roads, make land laws, and organize colonial militias.
- John Peter Zenger's trial in 1735 won support for the right to freedom of speech in the colonies.

THINK ABOUT IT
1. What were some of the colonies' earliest written plans for government?
2. Who could be elected to serve in the colonial assemblies?
3. **FOCUS** What were the major duties of the colonial assemblies? How would the jury

---

◀ Some lessons have features called **Links** or **Did You Know?**—activities to try and interesting information to share.

Look for a variety of lessons and features. **Infographics** bring you information with pictures, charts, graphs, and maps. You will build your **Skills**, learn about **Legacies** that connect us to the past, and meet people who show what **Citizenship** is. ▶

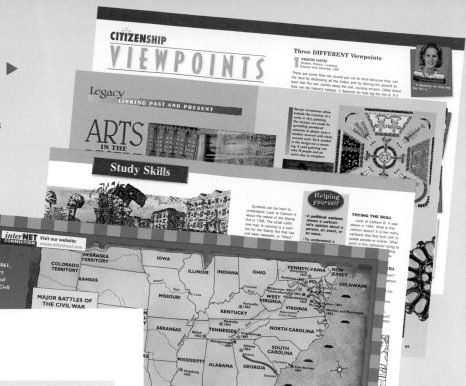

CITIZENSHIP
VIEWPOINTS

Three DIFFERENT Viewpoints

1 KRISTIN HAYES
Student, Pollock, Louisiana
Excerpt from interview, 1997

There are some fires we should put out at once because they ruin the land by destroying all the timber and by leaving the ground so bare that the rain carries away the soil, causing erosion. Other forest fires can be nature's helpers. It depends on how big the fire is. If a

It depends on how big the fire is…

Legacy
LINKING PAST AND PRESENT

ARTS
IN THE

Navajo ceremonies often include the creation of a sand, or dry, painting. The designs are made by sprinkling powdered minerals or plants onto a blanket covered with clean, smooth sand. Each symbol in the design has a meaning. A sand painting can take 18 people and an entire day to complete.

Study Skills

Symbols can be hard to understand. Look at Cartoon A about the repeal of the Stamp Act in 1766. The small coffin with this one man is carrying is a symbol for the Stamp Act that has just been repealed, or "killed."

• A political cartoon shows a cartoonist's opinion about a person, an event, or an issue.

• To understand a

Helping yourself

TRYING THE SKILL

Look at Cartoon B. It was drawn in 1994. What is this cartoon about? It is like many cartoons that find fault with or praise people or events. What point is this cartoonist trying to

Infographic

The Civil War

interNET CONNECTION Visit our website: www.mhschool.com

Early in the morning on April 12, 1861, Confederate troops attacked Fort Sumter, a Union fort off the coast of South Carolina. With this battle the Civil War between the Union and the Confederacy began. After several defeats in the beginning of the war, the

MAJOR BATTLES OF THE CIVIL WAR

BENJAMIN FRANKLIN

Ben Franklin, the grandson of an indentured servant, grew up to become the most famous person in the colonies. Born in 1706 into a large Boston family, Franklin learned at a young age that reading was a key to success. He read everything he could get his hands on.

At age 16 he wrote funny stories for his brother's newspaper under the name "Mrs. Silence Dogood." The stories were so good that his brother published them, not knowing that Ben had written them. This was the beginning of Franklin's work as a writer.

Franklin the Writer

In 1729 Franklin founded Philadelphia's first newspaper, the *Pennsylvania Gazette*. As a writer, one of Franklin's greatest successes was *Poor Richard's Almanack*. An almanac is a reference book that contains information about the stars and the weather. Franklin added jokes and sayings to his almanac. From 1732 to 1757 Franklin's almanac sold more copies than any other book in the colonies except for the Bible.

Franklin also wrote clever sayings to fill the blank spaces in his newspaper. The colonists loved the sayings, many of which are still popular today. Read some of Franklin's sayings on this page. What is Franklin trying to teach us?

MANY VOICES
PRIMARY SOURCE

Excerpts from *Poor Richard's Almanack* by Benjamin Franklin, published from 1732 to 1757.

Early to bed, early to rise, makes a man healthy, wealthy and wise.

Little strokes fell great oaks.

Glass, china, reputation, are easily cracked, and never well mended.

An open foe may prove a curse; but a pretended friend is worse.

One today is worth two tomorrows.

Haste makes waste.

Beware of little expenses. A small leak will sink a great ship.

The sleeping fox catches no poultry.

---

poultry: chicken
foe: enemy

Franklin the Scientist

As a scientist Franklin is best known for his experiments with electricity and his invention of the lightning rod. His other inventions still used today are bifocal eyeglasses and a wood-burning stove called the Franklin Stove.

Franklin's experiments caused excitement in the colonies and in Europe. He received many honors and prizes. His writings and experiments made him the best-known North American in Europe. When he visited Europe, people crowded in the streets to get a glimpse of him.

245

Use the **Reference Section** at the end of your book to look up words, people, and places. This section includes the **Constitution of the United States** and a **Time Line of Our Presidents**. ▼

Biographical Dictionary

This Biographical Dictionary tells you about the people you have learned about in this book. The Pronunciation

Dictionary of GEOGRAPHIC TERMS

▲

Lessons begin with a **Read Aloud** selection and **The Big Picture**. Study the **Read to Learn** question and list of words, people, and places. Enjoy **Many Voices**—writings, songs, and art by various people.

NATIONAL GEOGRAPHIC

Five Themes of Geography

Region
What are some things that help make the West a special region?

Human/Environment Interactions
How have people changed this landscape in Alaska?

Movement
How do people and goods travel from place to place?

Location
How do people know exactly where things are?

Place
What makes Niagara Falls different from other places?

GEOGRAPHY SKILLS

PART 1
Using Globes

VOCABULARY

continent	parallel
ocean	longitude
hemisphere	meridian
equator	prime meridian
latitude	

What is a globe? What does it show?

- A globe is a model of Earth. It is a useful tool for showing what Earth looks like.

- A globe shows Earth's seven continents, or large bodies of land. They are Africa, Antarctica, Asia, Australia, Europe, North America, and South America. What continents do you see on this globe?

- A globe also shows Earth's four oceans, or large bodies of salt water. They are the Atlantic, Arctic, Indian, and Pacific oceans. Look at the globe. On which continent do you live? What ocean is nearest to you?

What is a hemisphere?

- Like Earth, globes are spheres. A sphere is an object shaped like a ball. At any one time, you see only one half of a globe.

- Another word for half a sphere or globe is hemisphere. *Hemi* means half. Earth can be divided into four hemispheres.

- The equator is an imaginary line running halfway between the North Pole and South Pole. Into which two hemispheres does the equator divide Earth?

- Earth is also divided into the Eastern and Western hemispheres. Look at the maps at the top of the next page. Which two hemispheres show North America? Which hemispheres show South America?

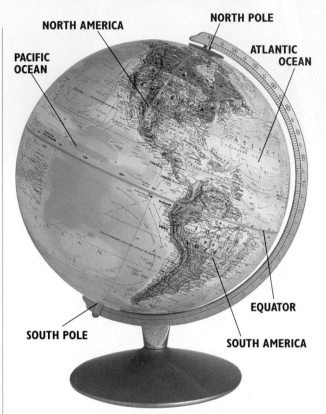

NORTH AMERICA — NORTH POLE — ATLANTIC OCEAN — PACIFIC OCEAN — EQUATOR — SOUTH POLE — SOUTH AMERICA

What are latitude and longitude?

- Maps and globes use a system of imaginary lines to help us locate places.

- Latitude lines run east and west. They measure the distance north or south of the equator. Latitude lines are also called parallels. Look at the lines of latitude at the bottom of the next page. What latitude line is shown just below the continent of South America?

- Longitude lines run north and south. Longitude lines are also called meridians. The starting line for measuring longitude is the prime meridian. Look at the lines of longitude. Where do they all meet?

More Practice

More maps in this book use lines of latitude and longitude. For examples, see pages 30, 33, and 37.

THE HEMISPHERES

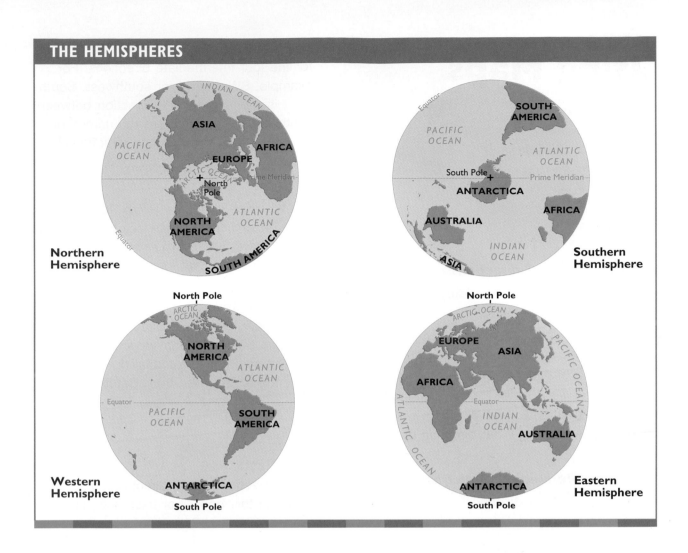

Northern Hemisphere

Southern Hemisphere

Western Hemisphere

Eastern Hemisphere

LINES OF LATITUDE (PARALLELS)

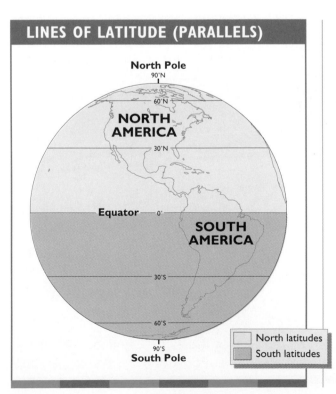

	North latitudes
	South latitudes

LINES OF LONGITUDE (MERIDIANS)

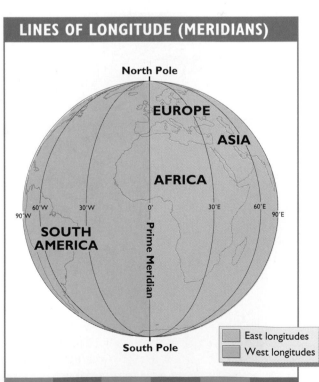

	East longitudes
	West longitudes

PART 2
Using Maps

VOCABULARY
cardinal directions
intermediate directions
compass rose
scale
symbol
map key
locator

What are cardinal directions?

- There are four main or cardinal directions.

- North is the direction you face when you stand facing the North Pole. South is behind you. East is to your right. What direction is to your left?

- The letters **N**, **S**, **E**, and **W** stand for these cardinal directions. What direction does **N** stand for?

What are intermediate directions?

- The intermediate directions are halfway between the cardinal directions.

- The letters **NE**, **SE**, **SW**, and **NW** stand for the four intermediate directions. For example, **SW** stands for southwest. Southwest is the intermediate direction between south and west. What are the names of the other three intermediate directions?

How can you find directions on a map?

- Not all maps show the North Pole. However, most maps you will see in this book have a compass rose. A compass rose is a small drawing that indicates directions on a map.

- A compass rose usually includes both cardinal and intermediate directions. Look at the map below. In what direction is Shreveport from Alexandria? In what direction is Lafayette from Baton Rouge?

More Practice

You can practice finding directions on almost any map in this book. For examples, see pages 65, 104, and 248.

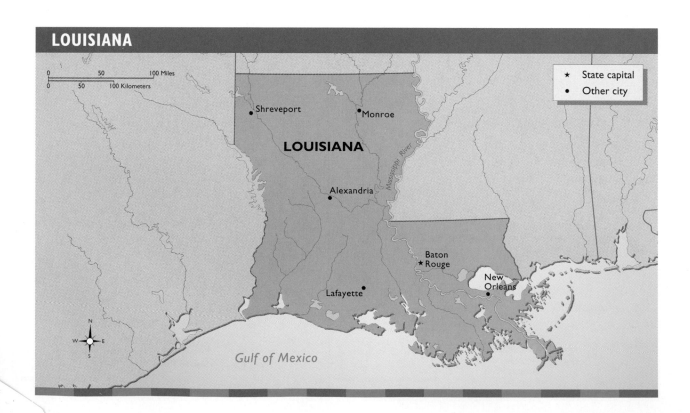

LOUISIANA

- State capital
- Other city

0   50   100 Miles
0   50   100 Kilometers

Shreveport
Monroe
LOUISIANA
Mississippi River
Alexandria
Baton Rouge
New Orleans
Lafayette
Gulf of Mexico

N
W   E
S

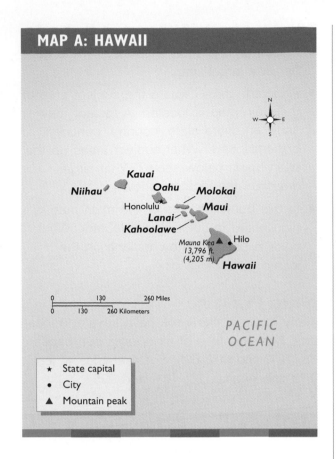

MAP A: HAWAII

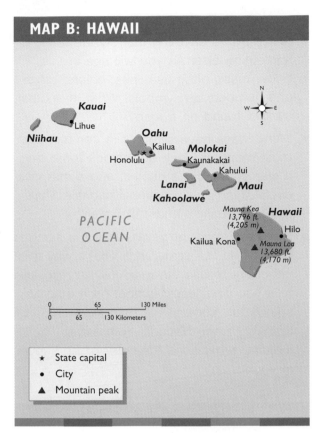

MAP B: HAWAII

What is a scale?

- Maps are much smaller than the actual places they show. The **scale** tells how much smaller. Scale explains the relationship between real distances on Earth and distances on the map.

- For the maps in this book, scale is indicated by two lines. One line shows miles. What does the other line show?

How can you use a scale? How are map scales different?

- To measure distances on a map, you can use a ruler. You can also make a scale strip like the one at right.

- Find the distance between the island of Molokai and the peak of Mauna Kea on Map A. First make a scale strip using the Map A scale. Place the edge of the strip on a line between the two places. The zero should be on Molokai. What is the distance in miles between the two places?

- Maps are drawn at different scales. Maps A and B both show the Hawaiian Islands,

but the islands look larger on Map B. They look larger because Map B has a larger scale. This means that it shows more detail.

- Even though the scales are different, the distance between places on both maps are the same. Make a scale strip using the Map B scale. What is the distance in miles between Molokai and Mauna Kea on Map B?

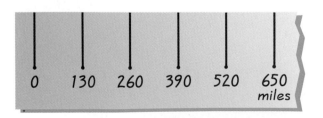

More Practice

You can practice using map scales on almost any map in this book. For examples, see pages 142, 179, and 376.

G7

How are symbols used on maps?

- A **symbol** is anything that stands for something else. As you will see in this book, maps often use lines, colors, stars, and numbers as symbols. What is another symbol found on a map?

- Many maps have symbols in common. On most maps, a black dot stands for a city, a star stands for a capital, and a star in a circle stands for a national capital. What symbol usually stands for water?

- Not every map, however, uses the same symbols in the same way. That's why it is important to use the **map key**. A map key tells you what each symbol on a map stands for. Look at the map keys of Francis Marion National Forest and Indiana. What does the color green show in each map?

What is a locator? What does it show?

- A **locator** is a small map inset in the corner of a larger map.

- A locator shows where the subject area of the main map is located. A locator may show an entire state, country, continent, or hemisphere. What subject areas do the main maps below show? What larger areas do the locators show?

- In this book the area of the main map is highlighted in color on the locator. What color is used to show Indiana on the locator?

More Practice

Many maps in this book have keys and locators. For examples of map keys, see pages 65, 121, and 602–603. For examples of locators, see pages 126, 161, and 205.

INDIANA: Corn and Dairy

Key:
- ★ State capital
- • Other city
- Corn-growing area
- Dairy-farming area

ILLINOIS

INDIANA

Hammond, Michigan City, South Bend, Elkhart, Gary, La Crosse, Warsaw, Rensselaer, Fort Wayne, Monticello, Lafayette, Marion, Portland, Muncie, Crawfordsville, Indianapolis, Richmond, Connersville, Shelbyville, Terre Haute, Columbus, Lawrenceburg, Bedford, Madison, Vincennes, Washington, Scottsburg, Paoli, New Harmony, Evansville, Corydon, Cannellton

KENTUCKY

Wabash River, White River, East Fork, Ohio River

0   25   50 Miles
0   25   50 Kilometers

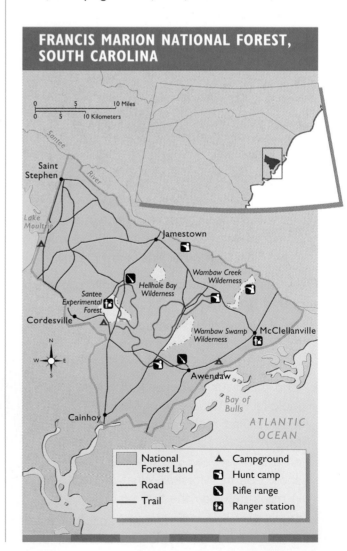

FRANCIS MARION NATIONAL FOREST, SOUTH CAROLINA

0   5   10 Miles
0   5   10 Kilometers

Santee River, Saint Stephen, Lake Moultrie, Jamestown, Wambaw Creek Wilderness, Hellhole Bay Wilderness, Santee Experimental Forest, Cordesville, Wambaw Swamp Wilderness, McClellanville, Awendaw, Cainhoy, Bay of Bulls, ATLANTIC OCEAN

Key:
- National Forest Land
- Road
- Trail
- ▲ Campground
- Hunt camp
- Rifle range
- Ranger station

PART 3
Different Kinds of Maps

VOCABULARY

political map   elevation map
physical map   road map
relief map   historical map

Why read a map title?

- There are many kinds of maps. This section discusses four kinds of maps.

- It is important to read the map title first. It may tell you what information the map shows and what the map's subject area is. What is the title of the map below?

- Sometimes a map includes areas that are not part of its subject area. For example, the map of the Middle West region, below, also shows part of Canada. In this book nonsubject areas are usually shown in gray. What colors are used in the subject area of the map below?

What is a political map?

- Many maps show borders between states or countries. As you can see below, a political map often uses colors to show the boundaries between states or countries.

- A political map usually labels capital cities. Look at the map below. How many states are in the Middle West? What is the capital of Iowa?

More Practice

To study other political maps in this book, see pages R8–9 and R14–R15.

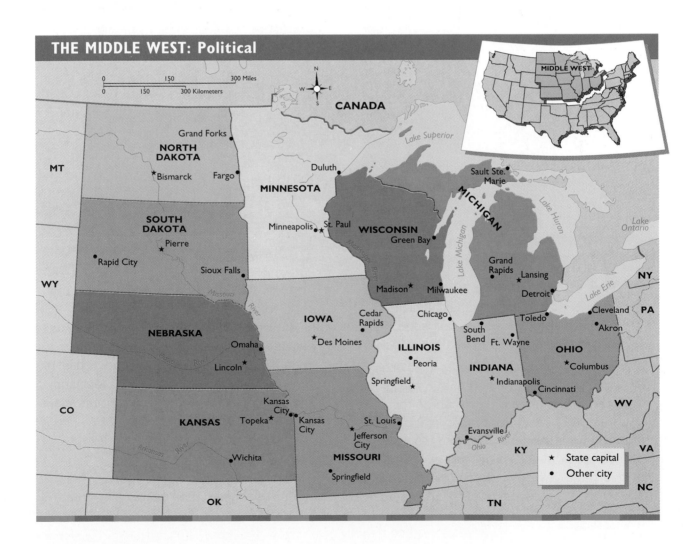

THE MIDDLE WEST: Political

★ State capital
• Other city

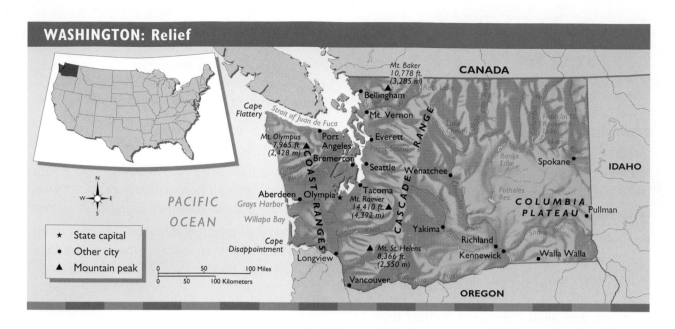

WASHINGTON: Relief

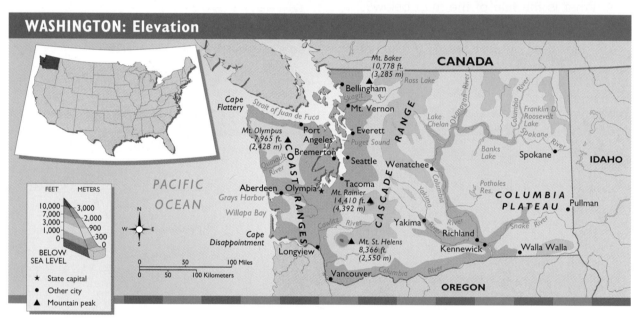

WASHINGTON: Elevation

What is a physical map?

- A **physical map** is a map that highlights Earth's natural features. You will see different types of physical maps in this book.

- A **relief map** is a physical map that uses shading to show the difference in height between areas of land. High landforms such as mountains are shaded to appear higher than lower land, such as plains or valleys. Look at the relief map at the top of this page. Which part of Washington state has the greatest relief? Which area has the least?

- An **elevation map** is a physical map that uses colors to show the elevation, or height of land above sea level. It is usually measured in feet or meters. What color does the elevation map just above use to show elevations between 3,000 feet and 7,000 feet? What is the approximate elevation of Spokane?

More Practice

You will find several physical maps in this book. For examples, see pages 34, 116, and R10–11.

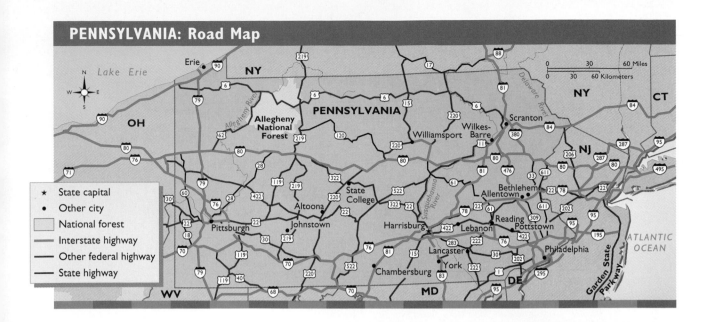

PENNSYLVANIA: Road Map

- ★ State capital
- • Other city
- National forest
- — Interstate highway
- — Other federal highway
- — State highway

What is a road map?

- A **road map** shows you how to get from one place to another. Road maps usually show cities and highways. They may also show natural features, points of interest, rest stops for drivers, and even the number of miles between places.

- Look at the road map above. What is the number of the road you would take to get from Chambersburg to Scranton? What type of road is it? If you travel west on federal highway 422 from Reading, what city would you pass through first?

What is an historical map?

- An **historical map** is a map that shows information about the past or where past events took place.

- The title of a map will help you determine that it is historical. Look at the historical map shown at right. What time in history does it show? The map key can give you more information. In which group of colonies is Virginia shown? What color is used to show the New England colonies?

More Practice

You will study a variety of maps in this book. For more practice using different kinds of maps, see pages 150, 474, and 521.

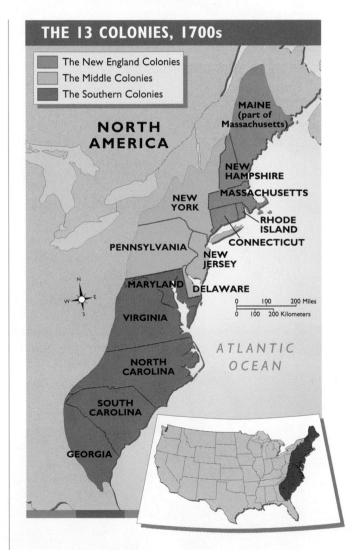

THE 13 COLONIES, 1700s

- The New England Colonies
- The Middle Colonies
- The Southern Colonies

CONNECTICUT FAMILY, 1942

WISCONSIN FAMILY, 1910

Americans and Our Environment

"America! . . . From sea to shining sea."

from *America, the Beautiful* by Katharine Lee Bates
See page 47.

Why Does it Matter?

We live in a country of great natural beauty. Breathtaking views delight the eye in every region of the United States. In fact, the quote above, from the song *America, the Beautiful,* was inspired by the American land. Katharine Lee Bates wrote of our country's mountains and deserts, its rolling hills and plains, the bounty and richness of its beautiful environment.

As rich and varied as our land is, so too is the population of the United States. Yet while we come from different backgrounds, we share many things in common. We are, for example, united by our belief in freedom and justice for all.

THEODORE ROOSE
SAN JUAN
ESIDENT 190

PEACE WITH HONOR
PREPAREDNESS
WILSON
WILSON
PROSPERITY

FIND OUT MORE!
Visit our website:
www.mhschool.com

CAMPAIGN BUTTONS OF
ROOSEVELT AND WILSON

*inter*NET
CONNECTION

3

Adventures with ☐ NATIONAL GEOGRAPHIC

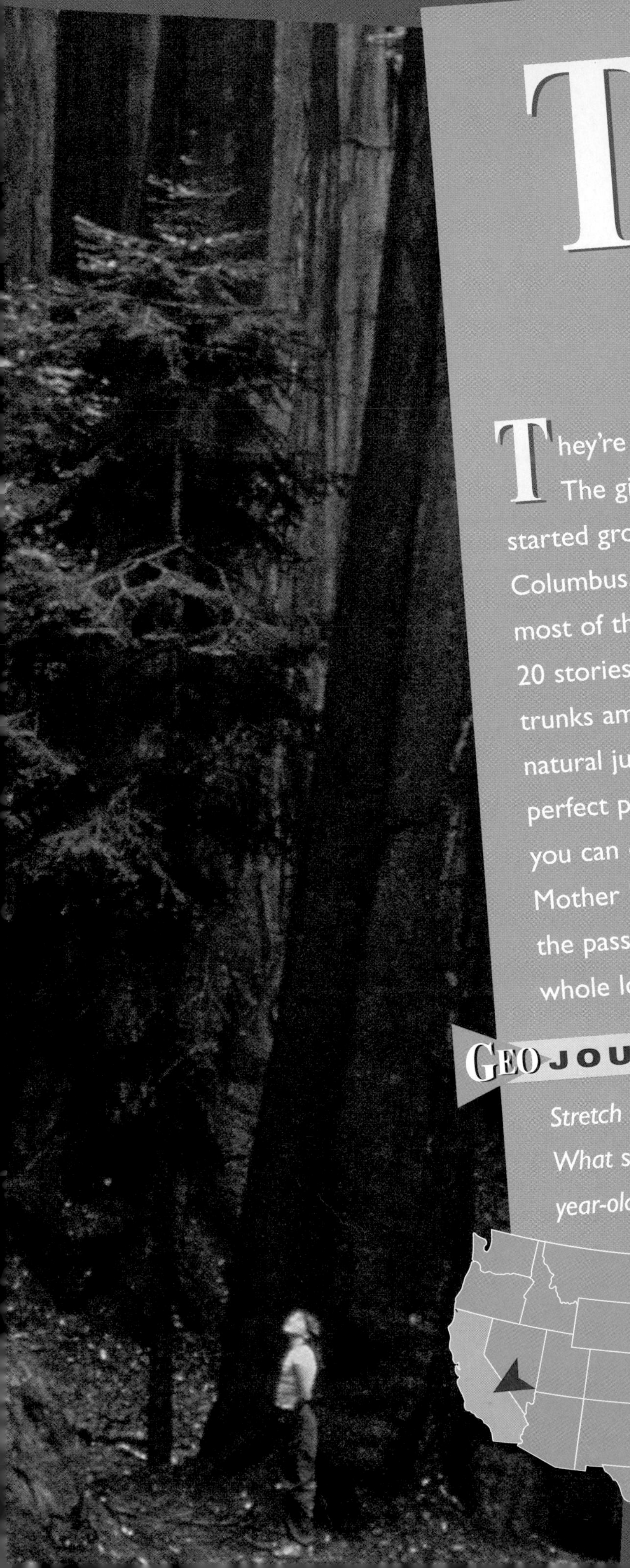

TALL TALES

They're even older than your teacher! The giant sequoias of California started growing centuries ago—before Columbus, before Washington, before most of the history in this book. Soaring 20 stories into the sky, their reddish trunks amaze visitors. Their roots make a natural jungle gym, and their stumps are a perfect place for a picnic. Between bites, you can digest a silent history lesson. Like Mother Nature's diary, the tree rings chart the passing years. And, as you'll learn, a whole lot happened during those years.

GEO JOURNAL

Stretch your imagination and listen real hard. What stories might you hear from a 2,000-year-old tree?

Life in the United States

THINKING ABOUT PEOPLE AND HISTORY

The history of the United States is the story of its people. In Chapter 1 you will begin to meet the people whose words and deeds have contributed to our history. Our country's people come from all over the world, yet we are united in our belief in freedom and equality for all.

ALASKA

CANADA

New York Harbor

UNITED STATES

PACIFIC OCEAN

MEXICO

HAWAII

New York Harbor, NEW YORK

The Statue of Liberty, or Miss Liberty as it is known, was a gift from the country of France to celebrate our country's first 100 years.

Americans Today

Read Aloud

E pluribus unum (EE PLUR uh bus YOO num). You may have heard these words before. What do they mean? They are Latin for "Out of many, one," the motto, or saying, of the United States for more than 200 years. This motto has defined an important goal of our country—that the many different peoples in our 50 states live together as one people.

Focus Activity

READ TO LEARN

Who are the people of the United States?

VOCABULARY

- culture
- diversity
- unity
- values
- immigrant
- ancestor
- ethnic group
- census
- population
- prejudice

THE BIG PICTURE

Today as in the past, the United States is home to people from many **cultures**. A culture is the entire way of life of a people—their customs, beliefs, and language.

People came to this country, and continue to come, from all over the world. Each group has brought its different ideas and traditions to the United States. These differences in cultures bring a great deal of **diversity** (dih VUR sih tee) to our country. Diversity is variety.

Although Americans come from different backgrounds, we share many basic beliefs. They include the freedom to worship and to earn a living as one chooses. Americans also believe in fairness and equal treatment of people. Such shared beliefs have helped to create a sense of **unity** among our country's people. Unity means being as one or being in agreement.

As you read this book, notice how people from many diverse cultures, places, and backgrounds have helped to make the United States a great and special country.

AMERICAN PEOPLE

Think about some Americans whom you know. Ask yourself, "What do we have in common?" You might note that most people in the United States speak English. Many Americans have a similar style of dress. Americans also enjoy similar sports, books, and movies.

Most important, you will probably find that people in the United States share similar values about the rights and freedoms they enjoy as Americans. Values are the beliefs or ideals that guide the way people live. Americans also respect the laws and the government that protect those rights.

Ancestors from Different Shores

Most people in the United States have someone in their family background who was an immigrant. An immigrant is a person who leaves one country to go and live in another land. Over the years people have come to the United States from just about every corner of the globe.

Many newcomers to the United States keep some of the traditional ways of their ancestors. Ancestors are the relatives who lived before you. We are all descended from many ancestors. In the United States you can see the influence of different cultures everywhere. Recent immigrants might speak Spanish, Arabic, or Korean. Americans who came here, whether recently or long ago, may celebrate the holidays of their ancestors such as the Chinese New Year or the Jewish holiday of Passover.

Our country's diversity is seen in its many ethnic groups— from Native Americans to people from almost every country in the world.

Ethnic Backgrounds

An example of our country's diversity is the variety of ethnic groups that live in the United States. An ethnic group includes people who share the same customs and language. Many also have a common history.

Some ethnic groups, such as Native Americans, have lived here for thousands of years. It was not until about 500 years ago that people from Europe and Africa began arriving here. Until after the Civil War, most African Americans were involuntary immigrants. They were forced to come to the United States in chains.

In recent years the largest numbers of immigrants have come from Asia and Latin America. Latin America includes Mexico, the Caribbean Islands, Central America, and South America. People whose ancestors are from Spanish-speaking countries in the Western Hemisphere are called Hispanics or Latinos. Asian Americans are descendants of people from China, Korea, Japan, Vietnam, India, and many other countries in Asia. You will read about people from many of our country's ethnic groups as you study this book.

Infographic

interNET CONNECTION Visit our website: www.mhschool.com

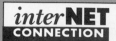

The People of the United States

How can we find out facts about our country's people? One way is to study the census that our government takes every ten years. A census is an official study of the people of a country. It provides information about the number of people in an area, where they live, and how they live. Such information helps the government plan for our future needs. Below are some facts about the American people today.

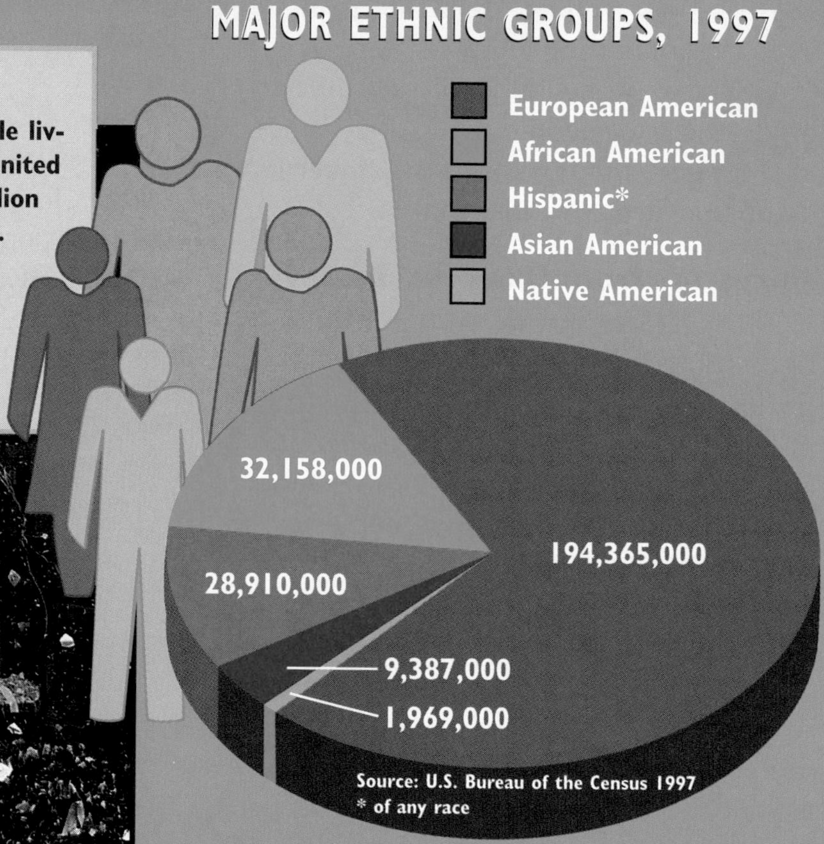

MAJOR ETHNIC GROUPS, 1997
European American
African American
Hispanic*
Asian American
Native American
32,158,000
194,365,000
28,910,000
9,387,000
1,969,000
Source: U.S. Bureau of the Census 1997
* of any race

POPULATION

The population is the number of people living in a place. The population of the United States has grown from less than 4 million people in 1790 to 267 million in 1997.

Population 1997: 267 million
Estimated population 2000: 273 million
Estimated population 2050: 381 million

Source: U.S. Bureau of the Census 1997

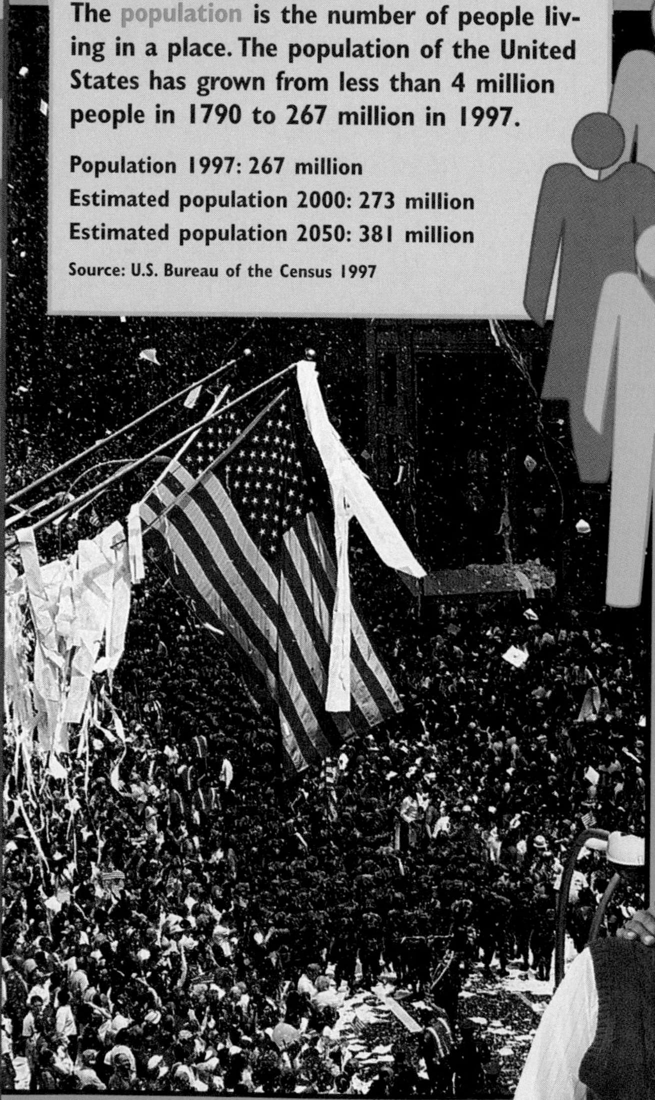

AGE

In a few families, members' ages span an entire century from newborn to more than 100 years of age.

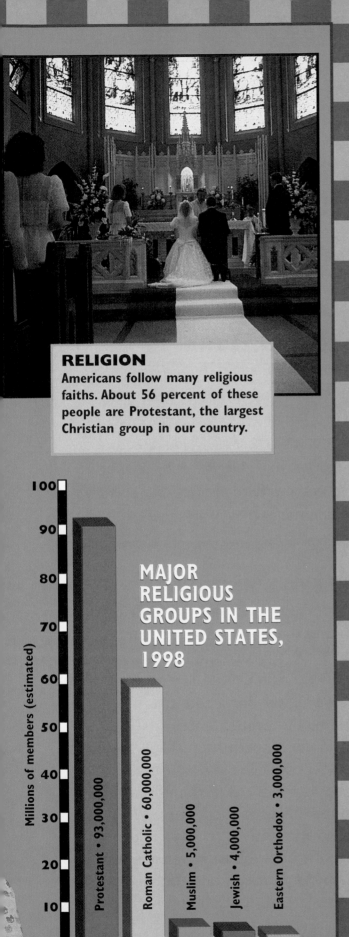

RELIGION
Americans follow many religious faiths. About 56 percent of these people are Protestant, the largest Christian group in our country.

MAJOR RELIGIOUS GROUPS IN THE UNITED STATES, 1998

Millions of members (estimated)

Protestant • 93,000,000
Roman Catholic • 60,000,000
Muslim • 5,000,000
Jewish • 4,000,000
Eastern Orthodox • 3,000,000

Source: *The World Almanac, 1998*

WHY IT MATTERS

Most of the people in our country are proud of their heritage. The writer Ishmael Reed has described the United States as a place "where the cultures of the world crisscross."

However, the acceptance of differences has not always come easily. Many ethnic groups have faced **prejudice** because their backgrounds, skin color, or beliefs were different from those of other groups. Prejudice is a negative opinion formed without proof.

Despite their differences, Americans share a common culture and values such as "liberty and justice for all," freedom of speech, religious freedom, and the hope for a better life.

✓ Reviewing Facts and Ideas

MAIN IDEAS

- The United States is a diverse country, but its people share a number of basic beliefs and values.
- Many ethnic groups have come together to form a rich variety of traditions and customs in our country.
- Many different religions are practiced in the United States.

THINK ABOUT IT

1. What is meant by the motto *E pluribus unum?*

2. What are some of the places in which our ancestors were born?

3. **FOCUS** Why is the United States home to many different peoples?

4. **THINKING SKILL** What *conclusions* might a newcomer to the United States make about its people today?

5. **WRITE** Write a paragraph explaining what immigrants might enjoy about the United States.

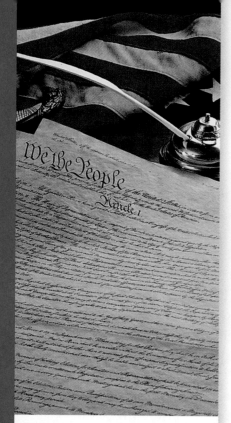

Our Country's Government

Focus Activity

READ TO LEARN

What is the role of citizens in our country's democratic republic?

VOCABULARY

- Constitution
- democracy
- republic
- federal
- citizen
- civil rights

PLACES

- Washington, D.C.

Read Aloud

"I pledge allegiance (uh LEE juhns) to the flag of the United States of America and to the Republic for which it stands, one Nation under God, indivisible, with liberty and justice for all." Most likely you already know these words to the Pledge of Allegiance. By reciting them, we promise our loyalty to our flag, our country's government, and the values they represent.

THE BIG PICTURE

In 1776 colonial leaders decided that the 13 British colonies should found their own country. Years later, many of the same leaders wrote the **Constitution** (kahn stih TOO shun) of the United States. A constitution is a plan of government for a country.

"We the People of the United States . . ." These famous words begin our Constitution. They show that our country's founders believed in **democracy**. In a democracy the people make the laws and run the government. The United States is also a **republic**. Here the people elect representatives to run the country.

Our country has three levels of government. The Constitution set up the **federal**, or national, government in **Washington, D.C.** It also explained the roles of the state and local governments. Like the federal government, all of our state and local governments are run by representatives elected by "we the people."

PEOPLE AND GOVERNMENT

Our government serves the people in many ways. We expect it to protect our lives and property, to enforce laws, to build highways, and to provide schools.

"The Consent of the Governed"

The government gets its power "from the consent of the governed," says the Declaration of Independence. Consent means approval. How do citizens give their consent? A citizen is a person who is born in a country or who chooses to become a member of that country by law. Citizens give their consent by voting. Americans vote in many kinds of elections. They vote for the President of the United States, for the governor of their state, and for the mayor of their city. They vote for local school-board members, as well.

Citizens often have different opinions about who should be elected or what the government should do. They get to voice their opinions in public meetings. Newspapers, radio, and television are also ways to speak out on issues. One big job that citizens have is staying informed about the issues.

DID YOU KNOW?

How many capital cities has our country had?

Today our country's capital is Washington, D.C. But early in our history, the capital was Philadelphia, Pennsylvania. It moved from there to Baltimore, Maryland, and then to New York City. Other cities, such as Trenton and Princeton in New Jersey, also served briefly as the national capital.

Government Responds

The government responds to citizens in a number of ways. When disaster strikes, Americans receive help from the federal, state, and local governments. They use tax money and can draw upon resources of the entire country in times of major crisis. How has our government helped people in your area in normal times and in times of need?

Federal rescue workers in Quins, Illinois, help to stack bales of hay to keep back flood waters.

RIGHTS AND RESPONSIBILITIES

The Constitution of the United States protects our basic rights such as freedom of speech, freedom of religion, and the right to earn a living as one chooses. Rights like these are called civil rights. Civil rights are the individual rights of a citizen under the law.

Citizenship

Citizenship includes both rights and responsibilities. Thomas Paine, an early writer, put it this way:

Those who expect to reap [receive] the blessings of freedom must . . . undergo the fatigue [weariness] of supporting it.

As citizens, we have important responsibilities, such as voting, obeying the law, taking part in government, and paying taxes to provide for the benefits that we receive. Respecting the rights of others is another responsibility that we all share.

Taking Part in Government

Citizens have many opportunities to take part in government. When you are 18 years old, you will be able to vote. Even now, you could help in a political campaign. Eventually you will pay taxes, or money that pays for the costs of running the government. Some citizens defend our country in times of peace as well as war. Others take a direct role by running for government office.

Ben Nighthorse Campbell was elected to represent the citizens of Colorado in the United States Senate in 1992. Read the following excerpt in which Senator Campbell talks about his job in Congress. What do you think about the Senator's view that our government is run by the people?

Excerpt from an Interview with Senator Ben Nighthorse Campbell in 1994.

We are lucky to live in a country that grants us rights in the Constitution such as freedom to speak, write, read, work, worship, and live as we choose. These freedoms place a responsibility on each of us to become involved in our system of government. America is run by the people—that includes you.

There are many reasons why I ran for the Senate. . . . I wanted this job because I care about my state and its people, and I wanted to ensure that the people's interests were well represented in Congress.

More than 500 men and women meet regularly in the United States Capitol Building to make our country's laws.

The Levels of Government

Our country's government works on three separate levels—federal, state, and local. The federal government handles issues that affect the entire country. As you have read, Senator Campbell works in the federal government—in Congress. Only the federal government can declare war or make peace agreements with other countries.

Our country's state governments deal with issues that affect an entire state or parts of a state. Their responsibilities include managing public schools and holding elections.

Like you, our country's people live in cities, counties, townships, and parishes. They have needs that are best met by local government. The people who work in local government are responsible for keeping law and order and building roads, among other duties.

Most important is how the levels of government work together. Issues such as energy and fuel use and highway and aircraft transportation involve the government at all levels—local, state, and federal.

WHY IT MATTERS

In our democratic republic the people are the government. We elect citizens like ourselves to speak for us at the local, state, and federal levels. If we do not approve of the views or actions of these representatives, we have the right to vote for others.

"The people's government, made for the people, made by the people, and answerable to the people." In those words, Daniel Webster, an American statesman, described how the people and the government are the same. Since our country's beginning, people have proudly taken part in running it. You will read in the next lesson how the words and deeds of American people have created our country's history.

✔️ Reviewing Facts and Ideas

MAIN IDEAS

- The Constitution of the United States organizes our government into a democratic republic.
- Americans give consent to the government by voting and by taking part in it themselves.
- Citizenship in a democratic republic involves rights and responsibilities.

THINK ABOUT IT

1. What kind of government does the United States have?
2. Describe the rights and responsibilities of American citizens.
3. **FOCUS** What are some jobs that citizens can do for our government?
4. **THINKING SKILL** What *effects* does the right to vote have on the people who hold government offices?
5. **WRITE** Write a paragraph explaining "consent of the governed."

alternatives to achieve your goal. An alternative is another way of doing something.

Sometimes decision making involves difficult choices. You might have to decide whether you should spend the night at a friend's house or stay home and celebrate your brother's birthday. Your decision in each case will affect other people.

Making the right decision will help you meet your goal. So you need to think carefully and evaluate the alternatives before you decide. To evaluate means to determine the value or meaning of something. Think about some of your recent decisions. Why did you make the decisions that you did?

In the last lesson you read that voting for government officials such as President or mayor is an important responsibility. In order to vote, citizens have to make a number of decisions. Each of these decisions helps a

Decision Making

VOCABULARY
decision
alternative
evaluate

WHY THE SKILL MATTERS

Every day you make dozens of decisions, or choices. You decide what clothes to wear and what kind of food to eat for lunch. You may also decide whether or not to try out for a class play. Decision making is choosing from a number of

voter to choose the candidate that he or she believes is best for the job.

USING THE SKILL

Look at the Helping Yourself box on this page. The hints there may help you as you make decisions of any kind.

Voters follow these same steps as they make informed decisions. Voters first decide what their goals are in choosing a candidate. What qualities would you look for in a candidate? Voters evaluate all the candidates. Then voters select the one candidate who will help them achieve their goals.

- **A decision is a choice that you make.**

- **Identify your goal. Always identify all possible alternatives before choosing one of them.**

- **Examine the immediate and long range consequences of each alternative before making your final decision.**

Why do you think it is important to choose a candidate who shares your views? Finally, voters choose the candidate they believe to be the best person for the job.

TRYING THE SKILL

Susan Kroczak is a fifth grader at Wilmont Elementary School. On Wednesday she must decide whom to vote for in a student council election. Two candidates are running for president of the student council. Susan wants a president who will work well with both students and teachers. She also wants a president who will help to do something about the problem with litter on the streets near the school.

Look at the campaign posters. What are Susan's goals for her school? What are the goals of Candidate A? Candidate B? If you shared Susan's goals, which candidate would probably get your vote?

REVIEWING THE SKILL

1. What does it mean to make a decision?

2. What would you do in order to decide who is the best candidate for the job?

3. Why is it important to evaluate carefully all of the alternatives when you are making a decision?

4. How do the campaign posters show you the importance of decision making?

TO CLEAN UP OUR SCHOOL

VOTE
MAX FOR PRESIDENT!

Our Country's History

Focus Activity

READ TO LEARN

How do the stories of many different people help us to understand our country's history?

VOCABULARY

- history
- historian
- primary source
- oral history
- secondary source
- perspective

Read Aloud

"All our stories are different," explained Tomo Shoji, as she spoke to a group of Asian Americans in 1988. Shoji urged children to listen to their ancestors' stories. Through those tales they can learn about their families' past. Such stories form part of our country's history, which includes the experiences of the many people who have settled on these shores.

THE BIG PICTURE

History is the study or record of what happened in the past. The history of the United States is rich and varied. But when does that story begin? What and whom does that story include?

It begins far back in time. The first people to shape this land were the Native Americans. Our story continues with later arrivals from Europe, Africa, Asia, and Latin America. A book like this cannot tell every story. Instead it will look at how some people—some famous, some not—contributed to our country's development.

When Minnie Miller, an immigrant from Europe, wrote of her life, she included her ancestors. "My history is bound up in their history, and the generations that follow should know where they came from to know better who they are." History helps us to see how the lives of our ancestors affect the way we live today.

HISTORY AND ITS CLUES

Think about what you did yesterday or last week or even last year. Can you remember all of the details? Historians have an even harder task. Historians are people who study the past. They examine clues and records left behind by others. Then they try to figure out what happened and why.

Primary and Secondary Sources

Historians, like detectives, comb through much written and unwritten evidence. By studying homes, pottery, or other objects, they learn about the people who made and used them.

Historians depend upon primary sources. A primary source is information that comes from the time being studied. Many are written documents such as letters. A film or photograph from the time an event happened is also a primary source. So are eyewitness accounts. An eyewitness is a person who saw an event happen.

Another kind of primary source is oral history, or spoken records. Stories passed from one generation to the next tell of our ancestors' hopes and fears.

Historians also use secondary sources. A secondary source is an account of the past written by someone who was not an eyewitness to those events. A history textbook like this one is a secondary source. So are encyclopedia articles or recent films about an event that occurred in the past.

A Matter of Perspective

Historians cannot list all the facts about past events. Instead they sort the evidence and try to make sense of what happened and why. As they weave the information into a story, they include some facts and leave out others.

Historians must also be careful about interpreting the clues that they find. *Interpret* means "to make understandable." Their own perspectives, or points of view, sometimes affect how they look at information. At other times they may get two or more different accounts of the same event. The responsibility of the historian is to be as accurate as possible.

George Catlin's 1834 painting, *Keokuk on Horseback,* shows one perspective on Native Americans. This Navajo mural in Canyon del Muerto, Arizona, is one on Europeans.

Smithsonian Institution

PEOPLE AND HISTORY

People are the chief participants in history. They make and experience it. They also record and interpret it. A book like this one is about people whose thoughts and actions formed our past.

Speaking of History

The following two historians have written about the part played by immigrants in our country's history.

Ronald Takaki wants to share stories of the people who helped make our country strong. In the first excerpt he gives his view of how different ethnic groups helped shape our country.

Arthur M. Schlesinger, Jr., has studied times in the past when our country was changing rapidly. In the second excerpt he discusses his perspective on American values. Read both excerpts. What similarities can you find in their views of America?

MANY VOICES
PRIMARY SOURCE

Excerpt from
A Different Mirror:
A Multicultural History of America
by Ronald Takaki, 1993.

The signs of America's ethnic diversity can be discerned [seen] across the continent. . . . Much of what is familiar in America's cultural landscape actually has ethnic origins. The Bing cherry was developed by an early Chinese immigrant named Ah Bing. American Indians were **cultivating** *corn, tomatoes, and tobacco long before the arrival of Columbus. . . . Jazz and blues as well as rock and roll have African-American origins. The "Forty-Niners" of the Gold Rush learned mining techniques from the Mexicans. . . . Songs like "God Bless America," "Easter Parade," and "White Christmas" were written by a Russian-Jewish immigrant named Israel Baline, more popularly known as Irving Berlin.*

cultivating: growing

MANY VOICES
PRIMARY SOURCE

Excerpt from
The Disuniting of America
by Arthur M. Schlesinger, Jr., 1991.

The genius [greatness] of America lies in its capacity to forge a single nation from peoples of remarkably diverse racial, religious, and ethnic origins.

Our democratic principles **contemplate** *an open society founded on tolerance of differences and on mutual respect. In practice, America has been more open to some than to others. But it is more open to all today than it was yesterday and is likely to be even more open tomorrow than today. The steady movement of American life has been from* **exclusion** *to* **inclusion.**

contemplate: think about
exclusion: not including
inclusion: including

The United States is a fascinating mixture of peoples and cultures. This is one of our country's greatest strengths.

WHY IT MATTERS

History is not only about famous people. It is about ordinary people as well. It is the story of men, women, and children of many ethnic groups. It is the story of people who worked ten-hour days in the factories and children who helped clear land for farms or labored underground in coal mines. It is the story of cowhands who slept on the hard ground of the trail. All these stories, like small creeks, flow into the great river of American history.

The story of the American past is your story. Today you are a participant in our history. You are creating the stories that future students will learn.

✓ Reviewing Facts and Ideas

MAIN IDEAS

- Our country's history is the story of many different people with many experiences.

- History is recorded in different ways. Historians gather, sort, and interpret all kinds of evidence about the past.

- By studying the past, we learn how our ancestors acted and how their experiences affect who we are today.

THINK ABOUT IT

1. Describe the job of historians.

2. When might historians use a primary source? A secondary source?

3. **FOCUS** Why do we listen to the stories of different peoples in order to understand our country's history?

4. **THINKING SKILL** How does an historian *decide* which facts to use and which to leave out?

5. **WRITE** Write a paragraph about how your history is linked to that of your parents and grandparents.

PRESERVING
HISTORIC PLACES

Is history a subject in a textbook? Or is it something we can see and touch? History is the study of the past, but its legacies are all around us. Legacies are traditions that are handed down from one generation to the next.

Almost everywhere in the United States, there are historic places that people have preserved. In preserving historic places we show future generations that the past is more than dates and names—it is, in fact, alive.

In 1963 First Lady Jacqueline Kennedy said that she wanted the White House to be a "museum of our country's heritage." The Diplomatic Reception Room (above) has changed little since she restored and redecorated it. This plate of china (right) was part of a set the Kennedys used during state dinners at the White House.

A nineteenth-century tenement building in New York City is now part of the Lower East Side Tenement Museum. In kitchens like the one above, immigrant families discussed their future in their new country.

Boley, Oklahoma, was settled by freed African Americans after the Civil War. Today the center of Boley is a National Historic District. Its residents celebrate Boley's past with a Black Rodeo held on Memorial Day.

CHAPTER 1 REVIEW

THINKING ABOUT VOCABULARY

Number a paper from 1 to 15. Beside each number write the word or term from the list below that matches the description.

ancestor	perspective
census	prejudice
citizen	primary source
civil rights	republic
Constitution	secondary source
culture	unity
ethnic group	values
immigrant	

1. A person who leaves one country to come and live in another
2. A country in which people elect representatives to serve in the government
3. A person who is born in a country or who chooses to become a member of that country by law
4. The rights of a citizen under the law
5. Historical information from the time that is being studied
6. The entire way of life of a people, their customs, beliefs, and language
7. The beliefs or ideals that guide the way people live
8. A negative opinion formed without proof
9. An official study of the people of a country
10. The plan of government for the United States
11. Being in agreement or being as one
12. The point of view a person brings to information and ideas
13. People who share, among other things, the same customs and language
14. An historical account written by someone who is not an eyewitness
15. A relative who lived before you

THINKING ABOUT FACTS

1. Why can the United States be considered a country of much diversity?
2. What was the population of the United States in 1997?
3. What are some of the basic beliefs or values that Americans share?
4. What are the three levels of government in the United States?
5. List two ways each level of government in the United States serves the people.
6. What famous words begin our Constitution? Why are these words important?
7. What is history? Is history only about famous people?
8. Why is it important to study history?
9. How does his or her perspective affect an historian's work?
10. How can the study of history help show our country's diversity?

THINK AND WRITE

WRITING A REPORT

Write a brief report in which you describe the government of the United States and the role a citizen plays in it.

WRITING AN ESSAY

Write an essay in which you discuss how the motto *E pluribus unum* applies to the United States.

WRITING FROM ORAL HISTORY

Write a paragraph that describes a true event from before you were born. Ask a relative, neighbor, or friend to tell you this piece of oral history.

APPLYING THINKING SKILLS

DECISION MAKING

To practice the thinking skill of decision making, answer the questions below.

1. What is a decision, and why is making good decisions important?

2. List three decisions you make during the course of a normal day.

3. What is the first step when you are making a decision?

4. When making a decision, why is it important to consider all the alternatives before choosing one?

5. What role does making decisions play in the duties of a citizen of the United States?

Summing Up the Chapter

Copy the main idea map on a separate piece of paper. Review the chapter to fill in the blank sections. After you have completed the map, use the information to write a short essay answering the question "How have historians helped us to learn about the people who made our country what it is today?"

Primary sources

The Study of History

MAIN IDEA
Historians use various sources to find out about the past of the United States—its people and government.

The People

Many different cultures

A federal system

Consent of the people

Geography of the United States

THINKING ABOUT
HISTORY AND GEOGRAPHY

Chapter 2 introduces you to the land and resources of the United States. From the Rocky Mountains of the West to the shores of the Atlantic Ocean in the East, our country has many different physical wonders. As you read this chapter, you will see how magnificent this land of ours is.

San Luis Valley
WEST

Colorado's Great Sand Dunes National Monument has the highest dunes in the Western Hemisphere.

Texas oil field
SOUTHWEST

Oil for fuel is one of the major natural resources of this region.

Wisconsin farmland
MIDDLE WEST

This region is one of our country's largest producers of grain, hay, and livestock.

New Orleans
SOUTHEAST

The sights and sounds of historic New Orleans bring many tourists to this region each year.

Niagara Falls
NORTHEAST

The rushing waters of these New York falls create low-cost electric energy for many industries.

The American Land

Focus Activity

READ TO LEARN

What are the five regions of the United States?

VOCABULARY

- geography
- region
- landform
- megalopolis
- interdependent

PLACES

- Rocky Mountains
- Continental Divide
- Grand Canyon
- Corn Belt
- Mississippi River
- Boswash

Read Aloud

Have you ever kept a scrapbook? A scrapbook holds photographs, ticket stubs, letters, post cards—things that remind us of special times or special places. It is also a way to hold on to memories of things we have done. You can visit a special place by taking a car trip, by gazing out the window of a plane, or by watching a movie. You can also visit a special place through the pages of a book. In the pages that follow, you will find a scrapbook of the United States.

THE BIG PICTURE

Every year millions of Americans take to the roads to see our land. They climb snow-capped mountains and explore deep canyons. They sail along rugged coasts or paddle in fish-filled lakes and rivers. They gaze in awe at waterfalls and deserts. They tour large cities and small towns. Although these vacationers might not realize it, they are studying our country's **geography**.

Geography is the study of Earth and the way people live on it and use it. Since earliest times the land has affected how people live. In turn, people have shaped the land to make houses for themselves or to earn a living. Geographers often divide the United States into smaller areas in order to study and compare these areas more closely. Read about these areas on the following pages. You may want to make a scrapbook of your own.

OUR COUNTRY'S REGIONS

The United States can be divided into several **regions**. A region is a large area that has common features that set it apart from other areas. Look at the map below. Into what five regions does it divide the United States?

Geographers, students, or teachers can divide a place into many kinds of regions. Suppose you want to learn about how people earn a living in the United States. You might divide our country into regions according to whether people work at large city jobs, in mines, or on farms. The regions shown on the map below have been created to help students such as you study our country's culture, history, and geography. Find the region in which you live. What similarities do the states in your region share?

Each **region**, such as the Middle West (top) and Northeast (above), is affected by how people use the land.

REGIONS OF THE UNITED STATES

WEST **MIDDLE WEST** **NORTHEAST**

ALASKA

WASHINGTON
OREGON
IDAHO
MONTANA
WYOMING
NEVADA
UTAH
COLORADO
CALIFORNIA

NORTH DAKOTA
MINNESOTA
SOUTH DAKOTA
WISCONSIN
MICHIGAN
NEBRASKA
IOWA
INDIANA
OHIO
ILLINOIS
KANSAS
MISSOURI

NEW HAMPSHIRE
VERMONT
MAINE
NEW YORK
MASSACHUSETTS
RHODE ISLAND
PENNSYLVANIA
CONNECTICUT
NEW JERSEY
DELAWARE
MARYLAND
WEST VIRGINIA
VIRGINIA
KENTUCKY
NORTH CAROLINA
TENNESSEE
SOUTH CAROLINA
ARKANSAS
GEORGIA
MISSISSIPPI
ALABAMA

ARIZONA
NEW MEXICO
OKLAHOMA
TEXAS
LOUISIANA

HAWAII

SOUTHWEST

SOUTHEAST

FLORIDA

MAP WORK

Each region in the United States has features that set it apart from the others. However, they work together to make our country strong.

1. How many states are part of the Southwest?

2. Which two regions have the most states?

3. Which regions do not border on the Atlantic coast or Pacific coast?

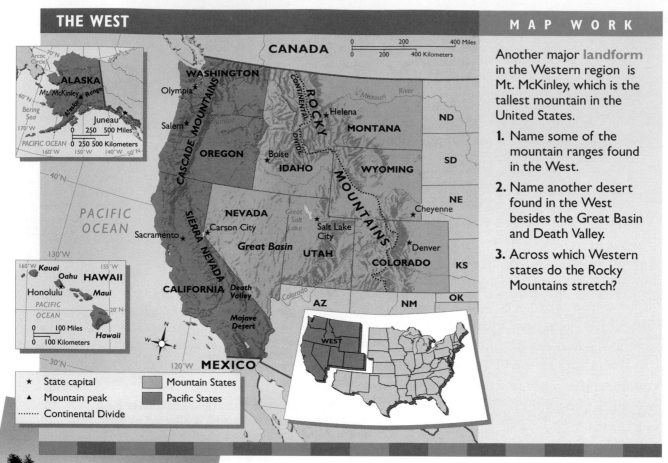

Another major **landform** in the Western region is Mt. McKinley, which is the tallest mountain in the United States.

1. Name some of the mountain ranges found in the West.

2. Name another desert found in the West besides the Great Basin and Death Valley.

3. Across which Western states do the Rocky Mountains stretch?

Map legend:
- ★ State capital
- ▲ Mountain peak
- .... Continental Divide
- Mountain States
- Pacific States

People in the Western Region enjoy gazing at beautiful views of the Pacific Coast (left) and skiing on the snowy Rocky Mountains (below).

THE WEST

Look at the map of the West above. It is a vast region of thick green forests, rugged ocean coastlines, bustling big cities, and, most of all, beautiful mountains. Mountains are a major **landform** of the West. A landform is a shape on Earth's surface. The **Rocky Mountains** are our longest mountain range. They attract millions of tourists each year.

There is an imaginary line in the Rockies that geographers call the **Continental Divide**. Rivers to the west of the Divide drain into the Pacific Ocean. Rivers to the east flow into the Atlantic Ocean or Gulf of Mexico. Imagine standing on the Continental Divide. You have one foot to the west and one foot to the east, and are looking down over the continent of North America.

THE SOUTHWEST

More people have moved to the Southwestern United States in recent years than to any other region of the country. As the map on this page shows, four very large states form this region. People from all over the United States and the world come to Arizona to gaze at the **Grand Canyon**. "It is the grandest of God's terrestrial [earthly] cities," said American geographer John Wesley Powell in 1869.

The fast-moving waters of the Colorado River carved out the Grand Canyon. You can look down at its blazing colors from the rim of the canyon. Or you can gaze up at the canyon walls from a raft in the Colorado River. You can even ride a mule down a narrow trail along the canyon.

Often visited places of the Southwest include the Grand Canyon (top) and buildings of sunbaked clay.

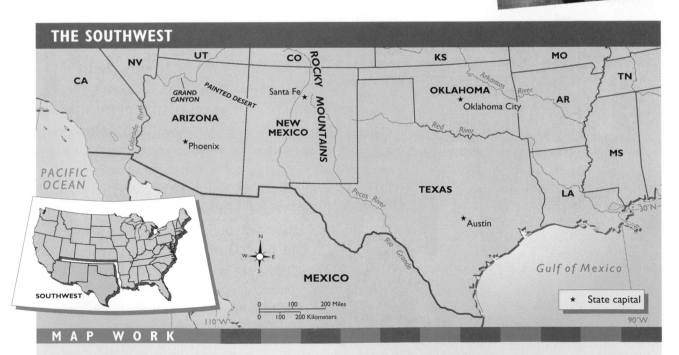

THE SOUTHWEST

CA · NV · UT · CO · ROCKY MOUNTAINS · KS · MO · TN
GRAND CANYON · PAINTED DESERT · Santa Fe ★ · OKLAHOMA ★ Oklahoma City · AR
ARIZONA · NEW MEXICO · Arkansas River · MS
★ Phoenix · Red River
PACIFIC OCEAN · Colorado River · Pecos River · TEXAS · LA · 30°N
★ Austin
Rio Grande · Gulf of Mexico
SOUTHWEST · MEXICO · ★ State capital
0 100 200 Miles
0 100 200 Kilometers
110°W · 90°W

MAP WORK

Besides the Grand Canyon, another place of note is the Painted Desert. Its hills and plateaus are in shades of blue, purple, red, and gold.

1. Which bodies of water border the Southwestern region?

2. Which states lie along the northern border of the Southwest?

3. How do you think the Southwest changes as you travel from west to east?

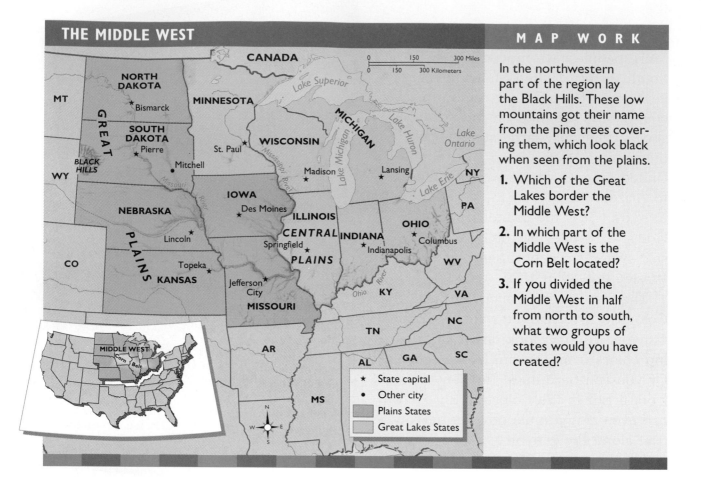

MAP WORK

In the northwestern part of the region lay the Black Hills. These low mountains got their name from the pine trees covering them, which look black when seen from the plains.

1. Which of the Great Lakes border the Middle West?

2. In which part of the Middle West is the Corn Belt located?

3. If you divided the Middle West in half from north to south, what two groups of states would you have created?

Map labels:
CANADA
0 150 300 Miles
0 150 300 Kilometers
MT
NORTH DAKOTA ★ Bismarck
MINNESOTA
Lake Superior
SOUTH DAKOTA ★ Pierre
MICHIGAN
Lake Huron
Lake Ontario
WISCONSIN
St. Paul
Madison ★
Lansing ★
Lake Michigan
NY
GREAT
BLACK HILLS
• Mitchell
Mississippi River
WY
IOWA
Des Moines ★
Lake Erie
PA
NEBRASKA
Missouri River
ILLINOIS
OHIO
Columbus ★
Lincoln ★
CENTRAL
INDIANA
Indianapolis ★
WV
PLAINS
Springfield ★
CO
Topeka ★
PLAINS
KANSAS
Jefferson City ★
Ohio River
KY
VA
MISSOURI
NC
TN
AR
VA
AL
GA
SC
MS

MIDDLE WEST
Corn Belt

★ State capital
• Other city
Plains States
Great Lakes States

N
W E
S

Chicago is the largest city in the Middle West, where many prize-winning farm animals are raised.

THE MIDDLE WEST

The Middle West has been called the breadbasket of the United States. Nowhere is that nickname more true than at the Corn Palace in Mitchell, South Dakota. Here people have put up a palace to honor a plant on which they have built their own way of life. People here are so proud of their corn that they tell and write stories about it.

The poet Carl Sandburg wrote about "the boy who climbed a cornstalk growing so fast he would have starved to death if they hadn't shot biscuits up to him."

Mitchell is in a part of the Middle West called the Corn Belt. Find the Corn Belt on the locator map. Here, on the flat land of the Great Plains, growing corn is a way of life.

THE SOUTHEAST

Big things sometimes start out little. In northern Minnesota, a stream so small you can almost jump across it flows out of Lake Itasca. As the stream flows south it gets bigger, much bigger. This is the mighty **Mississippi River**.

Native Americans who speak Algonkian (al GAHNG kee un) call it "big water" and "great river." It also is known as "the father of waters." Find the Mississippi River on the map on this page. People in the Southeast farm the rich lands along the Mississippi. Barges carry goods south to ports in New Orleans or north to cities such as Memphis and St. Louis. The Mississippi is both beautiful and valuable.

The Mississippi River (above) forms the western border of the state of Mississippi, birthplace of Charley Pride (left) and other country music singers.

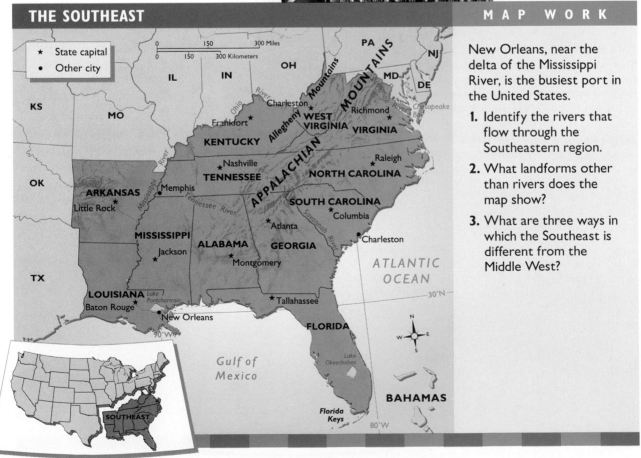

THE SOUTHEAST

Map legend:
★ State capital
● Other city

0 — 150 — 300 Miles
0 — 150 — 300 Kilometers

KS, MO, IL, IN, OH, PA, NJ, MD, DE

Charleston, Frankfort★, KENTUCKY, Nashville★, TENNESSEE, Ohio River, Allegheny Mountains, WEST VIRGINIA, VIRGINIA, Richmond★, Raleigh★, NORTH CAROLINA, APPALACHIAN MOUNTAINS, Chesapeake Bay

OK, ARKANSAS, Little Rock★, Memphis●, Mississippi River, Tennessee River, SOUTH CAROLINA, Columbia★, Savannah River, Charleston●

TX, MISSISSIPPI, Jackson★, ALABAMA, Montgomery★, GEORGIA, Atlanta●, ATLANTIC OCEAN

LOUISIANA, Baton Rouge★, Lake Pontchartrain, New Orleans●, Tallahassee★, FLORIDA, 30°N, 90°W

Gulf of Mexico, Lake Okeechobee, BAHAMAS, Florida Keys, 80°W

SOUTHEAST

MAP WORK

New Orleans, near the delta of the Mississippi River, is the busiest port in the United States.

1. Identify the rivers that flow through the Southeastern region.

2. What landforms other than rivers does the map show?

3. What are three ways in which the Southeast is different from the Middle West?

THE NORTHEAST

What is Boswash? No, it is not a new video game, or a new kind of laundry detergent. It is the name geographers have given to the Northeastern cities running south from Boston, Massachusetts, to Washington, D.C. These cities form a huge megalopolis (meg uh LAHP uh lis). A megalopolis is a group of cities that have grown so close together they seem to form one city. Find Boswash on the map. At night, pilots flying over the Northeast see an unbroken string of city lights.

From above, the nighttime view of Boswash may look like one big mass, but do not tell that to the people who live there! These cities have neighborhoods with their own foods and ways of life. You can almost travel to a different city by only going across town!

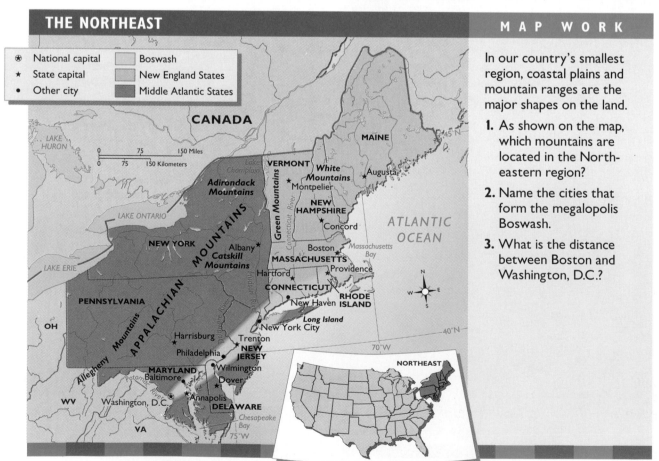

THE NORTHEAST

Legend
- ⊛ National capital
- ★ State capital
- • Other city
- Boswash
- New England States
- Middle Atlantic States

CANADA

LAKE HURON

0   75   150 Miles
0   75   150 Kilometers

Lake Champlain

MAINE
Augusta ★

VERMONT
White Mountains
Montpelier ★

Adirondack Mountains

Green Mountains

NEW HAMPSHIRE
Concord ★

LAKE ONTARIO

NEW YORK
Albany ★
Catskill Mountains

Connecticut River

ATLANTIC OCEAN

Boston
Massachusetts Bay

MASSACHUSETTS

LAKE ERIE

Hartford ★
Providence ★

CONNECTICUT
New Haven

RHODE ISLAND

APPALACHIAN MOUNTAINS

PENNSYLVANIA

Hudson River

Long Island
New York City

OH

Allegheny Mountains

Harrisburg ★
Trenton ★
Philadelphia

NEW JERSEY

70°W

40°N

45°N

Delaware River

MARYLAND
Baltimore
Wilmington
Dover ★

Potomac River

WV

Washington, D.C. ⊛
Annapolis ★

DELAWARE

VA

Chesapeake Bay

75°W

NORTHEAST

MAP WORK

In our country's smallest region, coastal plains and mountain ranges are the major shapes on the land.

1. As shown on the map, which mountains are located in the Northeastern region?

2. Name the cities that form the megalopolis Boswash.

3. What is the distance between Boston and Washington, D.C.?

The light that beams from this lighthouse (left) in the Northeast and the other lights from Boswash's large cities (above, rectangle) can be seen at night from outer space.

There are many other large cities in the Northeast. Some are hundreds of years old. There are also small towns and farms. A scrapbook of the Northeast would show that its people enjoy a variety of ways of life.

WHY IT MATTERS

This scrapbook has taken you all over the United States. It has also given you a look at some of the special places in each of our country's regions. As you read about the history of the United States in the pages ahead, you will revisit these regions.

Although each region of our country is special, all of our country's regions are becoming more interdependent. *Interdependent* means "depending on each other to meet needs and wants." Our country's regions depend on each other in many different ways. Metals

mined in the West are turned into tools and cars by Middle Western workers in factories. Fruits and vegetables grown in the Southeast feed city dwellers in other regions.

Often the weather will affect this interdependence. For example, a bad storm in Florida might cause a shortage of oranges in Boston markets. You will read more about weather in the United States and how it affects people's lives in the next lesson.

Reviewing Facts and Ideas

MAIN IDEAS

- A region is a large area with common features that set it apart from other areas.
- Regions discussed in this lesson are the West, Southwest, Middle West, Southeast, and Northeast. However, there are other ways to divide our country into regions.
- Our country's regions depend on each other to meet needs and wants.

THINK ABOUT IT

1. What are some of the features geographers can use to define a region?

2. Describe a landform that is located in the region where you live. Explain how the landform affects the way of life there.

3. **FOCUS** What are the five regions of the United States and what are some special features of each?

4. **THINKING SKILL** What *generalizations* can you make about each of the regions of the United States?

5. **WRITE** Suppose that you had visited the special places in this lesson. Prepare a scrapbook describing your visit to a friend.

Our Country's Climate

Focus Activity

READ TO LEARN

What kind of climates do Arid America and Humid America have?

VOCABULARY

- climate
- temperature
- precipitation
- arid
- humid

Read Aloud

"Everybody talks about the weather but nobody does anything about it," complained a witty writer named Mark Twain. How often have you said, "It's too hot!" or "It's too cold!" Perhaps you have also said, "I hope it doesn't rain on our game," or "I can hardly wait for the first snow day!"

THE BIG PICTURE

We talk a great deal about the weather because it affects our lives so much. It makes it possible for us to have fun on the beach or it can force us to spend a summer weekend indoors.

Weather in the United States differs a great deal from region to region. This means that each region also has a different **climate**. Climate is the weather an area has over a number of years. The climate of a place includes its general **temperature**, or the measurement of heat and cold. **Precipitation** (prih sihp ih TAY shun) is another important part of climate. Precipitation is the moisture that falls to Earth as rain or snow.

Climates vary for several reasons. One important factor that affects a region's climate is its distance from the equator. Places near the equator are usually warm or hot most of the year. Places farther away are colder. If you moved to a place near the equator, you could probably leave your scarf and gloves behind.

ARID AMERICA

Geographers study the climate of the United States by dividing it into two different areas of precipitation. They use two key words. One is arid, which means dry. The other is humid, which means wet. On the map on this page, find the line that divides Arid and Humid America. Most of Arid America receives less than 20 inches of precipitation a year. In Humid America, more than 20 inches of precipitation usually falls each year.

A Varied Climate

Much of Arid America lies in the Great Basin of the West and the deserts of the Southwest. The driest place in the United States is Death Valley, California. It receives less than two inches of precipitation a year. But you will also find other kinds of places with a variety of temperatures. In the Rocky Mountains the peaks are capped with snow all year. In Washington State and Oregon, a wetter, warmer climate allows vast forests of pine and fir to grow.

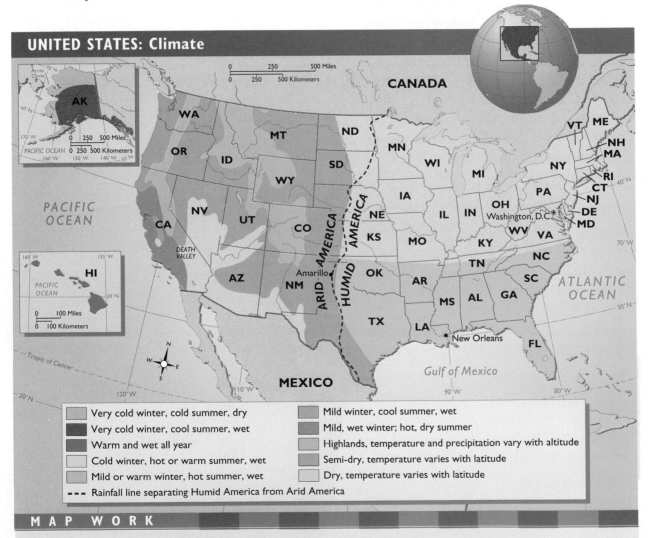

UNITED STATES: Climate

Legend:
- Very cold winter, cold summer, dry
- Very cold winter, cool summer, wet
- Warm and wet all year
- Cold winter, hot or warm summer, wet
- Mild or warm winter, hot summer, wet
- Mild winter, cool summer, wet
- Mild, wet winter; hot, dry summer
- Highlands, temperature and precipitation vary with altitude
- Semi-dry, temperature varies with latitude
- Dry, temperature varies with latitude
- - - Rainfall line separating Humid America from Arid America

MAP WORK

As the map above shows, the United States has a variety of climates, ranging from tropical heat to arctic cold.

1. Which states are found in both Arid America and Humid America?

2. Which states have a wet climate with warm winters and cool summers?

3. Which part of Humid America has a warmer climate?

HUMID AMERICA

How many times have you heard, "It's not the heat. It's the humidity"? You are more likely to have heard it in Humid America than Arid America.

The bar graph on this page shows precipitation in New Orleans, Louisiana, and Amarillo, Texas. Use the map on page 37 to find whether they are located in Arid or in Humid America.

A Moist Climate

Humid America stretches from the Atlantic Ocean in the East to the edges of the Great Plains in the West. From north to south, it extends from the Great Lakes to the Gulf of Mexico. People in the Northeast and around the Great Lakes have hot, steamy summers and cold, often snowy winters. In the Southeast frequent rains and warmer temperatures create a great deal of humid weather.

Contrasting Views

Down through the years Americans have written about our country's climates. In the 1940s the writer Marjory Stoneman Douglas described the climate of Florida's Everglades.

> *In the course of a single day so much rain will fall, as much sometimes as ten or twelve inches, that the glitter of rising water will be everywhere.*

Contrast her view of our country's climate with the following excerpt from a book written by Byrd Baylor.

> *Rain is a blessing*
> *counted*
> *drop*
> *by*
> *drop.*

Did you recognize the two areas of precipitation?

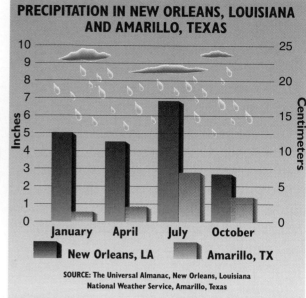

PRECIPITATION IN NEW ORLEANS, LOUISIANA AND AMARILLO, TEXAS

Inches / Centimeters — January, April, July, October

■ New Orleans, LA   ▧ Amarillo, TX

SOURCE: The Universal Almanac, New Orleans, Louisiana National Weather Service, Amarillo, Texas

GRAPH WORK

For the people of New Orleans, Louisiana, and Amarillo, Texas, **precipitation** is a major factor in their way of life.

1. Which city receives more precipitation?
2. During which month does Amarillo receive the least precipitation?

WHY IT MATTERS

As you have read, the different regions of the United States have different climates. If someday you were to travel across the country, you would have to be sure to pack the right kinds of clothes for each of the different climates. During your trip you would see how the different climates have influenced the way people work and play. You would also see the creative ways people have improved their lives in difficult climates.

In the next lesson, you will read about other ways people react to many different surroundings.

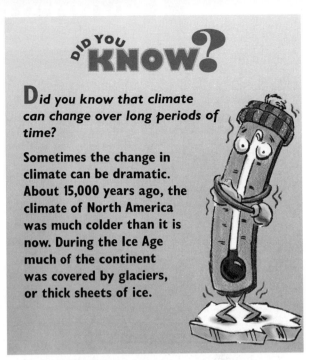

DID YOU KNOW?

Did you know that climate can change over long periods of time?

Sometimes the change in climate can be dramatic. About 15,000 years ago, the climate of North America was much colder than it is now. During the Ice Age much of the continent was covered by glaciers, or thick sheets of ice.

✓ Reviewing Facts and Ideas

MAIN IDEAS

- Climate is the weather an area has over a long period of time. It includes temperature and precipitation.
- Climate affects people's daily lives, as well as activities such as farming.
- Arid America is generally dry and receives less than 20 inches of precipitation a year.
- Humid America is generally wet and receives over 20 inches of precipitation a year.

The saguaro cactus (top left) is a common plant in the arid climate of the desert. In Humid America, on the other hand, rainfall is plentiful.

THINK ABOUT IT

1. What is the difference between weather and climate?

2. A man named Philander Johnson wrote this jingle about weather:

   *Oh, what a blamed uncertain thing
   This pesky weather is;
   It blew and snew and then it thew,
   And now, by jing, it friz.*

   Did he live in Arid America or Humid America? Explain your answer.

3. **FOCUS** What is climate and how does it affect people's lives?

4. **THINKING SKILL** What _conclusions_ would you make about how living in Arid America or Humid America would affect your way of life?

5. **GEOGRAPHY** Make a chart that describes each climate of the United States.

Understanding Latitude and Longitude

VOCABULARY

latitude   degree   prime meridian
longitude   meridian   grid
parallel

WHY THE SKILL MATTERS

You have been reading about the climates of the United States. As you know, places near the equator are warmer than places far from the equator. To locate places on Earth, geographers have drawn two sets of imaginary lines on maps and globes called latitude and longitude. Lines of latitude run east and west. Lines of longitude run north and south.

USING LATITUDE AND LONGITUDE

Lines of latitude measure distance north and south of the equator. Lines of latitude are also called parallels. *Parallel* means "always the same distance apart." Parallels never meet. Find the equator on the map below. The equator is labeled 0° latitude. The symbol ° stands for a degree. A degree is a unit of measurement.

Lines of latitude north of the equator are labeled **N**. Those south of the equator are labeled **S**. On the latitude map below, the lines of latitude running through the United States are 45°N and 30°N.

Longitude lines are also called meridians. They measure distance east and west of the prime meridian. The prime meridian is the line of longitude labeled 0° longitude. Any place east of the prime meridian is labeled **E**. Any place west of the prime meridian is labeled **W**.

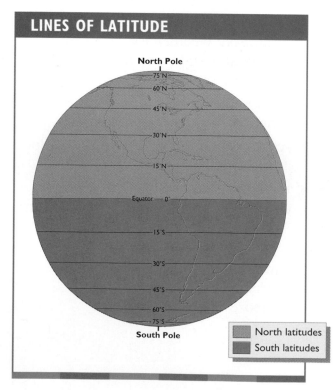

LINES OF LATITUDE

North latitudes
South latitudes

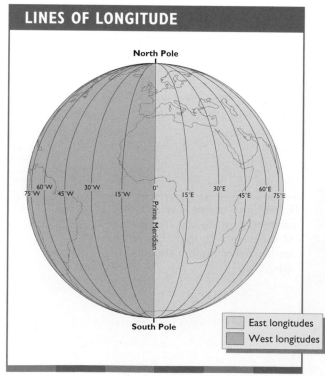

LINES OF LONGITUDE

East longitudes
West longitudes

Because 180°E and 180°W are the same, most maps do not mark it as east or west.

USING THE GRID

A grid helps you use lines of latitude and lines of longitude to find places on a map. A grid is a set of criss-crossing lines. On the map below, each line of latitude crosses the same line of longitude in a different place. Memphis, Tennessee, for example, is located at 35°N latitude and 90°W longitude. Its grid location is 35°N, 90°W.

TRYING THE SKILL

Now use the grid on the map to find New Orleans, Louisiana. At what lines of latitude and longitude is it located? The Helping Yourself box on this page gives a summary of how to use these lines.

Helping yourself

- Lines of **latitude** run north and south of the equator. Lines of **longitude** run east and west of the **prime meridian.**
- Use the **grid** to find where the lines intersect.

When cities are not shown exactly on a line of latitude or longitude on a particular map, use the lines that are closest. Find Springfield, Illinois. What are its closest lines of latitude and longitude?

REVIEWING THE SKILL

1. How do you find a place on a map using lines of latitude and longitude?

2. Between which lines of longitude is the state of Ohio located?

3. Give the grid location of Provo, Utah.

4. In which states do the following lines of latitude and longitude intersect:
   - 35°N, 105°W
   - 40°N, 80°W
   - 45°N, 100°W

5. When would it be helpful to be able to find latitude and longitude on a map?

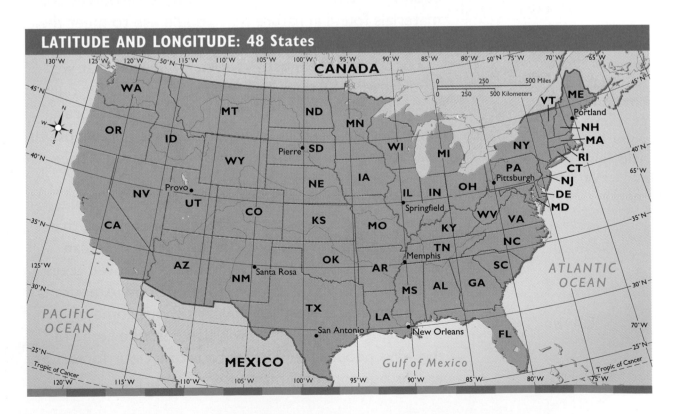

LATITUDE AND LONGITUDE: 48 States

Our Country's Natural Resources

Read Aloud

"When the well's dry, we know the worth of water," wrote Benjamin Franklin in the 1750s. His words are still true today. In the United States we have a great many valuable resources, including water. But we do not always appreciate their value until they become scarce.

Focus Activity

READ TO LEARN

What is a natural resource?

VOCABULARY

- natural resource
- nonrenewable resource
- renewable resource
- mineral
- fossil fuel
- environment
- economy
- pollution
- acid rain
- conservation
- recycle

THE BIG PICTURE

As you have read about our country's regions and its climates, you have also been introduced to many of our country's **natural resources**. Natural resources are materials found in nature that people use to meet their needs and wants.

For a long time most Americans believed that we would always have enough natural resources for our needs. But our country's resources will not last forever. Some, such as the coal, oil, and natural gas that we use to heat and light our homes, cannot be replaced. These resources are called **nonrenewable resources**.

Our forests, on the other hand, are **renewable resources**. Renewable resources are resources that can be replaced. When we cut down trees, we can plant new ones. Yet both old and newly planted trees face many dangers. As you read about how Americans use our forests, you will also learn about some of these dangers. This lesson will also describe some of the ways people are working to protect our forests as well as our country's many other resources.

RICH IN RESOURCES

As the chart on this page shows, all the regions of the United States have important natural resources. People use these resources to make a variety of goods. Some are as simple as bottled water taken from fresh mountain springs. Others, such as computers, can be complicated and made from many separate pieces. How many items in your classroom can you identify that came from natural resources?

Different Kinds of Resources

The United States has many, many natural resources. It can be confusing to identify and discuss resources. Where do they come from? How are they used? One easy way is to divide resources into groups, as shown on the chart on this page. You can see from the chart that some people in the Northeast earn their living by harvesting from the sea such animal resources as lobster. In all regions people use forests, a plant resource, to provide wood for building and paper.

The United States has vast mineral resources. A mineral is a substance found in the earth that is neither a plant nor an animal. Minerals include metals such as iron, copper, and zinc.

Among the most widely used mineral resources are fossil fuels. These fuels were formed over millions of years from fossils, which are the remains of ancient plants or animals. Fossil fuels include the nonrenewable resources oil, coal, and natural gas.

OUR COUNTRY'S NATURAL RESOURCES

REGION	MINERALS	FORESTS PLANTS	FISH WILDLIFE	FOSSIL FUELS
West	Zinc Lead	Cedar Birch	Salmon Tuna Deer	Oil
Southwest	Iron Copper	Oak Cacti	Shrimp Deer Rabbit	Natural Gas Oil
Middle West	Iron Copper	Maple Sunflowers	Bass Deer	Oil Coal
Southeast	Iron	Pine Mangrove	Shrimp Bears	Coal Natural Gas
Northeast	Granite Copper	Fir Maple	Lobster Scallops Deer	Coal

CHART WORK

The United States government has long been working to preserve our natural resources.

1. What wildlife is included among each region's natural resources?

2. What natural resources are found in the Western region?

3. In which region are mangroves found? In which regions is copper found?

FORESTS

The resources that you have been reading about are all part of Earth's **environment**. The environment is made up of all the surroundings in which people, plants, and animals live. One of the most important parts of the environment, and one of our greatest natural resources, is forests.

Forests contribute in important ways to the health of the environment. As trees soak up sunlight they keep the temperature of the air from getting too hot. A tree's roots hold together the soil in which they grow and prevent that soil from washing away. By producing oxygen and removing carbon dioxide from the air, the leaves of trees provide fresh air for us to breathe.

Using Forests

Most people do not think about oxygen and soil when they think about trees, however. You, for example, may think of the forest as a place to camp, to hike, to bird-watch, and to enjoy our country's natural beauty. Some of the most popular places in the United States are national and state parks. As you have read, many parks are covered with forests.

People use forests for many other purposes besides recreation. Forests are an important part of our **economy**. A country's economy is the way its people use natural resources, money, and knowledge to produce goods and services. Can you think of some ways that forests might play a role in our country's economy?

Chairs. Houses. Pencils. Desks. We use the trees of our forests to make a variety of goods. You are looking at one of the most important forest products right now as you read this page: paper. The flow chart on this page shows the many steps involved in turning a tree into paper.

Dangers to Our Forests

People called foresters work to understand how forests grow and how to take care of them. They often decide how many trees can be cut down—and

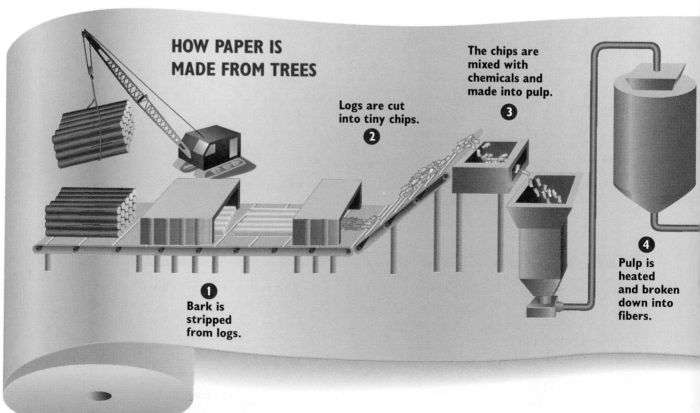

HOW PAPER IS MADE FROM TREES

1 Bark is stripped from logs.

2 Logs are cut into tiny chips.

3 The chips are mixed with chemicals and made into pulp.

4 Pulp is heated and broken down into fibers.

The lushness of this healthy green forest in North Carolina (left) seems remarkable when compared to the damage caused by acid rain (below).

when, where, and how many new trees to plant. They also work to protect forests from insects and diseases.

One of the most serious threats to our forests comes from pollution. Pollution is something—such as harmful chemicals—that makes our air, soil, and water dirty. Sometimes these chemicals mix with moisture in the air. When the polluted moisture falls to the ground, it is called acid rain. In spite of its name,

acid rain can take the form of snow, dew, or frost.

Acid rain can destroy trees and pollute the soil so it cannot support new growth. But the problem does not stop there. When forests die, animals must find new shelter. Acid rain can also pollute rivers and lakes and, therefore, kill fish as well.

How can we reduce the effects of acid rain? One thing that people can do is limit the amount of harmful chemicals that are released into the air. These chemicals often come from burning fossil fuels, such as gasoline in automobiles. Scientists and workers from business and government are studying cleaner ways to burn fossil fuels.

Chemicals and unwanted materials are removed from the fibers.
5

Dried sheets of paper are pressed smooth on rollers.
7

The paper is rolled onto reels and stored.
8

6
Fibers are poured onto a wire mesh, dried, and shaped into sheets.

The making of paper from trees involves a number of complex steps. By which step has the wood been turned into something else?

OTHER RESOURCES

You read on the chart on page 43 that the United States has many natural resources in addition to its forests. Such natural resources add to our country's beauty. Katharine Lee Bates wrote about this beauty as she traveled west to Colorado. Her poem, "America, the Beautiful," was published in 1910 as the song many know today. You also read about the effects of acid rain, and how our natural resources are related. There would be no forests without plentiful, clean water and rich, healthy soil.

Soil and Water

Soil, like forests, must be protected. Scientists are researching ways to use soil wisely. Using fewer harmful chemicals and growing different crops at different times help to restore the soil and to keep it healthy.

The water from our country's lakes, rivers, and streams is another valuable resource. Did you know that Americans use about 400 billion gallons of water each day? But only a small amount is used for washing and drinking. Most water is used to irrigate farmlands or to provide steam for power plants. People are working hard to find ways in which farms and factories can use water more wisely.

People Are a Resource

When people work to protect our environment and its natural resources, they are practicing conservation. Conservation is the protection and careful use of natural resources.

When people practice conservation they are using another important resource: themselves! Without people's creativity and skill, it would not be possible to make natural resources like forests into useful goods like paper.

Irrigation puts to use two valuable natural resources, water and soil (left). Scientists (below) looking for better ways to help such people as farmers are an important human resource.

America, the Beautiful

Words by Katharine Lee Bates, 1893;
music by Samuel Ward, 1882.

O beau - ti - ful for spa - cious skies, For am - ber waves of grain.

For pur - ple moun - tain maj - es - ties, A - bove the fruit - ed plain,

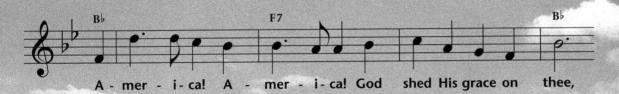

A - mer - i - ca! A - mer - i - ca! God shed His grace on thee,

And crown thy good with broth - er - hood, From sea to shin - ing sea.

RESOURCES FOR THE FUTURE

Americans work together to conserve our country's resources. One way that you can practice conservation is by **recycling**. Recycling means using something again. All over the country, people are no longer only throwing things away. They are saving them so that they can be used again. We can cut down fewer trees if, instead of throwing paper away, we recycle it to make cardboard or other paper products. Only by protecting and using natural resources carefully can we be sure they will be available in the future. Have you used any items that have been recycled?

WHY IT MATTERS

Natural resources are an important part of our country's economy. Many factors affect the types of goods and services people can afford. A plentiful supply of resources is one. If a resource were to be all used up, people might not be able to buy a particular product or service at all. We can prevent such harm to our country's economy by conserving and recycling natural resources today.

MAIN IDEAS

- The United States has many natural resources. Some are renewable, but others are nonrenewable.
- One of the most important natural resources is our forests. Forests serve the environment, provide recreation areas, and support our country's economy.
- People are also an important resource. They use their creativity and skill to practice conservation of natural resources.

THINK ABOUT IT

1. Name one natural resource for the headings *animal, plant,* and *mineral.*
2. Describe three products that people make out of trees.
3. **FOCUS** Why are forests one of our country's most important natural resources?
4. **THINKING SKILL** How would you *decide* which methods of recycling would work best in your community or your school?
5. **WRITE** Write a poem or song that celebrates the beauty of the United States or your region of the country.

Recycling is one way that all Americans can help to conserve our country's natural resources.

PLASTIC

MAKING A DIFFERENCE

Making the Land Green Again

NORTH ARLINGTON, NEW JERSEY—Little by little, seventh graders at North Arlington Middle School are turning land-fills—areas where garbage is buried—into wildlife garden parks where butterflies, birds, owls, and bats come to feed and nest. Since 1996, 118 student volunteers have planted 1,000 flowering plants and shrubs in an area that was once a landfill. So far their work has created three butterfly gardens on a half acre of land.

The land is located near the city of Newark, New Jersey, one of the most populated urban areas in the United States. "The former landfill," says teacher Lois Chen, "is one of the few remaining areas of open space around here. The students are helping to preserve it and make it into an area where people can enjoy bird watching, bicycling, walking, and jogging."

Before volunteers planted the flowers and shrubs, they researched what plants to buy. They wanted plants that would attract butterflies, bluebirds, and songbirds. "We chose" says volunteer Kathy Lam, "flowering plants like butterfly bush and butterfly weed and brown-eyed susan. They all make good food for caterpillars and for butterflies."

The town of North Arlington is on the flight path of birds that fly north to Canada from South America in the spring. Kathy says, "We wanted the birds to make our gardens a stopping place and nesting ground."

On Earth Day, April 22, 1996, the planting began. Four months later, students knew their gardens were a success. By August, volunteers had seen 12 different species of butterflies in the gardens and as many as 100 butterflies at a time.

The students' work is far from over. Many landfills remain. As each fills up, county workers will cover it with layers of new earth. Students will be adding a nature discovery center and planting trees. Kathy is looking forward to this new project. "Instead of just sitting around doing nothing for the environment, I feel good knowing that I am helping to make it green again."

"... I feel good knowing that I am helping ..."

Kathy Lam

CHAPTER 2 REVIEW

THINKING ABOUT VOCABULARY

Number a paper from 1 to 10. Beside each number write the word or term from the list below that correctly completes the sentence.

climate	interdependent
conservation	megalopolis
economy	nonrenewable resources
environment	precipitation
geography	regions

1. The study of the planet Earth and the way people live on it and use it is called _____.

2. _____ is the moisture that falls to Earth as rain or snow.

3. Coal, oil, and natural gas are all examples of _____.

4. Earth's _____ is made up of all the surroundings in which people, plants, and animals live.

5. _____ is the weather that an area has over a number of years, including its general temperature.

6. The United States can be divided into _____, or large areas with common features.

7. A _____ is a group of cities so close together that they seem to form one large city.

8. The protection and careful use of our planet's natural resources is called _____.

9. The way a country uses its natural resources, money, and knowledge to produce goods and services is called its _____.

10. To be _____ is to depend on each other for needs and wants.

THINKING ABOUT FACTS

1. Why do geographers divide the United States into regions?

2. This chapter divides the United States into regions of West, Southwest, Middle West, Southeast, and Northeast. Name another way to divide the United States into regions. Why might you want to do it that way?

3. What is the name of the large river that starts as a small stream in northern Minnesota?

4. What is Boswash?

5. What is the nickname of the Middle West? Why is this a good nickname for the region?

6. How are the regions of the United States interdependent?

7. In what ways does the distance of a country or region from the equator affect its climate?

8. What areas of the United States are included in Humid America? What areas are included in Arid America?

9. How does climate affect our daily lives?

10. What are natural resources? Name two categories into which natural resources can be divided.

11. What are fossil fuels? Name two examples of fossil fuels.

12. Use the chart on page 43 to name one natural resource from each region in the United States.

13. In what ways are forests important to our economy?

14. What is acid rain? How does it affect the environment?

15. How can people be considered a resource?

WRITING A TRAVEL BROCHURE

Choose a location in the United States, such as the Corn Palace or some spot you have visited. Write a brochure that describes the attractions of the place for visitors.

WRITING DIARY ENTRIES

Suppose that you are on a trip across the United States. Write a series of diary entries that describe what you might see in each region you visit.

WRITING A PARAGRAPH OF CONTRAST

Write a paragraph that summarizes the differences between Arid America and Humid America.

APPLYING GEOGRAPHY SKILLS

UNDERSTANDING LATITUDE AND LONGITUDE

Answer the following questions, using the grid map of the 48 states on page 41 to practice the skill of understanding latitude and longitude.

1. How can you recognize maps showing latitude and longitude?
2. Which steps would you follow to find 90°N, 120°W?
3. Locate Springfield, Illinois, on the grid map. At what line of latitude is it found?
4. Is the state of New Mexico east or west of 110°W?
5. How are maps showing latitude and longitude useful?

Summing Up the Chapter

Copy this chart on a separate piece of paper. Review the chapter to fill in the blank sections of the matrix chart below. After you have finished, use the information in the chart to answer the question "How would you describe the geography of the United States?"

REGION	CLIMATE	RESOURCES	LANDFORMS
West	Arid, rainy in northwest, varied		
Southwest			Painted Desert, Grand Canyon
Middle West			
Southeast		Minerals, forests, soil	
Northeast			

UNIT 1 REVIEW

THINKING ABOUT VOCABULARY

Number a paper from 1 to 15. Beside each number write the word or term from the list below that best matches the description.

alternative

ancestor

decision

democracy

economy

ethnic group

federal

landform

mineral

natural resource

oral history

pollution

temperature

unity

values

1. A shape on Earth's surface

2. Another word for choice

3. Something that makes air, soil, or water dirty

4. Beliefs or ideals that guide the way people live

5. Another word for *national*

6. A country in which the people create laws and run the government

7. People whose backgrounds include the same customs and language

8. Being as one

9. Another way of doing something

10. A relative who lived before you

11. A material found in nature that people use to meet needs and wants

12. Spoken records

13. The way a country's people use their natural resources, money, and knowledge to produce goods and services

14. The measurement of heat and cold

15. A substance found in the earth that is neither plant nor animal

THINK AND WRITE

WRITING AN EDITORIAL

Think about the issues affecting natural resources, such as the dangers forests face from acid rain. Write a newspaper editorial in which you discuss the need to pay closer attention to conserving natural resources.

WRITING A REPORT

Choose a culture different from your own, and find out about one of its holidays. You may find your information in a book or by speaking to someone who celebrates the holiday you choose. Write a report about what the holiday means and when and how it is celebrated.

WRITING ABOUT PERSPECTIVES

Think of a place in the United States in which the climate is completely different from that in the area in which you live. Write a letter from the point of view of a fifth grader who lives there in which you describe a typical day.

BUILDING SKILLS

1. **Decision making** How do you decide what to do on a day off from school?

2. **Decision making** What are the results of decision making?

3. **Decision making** How might a speech or commercial affect a voter's decision on whom to vote for in an election?

4. **Latitude and longitude** What lines of latitude and longitude run through the state in which you live? Refer to the atlas map on pages R8–R9.

5. **Latitude and longitude** How can a grid map help you locate a city or a specific area?

YESTERDAY, TODAY & *TOMORROW*

Historic places help us to keep history alive. Are there any historic places in your area that have been preserved for the future? Think of a place, like your school, that you use or visit every day. What would people from the future learn about daily life today if that place were preserved?

READING ON YOUR OWN

Here are some books you might find at the library to help you learn more.

. . . IF YOUR NAME WAS CHANGED AT ELLIS ISLAND
by Ellen Levine
This book explains the experience of coming to the United States for various immigrants.

OUR NATIONAL PARKS
by Donald Young
This guided tour of our nation's parks highlights their history and describes their main attractions.

WHO BELONGS HERE: AN AMERICAN STORY
by Margy Burns Knight
The author describes the story of a ten-year-old who comes to live in a new country.

UNIT 1 REVIEW PROJECT

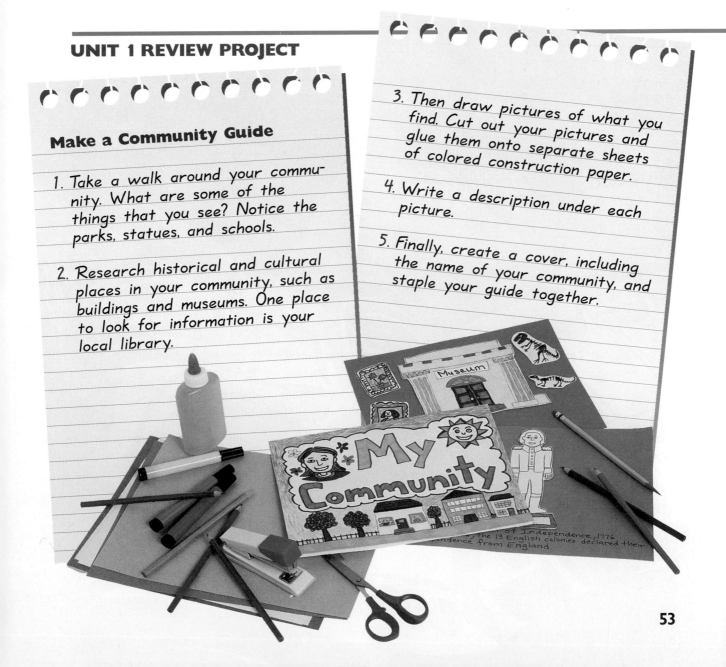

Make a Community Guide

1. Take a walk around your community. What are some of the things that you see? Notice the parks, statues, and schools.

2. Research historical and cultural places in your community, such as buildings and museums. One place to look for information is your local library.

3. Then draw pictures of what you find. Cut out your pictures and glue them onto separate sheets of colored construction paper.

4. Write a description under each picture.

5. Finally, create a cover, including the name of your community, and staple your guide together.

MAYA MURAL

AZTEC KNIGHT CARVING;
NORTHWEST COAST
TOTEM POLE

Culture West and East

"We must have but one voice."

from a speech by Hiawatha
See page 106.

Why Does it Matter?

Many thousands of years ago, a land bridge rose out of the cold northern sea, connecting the Western and Eastern hemispheres. People and animals crossed back and forth between the continents of North America and Asia.

Many centuries later, the people of the Western and Eastern hemispheres were building great cities, farming, trading, and developing unique cultures. The quote above from Hiawatha, an Iroquois leader, explains why different Iroquois groups united to form a representative government. This government is one example of the ways in which many cultures have shaped our country.

CHINESE PORCELAIN VASE

FIND OUT MORE!

Visit our website:
www.mhschool.com

*inter*NET
CONNECTION

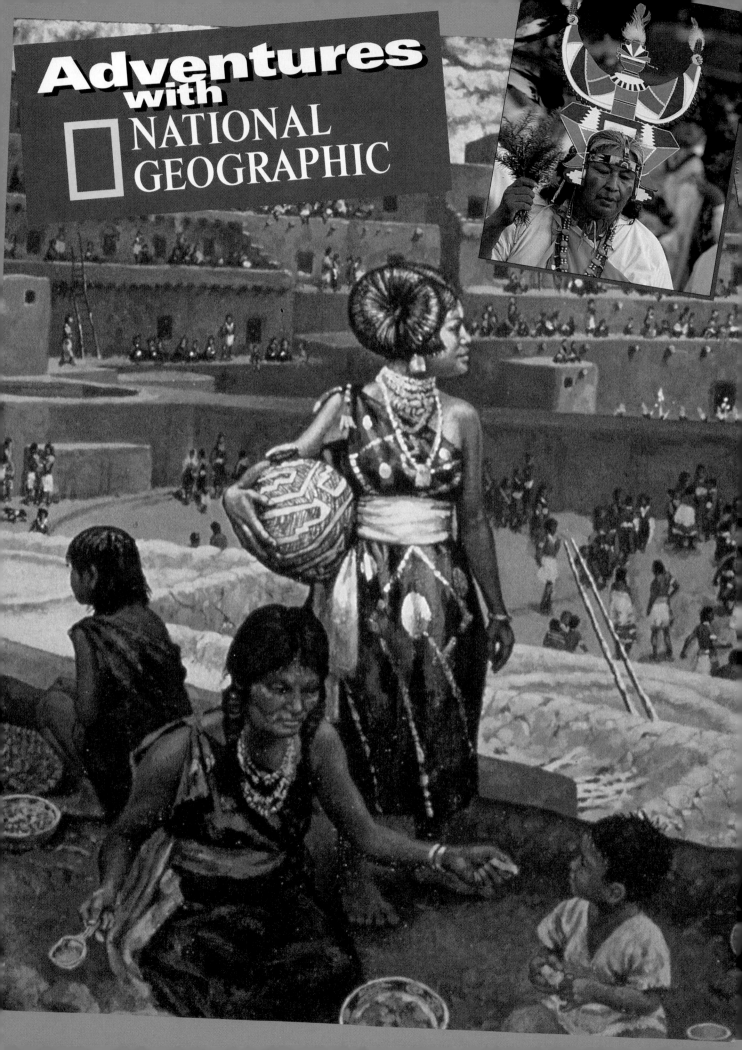

Adventures
with
NATIONAL
GEOGRAPHIC

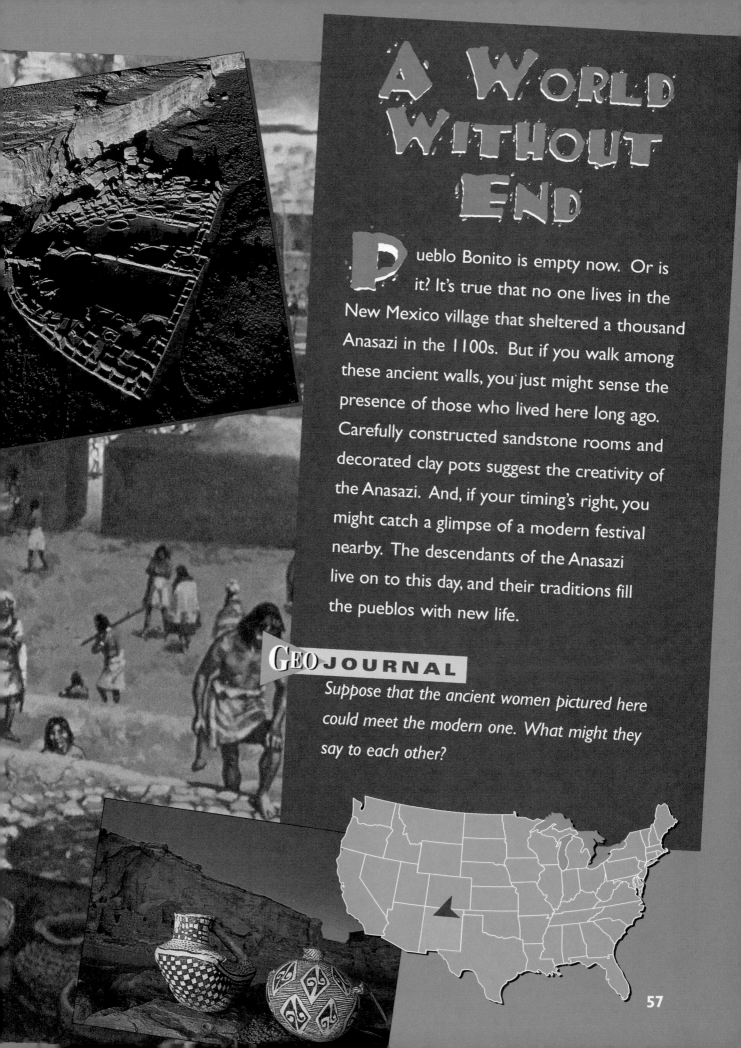

A World Without End

Pueblo Bonito is empty now. Or is it? It's true that no one lives in the New Mexico village that sheltered a thousand Anasazi in the 1100s. But if you walk among these ancient walls, you just might sense the presence of those who lived here long ago. Carefully constructed sandstone rooms and decorated clay pots suggest the creativity of the Anasazi. And, if your timing's right, you might catch a glimpse of a modern festival nearby. The descendants of the Anasazi live on to this day, and their traditions fill the pueblos with new life.

GEOJOURNAL

Suppose that the ancient women pictured here could meet the modern one. What might they say to each other?

CHAPTER 3

Early Peoples of the Western Hemisphere

THINKING ABOUT HISTORY AND GEOGRAPHY

The story of Chapter 3 begins in Central America nearly 2,000 years ago. Read the time line below to follow the major events of this chapter. Notice that the background color of each event is the same color as a square on the map. Each square marks the location of that event. As you read the chapter, you will learn more about the different groups of people that lived throughout the Western Hemisphere.

195

TIKAL
The Maya build cities in Mexico and Central America

900s

PUEBLO BONITO
The Anasazi build large towns

1200s

CAHOKIA
The Mound Builders establish a trade center along the Mississippi River

195

900

1100

NORTH AMERICA

Pueblo Bonito

Cahokia

ATLANTIC OCEAN

Gulf of Mexico

Tenochtitlán

PACIFIC OCEAN

Tikal

CENTRAL AMERICA

Caribbean Sea

1440

TENOCHTITLÁN
The Aztec rule central Mexico

1471

CUZCO
The Inca carve roads out of the steep Andes Mountains

SOUTH AMERICA

Cuzco

1300

1500

| 250 | 900 | 1200 | 1500 |

The Maya

Read Aloud

An ancient story describes Maya beliefs about how human beings were created. In this story, people were made first of clay, then of wood, and then of reeds, but they did not survive. The fourth people, who were made of corn dough, did survive. They became the Maya. This creation story helps to explain the importance of corn to the Maya. Corn was the key to life itself.

Focus Activity

READ TO LEARN

What did the Maya civilization achieve?

VOCABULARY

- civilization
- surplus
- specialize
- archaeologist

PLACES

- Tikal

THE BIG PICTURE

You have read in the last chapter that people are an important resource. In this chapter you will read about how ancient peoples used their skills and creativity to form some of the major **civilizations** in the Western Hemisphere. Civilization is a word used to describe a kind of culture. A civilization is a culture that has developed complex systems of government, education, and religion. Often it has large populations, with some people living in large cities. One reason that scholars and students like you study past civilizations is that they leave lasting legacies for people today.

Farming was the key to the development of most civilizations. About 7,000 years ago people in the Western Hemisphere learned to plant seeds from foods they ate. As they learned about farming, people were able to grow a **surplus** of food. A surplus is an amount greater than what is needed. People no longer had to spend all their time hunting for food. They could **specialize**, or spend most of their time doing one kind of job. Some people took up jobs such as weaving, building, and making pottery. The Maya were an ancient civilization in what are now southern Mexico and Central America.

MAYA CITIES

Imagine walking through the dense rain forest of what is now Guatemala 1,700 years ago. Suddenly, like a snow-capped mountain range, bright white shapes appear. This is not a mountain range, though. It is the Maya city of **Tikal** (ti KAHL).

Tikal, one of the oldest Maya cities, was first built about 1,800 years ago. It had a population of about 50,000. Find other Maya cities, such as Copán (koh PAHN), Palenque (puh LENG kay), and Bonampak (boh nahm PAHK) on the map below.

The Abandoned Cities

If you visit Tikal today, its buildings still seem to rise out of nowhere. But now the buildings are empty. Once they were the center of a civilization. What happened to the people of Tikal and the other Maya cities?

This is one of the most puzzling questions in history. **Archaeologists** (ar kee AHL uh jists) have studied monuments that the Maya have left behind in their cities. An archaeologist is a scientist who looks for and studies

This is one of two temples the Maya built in the main plaza at Tikal in the present-day country of Guatemala. Thousands visit the site each year.

evidence from long ago. Beginning about the year 292, the Maya built many monuments. Some, shaped like tall columns, have pictures of rulers. Others were built to ask their gods for success in battle and for good corn harvests. But in the year 909, the Maya built the last of their monuments.

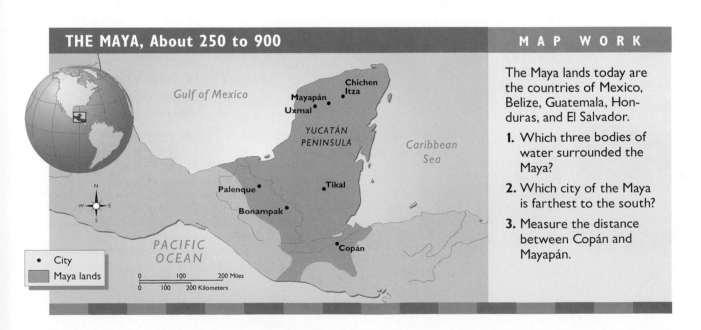

THE MAYA, About 250 to 900

Gulf of Mexico

Chichen Itza

Mayapán

Uxmal

YUCATÁN PENINSULA

Caribbean Sea

Palenque

Tikal

Bonampak

PACIFIC OCEAN

Copán

- City
- Maya lands

0   100   200 Miles
0   100   200 Kilometers

M A P   W O R K

The Maya lands today are the countries of Mexico, Belize, Guatemala, Honduras, and El Salvador.

1. Which three bodies of water surrounded the Maya?

2. Which city of the Maya is farthest to the south?

3. Measure the distance between Copán and Mayapán.

THE RISE OF THE MAYA

Archaeologists believe that the Maya civilization began about 2,300 years ago in what is now southern Mexico and the country of Guatemala. The Maya built stone temples that were hundreds of feet tall. They were one of the first people in the Western Hemisphere to do so.

Maya Farmers

Maya farmers grew a plentiful supply of food for a large population. They used their knowledge of the environment to get the most out of their land. In hilly areas farmers built terraces to make level surfaces for planting. In swampy areas they built raised islands by piling up soil above the water. Farmers also moved their fields from place to place to help keep the soil from wearing out.

Although the Maya grew a variety of crops, corn was their main source of food. People made corn dough into flat cakes, like tortillas people eat today.

The Granger Collection

This statue of a Maya corn god was probably used by farmers during both planting and harvesting ceremonies.

Maya Writing

The Maya were not only good farmers. They were artists, scientists, and historians. The Maya also wrote a large number of books. Archaeologists have found written records of dates, times, and events on the Maya calendar. The Maya's invention of the idea of the number zero helped to keep their calendar accurate.

The Maya were one of the first people in the Western Hemisphere to develop an advanced form of writing. Their writing system used symbols that stood for both pictures and sounds in place of written words. The photograph below shows how the Maya language was written. Three of the symbols are translated. Why do you think it might have taken the Maya a long time to learn how to write these symbols?

BUNDLE

ENTERED THE ROAD

BUILDING

MANY VOICES
PRIMARY SOURCE

Maya writing symbols from a wall inside Temple 18 at Palenque, Mexico.

The symbols on this wall are plaster copies of the originals. They were assembled by archaeologists who could not read Maya writing. The symbols do not appear in the order in which the Maya wrote them.

Looking for Answers

What happened to the Maya civilization after 909? One of their ancient books says that foreigners arrived and "there were no more lucky days for us." Did invaders conquer the Maya?

Scholars believe that wars helped cause the end of Maya civilization. Scholars had thought that the Maya were peaceful. New evidence shows that they carried out human sacrifice, or killed people in special ceremonies. Some experts believe that food shortages *and* wars caused Maya civilization to end. All these problems probably weakened the Maya. The disappearance of the Maya civilization, although still a mystery, is slowly being made clear.

WHY IT MATTERS

The Maya cities were abandoned, but the Maya people lived on in the surrounding countryside. Descendants of the Maya live today in present-day Guatemala and Mexico. They still speak a Maya language and follow many customs and traditions that are similar to those of the ancient Maya. Later Indian people, such as the Aztec, also carried on Maya traditions in art, science, and mathematics.

A present-day Maya woman weaves cloth using a traditional loom in Chiapas, Mexico.

DID YOU KNOW?

What sports did the Maya play?

A Maya ball game called pokta-pok seems to have been a combination of basketball, volleyball, and soccer. Great crowds came to see the game. The object of pokta-pok was to put a heavy rubber ball through a stone hoop. Winners of the game were rewarded with clothing or with money in the form of cacao (kuh KAH oh) beans. Cacao beans are used to make chocolate.

✓✓ Reviewing Facts and Ideas

MAIN IDEAS

- Farming enabled the ancient people of the Western Hemisphere, such as the Maya, to develop civilizations.
- The Maya began building cities about 1,800 years ago. They also developed a system of writing that was unique in the Western Hemisphere.

THINK ABOUT IT

1. How did farming lead to the development of civilizations?

2. What kind of activities took place in the Maya cities?

3. **FOCUS** What accomplishments did the Maya achieve in mathematics?

4. **THINKING SKILL** *Predict* what might have happened if the Maya civilization had continued into the present day. Explain.

5. **WRITE** Write a story about what you think happened when the Maya left their cities.

National Geographic Society

300   600   900   1100   1440   1500

The Aztec

Focus Activity

READ TO LEARN

How did the Aztec create their empire?

VOCABULARY

- empire
- tribute
- slavery

PLACES

- Valley of Mexico
- Tenochtitlán

Read Aloud

The following poem is translated from an Aztec language called Nahuatl (NAH wah tuhl). First written down in the 1500s, it explains why the quetzal (ket SAHL) bird is important to the Aztec.

> *Listen!*
> *I am the singer*
> *I am singing*
> *the pictures of the book*
> *I am the blue-and-green bird*
> *I make the [books] speak*
> *I am the quetzal.*

THE BIG PICTURE

After the Maya civilization ended, other civilizations in the Western Hemisphere rose and fell. None, however, was able to gain power over a very large area. Then, in the 1100s and 1200s, two civilizations began to succeed in gaining power.

By the 1500s the Inca people had built an **empire** that stretched over 1,000 miles. An empire is a large area of different groups of people controlled by one ruler or government. The Inca empire was located mostly in the Andes Mountains, along the west coast of South America. Farther north lay the empire of the Aztec people. It controlled much of the southern part of what is now Mexico.

Both the Aztec and the Inca had strong armies, powerful leaders, and expert builders. These qualities helped to make their empires strong. This lesson will focus on how the Aztec empire was formed.

THE VALLEY OF MEXICO

In the 1100s the Aztec came to the Valley of Mexico. They had not yet formed an empire. They were one of many newcomers in the area seeking a home. Much of inland Mexico is dry. But in the valley are several lakes. Around 1325 the Aztec settled on the shores of Lake Texcoco and on a small island in the lake.

"Land of the Prickly Pear Cactus"

According to legend the Aztec had seen an eagle standing on a cactus with a snake in its beak. They believed this was a sign from their main god, Huitzilopochtli (weet si loh POCH tlee). It meant their search for a homeland was over. The Aztec named the place Tenochtitlán (te noch tee TLAHN). This name means "land of the prickly pear cactus." Find Tenochtitlán on the map on this page.

At first life was hard on the swampy land of Tenochtitlán. Gradually the Aztec built up their city. They soon found the lake to be rich in resources.

They built reed boats for fishing and traveling. To connect the island to the rest of the valley, they built causeways and bridges. A causeway is a raised road or path usually built across a body of water.

To grow the large amounts of food they needed, the Aztec built chinampas, or "floating gardens." These gardens only appeared to float. To create them the Aztec stuck rows of thick posts into the marsh. Then they filled the spaces between the posts with mud from the lake. These gardens became rich farm land. Eventually, the chinampas provided chili peppers, squash, tomatoes, corn, and beans for the entire city.

The prickly pear cactus is one of the national symbols of Mexico. It represents part of the legend of how the ancient Aztec found their new homeland.

THE AZTEC AND THEIR NEIGHBORS, About 1440

MAP WORK

0   100   200 Miles
0   100   200 Kilometers

N
W · E
S

Gulf of Mexico

TOTONAC

TARASCA
Tenochtitlán
· TLAXCALA
TEPANEC   AZTEC

MIXTEC
ZAPOTEC

PACIFIC OCEAN

- City
- Aztec lands
- Neighboring lands

Many of the Aztec cities were close together, as the Valley of Mexico provided rich farm land.

1. Which people were surrounded by the Aztec **empire**?

2. Did the Mixtec live north or south of Tenochtitlán?

3. Which two peoples were farthest away from Tenochtitlán?

THE AZTEC EMPIRE

In the early l400s a people called the Tepanec (tay pah NAYK) ruled the Valley of Mexico. They forced the Aztec to give them **tribute**, or payment in the form of valuable goods. Around 1430, however, the Aztec joined with other people of Lake Texcoco to defeat the Tepanec. This victory was the beginning of Aztec control over the Valley.

Mighty Tenochtitlán

By 1440 Tenochtitlán was the capital of a mighty empire. An Aztec poem tells of the power of Tenochtitlán:

Who could conquer Tenochtitlán?
Who could shake the foundation of
heaven . . . ?

Tenochtitlán's broad avenues, beautiful plazas, and markets served a population of over 200,000. The city even had a zoo, which contained animals from all over the empire.

The diagram on the next page shows how the city's main palaces and temples were laid out. The Aztec planned their city in honor of the sun and their gods. Each building was put in a special location. Each location marked the position of the sun during an important time of the year, such as planting time.

Growing Up Aztec

From birth to death, Aztec life was guided by their calendar. Each day was special. Children were given names in honor of the date on which they were born.

Most Aztec children went to school. All schools were strict. But the one for the sons of Aztec leaders was the most difficult. It was known as the "house of

It is easy to see why the bright green feathers of the quetzal (left) were used for decoration. Today quetzals are found throughout Central America.

tears." Both boys and girls learned Aztec history and religion in school. They were also taught to be honest and respectful. This advice from an Aztec book was given by a father.

1. *Do not sleep too much, or you will become a sleeper, a dreamer.*
2. *Speak very slowly. Do not speak fast, do not pant or squeak or you will be called a groaner, a growler, a squeaker.*
3. *Do not stare into another person's face.*
4. *Do not eavesdrop or gossip.*
5. *When you are called, do not be called twice or you will be thought lazy or rebellious.*

The Aztec Market

On market day the Aztec and other people met and exchanged news. They also danced, played music, and performed juggling tricks.

Some scholars believe the Aztec market was one of the largest in the world at that time. Some foods for sale were chili peppers, squash, beans, corn, tomatoes, potatoes, fish, and cactus. Many beautiful items were also sold at the market. Most highly prized were items made from the feathers of the quetzal. As you have read on page 64, quetzals were special to the Aztec. Poets wrote about them. Hunters usually captured the bird, plucked a few feathers, and then set it free.

66

TENOCHTITLÁN

PALACES

GREAT PLAZA

GREAT TEMPLE

TEMPLE

CAUSEWAY

BRIDGE

CHINAMPAS

THE IMPORTANCE OF WAR

War was an important part of Aztec life. Emperor Moctezuma I once remarked, "If war is not going on, the Aztec consider themselves idle." The Aztec were in battles from 1430 through most of the next 90 years. The Aztec conquered over 400 cities in central Mexico. One purpose for conquering the cities was to obtain tribute from the people. The Aztec had other reasons for conquering peoples as well.

The mural, or large painting (below), is one image of a jaguar knight. The chacmool (chahk MOOL), or altar (bottom), was used to make human sacrifices. Many Aztec believed the chacmools represented dead soldiers.

Antochin Collection

The Aztec Army

From an early age boys were trained as soldiers. At age ten they shaved their heads, leaving one lock of hair. A boy could not cut that lock until he had captured a prisoner in battle.

The goal of every soldier was to become a knight. Jaguar and Eagle knights were the leaders of the Aztec army. During war they wore suits made of feathers or animal skins that were meant to terrify the enemy.

Soldiers were sent to fight but not to kill the enemy. Instead they took prisoners. Some prisoners were forced into slavery. Slavery is the practice of owning people and forcing them to work. Other prisoners were sacrificed to Aztec gods. To sacrifice means to give up or destroy for the sake of something else. Human sacrifice as well as slavery was a part of Aztec life.

People of the Sun

The Aztec believed that every morning the god Huitzilopochtli brought out the sun and chased away the moon and

68

The Metropolitan Cathedral of Mexico City sits on the north side of the Zócalo, or Constitution Plaza. In 1573 building began on the church, which is now the oldest and largest church in Latin America.

stars. They also believed the god needed energy to do his work and that he got energy from human blood.

To make sure that the sun would rise another day, the Aztec sacrificed thousands of prisoners and slaves each year. The sacrifices were done by priests in the Great Temple. The Aztec believed they were wealthy enough to give their gods human lives.

WHY IT MATTERS

Like many other civilizations, the Aztec's was full of contrasts. It was a civilization of both great beauty and great cruelty. Aztec attempts to conquer and enslave other peoples created many enemies. As you will read later, these enemies would help bring about the end of the Aztec empire.

Aztec culture remains alive even today. Many Mexicans still speak the Nahuatl language of the Aztec and follow Aztec traditions. In fact, words we use today, such as *avocado, chocolate,* and *Mexico,* were spoken by the Aztec and other early peoples of Mexico hundreds of years ago.

Reviewing Facts and Ideas

MAIN IDEAS

- After the Maya civilization ended, the Aztec and the Inca formed two great empires in the Western Hemisphere.
- By 1440 the Aztec had developed a powerful civilization in the Valley of Mexico.
- War was the main way that the Aztec captured prisoners to sacrifice to their gods.

THINK ABOUT IT

1. Describe how the city of Tenochtitlán was founded.

2. How did the Aztec increase the amount of land that could be used for farming in Tenochtitlán?

3. **FOCUS** What events led to the creation of the Aztec empire?

4. **THINKING SKILL** What *similarities* do you see between the civilizations of the Maya and the Aztec? Explain the reasons for any differences you find.

5. **GEOGRAPHY** How do you think the location of Tenochtitlán helped the Aztec to maintain their empire?

Study Skills

Reading Time Lines

VOCABULARY

time line
century
decade
B.C.
A.D.

WHY THE SKILL MATTERS

By the time the Aztec were forming their empire in the middle of the 1400s, the Inca had already established their civilization in South America. One way to understand the history of these early civilizations is to use a time line. A time line is a diagram of a series of events in time. It shows events in the order in which they took place. Dates are marked to identify these events. Putting events in correct time order helps you to see relationships between events.

USING TIME LINES

As you have read, the Inca settlement was founded at about the same time that the Aztec arrived in the Valley of Mexico. In about 1100 the Inca settled in a village called Cuzco (KOOS koh) in the country now called Peru. This is the first event shown on the Inca history time line.

Over the next 200 years, the Inca slowly gained power over other groups in the area. About 1300, a leader named Inca Roca (een kah ROH kah) used the word *Inca* as a noble title. Historians date the Inca empire as beginning in 1438, under the ruler Pachacuti (pah chah KOO tee). By 1450 the Inca had conquered the Chimu people and increased the size of the empire. This is the fourth event shown on the time line.

The Inca were expert builders who paved roads in the steep Andes Mountains. Find when this occurred on the time line. In what year did the Inca begin building roads?

The Inca were also very skilled at making gold jewelry and other items. When the

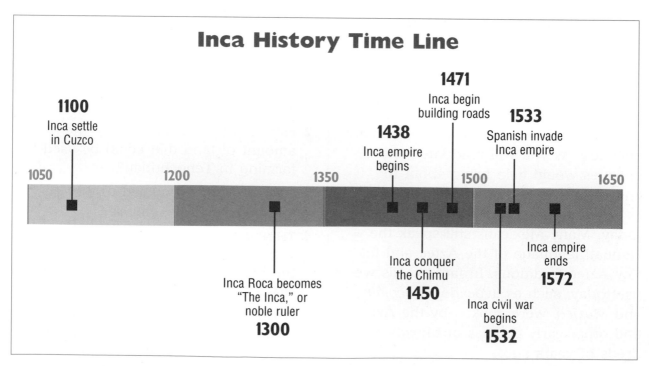

Inca History Time Line

1100 — Inca settle in Cuzco

1438 — Inca empire begins

1471 — Inca begin building roads

1533 — Spanish invade Inca empire

1050   1200   1350   1500   1650

Inca Roca becomes "The Inca," or noble ruler — 1300

Inca conquer the Chimu — 1450

Inca civil war begins — 1532

Inca empire ends — 1572

Spanish explorers who came to the Americas heard this information, they invaded the Inca's lands. When did this event occur? What event might have helped the Spanish to be successful in 1533?

USING DECADES AND CENTURIES

All time lines are divided into time periods. The time line on this page shows time in periods of 100 years, or centuries. To many people the years 1 to 100 are called the first century. The second century includes the years 101 to 200. The jagged line shows that a long period of time has been left out.

A ten-year time period is called a decade. The years 1981 to 1990 make up the decade of the 1980s. In what decade do we now live?

We use a system of dating events that divides time into two periods called B.C. and A.D. The letters B.C. stand for time "before Christ," or before Jesus Christ was born. It marks events that took place before the year 1. The letters A.D. stand for the Latin phrase *Anno Domini* or "in the year of the Lord." We use A.D. before a date to mark the events that took place after the birth of Christ.

Helping yourself

● **A time line is a diagram of a series of events in time.**

● **Find the first and last dates on the time line.**

● **Identify any connections between the events.**

When reading B.C. dates, the numbers get lower as you read from left to right. For example, the year 100 B.C. is followed by the year 99 B.C. Dates after the year 1 are much simpler to read because the numbers get higher. For example, the year A.D. 100 is followed by the year A.D. 101.

TRYING THE SKILL

Now try reading the Inca history time line on your own. If you need help, use the Helping Yourself box on this page. How many entire centuries does the time line show? What is the last event on the time line? Which event on the time line took place first?

REVIEWING THE SKILL

1. What is a time line? What type of information does it show?

2. In which century did the Inca empire begin? How do you know?

3. How many centuries passed between the time the Inca conquered the Chimu and the time the Inca civil war began? How do you know?

4. What are some things that reading time lines can help you to do?

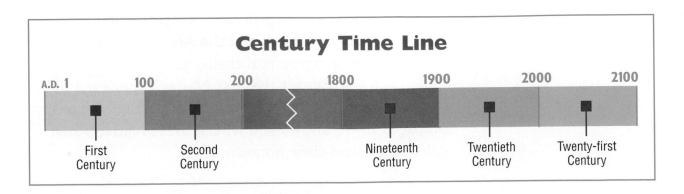

Century Time Line

| A.D. 1 | 100 | 200 | 1800 | 1900 | 2000 | 2100 |

First Century   Second Century   Nineteenth Century   Twentieth Century   Twenty-first Century

300   500   1300 1500

The Anasazi

Read Aloud

On January 22, 1941, the New Mexico desert stood silent. Suddenly, there was a crash. A giant boulder called Threatening Rock had fallen on the village of Pueblo Bonito. No one was injured because the village had been empty for over 600 years. Who had lived there? What made these people leave, and where did they go?

Focus Activity

READ TO LEARN

Who were the Anasazi people?

VOCABULARY

- artifact
- drought
- irrigation

PLACES

- Cahokia
- Four Corners
- Pueblo Bonito
- Mesa Verde
- Beringia

THE BIG PICTURE

As you have read, the Maya were among the first people to develop a civilization in the Western Hemisphere. Other early North Americans also formed civilizations in what is now the United States. They lived mostly in two regions—the Southeast and the Southwest.

The Southeast was populated by people whom scholars today call the Mound Builders. The Hohokam (ho ho KAHM) and the Anasazi (ah nuh SAH zee) peoples lived in the Southwest. These early Native Americans started farming and settling in permanent villages in both regions about 3000 B.C.

The geography of these regions had a great effect on each people's way of life. The Mound Builders' land received much rainfall. The Hohokam and the Anasazi lived in a much drier region, where farming was difficult. The Mound Builders and the Anasazi had to meet very different geographical challenges.

You will learn about the first Native Americans to live in what is now the United States. The Infographic on pages 76–77 shows you where these Native Americans established their homelands.

EARLY NORTH AMERICA

As you have read, the environment affects people's lives. The reverse is also true. People also affect their environment. Many of the people who met difficult challenges in the past went on to build large civilizations.

The Mound Builders

About 2,000 years ago, groups of people lived along the Mississippi River and in part of the Middle West near where the Ohio and Mississippi rivers meet. Today we know them as Mound Builders because of the large mounds they built. No one knows what name they called themselves. Yet later, Mound Builders were called Mississippians.

The Mound Builders lived in an area of plentiful rainfall and plant and animal life. Their land was also crossed by many rivers, which served as major routes of trade. Think about what items the Mound Builders might have obtained through trade.

At first, the Mound Builders built small, rounded piles of earth to bury their dead. Workers carried loads of earth on their backs to the spot chosen for the mound. They often built one mound on top of another. As time passed, larger mounds were built. Archaeologists have found burial mounds containing cloth, jewelry, and pottery. One young woman was buried wearing necklaces made with almost 2,000 shells.

Later, mounds were also used for religious purposes. The largest, Great Serpent Mound, is found near present-day Cincinnati, Ohio. It measures over 1,000 feet in length and is 100 feet tall. Other large mounds were built in Cahokia (kuh HOH kee uh) in what is now Illinois. The Mound Builders also built pyramid-shaped structures similar to those of Maya and Aztec temples.

From the air, Great Serpent Mound (below) looks like a snake. The etched shell (left) was found in Hohokam lands in Arizona.

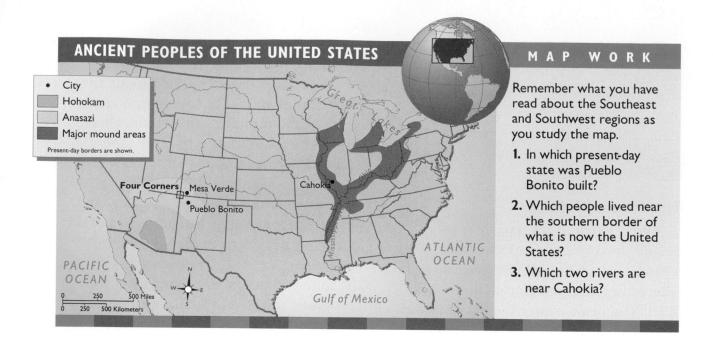

- • City
- Hohokam
- Anasazi
- Major mound areas

Present-day borders are shown.

Great Lakes

Four Corners
Mesa Verde
Cahokia
Pueblo Bonito

Ohio River

Mississippi River

ATLANTIC
OCEAN

PACIFIC
OCEAN

Gulf of Mexico

0   250   500 Miles
0   250   500 Kilometers

Remember what you have read about the Southeast and Southwest regions as you study the map.

1. In which present-day state was Pueblo Bonito built?

2. Which people lived near the southern border of what is now the United States?

3. Which two rivers are near Cahokia?

THE ANASAZI

As desert dwellers, the Anasazi people faced many challenges caused by geography. However, geography has also been a friend to archaeologists who choose to study the Anasazi.

A Preserved Past

Archaeologists know about the Anasazi mostly because of the dry climate in which they lived. Pottery and baskets found buried in the arid Southwest have been preserved for hundreds or even thousands of years. In moist climates, most artifacts rot, or decay, quickly. An artifact is an object left behind by people who lived long ago.

Many artifacts have been found in an area known as the Four Corners. The map on this page shows that the Four Corners is the place where today the borders of four states—Colorado, New Mexico, Arizona, and Utah—meet.

The "Ancient Ones"

The Anasazi lived in the Four Corners area about 2,000 years ago. Until A.D. 600, the Anasazi lived in simple underground houses. Gradually, they developed villages that looked like large apartment houses. Some built their villages beneath rock cliffs, on the sides of canyons, and on the tops of tall, flat hills called mesas.

Although Anasazi building methods and styles changed, they continued to make kivas (KEE vuhz). A kiva is an underground room used usually by Native American men for religious ceremonies. The men painted the walls of the kiva with special symbols in red, green, white, and yellow.

74

About A.D. 900, the Anasazi began building Pueblo Bonito, a huge 800-room town. It towered over the desert in what is now New Mexico. In the town of Mesa Verde, they built Cliff Palace, which had 217 rooms carved out of the side of a steep cliff.

The Anasazi Mystery

The Anasazi's population had reached into the thousands by about A.D. 900. But in the late 1200s something happened. The Anasazi started to leave their towns and villages. Many archaeologists believe that a long drought drove them from their homes. A drought is a long period with very little rainfall.

But the Anasazi were used to the dry climate. They had been using irrigation to water their crops. Irrigation is a method by which water is brought into dry areas. The Anasazi irrigation system guided rain water through a series of channels to their crops of squash, beans, corn, and cotton. Still, irrigation could not provide enough water for the crops during droughts.

Other archaeologists believe that enemies, quarrels among the Anasazi, or other reasons may have caused some to leave their homes. By about A.D. 1300 most of the Anasazi towns and villages were empty. Over time, the Anasazi moved or joined with other Native Americans in the Southwest. Today many historians believe that the Hopi and Pueblo peoples are descendants of the Anasazi. You will read about the Hopi and Pueblo in the next chapter.

Much of the Anasazi's black-on-white pottery (far left) survives. Looking at Mesa Verde (left) and its environment, one can imagine the role climate has played in preserving such artifacts. Today a Pueblo girl (above) might be learning about her Anasazi ancestors from her grandmother.

75

Infographic

interNET CONNECTION Visit our website: www.mhschool.com

Native Americans, 1500s

Some scholars believe that about 40,000 years ago, people first came to what is now the United States. Many may have crossed a land bridge called **Beringia** (buh RIN jee uh), which once connected Asia to North America. By 1500, millions of Native Americans lived throughout North America. Which Native Americans made their home in what is now your region?

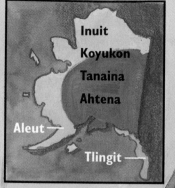

Inuit
Koyukon
Tanaina
Ahtena
Aleut
Tlingit

Alaska

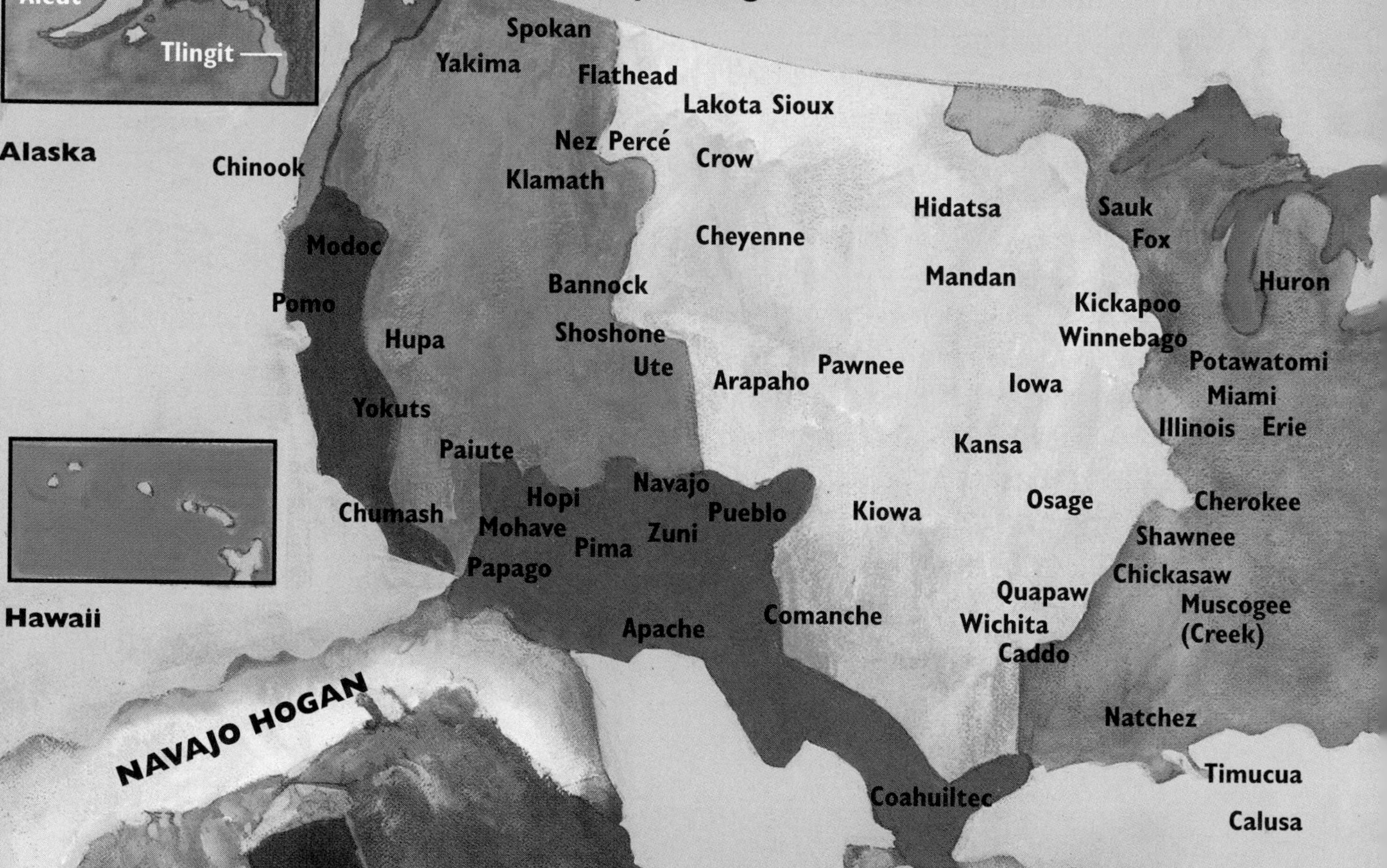

Spokan
Yakima
Flathead
Lakota Sioux
Nez Percé
Crow
Chinook
Klamath
Hidatsa
Sauk
Fox
Cheyenne
Modoc
Mandan
Huron
Bannock
Kickapoo
Pomo
Winnebago
Hupa
Shoshone
Potawatomi
Ute
Arapaho
Pawnee
Iowa
Miami
Yokuts
Illinois
Erie
Kansa
Paiute
Navajo
Hopi
Pueblo
Kiowa
Osage
Cherokee
Chumash
Mohave
Zuni
Shawnee
Pima
Papago
Chickasaw
Quapaw
Muscogee (Creek)
Comanche
Wichita
Apache
Caddo
Natchez
Timucua
Coahuiltec
Calusa

Hawaii

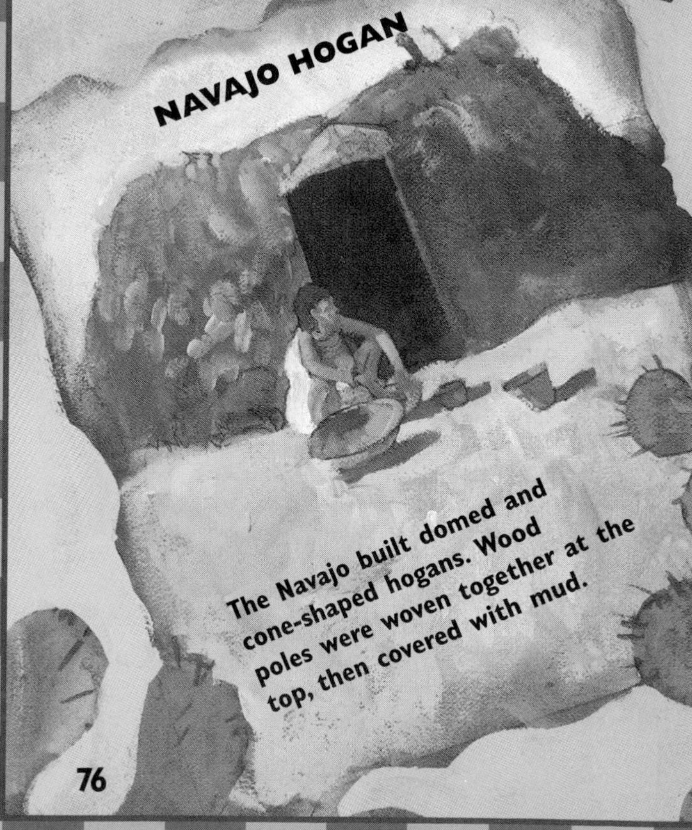

NAVAJO HOGAN

The Navajo built domed and cone-shaped hogans. Wood poles were woven together at the top, then covered with mud.

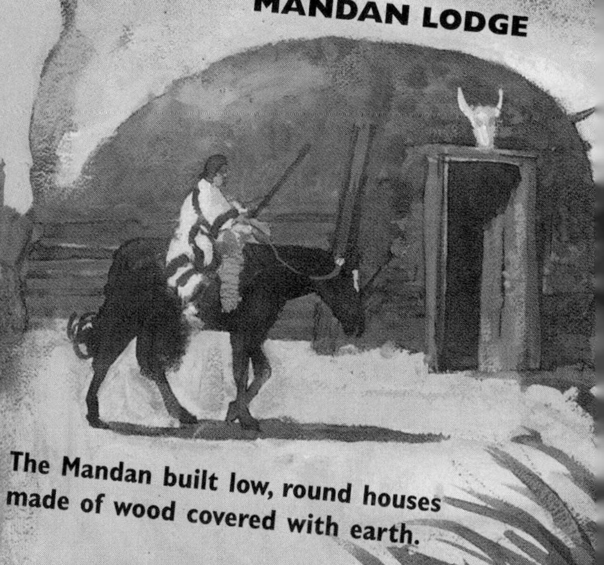

MANDAN LODGE

The Mandan built low, round houses made of wood covered with earth.

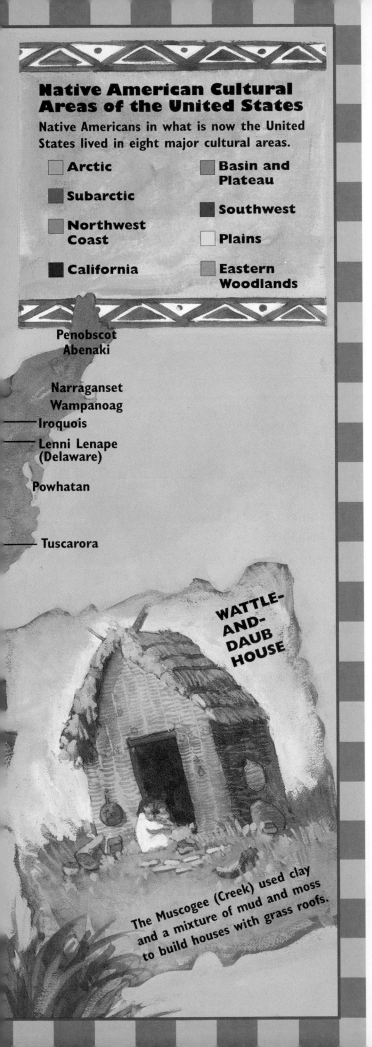

Native American Cultural Areas of the United States

Native Americans in what is now the United States lived in eight major cultural areas.

- Arctic
- Subarctic
- Northwest Coast
- California
- Basin and Plateau
- Southwest
- Plains
- Eastern Woodlands

Penobscot
Abenaki

Narraganset
Wampanoag
Iroquois
Lenni Lenape (Delaware)

Powhatan

Tuscarora

WATTLE-AND-DAUB HOUSE

The Muscogee (Creek) used clay and a mixture of mud and moss to build houses with grass roofs.

WHY IT MATTERS

In chapters to come, you will learn how Native Americans have played important roles in the history of the United States. As you read about our country's history, keep your knowledge of the early North Americans in mind.

✓✓ Reviewing Facts and Ideas

MAIN IDEAS

- In what is now the United States, Native Americans farmed and lived in permanent villages for thousands of years.
- The Anasazi left their towns and villages around 1300 for reasons scholars cannot fully explain.

THINK ABOUT IT

1. What problems did people living in the Southwest have? What solutions did they find?

2. Why might an archaeologist believe the Mound Builders traded with people from distant areas?

3. **FOCUS** List in time order the events that probably led to the Anasazi leaving Pueblo Bonito.

4. **THINKING SKILL** _Compare_ the Mound Builders to the Maya and Aztec. What possible connections might there have been among them?

5. **GEOGRAPHY** Using this Infographic, name at least three Native American peoples that lived in each of the five regions of the present-day United States.

CHAPTER 3 REVIEW

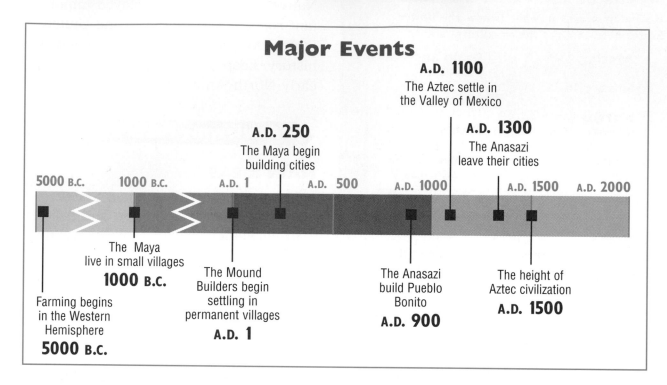

Major Events

A.D. 1100
The Aztec settle in
the Valley of Mexico

A.D. 250
The Maya begin
building cities

A.D. 1300
The Anasazi
leave their cities

5000 B.C.   1000 B.C.   A.D. 1   A.D. 500   A.D. 1000   A.D. 1500   A.D. 2000

The Maya
live in small villages
1000 B.C.

The Mound
Builders begin
settling in
permanent villages
A.D. 1

The Anasazi
build Pueblo
Bonito
A.D. 900

The height of
Aztec civilization
A.D. 1500

Farming begins
in the Western
Hemisphere
5000 B.C.

THINKING ABOUT VOCABULARY

Number a paper from 1 to 10. Beside each number write the word that best matches the description.

archaeologist	irrigation
artifact	slavery
civilization	specialize
drought	surplus
empire	tribute

1. A large area of different peoples controlled by one ruler or government

2. An object left behind by people from long ago

3. An amount greater than what is needed

4. A long period with very little rain

5. A scientist who looks for and studies evidence from long ago

6. A culture that has developed complex systems of government, education, and religion

7. Payment in the form of valuable goods

8. The practice of people owning other people

9. A method by which water is brought into dry areas

10. Spend most of the time doing one job

THINKING ABOUT FACTS

1. What is an archaeologist? How have archaeologists found information about the Maya?

2. What other achievements besides farming marked Maya civilization?

3. Who were the Aztec? In what area did their civilization form?

4. What early civilization lived in what is now the Southeast region of the United States? What were its major routes of trade?

5. Look at the time line above. How many years passed between the Aztec settlement of the Valley of Mexico and the height of their civilization?

THINK AND WRITE

WRITING INTERVIEW QUESTIONS
Suppose that you are interviewing a descendant of the Maya. Write a series of questions about what customs or traditions can be traced back to his or her ancestors.

WRITING A DESCRIPTION
Use the information in the lesson and the diagram on page 67 to write a description of Tenochtitlán.

WRITING A PROPOSAL
Suppose that you are a member of a group that has recently begun to farm. Write a description for another group that has not yet begun farming telling what farming is and why it would improve their lives.

APPLYING STUDY SKILLS

READING TIME LINES
To practice the skill of reading time lines, use the time line on page 70 to answer the questions below.

1. What do the different dates on a time line mean?
2. When does the time line begin? When does it end?
3. When did the Spanish invade the Inca empire?
4. What happened in the year A.D. 1572?
5. Think about the last two questions. How can a time line help you understand historical events?

Summing Up the Chapter

Copy this chart on a separate piece of paper to help you organize the information you have read about the early peoples of the Western Hemisphere. Review the chapter to fill in the blank parts of the chart. After you have filled in the chart, write a paragraph that answers the question "Which civilization did you find the most interesting and why?"

THE FIRST AMERICANS	IMPORTANT DATES	TYPES OF BUILDINGS	WAYS OF FARMING
Maya	• A.D. 250 Begin building cities • A.D. 909 Last monuments built		
Aztec		• Palaces • Temples	
Anasazi			• Irrigation

Native Americans of North America

THINKING ABOUT HISTORY AND GEOGRAPHY

Chapter 4 tells the story of some of the many Native Americans of North America. From the Tlingit in the West to the Iroquois of the Northeast, Native American culture stretched from the Atlantic coast to the Pacific coast. Read the time line below to follow the major events of this chapter. The background color of each event on the time line matches a square marker on the map.

1400s

OLD ORAIBI
The Hopi live in a large pueblo now known as Old Oraibi

1500s

HODENOSAUNEE TRAIL
The Iroquois trade and hunt in the Eastern Woodlands

1600s

MISSISSIPPI RIVER
The Natchez raise crops in the Southeast

1400

1500

1600

Sitka

PACIFIC
OCEAN

Black Hills

Hodenosaunee
Trail

NORTH
AMERICA

Old Oraibi

Mississippi
River

ATLANTIC
OCEAN

Gulf of
Mexico

Caribbean
Sea

1600s

SITKA
The Tlingit of Alaska
hold celebrations to honor
leaders and family
members

1700s

BLACK HILLS
The Lakota Sioux hunt on
the Great Plains

Native Americans of the West

Read Aloud

"When I was growing up," says Marie Olson, whose Tlingit (KLIHNG iht) name is Kaayistaan (KĪ yih stan), "I was taught to treat the environment with respect. . . . A fisherman would talk to a fish before catching it. He would say thank you for coming to his net."

Focus Activity

READ TO LEARN

How did the Tlingit use their environment?

VOCABULARY

- technology
- totem pole
- potlatch

PLACES

- Sitka

THE BIG PICTURE

As you read in Chapter 3, Native Americans have lived for thousands of years in what is now the United States. In each of the five regions of the United States, Native American peoples created distinctive ways of life that were strongly influenced by their environment.

The Western region of the United States provides an example of varied environments. Many Native Americans, such as the Mohave (moh HAH vee), lived in the mild climate of present-day southern California. Others, such as the Paiute (pi OOT), lived in the deserts of the Great Basin. Farming was so difficult there that these peoples had to move from place to place to get food. After about 1000 B.C., however, most people in the Western Hemisphere relied on farming as their main source of food.

The Northwest Coast of the Western region had yet another type of environment. Native Americans such as the Tsimshian (TSIHM shee un) and Chinook lived in villages all year round without farming. In this lesson you will learn how one people, the Tlingit, use the resources of the sea. You will learn about how the Tlingit lived before the Europeans arrived in the 1700s.

GEOGRAPHY OF THE NORTHWEST COAST

The Northwest Coast is a narrow area of land that extends roughly south from Anchorage, Alaska, to San Francisco, California. To the area's east are forests, plateaus, basins, and rivers. To the west is the Pacific Ocean. As you saw on the United States climates map on page 37, this area has a wet climate with mild winters and cool summers.

Riches from the Forest and the Sea

How did the people of the Northwest Coast live without farming? First, the wet climate of the Northwest Coast helps a rich variety of plants to grow. So, the peoples of the Northwest Coast gathered roots and berries from the dense forests that lined the shore. Second, the forest was also home to such animals as deer, elk, beaver, and bears. Third, Native Americans of this area got almost everything else they needed from the sea.

Many kinds of fish—salmon, cod, herring, trout, halibut—lived in the nearby streams, rivers, and the ocean.

On the open sea, fishers in huge canoes caught large sea animals including sea lions and sea otters. From the shore people gathered mussels, clams, and the eggs of seabirds. Salmon, however, was the most important source of food to the Northwest Coast peoples. Salmon became important because the Native Americans always knew when and where large numbers of the fish could be caught.

The Salmon Run

The salmon run was and still is an important event in the lives of the Native Americans of the Northwest Coast. The salmon run is the yearly return of salmon to lay eggs in the freshwater rivers where they were born. From early spring to late summer, millions of salmon swam from the Pacific Ocean to rivers, such as the Columbia.

During the salmon run a family could catch over 1,000 pounds of fish. Men and women set aside their daily tasks to go to the river to catch the plentiful fish. Some of the salmon was eaten. Most was dried or smoked then stored for meals throughout the year.

On Washington State's Columbia River, a present-day Native American fisher catches a salmon.

THE TLINGIT

Today if you visited Sitka, Alaska, you would find a busy American city. You might not guess that this city stands in the heart of the Tlingit homeland of long ago. As you can see on the Infographic on page 76, the Tlingit lived in the northernmost part of the Northwest Coast. Like many Native Americans in this area, the Tlingit got most of their food from the sea. In addition to fish, they and their neighbors caught seals, porpoises, and even whales. During the winter they hunted animals from the forests and mountains.

The Tlingit had direct water routes from the coast to other parts of the country. This enabled them to trade their surplus food for other goods they needed. The Tlingit also helped other Native Americans to the north, south, and east trade with each other and with the Inuit in the far north. Trade helped to make the Tlingit a wealthy people.

Technology and Art

Because food was plentiful, the Tlingit were able to specialize in making art and developing technology. Technology is the design and use of tools, ideas, and methods to solve problems. The Tlingit used their technology to build dams and traps for catching salmon. They also made large canoes that could hold up to 50 people.

As highly skilled woodworkers, the Tlingit built large homes. In front of most houses stood a totem pole. Totem poles are tall logs carved with many designs. Most totem poles were 40 to 60 feet tall, but some were as high as 150 feet. Many totem poles were built to honor family members or new chiefs, or to mark special events.

Even everyday objects made by the Tlingit were often as beautiful as they were useful. Almost everything—from spoons to blankets to wooden storage boxes—was highly decorated.

The Potlatch

To mark an important event, a family sometimes held a potlatch (PAHT lach). Potlatches are special feasts at which the guests, not the hosts, receive

A Tlingit father teaches his daughter to carve a totem pole (far left). Someday her carvings may come to look like this totem pole (near left) in Haines, Alaska.

A **Northwest Coast** potlatch (above) was an elaborate event. Handmade baskets such as those shown below were often given as gifts by the Native American hosts of the feasts.

gifts. A potlatch, for example, might be held to honor a new chief or to celebrate a wedding.

It could take years for the host's family to prepare for a potlatch. A special gift was collected or made for each guest. A guest's importance in the community determined what kind of gift the host gave.

Suppose that you could attend a wedding potlatch. Everyone would be dressed in his or her finest clothing. The host would wear one of the family's best woven blankets. The ceremony, which could last for days, would include songs and dances. Each person would contribute in some way. Excitement would mount as guests waited to see what each gift would be.

An important guest might receive a canoe or fur robe. The host might distribute hundreds of valuable gifts. In return, the host received the respect of the community.

To show their generosity, each host's family tried to give more gifts than the hosts of the last potlatch they attended. Sometimes the host's family gave away all of their valuables. But over time, wealth would return when the potlatch was held by another host. Potlatches may have been a way of sharing wealth and determining social standing. They were also happy times of celebration and togetherness.

CHANGE COMES TO THE TLINGIT

As you will learn in Chapter 6, contact with Europeans led to great changes in the cultures of many Native Americans. Since Alaska is so far north, Europeans arrived there later than in other parts of North America. Russians were the first Europeans to become interested in the area. An explorer named Vitus Bering sailed from Russia to Alaska in the middle of the 1700s across what is now called the Bering Strait.

Russian, English, Spanish, and French people traded with the Tlingit for fur. The traders also built settlements in the area. In 1867 the United States government bought Alaska from Russia, which had claimed it earlier. Sitka was the place where the Russians officially handed over control of Alaska to the United States. Alaska became our country's 49th state in 1959.

Conflict with the Government

When their homeland became part of the United States, the Tlingit found it hard to keep their way of life alive. In some places, the United States government forced Northwest Coast peoples to move far from the ocean.

The Tlingit and other Native Americans in the area struggled to preserve their culture. As a result of efforts by Native Americans and the Inuit, the United States government passed the Alaska Native Claims Settlement Act in 1971. This law gave them back control of over 44 million acres of their original homelands in Alaska.

The Granger Collection

Many Northwest Coast villages looked like this one (above) in the early 1900s. The fishing boats (right) are owned by present-day Tlingit fishers.

WHY IT MATTERS

Today Sitka is a major business center. Many of our country's 15,000 Tlingit work at logging and fishing. Some have moved to large cities. But the creation of beautiful artwork and the giving of potlatches are still an important part of Tlingit life.

Looking at how the Tlingit lived in the early 1700s, you can see how important environment is to people. To understand our country's history, it helps to learn about people and their environments all over the United States. The next lesson continues this story.

These members of a Tlingit dance group wear traditional dress during performances.

✓ Reviewing Facts and Ideas

MAIN IDEAS

- The West includes many types of environments in which many different Native American peoples live.
- Native Americans of the Northwest Coast of North America developed a rich way of life that was based on resources from the sea.
- Because food was plentiful in their region, the Tlingit were able to spend time developing their technology and art.
- The potlatch is a feast at which the host gives away many valuable gifts to the guests. It is still an important part of Tlingit life.

THINK ABOUT IT

1. What role did salmon fishing play in the life of Native Americans of the Northwest Coast?

2. What purposes does a potlatch serve?

3. **FOCUS** How did the Tlingit make use of the natural resources in their environment?

4. **THINKING SKILL** What _conclusions_ can you make about the effect of trade on the Tlingit? On what information did you base your conclusions?

5. **WRITE** Suppose your class was giving a potlatch. What would be your reason for holding the potlatch? Whom would you invite? What activities would you plan? What gift would you give to each person?

ARTS
IN THE
DESERT

The Navajo people have been master artists and craftworkers for hundreds of years. From materials in their environment, the Navajo made blankets, baskets, pottery, clothing, and other useful objects. They also made art for religious purposes. It was important to the Navajo that the objects they made were beautiful as well as useful.

Navajos continue to be known for their artwork. Their woven rugs and silver jewelry attract buyers from all over the world. Today Navajo art can be seen in many museums. The creation of art by the Navajo is a legacy from the past that continues to enrich our present.

The Navajo are world famous for their skill as weavers. Since many Navajo are sheep herders, wool from their sheep is often used to make blankets. Today machine-made yarns are also used by Navajo women, who do most of the weaving.

Navajo ceremonies often include the creation of a sand, or dry, painting. The designs are made by sprinkling powdered minerals or plants onto a blanket covered with clean, smooth sand. Each symbol in the design has a meaning. A sand painting can take 15 people and an entire day to complete.

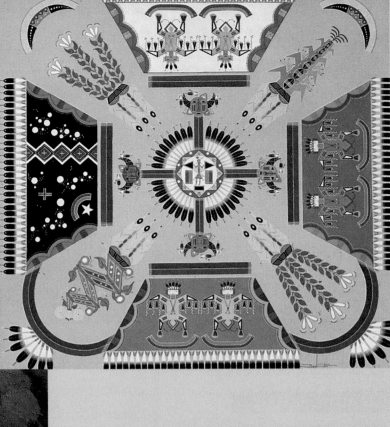

Squash-blossom necklaces, concha belts, and bracelets made of silver are the major types of jewelry created by Navajo artisans. The Navajo learned the art of working with silver from their neighbors, the Mexicans. They passed on this knowledge to the Hopi and Zuni, who are also known for their skill as jewelry makers.

89

1300	1400	1500	1600	1700

Native Americans of the Southwest

Focus Activity

READ TO LEARN

What traditions have helped shape Hopi life?

VOCABULARY

- pueblo
- adobe
- kachina

PEOPLE

- Nampeyo

PLACES

- Old Oraibi

Read Aloud

"Before dancing, I get a little nervous," says Timmy Roybal, a 10-year-old from the San Ildefonso Pueblo in New Mexico. "My legs start shaking, but they settle down once I am dancing. When I am dancing, I feel I am part of everything." Timmy is talking about the Green Corn Dance, in which Pueblo peoples give thanks for all that nature has given them.

THE BIG PICTURE

In Chapter 3 you read about the Anasazi, who lived in the Southwestern United States. Many historians think that the Anasazi were the ancestors of today's Pueblo peoples, Native Americans who live in the Southwest.

Also living in the region are non-Pueblo Native Americans such as the Navajo (NAHV uh hoh) and Apache (uh PACH ee). Historians believe the Navajo and Apache are fairly new to the Southwest. They probably began arriving from present-day Alaska and the north-western part of Canada around a.d. 1000.

Scholars often divide Native Americans in the Southwest into two groups. The first includes the Navajo and Apache, who were mainly hunters and herders. The second includes Pueblo peoples such as the Hopi and the Zuni (ZOO nee), who were mainly farmers. In this lesson, you will read about the Hopi, who became skilled farmers of the desert.

THE LAND OF THE HOPI

The Hopi call themselves *Hopiti,* which in their own language means "the gentle people." When the Spanish arrived in the 1500s, they called the Hopi apartment-style homes pueblos which means "villages" in Spanish. The Spanish used the word *pueblo* to describe both the people and the type of home in which they lived. Over time Native Americans living in pueblos have become known as the Pueblo people. The Hopi pueblo of Old Oraibi (oh rah EE bee) is one of the oldest settlements in the United States. The Hopi have lived there for about 800 years.

Farmers of the Desert

The land of the Hopi is mostly made up of tall mountains, deep canyons, and steep mesas. This dry land is not a place where you would expect to find farming people. Yet the Hopi were among the most successful farmers in North America.

The Hopi have been growing crops in the Southwest for hundreds of years. Some of their farming methods were passed down to them by the Anasazi. To grow their crops, the Hopi use a method called *dry farming.* Dry farming is a way of growing crops in places where there is little water. To water their crops, the Hopi built dams and irrigation canals. They also grew special corn plants with long roots to reach the water underground.

Farming was sacred to the Hopi. Each plant had to be tended according to ancient religious practices. Every person in the community performed a task. Some planted, some weeded, some kept pests away. Success depended on everyone working together and carefully observing nature. As you can tell from the Hopi poem below, respect for nature is important to the Hopi and other Native Americans.

> *Power is very mysterious.*
> *Power is all around us*
> *in the wind*
> *and the clouds*
> *and the earth.*

A Hopi uses dry farming to grow corn (above) in Oraibi, Arizona. The Taos Pueblo (left) looks much the same today as it did long ago.

This piece of Zuni jewelry shows a kachina called Long Hair (below). In this painting (right) the kachina dancers perform in a Hopi village.

The Heard Museum

HOPI LIFE

The Hopi built homes made of adobe (uh DOH bee). Adobe is a type of clay found in the earth. It protected the house from the desert's blistering heat and extreme cold as well as floods and blizzards. In summer the roof of an adobe house could get as hot as 140°F. Even then, the temperature inside remained between 75°F and 85°F.

To keep invaders out, the Hopi built the first floor of most pueblos without doors or windows. To get in and out, people climbed ladders up to and down from doors in the roofs. Like the Anasazi towns, most pueblo towns had kivas for religious ceremonies.

The Kachinas

Kachina ceremonies are an important part of Hopi religion. The Hopi kachinas are spirits who can visit Hopi villages for half of every year. The Hopi believe the kachinas bring the rains and help the crops to grow. They also show people how to live and behave, and bring peace and prosperity.

Kachina ceremonies are held throughout the six months the kachinas are said to dwell in the Hopi villages. Kachina dances are an important part of these ceremonies. Each kachina dancer represents one of the hundreds of different kachinas. For example, one dancer might become the kachina Crow Mother. Crow Mother is the mother of all kachinas. Other dancers represent clowns who follow the kachinas and cause mischief. One clown named Tcutckutu (koot KOO too) is known for his love of food. It takes years of training to become a kachina dancer, which is a position of honor among the Hopi.

During the kachina festivals, some kachina dancers give out colorful wooden dolls that look like the kachinas they represent. Kachina dolls are used to teach Hopi children about the powers and abilities of each of the hundreds of different kachinas.

Generations of Artists

The skill of Hopi artists can also be seen in their pottery. A Hopi woman named **Nampeyo** (nahm PAY oh) was one of these artists. In 1895 Nampeyo's husband was working with an archaeologist digging up the ruins of an ancient Hopi pueblo. When Nampeyo saw the pottery that had been found there, she was struck by its beauty. She thought the ancient designs were more beautiful than the designs she and other artists of her time were creating. She began to visit the digging site to study the ancient pottery.

At first she tried to copy the designs she saw. Then she began to create her own designs in the ancient style. Over the next 20 years, Nampeyo made many beautiful pots. Her work soon gained wide recognition. Determined to spread interest in the traditional Hopi pottery, Nampeyo taught her skill to her daughters. Today many Hopi potters, including Nampeyo's grandchildren, carry on her work.

Southwest Museum

The Hopi artist Nampeyo (above) displays her pottery. The pottery shown at right includes many of the traditional designs that were brought back into use by Nampeyo.

The Heard Museum

WHY IT MATTERS

Today the Pueblo peoples' way of life includes a mix of the old and the new. Adobe homes exist alongside buildings made of other materials. Some of the irrigation canals built hundreds of years ago are now used by big cities like Phoenix, Arizona.

The Hopi have worked hard to maintain their traditional way of life. Hopi ceremonies, government, and social organizations continue to exist much as they always have. Kachina dances are still being held. Visitors come from all over the world to watch these ceremonies and to buy Hopi artwork.

This Zuni necklace uses the traditional Pueblo materials of silver, turquoise, and other stones.

✓// Reviewing Facts and Ideas

MAIN IDEAS

- Native Americans in the Southwest include such Pueblo peoples as the Hopi and the Zuni, and such non-Pueblo peoples as the Apache and the Navajo.

- The Hopi were skilled dry farmers in a harsh, desert climate.

- Art and tradition have been and still are central to Hopi life.

- In 1895 a Hopi artist named Nampeyo revived the art of making traditional Hopi pottery.

THINK ABOUT IT

1. Name some of the Native American peoples who live in the Southwestern region. How and when did they come here?

2. How did the Hopi succeed at farming in their dry environment?

3. **FOCUS** Explain how art and tradition influence and enrich the life of the Hopi people.

4. **THINKING SKILL** How did Nampeyo become interested in traditional Hopi pottery? What _effect_ did this have on Hopi art? Explain the reasons for your answer.

5. **GEOGRAPHY** What might the Hopi's belief in kachinas show about the effect of geography on their lives? Explain your answer.

MAKING A DIFFERENCE

Sharing the Old Ways

LAGUNA PUEBLO, NEW MEXICO, is one of 19 Pueblo communities in the state. At Laguna Elementary School, Ron Sarracino's students begin the day with the greeting "Guwatzi" (guh WAHT zee). In the Keres (KE rez) language, this word means "How are things here?"

Today English has replaced Keres as the main language spoken in many pueblos. Because of this, few young people have learned to speak Keres. To Mr. Sarracino, the Keres language plays an important part in the Laguna community. He explains:

All our ceremonies are based on our traditional language. The elders of our pueblo are telling us that if the young people do not learn the language, then our culture, ceremonies, and everything else that goes with it will be lost.

Mr. Sarracino learned Keres from his parents as he was growing up in Laguna. Today, in his classroom, the learning continues. The older people, or elders, in the community are helping Mr. Sarracino and his students. He explains that during Native American Week, which is held each April, "the elders share the old ways with our children." They tell traditional stories of long ago and talk about events from their own childhoods. "The students are surprised," says Mr. Sarracino, "at how different life in Laguna was then. Children herded sheep and went to the river for water for cooking and drinking."

Dancing is also an important part of the festivities. Students dance the arrow dance or the deer dance to songs Mr. Sarracino sings in Keres. One of the dancers is fifth grader Samantha Fernando. She has been learning Keres at home from her grandparents, as well as from Mr. Sarracino in school. "I'm glad we're learning our Laguna language," she says. "When we grow up, we don't want our traditions to be forgotten." Thanks to the efforts of the elders and people like Mr. Sarracino, they will be remembered.

"All our ceremonies are based on our traditional language."

Ron J. Sarracino

1300   1400   1500   1800

Native Americans of the Plains

Focus Activity

READ TO LEARN

How did the Lakota adapt the horse to their culture?

VOCABULARY

- lodge
- prairie
- teepee
- travois
- coup stick
- jerky

PLACES

- Black Hills

Read Aloud

Iron Teeth, a woman from the Plains, described how the horse changed the lives of her people: "My grandmother told me that when she was young . . . people themselves had to walk. In those times they did not travel far or often. But when they got horses, they could move more easily from place to place. Then they could kill more of the buffalo and other animals, and so they got more meat for food and gathered more skins for [homes] and clothing."

THE BIG PICTURE

For thousands of years Native Americans who lived on the plains of the Middle West lived mostly in villages. The villages were usually located near rivers, where there was plenty of water for farming. The Plains peoples lived in **lodges**. Lodges are homes made of logs covered with grasses, sticks, and soil. During the summer, the men left their villages to hunt buffalo. They returned in the fall to harvest their crops.

In the 1500s the Spanish arrived in North America. They brought something that would change the Plains peoples' lives forever—the horse. In this lesson you will read about the Lakota Sioux (luh KOH tah SOO), one of the peoples of the Plains, from about 1500 to 1800. You will read about how their taming of the horse led to major changes in their way of life.

LIFE ON THE GREAT PLAINS

The Great Plains are made up of dry **prairies** that cover much of the Middle West. A prairie is flat or gently rolling land covered mostly with grasses and wildflowers. Summers can be extremely hot, and winters extremely cold. The lack of rain makes growing corn and other crops difficult except in river areas. Until the late 1800s, herds of buffalo roamed the Great Plains.

When they were hunting buffalo, the Plains people lived in **teepees** (TEE peez). Teepees are cone-shaped tents made of animal skins. Some Plains people still use teepees today. Jerry Flute says this about the teepee:

> *We live in a very harsh climate. . . . It's not unusual to hear the [reporter] say it's going to be 85°F below zero with the wind chill. . . . [The teepee is] a dwelling that is cool in the summer, that is warm in the winter, and that is extremely mobile.*

When it was time to move, the teepee was folded up and loaded onto the **travois** (truh VOY). A travois was a sled-like device used for carrying people and belongings. Plains people used the travois to carry buffalo meat home after a hunt. Before the arrival of the horse, the travois was often pulled by dogs.

Taming the Horse

By the 1600s horses that had run away from their Spanish owners roamed freely across the Plains. By the 1700s the Lakota were taming these wild horses and adapting them to their way of life. Many Plains peoples became expert riders, breeders, and trainers. The most important change the horse brought was in the economy of the Plains people. The buffalo replaced farming as the Lakota's main source of food. Many stopped living in permanent settlements. Instead, they moved from one campsite to another to hunt the buffalo.

This doll (right) was made from deerskin and horsehair. The Plains rider (below) is using a **travois** in the early 1900s.

Buffalo Bill Historical Center

THE LAKOTA

The Lakota Sioux, who are also known as the Dakota, live in the northern part of the Great Plains. The time is 1800. You are about to meet Standing Bear and Red Deer, young members of the Lakota people. They live in the Black Hills of South Dakota. The Black Hills were and still are a sacred area to the Lakota people.

A Young Lakota Boy

Standing Bear, an 11-year-old boy, is at a buffalo hunt with his father and other men from their camp. First the hunters ride straight into the buffalo herd to create confusion. Then they go after a single buffalo using a lance, bow and arrow, or rifle. Standing Bear admires the great courage and skill it takes to do this. He is only here to help, but someday he will kill his own buffalo. His father cuts out the liver of a buffalo that has just been killed. It is the most nutritious part, so he and Standing Bear eat some of it now. They save the rest for Standing Bear's mother and sister.

After the hunt Standing Bear practices riding. Someday he would like to

The Buffalo Hunt, a painting by Edgar S. Paxon, shows hunters using their skill and their knowledge of the horse and the buffalo.

become one of the leaders who govern his community. To do this he must show courage in the face of danger—during the buffalo hunt and in battle. Standing Bear knows the bravest act that he can make in battle is to touch an enemy without killing him. To do this, Standing Bear would have to use a special weapon called a coup (KOO) stick. *Coup* is a French word that means "strike" or "hit."

Standing Bear can also bring honor to himself in other ways. Being a good speaker and generosity are other qualities that the Lakota admire.

A Young Lakota Girl

Red Deer, Standing Bear's older sister, works hard beside her mother. The hunt is over, but Red Deer's tasks have just begun. As you can see in the diagram on the next page, the buffalo serves many purposes. Thousands of pounds of buffalo meat lie in the field. If the meat is not cut and cured quickly, it will spoil.

Red Deer and her mother slice the buffalo meat in thin strips and leave it to dry in the sun. This dried meat is called jerky. Sometimes they make pemmican by adding berries and fat to jerky. Red Deer's family will eat this food all through the winter.

After the buffalo meat is prepared, Red Deer helps her mother make a teepee. The teepee will use about ten buffalo skins. First the skins must be cleaned and scraped. Then Red Deer and her mother will cut them and sew them together. Finally they will stretch the skins over several wooden poles.

Tomorrow Red Deer might go with her mother to search for herbs. Many Native Americans use herbs to cure common sicknesses. The major ingredient in aspirin today, for example, comes from an herb used by many Native Americans to treat illnesses.

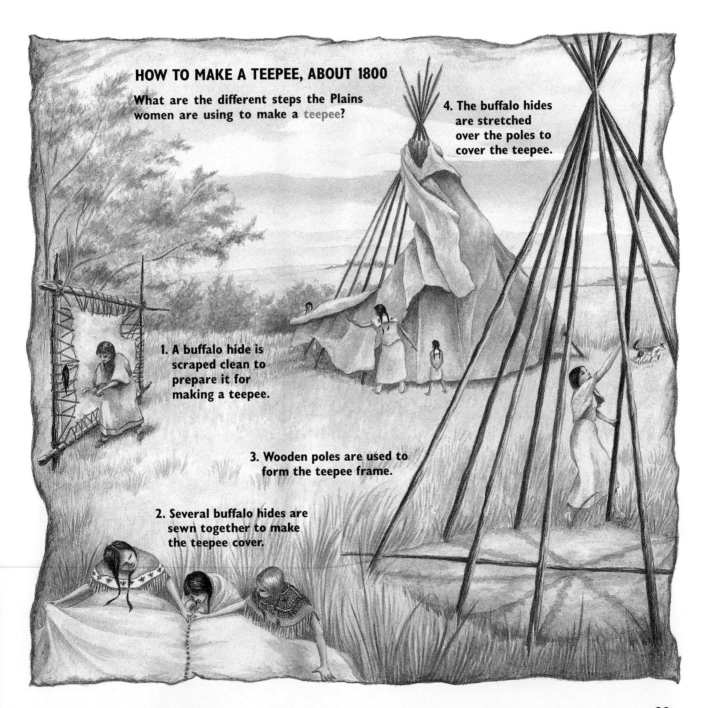

HOW TO MAKE A TEEPEE, ABOUT 1800

What are the different steps the Plains women are using to make a teepee?

4. The buffalo hides are stretched over the poles to cover the teepee.

1. A buffalo hide is scraped clean to prepare it for making a teepee.

3. Wooden poles are used to form the teepee frame.

2. Several buffalo hides are sewn together to make the teepee cover.

THE WINTER COUNT

The Lakota kept track of time with calendars called winter counts. Each winter the Lakota met to choose an important event of the past year. An artist then recorded this event by drawing a symbol, or picture of it, on the hide of an animal.

Studying winter counts has helped historians understand the history of the Lakota. On this page is a winter count from the 1800s. What other means do people use to record important events from their past?

MANY VOICES
PRIMARY SOURCE

An 1801–1870 winter count by Lone Dog, published by the Smithsonian Institution.

Most of this winter count was recorded on a buffalo hide by a Lakota who lived in what is today Montana. The symbols are read in a counterclockwise spiral. The key tells the meaning of some of the symbols.

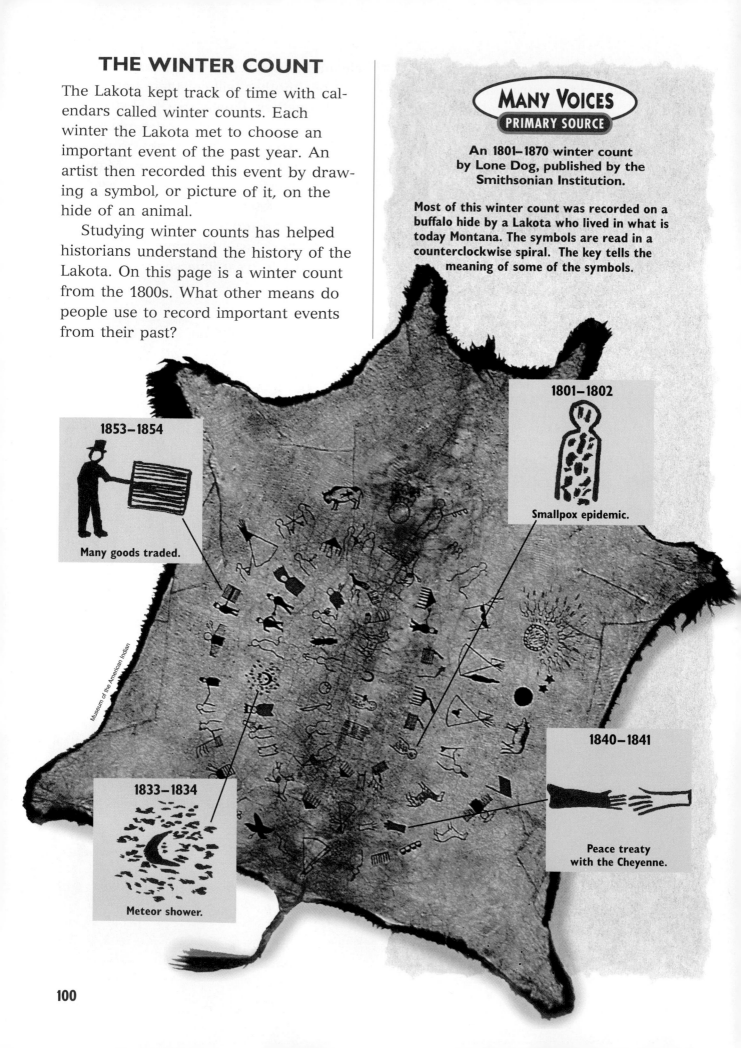

1801–1802

Smallpox epidemic.

1853–1854

Many goods traded.

Museum of the American Indian

1833–1834

Meteor shower.

1840–1841

Peace treaty with the Cheyenne.

WHY IT MATTERS

The arrival of the horse on the Great Plains changed the lives of the Native Americans of the Plains in many ways. It made buffalo hunting easier and helped the Lakota become a powerful people. It also made them much more dependent on the buffalo than they had ever been before.

The buffalo, in fact, became central to the Plains peoples' way of life. Their very existence now depended on their maintaining large buffalo herds on the Great Plains.

When Europeans started moving to the Plains, problems arose. Would there still be enough land for the buffalo to graze? You will learn more about these developments on the Great Plains in Chapter 18 of this book.

How did the different Plains peoples communicate with each other?

Native Americans on the Great Plains spoke at least 20 different languages. They developed a special sign language to communicate. When they met people from another group, they used hand signals for important words. For example, to express the word *buffalo*, a person would raise an index finger to each side of his or her head to show horns.

✓ Reviewing Facts and Ideas

MAIN IDEAS

- Before they learned to tame the horse, most Native Americans on the Great Plains were farmers who lived in permanent villages.

- With the horse, many Plains peoples began moving from place to place to hunt the buffalo herds.

- The Lakota began to depend on the buffalo about 1700. They used the animal for food such as jerky and pemmican, for clothing, and as a covering for the teepee. They kept a record of their history by making a winter count each year.

- The Lakota kept a record of important events in their history with a calendar called a winter count.

THINK ABOUT IT

1. For what purposes did the Lakota people use the different parts of the buffalo?

2. What qualities did the Lakota value in a person? Why were they important?

3. **FOCUS** How did the Lakota's taming of the horse lead to changes in their way of life?

4. **THINKING SKILL** *Compare* the roles of the Lakota children Standing Bear and Red Deer, described in this lesson. How might you expect these roles to be different today?

5. **WRITE** Write your own version of a winter count. Pick one event from each year of your life and draw a symbol for it. Write down the meaning of each symbol.

Rochester Museum

Focus Activity

READ TO LEARN

How did the Iroquois bring peace among their people?

VOCABULARY

- longhouse
- wampum
- clan
- Iroquois Confederacy
- compromise

PEOPLE

- Deganawida
- Hiawatha

PLACES

- Hodenosaunee Trail

1300   1600   1700

Native Americans of the Eastern Woodlands

Read Aloud

"Into our bundle we have gathered the causes of war. We have cast this bundle away. . . . Our great-grand-children shall not see them," spoke the Mohawk leader Hiawatha (hī uh WAH thuh). Hiawatha helped to bring peace to the Iroquois (IHR uh kwah).

THE BIG PICTURE

In Chapter 2 you read about Arid and Humid America. Because of its fertile soil and plentiful rainfall, hundreds of years ago Humid America was almost completely covered by forest. This region was home to many Native Americans. Today these people are known as Native Americans of the Eastern Woodlands.

Among the peoples of the southern woodlands were the Cherokee and the Creek. Today the Creek also call themselves Muscogee (mus KOH gee). In the northern woodlands lived the Penobscot (puh NAHB skaht), the Lenni Lenape (LEN ee LEN nah pee), and others. The Potawatomi (poh tuh WAH tuh mee) and the Winnebago (wihn uh BAY goh) lived near the Great Lakes.

Scholars usually divide the Native Americans in the Eastern Woodlands into two major language groups. The larger of the two groups spoke a language called Algonkian (al GAHNG kee un). In this lesson you will learn about the second group, the Iroquois, who spoke Iroquoian. By the 1700s the Iroquois had become a major power in the Eastern Woodlands.

THE EASTERN WOODLANDS

As you saw on the Infographic on page 76, the Eastern Woodlands is a vast area that extends roughly from the Atlantic Coast to west of the Mississippi River. In addition to forests, the area has many lakes and rivers. In most of the Eastern Woodlands there are four distinct seasons.

Natural resources are plentiful. The Atlantic Ocean, the lakes, and the rivers are rich sources of fish. The forests provide animals for food and wood for building homes and canoes. Wild rice grows in the Great Lakes area. Along the coastal plains and river valleys, the soil is excellent for farming.

North and South

Like other Native Americans discussed in this chapter, the peoples of the Eastern Woodlands used and changed their environments. In what is now Maine, the Penobscot lived in mountainous areas where farming was difficult. They moved from place to place, hunting animals for food. The Penobscot also gathered fruits, nuts, and berries from the forests. To protect themselves from the cold and snowy winters, the Penobscot wore warm clothes made from deerskin.

The Natchez, who were descendants of the Mound Builders, lived in what is now the state of Mississippi. In the south, where the climate is mild much of the year, the Natchez and other peoples depended mostly on farming. To keep cool in their warm climate, the Natchez wore light clothes woven from the fibers of plants.

Overall, Native American peoples throughout the Eastern Woodlands had much in common. Most were farming people who lived in permanent villages. They built homes out of wood and grew crops of corn, squash, and beans. In addition to farming, they hunted and fished. Using the area's many lakes, rivers, and streams, Native Americans of the Eastern Woodlands traveled far in their canoes. Most importantly, they shared similar beliefs and traditions.

In Iroquois culture, women (below) were mainly responsible for growing and harvesting crops.

Rochester Museum

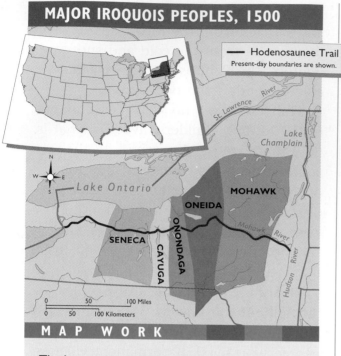

Hodenosaunee Trail
Present-day boundaries are shown.

Lake Champlain

St. Lawrence River

Lake Ontario

MOHAWK

ONEIDA

SENECA

ONONDAGA

CAYUGA

Mohawk River

Hudson River

0   50   100 Miles
0   50   100 Kilometers

MAP WORK

The hunting grounds of the five major Iroquois peoples once extended well beyond present-day New York State to the Mississippi River.

1. Which people lived near Lake Champlain?

2. Which peoples lived closest to the Onondaga?

THE IROQUOIS

In the 1500s the Iroquois lived mostly in what is now New York State. The map on this page shows the location of the five Iroquois peoples in this area. Historians have called them the Iroquois because of the Iroquoian language they spoke. But the Iroquois call themselves *Hodenosaunee* (hoh den oh SAH nee). In Iroquoian this means "people of the longhouse." Longhouses are long buildings made of poles covered with sheets of bark.

A longhouse can be over 200 feet long. In the 1500s each longhouse provided a home for several families. A central aisle with cooking fires ran the length of the building. Each family had its own living space on either side of the aisle. Goods were stored overhead.

The diagram on the next page shows what a longhouse looked like during this time period.

The Iroquois Homeland

During the 1500s the homelands of the Iroquois were connected by well-used trails. One central route, the Hodenosaunee Trail, ran through the main villages of all five peoples. This winding path ran 250 miles through Iroquois territory.

The Iroquois were expert farmers. Women did most of the farming. They grew 15 types of corn and over 60 different kinds of beans. From the forest, the Iroquois obtained animals for meat, maple syrup, nuts, roots, vegetables, oils, fruits, all kinds of berries, teas, and herbs for medicines.

Wampum

Wampum (WAHM pum) was one thing the Iroquois could not get from the forest. Wampum consisted of small, polished beads that were usually made from shells and then strung or woven together. These beads took a long time to make by hand. First a bead had to be carefully carved out of part of a shell. A small, slender drill was used to create a hole. Sand was then used to polish the bead. The finished beads were woven into belts or strung into necklaces. You can see an example of wampum on page 106.

Every belt of wampum was different. Often a wampum maker would create a piece to remember an important event. The time and effort that went into creating wampum made it very valuable. It was often given as a gift on special occasions. In the early 1600s the Iroquois began trading wampum to the Europeans for other goods.

The Clan Mother

Women held a great deal of power in the Iroquois world. They decided how the land would be used and who would use it. They were also the leaders of the clans. A clan is a group of families who share the same ancestor.

Almost all Iroquois property was controlled by clans. This meant that women were the owners of the land. They owned the longhouses and everything in them. When a man married, he moved into his wife's longhouse and lived with her family. The head of each clan was called a *clan mother*.

No important decision could be made without the consent of the clan mother. Although the leaders of each village were men, they were chosen by the clan mothers. If a leader failed in his duties, the clan mother would meet with other clan women. They would then decide who would replace him.

Conflicts Among the Iroquois

As long as the Iroquois peoples remained small in number, they cooperated on many matters. Then, around 1300, when their numbers began to grow, arguments arose and fighting broke out. They also fought other Eastern Woodlands peoples. These conflicts were often over hunting grounds.

The Iroquois believed that if one person was wronged, it hurt the peace of the whole clan. For this reason, wrongs had to be punished. Warfare soon became a constant problem for the Iroquois peoples.

IROQUOIS LONGHOUSE, 1500s

What kinds of activities took place inside an Iroquois longhouse?

ONE FAMILY'S LIVING SPACE

SMOKE HOLE

CENTRAL AISLE

STORAGE AREA

COOKING FIRE

SLEEPING PLATFORM

ANOTHER FAMILY'S LIVING SPACE

IROQUOIS CONFEDERACY

According to the Iroquois legend, two Iroquois leaders, Deganawida (day gahn uh WEE duh) and Hiawatha, saw that fighting was destroying their people. Read Hiawatha's speech below. How does Hiawatha think uniting will help the Iroquois?

MANY VOICES
PRIMARY SOURCE

Excerpt from a speech by Hiawatha in about 1570, as told by Iroquois chief Elias Johnson, 1881.

Friends and Brothers: You being members of many tribes, you have come from a great distance; the voice of war has aroused you up; you are afraid . . . [for] your homes, your wives and your children; you tremble for your safety. Believe me, I am with you. My heart beats with your hearts. We are one. We have one common object. We come to promote our common interest, and to determine how this can be best done.

*To oppose those **hordes** of northern tribes, singly and alone, would prove certain destruction. We can make no progress in that way. We must unite ourselves into one common band of brothers. We must have but one voice. Many voices makes confusion. We must have one fire, one pipe [of peace] and one war club. This will give us strength.*

hordes: crowds

The Great Laws

In about 1570 five separate Iroquois peoples banded together to form the Iroquois Confederacy, also known as the Iroquois League. A confederacy is a union of people who join together for a common purpose. The five peoples that made up the Iroquois Confederacy were the Onondaga (ahn un DAW gah), the Mohawk, the Oneida (oh NĪ duh), the Seneca (SE nih kuh), and the Cayuga (kah YOO guh).

Deganawida became known as the Peace Maker. Deganawida and Hiawatha developed rules for the Iroquois to follow. These were called the Great Laws. The Great Laws were not only rules, though. They were also guidelines for living together in peace.

The Grand Council

Deganawida described the Iroquois Confederacy as a great longhouse that stretched the length of the Hodenosaunee Trail. To keep peace within the confederacy, Deganawida set up a Grand Council.

The Granger Collection

This Iroquois wampum belt (above) was made in the early 1800s. It was made to honor the founding of the Iroquois Confederacy.

Representatives to the council were chosen by the clan mothers from each of the Iroquois peoples. The Grand Council made decisions through discussion and **compromise**. A compromise is the settling of a dispute by agreeing that each side will give up something.

WHY IT MATTERS

Deganawida's ideas brought peace to the Iroquois and helped make them powerful. By the 1700s they had influence over Native Americans from the St. Lawrence River in the north to present-day Tennessee in the south and to Michigan in the west. In the early 1700s the Tuscarora (tus kuh RAWR uh), an Iroquoian-speaking people from the southern woodlands, moved to New York State. The Tuscarora joined the

Iroquois Confederacy about 1722. Today the Grand Council governs the Iroquois, using discussion and compromise.

✓✓ Reviewing Facts and Ideas

MAIN IDEAS

- Algonkian and Iroquoian were two major language groups in the Eastern Woodlands.

- Most Native Americans in the Eastern Woodlands, such as the Iroquois, were farming peoples living in permanent villages.

- Women had a great deal of power in Iroquois communities of the 1500s, and still do today.

- According to Iroquois legend, Deganawida and Hiawatha formed the Iroquois Confederacy in around 1570. The Confederacy brought peace and unity to the Iroquois.

THINK ABOUT IT

1. How did Native Americans of the Eastern Woodlands use the natural resources in their environment?

2. What role do clan mothers play in Iroquois communities?

3. **FOCUS** How did the Iroquois Confederacy bring peace to its members?

4. **THINKING SKILL** Based on what you have read, what *generalizations* might you make about the different Eastern Woodlands peoples in about 1500?

5. **GEOGRAPHY** Referring to the Infographic on page 76, make two lists: one of Native American peoples of the northern woodlands and one of peoples of the southern woodlands.

A present-day Iroquois couple (left) joins in a traditional community dance.

107

Thinking Skills

Rochester Museum

This Iroquois council meeting took place in New York State in the early 1900s.

Identifying Cause and Effect

VOCABULARY
cause
effect

WHY THE SKILL MATTERS

As you study history, you will notice that one event often follows another. Some of these events, but not all, are related to each other. One of the most important of these relationships is **cause** and **effect**.

A cause is something that makes something else happen. The event that happens as a result of a cause is the effect. For example, on a cold winter night, you might close your window. This cause, the closing of the window, produces an effect—your room gets warmer.

USING THE SKILL

A cause-and-effect connection exists when something causes another thing to happen. How can you find this connection? Looking for word clues can help you.

Words such as *because, caused by,* and *as a result of* are clues to causes and effects. *Because, since,* or *caused by* signal a cause. *As a result, therefore,* and *so* usually signal an effect.

You learned about cause and effect in the last lesson. For example, in the 1500s the Iroquois peoples were fighting among themselves. Iroquois leaders urged them to unite. As a result of these events, the Iroquois Confederacy was formed.

These historical events, which follow each other, have a cause-and-effect relationship. Which were causes? What was the effect?

The word clues *as a result* signal that the formation of the Iroquois Confederacy was an effect. The constant warfare and the urging of Iroquois leaders caused the Iroquois to unite.

TRYING THE SKILL

Read the following paragraph. Try to identify the cause-and-effect connections. Refer to the Helping Yourself box for a reminder of what causes and effects are.

The Iroquois prided themselves on being able to travel great distances. In the winter, however, snow slowed them down. If you have ever walked through deep snow, you know why. Your weight causes you to sink into the snow. To keep that from happening, the Iroquois made snowshoes that helped keep their feet on top of the snow. As a result, they were able to walk quickly in the snow. Some even claimed to walk faster in snow than on dry land.

Think about the events described in this paragraph. What is the effect that results from walking in deep snow without snowshoes? If you are having trouble finding the cause and effect, look for a clue word.

Helping yourself

- A **cause** is something that makes something else happen. An **effect** is the result of a cause.

- Look for clue words that show causes— *because, since, caused by*.

- Look for clue words that show effects— *so, therefore, as a result*.

REVIEWING THE SKILL

1. What is a cause? An effect?

2. What clue words signal that you are talking about a cause? What clue words signal that you are talking about an effect?

3. What was the cause of the Iroquois slowing down when they walked in the snow without snowshoes? How do you know?

4. Name two effects that occurred as a result of the Iroquois wearing snowshoes. How do you know?

5. When might finding cause-and-effect connections be useful to you?

CHAPTER 4 REVIEW

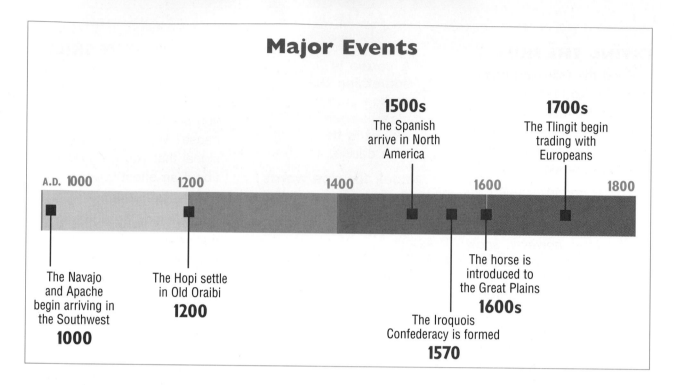

Major Events

1500s
The Spanish arrive in North America

1700s
The Tlingit begin trading with Europeans

A.D. **1000**   1200   1400   1600   1800

The Navajo and Apache begin arriving in the Southwest
1000

The Hopi settle in Old Oraibi
1200

The horse is introduced to the Great Plains
1600s

The Iroquois Confederacy is formed
1570

THINKING ABOUT VOCABULARY

Number a paper from 1 to 5. Beside each number write the word from the list below that matches the description.

adobe
clan
compromise
prairie
technology

1. A group of families who share the same ancestor

2. A type of clay found in the earth

3. The settlement of a dispute in which each side agrees to give up part of its demands

4. The design and use of tools, ideas, and methods to solve problems

5. Flat or gently rolling land covered with grasses and wildflowers

THINKING ABOUT FACTS

1. How did the Native Americans of the Northwest Coast make use of the resources of the sea? How did this affect other areas of their lives?

2. What did the Alaska Native Claims Settlement Act say?

3. What is a kachina? What role does the kachina play in Hopi life?

4. What material did the Hopi use to build their homes? Describe this material.

5. What is the role of women among the Iroquois?

6. How do the Lakota use a coup stick?

7. What were the two major language groups in the Eastern Woodlands?

8. Where did the Penobscot live?

9. Who are the ancestors of the Natchez?

10. Look at the time line above. Name the event that eventually led to the appearance of the horse on the Great Plains by the 1600s.

THINK AND WRITE ◄▤▤►

WRITING A STORY
Write a story of your own in which you show the importance of the natural environment to one of the Native American peoples you have read about.

WRITING AN ACCOUNT
Suppose that you are the Lakota who made the winter count pictured on page 100. Choose one of the events the picture shows and write an account of what happened.

WRITING A NEWSPAPER STORY
Suppose that you are a newspaper reporter assigned to write about the founding of the Iroquois Confederacy. You might wish to include a quote from Hiawatha's speech in the story you write.

APPLYING THINKING SKILLS

IDENTIFYING CAUSE AND EFFECT
Answer the questions below to practice the skill of identifying cause and effect.

1. What is a cause? What is an effect?
2. What are some clue words that can help you identify cause and effect?
3. What caused the Hopi to use the dry farming method?
4. What was the effect of the horses from Spain arriving on the Great Plains?
5. How is understanding the connections between cause and effect important in the study of history?

Summing Up the Chapter

Copy the cause-and-effect chains on a separate piece of paper. Review the chapter to complete the blank sections. When you have finished, write a paragraph describing how life might have changed if a cause in the first part of the chain had been different. For example, what might have happened to the peoples of the Great Plains if the horse had not been introduced to North America?

CAUSE		EFFECT
The peoples of the Northwest Coast get most of what they need from the sea.	As a Result	
	As a Result	The Hopi use dry farming methods, irrigating their farmlands.
	As a Result	The Great Plains peoples tame the horse, and their way of life is changed.
The Iroquois Confederacy is formed.	As a Result	

CHAPTER 5

Life in the Eastern Hemisphere

THINKING ABOUT HISTORY AND GEOGRAPHY

The story of Chapter 5 stretches across Europe, Africa, and Asia before the peoples of the Eastern and Western hemispheres met. Following the time line, you see that throughout the world people were exploring and trading. It would be only a few years before Europeans began making voyages to the Americas.

Portugal

Sahara

Timbuktu

1300s

SAHARA
Traders crisscross the Sahara in West Africa

1400s

TIMBUKTU
Gold and valuable goods are sold at markets in West Africa

1430s

CHINA
Zheng He explores the coasts of Asia and Africa

1300

1400

1420

Germany

EUROPE

Mediterranean
Sea

China

ASIA

INDIAN
OCEAN

1436

GERMANY
Johannes Gutenberg
invents the printing press

1440s

PORTUGAL
Prince Henry's ships
explore the African coast

1440

1460

1300   1350 **1368**   **1433** 1450   1500

Asian Emperors and Traders

Read Aloud

"Let the dark water dragons go down into the sea and leave us free from calamity," prayed the Chinese sea captains.* *In the autumn of 1405 over 300 Chinese ships were made ready to sail to the east coast of India. The captains' prayer asked their gods to protect them from danger. They were worried about what lay ahead.*

Focus Activity

READ TO LEARN

How did the Chinese increase trade in the East?

VOCABULARY

- magnetic compass

PEOPLE

- Zhu Di
- Zheng He

PLACES

- China
- Great Wall
- Silk Road
- Persia
- India

THE BIG PICTURE

You have been reading about the peoples of the Western Hemisphere. Now you are going to read about the peoples of the Eastern Hemisphere. In the late 1400s, the century of contact, the peoples of the West met the peoples of the East. The lives of each of these peoples were changed forever. You will begin by looking at life in Asia at a time when people there were meeting people from Africa and Europe for the first time.

In the eastern part of Asia, northeast of the towering Himalaya Mountains, is the country of **China**. At about the same time that the Aztec and Inca were building their empires in the Western Hemisphere, the Chinese had enlarged their empire in the Eastern Hemisphere.

*Mariner's prayer from "When China Ruled the Seas" (1994), translated by Chu Hung-lam and James Geiss.

114

THE CHINESE EMPIRE

The people of China viewed their land as the great empire. As you will see from the map on page 116, this huge land was protected by the Himalayas to the west, the Gobi Desert to the north, and the Pacific Ocean to the east. Despite these protections, invaders sometimes broke through. In the late 1200s, after years of fighting the Chinese, the Mongols from northern Asia gained control of the empire.

The Chinese pushed the Mongols out in 1368. In 1402 the new emperor, Zhu Di (ZHOO DEE), set out to rebuild China. The Great Wall, which began as several older walls built around 200 B.C., was repaired. New bridges and roads were also built.

The Silk Road

Zhu Di also increased trade on the ancient Silk Road. The Silk Road was a network of overland trade routes that stretched from China to Persia, which is today the country of Iran. During the late 1200s, Europe's demand for Chinese silk was so high that the ancient trade route became known as the Silk Road. Find the Silk Road on the map on the next page.

The most important item carried on the Silk Road was, of course, silk. Through a chain of Chinese, Indian, Arab, and Italian traders, the silk made its long journey over Asia's mountains and deserts to Europe. In exchange, oranges, gold, and horses were brought to China. However, few traders traveled the entire Silk Road. Most of them passed goods from one trading post to the next.

The Great Wall of China (below) is the longest human-made feature ever built. It is 4,600 miles long and was built mostly by hand. The wall can be seen by astronauts in outer space.

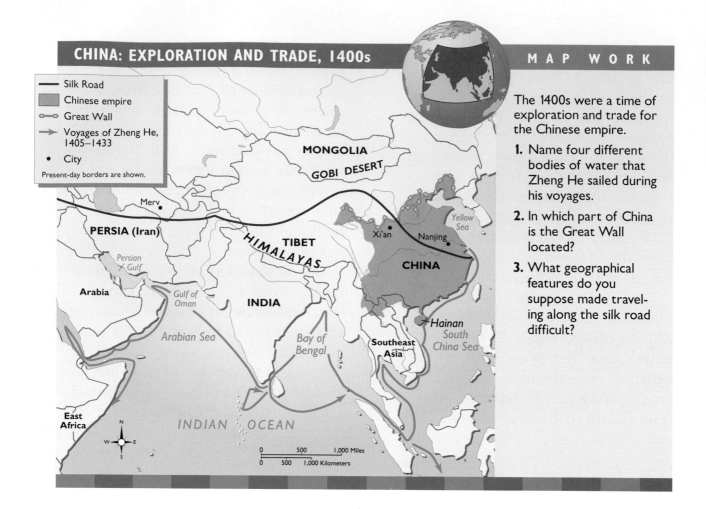

Legend:
— Silk Road
▨ Chinese empire
⊏⊐ Great Wall
→ Voyages of Zheng He, 1405–1433
• City
Present-day borders are shown.

MONGOLIA
GOBI DESERT

Merv •

PERSIA (Iran)

Persian Gulf

Arabia

Gulf of Oman

HIMALAYAS

TIBET

INDIA

Xi'an •

Yellow Sea

Nanjing •

CHINA

Hainan

South China Sea

Southeast Asia

Arabian Sea

Bay of Bengal

East Africa

INDIAN OCEAN

0   500   1,000 Miles
0   500   1,000 Kilometers

The 1400s were a time of exploration and trade for the Chinese empire.

1. Name four different bodies of water that Zheng He sailed during his voyages.

2. In which part of China is the Great Wall located?

3. What geographical features do you suppose made traveling along the silk road difficult?

ZHENG HE'S VOYAGES

In 1403 emperor Zhu Di ordered the building of thousands of sailing ships. He put Zheng He (ZHAHNG HUH), a Chinese Muslim sea captain, in command of the huge fleet. Muslims are followers of the religion of Islam. From 1405 to 1433 Zheng He made seven voyages. He explored India, southeast Asia, Arabia, and the coast of East Africa.

The Ships of Zheng He

Over 300 ships were part of Zheng He's fleet. Several ships were over 400 feet long—the largest ever built at that time. To help them find the cardinal directions on the open seas, the sailors used a magnetic compass. The Chinese invented the magnetic compass about A.D. 100. Traders used the compass to guide them across the vast deserts along

the Silk Road. The sailors used a compass that floated in a container of water so that the compass needle was not upset by the movement of the ship.

Scholars today do not agree on why Zheng He made these voyages. The emperor might have wanted to find new trading centers or to show outsiders the power of the Chinese empire. In 1433 Zheng He's ships were called home. China's days of exploration ended in 1525 when a new emperor ordered that the empire's sailing ships be destroyed. China's chances for becoming a sea power were over.

A Chinese Tale

Over many centuries, tales have been exchanged among different peoples in the Eastern Hemisphere. Zheng He's voyages helped to bring new tales to

Asia. In fact the Chinese may have been the first to write down a tale about the young woman who lost her shoe. Following is an excerpt from the Chinese tale of Yeh-hsien (YE SHEN). How is her story like the Cinderella tale that you know?

PRIMARY SOURCE

Excerpt from *Yeh-hsien* translated by Arthur Waley, in *The Chinese Cinderella Story*, adapted by Judy Sierra, 1992.

*The man who had picked up the gold shoe sold it in **T'o-han**. (TOH HAHN), and it was brought to the king. He ordered all the women of the court to put it on, but it was too small even for the one among them that had the smallest foot. He then ordered all the women in his kingdom to try it on, but there was not one that it fitted. It was as light as **down**, and it made no noise even when **treading** on stone. His search finally took him to the place where Yeh-hsien lived with her stepmother, and the shoe fitted her perfectly.*

T'o-han: an imaginary kingdom
down: fine, soft feathers
treading: walking

WHY IT MATTERS

China is one of the world's oldest civilizations. Its roots go back more than 3,000 years. Today China has the world's largest number of people. Over 1 billion live within its borders. Until about the 1400s, China had done little trading with Europe. During the voyages of Zheng He, China began exploring countries in the Eastern Hemisphere before Europe had started exploring the Western Hemisphere. China's voyages soon ended, which prevented it from competing with Europe.

✓ Reviewing Facts and Ideas

MAIN IDEAS
- In the 1400s, while the Aztec and Inca empires were growing, the Chinese were strengthening their already powerful empire.
- Traders on the Silk Road carried silk and other goods from China to Europe. Oranges and horses were brought back to China.
- From 1405 to 1433, Zheng He explored India, southeast Asia, Arabia, and the east coast of Africa.

THINK ABOUT IT
1. What natural and human-made features helped protect China from invasions? Which group broke through in the late 1200s?
2. How did the Silk Road get its name?
3. **FOCUS** What did Zheng He's voyages accomplish for the Chinese empire?
4. **THINKING SKILL** List the *cause* and *effect* connections between the Chinese invention of the magnetic compass and Zheng He's voyages.
5. **WRITE** Write a tale about the special shoes Cinderella might wear today.

Reading Line and Circle Graphs

VOCABULARY

graph   circle graph

line graph

WHY THE SKILL MATTERS

As you have read, the Chinese empire went through a great period of shipbuilding in the early 1400s. The Chinese built warships, passenger ships, and transport ships for the empire's fleet. A fleet is a group of ships under one command. Some of these ships took part in Zheng He's voyages.

One way to picture how large the Chinese fleet was is by using a **graph**. A graph is a diagram that presents information in a way that makes it easy to understand. Graphs are especially useful for showing such things as patterns, trends, amounts, or how things change over time.

USING LINE GRAPHS

Line graphs show changes over time. The graph below shows how the size of the Chinese fleet changed during the 1400s through the middle 1500s.

To read a line graph, first look at its title. What is the title of the line graph on this page? Then read the years shown on the bottom of the graph. The numerals on the left side show the number of ships that made up the Chinese fleet.

For each year, a dot is placed on the graph to match the number of ships. The first dot shows that in 1410 China had about 3,500 ships. Trace the line of dots to see how the number of ships changed. How many ships were there in 1470?

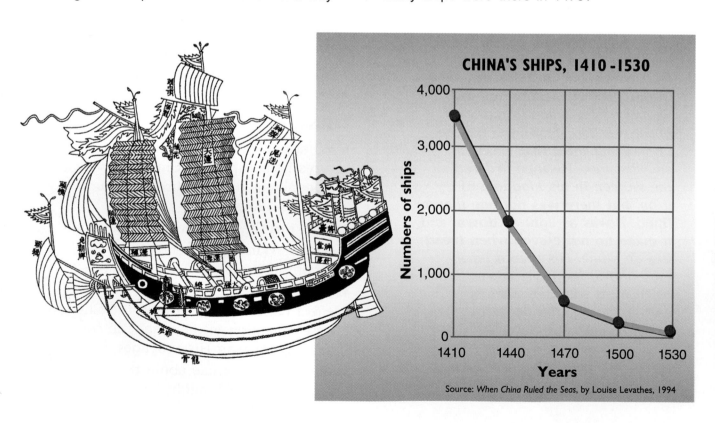

CHINA'S SHIPS, 1410 – 1530

Numbers of ships / Years

Source: *When China Ruled the Seas*, by Louise Levathes, 1994

When you look at a line graph, pay special attention to patterns. For example, in the graph on page 118 you can see that the number of ships decreased over time. When did the empire have the highest number of ships?

USING CIRCLE GRAPHS

A circle graph shows how something can be divided into parts. All of these parts together make up the whole. Circle graphs are also called pie graphs because the parts look like slices of a pie. The circle graph on this page shows what kinds of ships China had in the early 1400s.

Looking at the graph, you can get a picture of how many of each type of ship there

Helping yourself

- **Line graphs** show how information changes over time. Trace the line of dots to see how the information changes.

- **Circle graphs** show how something can be divided into parts. Look at the sizes of the parts of the circle graph to see how they compare.

were in the Chinese fleet. For example, you can see that there were 400 transport ships. Look at the sizes of each part of the graph to see how they compare to each other. Of which ships did the Chinese have the largest number?

TRYING THE SKILL

Take another look at each of the graphs. Then answer the following questions about the Chinese fleet. The Helping Yourself box on this page can give you hints about how to read circle graphs and line graphs.

Which graph or graphs would you use to find out the size of the fleet in 1410? In 1450? Which graph tells you how many warships were built? Which graph shows how many ships existed over time?

REVIEWING THE SKILL

1. How are line graphs different from circle graphs? How are they the same?

2. In which year did the greatest drop in the number of Chinese ships occur? How do you know?

3. Which kind of graph is better for showing how the population of your school changed over several years?

4. Which kind of graph would be better for showing the number of boys and the number of girls in your school this year? How do you know?

5. When might it be useful to know how to read line graphs and circle graphs?

THE CHINESE FLEET, EARLY 1400s

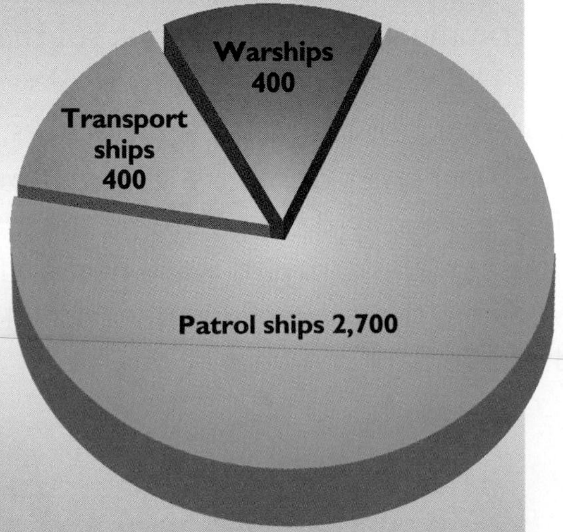

Warships 400

Transport ships 400

Patrol ships 2,700

Source: *When China Ruled the Seas,* by Louise Levathes, 1994

1300　1350　1400　1450　1464　1492　1500

African Kingdoms

Read Aloud

"Life is a perpetual coming and going," says a West African song. The endless comings and goings of trade have long been a part of life in Africa. Many great kingdoms that began as villages became powerful because of trade.

Focus Activity

READ TO LEARN

How did trade help the Songhai kingdom to grow?

VOCABULARY

- caravan
- malaria

PEOPLE

- Sunni Ali
- Leo Africanus

PLACES

- Sahara Desert
- Songhai
- Timbuktu
- Jenne
- Gao

THE BIG PICTURE

Zheng He's voyages during the early 1400s brought China into contact with Africa. Africa is home to many peoples. It is also the second largest continent in the world. Stretching across most of North Africa up to the Mediterranean Sea is the Sahara Desert. The Sahara is the largest desert in the world.

People called Berbers lived in the Sahara and along the Mediterranean coast. They had been in contact with Europe for centuries. Yet the Sahara made it difficult for them to communicate with regions south of the desert. In the 1200s, however, caravans of traders from Arabia began riding south on horses, donkeys, and camels across the Sahara. A caravan is a group of people traveling together, especially through desert areas. In the late 1400s most of the caravans were headed for Songhai (SAWNG hi), the powerful and wealthy kingdom that ruled a large part of West Africa.

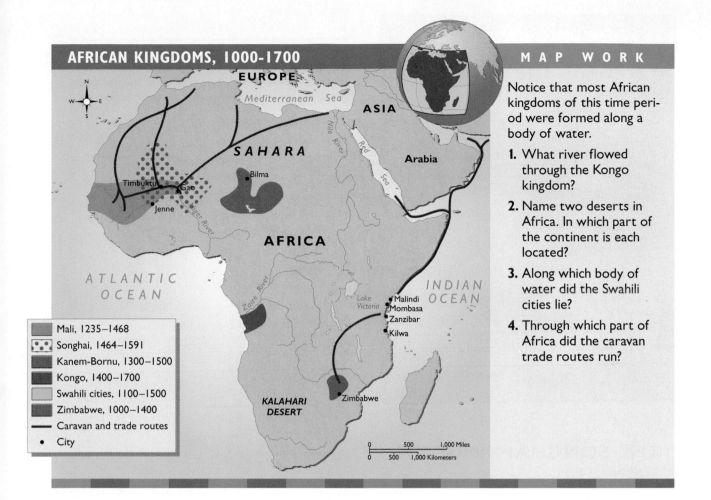

EUROPE

Mediterranean Sea

ASIA

Arabia

SAHARA

Bilma

Timbuktu

Gao

Jenne

Niger River

Nile River

Red Sea

AFRICA

ATLANTIC OCEAN

Zaire River

Lake Victoria

INDIAN OCEAN

Malindi
Mombasa
Zanzibar
Kilwa

KALAHARI DESERT

Zimbabwe

Mali, 1235–1468
Songhai, 1464–1591
Kanem-Bornu, 1300–1500
Kongo, 1400–1700
Swahili cities, 1100–1500
Zimbabwe, 1000–1400
— Caravan and trade routes
• City

0   500   1,000 Miles
0   500   1,000 Kilometers

Notice that most African kingdoms of this time period were formed along a body of water.

1. What river flowed through the Kongo kingdom?

2. Name two deserts in Africa. In which part of the continent is each located?

3. Along which body of water did the Swahili cities lie?

4. Through which part of Africa did the caravan trade routes run?

KING SUNNI ALI

In 1464 Sunni Ali became king of Songhai. He captured Timbuktu from the Berbers in 1468 and Jenne (je NAY) about 1475. Find them on the map on this page. Both cities are located along the Niger River, which runs mostly through the present-day country of Mali.

Ruling Songhai

At its peak Songhai stretched over 1,000 miles across West Africa. To maintain power, Sunni Ali enslaved the people he conquered. Many African rulers did this. In Africa criminals and prisoners of war were often enslaved. African rulers traded slaves with Arab sailors in the 1400s. Although they could be sold, African slaves were often given food and shelter in difficult times and even treated as family members rather than as property.

Sunni Ali's tolerance of different religions encouraged traders of gold, ivory, cloth, and salt to come to Songhai. Diversity brought a great variety of goods to the kingdom.

A man and children travel in a caravan through the Sahara in the northern part of Nigeria.

A brass smith in Nigeria (left) sells his work. The leopard carvings (below) were done by an artist from the ancient kingdom of Benin. In Timbuktu (bottom) women carry goods to the market.

THE SONGHAI KINGDOM

Sunni Ali ruled until his death in 1492. Songhai had become one of the largest kingdoms in West Africa during the 1400s. It controlled almost all trade coming south from the Sahara to the Niger River valley. It also controlled the valuable salt and gold mines of central Africa. The trading of salt and gold with people from North Africa helped make Songhai a wealthy kingdom.

Songhai's Cities

Gao, Timbuktu, and Jenne were the major centers of trade in Songhai. But each also had its own special character. Gao was a city full of skilled workers, craftworkers, and artists. The historian al-Kati called Gao an "artist's paradise." Leo Africanus, an Arab historian born in Spain, wrote that in Gao "it is a wonder to see . . . how costly and sumptuous [rich] all things be." Gold was so plentiful that miners sometimes had trouble finding a buyer.

Timbuktu, on the other hand, was a great cultural center. Scholars from far and wide studied astronomy, mathematics, music, and literature at Timbuktu's university. Arabic was the main language used by most people at the university. Leo Africanus was deeply impressed with the value the Songhai people placed on learning. Books, he reported, were "sold for more money than any other merchandise."

While Timbuktu was a place of learning, scholars at Jenne were known for their knowledge of medicine. Doctors there performed operations on the human eye. They also made the discovery that mosquitoes cause malaria, a disease caused by the bite of certain mosquitoes.

WHY IT MATTERS

In the 1400s Songhai, one of Africa's wealthy kingdoms, increased trade with other peoples in the Eastern Hemisphere. Over the centuries, traders and explorers from Europe came seeking Africa's gold, ivory, and other riches. Arab traders sailing off the east coast of Africa would bring the religion of Islam to the people there. Today people in many countries throughout Africa are Muslim.

DID YOU KNOW?

How did African gold miners trade without giving away the location of their secret gold mines?

A tenth-century Arab writer described how silent trading took place in Africa. Traders spread out goods such as salt and ivory near a stream. Then they left. Later gold miners crept in and put down bags filled with gold. Then they left also. The trading continued until both sides were satisfied with the amount the other group had left behind. Neither group of traders ever saw the other. In this way the gold miners did not fear that they would be kidnapped and forced to tell the location of the secret gold mines.

✓ Reviewing Facts and Ideas

MAIN IDEAS

- In the 1400s caravans helped connect parts of Africa south of the Sahara Desert with Arab traders coming from North Africa.

- Sunni Ali ruled the Songhai kingdom in West Africa from 1464 to 1492.

- Trade brought great wealth to Songhai. Artists, scholars, and people of medicine flocked to its cities.

THINK ABOUT IT

1. Why might people have traveled in caravans when crossing the Sahara Desert?

2. What did Sunni Ali accomplish as king of Songhai?

3. **FOCUS** How did trade help the Songhai kingdom to grow?

4. **THINKING SKILL** _Compare_ the features of Songhai's three major cities. How are they different?

5. **GEOGRAPHY** Look at the map on page 121. Why might you think that the Songhai culture was different from that in North Africa?

The Granger Collection

Europe's Age of Exploration

Read Aloud

In 1274 Marco Polo was one of the first Europeans to reach Asia. When he returned 20 years later, he brought back many treasures, among them ivory, jade, and silk. Marco Polo also wrote a book about his travels. Stories about China's emperor and his pet leopard, for example, buzzed all over Europe. Like people elsewhere, Europeans wanted to learn about the rest of the world.

Focus Activity

READ TO LEARN

What was Portugal's role in European exploration?

VOCABULARY

* Renaissance
* navigation
* caravel

PEOPLE

* Marco Polo
* Johannes Gutenberg
* Prince Henry
* Bartholomeu Dias
* Vasco da Gama

PLACES

* Portugal
* Spain
* Italy
* England
* France
* Cape of Good Hope

THE BIG PICTURE

Starting out in 1271, **Marco Polo** traveled from Persia to China along the Silk Road. The voyage took three years. When he returned to Europe in 1292, he knew more about China than any European of his time. Before then few Europeans were interested in China or any other part of Asia.

Europeans eventually developed contacts with Asia. By the 1400s an important link between the two continents was trade. When Europeans saw what kinds of goods Asia had to offer, they began searching to find a direct sea route there. In the middle of the 1400s the countries of **Portugal** and **Spain** sent explorers throughout the world in search of this route.

124

EUROPE'S RENAISSANCE

Why were Europeans looking beyond their own borders? One reason is that the people were influenced by the Renaissance (ren uh SAHNS). The Renaissance was a period of cultural and artistic growth that began in Italy in the 1300s. It spread throughout Europe in the 1400s and 1500s.

Renaissance is a French word that means "rebirth." In Europe there was a rebirth in learning about the past. The invention of the printing press by Johannes Gutenberg about 1436 helped to spread learning through books. Probably about 100,000 books existed in Europe at the time—all hand-copied. By 1500 Europe had close to 6 million printed books.

Science was one kind of learning that people read about. New knowledge about science encouraged people to try new ideas. New inventions enabled them to explore places that were new to them.

Trade with Asia

In Europe, as you have read, the demand for Asian silk was very strong. But Europeans also wanted spices. Without refrigeration, people wanted especially pepper and cloves to preserve food over the winter.

Europeans paid high prices for their spices. A single pound of pepper from India, for example, was traded dozens of times before it reached England or France. With each trade along the Silk Road, the price would rise. European traders decided to find another, cheaper route by which they could get goods from Asia.

The *Pietà* (below) was carved by the great Renaissance artist Michelangelo in 1498. The Gutenberg Bible (left) was one of the first books made using the new printing press.

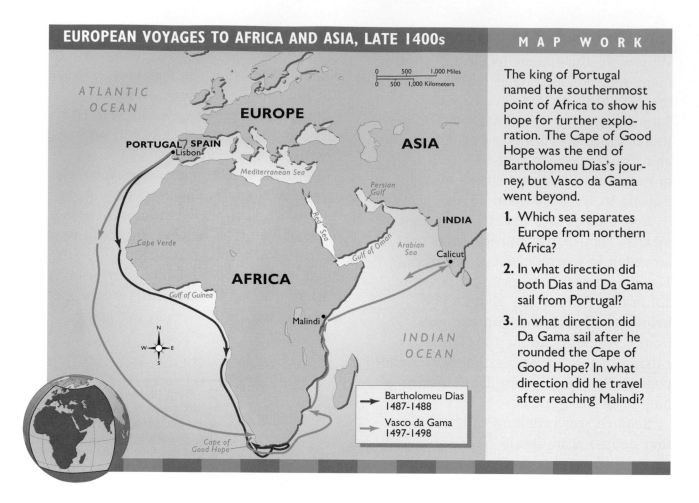

The king of Portugal named the southernmost point of Africa to show his hope for further exploration. The Cape of Good Hope was the end of Bartholomeu Dias's journey, but Vasco da Gama went beyond.

1. Which sea separates Europe from northern Africa?

2. In what direction did both Dias and Da Gama sail from Portugal?

3. In what direction did Da Gama sail after he rounded the Cape of Good Hope? In what direction did he travel after reaching Malindi?

Bartholomeu Dias
1487-1488

Vasco da Gama
1497-1498

PRINCE HENRY

To find another route to Asia, Europeans could only look to the sea. Study the map on this page. Was it possible to reach the shores of Asia by ship? Prince Henry of Portugal proved that it was. Although Henry never went on any explorations himself, he became known as Prince Henry the Navigator.

Portuguese Exploration

Prince Henry got his name from the improvements in navigation he made. Navigation is the science of determining a ship's sailing direction and location. Scientists working for Henry improved such inventions as the astrolabe and magnetic compass.

In the early 1400s Prince Henry also brought together shipbuilders, scientists, mapmakers, and ship captains in Europe. Together they created a new type of ship called the caravel. The caravel was about 70 feet long and could be steered more easily than other ships. It could sail at fast speeds through dangerous waters, even against the wind. The caravel also had a hold for carrying large amounts of cargo.

Using these new technologies, Henry's caravels first sailed the coast of West Africa. In 1445 he paid for voyages that

This is a model of a caravel that was used during the 1400s.

reached Cape Verde, the westernmost point of Africa. By 1460, when Henry died, his ships still had not reached southern Africa. As you can see on the map, though, other explorers achieved Henry's goal. In 1488 a Portuguese explorer named Bartholomeu Dias (bar TOH loh myoo DEE ush) rounded the tip of southern Africa, which was later named the Cape of Good Hope. In 1498 Vasco da Gama, a Portuguese sea captain, reached Asia when he arrived in Calicut, India.

This figure of Prince Henry (below) is part of a statue titled "Monument to Discoveries," which is located in Lisbon, Portugal.

WHY IT MATTERS

Vasco da Gama's 1498 voyage to India showed Europe a way to Asia without using the Silk Road. By 1503 the price of pepper in Portugal dropped to less than half of what it had been when Portugal's explorations first began.

Portugal made huge profits from the new sea routes. Its captains explored the Congo region of Africa, and they enslaved prisoners there. Spain, seeking a much shorter route to Asia, began to sail the Atlantic Ocean—leading one of the most important voyages of Europe's age of exploration.

✔// Reviewing Facts and Ideas

MAIN IDEAS

- Marco Polo's visit to China in 1274 made Europeans interested in Asia.

- The demand for Asian goods and the expense of goods traded on the Silk Road caused Europeans to seek a sea route to Asia.

- Prince Henry of Portugal built up a fleet of ships in the early 1400s that eventually reached Africa and Asia.

THINK ABOUT IT

1. What navigation equipment did European sailors use in the 1400s?

2. Why had Europeans become interested in finding a sea route to Asia?

3. **FOCUS** What did Prince Henry do to find a sea route to Asia?

4. **THINKING SKILL** List the _cause_ and _effect_ connections between the beginning of the Renaissance and Vasco da Gama's arrival in India.

5. **GEOGRAPHY** Use the map on page 126 to find the land and sea routes from Europe to Asia. Which route is longer?

CHAPTER 5 REVIEW

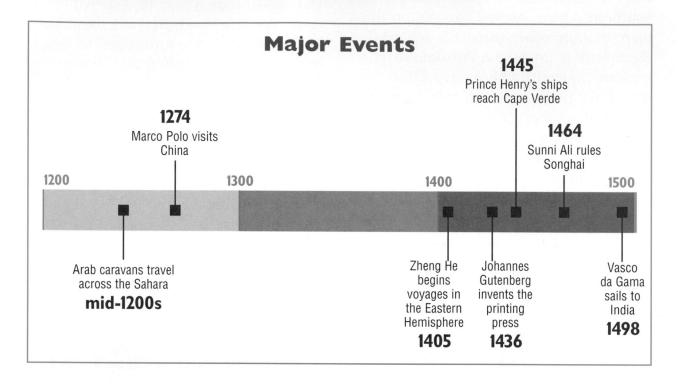

Major Events

1445
Prince Henry's ships
reach Cape Verde

1274
Marco Polo visits
China

1464
Sunni Ali rules
Songhai

1200   1300   1400   1500

Arab caravans travel
across the Sahara
mid-1200s

Zheng He
begins
voyages in
the Eastern
Hemisphere
1405

Johannes
Gutenberg
invents the
printing
press
1436

Vasco
da Gama
sails to
India
1498

THINKING ABOUT VOCABULARY

Number a paper from 1 to 5. Beside each number write the word from the list below that best matches the description.

astrolabe   navigation
caravan   Renaissance
caravel

1. A period of great cultural and artistic rebirth in Europe

2. The science of determining a ship's location and direction

3. An instrument used to find direction by the stars

4. A kind of small, fast-sailing ship that can be steered easily

5. A group of people traveling together for safety, especially through desert areas

THINKING ABOUT FACTS

1. What geographical features protected China from invaders?

2. What was the Silk Road?

3. Who was Zheng He?

4. What instruments did Zheng He use?

5. What is the largest desert in the world? What is the name of the people that lived there in the early 1400s?

6. Name and describe the three great cities of the Songhai kingdom.

7. What are some of the goods that were traded in the Songhai kingdom?

8. Which European countries sent explorers to find a sea route to Asia in the 1400s?

9. What kind of people did Prince Henry bring together in the early 1400s? What was their goal?

10. In 1503 the price of pepper in Portugal had dropped by more than half of what it had been in the 1400s. What event on the time line led to this drop in price?

THINK AND WRITE

WRITING A PARAGRAPH OF COMPARISON & CONTRAST

Reread the sections in the chapter about Prince Henry and Zheng He. Write a paragraph in which you compare and contrast the ocean explorations involving them.

WRITING A REPORT

Research more information about the early explorers' instruments. Write a brief report explaining these inventions and how they helped sea travel.

WRITING LOG ENTRIES

Suppose that you are on Da Gama's trip to India in 1498. Write three log entries that describe your expedition. One entry should describe the beginning of your trip, another some time in the middle, and the third the day you reach India.

APPLYING STUDY SKILLS

READING CIRCLE GRAPHS

To practice the skill of reading circle graphs, answer the questions below. Use the circle graph on page 119.

1. What do circle graphs show?
2. How many types of ships did China have in the early 1400s? What types were they?
3. What type of ship made up the greatest part of the Chinese fleet?
4. What kind of ship made up the smallest part of the graph?
5. How are circle graphs useful?

Summing Up the Chapter

Copy the main idea map on a separate piece of paper. Review the chapter to find details that will complete the blank sections. After you have finished, use the map to write a few short paragraphs that answer the question "How would you describe each person in the chart?"

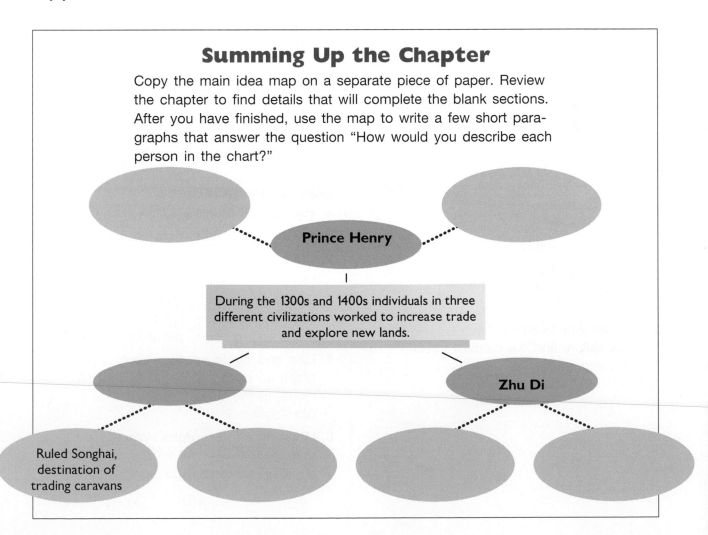

Prince Henry

During the 1300s and 1400s individuals in three different civilizations worked to increase trade and explore new lands.

Zhu Di

Ruled Songhai, destination of trading caravans

UNIT 2 REVIEW

THINKING ABOUT VOCABULARY

A. On a separate piece of paper write sentences for the word pairs below.

1. specialize	archaeologist
2. teepee	travois
3. magnetic compass	navigation
4. pueblo	kachina
5. Iroquois Confederacy	compromise
6. totem pole	wampum
7. jerky	coup stick
8. technology	irrigation
9. kiva	lodge
10. clan	longhouse

B. Number a paper from 1 to 10. Beside each number write the term that best completes the sentence.

astrolabe	navigation
caravel	Renaissance
magnetic compass	

1. If you were traveling through the desert and wanted to find your way by the stars, you might use a(n) _____.

2. The _____, which was a period of cultural and artistic growth, began in Italy in the 1300s.

3. In the 1400s a small, fast ship called the _____ was created.

4. Prince Henry had a nickname that came from the science of determining a ship's direction, or _____.

5. The Chinese invented the _____, which helps sailors find the cardinal directions of north and south.

THINK AND WRITE ◄═══▶

WRITING A LETTER
Suppose that you are an archaeologist. What from this unit would you like to study? A Maya ruin? The remains of an Iroquois longhouse? Write a letter to a fellow archaeologist in which you use facts to help describe your area of study.

WRITING A PARAGRAPH OF COMPARISON AND CONTRAST
In this unit you have read about many different people and their ways of life. Choose one group of people from Chapter 3 and another group from Chapter 4. Write a paragraph describing the similarities and differences in the way that they lived.

WRITING ABOUT PERSPECTIVES
What would Zheng He have thought about people traveling through outer space? How might Sunni Ali compare Gao to present-day Chicago? Write a description of an aspect of present-day life from the perspective of a person you read about in this unit.

BUILDING SKILLS

1. **Time lines** How can you tell which events happened earliest on a time line?

2. **Cause and effect** What clue words signal causes? Which signal effects?

3. **Cause and effect** Think about Chapter 4. What caused some Indian peoples to move from place to place to get food?

4. **Line and circle graphs** Look at the graph on page 119. What kind of ship made up the largest portion of the Chinese fleet?

5. **Line and circle graphs** What kind of graph would you use to show attendance at school basketball games over time?

YESTERDAY, TODAY & *TOMORROW*

Nampeyo, the woman who helped bring back the art of traditional Hopi pottery, at first tried to copy ancient designs. Then she created her own designs in the ancient style. What do you think of what Nampeyo did? Should she have continued copying designs? Why is remembering the past important for the future?

READING ON YOUR OWN

Here are some books you might find at the library to help you learn more.

MARCO POLO: HIS NOTEBOOK
by Susan L. Roth
This fact-based journal describes Marco Polo's journeys as though he wrote it himself.

PUEBLO BOY: GROWING UP IN TWO WORLDS
by Marcia Keegan
A young boy's life includes both ancient traditions and present-day activities.

RAIN PLAYER
by David Wisnlewski
A young Mayan boy attempts to bring rain to his village.

UNIT 2 REVIEW PROJECT

Design a Civilization Mural

1. Work in a group. Choose a civilization that you learned about in this unit, such as the Maya or the Aztec.

2. Have each group member list the civilization's achievements. For example, the Maya developed a unique writing system.

3. Create your mural on a sheet of oak tag. Choose at least one achievement from each group member's list. Paint, glitter, colorful streamers, beans, pasta, and seeds will make your mural come alive.

4. Be sure to label your mural and write a description under each picture.

5. Share your mural with the class.

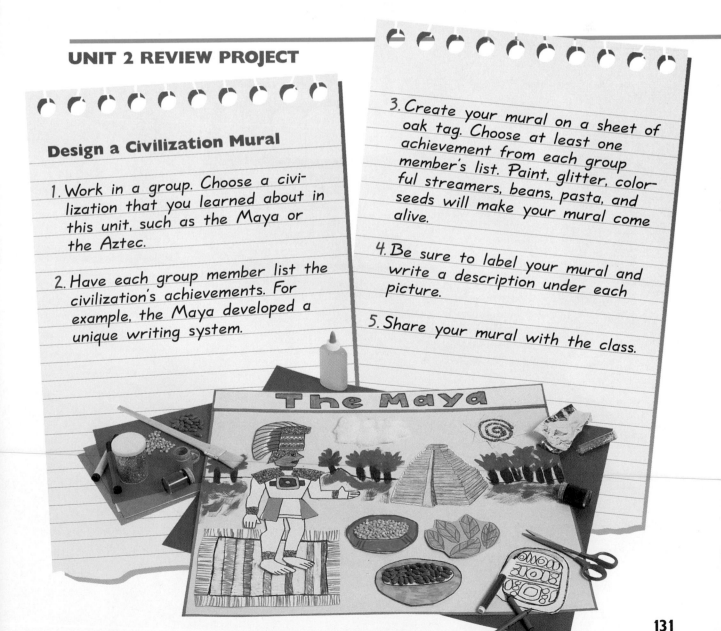

The Maya

The British Museum

The British Museum

**TURQUOISE MASK;
COPY OF THE
HEADDRESS MOCTEZUMA
PROBABLY WORE**

AZTEC ATLATL

Contact and Exploration

"At dawn we saw people."

from the log of Christopher Columbus
See page 141.

National Museum, Mexico City

Why Does it Matter?

A European sea captain named Christopher Columbus wrote the words above about one of the most important meetings in history. On an October morning in 1492, Columbus arrived in the Americas and was greeted by the Taino people. The peoples of two hemispheres—east and west—were now in contact, and neither would ever again be the same.

This meeting started a chain of events that would reshape lives around the world. European ships raced westward across the Atlantic Ocean. Their captains claimed Native American lands and new riches for their countries. Many of the Native Americans lost their freedom and their lives. Before the end of the 1500s, a different America—not quite Indian, not quite European—was beginning to take shape.

CHRISTOPHER COLUMBUS

FIND OUT MORE!
Visit our website:
www.mhschool.com

*inter*NET
CONNECTION

Adventures
with
NATIONAL
GEOGRAPHIC

MAN OF MYSTERY

You sail across an uncharted sea and bump into a world unknown back home. You become one of the most famous men in history. Everyone remembers your face, right? Wrong. The only portraits we have of Columbus were painted after his death; the artists could only guess what he looked like. But we have a much better idea of what his ships looked like. Thanks to careful work by historians and shipbuilders, modern sailors now re-create Columbus's journey aboard reproductions of the *Niña*, the *Pinta*, and the *Santa María*.

GEOJOURNAL

Describe what you think it would be like to sail on one of the reconstructed ships.

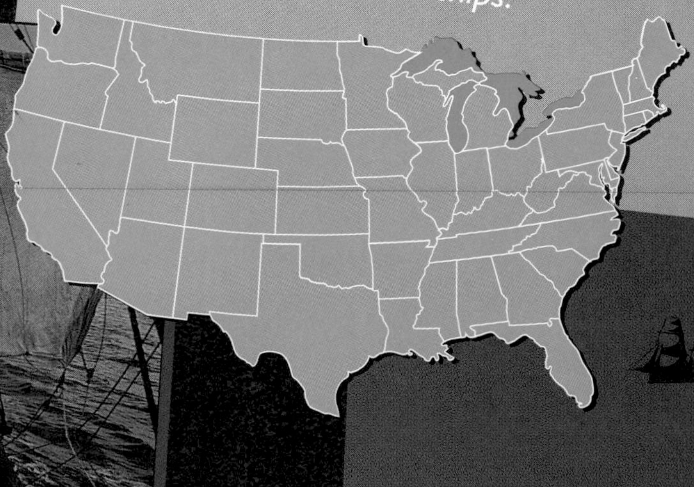

135

Contact: East Meets West

THINKING ABOUT HISTORY AND GEOGRAPHY

The story of Chapter 6 begins in 1492, the year Christopher Columbus reached the Americas. Read the time line below. Notice the different ways in which Europeans interacted with the many peoples of the Americas. Europe had brought many changes to the Western Hemisphere. Out of these changes came the world we know today.

1492

BAHAMA ISLANDS
The Taino and Columbus meet

1519

TENOCHTITLÁN
Cortés is greeted by Moctezuma in Mexico

1533

CUZCO
Pizarro conquers the Inca in the Andes Mountains

1490

1517

1542

NORTH AMERICA

Veracruz

Gulf of Mexico

Bahama
Islands

ATLANTIC
OCEAN

Tenochtitlán

Chiapas

CENTRAL
AMERICA

Caribbean Sea

PACIFIC
OCEAN

SOUTH
AMERICA

Cuzco

1542

CHIAPAS
The Spanish priest, Bartolomé de Las Casas, defends the rights of Indians in Mexico

1609

VERACRUZ
Yanga, an African captive, leads other captives in a slave rebellion in Mexico

North Wind Picture Archives

Focus Activity

READ TO LEARN

How did the meeting of Columbus and the Taino people change the world?

VOCABULARY

- expedition
- colony
- Columbian exchange

PEOPLE

- Leif Ericson
- Christopher Columbus
- King Ferdinand
- Queen Isabella

PLACES

- Bahama Islands
- San Salvador

1450   1492 1502   1550   1600   1650

Europeans Come to the Americas

Read Aloud

October 12, 1492. On this fall morning, three ships landed near a small island in the Western Hemisphere. The island was home to the Taino (TĪ noh) people. A sea captain named Christopher Columbus, who was sailing under the flag of Spain, waded ashore. Neither the Taino nor Columbus knew that their meeting would change the world.

THE BIG PICTURE

As you have read, the 1400s was a time of human movement and exploration. In the Western Hemisphere the Aztec were conquering other peoples in what is today Central America and the country of Mexico. The Inca were building an empire in South America. In the Eastern Hemisphere, European explorers were searching for new routes to Asia's rich markets. Chinese sailors were exploring Africa's east coast. African traders were exchanging goods with people from Asia and Europe.

The people of one hemisphere hardly knew that people of the other hemisphere existed. In about A.D. 1000, the Vikings, led by **Leif Ericson**, came from northern Europe and started a small settlement in northeastern Canada. They called it Vinland. Vinland did not survive long, and memory of it soon faded.

Nearly 500 years later the worlds of the West and the East came together again, this time forever.

THE TAINO

You read that by 1492 many peoples were living throughout the Americas. The Taino were one of the peoples living on islands in the Atlantic Ocean. Find the Taino's home islands on the map on this page.

On the morning of October 12, 1492, explorers from Spain arrived on one of the Taino's islands. We do not know what the Taino thought about their visitors. In fact, very little is known today about the Taino. What we know comes from artifacts the Taino left behind. Their stories of that first meeting with Europeans died with them.

The Taino Language

Some of the words from the Taino language, however, have survived. By studying these words and by examining other clues and artifacts from their lives, we can learn something about how the Taino lived.

One Taino word that we use in English is *canoe*. The Taino made sturdy boats by hollowing out the centers of tree trunks with special tools. Since the Taino lived on islands, canoes were their lifelines. They used the boats to fish, to trade with their neighbors, and sometimes to make war.

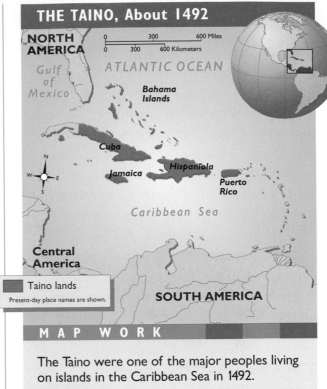

THE TAINO, About 1492

NORTH AMERICA

ATLANTIC OCEAN

Gulf of Mexico

Bahama Islands

Cuba

Jamaica

Hispaniola

Puerto Rico

Caribbean Sea

Central America

SOUTH AMERICA

Taino lands
Present-day place names are shown.

0   300   600 Miles
0   300   600 Kilometers

MAP WORK

The Taino were one of the major peoples living on islands in the Caribbean Sea in 1492.

1. What are some of the islands on which the Taino lived?

2. Between which continents was the Taino homeland located?

Some Taino canoes could hold over 30 people and could travel for hundreds of miles over the open sea.

Another word from the Taino language is *hamaca,* or *hammock.* This simple bed was perfect for the Taino's tropical climate. Made from woven cotton or other plant fibers, a hammock was easy to set up between two posts or trees. It did not take up much room in the Taino's small houses, and it was cool in the warm night air.

The Granger Collection

Taino hammocks might have looked like the one in this Spanish drawing (left). They have changed little since then.

139

CHRISTOPHER COLUMBUS

Although we do not know what the Taino thought about the strangers who arrived that October morning in 1492, we do know who the strangers were and where they came from. They had left Spain two months earlier in three small ships, the *Niña,* the *Pinta,* and the *Santa María.* This Spanish expedition was led by an Italian seaman named Christopher Columbus. An expedition is a journey made for a special purpose. Columbus's purpose was to find a sea route to the Indies, or the islands of Southeast Asia, by sailing west instead of east.

A Sea Route to the Indies

You read that Europeans were eager to trade for Asian spices, silks, gold, and jewels. But the cost of bringing Asian goods to Europe by land was very high. Columbus thought there might be a way to reach the Indies by sailing west across the Atlantic Ocean. Then the cost of trade with Asia would drop. In Europe, the price of spices from Asia would become cheaper.

Museo Navale, Genoa

This painting of Christopher Columbus was done in the early 1500s. No one really knows what he looked like because none of his portraits were painted during his lifetime.

Links to MATHEMATICS

Columbus Miscalculates!

Why was Columbus confused about where he was in 1492?

One reason is that he thought Asia lay about 3,000 miles (4,827 km) west of Europe. Use the scale of miles on the world map in your Atlas to figure out how great this distance actually is.

How much farther would Columbus have had to sail to reach Asia if he had not run into the Americas first?

Money for Columbus's Expedition

For years Columbus tried to raise money for an expedition across the Atlantic. The king of Portugal listened to Columbus's plan and turned him down. The distance to Asia sailing west, the king said, was much greater than Columbus thought. Next, Columbus took his plan to King Ferdinand and Queen Isabella of Spain. They made him wait six years before giving him money for his first expedition.

Reaching the Americas

On August 3, 1492, Columbus left Spain with three ships and sailed west into the unknown. Week after week dragged by with no sight of land. His men began to grumble, afraid they would never see home again. To calm their fears Columbus kept two records, or ship's logs. In the first he recorded the actual distance sailed each day. In the second he recorded a shorter distance. He showed his crew the second log so they would not know how far they really were from Spain.

Still the men worried, demanding that he turn back. Columbus asked them to wait two more days. If no land was sighted by then, he would return to Spain.

It was just enough time. Early on October 12, 1492, a lookout shouted "¡Tierra! ¡Tierra!" (Land! Land!). Ahead a small island rose out of the blue sea.

Columbus was certain that he was near the coast of Asia. Instead, his ships had sailed to the Bahama Islands off the coast of North America.

Columbus Describes the Meeting

The next morning Columbus visited the island first seen the night before. In his log he wrote that he named the island San Salvador, or Holy Savior, and claimed it for Spain. Today many historians believe that Columbus may have landed at Watling Island. Read Columbus's description of his meeting with the Taino people. Believing he had reached the Indies, Columbus called these people "Indios," or Indians. What opinions did Columbus have about the Taino?

One of the tools Christopher Columbus used to guide him across the Atlantic Ocean was an astrolabe (above). It helped him to find his latitude and to sail a straight course. The hawks' bells that Columbus wrote about in his log looked like these (right).

MANY VOICES

PRIMARY SOURCE

Excerpt from
The Log of Christopher Columbus,
presented to Queen Isabella in 1493.

At dawn we saw . . . people, and I went ashore in the ship's boat. . . .

*The people here call this island Guanahani (gwah uh HAHN ee) in their language, and their speech is very **fluent**, although I do not understand any of it. They are friendly . . . people who [carry no weapons] except for small spears, and they have no iron. I showed one my sword, and through **ignorance** he grabbed it by the blade and cut himself. Their spears are made of wood, to which they attach a fish tooth at one end, or some other sharp thing.*

. . . They traded and gave everything they had with good will, but it seems to me that they have very little and are poor in everything. . . .

*This afternoon the people . . . came swimming to our ships and in boats made from one log. They brought us parrots, balls of cotton thread, spears, and many other things, . . . For these items we traded them little glass beads and **hawks' bells**.*

. . . They ought to make good and skilled servants, for they repeat very quickly whatever we say to them. . . . I will take six of them to Your Highnesses when I depart.

---

fluent: smooth and rapid
ignorance: not knowing
hawks' bells: small bells that are attached to the legs of a captive hawk

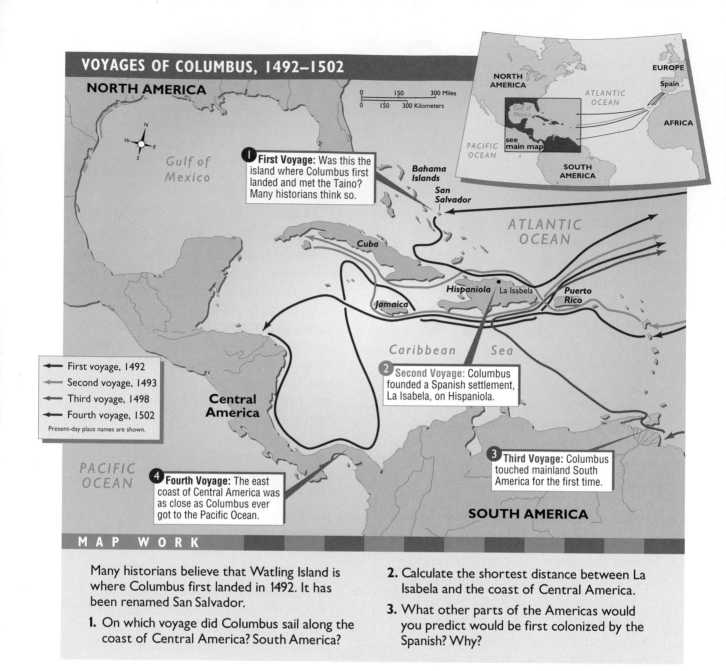

VOYAGES OF COLUMBUS, 1492–1502

NORTH AMERICA

Gulf of Mexico

0 150 300 Miles
0 150 300 Kilometers

1 First Voyage: Was this the island where Columbus first landed and met the Taino? Many historians think so.

Bahama Islands

San Salvador

ATLANTIC OCEAN

Cuba

Hispaniola | La Isabela

Puerto Rico

Jamaica

Caribbean Sea

2 Second Voyage: Columbus founded a Spanish settlement, La Isabela, on Hispaniola.

← First voyage, 1492
← Second voyage, 1493
← Third voyage, 1498
← Fourth voyage, 1502
Present-day place names are shown.

Central America

3 Third Voyage: Columbus touched mainland South America for the first time.

PACIFIC OCEAN

4 Fourth Voyage: The east coast of Central America was as close as Columbus ever got to the Pacific Ocean.

SOUTH AMERICA

NORTH AMERICA

EUROPE
Spain

ATLANTIC OCEAN

AFRICA

PACIFIC OCEAN

Gulf of Mexico
see main map

SOUTH AMERICA

MAP WORK

Many historians believe that Watling Island is where Columbus first landed in 1492. It has been renamed San Salvador.

1. On which voyage did Columbus sail along the coast of Central America? South America?

2. Calculate the shortest distance between La Isabela and the coast of Central America.

3. What other parts of the Americas would you predict would be first colonized by the Spanish? Why?

THE COLUMBIAN EXCHANGE

From San Salvador, Columbus sailed south to islands in the Caribbean Sea. A few months later he returned to Spain with parrots and plants unknown in Europe. He had also kidnapped six Taino and taken them back to Spain. King Ferdinand and Queen Isabella were pleased. They asked Columbus to return to the Caribbean to found a colony. A colony is a settlement far away from the country that rules it.

The **Columbian exchange** brought American plants and animals to Europe, including chili peppers, tomatoes, corn, pineapples, and turkeys.

142

Contact Brings Change

In 1493 Columbus set off on his second voyage. You can trace his route on the map on page 142. With him were 17 ships full of colonists. The colonists brought horses, cattle, and sheep as well as seeds and cuttings for growing wheat, onions, sugar, and other crops from the Eastern Hemisphere. The colonists also unknowingly carried germs that caused smallpox, measles, and other diseases.

Columbus also took more American plants and animals back to Spain. Colonists loaded ships with turkeys, corn, potatoes, tomatoes, chili peppers, pumpkins, beans, peanuts, avocados, tobacco, and pineapples and sent them back with him.

Historians call this movement of people, plants, animals, and germs across the Atlantic Ocean the Columbian exchange. Historians often use a form of Columbus's name to describe events that happened in the Americas before and after his arrival. Why do you think his name is used in this way?

The Columbian exchange changed life around the world. It affected the population of five continents. Some

The Columbian exchange brought wheat and horses to the Americas. But as this drawing (above) by a Spanish priest shows, previously unknown diseases such as smallpox had a terrible effect on the Indians.

of these changes were welcome. American foods, for example, improved the diets of people in the Eastern Hemisphere. New crops from the Americas grew so well in the Eastern Hemisphere that they increased food supplies in Europe, Africa, and Asia. As a result, the population of those continents increased more rapidly than before.

For the peoples of the Americas, the Columbian exchange had both good effects and bad effects. The horse, as you have read, changed the lives of Native Americans on the Great Plains. But diseases that were brought unknowingly by Europeans killed millions of Caribbean Indians, who had not built up a strong resistance to such diseases.

THE SEEDS OF CHANGE

Among all of the items included in the Columbian exchange, five were especially important. Once planted on distant shores, they changed the lives of countless people. All five still have an effect on our lives today. For this reason they have been called the "seeds of change." Look at the chart on this page to find out what effect the seeds of change had on the peoples of the world.

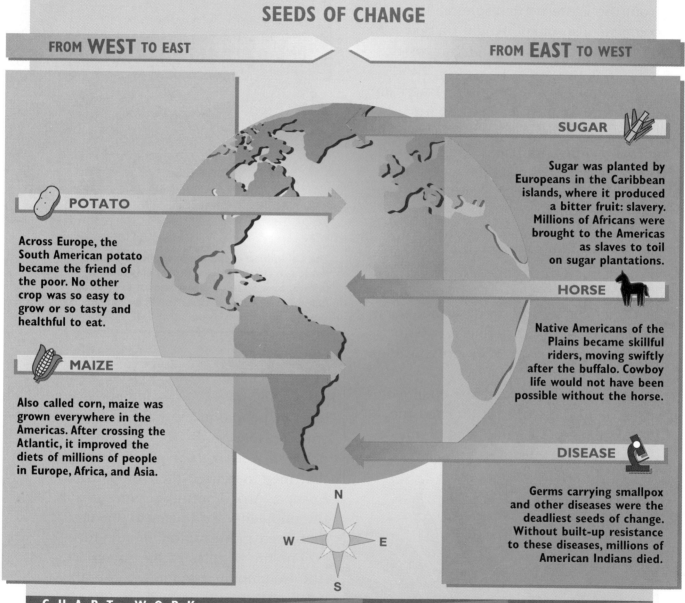

SEEDS OF CHANGE

FROM WEST TO EAST

FROM EAST TO WEST

POTATO

Across Europe, the South American potato became the friend of the poor. No other crop was so easy to grow or so tasty and healthful to eat.

MAIZE

Also called corn, maize was grown everywhere in the Americas. After crossing the Atlantic, it improved the diets of millions of people in Europe, Africa, and Asia.

SUGAR

Sugar was planted by Europeans in the Caribbean islands, where it produced a bitter fruit: slavery. Millions of Africans were brought to the Americas as slaves to toil on sugar plantations.

HORSE

Native Americans of the Plains became skillful riders, moving swiftly after the buffalo. Cowboy life would not have been possible without the horse.

DISEASE

Germs carrying smallpox and other diseases were the deadliest seeds of change. Without built-up resistance to these diseases, millions of American Indians died.

N
W E
S

CHART WORK

The Columbian exchange was a major event in the worldwide movement of living things.

1. Which seeds of change moved from east to west? West to east?

2. Which seeds of change moved to the Caribbean? To Europe, Asia, and Africa?

3. How did the introduction of sugar affect the lives of Africans and Spanish colonists in the Americas?

4. Why did the Indians have no resistance to European diseases?

144

WHY IT MATTERS

When Christopher Columbus brought six Tainos back to Spain, people in Europe thought that he had "discovered a new world." They began calling the Americas the "New World." But people had been living in both the Western Hemisphere and the Eastern Hemisphere for thousands of years. A new world did begin when Columbus and the Taino met. It was the new world created by a joining of two old worlds, west and east.

Columbus was determined to take great risks to cross the Atlantic. He knew of shipwrecks, drownings, and storms. But he faced them and showed Europe the way to the Americas. People from Spain and other European countries soon began sailing to the Americas. In the next lessons you will read about some of the people who followed Columbus. You will also find out what happened to the native peoples of the Americas.

Links to CURRENT EVENTS

Taino News Flash!

In 1997 in a jungle in the Dominican Republic, archaeologists uncovered an ancient Taino city. Scientists believe many of these cities existed at the time Columbus arrived in the Americas.

Huge limestone plazas were discovered where scientists believe ceremonies took place and a soccer-like game was played. But that's not all! Months earlier at the site, scuba divers were investigating a natural well. Carved axes, baskets, and decorative pottery believed to have been used in Taino ceremonies were found 150 feet deep within the well. Ask your teacher or librarian to help you search the Internet for more information about this discovery. Then write a paragraph about it.

✓✓ Reviewing Facts and Ideas

MAIN IDEAS

- In both the Western and Eastern hemispheres people were moving into and exploring new lands.

- In 1492 the Taino lived on many islands between the Caribbean Sea and the Atlantic Ocean. That same year Christopher Columbus left Spain to sail west across the Atlantic. After two months at sea his ships reached the Bahama Islands, home to the Taino people.

- The Columbian exchange of people, plants, animals, and diseases changed life west and east of the Atlantic Ocean forever.

THINK ABOUT IT

1. What do we know about the Taino way of life, and how do we know it?

2. What was the Columbian exchange? Why is it called this?

3. **FOCUS** How did the meeting between the Taino and Christopher Columbus change the world?

4. **THINKING SKILL** _Compare_ the effects of the Columbian exchange on the peoples of Europe, Africa, and the Americas.

5. **WRITE** Suppose you were there at the first meeting of Columbus and the Taino. Describe the meeting from the point of view of a Taino.

CITIZENSHIP
VIEWPOINTS

This painting by John Vanderlyn, *The Landing of Columbus*, hangs in the Capitol Building in Washington, D.C. Painted in 1846, it shows Columbus as discoverer of the Americas, a view that was common at the time.

1492: What did the Spanish think about paying for Columbus's voyage?

Christopher Columbus went to the royal court of Spain in 1486. He wanted to ask Queen Isabella and King Ferdinand to pay for a voyage of exploration. Columbus spread out his map of the world. He spoke of the riches and fame his voyage to Asia would bring to Spain. Knowing of Queen Isabella's deep Catholic faith, he also said his voyage would bring Christianity to distant parts of the world. The rulers listened carefully. When Columbus finished, the rulers decided they needed to study seriously whether or not to support him.

Isabella and Ferdinand asked a committee of learned men to examine Columbus's proposal. The leader of this group was an official in the Catholic Church named Fernando de Talavera. The group became known as the Talavera Commission. As you will read in the third viewpoint, the commission advised the rulers to reject Columbus's project. Other advisers believed that Columbus offered the rulers an opportunity that should not be missed. Read and consider the three viewpoints. Then answer the questions that follow.

Three DIFFERENT Viewpoints

1 DON LUIS DE LA CERDA
Duke of Medina Celi
Excerpt from Letter to the Grand Cardinal of Spain, 1492

For some time I had staying in my house Christopher Columbus, who came here . . . to get the king's backing for a voyage in search of the Indies. Having three or four caravels available, I was minded to take a chance on this myself, . . . but it occurred to me that the Queen . . . might be interested, so I wrote to Her Highness about it. . . . She wrote back telling me to send Columbus to Her, so I did.

". . . take a chance on this myself . . ."

2 LUIS DE SANTANGEL
King Ferdinand's Treasurer and Chief Tax Collector
Excerpt adapted from Conversation recorded in
The Life of Christopher Columbus by His Son Ferdinand in the 1500s

Queen Isabella has always shown bravery and firmness in matters of great importance. Why should she lack it now for a project of so little risk, yet which could be of such great service to God and the glory of Spain? Columbus's project is so important that if any other ruler agrees to do what Columbus offers the Queen, it will greatly hurt her Crown, disappoint her friends, and cause her enemies to criticize her.

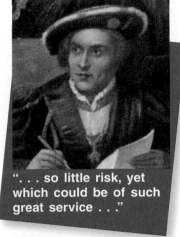

". . . so little risk, yet which could be of such great service . . ."

3 FERNANDO DE TALAVERA
Excerpt from Report of the Talavera Commission,
made public about 1490

We can find no justification [reason] for their Highnesses' supporting a project that rests on extremely weak foundations and appears impossible to translate into reality to any person with any knowledge, however modest, of these questions.

". . .appears impossible . . ."

BUILDING CITIZENSHIP

1. What was the viewpoint of each person? How did each support his opinion?

2. In what ways did some of the viewpoints agree? In what cases did they disagree?

3. What other viewpoints might people have had on this issue? What are some cases in which the issue of paying for explorations might be discussed today?

SHARING VIEWPOINTS

Discuss why groups such as the Talavera Commission might have argued against supporting Columbus while others might have favored helping him. Write a letter to King Ferdinand and Queen Isabella describing the risks and possible rewards of paying for Columbus's voyage.

1450 1502 1542 1600 1650

Explorers and Conquerors

National Geographic Society

Focus Activity

READ TO LEARN

How did the battle for Tenochtitlán change the Americas?

VOCABULARY

- conquistador

PEOPLE

- Moctezuma
- Hernando Cortés
- Doña Marina
- Cuauhtémoc
- Francisco Coronado
- Francisco Pizarro
- Ferdinand Magellan
- Hernando De Soto
- Juan Ponce de León
- Vasco Núñez de Balboa
- Álvar Núñez Cabeza de Vaca

PLACES

- Tenochtitlán
- New Spain

Read Aloud

On a bright November day in 1519, two men faced each other at the entrance to Tenochtitlán, one of the world's great cities. Moctezuma (mahk tuh zoo muh) II, the ruler of Mexico's mighty Aztec empire, looked into the eyes of Hernando Cortés, the leader of a small Spanish army. Their meeting was the painful joining of two civilizations.

THE BIG PICTURE

In the 20 years after Christopher Columbus's meeting with the Taino, Spain claimed most of the islands in the Caribbean Sea. Its soldiers, who hoped to find gold and other riches, conquered new lands for Spain. They were known as **conquistadors** (kahn KEES tuh dohrz), from a Spanish word that means "to conquer."

During this time, Spanish and Portuguese explorers also began traveling to other parts of the Americas. The conquistadors claimed lands throughout present-day Mexico and explored what is now the southeastern United States. The Portuguese reached South America and landed at present-day Brazil. You can locate the areas of Spanish exploration on the Infographic on pages 152–153.

In the 1400s, as you have read, Spain and Portugal led the way for European exploration of Asia and Africa. Now, in the 1500s, Spain was beginning to take the lead in exploring the Americas.

MOCTEZUMA'S AZTEC EMPIRE

Tenochtitlán had been the capital of the Aztec empire since the early 1300s. Under Moctezuma I, who ruled from 1440 to 1468, the Aztec conquered their neighbors to the south and east. Under the following three rulers, the empire expanded to include most of present-day Mexico.

Ruling an Empire

In 1502 the great-grandson of Moctezuma I was chosen emperor. A strong leader in his own right, he was called Moctezuma II, or Moctezuma the Younger. In Aztec tradition the title of emperor was not passed on from father to son to grandson. Nobles chose from the royal families one male thought to be best suited for the job.

Early in his rule Moctezuma II faced challenges to his power. People inside the empire were beginning to rebel against those in control. They no longer wanted to pay tribute or give up prisoners to the Aztec.

Moctezuma also had enemies outside his empire. The Aztec were bitterly hated by the Tlaxcalan (tlahs KAH lahn) people, who lived less than 100 miles east of Tenochtitlán. For years the Tlaxcalan had been fighting to keep from being conquered by their powerful neighbors. Despite these problems, however, Moctezuma was still firmly in control of his empire.

News of Strangers

Early in 1519 over 500 Spanish troops landed on the east coast of Mexico. Rumors of gold had brought them there. From the moment the Spaniards landed, Aztec messengers began reporting their movements to Moctezuma.

Moctezuma sent the Spaniards two disks of solid gold and silver. He did not know whether they were enemies to be feared or friends to be respected. In either case Moctezuma hoped that his gifts would persuade the Spaniards to return home. This was a mistake. Moctezuma did not know the men were looking for gold. Nothing would keep the Spanish from trying to reach Tenochtitlán now.

Moctezuma probably wore a headdress like this one made from feathers of the quetzal bird. The Spanish melted down Aztec artworks like the gold mask and made them into coins.

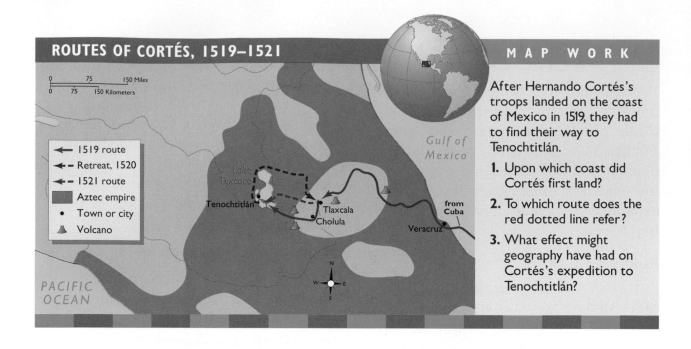

0   75   150 Miles
0   75   150 Kilometers

← 1519 route
←- Retreat, 1520
←- 1521 route
▨ Aztec empire
• Town or city
▲ Volcano

Gulf of Mexico

Lake Texcoco

Tenochtitlán

Tlaxcala
Cholula

from Cuba

Veracruz

PACIFIC OCEAN

After Hernando Cortés's troops landed on the coast of Mexico in 1519, they had to find their way to Tenochtitlán.

1. Upon which coast did Cortés first land?

2. To which route does the red dotted line refer?

3. What effect might geography have had on Cortés's expedition to Tenochtitlán?

CORTÉS DEFEATS THE EMPIRE

At the age of 19, Hernando Cortés came from Spain to the Caribbean island of Cuba. Cortés was given land to farm. But he had other ideas. "I don't want land," he wrote. "I came for gold." When the governor of Cuba asked Cortés to lead an expedition to Mexico, he jumped at the chance.

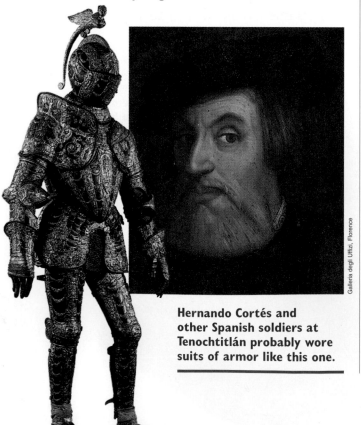

Hernando Cortés and other Spanish soldiers at Tenochtitlán probably wore suits of armor like this one.

Galleria degli Uffizi, Florence

Heading for Tenochtitlán

Cortés came upon several Indian cities as he made his way inland from the coast to Tenochtitlán. You can trace his route on the map above. The people of these cities were enemies of the Aztec. At one city Cortés met an Indian woman who was called Doña Marina (DOHN yah mah REE nah) by the Spanish and Malinche (mah LEEN chay) by the Indians.

Doña Marina was the daughter of a chief but had been sold as a captive after her father died. She knew several languages including those of the Aztec and Maya. Doña Marina helped Cortés convince many Indians to join him. Soon his small army grew into a force big enough to challenge the Aztec.

When the two leaders finally met in 1519, Moctezuma welcomed Cortés to Tenochtitlán. The Spaniards could hardly believe their eyes when they first saw the city. One of them wrote:

We were amazed because of the huge towers, temples, and buildings. . . . We were seeing things which had never been heard of or seen before, nor even dreamed about.

For reasons that are not understood today, Moctezuma did not resist the Spaniards. Cortés took Moctezuma prisoner and gained control of the city. Then the Aztec fought back. In a furious attack they drove the Spaniards out of their city. Moctezuma was killed during the fighting.

Tenochtitlán Falls

Cortés returned to Tenochtitlán in 1521 with more soldiers. His goal was to recapture the city. A young man named Cuauhtémoc (kwah TAY mahk) was now ruler of the Aztec. He led them in the battle for Tenochtitlán. But again Cortés was helped by the Aztec's enemies. The Spaniards and their Indian supporters blocked all the entrances to the city. No food or water could be taken inside. An Aztec who survived this battle later reported that

[m]any died of hunger. . . . The people ate anything—lizards, barn swallows, corn leaves, saltgrass. They gnawed . . . leather and buckskin, cooked or toasted; or . . . adobe bricks. Never had such suffering been seen.

After 75 days Tenochtitlán fell to Cortés. Cuauhtémoc was captured and later killed. Then the Spaniards and their Indian allies destroyed Aztec temples and pulled down statues of Aztec gods. They also burned the Aztec sacred books. The Spaniards had conquered a great city. They then set out to control a vast empire. They called their new colony New Spain.

How the Spanish Won

How was a small group of Spaniards fighting in a strange land able to conquer an empire? One important reason was the thousands of Indian supporters who fought with the Spanish.

Another reason for the success of the Spaniards was their deadlier weapons. The Aztec fought with wooden spears and arrows tipped with stone points. They used wooden shields and wore armor made of thick, tightly woven cotton. These weapons were no match for Spanish steel and gunpowder. Study the drawing below. What were some differences between Spanish and Aztec weapons?

Biblioteca Nacional, Madrid

MANY VOICES
PRIMARY SOURCE

Drawing by an unknown artist, created during the late 1500s.

As the drawing of the battle for Tenochtitlán shows, the Spanish musket, or rifle, was one of the main weapons used by the Spanish.

Spanish Explorers and Conquistadors

After Columbus's voyage in 1492, other Spanish explorers and conquistadors sailed across the Atlantic Ocean. Some came in search of routes to Asia. Others came to seek gold or to achieve glory for God. Study the Infographic to learn about the expeditions of the Spanish explorers and conquistadors in the Americas.

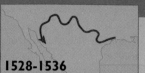

1528–1536

ÁLVAR NÚÑEZ CABEZA DE VACA

Shipwrecked during an expedition from Cuba, he reached what is now Texas in 1528. He became the first Spaniard to explore Texas.

1540–1542

FRANCISCO CORONADO

With a small group, he began to explore the American Southwest in search of the rumored Seven Cities of Gold.

HERNANDO CORTÉS

He led an expedition from Cuba to Mexico that ended with the conquest of Moctezuma and the Aztec.

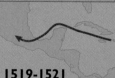

1519–1521

1513

VASCO NÚÑEZ DE BALBOA

He led an expedition across Central America to what later was named the Pacific Ocean.

FRANCISCO PIZARRO

His forces conquered the Inca empire ruled by Atahualpa.

1531–1533

HERNANDO DE SOTO

He led an expedition through the American Southeast in search of gold. He became the first European to see the Mississippi River.

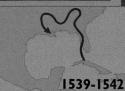

1539-1542

JUAN PONCE DE LEÓN

Stories of a fountain of youth led him to sail north from Puerto Rico. He reached a land he called Florida.

1513

CHRISTOPHER COLUMBUS

Sailing under the flag of Spain, he reached a group of islands in the Atlantic Ocean while seeking a route to Asia.

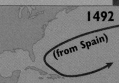

1492

(from Spain)

FERDINAND MAGELLAN

Sailing for the Spanish, he set out to find a route to the Indies by sailing around the southern tip of South America. Although he was killed, some of his crew returned to Spain, completing the first known voyage around the world.

(from Spain)

1519-1522

WHY IT MATTERS

By the middle of the 1500s, the peoples of the Western and Eastern hemispheres were bonded together in many ways. Spaniards and other Europeans explored and conquered much of the Americas. They forever changed the land and the peoples they met. But they, too, were changed. The king of Spain became the ruler of New Spain. And Tenochtitlán became known as Mexico City. As you will read, from all of these changes a very different culture was born.

✓// Reviewing Facts and Ideas

MAIN IDEAS

- Other European explorers and conquerors soon followed Columbus to the Americas.
- By the 1500s the Aztec had built a large and powerful empire in Mexico.
- In 1521 the conquistador Hernando Cortés conquered the Aztec empire.
- After the Aztec's defeat, Mexico became a colony called New Spain.

THINK ABOUT IT

1. In what way did Doña Marina help Hernando Cortés?

2. How did Moctezuma and Cortés treat each other when they met? What other options might Moctezuma have chosen?

3. **FOCUS** How did the fall of Tenochtitlán change the Americas?

4. **THINKING SKILL** _Predict_ how Mexico might be different today if Moctezuma had defeated Cortés.

5. **GEOGRAPHY** Use the map on page 150 to evaluate the advantages and disadvantages of other routes Cortés might have taken to Tenochtitlán.

Geography Skills

Reading Historical Maps

VOCABULARY

historical map

WHY THE SKILL MATTERS

When Hernando Cortés marched to Tenochtitlán in 1519, a Portuguese sea captain named Ferdinand Magellan was beginning a different expedition. With help from the king of Spain, Magellan's crew made an unforgettable voyage around the world.

One way to study an historical event, such as Magellan's expedition, is by using an historical map. Historical maps show information about the past or where past events took place. For example, the map below traces a voyage that took place nearly 500 years ago. Use the Helping Yourself box on the next page to guide you in reading historical maps.

USING HISTORICAL MAPS

Study the map on this page. What is its title? What clues help you to know that it is an historical map?

In September Magellan started out with 250 men and 5 ships. He hoped to find a route from Europe to Asia

North Wind Picture Archives

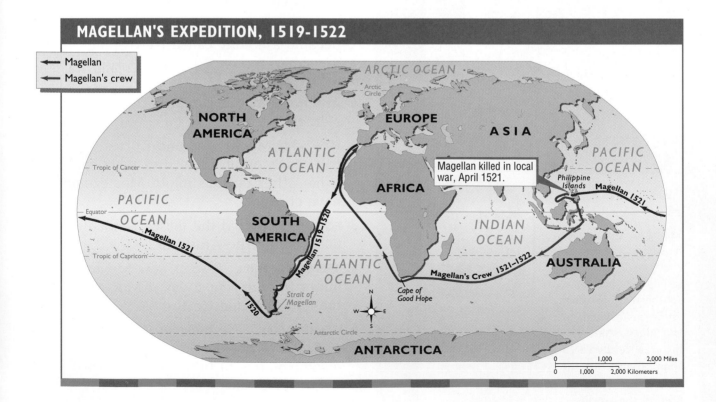

MAGELLAN'S EXPEDITION, 1519-1522

154

that was shorter than the route around Africa. Magellan believed that he could sail south around the tip of South America and then sail west until he reached Asia.

At the southern tip of South America, Magellan reached a strait, or narrow waterway. This stormy passage, which caused one of his ships to sink, is now named for Magellan. Find it on the map.

His tiny fleet traveled for almost four more months before it reached land. Food and water ran low. One of the men, Antonio Pigafetta, wrote in his journal:

We ate only old biscuits turned to powder, all full of worms.... And we drank water impure [dirty] and yellow.

Finally Magellan reached the Philippine Islands. He thought his expedition had failed. He had not found a shorter route to Asia. But Magellan had proved that a ship could circumnavigate (sur kum NAV uh gayt), or entirely circle, the world. What happened to Magellan in the Philippines?

Magellan's death did not end the first known voyage around the world. In September 1522 a single ship with 18 men finally returned to Spain.

TRYING THE SKILL

You have practiced reading an historical map about Magellan's expedition. Try reading this one about the Spanish conquest of the Inca. In 1531 the conquistador known as Francisco Pizarro (pih ZAH roh) set out to capture the Inca's riches in South America. He met and defeated the Inca ruler Atahualpa (ah tuh WAHL puh), who was travelling to the Inca's capital city, Cuzco.

Helping yourself

- An **historical map** shows places or events from the past.
- Study the title, date, and map key.
- Look for other information on the map.

Pizarro and his 180 men were lucky. Fighting between Atahualpa and his brother had weakened the Inca. Atahualpa, the victor, was heading to Cuzco to be crowned when Pizarro captured him. In what city did Pizarro and Atahualpa meet? In time Spain controlled all of the Inca empire.

REVIEWING THE SKILL

1. What is an historical map?
2. Where was the Inca empire located? How do you know?
3. In what direction did Atahualpa's forces travel? Pizarro's? How do you know?
4. Who traveled part of the way by water? Why do you think he used a water route?
5. What are some ways in which reading historical maps can be useful to you?

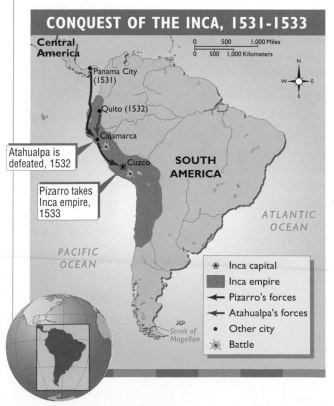

CONQUEST OF THE INCA, 1531-1533

Central America

Panama City (1531)

Quito (1532)

Cajamarca

Atahualpa is defeated, 1532

Cuzco

Pizarro takes Inca empire, 1533

SOUTH AMERICA

ATLANTIC OCEAN

PACIFIC OCEAN

Strait of Magellan

0   500   1,000 Miles
0   500   1,000 Kilometers

- ✹ Inca capital
- Inca empire
- ← Pizarro's forces
- ← Atahualpa's forces
- • Other city
- ✵ Battle

155

Museo de América, Madrid

Focus Activity

READ TO LEARN

What was life like in New Spain?

VOCABULARY

- encomienda
- missionary

PEOPLE

- Estevanico
- Fray Marcos de Niza
- Bartolomé de Las Casas
- Yanga

PLACES

- New Spain
- Mexico City

1450   1500   1521   1609   1650

The Spanish Build an Empire

Read Aloud

On an October night in 1521, Spaniards destroyed the city of Tenochtitlán. A large and powerful empire had come to an end. What would take its place? What would life be like for the conquerors and the people they now ruled?

THE BIG PICTURE

In the early 1500s the colony of New Spain included the lands of the Aztec, the Maya, and other peoples of the Americas. Mexico City, the new name for Tenochtitlán, was the capital of the colony.

New Spain covered much of the Caribbean islands, Central America, and the present-day country of Mexico. It stretched north into what are now the southwestern United States and the state of Florida.

As a way of settling and controlling this huge region, the government of Spain began granting encomiendas (en koh mee EN dahs) to certain Spanish colonists. An encomienda was a very large piece of land that often included several Indian villages. The encomienda system helped New Spain to grow and its colonists to prosper. It also caused much suffering to the Indians who lived there and to the Africans later brought by force from their homes across the Atlantic Ocean. As you read the lesson, you will also find out what kind of life the Spanish colonists made for themselves in New Spain.

THE GROWTH OF NEW SPAIN

After Spain's defeat of the Aztec empire, conquistadors spread through much of North America and South America to win more land and find more riches for Spain. The map on this page shows which areas became part of New Spain. As they traveled north and south of Mexico City, the Spanish brought more Indian cities and villages into the colony.

Spain Conquers the Maya

About five years after Tenochtitlán fell, Spanish soldiers headed southeast to the Yucatán peninsula to find Maya treasures. You read about the Maya in Chapter 3. Their determined fighters and the thick rain forest environment helped the Maya to defend parts of their land for 20 years. But by 1546 the Maya, like the Aztec, fell under Spanish rule.

To the Maya's horror the Spanish burned their valuable collection of books—books that contained their knowledge of history, math, and science. In one act much of Maya civilization went up in smoke. Only three Maya books written before the Spanish conquest survive today.

Francisco Coronado Searches for Gold

In 1540 the young conquistador Francisco Coronado led a group of Spaniards, Africans, and Indians on a search for gold in what is now the southwestern United States. For two years Coronado looked for the rumored Seven Cities of Gold. An African scout, Estevanico (ays tay VAH nee koh), and a Spanish priest called Fray Marcos de Niza had heard stories about the golden cities during an earlier expedition. But before they could find the cities, Estevanico was killed.

Fray Marcos lived to tell what had happened and went on to join Coronado on his expedition. Coronado did not find the golden cities either. The Seven Cities of Gold did not really exist. But during their expedition, Coronado's men gazed down the cliffs of the Grand Canyon.

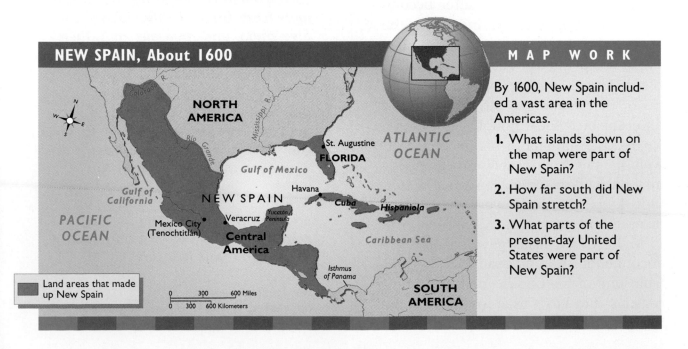

NEW SPAIN, About 1600

NORTH AMERICA

Colorado R.
Rio Grande
Mississippi R.

St. Augustine
FLORIDA
ATLANTIC OCEAN

Gulf of Mexico

Gulf of California

NEW SPAIN

Havana

Cuba

Hispaniola

PACIFIC OCEAN

Mexico City (Tenochtitlán)
Veracruz
Yucatán Peninsula

Central America

Caribbean Sea

Isthmus of Panama

SOUTH AMERICA

Land areas that made up New Spain

0 300 600 Miles
0 300 600 Kilometers

MAP WORK

By 1600, New Spain included a vast area in the Americas.

1. What islands shown on the map were part of New Spain?

2. How far south did New Spain stretch?

3. What parts of the present-day United States were part of New Spain?

BUILDING NEW SPAIN

For the Indians who stayed on their homelands after New Spain was formed, life became very harsh. The harshness began with the encomienda system. This system was similar to slavery, but it had an important difference. In exchange for the Indians' work, the colonists agreed to care for the Indians and to teach them about Christianity.

Whether constructing buildings, tending cattle, or growing corn, Indians worked from dawn to dusk. Sometimes they were whipped. Often they went hungry. When the Spanish found silver in the mountains of northern Mexico, Indians were put to work in the mines. The silver the Indians mined helped to make Spain one of the richest and most powerful countries in Europe.

"Protector of the Indians"

One of New Spain's strongest defenders of Indian rights was a Catholic priest named Bartolomé de Las Casas. Las Casas came to New Spain to run an encomienda. A few years after becoming a missionary to the Indians in the early 1500s, Las Casas was given his own encomienda in Hispaniola in 1513. A missionary is a person who teaches his or her religion to others who have different beliefs. Although Las Casas treated the Indians in his encomienda well, he saw how cruelly other encomienda owners acted. He knew that thousands of Indians were dying from disease and overwork.

In 1514 Las Casas gave up his encomienda. As you read this excerpt from one of his books, identify some reasons that Las Casas gives for opposing the encomiendas.

Biblioteca Colombina, Seville

MANY VOICES
PRIMARY SOURCE

Excerpt from
History of the Indies,
completed by
Bartolomé de Las Casas in 1563.

*Tell me, by what right or justice do you hold these Indians in such a cruel and horrible **servitude**? On what authority have you [tried to destroy] these peoples, who dwelt quietly and peacefully on their own land? . . . Why do you keep them so **oppressed** and exhausted, without giving them enough to eat or curing them of the sicknesses they [get] from the excessive labor you give them, and they die, or rather, you kill them, in order to extract and acquire gold every day?*

And what care do you take that they should be instructed in religion, so that they may know their God and creator, may be baptized, may hear Mass, and may keep [observe] Sundays and feast days? Are these not men? . . . Are you not bound to love them as you love yourselves? Do you not understand this? Don't you feel this?

---

servitude: slavery
oppressed: cruelly, or unjustly, controlled

For the next 50 years Las Casas devoted himself to ending the encomiendas. He soon became known as the "Protector of the Indians." Because of Las Casas's work, the king of Spain passed the "New Laws of 1542," which said that Indians could no longer be made to work without pay. The encomienda system lasted until the end of the 1700s. Sadly, until late in his life, Las Casas failed to see the similarity in the enslaving of Indians and Africans.

Slavery in New Spain

Scholars disagree about the number of Indians that were living in Mexico in 1519. Their estimates range from about 8 to 30 million. By 1568 the population had dropped to less than 3 million. Much of this human tragedy was due to disease as well as overwork. Enslaving Africans became the cruel solution to the desire for workers.

African captives had been a part of Spain's empire since its earliest days. Yet enslaved Africans were not brought to New Spain in large numbers until the Indians began to die out. By 1570 over 200,000 Africans had been bought and taken to New Spain. Most were brought to such Caribbean islands as Cuba and Hispaniola to grow sugarcane.

Enslaved Africans also worked in the mines. At the ports of Veracruz and Acapulco, they loaded silver and other goods onto the treasure ships bound for Spain.

Some Captives Break Free

By law, enslaved Africans in New Spain could make money in their spare time to buy their freedom. But African captives also escaped. In the 1560s and 1570s, Africans and Indians rose up against the Spanish.

In 1609 about 600 Spanish soldiers were sent to the mountains around Veracruz to recapture an elderly African slave named Yanga and over 80 of his followers. After 30 years the Africans still had not been captured. The government then left Yanga and his followers alone. They later established a town, San Lorenzo de los Negros.

Diego Rivera, a Mexican artist, painted *Disembarkation of the Spanish at Vera Cruz* in 1951. Many captive Indians and Africans were held in shackles (above, right).

The Detroit Institute of Art

159

COLONIAL MEXICO CITY

In addition to working on farms and ranches and in mines, Indians were also forced to build New Spain's capital, Mexico City. In early 1522 Hernando Cortés decided that "it was well to rebuild" Tenochtitlán. In the process almost all the Aztec features of the city were destroyed.

Upon the rubble where the Great Temple had stood, Cortés began building a cathedral, or huge church. Most cities in Spain had a cathedral and government buildings arranged around a central plaza. Cortés saw to it that Mexico City also had these buildings. Wide streets fanned out from the Great Plaza. At first only the streets on which conquistadors, lawyers, and merchants lived were paved.

A Walk Through Mexico City

Beginning at dawn, Mexico City was full of activity. Through the morning mist Indians paddled across Lake Texcoco in long boats loaded with goods. They carried vegetables, hay for horses, pottery, firewood, and other goods to the markets and shops. Most of the local goods were sold at the market on the Great Plaza together with goods from Spain, China, and the Netherlands. "[E]verything that is best in Spain comes to this square," wrote one Spaniard.

Spaniards first arriving in Mexico City marveled at the fine houses and wide streets. These sights were often found on Calle del Reloj (KAH yay dayl RAY loh), or Clock Street, and on La Moneda (lah mohn AY dah). *Moneda* means "coin" in Spanish. La Moneda is a place where coins are made. Look at the map of today's Mexico City on page 161. Find Constitution Plaza. Today Mexicans call it the Zócalo (ZOH kah loh), an Aztec word for "plaza."

By 1554 Mexico City had many of the features of a European city. Spaniards of the time compared it to Venice, Italy, because it, too, had been built on water. There were mansions, flowering parks, schools, and a university. Mexico City also had a theater, post office, and printing press. The city's most widely published books had to do with Catholic teachings.

The National Palace is one of the buildings the Spanish erected during colonial times. It is located on the Zócalo on the former site of Moctezuma's palace.

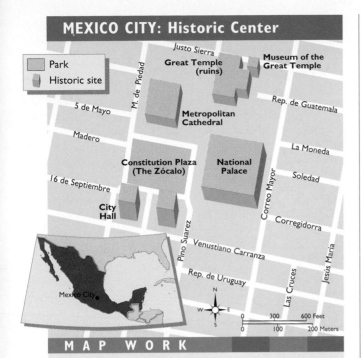

MEXICO CITY: Historic Center

Park

Historic site

Justo Sierra

Great Temple (ruins)

Museum of the Great Temple

M. de Piedad

Rep. de Guatemala

5 de Mayo

Metropolitan Cathedral

Madero

La Moneda

Constitution Plaza (The Zócalo)

National Palace

Soledad

16 de Septiembre

Correo Mayor

City Hall

Corregidorra

Pino Suárez

Venustiano Carranza

Jesús María

Rep. de Uruguay

Las Cruces

Mexico City

0   300   600 Feet

0   100   200 Meters

M A P   W O R K

The Historic Center of Mexico City surrounds the largest plaza in the Western Hemisphere.

1. What are the names of the government buildings surrounding the Zócalo?

2. Which side of the Zócalo is next to the Metropolitan Cathedral?

Mexico City contained schools and many other buildings owned by the Catholic Church. Within the walls of the convents, nuns cared for lemon, orange, and apple orchards. To many colonists, as a Catholic friar wrote, Mexico City was "the noblest and most imposing [city] in New Spain."

WHY IT MATTERS

From the ashes of the Aztec empire arose a different civilization—New Spain. Spain built an empire in the Americas, and the cost in suffering was high. The Indian land and people gave way to much of the culture of Spain. But as you will read in the Legacy on pages 162–163, Indian ways can still be found in Mexico City today.

✓✓ Reviewing Facts and Ideas

MAIN IDEAS

- As the conquistadors searched for land and gold, they helped to expand New Spain to include the Caribbean islands, Central America, the land now called Mexico, and those areas now part of the southwestern and southeastern United States.

- The government of Spain began the encomienda system in which thousands of Indians died from overwork. The priest Bartolomé de Las Casas called for the end of the encomiendas. Thousands of African captives were brought to New Spain to replace the dying Indians.

- Colonial Mexico City was built to resemble cities in Spain. Some buildings and streets from this time can still be found today.

THINK ABOUT IT

1. Who benefited the most from the encomiendas? Who was hurt? Why?

2. How did enslaved Africans contribute to life in New Spain?

3. **FOCUS** What was life like in New Spain for the Indians, their Spanish conquerors, and the Africans brought as slaves?

4. **THINKING SKILL** What *effect* did Las Casas have on life in New Spain? What else could have been done by him or others to help the Indians? Give reasons for your answer.

5. **WRITE** Suppose that you are Las Casas, a colonist running an encomienda, or an Indian working on one. Write a letter to the king of Spain explaining what you think about the encomienda system.

MEXICAN ART

Almost 500 years ago one empire conquered another in what is now Mexico. The conquerors came from Spain. The land they took was home to the Aztec and other Indians. Over time the Spanish forever changed Mexico. But many Indians and their cultures have survived.

The past that all Mexicans share lives on in the paintings of today's artists. Mexico's art links past, present, and future and is a special part of the country's legacy. As you look at the art on these pages, think about how the use of certain symbols shows connections between past and present.

This is a scene from Juan O'Gorman's 1949 painting *The City of Mexico*. It shows both a feathered snake and an eagle above modern Mexico City. Read the next page to find out why O'Gorman might have included these symbols in his painting.

Codex Telleriano-Remensis, M.N.A.H., Biblioteca

The serpent, or snake, has been an important symbol in Mexico for many centuries. The Aztec ornament (above) was worn on the chest. The serpent with feathers represented the god Quetzalcoatl (ket ZUL kuh waht ul), who was worshiped by many Indian peoples. This drawing of Quetzalcoatl (right) is from a calendar created around 1389.

Codex Mendoza, M.N.A.H., Biblioteca

The eagle is another important Mexican symbol. According to Aztec tradition, Tenochtitlán was founded at the site where an eagle had landed on a cactus. This drawing appeared in a book created around 1540. A similar eagle appears on the Mexican flag today (above).

CHAPTER 6 REVIEW

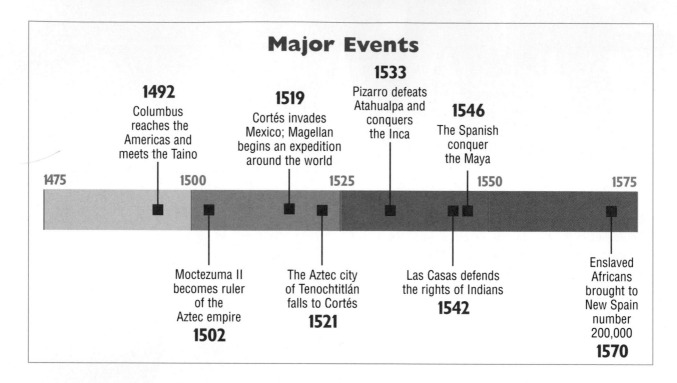

Major Events

1492
Columbus reaches the Americas and meets the Taino

1519
Cortés invades Mexico; Magellan begins an expedition around the world

1533
Pizarro defeats Atahualpa and conquers the Inca

1546
The Spanish conquer the Maya

1475   1500   1525   1550   1575

Moctezuma II becomes ruler of the Aztec empire
1502

The Aztec city of Tenochtitlán falls to Cortés
1521

Las Casas defends the rights of Indians
1542

Enslaved Africans brought to New Spain number 200,000
1570

THINKING ABOUT VOCABULARY

Number a paper from 1 to 5. Beside each number write the word or term from the list below that matches the description.

colony
Columbian exchange
conquistador
encomienda
expedition

1. A soldier who conquered lands for Spain

2. A journey made for a special purpose

3. A settlement that is ruled by another country

4. A huge piece of land, often including several Indian villages, that the Spanish government gave to its colonists

5. The movement of people, plants, animals, and germs across the Atlantic Ocean that began after Christopher Columbus arrived in the Americas

THINKING ABOUT FACTS

1. Who were the Taino? What had happened to them by the 1500s?

2. How did Christopher Columbus get the money he needed for his journey?

3. Why do people remember Christopher Columbus today?

4. What was one good effect of the Columbian exchange for the peoples of the Americas? What was one bad effect?

5. What were the Spanish troops looking for in Mexico?

6. How was Hernando Cortés able to conquer the Aztec on their own land?

7. What lands made up New Spain?

8. What is a missionary?

9. Why did Bartolomé de Las Casas come to New Spain? What did he do there?

10. What events shown on the time line occurred in 1519?

WRITING A PARAGRAPH OF COMPARISON

Write a paragraph comparing Columbus's meeting with the Taino to Cortés's first meeting with Moctezuma.

WRITING A JOURNAL ENTRY

Suppose that you are either an Aztec or a Spanish soldier at the battle for Tenochtitlán. Write an entry in your journal in which you describe the experience.

WRITING A LETTER

Suppose that you are an Indian living in New Spain. Write a letter to the king of Spain describing the cruelty you believe your people have suffered under the Spanish colonists. Explain why you think the encomienda system should be ended.

APPLYING GEOGRAPHY SKILLS

HISTORICAL MAPS

To practice your skill in reading historical maps, answer the following questions about the map on page 155.

1. How do you know that the map on this page is an historical map?

2. What does the map key tell you?

3. Across which ocean did Pizarro travel to reach the Inca empire?

4. Where is Cuzco? Why is this an important city?

5. What makes historical maps useful?

Summing Up the Chapter

Copy the main-idea map on a separate piece of paper. Review the chapter to complete the blank sections. When you have completed the map, use the information to write a paragraph that answers the question "What changes came to the Americas in the 1500s?"

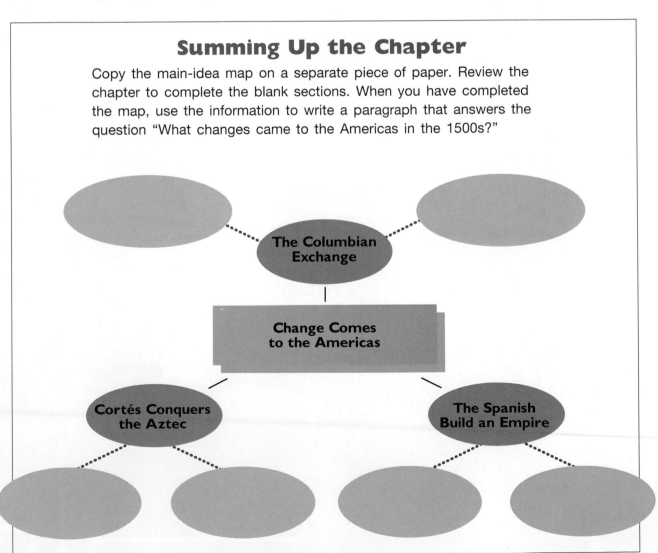

The Columbian Exchange

Change Comes to the Americas

Cortés Conquers the Aztec

The Spanish Build an Empire

Early European Settlements of North America

THINKING ABOUT HISTORY AND GEOGRAPHY

The story of Chapter 7 begins in North America in the year 1587 . Read the time line below. By the last date, Europeans had established a growing colony in New England. By the middle 1600s, the English, French, and Dutch each had their own settlements in North America.

PACIFIC OCEAN

1587

ROANOKE ISLAND
John White leads English colonists to Roanoke Island

1607

JAMESTOWN
The English build a new settlement in Virginia

1608

QUEBEC
Samuel de Champlain of France explores the St. Lawrence River

1587

1597

1607

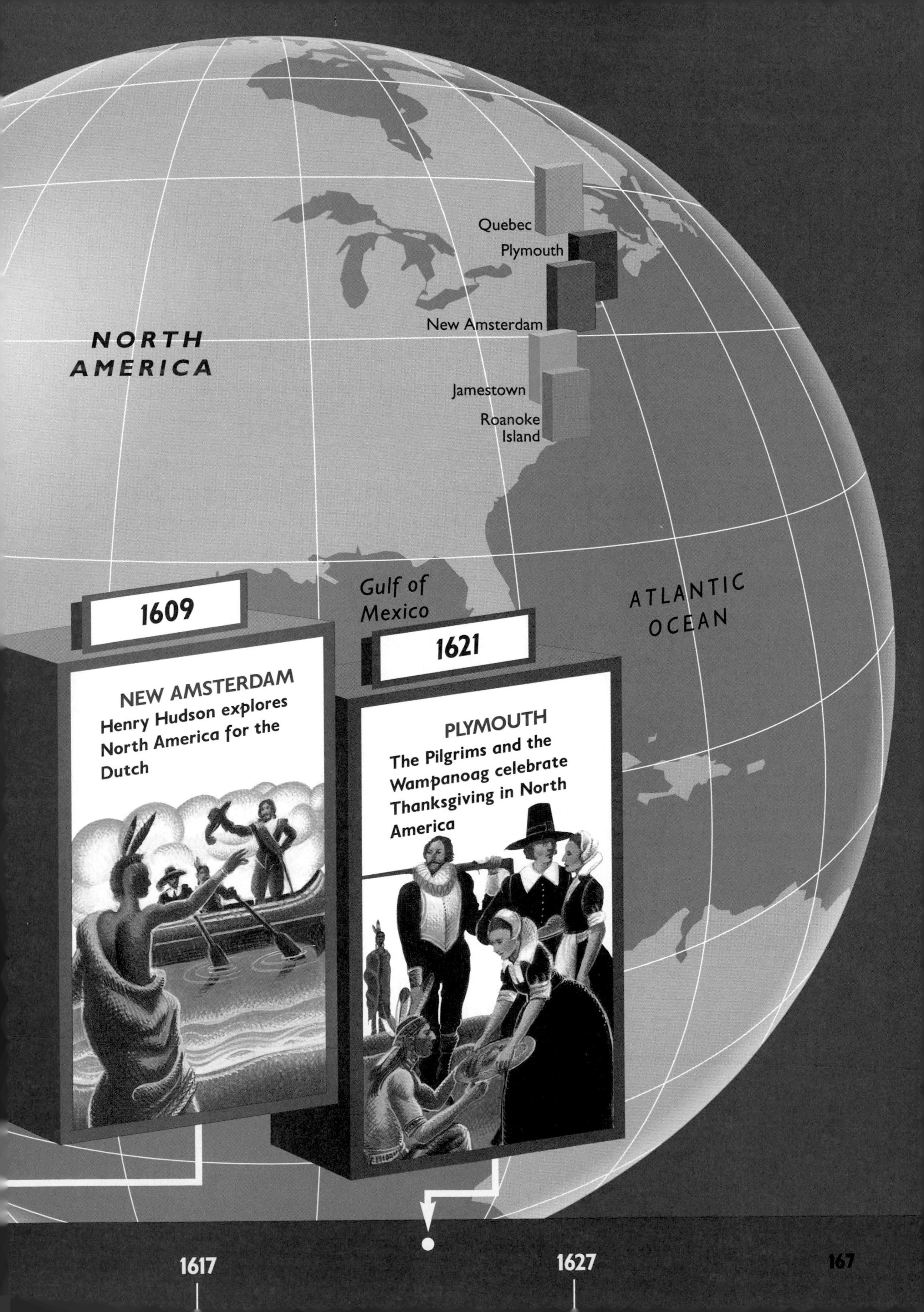
Quebec
Plymouth
New Amsterdam
Jamestown
Roanoke Island
NORTH AMERICA
Gulf of Mexico
ATLANTIC OCEAN
1609
NEW AMSTERDAM
Henry Hudson explores North America for the Dutch
1621
PLYMOUTH
The Pilgrims and the Wampanoag celebrate Thanksgiving in North America
1617
1627

1500　　1540　　1585　1590　　1620　　1660

Early European Settlements

Focus Activity

READ TO LEARN

What is the mystery of the "Lost Colony" of Roanoke?

VOCABULARY

- charter
- armada

PEOPLE

- Queen Elizabeth I
- Sir Walter Raleigh
- John White
- King Philip II

PLACES

- Virginia
- Roanoke Island

Read Aloud

The word CROATOAN (kroh uh TOH un) was one of the last messages left by a small group of English colonists before they disappeared. In 1587 over 100 English people had begun new lives on Roanoke Island off the coast of present-day North Carolina. Three years later, they were gone. Eight letters, which were carved into a tree, provide a clue to their whereabouts. But we still do not know what happened to them.

THE BIG PICTURE

By the late 1500s Spain claimed most of South America and North America. But other European countries ignored Spain's claims to these lands. They too wanted to share in the riches of the Americas.

England challenged Spain in several ways. English sea captains called "sea dogs" raided Spain's colonies and seized its treasure ships. England also planned to plant colonies in North America. The English claimed a region north of Florida that was also claimed by the Spanish. The English called their claim the **Virginia** colony in honor of **Queen Elizabeth I**, who was known as the "Virgin Queen."

The early English colonists in Virginia faced many hardships. On their first attempt to start a colony in 1585, they returned home after one year. Colonists in England's second attempt were never heard from again.

ROANOKE ISLAND

Sir Walter Raleigh was one of the first people in England who told Queen Elizabeth to begin a colony in North America. Elizabeth had made Raleigh a knight because of battles he had won for England in Europe. He was one of her most trusted advisers.

English explorers told Raleigh about **Roanoke Island** off the Atlantic Coast of North America. Find Roanoke Island on the map on this page. The island was "sweet, fruitful and wholesome," they said. It was also in a location difficult for passing Spanish sailors to see. Elizabeth granted Raleigh a **charter** to establish a colony in Virginia. A charter was a document that permitted colonists to settle on land claimed by their ruler.

The First Try

Roanoke, an Algonkian word, comes from the Roanoac (ROH uh noh uk) people. They and the Hatteras (HAT ur as) and the Tuscarora (tus kuh ROHR uh) lived on the Atlantic Coast. They built their villages along its many streams and rivers.

In 1585 the first English people came to Roanoke Island to start a settlement. They faced hunger and hardship. After a colonist killed the Roanoac's leader, Wingina (WIHN jih nuh), the Roanoac stopped helping the English. The colonists soon returned to England.

A Second Try

In 1587 Raleigh again sent colonists across the Atlantic Ocean. He chose **John White** to be the colony's governor.

Sir Walter Raleigh's interests included military fighting, navigation, and writing history and poetry.

White, a skillful painter, had gone with the first settlers to Roanoke. While there, he sketched the Native Americans he met and drew pictures of plants and animals.

In July White and more than 100 men, women, and children landed at Roanoke. His granddaughter, Virginia Dare, was born after they arrived. Her family named the baby Virginia after the colony.

The colonists asked White to return to England for more food and tools. White sadly bid farewell to the colony in 1587. He promised to return as soon as possible. He told the colonists to carve a message on a tree trunk if they should move. "Mark a cross if you are in danger," he added.

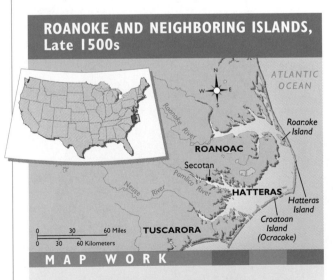

ROANOKE AND NEIGHBORING ISLANDS, Late 1500s

ATLANTIC OCEAN

Roanoke River

Roanoke Island

ROANOAC

Secotan

Neuse River

Pamlico River

HATTERAS

Hatteras Island

Croatoan Island (Ocracoke)

0 30 60 Miles

0 30 60 Kilometers

TUSCARORA

MAP WORK

"Secotan" was the name of the village and the people White met on his first voyage.

1. Not including the Secotan people, which Native Americans lived near Roanoke Island?

2. How far is Roanoke Island from Secotan village?

THE LOST COLONY

White reached England in November to find the country caught by war fever. Spain was preparing an armada, or large fleet of ships, to invade England. Queen Elizabeth needed all her ships and sailors for the war. White would have to delay returning to Roanoke.

The Spanish Armada

Spain's King Philip II wanted to punish England for attacking Spanish colonies and ships. In 1588 the Spanish Armada set sail for England. The "sea dog," Sir Francis Drake, led the English fleet. England's smaller, better armed ships darted around Spain's larger, slower ships. The English set many Spanish ships on fire. Then the weather took a bad turn. A violent storm pounded and sank much of the badly damaged Spanish Armada. The surviving ships fled home to Spain. The English celebrated an important victory.

The Mystery and Its Clues

John White was finally able to return to Roanoke in August 1590. His hopes soared as he neared land.

We let fall our grapnel [anchor] near the shore and sounded with a trumpet a call, and afterwards many familiar English tunes.

No one appeared on land. White went ashore. There he found some clues.

One of the chief trees . . . had the bark taken off, and five [feet] from the ground in fair capital letters was [engraved] CROATOAN without any cross or sign of distress,

White wrote. *Croatoan* was the name of an island south of Roanoke. It was also the name of Native Americans who might have been living on the island.

Storms, low supplies, and complaints from his crew forced White to end his search. He had to sail back to England.

People still wonder what happened to the "lost colonists." Did they fight with the nearby Roanoac or with Spanish soldiers from Florida? White

John White's watercolor (left) shows the Secotan people's village in what is now North Carolina. Below is a nineteenth-century artist's painting of John White's return to Roanoke.

The Granger Collection

The Granger Collection

thought the colonists might be safe among the Croatoan people. Today, the Lumbee people of North Carolina believe they are descendants of the "lost colonists." No one knows for sure.

WHY IT MATTERS

England's efforts in the 1500s to start colonies in North America seemed doomed at first. But the defeat of the Spanish Armada boosted English confidence. Spain was still the strongest country in Europe. However, English sea power was growing. In the 1600s England would soon plant permanent colonies of its own along the Atlantic Coast of North America.

Yet England would not be the only European country to dot the coast with colonies. The Netherlands, Sweden, and France would also send colonists across the Atlantic Ocean.

Links to **LANGUAGE ARTS**

A Play About the Lost Colony

How do people today remember the 400-year-old lost colony of Roanoke?

Paul Green wrote the play *The Lost Colony*, which is performed every year on Roanoke Island. Using songs, dances, and drama, it tells the story of the colonists who disappeared.

In groups, use what you have read about the colony to choose an event that may have happened at the Roanoke colony. Then work together to write a play, poem, or television or film script that brings that event to life.

✓ Reviewing Facts and Ideas

MAIN IDEAS

- By the late 1500s England was challenging Spanish claims to North America by trying to plant its own colonies there.

- When the English first tried to establish a colony on Roanoke Island, they met the Roanoac, who had lived there for many years.

- John White brought a second group of colonists to Roanoke, but they disappeared—a mystery still unsolved today.

THINK ABOUT IT

1. Which Native Americans were living near the coast of present-day North Carolina in the late 1500s?

2. What were some reasons that the first English colonists on Roanoke Island returned to England?

3. **FOCUS** Why do you think the story of the "Lost Colony" of Roanoke still interests people?

4. **THINKING SKILL** What *effect* did the war between Spain and England have on England's attempts to colonize Roanoke Island?

5. **GEOGRAPHY** What natural features off the coast of Virginia might have helped to hide the Roanoke settlement from Spanish sailors?

Distinguishing Fact from Opinion

VOCABULARY
fact   opinion

WHY THE SKILL MATTERS

In the last lesson you read that John White searched for the "lost colonists" of Roanoke. When White wrote about this event he gave the **facts** of what he saw. A fact is a statement that can be checked and proved true. He also had an **opinion** about what happened to the missing colonists. An opinion is a personal view or belief. As you studied White's account of this mystery, you may have tried to figure out which of his statements could have been checked by the people who accompanied him and which were his personal beliefs or judgments.

USING THE SKILL

Being able to distinguish facts from opinions is important in your study of history. Many of the primary and secondary sources you read contain both facts and opinions. In statements that have both, you must first distinguish the facts from the opinions. Then check the facts before you decide whether or not the statement is correct.

An opinion is often based on a feeling or personal liking, and, therefore, cannot be proved. One way to identify such opinions is to look for clue words like *I believe, I think, I feel that,* or *it seems.* Sometimes sentences use descriptive words such as *good, the best,* or *wonderful.* These words express beliefs that cannot be proven. Therefore, they, too, are clues that the writer is giving an opinion.

During the 1500s people in England were thinking about settling in Virginia. They needed to distinguish fact from opinion when they read explorers' accounts of the unfamiliar land. One of the most famous of these accounts was written by Thomas Hariot. Hariot spent the year of 1585 in Roanoke. During his stay, Hariot took notes on the plants, animals, and people that he found there. When he returned to England, he wrote *A Brief and True Report of the New Found Land of Virginia.* His book includes both facts and opinions about Virginia.

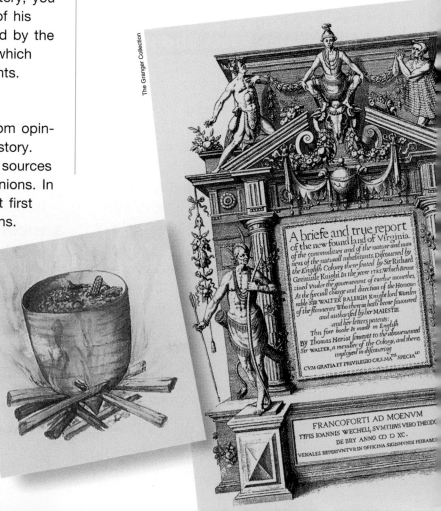

The Granger Collection

In the following excerpts, Hariot talks about the Powhatan (pow uh TAN) people.

It remains for me to speak a word or two of the inhabitants of the country. They dress in loose mantles [capes] *made of deerskins. They have no . . . tools of iron or steel. Their only weapons are bows made of witch-hazel* [a kind of wood] *and arrows of reeds.*

[The Powhatan] seem very ingenious [good at inventing things]. *For although they have no such tools, crafts, sciences, and arts as we, yet in those things they do, they show excellence of wit* [they are very smart].

Which statements in the first paragraph are facts? Which word clues that show opinions can you find in the second paragraph?

Helping yourself

- **A fact** can be proven true; an **opinion** cannot.
- Look for word clues that show an opinion, such as *believe* or *think.*
- Decide whether each statement is a fact or an opinion.

TRYING THE SKILL

Read the following description of early Virginia by an English sea captain, Ralph Lane. Then use the Helping Yourself box to distinguish facts from opinions.

We have discovered the mainland to be the goodliest soil under . . . heaven. So abounding with trees . . . and . . . grapes that France, Spain nor Italy have no greater; so many kinds of apothecary drugs [medicines], *several kinds of flax* [a kind of plant]. . . . *Within these few days we have found here maize . . . whose ear yields corn . . . four hundred upon one ear.*

Which statement is an opinion? How can you tell?

REVIEWING THE SKILL

1. What is a fact? What is an opinion?

2. What facts does Ralph Lane give to back up his opinion? How do you know?

3. What do you think Lane wants people in England to believe about Virginia?

4. Do you think the facts that Lane gives back up his opinion? Explain.

5. Why would it be important for you to be able to distinguish facts from opinions?

NOVA BRITANNIA.
OFFRING MOST
Excellent fruites by Planting in
VIRGINIA.
Exciting all such as be well affected to further the same.

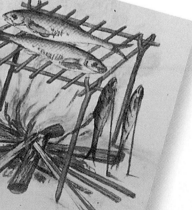

John White's paintings (far left and left) show cooking methods of the Southeastern Indians. Books and advertisements encouraged people to come to Virginia.

The Granger Collection

The Granger Collection

1497   1625   1660

The Search for a Northwest Passage

Read Aloud

No one knows exactly what happened to the English sea captain for whom some of the north Atlantic Coast's great waterways are named. On his final expedition to North America in 1611, the captain's men set him, his son, and a few loyal crew members adrift in a small boat. Their fate was left to the frigid waters near the Arctic Circle. Who would have risked the dangers of sailing so far north? What would be the purpose of such an expedition?

Focus Activity

READ TO LEARN

What did Henry Hudson's voyage show Europeans about North America's Atlantic Coast?

VOCABULARY

- Northwest Passage
- profit

PEOPLE

- Henry Hudson
- John Cabot
- Giovanni da Verrazano
- Jacques Cartier
- Samuel de Champlain

PLACES

- Hudson River

THE BIG PICTURE

The English had tried to set up a colony on Roanoke Island. But another quest kept Europeans searching for over one hundred years. Like Christopher Columbus, other Europeans searched for a western water route to Asia. In the early 1500s the Spanish had found that a southern sea route through Central America and South America did not exist.

English, French, and Dutch explorers continued to search for what they called a **Northwest Passage**, a water route through North America to Asia. You can see what these explorers achieved on the Infographic on pages 176–177. In 1609 **Henry Hudson** believed he had come close to finding such a Northwest Passage on his first voyage to North America.

THE VOYAGE OF HENRY HUDSON

Exploring the Americas was costly. Europe's rulers were not always willing to pay for expeditions. But the Dutch found their own way to pay for them. A group of merchants who wanted to trade with Asia formed the Dutch East India Company. The merchants agreed to pay for expeditions in return for the **profits** each might bring. Profit is the amount of money remaining after the costs of a business have been paid. In 1609 the Dutch East India Company hired Henry Hudson, an English captain, to search for a Northwest Passage to Asia.

Exploring New York Harbor

That summer Hudson and his crew on the *Half Moon* explored the coast of North America. They traveled north from present-day South Carolina to Maine. In August Hudson saw Chesapeake Bay and then Delaware Bay. Continuing north, Hudson reached what is today New York Harbor. Had he found a route to Asia?

Hudson mapped the harbor. He traded with the local Native Americans who were known as the Mannahata. "They go in deerskins loose, well dressed," wrote a crew member. "They have a great store [supply] of maize or Indian wheat, whereof they make good bread." But times were not always peaceful between the Dutch and the Mannahata. Hudson's crew also wrote of drunken fights and armed battles.

"Great River of the Mountains"

In September Hudson sailed north up the river that empties into New York Harbor. Today it is called the Hudson River. He felt sure the river was the Northwest Passage. Hudson called it "Great River of the Mountains." After about 150 miles, near what is today Albany, New York, the river narrowed and became shallow. Hudson realized this was not the Northwest Passage.

At present-day Albany, Hudson reached a large settlement that was home to the Delaware people. Hudson was amazed at the amount of surplus corn and beans the Delaware were preparing to store. There was "enough to load three ships," he wrote.

Hudson failed to find a Northwest Passage. But his voyage led to the beginning of trade between the Dutch and Native Americans.

Hudson the Dreamer, J. L. G. Ferris/Superstock Fine Arts Division

The Delaware met Henry Hudson in 1609. They call themselves the Lenni Lenape, which means "the People" in Algonkian.

Infographic

interNET CONNECTION Visit our website: www.mhschool.com

The Search for a Northwest Passage

Europeans slowly explored the east coast of North America, searching for a Northwest Passage to Asia. The search failed. However, it did lead Europeans to begin colonies on the coast. Look at the map below and locate the Swedish, Dutch, English, French, and Spanish settlements.

Quebec (1608)
Montreal (1642)
Plymouth (1620)
Fort Orange (1624)
New Amsterdam (1624)
New Sweden (1638–1655)
Jamestown (1607)
Roanoke (1585–1587)
Verrazan
1524
Santa Elena (1566–1587)
Fort Caroline (1564)
St. Augustine (1565)

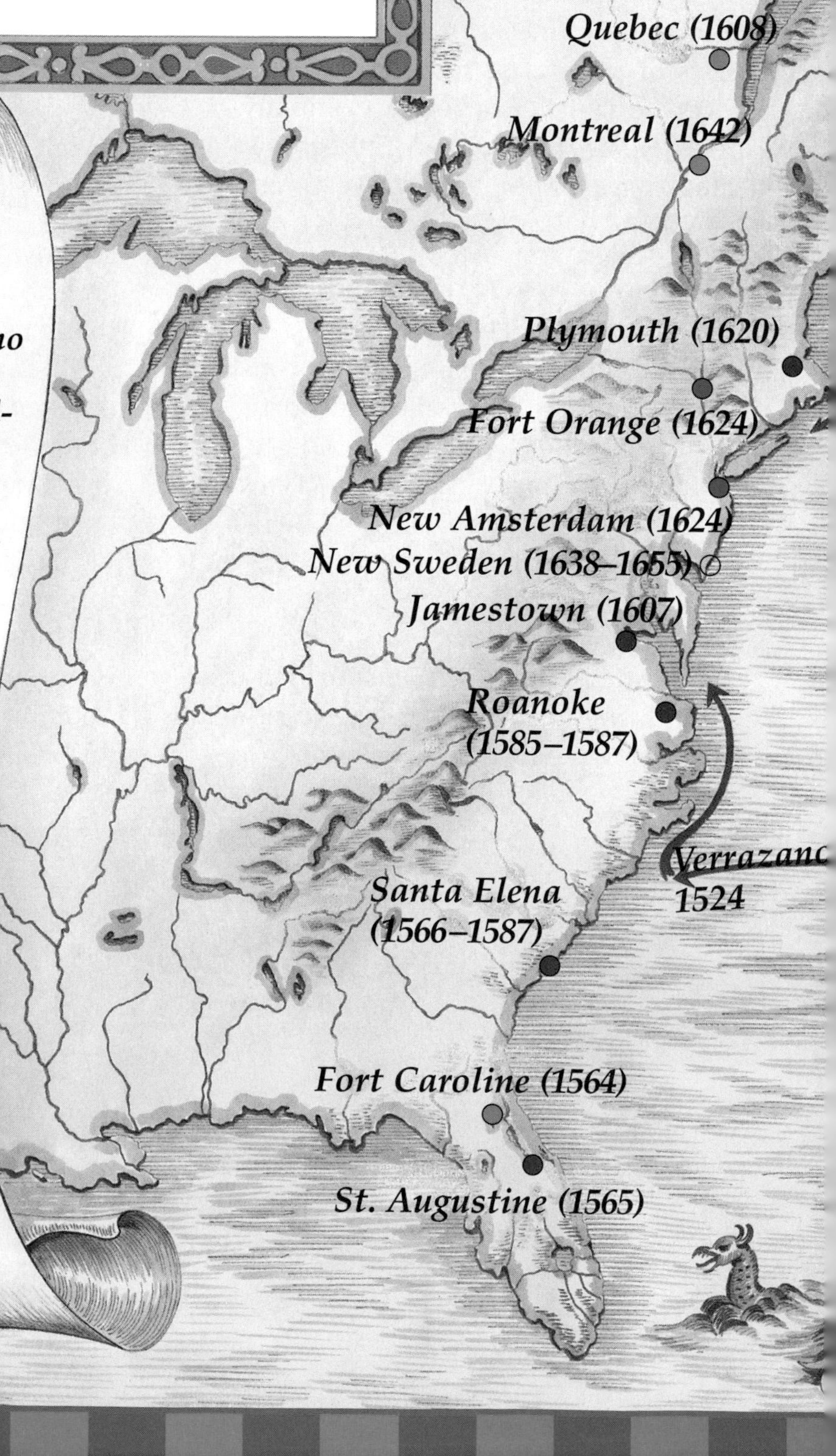

Explorers

John Cabot, *an Italian who sailed under the flag of England, reached Newfoundland via present-day Nova Scotia in 1497.*

Giovanni da Verrazano, *an Italian sailing under the flag of France, explored the Outer Banks of present–day North Carolina in 1524.*

Jacques Cartier, *who sailed under the flag of France, reached Newfoundland in 1534.*

Samuel de Champlain, *sailing under the flag of France, founded Port Royal in present–day Nova Scotia in 1604 and took colonists to Quebec in 1608.*

Henry Hudson, *an Englishman sailing under the flag of the Netherlands, explored the north Atlantic Coast in 1609.*

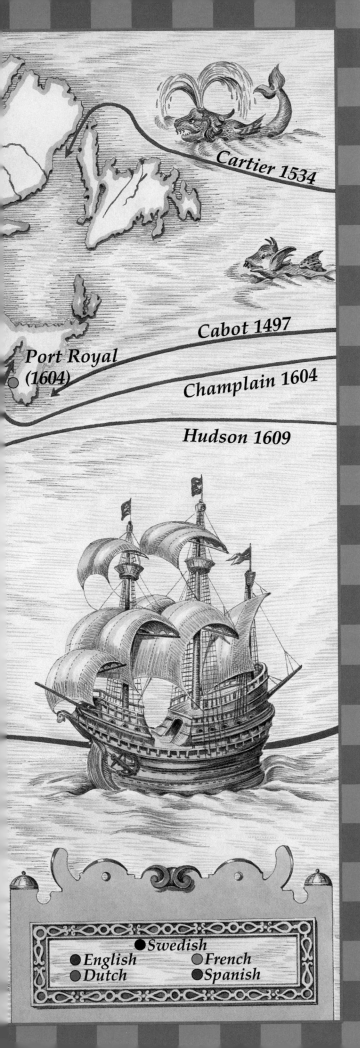

Cartier 1534

Cabot 1497

Port Royal
(1604)

Champlain 1604

Hudson 1609

●Swedish
●English   ○French
●Dutch   ●Spanish

WHY IT MATTERS

The search for a Northwest Passage continued for about another 200 years. It was not until the 1800s that Europeans finally carved a path through the frozen seas of the far north. However, in the 1600s the explorations made it possible for England, France, and the Netherlands to begin building colonies in North America. Like Spain, they also looked for ways to make a profit from their new colonies

✓ Reviewing Facts and Ideas

MAIN IDEAS

- In the 1500s and 1600s, English, Dutch, and French explorers searched for a Northwest Passage to Asia.
- In 1609 Henry Hudson first sailed up the Hudson River, hoping it might be a waterway to Asia.
- During the search for a Northwest Passage, Europeans began to claim land and plant colonies along the Atlantic Coast of North America.

THINK ABOUT IT

1. Why did European explorers want to find a Northwest Passage?

2. How did Dutch explorers pay for their explorations?

3. **FOCUS** What did Henry Hudson's 1609 voyage accomplish?

4. **THINKING SKILL** Identify the _facts_ and _opinions_ that led to the search for a Northwest Passage.

5. **GEOGRAPHY** Use the Infographic on pages 76–77 in order to locate and list the Native Americans who lived along the waterways that Hudson explored in 1609.

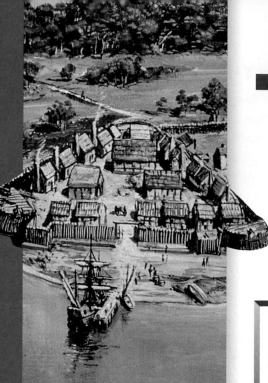

1500   1540   1580   1607   1624   1660

The Jamestown Colony

Read Aloud

In April 1607, 104 men and boys landed at Jamestown, Virginia, to set up another English colony. Fish filled the rivers. Deer wandered everywhere. The strawberries, wrote one colonist, were "four times bigger and better than ours in England." By September only 46 settlers were still alive. What happened to cloud the bright beginning of England's first permanent colony in North America?

Focus Activity

READ TO LEARN

Who helped the colony of Jamestown survive?

VOCABULARY

- stock
- cash crop
- indentured servant
- House of Burgesses

PEOPLE

- Chief Powhatan
- John Smith
- Pocahontas
- John Rolfe
- Openchancanough

PLACES

- Chesapeake Bay
- Tsenacomacoh
- Jamestown

THE BIG PICTURE

The English had faced setbacks like those on Roanoke Island. But they still wanted to build colonies in North America. Explorers told stories about its rich land. Others brought home valuable cargoes of fur and fish. In 1606 a group of London merchants asked King James I for a charter to plant a colony in Virginia again. The king agreed.

The English thought the best place to settle was around **Chesapeake Bay**. The bay had plentiful fish and good hunting. Historians disagree about the number of Native Americans living in eastern Virginia at that time. Whatever their population was, they called their homeland **Tsenacomacoh** (sen uh KAHM uh koh). The center of Tsenacomacoh was Chesapeake Bay.

At first the English and the Native Americans found a way to live on the land together. That changed as peace gave way to conflict.

THE POWHATAN

For over 1,000 years Native Americans had lived in the area the English now called Virginia. Algonkian-speaking peoples there had joined together to form the Powhatan chiefdom. This chiefdom was a group of Native Americans, including the Powhatan people, who united under one main chief. The chief was known as the Powhatan. When the English heard this, they also gave the name *Powhatan* to all the peoples the chief ruled.

Chief Powhatan was called Wahunsonacock (wah hun SAHN uh kahk) by his people. He ruled hundreds of villages in Tsenacomacoh. The Powhatan people paid him tribute with deerskins, pearls, corn, and other valuables. Chief Powhatan was a respected leader whose orders were obeyed.

The Powhatan Chiefdom

By the early 1600s the Powhatan chiefdom included many other Native Americans besides the Powhatan people. The map on this page shows where some of the other members of the chiefdom lived. Their enemies spoke Iroquoian and Siouan languages. They lived on all sides of the chiefdom. The people of the chiefdom had united probably in order to protect their hunting grounds as well as because they shared a language.

In addition to Chief Powhatan, each town and village also had its own chief, or leader. Both men and women could become either the chief of the village or the Chief Powhatan. All this would change after the English arrived.

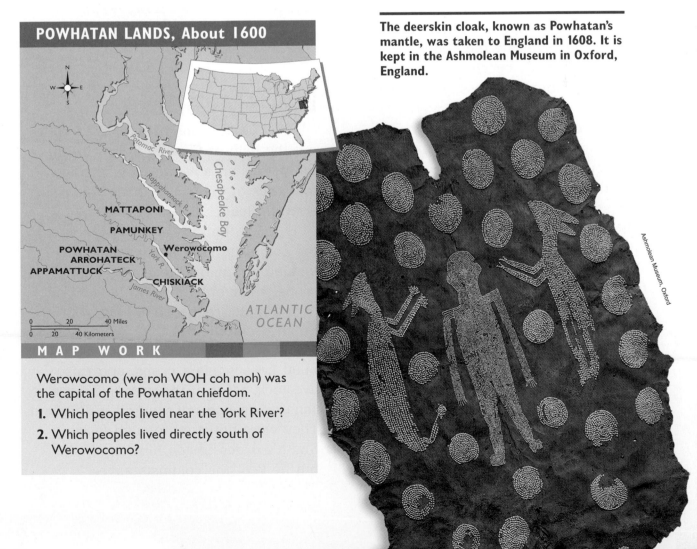

POWHATAN LANDS, About 1600

Potomac River
Rappahannock R.
Chesapeake Bay
MATTAPONI
PAMUNKEY
POWHATAN
ARROHATECK
Werowocomo
York R.
APPAMATTUCK
CHISKIACK
James River
ATLANTIC OCEAN

0   20   40 Miles
0   20   40 Kilometers

MAP WORK

Werowocomo (we roh WOH coh moh) was the capital of the Powhatan chiefdom.

1. Which peoples lived near the York River?
2. Which peoples lived directly south of Werowocomo?

The deerskin cloak, known as Powhatan's mantle, was taken to England in 1608. It is kept in the Ashmolean Museum in Oxford, England.

Ashmolean Museum, Oxford

THE ENGLISH

Across the ocean from the Powhatan chiefdom, in England, merchants and landowners started a business called the Virginia Company of London. They set up the company to start a colony in Virginia. The merchants sold shares of ownership, or stock, in the company. Any profits the company made from the colony would be divided among the people who had bought stock.

The Virginia Company offered to send colonists to North America. It gave them tools, weapons, medicine, seed, and other goods. In return, the colonists had to repay the company. Repayment was made with a share of any gold the colonists found or any crops they grew.

The Jamestown Colony

In 1607 three small ships paid for by the Virginia Company entered Chesapeake Bay. "We saw the goodliest woods—[such] as beech, oak, cedar, cypress, walnut, and sassafras," wrote one colonist named George Percy. Percy became one of the colony's first planters.

After much debate, the newcomers settled near a large river. They called it the James River, after England's King James I. They built houses, a church, and a fort. Unknown to them, this was Tsenacomacoh. The colonists named their tiny settlement Jamestown.

Jamestown sat on a peninsula a few miles from the ocean into Chesapeake Bay. The location seemed to be safe from Spanish ships. But the water was salty and dangerous to drink. The swampy land held another danger, disease-carrying mosquitoes. That summer almost half of the colonists died. By winter the survivors were desperate.

Scholars have found that while John Smith stretched the truth about some events in Virginia, his writings have proved to be a valuable source on colonial history.

John Smith Leads the Colony

The colonists might have died without the help of Captain John Smith. Smith was an adventurer who often told tales of his past. But he was also a strong leader.

By 1608 Smith was disgusted with the colonists. They spent their time looking for gold instead of planting crops. Their only interest, he said, was to "dig gold, refine gold, load gold." So Smith declared, "He that will not work shall not eat." He forced colonists to build houses, plant crops, and raise livestock. Most of the men and boys at Jamestown had not worked in England. They were not used to such tasks. Smith's orders made him unpopular, but he kept the colonists alive.

The Granger Collection

Smith later wrote a book about Virginia. In it he tells how he was taken captive by Chief Powhatan and saved by the chief's daughter, Pocahontas (poh kuh HAHN tus). Read the excerpt from Smith's *A General History of Virginia*. Today, many historians believe that Smith's account of this event was not completely accurate.

> [T]wo great stones were brought before Powhatan, then as many as could laid hands on [Smith], dragged him to [the stones], and thereon laid his head. And being ready with their clubs to beat out his brains, Pocahontas, [Powhatan]'s dearest daughter, . . . got his head in her arms and laid her own upon his to save him from death. Whereat [Powhatan] was contented he should live.

Trading with the Powhatan

Sometimes Smith traded with the Powhatan people for food. Other times the colonists and the Native Americans fought with one another. From Smith's writings we know that he and Chief

Powhatan spoke about the fighting. Powhatan said:

> *Think you I am so simple not to know it is better . . . being your friend, than . . . being so hunted that . . . I can neither rest, eat, nor sleep . . . [E]very year our friendly trade shall furnish you with corn.*

In 1609 Smith was hurt in a gunpowder explosion. He had to return to England. Without his leadership, the colony again faced hard times. One colonist called the winter of 1609–1610 the starving time. "Our food was but a small can of barley shared among five men each day," he wrote.

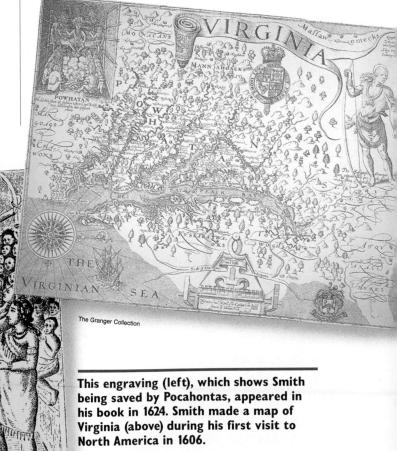

The Granger Collection

This engraving (left), which shows Smith being saved by Pocahontas, appeared in his book in 1624. Smith made a map of Virginia (above) during his first visit to North America in 1606.

National Portrait Gallery, Smithsonian Institution/Art Resource

Ætatis suæ 21. Aº.1616.

The 1614 wedding of John Rolfe and Pocahontas (right) was a turning point for Jamestown. That same year Rolfe began growing tobacco (above). The painting of Pocahontas in English clothes (left) hangs in the National Portrait Gallery in Washington, D.C.

NEW VIRGINIANS

The colony barely survived. Then in 1614 John Rolfe found a solution. He harvested a crop of tobacco. This plant is native to the Americas. People were already smoking tobacco in England. As demand grew, tobacco became a cash crop, or a crop that is sold for money. Colonists hoped to become wealthy from growing tobacco.

King James I called tobacco a "stinking weed." To him, smoking was "hateful to the nose, harmful to the brain, dangerous to the lungs." But the Virginia Company ignored the king's views. It began to give colonists land that they could own and grow tobacco on. The colonists worked harder than ever. Before tobacco, wrote one colonist, "glad was he who could slip from his labor or slumber over his task." Now the colonists did more work in a day than they had done in a week.

The "Peace of Pocahontas"

John Rolfe took another important step in 1614. He married Pocahontas. She had become a Christian and taken the name Rebecca. Two of Pocahontas's brothers and her uncle attended the wedding at Jamestown's church.

The marriage helped keep peace between the English and the Powhatan people. The "Peace of Pocahontas" lasted for about eight years. In 1617 the Rolfes sailed to England with their baby boy Thomas. In London Pocahontas met Sir Walter Raleigh. As she was about to return to Virginia she became ill and died.

Jamestown were indentured servants. After working for some years as indentured servants, they became farmers and planters. Over the next few decades, the population of the colony included both free Africans and those who worked as indentured servants.

An African named Anthony Johnson arrived in Jamestown in about 1621 and worked there as an indentured servant. After working off his debt, he later became a landowner. By 1651 he had over 250 acres of land in present-day North Hampton County on the Pungoteague (PUN goh teeg) River. The area soon became home to a successful African American community.

However, by 1661 a very different life had begun for most Africans in Virginia. By then large numbers were enslaved and forced to work on large farms.

Africans Arrive in Jamestown

When John Rolfe returned to Jamestown, he found people growing tobacco in "the marketplace, the streets, and all other spare places." Tobacco growing attracted more colonists. In 1619 new people arrived.

Many newcomers to Virginia were **indentured** (ihn DEN churd) **servants**. Some people could not afford the trip to North America. In these cases, the Virginia Company paid for them. To repay the debt, each person agreed to work about five to seven years. In following years, thousands of people came to Virginia as indentured servants.

Also in 1619 a Dutch ship anchored off Jamestown. Its captain sent about 20 captive Africans ashore, with the hope of trading them for supplies. Although they were held as captives on the ship, these first Africans to arrive in

Probably because they had become Christians, the first Africans brought to Jamestown were not enslaved. Christians could not be enslaved under English law.

VIRGINIA GROWS

Two other major events helped Virginia to grow. These events both took place in 1619. As you have read, the first Jamestown colonists were mostly men. Then the Virginia Company brought women to the colony. The men paid for the voyage of their future wives. At last Jamestown was becoming a place for families to live.

The last major event to occur in 1619 took place in Jamestown's small church. There, the House of Burgesses met for the first time. The House of Burgesses made laws for the colony. Its members were white men who owned land.

The House of Burgesses did not represent all people, but it did give some Virginia colonists a voice in their government. It is important because it was one of the first steps European colonists took toward governing themselves. You will read more about the House of Burgesses in later chapters.

The Granger Collection

Conflict with the Powhatan

After 1619 the colonists faced the future with more hope. Even so, Virginia's growth brought problems. Planters were moving up the James River. They were clearing new land for tobacco. The Powhatan chiefdom saw the English taking more and more of their hunting grounds.

Chief Powhatan had died in 1618. His brother, Openchancanough (oh pun CHAN kun awf), became the new Powhatan. He was determined to force the English to leave. Early one March morning in 1622, the Powhatan chiefdom attacked. They killed about 350 colonists. This was one of the last major battles between Native Americans and the English in Virginia.

The first women to come to Jamestown (above) married the male colonists who paid for their voyage or became indentured servants. Scholars are not sure how women wore bonnets such as this one from the early 1600s (right).

The first male landowners at Jamestown learned how to govern themselves in the House of Burgesses.

A New Governor

In 1624 King James I took control of Virginia from the House of Burgesses. He named a governor to rule the colony. The king did not like the idea of the colonists governing themselves. As you will read later, the colonists battled with the new governor. They did not like outside control, especially following laws made in far-off England.

WHY IT MATTERS

The English finally established a colony in 1607. Jamestown, the first permanent English colony in North America, helped set a pattern that later European colonists followed. Each colony had a brief period of help from Native Americans until the colonists began taking more and more land. Conflict soon followed as the colonists came to value land more than good relations with Native Americans. The colonists' desire for self-government also became more important to them as their colonies grew.

Other English colonies followed. You will read in the next lesson about colonists who formed a strong friendship with the Native Americans.

✔ Reviewing Facts and Ideas

MAIN IDEAS

- In the early 1600s the English again tried to build a permanent colony in North America.

- The Powhatan chiefdom had established its own way of life on the east coast of North America, where the English planned to colonize.

- In 1607 English newcomers to Jamestown suffered many terrible hardships until Captain John Smith brought order to the colony.

- When the colonists began growing tobacco for money, the Virginia colony finally began to grow. In 1619 Africans and women settled in the new colony.

THINK ABOUT IT

1. What was the Powhatan chiefdom?

2. What problems did the colonists face in Jamestown?

3. **FOCUS** Identify the key contributions made by both Powhatan and English peoples that helped the Jamestown colony to survive.

4. **THINKING SKILL** What *effects* did Virginia's "stinking weed" have on the growth of the colony?

5. **WRITE** Write a scene that shows how John Smith might have told his men, "He that will not work shall not eat."

1500   1540   1580   1615   1621   1660

The Plymouth Colony

Read Aloud

In December 1620 weary and cold passengers on board a ship called the Mayflower landed near what is now Plymouth, Massachusetts. In their first years, the new-comers might have starved without help from the Wampanoag (wahm puh NOH ahg) people who helped to keep the little English colony alive.

Focus Activity

READ TO LEARN

How did the Wampanoag people help the Pilgrims at Plymouth?

VOCABULARY

- Mayflower Compact
- sachem

PEOPLE

- Massasoit
- Squanto
- Samoset
- William Bradford
- Miles Standish

PLACES

- Cape Cod
- New England
- Plymouth

THE BIG PICTURE

Early in the 1500s much of Europe was divided over religion. The king of England, Henry VIII, broke away from the Roman Catholic Church and set up another Christian church called the Church of England. The members of the Church of England were called Protestants because they had protested against practices of the Catholic Church. Protestants' beliefs and practices were different from those of Catholics.

Within England, however, some Protestants felt that the Church of England had kept too many Catholic ways. They set up their own Protestants churches.

In the early 1600s these Protestants moved to the Netherlands, where they could worship in peace. Life was difficult in a foreign land. Parents worried that their children were growing up too much like the Dutch, not like the English. These people, who became known as the Pilgrims, decided to start a colony in North America. This is the story of the Pilgrims, who hoped to find religious freedom in a new land.

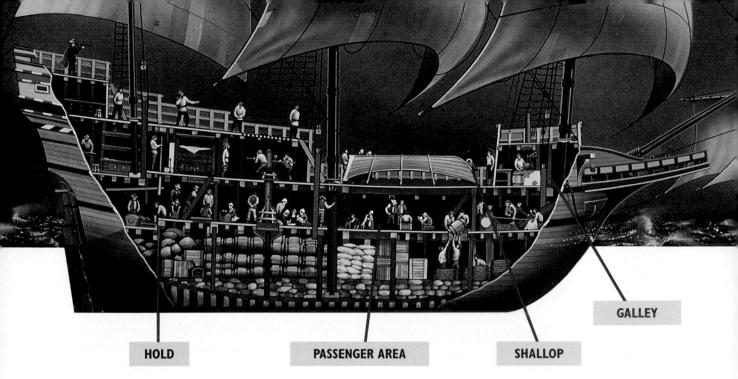

GALLEY

HOLD

PASSENGER AREA

SHALLOP

VOYAGE OF THE MAYFLOWER

In 1620 King James I allowed the Pilgrims to settle in Virginia. In London merchants agreed to pay for the voyage. The Pilgrims agreed to repay the debt by sending back lumber and furs.

On September 16 the Pilgrims and other colonists hired by the London merchants set sail from Plymouth, England, in the *Mayflower*. The holds below the deck of the *Mayflower* were stuffed with barrels of salted beef and bread. The holds also contained pigs, chickens, and goats. The diagram above shows that the space below was very cramped for the more than 100 passengers on board. They planned to reach Virginia just as winter set in.

For 66 days the *Mayflower* tossed in the stormy Atlantic. One passenger, a servant boy, died. Another passenger, Mrs. Hopkins, gave birth to a boy. He was named Oceanus.

In November lookouts finally saw land. The *Mayflower* was far off course. The land was not Virginia but Cape Cod, in what is today New England. A

This diagram shows how the inside of the *Mayflower* might have looked. Supplies were stored in the hold; a shallop is a small boat; meals were prepared in the galley. In what space did the Pilgrims stay during their trip?

small group went ashore to explore. They "fell upon their knees and blessed the God of Heaven, who had brought them over the vast and furious ocean," wrote one of the passengers.

The Mayflower Compact

The Pilgrims were supposed to settle in Virginia, not in New England. Before setting foot on land, the Pilgrims wrote a compact, or agreement. The compact would serve as a form of government for their colony. In the Mayflower Compact, the Pilgrims agreed to make and obey the colony's "just and equal laws." Forty-one men signed the compact. Having few legal rights, women were not asked to sign. But they were still expected to obey the laws.

The Mayflower Compact was an important step. It helped plant the idea of self-government among the colonists in North America.

187

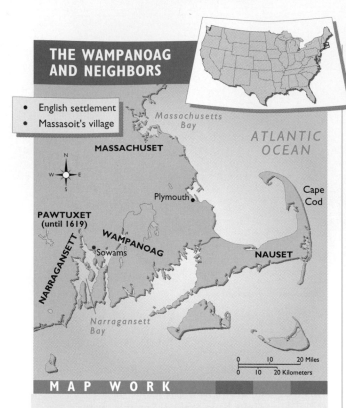

- English settlement
- Massasoit's village

Massachusetts Bay

ATLANTIC OCEAN

MASSACHUSET

Plymouth

Cape Cod

PAWTUXET (until 1619)

WAMPANOAG

Sowams

NARRAGANSETT

NAUSET

Narragansett Bay

0   10   20 Miles
0   10   20 Kilometers

MAP WORK

The Native Americans of New England included many more smaller groups of peoples than those shown on the map.

1. How many Native American peoples are shown on the map? Who are they?

2. What was the name of Massasoit's village?

THE WAMPANOAG

Like the Jamestown colonists, the Pilgrims settled on land already home to many Native Americans. In New England they first met the Wampanoag people. The Wampanoag hunted, farmed, and fished on the east coast of present-day Massachusetts and Rhode Island, as the map on this page shows.

Native Americans of New England

Many other Native Americans besides the Wampanoag lived in New England. Among them were the Narragansett, the Pequot (PEE kwaht), and the Mohegan. Each spoke a form of the Algonkian language. In Algonkian, *Wampanoag* means "people of the east

(or dawn)." Many Algonkian words are now part of English. Words such as *moose, woodchuck, hickory, moccasin, squash,* and *toboggan* are all from the Algonkian language.

Each of the Native American peoples had a sachem (SAY chum), or leader. In the early 1600s, Massasoit (MAS uh soyt) was the sachem of the Wampanoag. He probably ruled about 30 different communities. Even before the Pilgrims arrived, Massasoit knew about the strange ships that were reaching the New England coast.

Massasoit had also heard the story of a man named Squanto. Squanto belonged to a Wampanoag community called the Pawtuxet (paw TUK sut). In 1615 he was captured by an English fishing captain and was enslaved in Spain. Squanto escaped to England and returned home in 1619. He found his village empty. His family and friends had all died. Squanto then found a home with the Wampanoag. Another Native American, the sachem called Samoset, had learned a little English from sailors and traders. Massasoit, Squanto, and Samoset helped to save the Pilgrims' lives in their first hard years in New England.

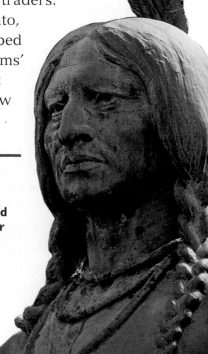

This statue of chief Massasoit stands in Plymouth, Massachusetts. It was carved by the sculptor Walter Meayers Edwards.

THE PILGRIMS

For a month after reaching Cape Cod, the Pilgrims looked for a place to settle. They decided on a place the English called Plymouth. Captain John Smith had visited and named Plymouth Harbor six years earlier.

Plymouth Colony

Once on shore, the Pilgrims faced a lonely future. One of the Pilgrims, William Bradford wrote a book about the Plymouth colony. How did the Pilgrims feel after they arrived?

The Granger Collection

MANY VOICES
PRIMARY SOURCE

Excerpt from
Of Plymouth Plantation,
written by William Bradford
in 1646.

It was winter, and they that know the winters of the country know them to be sharp and violent, and subject to cruel and fierce storms, dangerous to travel to known places, much more to search an unknown coast.

For summer being done, all things stand upon them with a weather-beaten face, . . . If they looked behind them, there was the mighty ocean which they had passed and was now as a main bar and gulf to separate them from all the civil parts of the world. . . .

What could now sustain them but the spirit of God and His grace?

civil: having to do with cities

The Pilgrims' first winter was cold and harsh. Everyone went hungry. Without the right kind of food, many died from disease. By spring, only about half of the Pilgrims were still alive. When their governor died, the Pilgrims elected William Bradford to be the colony's new leader.

Meeting the Wampanoag

With spring, the Pilgrims' hope returned. They started planting crops. One March morning, Samoset entered their settlement. "Welcome, Englishmen!" he declared. He told the surprised newcomers how he had learned to speak their language. A few days later, Samoset returned. With him were Massasoit and Squanto. With Squanto's help, the sachem Massasoit and the Pilgrims' leaders worked out a lasting peace agreement.

Help from Squanto

Squanto decided to stay with the Pilgrims. The land on which the Pilgrims had settled was once the home of Squanto's people, the Pawtuxet. Squanto showed the Pilgrims how to plant corn in the traditional Native American manner, using fish to fertilize the soil. He also shared his knowledge of the woodlands. The newcomers learned how to trap rabbits, deer and other wild animals.

With Squanto's help, the Pilgrims began to eat better. The sickness of the past winter finally ended. Squanto was so helpful to the Pilgrims that Bradford called him "a special instrument sent of God for their good."

Painting by Jerome Brownscombe/The Bettmann Archive

According to tradition, the Pilgrims landed at Plymouth Rock (left) in 1620. A year later they celebrated Thanksgiving with the Wampanoag.

PLYMOUTH, 1621

By the autumn of 1621, the Pilgrims had some important successes. Governor Bradford noted that "they began now to gather in the small harvest they had, and to fit up their houses and dwellings against winter." Besides homes and crops, they had made friends with the Wampanoag.

The Pilgrims invited Massasoit to a great feast. He and 90 of his followers arrived. The Pilgrims had suffered much hardship, but they still had good reason to celebrate and thank God. This feast would later be considered by many as our country's first "thanksgiving." But the idea of celebrating good harvests was not new. Both the English and the Wampanoag had held such celebrations long before.

A Thanksgiving Feast

For three days in October, as the leaves sparkled red, orange, and yellow, the English and their Wampanoag guests feasted. The Indians brought five deer. The Pilgrims added other foods, including wild turkey, geese, and duck.

We do not know exactly what people ate at that Thanksgiving. Lobster, eels, oysters, and fish were plentiful. There was also corn, which could be made into bread and puddings. Pumpkin may have been served, but not pumpkin pie. Seeds from England would have given the Pilgrims cabbage, carrots, turnips, and onions. Other treats were fruits such as plums, gooseberries, and strawberries that were picked and dried in the spring.

At meal time, the Wampanoag sat on the ground. The Pilgrims probably sat on stools around tables made of wooden planks.

The days were filled with games, races, and wrestling contests. Under the command of Pilgrim Miles Standish, men paraded and fired off their guns. The Wampanoag in turn showed their skills with bows and arrows. They also performed their own harvest dances. It was, indeed, a celebration.

WHY IT MATTERS

At first relations between the Wampanoag and Pilgrims were friendly. But the English took over more and more land. Soon the Native Americans of New England and the English became bitter enemies. Today several Wampanoag communities survive. Through traditional ceremonies they preserve their values and culture.

Despite the constant struggles the Plymouth colony survived and grew. Before long, other English Protestants would seek religious freedom in North America. Among them were the Puritans. Like the Pilgrims, the Puritans were treated badly in England for their beliefs. They, too, hoped to make a safe home on the wooded shores of New England. And as in Plymouth, the idea of self-government also took root.

How did Thanksgiving become a national holiday?

For many years the United States as a country had no regular date on which to celebrate Thanksgiving. Then in 1863 President Abraham Lincoln officially made the last Thursday of November Thanksgiving Day. In 1941, the United States Congress made Thanksgiving the fourth Thursday of November. Thanksgiving also became a legal federal holiday.

✔ Reviewing Facts and Ideas

MAIN IDEAS

- Religious conflict led the Pilgrims to leave England for the Netherlands and then to settle in North America.

- In 1620, the Pilgrims sailed for Virginia on the *Mayflower* but landed instead in New England. There, they drew up the Mayflower Compact to set up a government for their colony.

- The Wampanoag were one of many Native American groups living in New England. Their leader, Massasoit, became a loyal friend of the Pilgrims.

- Almost a year after landing, in 1621 the Pilgrims and their Wampanoag friends celebrated a great harvest. Today many people in the United States count that feast as our country's first Thanksgiving.

THINK ABOUT IT

1. Why did the Pilgrims draw up the Mayflower Compact? Why was it an important document?

2. What hardships did the Pilgrims face during their first year at Plymouth?

3. **FOCUS** Describe three ways that the Wampanoag helped the Pilgrims.

4. **THINKING SKILL** Read the excerpt on page 189 from *Of Plymouth Plantation*. Then list the _facts_ Bradford gives in one column and the _opinions_ in another.

5. **GEOGRAPHY** How did the New England climate affect the Pilgrims' attempts to settle there? How might the climate of Virginia have affected their settling there?

Thanksgiving

How do you picture Thanksgiving? Perhaps you imagine a warm house filled with the delicious smell of turkey, where a family such as the one in this painting sits around the dinner table. Perhaps you think of it as a day on which to worship God and to help others. Both images of Thanksgiving have been around a long time.

Thanksgiving has been a national American holiday since 1863. The holiday's roots go back directly to the Pilgrims' feast in the fall of 1621.

Giving thanks is a legacy shared by many cultures. For hundreds of years people have come together for at least one day to give thanks for plentiful food and safe homes.

The Norman Rockwell Museum, Stockbridge

This painting, *Freedom from Want*, was created by Norman Rockwell in 1943.

This painting shows English colonists giving thanks to God for their safe arrival in Virginia on December 14, 1619. Similar ceremonies were held by the Pilgrims in Massachusetts, French colonists in Florida, and Spanish settlers in Texas. Many Native Americans in these places held thanksgiving celebrations long before Europeans arrived.

Thanksgiving reminds many people that their community is made up of more than family and friends. Every Thanksgiving state workers serve Thanksgiving dinner to homeless people in Austin, Texas.

Painting by Sidney King/Courtesy of the Berkeley Plantation and Bicast Publishing Co., Williamsburg

The people of Santa Clara Pueblo in New Mexico hold the ceremonial Rainbow Dance to show thanks for the season's corn crop.

CHAPTER 7 REVIEW

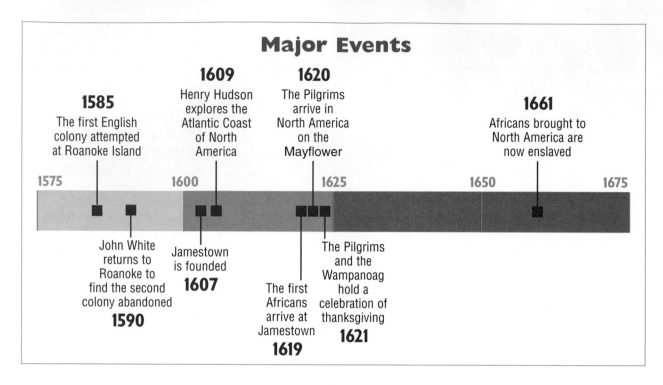

Major Events

1585
The first English colony attempted at Roanoke Island

1609
Henry Hudson explores the Atlantic Coast of North America

1620
The Pilgrims arrive in North America on the Mayflower

1661
Africans brought to North America are now enslaved

1575   1600   1625   1650   1675

John White returns to Roanoke to find the second colony abandoned
1590

Jamestown is founded
1607

The first Africans arrive at Jamestown
1619

The Pilgrims and the Wampanoag hold a celebration of thanksgiving
1621

THINKING ABOUT VOCABULARY

Number a paper from 1 to 10. Beside each number write the word or term below that best completes the sentence.

armada
cash crop
House of Burgesses
indentured servant
Mayflower Compact

Northwest Passage
profit
sachem
stock

1. Henry Hudson sailed in search of the _____, a water route through North America to Asia.

2. A successful trading company makes a great deal of _____ .

3. The merchant bought _____, or a share of ownership, in the Virginia Company.

4. Each of the Native American peoples had a _____, or leader.

5. Demand for tobacco in England made it a good _____ for the Virginia colonists.

6. Spain tried to invade England with a large fleet of ships called an _____ .

7. The Pilgrims wrote the _____ to serve as a form of government for the Plymouth colony.

8. An _____ worked in exchange for the trip to North America.

9. The Virginia _____ was the first lawmaking body in North America established by Europeans.

10. The Spanish _____ was badly damaged by fire and stormy weather.

THINKING ABOUT FACTS

1. What did Sir Walter Raleigh convince Queen Elizabeth to do in the late 1500s?

2. What was the purpose of Henry Hudson's explorations in 1609?

3. Who was John Rolfe?

4. Why did the Pilgrims come to North America on the *Mayflower*?

5. Look at the time line above. How many years passed from when the first Africans arrived at Jamestown to when large numbers of Africans were enslaved?

THINK AND WRITE

WRITING AN EXPEDITION PROPOSAL

Write a proposal in which you attempt to convince a ruler or company to pay for your expedition across the Atlantic.

WRITING A DIARY

Suppose that you are Pocahontas traveling in England for the first time. Write a series of diary entries in which you record your thoughts about the country.

WRITING A REPORT

Write a report in which you describe the various Native American peoples that Europeans met as they began colonies in North America. Include facts about their way of life, as well as government.

APPLYING THINKING SKILLS

DISTINGUISHING FACT FROM OPINION

Answer the following questions to apply the skill of distinguishing facts from opinions.

1. What is a fact? What is an opinion?

2. What are some clues that you can look for to help recognize an opinion?

3. Which of the following states a fact?

   a. John White returned to the Roanoke colony in 1590.

   b. The English defeated the Spanish armada in 1588.

   c. The Roanoac killed all the English.

4. At first Henry Hudson believed that he had found the Northwest Passage as he sailed up the Hudson River. Is this a fact or an opinion?

5. Why is distinguishing facts from opinions an important skill?

Summing Up the Chapter

Copy the matrix chart on a separate piece of paper. Fill in the blank sections to help summarize the information in this chapter. After you have finished, use the information in the chart to write a few paragraphs in which you answer the question "How would you compare and contrast the early European settlements and expeditions in the Americas?"

COLONY/EXPEDITION	YEARS	LEADER	RESULTS
Roanoke			
Jamestown			
Hudson's Expedition			
Plymouth			

UNIT 3 REVIEW

THINKING ABOUT VOCABULARY

Number a paper from 1 to 10. Beside each number write the word or term from the list below that best completes the sentence.

armada
cash crop
colony
conquistador
expedition

historical map
indentured servant
Mayflower Compact
missionary
Northwest Passage

1. When the young woman agreed to work for a period of time in exchange for passage to the Americas, she became an ____.

2. Spain's strong ____ was defeated by England's fast ships.

3. European explorers from many countries began looking for a ____ to Asia.

4. The explorer's ____, or journey for a special purpose, took him through lands unknown to him.

5. The ____ came to New Spain to teach the Roman Catholic religion to the Indians of Mexico.

6. Only male Pilgrims could sign the ____ when they reached North America.

7. A ____ is a place ruled by another country.

8. Tobacco is an example of a ____.

9. The ____ came to the Americas to conquer land for Spain.

10. To find information about places where past events occurred, you can use an ____.

THINK AND WRITE

WRITING A SUMMARIZING PARAGRAPH

Write a summarizing paragraph that explains the cause-and-effect connections between Columbus's contact with the Taino in 1492 and the founding of European colonies in the Americas.

WRITING A DIALOGUE

Think about what the Wampanoag and the Pilgrims might have said to each other when they first met in the Plymouth Colony. Write a dialogue that you think could have taken place between one of the Pilgrims and one of the Wampanoag. For example, you might want to write a conversation between Samoset and William Bradford.

WRITING ABOUT PERSPECTIVES

Select a person you have read about in the unit. Compare what people thought about that person during his or her lifetime with what people may think about that person today. Explain why there might be differences between the two perspectives.

BUILDING SKILLS

1. **Historical maps** What does an historical map show?

2. **Historical maps** How can you tell if a map is an historical map?

3. **Fact and opinion** What are the clue words that help you know that something is an opinion?

4. **Fact and opinion** Is the following sentence a fact or an opinion? *Columbus made four voyages to the Americas.*

5. **Fact and opinion** What is one way to check the statement above?

YESTERDAY, TODAY &
TOMORROW

The explorers of the 1500s needed courage, knowledge, and creativity to invent new technologies and to journey to places unknown to them. Would an explorer today need the same qualities? What kind of technology would he or she use? Where might an explorer of the future travel?

READING ON YOUR OWN
Here are some books you might find at the library to help you learn more.

THE LOG OF CHRISTOPHER COLUMBUS
by Christopher Columbus, sel. by Steve Low
This is an illustrated adaptation of excerpts from Columbus's log.

THE SPANISH PIONEERS OF THE SOUTHWEST
by Joan Anderson
This photographic essay shows the Latino culture of the Southwest region.

THREE YOUNG PILGRIMS
by Cheryl Harness
This story, based upon actual events, is about three Pilgrim children who sailed on the *Mayflower*.

UNIT 3 REVIEW PROJECT

Make an Explorers' Map

1. Think about all the explorers you read about in this unit.

2. On a large piece of oak tag, trace a map that shows the Eastern and Western hemispheres.

3. Draw each explorer's route on the map. You can use a different color marker for each one.

4. Present your map to the class.

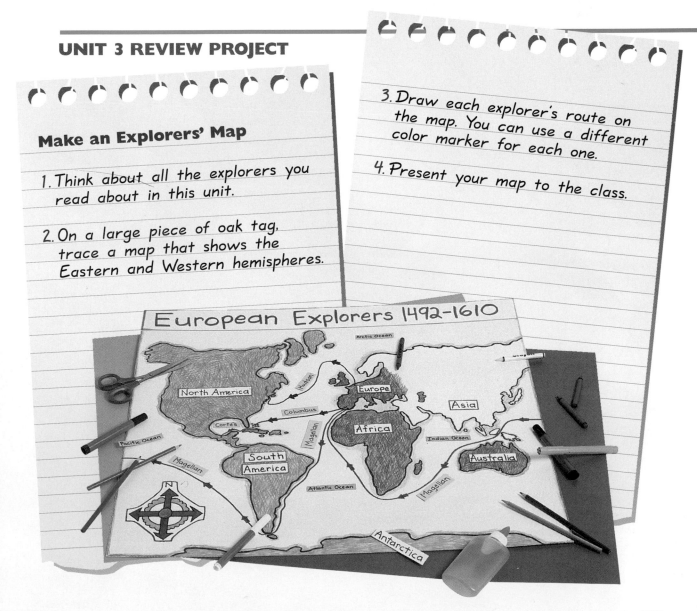

Colonial Williamsburg Foundation

**MIDDLE COLONIES TAPESTRY;
BENJAMIN FRANKLIN;
PEWTER CREAM PITCHER**

National Protrait Gallery London

Metropolitan Museum of Art

Colonization and Conflict

"One today is worth two tomorrows."

from *Poor Richard's Almanac* by Benjamin Franklin
See page 245.

Why Does it Matter?

The words above, written by an industrious colonist named Benjamin Franklin, described how many English colonists felt about settling and building new homes in North America. The colonists faced many hardships, but they worked hard to overcome them.

Colonial settlements and cities developed along the Atlantic Coast and eventually reached the foothills of the Appalachian Mountains. Some Native Americans who had been living on these lands found a way to live in peace with the colonists. Others fought to protect their way of life. In time England would succeed as the major European power in North America.

The Granger Collection

PURITAN HORNBOOK

FIND OUT MORE!
Visit our website:
www.mhschool.com

*inter*NET
CONNECTION

Adventures with
NATIONAL GEOGRAPHIC

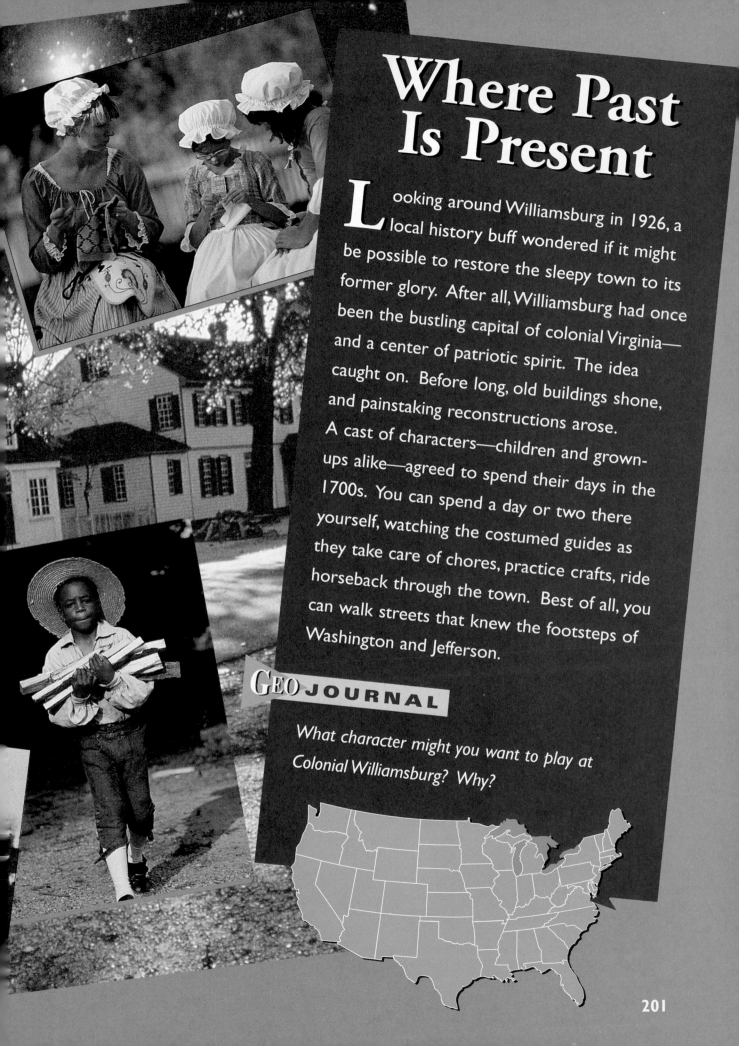

Where Past Is Present

Looking around Williamsburg in 1926, a local history buff wondered if it might be possible to restore the sleepy town to its former glory. After all, Williamsburg had once been the bustling capital of colonial Virginia— and a center of patriotic spirit. The idea caught on. Before long, old buildings shone, and painstaking reconstructions arose.

A cast of characters—children and grown-ups alike—agreed to spend their days in the 1700s. You can spend a day or two there yourself, watching the costumed guides as they take care of chores, practice crafts, ride horseback through the town. Best of all, you can walk streets that knew the footsteps of Washington and Jefferson.

GEOJOURNAL

What character might you want to play at Colonial Williamsburg? Why?

The English Establish 13 Colonies

THINKING ABOUT HISTORY AND GEOGRAPHY

From the time line you can see that Chapter 8 begins with the Puritans' arrival at Massachusetts Bay in 1630. Out of this settlement grew the New England Colonies. To the south the natural resources of the Middle and Southern colonies also attracted colonists. As you read the chapter you will learn more about the first colonists and how they used the land and resources they found.

1675

CONNECTICUT
Native Americans of New England battle the English colonists

1630

MASSACHUSETTS BAY
John Winthrop and the Puritans found a new colony

1638

RHODE ISLAND
Anne Hutchinson settles Portsmouth

1630

1655

1680

NORTH
AMERICA

THE ENGLISH
COLONIES

ATLANTIC
OCEAN

Pennsylvania

Connecticut   Rhode Island

Massachusetts
Bay

Georgia

1682

PENNSYLVANIA

William Penn and the
Lenape sign a treaty

1733

GEORGIA

Tomochichi grants James
Oglethorpe land for a
settlement

1600   1630 1639   1660   1690   1720

The New England Colonies

Read Aloud

John Winthrop, the Puritan leader, saw Massachusetts for the first time from the ship Arbella. "We must be knit together as one," he said to the passengers. "We must rejoice together, mourn together, labor and suffer together." The year was 1630. The Puritans had arrived in North America.

Focus Activity

READ TO LEARN

Who were the Puritans?

VOCABULARY

- covenant
- tolerate

PEOPLE

- King Charles I
- John Winthrop
- Roger Williams
- Anne Hutchinson
- Thomas Hooker
- Metacomet

PLACES

- Massachusetts
- Boston
- Providence
- Rhode Island
- Portsmouth
- Connecticut
- New Hampshire
- Vermont
- Maine

THE BIG PICTURE

During the time that the Pilgrims were first settling in Plymouth, the Puritans were growing in numbers in England. The Puritans were a group of English Protestants. They felt the Church of England followed too many practices of the Roman Catholic Church.

Like the Pilgrims, the Puritans had been thrown into jail because of their religious beliefs. Also like the Pilgrims, some Puritans decided to leave England in order to practice their religion in peace.

In 1629 a group of wealthy Puritans formed the Massachusetts Bay Company. **King Charles I** of England gave them a charter to settle in North America. The charter was like a permit that gave them permission to settle in areas claimed by England. In 1630 the Puritans sailed to North America. They landed in an area that John Smith had reached in 1614. Smith later named the region New England. The Puritans settled in a part of New England called Massachusetts Bay. Their settlement later became known as **Massachusetts**.

THE PURITANS ARRIVE

Compared to the Pilgrims, the Puritans arrived in North America in great numbers. Instead of one ship, the Puritans sailed to North America in a fleet of 11 ships. Instead of 100 people, the Puritans brought close to 700. They also brought supplies, equipment, a herd of cows, and about 60 horses.

John Winthrop

The leader of the Puritans was a successful lawyer named John Winthrop.

It was Winthrop who led the Puritans to Massachusetts Bay on the coast of New England in 1630. The word *Massachusetts* means "at or near the great hill" in Algonkian, the language of the Native Americans who lived in the area.

The Puritans founded Massachusetts Bay Colony along the Charles River. The colony's first settlement was named Boston. Find Boston on the map on this page. John Winthrop was elected the first governor by Puritan men, who were the only colonists allowed to vote.

The Geography of New England

At first, life in Massachusetts Bay Colony was hard. Much of the land is hilly. The soil is also thin and rocky. These conditions made farming difficult.

Still the area had many other natural resources that the Puritans needed to survive. The forests supplied the colonists with wood to make homes, fences, and tools. The Charles River as well as the Atlantic Ocean also provided many kinds of fish. New England had much to offer its colonists.

THE NEW ENGLAND COLONIES

St. Lawrence R.

0   100   200 Miles
0   100   200 Kilometers

MAINE
(part of Massachusetts)

St. Croix River

NEW FRANCE

Lake Champlain

Kennebec River

VERMONT
(claimed by New Hampshire & New York)

NEW HAMPSHIRE
(1680)

Connecticut R.

Merrimack River

ATLANTIC OCEAN

MASSACHUSETTS (1630)

Massachusetts Bay

Boston
Plymouth

Cape Cod

Cape Cod Bay

CONNECTICUT
(1636)   Hartford

Providence
Portsmouth

RHODE ISLAND (1636)

Long Island Sound

Long Island

MAP WORK

Dates after the names of most New England colonies are the years they were founded.

1. Which colony was claimed by both New Hampshire and New York?
2. Which colonies were founded after 1630?

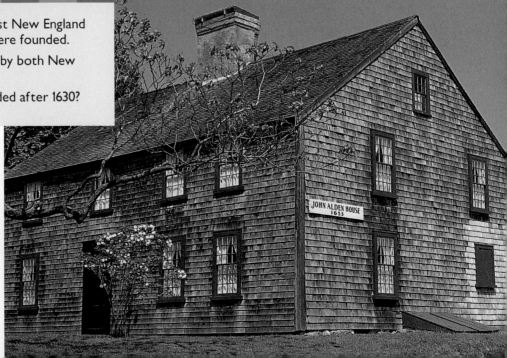

This is the Duxbury, Massachusetts, home of John and Priscilla Alden. They and other New Englanders moved to Duxbury in the late 1620s.

JOHN ALDEN HOUSE
1653

"A CITY UPON A HILL"

The Puritans wanted to create a colony that would be a model for all the world to see and follow. John Winthrop used words from the Bible to describe their colony as a "city upon a hill." In many ways their dream came true. Massachusetts Bay Colony began with about 700 people in 1630. Ten years later the population had grown to over 20,000. Massachusetts Bay had one of the largest populations of any European colony in North America at that time.

The Puritan Way of Life

In the Puritan community, each "free man," as a male colonist was called, signed a covenant. A covenant is a special promise or agreement. In the covenant, each free man promised that his family would live by the rules of the Puritan church.

The Puritans believed that the success of their colony was a result of their belief in God and the Bible. They also believed in hard work. This meant that everyone—rich and poor alike—had to help build the community.

The Puritans built their villages according to a plan. You can see a diagram of a New England village of the middle 1600s on the next page. In the center of each village was the meeting house and the village common. In earlier villages the meeting house also served as the church.

Education was important to the Puritans. They believed that people should be able to read the Bible. The Puritans built schools that were free to all the children of the community. Free education was unheard of in Europe at that time. To imagine what school was like then, read the excerpt from the Puritan schoolbook. How does it compare to those of today?

MANY VOICES
PRIMARY SOURCE

Excerpt from
The New England Primer,
a schoolbook first published in 1689
for Puritan children.

A *In Adam's Fall
We Sinned All.*

B *Thy Life to Mend
This Book Attend.*

C *The Cat doth play
And after slay.*

D *A Dog will bite
A Thief at night.*

E *An Eagle's flight
Is out of sight.*

F *The Idle Fool
Is whipt at School.*

Colonial students learned to read using a hornbook, a page under clear horn.

A New England Village, 1630–1650

MILL

WOOD LOT

FIELDS

MINISTER'S HOUSE

SCHOOL

MEETING HOUSE

INN

STOCKS

COMMON

WELL

SHOEMAKER

BLACKSMITH

BARREL MAKER

NEW ENGLAND GROWS

At first the Puritans lived in and around Boston. Soon they started new colonies in the region. Some of these colonies were founded as a result of religious disagreements between the Puritans and their leaders.

Puritans Speak Out

Puritan leaders wanted everyone in the community to share their beliefs. One Puritan who disagreed with them was the minister Roger Williams. Williams believed that the colony needed to tolerate different religious beliefs. To tolerate means to allow people to have beliefs different from your own.

Anne Hutchinson was another Puritan who disagreed with the leaders. She believed people should pray directly to God rather than depend upon church teachings. John Winthrop described her as "a woman of active spirit . . . more bold than a man."

Both Williams and Hutchinson were brought to trial. Puritan leaders tried to convince Williams to change his views. Instead Williams fled Massachusetts in 1636. He founded the settlement of Providence in what became Rhode Island. Rhode Island was the first European colony in the Americas to allow freedom of religion.

After her trial, Anne Hutchinson was forced to leave Massachusetts. In 1638 she traveled south to Rhode Island. Her family and supporters started the settlement of Portsmouth.

Another Puritan minister, Thomas Hooker, also left Massachusetts. Hooker believed that each church should be independent and should choose its own leaders. In 1636 he and about 100 followers founded the colony of Connecticut.

Changes for the Native Americans

As the New England colonies grew, the Native Americans lost their land. At first some Native Americans helped the colonists. When Roger Williams fled Massachusetts, for example, the Narragansett allowed him to live on their land. In turn Williams paid them for land on Narragansett Bay, where he started his colony.

As the colonists settled more land, disagreements arose with the Native Americans. In what later became the Connecticut colony, bitter fighting broke out between the Pequot (PEE kwaht) and the English colonists. In the Pequot War of 1637, as the fighting was called, hundreds of the Pequot and colonists were killed.

The Granger Collection

John Winthrop (above), Governor of Massachusetts, disagreed with colonists such as Anne Hutchinson (right).

Metacomet (above) wanted to force the colonists out of New England. He had a very different perspective on the English than his father, Massasoit, who had helped the Pilgrims.

Shelburne Museum, Vermont

After the Pequot War there was no fighting between colonists and Native Americans for almost 40 years. During that time colonists moved to what is now **New Hampshire**. They also moved to the regions that later became the colonies of **Vermont** and **Maine**.

Metacomet

By 1675 the Wampanoag leader **Metacomet** (met uh KAHM uht), whom the English called King Philip, was preparing to fight to keep Wampanoag lands. Many Native Americans joined Metacomet, including the Narragansett. Years earlier Metacomet's father, Massasoit, had helped the Pilgrims.

King Philip's War, as the struggle was called, was fierce. In Massachusetts alone, Native Americans destroyed 16 towns. In 1676 Metacomet was captured and killed. His family was sold into slavery in the West Indies. This defeat marked the end of strong Native American resistance in New England.

WHY IT MATTERS

The way of life that the Puritans brought to New England can still be seen as you travel through its many towns and small villages. Some Puritan ideas also continue to affect life in the United States. Part of our country's system of public education was modeled after Puritan schools.

✔️ Reviewing Facts and Ideas

MAIN IDEAS

- The Puritans, led by John Winthrop, arrived in New England and founded the settlement of Boston in 1630.

- Roger Williams founded Providence in 1636, the first settlement in Rhode Island. In 1638 Anne Hutchinson founded Portsmouth, also in Rhode Island. Connecticut was founded in 1636 by Thomas Hooker.

- The Wampanoag leader Metacomet led King Philip's War against the English in 1675. His defeat ended most Native American resistance to the colonists of New England.

THINK ABOUT IT

1. Why did the Puritans decide to come to North America?

2. Why were Roger Williams and Anne Hutchinson brought to trial?

3. **FOCUS** How did Puritan beliefs influence the type of colony they built?

4. **THINKING SKILL** *Compare* Massasoit's feelings toward the English with those of his son Metacomet. What might have *caused* any differences in how they felt?

5. **WRITE** Suppose you are a young child from Massachusetts Bay Colony. Write a letter to a friend in England that describes what your new life is like.

1600   1630   1660   **1681**   **1704**   1720

The Middle Colonies

Read Aloud

The word was out. All over Europe, people were reading William Penn's advertisements for a colony called Pennsylvania. Here was a place where "the Air is sweet and clear," the ads said. Who was William Penn? Could his promises really be believed?

Focus Activity

READ TO LEARN

How did William Penn help to build the colony of Pennsylvania?

VOCABULARY

- Conestoga

PEOPLE

- King Charles II
- William Penn

PLACES

- New Netherland
- New Amsterdam
- New York
- New York City
- New Jersey
- Pennsylvania
- Delaware
- Middle Colonies
- Philadelphia

THE BIG PICTURE

In the middle 1600s, the Dutch founded their colony of New Netherland. As you have read, Henry Hudson first claimed this area along the Hudson River for the Dutch in 1609. On Manhattan Island, which they bought from the Mannahata, the Dutch built a port that soon grew into a bustling center of trade. They called it New Amsterdam. Amsterdam was the name of their capital city in Holland.

In 1664 King Charles II of England wanted to make New Netherland an English colony. New Amsterdam's leader, Peter Stuyvesant, protested. Yet Stuyvesant was so unpopular that the English were able to take the port and the rest of New Netherland without firing a shot.

The English renamed New Netherland New York in honor of King Charles's brother, the Duke of York. New Amsterdam was renamed New York City. Later the Duke gave part of New York to two friends, Lord John Berkeley and Sir George Carteret. This land became the English colony of New Jersey. By 1704 Pennsylvania, Delaware, New York, and New Jersey had become the English Middle Colonies.

The Granger Collection

William Penn (left) made a treaty with the Lenni Lenape (above) and built a colony on the land that became Pennsylvania.

WILLIAM PENN

In 1681 King Charles II granted land in the Middle Colonies to William Penn, a Quaker. The Quakers are a religious group whose nickname comes from their belief that people should "quake before the power of the Lord."

Like the Puritans, some Quakers had been put in jail because of their religious beliefs. Penn hoped to establish a colony where Quakers could practice their religion in freedom.

Quaker Beliefs

The Quakers called themselves the Society of Friends. The Friends were started in England by George Fox in 1652. Fox told his followers that in order to know God, they had only to listen to His voice in their heart. They did not need to rely on ministers.

Penn's plans for his colony were based upon Quaker beliefs. "Be plain in clothes, furniture, and food," he said.

The Friends believed that people should be treated fairly. Many were against slavery. Most, like William Penn, believed in treating the Native Americans with respect.

The Lenni Lenape

In 1682 Penn arrived in North America with about 100 colonists. He named the colony *Pennsylvania,* which means "Penn's Woods." His settlement was called Philadelphia. In Greek, the word *Philadelphia* means "brotherly love."

Penn planned for Pennsylvania to be a place of peace where people would treat each other fairly. He believed that the Lenni Lenape (LEN nee LEN nah pee), who were also known as the Delaware, should be included in his plan.

In a letter to the Lenni Lenape, Penn wrote that everyone could "live together as neighbors and friends." Unlike most European colonists, Penn paid the Native Americans for their land. Because of Penn's actions, relations between Native Americans and the colonists in Pennsylvania remained peaceful for many years.

THE MIDDLE COLONIES

The Middle Colonies grew rapidly during the 1700s. Colonists started the new colony of Delaware by settling on land that had also been part of Pennsylvania.

Many Europeans moved to the Middle Colonies in hope of finding a better life. In 1720 about 10,000 colonists lived in Philadelphia. By 1760 the city's population had grown to over 22,000, making Philadelphia the largest city in the English colonies. Locate Philadelphia on the map on this page.

Geography of the Middle Colonies

The Middle Colonies reached west from the Atlantic Coastal Plain to the foothills of the Appalachian Mountains.

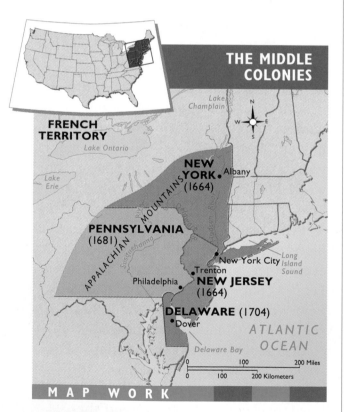

THE MIDDLE COLONIES

FRENCH TERRITORY

Lake Champlain
Lake Ontario
Lake Erie

NEW YORK (1664) • Albany

PENNSYLVANIA (1681)

APPALACHIAN MOUNTAINS

Susquehanna River
Hudson River

New York City
Trenton
Philadelphia •
NEW JERSEY (1664)

Long Island Sound

DELAWARE (1704) • Dover

ATLANTIC OCEAN

Delaware Bay

0   100   200 Miles
0   100   200 Kilometers

MAP WORK

Some colonies were smaller than the present-day states of the same name.

1. Which city was located farthest north?

2. Which two Middle Colonies were founded first? Which one was founded last?

Rivers and lakes crisscrossed much of the Middle Colonies. Colonists used these waterways to send their lumber, crops, and animal furs to markets in coastal cities. New York Harbor, at the southern end of Manhattan Island, was one of the busiest ports in the 13 English colonies.

For colonial farmers, the land was much richer in the Middle Colonies than in New England. Within several years, hard-working farmers turned the Middle Colonies into the main food-growing region in colonial North America. People called the Middle Colonies the "breadbasket of the colonies."

Many Different People

Colonists from all over Europe were welcomed to the Middle Colonies. Jewish people from Portugal had begun arriving in the late 1600s. A large number of Dutch people were already living in the area. By the early 1700s many German immigrants had come as well and become farmers. Since the German word for their language is *Deutsch* (DOYTCH), the Germans became known as the Pennsylvania Dutch. The Pennsylvania Dutch built the first Conestoga (kahn uh STOH guh) wagons. These large wagons carried farm goods to city markets.

Another group of colonists was the Scots-Irish. They were Scottish people who had settled in Northern Ireland before coming to North America.

One group that was not treated equally in the Middle Colonies was the Africans. Many of them were enslaved. Some were free, but few African colonists enjoyed the same rights that European colonists did. You will read more about Africans in the English colonies in the next chapter.

Penn's statue stands atop City Hall, one of Philadelphia's tallest buildings (below). The statue (right) was on view before being put on the building.

WHY IT MATTERS

Many different people came to the Middle Colonies. They brought with them a wide variety of skills and trades. This great mix of people and abilities was important to the Middle Colonies.

The blending of different peoples and cultures started in colonial times. It continues today. From its earliest days, the United States has depended on the contributions made by all of its people to build the country.

Reviewing Facts and Ideas

MAIN IDEAS

- The Dutch colony of New Netherland became the English colony of New York in 1664.

- In 1681 William Penn founded the Pennsylvania Colony. In Pennsylvania Quakers and other religious groups could worship freely.

- The variety of people in the Middle Colonies helped the region to succeed at farming and trading.

THINK ABOUT IT

1. How did New York and New Jersey become English colonies?

2. How did William Penn show that he wanted to treat Native Americans with fairness?

3. **FOCUS** Describe how the Middle Colonies were different from the New England Colonies.

4. **THINKING SKILL** What were some of the beliefs held by the Quakers? What *effects* did these beliefs have on William Penn's colony?

5. **WRITE** Suppose that you are a Lenni Lenape. Write a short paragraph that describes what you think about the colonists and their ways.

Reading Elevation and Relief Maps

VOCABULARY

elevation

relief

WHY THE SKILL MATTERS

As you saw on the map of the Middle Colonies on page 212, Delaware and New Jersey lie along the Atlantic Coastal Plain, which is mostly flat. Colonists arriving in the Middle Colonies often used maps to study the geography of a place.

Different kinds of maps used today can show different kinds of geographical information. The elevation of a place, for example, is shown on an elevation map. Elevation is the height of land above sea level. Mountain climbers often use maps that show elevation. Why do you think they need them?

USING ELEVATION MAPS

Elevation maps show how high, or elevated, the land is. Elevation is measured in feet or meters above sea level. Sea level is measured as 0 feet all around the world. Places close to sea level have low elevations.

Elevation maps use color to show the difference in height of land areas. In the elevation map of New York on this page, red shows areas with the highest elevation. The key tells you that red represents areas higher than 2,000 feet, or 600 meters, above sea level. The other colors on the map each show different elevations.

You know that as you travel southeast from the Catskill Mountains to the coast, the land drops suddenly in elevation. The drop in elevation from the foothills of the Catskill

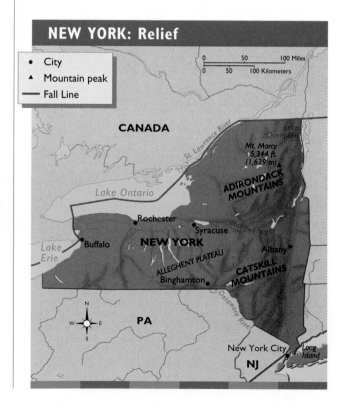

NEW YORK: Elevation

FEET	METERS
2,000	600
1,500	450
1,000	
500	300
0	150
	0

BELOW SEA LEVEL

0   50   100 Miles
0   50   100 Kilometers

CANADA

St. Lawrence River

Lake Champlain

Mt. Marcy 5,344 ft. (1,629 m)

ADIRONDACK MOUNTAINS

Lake Ontario

Rochester

Syracuse

Mohawk River

Buffalo

NEW YORK

Albany

Lake Erie

ALLEGHENY PLATEAU

CATSKILL MOUNTAINS

Binghamton

Delaware River

Hudson River

PENNSYLVANIA

New York City

Long Island

NJ

- City
- ▲ Mountain Peak

NEW YORK: Relief

- City
- ▲ Mountain peak
- — Fall Line

0   50   100 Miles
0   50   100 Kilometers

CANADA

St. Lawrence River

Lake Champlain

Mt. Marcy 5,344 ft. (1,629 m)

ADIRONDACK MOUNTAINS

Lake Ontario

Rochester

Syracuse

Mohawk River

Buffalo

NEW YORK

Albany

Lake Erie

ALLEGHENY PLATEAU

CATSKILL MOUNTAINS

Binghamton

Delaware River

PA

New York City

Long Island

NJ

to the flatter land along the coast is called the fall line. On the relief map on page 214 the fall line is east of the Piedmont.

USING RELIEF MAPS

Elevation maps show the height of land areas. A relief map shows how elevation changes from place to place. Relief is the difference in height between land areas. Level or flat, land that stretches for long distances has low or little relief. Land that rises and then drops off within short distances has high, or more, relief. Mountains are landforms with both a high elevation and high relief. Plains and plateaus are landforms with low relief.

Helping yourself

- **Elevation** is the height of land above sea level. Use the map key colors to find the ranges of elevation.

- **Relief** is the difference in height between areas. Heavy or light shading shows changes in elevation.

On a relief map the difference in height between land areas is shown by using light to heavy shading. Look at the relief map on page 214. The heavy shading shows high elevation areas. The light shading indicates low elevation.

The relief map on page 214 tells us the Adirondack Mountains have high relief because they are heavily shaded.

TRYING THE SKILL

Look at the map of the Middle Colonies on this page. It shows both elevation and relief. Both color and shading are used to show what the landforms in the Middle Colonies are like. The highest mountains are heavily shaded and colored red. What does this map tell about these mountains?

Look at the area around the Appalachian Mountains. What does the map tell you about the elevation as you move east of the mountains? How do you think elevation affected the settling of this region?

REVIEWING THE SKILL

1. What is elevation? What is relief?

2. Which map is better for showing the height of a mountain above sea level—an elevation map or a relief map? Why?

3. Suppose you were planning a bicycle trip. Which kind of map would you use to avoid pedaling up steep hills? Why?

4. Using the map on this page, compare the elevation and relief of the Middle Colonies. Which colony do you think would have the best land for farming? Explain.

5. How would you use an elevation and relief map to find a place in which to settle?

THE MIDDLE COLONIES: Elevation and Relief

FEET	METERS
2,000	600
1,500	450
1,000	300
500	150
0	0
BELOW SEA LEVEL	

FRENCH TERRITORY
St. Lawrence River
Lake Champlain
Lake Ontario
ADIRONDACK MOUNTAINS
(VT)
NH
Albany
NEW YORK
ALLEGHENY PLATEAU
CATSKILL MOUNTAINS
MA
CT
Long Island Sound
APPALACHIAN MOUNTAINS
New York City
PENNSYLVANIA
Trenton
Philadelphia
NEW JERSEY
MARYLAND
ATLANTIC OCEAN
VIRGINIA
0 50 100 Miles
0 50 100 Kilometers
Delaware Bay
DELAWARE
40°N
70°W

Metropolitan Museum of Art, Gift of Mr. and Mrs. Samuel Schwartz, 1979

Focus Activity

READ TO LEARN

Why was the founding of Georgia important to the Southern Colonies?

VOCABULARY

- proprietor
- debtor
- indigo

PEOPLE

- Tomochichi
- James Oglethorpe
- King George II

PLACES

- Maryland
- Virginia
- North Carolina
- South Carolina
- Georgia
- Southern Colonies
- Savannah

1600 1630 1660 1690 1729 1733

The Southern Colonies

Read Aloud

The king of England hoped that England's new colony of Georgia would protect the English Carolinas. South of the Carolinas the Spanish had built several settlements. To the west, the French had established a large colony, but few colonists lived there. In 1732 the founding of Georgia became the king's best plan for keeping the Carolinas under English control.

THE BIG PICTURE

The Pilgrims, Puritans, and Quakers were not the only groups who could not practice their religions freely in England. Many Roman Catholics were treated badly as well. In 1634 King Charles I of England gave a Catholic, Lord Baltimore, a charter to start a new colony for Catholics. He called the colony **Maryland**, after Queen Henrietta Maria of England. Maryland was controlled by a group of people called **proprietors**. The proprietors were men who owned all the land of the colony.

South of Maryland, **Virginia** was growing. Good land was becoming harder to locate. In 1663 King Charles II gave eight proprietors a charter to found Carolina, a new colony south of Virginia. Carolina was later divided into **North Carolina** and **South Carolina**. In 1732 Georgia was founded. Georgia was the last of the group of settlements that became known as England's **Southern Colonies**.

THE MUSCOGEE AND THE ENGLISH

The area the English called the Southern Colonies was home to the Muscogee (Creek), Cherokee, Choctaw, and Chickasaw. Of these, the Creek were the largest group. All the Creek spoke one language. Each of their villages was independent. Before Europeans arrived, the independent Creek villages joined together to form the Creek Confederacy. As a confederacy, the Creek were better able to protect their lands.

The Granger Collection

Chief Tomochichi

Another group of Creek people lived along the Savannah River in what is now eastern Georgia. They were separate from the Creek Confederacy. They called themselves the Yamacraw and built their village in a place called Yamacraw Bluff. Most Creek villages were located along rivers and streams or in treeless areas. These locations were well suited to farming.

In the early 1700s the chief of the Yamacraw was a man named Tomochichi (toh mah CHEE chee). Tomochichi led the Yamacraw in their first meetings with the English colonists and their leader, James Oglethorpe.

General James Oglethorpe

James Oglethorpe was a wealthy English army general. In 1729 he formed a committee to examine England's prisons for debtors. A debtor is a person who owes money. Oglethorpe was shocked by the number of debtors who were locked away in prison. He asked for and received a charter to start a colony for debtors and poor people in North America. Oglethorpe named the new colony that he founded there *Georgia* after King George II.

James Oglethorpe (above) and Chief Tomochichi met in London, England (below), to sign a treaty giving the English land on which to build Savannah, Georgia.

Courtesy, Winterthur Museum

THE GEORGIA COLONY

King George liked Oglethorpe's plan to start the colony of Georgia. Because of its location, Georgia would separate the Carolinas from the Spanish and French claims. You can see this by finding Georgia on the map on this page. Also, Georgia would be a place to send England's debtors. "England will grow rich by sending her poor abroad," Oglethorpe explained.

Oglethorpe gave each colonist land for growing grapes and raising silkworms. Georgia's climate was not suitable for raising silkworms, though.

Geography of the Southern Colonies

Farmers in the other Southern Colonies found that the red clay soil of the Appalachian foothills was good for growing corn and tobacco. Along part of the Atlantic Coastal Plain the growing season lasts seven months. Planters there grew rice and indigo on large farms. Indigo is a plant that produces a blue dye.

The Creek Assist the Colonists

In 1733 Oglethorpe planned Georgia's first settlement, Savannah. The site for the new settlement was located next to Tomochichi's village. The two leaders met. Tomochichi agreed to give Oglethorpe a large area of land on Yamacraw Bluff for the settlement.

Change Comes to Georgia

The debtors who came to Georgia were soon outnumbered by other colonists. Oglethorpe had not allowed slavery. So these colonists pretended to "rent" enslaved Africans from South Carolina.

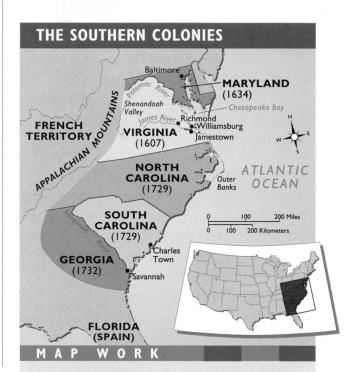

THE SOUTHERN COLONIES

Baltimore
Potomac River
MARYLAND (1634)
Shenandoah Valley
Chesapeake Bay
James River
Richmond
Williamsburg
FRENCH TERRITORY
VIRGINIA (1607)
Jamestown
APPALACHIAN MOUNTAINS
NORTH CAROLINA (1729)
Outer Banks
ATLANTIC OCEAN
SOUTH CAROLINA (1729)
Savannah River
0 100 200 Miles
0 100 200 Kilometers
GEORGIA (1732)
Charles Town
Savannah
FLORIDA (SPAIN)

M A P   W O R K

The Southern Colonies were located between the French territory to the west and Spanish Florida to the south.

1. Which colonies were founded after 1607 and before 1732?

2. Name some of the Southern Colonies' cities.

In the spring tourists often take a carriage ride through the historic section of downtown Savannah, Georgia.

By the 1750s slavery was well established in Georgia. Between the years of 1750 and 1760 the number of enslaved Africans in Georgia grew from about 1,000 to 4,000. By 1760 there were about 10,000 people living in Georgia. Of these 10,000 people, about 4,000 lived in slavery.

WHY IT MATTERS

Founded by James Oglethorpe in 1732, Georgia became the thirteenth English Colony. From the forests of present-day Maine in the north to the coastal plains of Georgia in the south, all of the 13 English Colonies were developing and expanding. It had been over 100 years since England had established its first colony in North America. In less than 50 years the 13 English colonies would become the United States of America.

Links to MATHEMATICS

Savannah's Squares

How did Oglethorpe plan the first settlement in Georgia? Savannah was laid out on Yamacraw Bluff as a series of squares. Each square measured 1 mile by 1 mile. Some squares were broken up into rectangular farms. There were 12 rectangular farms in each square mile.

Oglethorpe laid out 23 of the square miles with rectangular farms. How many of such farms did Savannah have?

Reviewing Facts and Ideas

MAIN IDEAS

- The colony of Maryland was founded in 1634 by Lord Baltimore as a place for Catholics to worship in freedom.

- In 1663 the English established what became the colonies of North Carolina and South Carolina.

- Before the arrival of Europeans, the Creek, one of the largest Native American groups in the Southern Colonies, formed a Confederacy.

- In 1732 James Oglethorpe, an English general, established Georgia as a colony for debtors and poor people. Later wealthy newcomers began forcing people to work as slaves on large rice and indigo farms.

THINK ABOUT IT

1. What were the names of the Southern Colonies?
2. How did Chief Tomochichi help the colonists to found Savannah?
3. **FOCUS** What reasons did King George II have for allowing Oglethorpe to found Georgia?
4. **THINKING SKILL** *Compare* the relations between Tomochichi and Oglethorpe with relations between colonists and Native Americans in the other colonies. How were they similar? How were they different?
5. **GEOGRAPHY** Identify the major landforms of the Southern Colonies shown on the map on page 218. Which landforms were helpful to the colonists?

CHAPTER 8 REVIEW

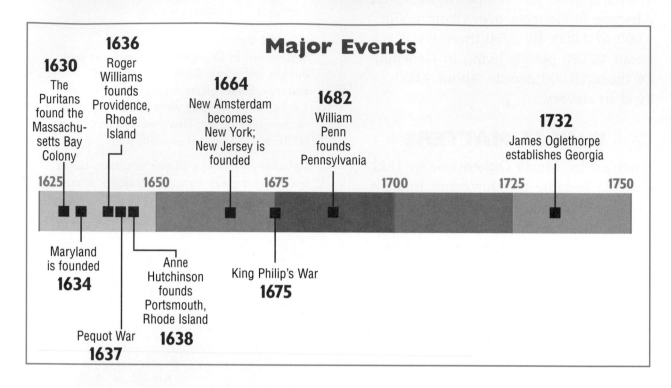

Major Events

1630 The Puritans found the Massachu-setts Bay Colony

1636 Roger Williams founds Providence, Rhode Island

1664 New Amsterdam becomes New York; New Jersey is founded

1682 William Penn founds Pennsylvania

1732 James Oglethorpe establishes Georgia

1625 — 1650 — 1675 — 1700 — 1725 — 1750

Maryland is founded **1634**

Anne Hutchinson founds Portsmouth, Rhode Island **1638**

King Philip's War **1675**

Pequot War **1637**

THINKING ABOUT VOCABULARY

Number a paper from 1 to 5. Beside each number write the word from the list below that matches the description.

debtor   relief
elevation   tolerate
proprietors

1. The men who owned all the land of a colony

2. The difference in height between land areas

3. The height of land above sea level

4. A person who owes money

5. To allow people to have beliefs that are different from one's own

THINKING ABOUT FACTS

1. Why did Roger Williams, Anne Hutchinson, and Thomas Hooker leave the Massachusetts Bay Colony?

2. Why was education important to the Puritans? How did the Puritan colonists provide for education in a way that no European country had done before?

3. Who led the Native Americans of New England in King Philip's War? Why was this war fought?

4. Why did the Quakers come to North America? In which colony did they settle?

5. What different groups of people lived in the Middle Colonies?

6. Who founded the colony of Maryland? What religious group settled there?

7. Why were the Southern Colonies good for farming?

8. What role did Native Americans play in the founding of Georgia?

9. What is indigo? Where was it grown?

10. Look at the time line above. Which colony was founded last? Which is the earliest colony shown on the time line?

WRITING A NEWSPAPER ARTICLE

Suppose that you are a newspaper reporter in the Massachusetts Bay Colony. Write an article about the trial of Anne Hutchinson.

WRITING AN ADVERTISEMENT

Suppose that William Penn has asked you to help him bring people to his colony. Write an advertisement in which you try to persuade people to settle in Pennsylvania.

WRITING A DIALOGUE

Write a dialogue in which you present the first meeting between Chief Tomochichi and General James Oglethorpe.

APPLYING GEOGRAPHY SKILLS

USING ELEVATION AND RELIEF MAPS

Answer the questions below to practice the skill of using elevation maps and relief maps.

1. What is the difference between elevation and relief?

2. How can you identify an elevation map? How can you identify a relief map?

3. What is the fall line?

4. Look at the elevation map of New York on page 214. What is the highest point in New York?

5. If you were the leader of a colony and were searching for a good spot to build a settlement, how might a map showing both elevation and relief help you?

Summing Up the Chapter

Copy the comparison chart on a separate piece of paper. Then review the chapter to complete the chart. After you have finished, use the information to write three paragraphs that answer the question "How were the colonies in each area founded?"

FOUNDER/COLONY	REASON FOR FOUNDING	AREA	CHARACTERISTICS OF AREA
John Winthrop Massachusetts Bay			
William Penn			
James Oglethorpe			

Life in the 13 English Colonies

THINKING ABOUT HISTORY AND GEOGRAPHY

The story of Chapter 9 takes place in the growing English Colonies. Since the early 1600s, people had been arriving from all over the world. Some came as colonists. As you can see on the time line, others came as captives. As you read the chapter, you will learn more about the people who came to the 13 English Colonies and their ways of life.

EARLY 1700s

CHARLES TOWN
The plantation system develops in the Southern Colonies

1740s

MIDDLE PASSAGE
African captives are brought to the 13 Colonies

1740s

PHILADELPHIA
Ben Franklin writes Poor Richard's Almanack

1700   1720   1740

NORTH
AMERICA

THE ENGLISH
COLONIES

Boston

Philadelphia

Shenandoah
Valley

Charles Town

Middle
Passage

ATLANTIC
OCEAN

1740s

BOSTON
Fishing is an important part of New England economy

1760s

SHENANDOAH VALLEY
English colonists begin moving to the backcountry

1760

1780

The Granger Collection

LESSON 1

1640 1670 1700 1750 1760

Why They Came

The Granger Collection

Read Aloud

By the middle of the 1600s, Europeans were streaming into North America by the thousands. They left the homes they had grown up in and their friends to go to a new land. They began new lives, often with only the contents of one small trunk. Why would so many people leave everything they had known to come to the English colonies?

Focus Activity

READ TO LEARN

Who came to the English colonies and why?

VOCABULARY

- **autobiography**
- **slave trade**

PEOPLE

- **Jane Hoskens**
- **Olaudah Equiano**

THE BIG PICTURE

In the 1600s many groups of people came to the English colonies. The Pilgrims and the Puritans came seeking religious freedom. Others came in search of wealth. In the 1700s more people began making the trip on their own instead of coming to North America as part of a group. Times were so hard in Europe that, by 1760, "colony fever" had hit England. The English government began passing laws forbidding people to leave the country. Yet they still came to the colonies.

What kind of people moved to the colonies? Some were wealthy. Most were not. Many people sold everything they had in order to pay for the voyage. Others could not afford to pay for the trip. They wanted to come so badly that they agreed to become servants in exchange for the cost of the voyage. Still others came against their will. Thousands of Africans were kidnapped from their homes and forced to come to the English colonies as slaves. Whether people came as free persons, captives, or servants, they all made the dangerous voyage across the Atlantic Ocean. Many of these people did not survive.

FREEDOM AND OPPORTUNITY

The voyage to the English colonies was dangerous and uncomfortable. Even people who traveled in the best quarters suffered hardships. Passengers were trapped for weeks in crowded conditions. Sicknesses spread quickly from one person to another. Many people did not survive the trip. Yet the ones who did survive encouraged others to follow them.

Pulling Up Stakes

The colonies usually offered a better way of life for those Europeans who chose to come. The promise of cheap land, greater opportunity to earn a living, and religious freedom made the hardship of the trip worth it for most of the immigrants.

Once they arrived, many newcomers wrote home to tell friends and relatives about what they had found in the colonies. In a letter to his cousin in Scotland, a colonist wrote, "You would do well to advise all poor people . . . to take courage and come to this country." Another Scotsman, William MacKay, told a friend that most hard-working people "could not fail of living comfortably" in the colonies. Look at the graph on this page to see how the population in the colonies grew.

The Voyage to America

"On the eighth of June . . . we left home at four o'clock in the morning," wrote two Dutch newcomers, Jaspar Dankers and Peter Sluyter. The voyage to the colonies usually lasted four

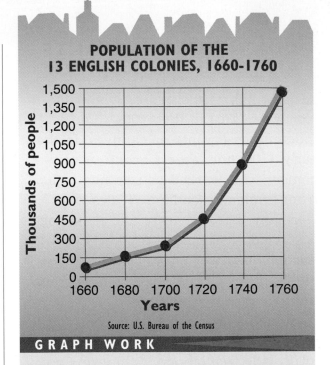

POPULATION OF THE 13 ENGLISH COLONIES, 1660-1760

Source: U.S. Bureau of the Census

GRAPH WORK

The population of the colonies grew quickly.

1. How many more people were living in the colonies in 1740 than in 1720?

2. Between which two years did the greatest increase in population occur?

months. Their trip was long and hard. Passengers in "great number [were] lodged between the two decks" of the ship. Inside there was little air or light. The ceiling measured only 4 1/2 feet in height. Dankers and Sluyter said that the "meat was old and tainted, . . . the bread mouldy or wormy, . . . the water smelt very bad."

Not everything was bad, though. At times, they saw remarkable things. One night, Dankers and Sluyter were awakened by the splashing of porpoises and two large whales that swam up close to the ship.

The Granger Collection

Some colonists brought their belongings in beautiful carved boxes such as the one shown here.

225

INDENTURED SERVANTS AND AFRICAN CAPTIVES

At least half of the people who came to North America in the 1700s came as indentured servants or captives. In the early 1700s the largest group of new-comers who worked as servants came from England, Scotland, Wales, and Germany. Because wars and poor harvests had weakened many parts of Europe, jobs were few. Taxes were high, and landlords often charged rents that people could not afford.

Some of the people who came to the colonies were convicts. They were sent to provide free labor for the growing colonial settlements. Others left their homes because they were forced to leave. By 1750 over 250,000 people had been taken from their homes in Africa and brought to the English colonies. Once here, most African people were forced to work as slaves in the Southern Colonies.

Indentured Servants

To pay the price of their passage to the colonies, many Europeans became indentured servants. In the 1700s, four out of every five immigrants in Maryland and Virginia were indentured servants. There were fewer indentured servants working in New England. Some indentured servants had hard lives with little food and harsh treatment. They often ran away from their employers to escape such treatment.

Others, like Jane Hoskens, were treated very well. Hoskens arrived in Philadelphia from London in 1719. Read this excerpt from her autobiography. An autobiography is the story of a person's life, written by that person. How did Hoskens feel about her new job as a teacher?

MANY VOICES
PRIMARY SOURCE

Excerpt from
the Autobiography of
Jane Hoskens,
published in 1837.

*The [heads] of four families living in Plymouth, who had several children, agreed to **procure** a sober young woman, as a school-mistress to instruct them in reading. . . . And on their applying to their friends in town, I was recommended for that service. When we saw each other I **perceived** it my place to go with them; wherefore . . . I bound myself to them by indenture for three years, and went cheerfully with them. . . . The children learned very fast, which afforded comfort to me and satisfaction to their parents.*

procure: get
perceived: thought

The Granger Collection

The Slave Trade

Many of the crops grown in the colonies required a great deal of labor before they could be sold. Some farmers in the colonies could not hire enough workers to tend their crops.

Instead, they bought captives from the **slave trade** in Africa. The slave trade was the business of buying and selling people for profit.

Read the following excerpt from the autobiography of Olaudah Equiano (AHL uh dah ih kwee AH nah), a West African who was enslaved in 1756 when he was 11 years old. Why did many captives get sick and die?

MANY VOICES
PRIMARY SOURCE

Excerpt from the Autobiography of Olaudah Equiano, published in 1789.

The first thing I saw when I arrived at the coast was the sea and the slave ship waiting to pick up its cargo. The sight of the slave ship amazed me. This amazement turned to terror when I was carried on board. . . . We were packed together in chains so tightly we could hardly move or turn over. The cramped surroundings and the deadly heat almost suffocated us. Many slaves fell sick and died—a result of being packed so closely. The only reason they were packed so closely was to increase the profits of the slave dealers.

suffocated: prevented from breathing

One out of seven captives did not survive the ocean voyage. You can see from the illustration on page 231 how Africans were packed into ships. Those who survived would begin difficult lives held in slavery.

WHY IT MATTERS

Many different peoples came to North America in the 1700s. These workers played an important role in the development of the English colonies. They helped build the new cities, towns, and farms. Their arrival was part of our country's long history of newcomers coming to these shores.

✓ Reviewing Facts and Ideas

MAIN IDEAS

- Beginning in the 1600s, many Europeans came to the English colonies seeking a better life for themselves.

- For many the voyage to the colonies was long, terrifying, and difficult.

- In the 1700s both indentured servants from Europe and captives from Africa came or were brought to the colonies.

THINK ABOUT IT

1. What hardships did people suffer to reach the English colonies?

2. What was the slave trade?

3. **FOCUS** For what reasons did people make the voyage to North America?

4. **THINKING SKILL** What _conclusions_ can you make from the population graph on page 225? What information did you use?

5. **WRITE** Suppose you are a young person who wants to become an indentured servant to pay for your passage to the colonies. Write a letter to your parents explaining your reasons.

1640   1670   1700   1752   1760

The Colonial Economy

Read Aloud

The riches of the 13 English colonies poured into England. Fat bundles of tobacco, bulging bags of rice, soft furs, and crates of deep blue indigo dye rolled off of the ships, all for England's profit.

Focus Activity

READ TO LEARN

How did New Englanders use the sea?

VOCABULARY

- export
- import
- agriculture
- free enterprise
- industry
- triangular trade
- Middle Passage

PEOPLE

- Elizabeth Lucas Pinckney

PLACES

- West Indies

THE BIG PICTURE

As more people arrived in the English colonies, their economy grew. Some of the products the colonies produced appear in the Infographic on page 232. During this time, England tried to control trade with its colonies. England's rulers said that some products from the colonies could only be **exported** to England. To export means to send goods to other countries for sale or trade.

In exchange for the colonies' products, the colonists **imported** cloth, metal tools, glass, and machines. To import means to bring goods from another country for sale or use. The English paid low prices for the colonies' goods, which they later sold to other Europeans at much higher prices. Yet England did not have complete control over colonial trade. Some colonies were able to trade with other countries and make a profit.

DIFFERENT ECONOMIES

In the early 1700s, agriculture, or the business of farming, was the major way of life in the English colonies. About nine out of ten colonists made a living from agriculture. Some farms were so successful that they had surplus crops to sell. By selling crops and other products, colonists were following a system of free enterprise. In a free enterprise system, people can start any business they want. They decide what to make, how much to produce, and what price to charge.

As you have read, each region of the colonies had different natural resources. Now you will read how those resources helped each region to develop its own special economy.

The Southern Colonies

The hot, humid climate and good soil of the Southern Colonies were well-suited to growing crops. Farmers and planters used much of their land for cash crops. They grew and exported tobacco, rice, and indigo to England.

In 1744 Elizabeth Lucas Pinckney succeeded in growing indigo on the three farms she managed in South Carolina. English merchants needed the blue dye from the indigo plant for their huge cloth-making businesses. Indigo quickly became a major cash crop of the Southern Colonies.

The Middle Colonies

As you have read, farmers in the Middle Colonies grew so much wheat and corn that people called their region the "breadbasket of the colonies." These farmers looked south to the English colonies in the West Indies for a place to sell their surplus grain.

The colonists of the West Indies needed to import grain to feed the people they held in slavery. Little land was available to grow food because the colonial planters used most of it to plant cash crops, such as sugarcane. On such islands as Jamaica and Barbados, colonists ran huge farms with hundreds of enslaved African workers.

This oil painting of a colonial farm (below) was probably done about 1732. The indigo plant (right) probably came from South Carolina.

Charleston Library Society

New York State Historical Association, Cooperstown

New England harbors in the 1700s (left) were busy fishing centers. Today they attract many tourists (below).

NEW ENGLANDERS AND THE SEA

In the rocky soil of New England, farmers barely grew enough crops to feed themselves. As a result, many New Englanders turned to the thick forests or the sea to make a living. In the 1700s waters off the coast of Massachusetts were among the richest fishing areas in the world. Some New Englanders became fishers. Others became builders of ships.

Profits from the Sea

To create a fishing fleet, New England needed ships. English ships were too expensive for the colonists to buy. So workers began cutting down trees from New England's large forests to build their own ships. By 1741 New England had a fleet of more than 800 fishing boats. New England ships were built so well that soon the English companies were buying them.

New Englanders sold their fish to Spain, Portugal, and the West Indies. New England's fishing and whaling industries made large profits. An industry is all the businesses that make one kind of product or provide one kind of service.

Fishing and shipbuilding helped create other industries in New England. Ships needed ropes, sails, and other equipment. These were also made in New England. Before long, Boston, the largest city in New England, became a busy trade center. Merchants and tradespeople from all over New England and the Middle Colonies came there to sell their products.

The Triangular Trade

Many New England merchants and sea captains also became rich in the triangular trade. The map on page 231 shows how the colonial trade routes formed a triangle. The first leg of the triangle started at such ports as Boston and New York. Traders sailed from these ports to the coast of West Africa, where they traded rum and guns for gold, ivory, and captive Africans.

The second leg of the triangle began in Africa. This part of the voyage was called the **Middle Passage** because it was the middle part of the triangular trade route. Thousands of Africans died on the voyage to the Americas, which lasted six to eight weeks.

In the West Indies the sea captains traded Africans for molasses, a thick syrup made from sugarcane. Then they returned to New England, where the molasses was made into rum. This was the last leg of the triangular trade route. Port cities such as Boston grew very quickly on the money earned in the triangular trade.

This drawing (right) shows how captive Africans were crowded into ships on the **Middle Passage**.

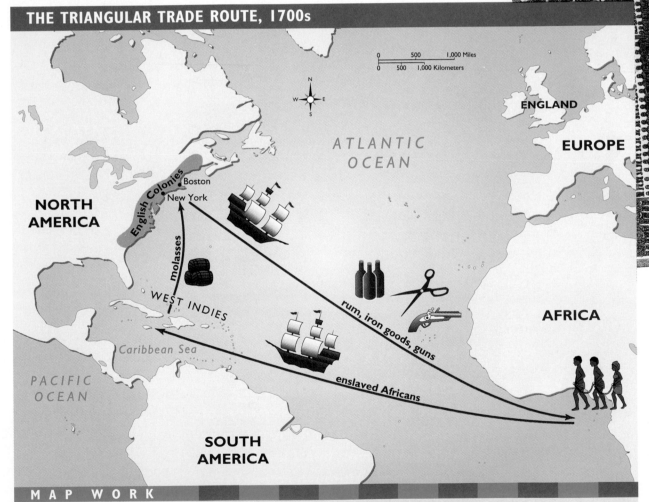

THE TRIANGULAR TRADE ROUTE, 1700s

ENGLAND
EUROPE
ATLANTIC OCEAN
NORTH AMERICA
English Colonies
Boston
New York
molasses
WEST INDIES
Caribbean Sea
PACIFIC OCEAN
rum, iron goods, guns
AFRICA
enslaved Africans
SOUTH AMERICA
Store Room.

MAP WORK

Trace the colonial routes of the **triangular trade** on the map.

1. How long was the route between Africa and the West Indies?

2. What was the destination of most of the enslaved Africans?

3. What products were shipped from New England to Africa? From the West Indies to Boston and New York?

231

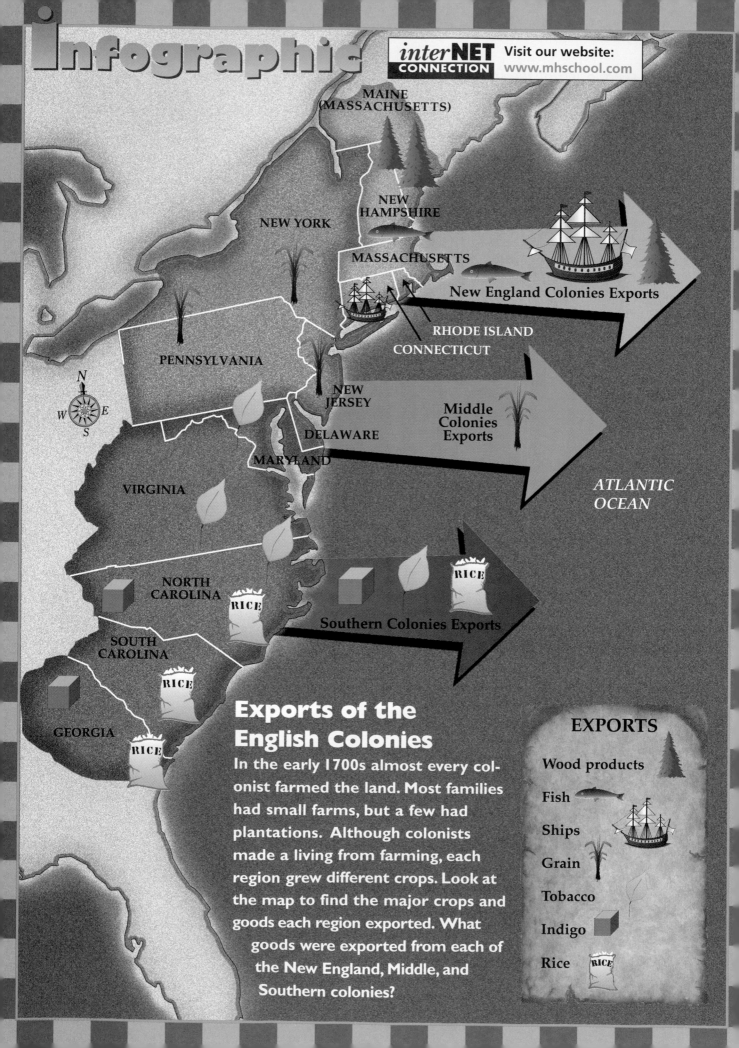

Infographic

interNET CONNECTION Visit our website: www.mhschool.com

MAINE
(MASSACHUSETTS)

NEW HAMPSHIRE

NEW YORK

MASSACHUSETTS

New England Colonies Exports

RHODE ISLAND
CONNECTICUT

PENNSYLVANIA

N
W   E
S

NEW JERSEY

DELAWARE

Middle Colonies Exports

MARYLAND

VIRGINIA

ATLANTIC OCEAN

NORTH CAROLINA

RICE

RICE

Southern Colonies Exports

SOUTH CAROLINA

RICE

GEORGIA

RICE

Exports of the English Colonies

In the early 1700s almost every colonist farmed the land. Most families had small farms, but a few had plantations. Although colonists made a living from farming, each region grew different crops. Look at the map to find the major crops and goods each region exported. What goods were exported from each of the New England, Middle, and Southern colonies?

EXPORTS

Wood products

Fish

Ships

Grain

Tobacco

Indigo

Rice   RICE

WHY IT MATTERS

Farming, fishing, and trading—these were only a few of the ways colonists made a living. In the busy towns and cities, craftsworkers such as blacksmiths and carpenters produced all kinds of goods. As the colonial economy grew, colonists were more and more able to support themselves without importing goods from England. By the middle of the 1700s, the colonists had developed a strong free enterprise economy. Over time the colonists became unhappy with the English laws that controlled trade. The colonists' desire to run their own economy eventually led to conflict with England. Today the economy of the United States remains a free enterprise system in which people run many types of businesses. This legacy of colonial times has drawn people to our country for well over two hundred years.

DID YOU KNOW?

Where does the phrase "two bits" come from?

The phrase *two bits* is as old as the English colonies. Often the colonists used whatever foreign coins they could get in exchange for their goods—English shillings, Spanish dollars, and Dutch guilders (GIHL durz).

The large silver Spanish dollars were most common because of trade with the West Indies. The dollars were called "pieces of eight." To make change, people cut the coin into eight equal pie-shaped pieces, or bits. Two bits were worth a quarter of a dollar. Some people still use the phrase *two bits* to mean 25 cents.

✓ Reviewing Facts and Ideas

MAIN IDEAS

- In the 1700s England tried to control the trade of the English colonies, but independent trading still developed.

- The economy in each of the colonies' three regions developed differently, although all were based mostly upon agriculture.

- Some New Englanders relied on fishing, shipbuilding, and trading. The triangular trade of the 1700s enabled a good many New Englanders to become wealthy.

- By the middle of the 1700s English colonists were following a free enterprise system.

THINK ABOUT IT

1. What kinds of resources did the New England colonies have?

2. Select three crops or products shown on the Infographic on page 232. Explain how each contributed to the economy of the English colonies.

3. **FOCUS** How did using the ocean help New England to grow and become successful?

4. **THINKING SKILL** What *caused* English colonists to begin looking for new places to trade their goods? What were some *effects* of the new trade?

5. **GEOGRAPHY** Look at the map of triangular trade on page 231. How many miles did the Middle Passage cover? Compare its distance with those of the other legs of the route.

FREE ENTERPRISE

Do you know someone who owns a business? Business owners in the United States take part in our country's system of free enterprise. Since colonial times, people have worked hard in their own businesses, making and selling goods.

Colonial business people strained their eyes to see in the flickering candlelight. Through patience and determination, they built a legacy of independence and hard work—a legacy that is still an important part of our country's free enterprise economy.

Museum of Fine Arts, Boston

These houses of Cornhill Street (bottom) in Annapolis, Maryland, were the homes and businesses of such colonial tradespeople as the tinsmith, the carpenter, the blacksmith, and the shoemaker.

National Geographic

Mary Provoost Alexander (below) had a shop in New York City. It was crammed with goods from Europe and the colonies. It probably looked like this one (left) in colonial Williamsburg.

Museum of the City of New York

Colonial craft workers such as Paul Revere (far left) took great pride in their work. Revere is famous for his skill in silversmithing, as the teapot (near left) shows. His shop also produced iron products, such as cannons, bells, stoves, and bolts for ships.

The Minneapolis Institute of the Arts

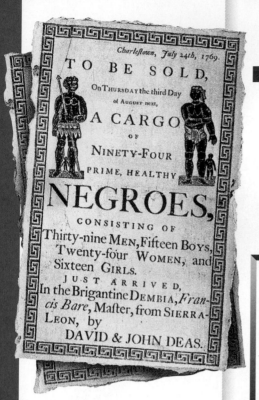

Charleftown, July 24th, 1769.
TO BE SOLD,
On Thursday the third Day
of August next,
A CARGO
OF
NINETY-FOUR
PRIME, HEALTHY
NEGROES,
CONSISTING OF
Thirty-nine MEN, Fifteen Boys,
Twenty-four WOMEN, and
Sixteen GIRLS.
JUST ARRIVED,
In the Brigantine DEMBIA, Francis Bare, Mafter, from SIERRA-LEON, by
DAVID & JOHN DEAS.

Focus Activity

READ TO LEARN

What was the plantation system?

VOCABULARY

- plantation
- slave codes
- overseer

PEOPLE

- John Woolman
- Robert Carter III

1640   1670   1700   1760

Slavery in the Colonies

Read Aloud

"My poor mother," wrote Charles Ball about his time as a captive in the colonies during the 1700s. "When she saw me leaving her for the last time, [she] ran after me, took me down from the horse, clasped me in her arms, and wept loudly and bitterly over me."

THE BIG PICTURE

Slavery was not a new idea in the 1700s. It had been practiced all over the world for thousands of years. The Aztec and Maya, whom you read about in Chapter 3, had practiced slavery. So did the Native Americans in what is now the United States. People in Europe, Africa, and Asia also forced people to work as slaves. Before the 1500s, however, enslaved people were mainly war prisoners. They lost their freedom when they lost in battle.

Slavery practiced by Europeans in the Americas was different because it was often based on skin color. African captives were bought and sold like property. They had no rights. Family members, such as Charles Ball, were often separated and sold to different owners. The children of captives were also the property of the slave owners.

Slave traders brought Africans to such places in the Americas as Brazil and the West Indies as well as to the 13 colonies. However, over time, most Africans who came to North America toiled in the Southern Colonies on large farms that grew one crop. In the South these large farms were called **plantations** (plan TAY shunz).

SLAVERY IN THE ENGLISH COLONIES

In the English colonies slavery grew slowly. There were only about 300 captives in Virginia in 1650. By 1671 there were 2,000.

In the early 1700s the economy of the colonies was beginning to grow. Yet colonists who worked for wages were scarce and expensive. Colonial farmers, merchants, lawyers, and shop owners instead bought enslaved people and hired indentured servants. In 1708, the number of enslaved people in the colonies reached 12,000.

In the North

The population of enslaved people in the North, however, remained small. Most farms in New England and the Middle Colonies were not very large. Without a lot of land, farmers did not use many workers to run their farms.

Most Africans who were enslaved in the North became servants or skilled workers. They often worked side by side with their owner, who was a baker, sailmaker, carpenter, printer, or innkeeper.

In the South

Small farms and plantations made up the largest part of the Southern Colonies' economy. While enslaved men, women, and children worked on both types of farms, the greatest number of them toiled on large plantations.

Planters bought Africans to tend important cash crops, such as tobacco and rice. Most people in slavery were owned by a small number of planters. Only about one of every four whites owned slaves or were members of a slave-owning family. In fact, the planters owned over half of the people held in slavery.

To keep the growing population of enslaved workers under control, the planters made rules called slave codes. These rules took from the captives many of the rights that most free people in the colonies enjoyed. Under the slave codes, for example, enslaved people were not allowed to practice their own religion, learn to read, marry, or own property.

This way of controlling enslaved Africans spread throughout the South. In time, the slave codes made it legal to treat enslaved people as if they were not equal to the other colonists.

In 1655, the first slave auction in the colonies took place in what is now New York City.

The Granger Collection

DAILY LIFE ON A PLANTATION

A plantation was much like a small village. Sometimes hundreds of people lived and worked on one plantation. The diagram on the next page shows how a plantation was set up. The center of the plantation was called the "big house," where the planter and the planter's family lived. The big house was built with high ceilings and thick walls to help it stay cool in the summer.

Many enslaved people worked in the big house as "house slaves." All of the captives lived in small, often run-down cabins near the crop fields. The people on the plantation sometimes called this area "slave row." Life on the plantation depended on who you were.

The Planter's Life

Wealthy planters and their families enjoyed many goods and products that most colonists could not afford to buy. For example, the big house had fine furniture from England, crystal glasses, china dishes, and silver platters.

Most planters were men, but women also owned plantations. The planter held an important position in the colonies. The courts as well as government and business leaders, accepted the planters' view that the economy of the Southern Colonies would grow weak without slavery.

The Slave's Life

The day began early and ended late for the enslaved people on the plantation. There was no time for rest under the rule of the overseer. The overseer was the boss of the plantation. He told the slaves where to work and what to do. He was usually the one who punished them.

The overseer was often an indentured servant or even an enslaved person. The overseer sometimes got a share of the plantation's profits. He, therefore, pushed the "field slaves" to work hard from sunrise to sundown. Sometimes, when there was a full moon, enslaved people worked in the crop fields at night, too.

In the fields, Africans did the dirty, back-breaking work of planting and harvesting tobacco, rice, and indigo. They also took care of animals, cooked, cleaned, and repaired tools.

Not all work on the plantation was done in the fields. Africans who were skilled workers made furniture, shoes, or glass. Some of these skills the Africans had learned in their homeland. These skilled workers built many beautiful churches and other buildings all over the Southern Colonies. Some of these buildings still stand today.

The Plantation at Night

Most people in slavery said the day "never really ended" on the plantation. After working in the fields or in the big house, slaves had to do their own chores. They fed animals, cut firewood, and tended their own gardens. Then they went to their cabins to make supper.

After supper, enslaved people finally got to rest. They were tired, but they made time to talk, tell stories, and sing songs with their family members. Story-telling has a long tradition in Africa. Most stories were used mainly to teach values and beliefs.

Some of the slaves' songs were a signal to meet after work. At the secret meetings a number of them planned their escape. Some enslaved people also secretly learned to read and later wrote about their experiences.

"BIG HOUSE"

SMOKEHOUSE

KITCHEN

OVERSEER'S HOUSE

LAUNDRY

FRUIT TREES

SLAVE QUARTERS

WHIPPING POST

STABLE

VEGETABLE GARDEN

HEN HOUSE

TOBACCO BARN

CARPENTRY SHOP

BLACKSMITH SHOP

DOCK

TOBACCO FIELDS

A Colonial Southern Plantation

STRUGGLING AGAINST SLAVERY

Most enslaved workers were brought from the present-day countries of Ghana and Nigeria in West Africa. They spoke different languages and had different cultures. The major ethnic groups from Nigeria were the Hausa (HOW sah) and the Yoruba (YOH ru bah). The Ashanti (uh SHAHN tee) and the Fante (FAHN tee) came from Ghana.

To keep them from communicating with each other, slave traders and slave owners separated captives who spoke the same language. As Captain William Smith wrote in 1744, "By having some of every sort on board, there will be no more likelihood of their succeeding in a plot." Still, enslaved people found ways to communicate with each other. In fact, some African words that they used, such as *banana* and *boss*, became part of the English language.

Rebellion

Captives showed their anger toward the slave owner in different ways. Many enslaved people refused to work. "They often die before they can be conquer'd *[forced to work]*," wrote one Englishman visiting the colonies.

Other captives worked slowly or purposely broke tools. Still others escaped. Escaping captives were hunted down. When caught, they were usually beaten, whipped, and sometimes killed. Even so, many kept trying to escape.

One thing the planters feared most was rebellion. When they got the chance, some captives were willing to die for their freedom. In many rebellions enslaved people organized raids, burned houses, and killed people. In the Stono Rebellion of 1739, a captive named Cato led a rebellion in which 30 colonists of South Carolina were killed. To stop the rebellions the planters strengthened the slave codes.

Stratford Hall (below left) in Virginia was built with the help of enslaved African workers. Most enslaved Africans had little time to create artwork, such as this sculpture from the eighteenth century (below).

Smithsonian Institution

The New Jersey Quaker John Woolman visited many of the English colonies as a traveling preacher.

The Family

The main thing that kept enslaved Africans from giving up hope was their families. Family members tried to keep in contact with one another, even when they were separated. On the one day that they did not have to work, usually Sunday, enslaved parents often visited their children. Some parents walked miles to see children who had been sold away from them. One such child was Charles Ball whose words you read at the beginning of the lesson.

WHY IT MATTERS

Enslaved Africans had a major effect on the English colonies. Slave labor played a large part in building much of the South and some of the North. Profits from slavery helped all the Southern Colonies become wealthy and successful.

In a land that offered much freedom and opportunity to its European colonists, the plantation system denied such freedom to enslaved Africans. One of the few European colonists who spoke out against slavery in the 1700s was John Woolman, a Quaker. In 1754 he wrote, "the color of a man [means] nothing in matters of right and [equality]." Woolman traveled through much of the Southern Colonies and gained first-hand knowledge about slavery.

Woolman also asked slave-owning Quakers to release their captives. Quakers and other colonists did begin to free their slaves. In 1791 the Virginia planter and slave owner Robert Carter III said that slavery was against "the true principles of religion and justice." He began freeing the 500 enslaved people on his plantation. Yet these efforts did not end slavery. The struggle by African Americans to gain the same rights of most Americans continued.

✔ Reviewing Facts and Ideas

MAIN IDEAS

- Slavery was practiced throughout North America and in the English colonies. But most enslaved people worked on large plantations in the Southern Colonies.

- A plantation was like a small village in which enslaved people did almost all the work.

- African captives rebelled against slavery in many ways. Strong family ties kept many from giving up hope.

THINK ABOUT IT

1. What kinds of work did enslaved people do on the plantations?

2. From where did the majority of the African captives come? What kind of work did they do?

3. **FOCUS** What was life like for the enslaved people on plantations in the Southern Colonies?

4. **THINKING SKILL** Explain why the following sentence is a _fact_ or an _opinion_: "The overseer was often an indentured servant or sometimes an enslaved person."

5. **WRITE** Read again the words of John Woolman. Write a paragraph that explains Woolman's statement.

241

Reading Climographs

VOCABULARY
climograph

WHY THE SKILL MATTERS

In the last lesson you read that many people came to the English colonies in the early 1700s. The climate in the colonies was sometimes very different from the climate that the newcomers from Europe were used to.

One way they could have compared climates would have been by looking at a climograph (KLI muh graf). A climograph is a graph that shows information about the temperature and precipitation of a place over time.

A climograph is useful because it gives a picture of the weather for each month. Today, farmers use climographs to decide when the climate will most likely be right for planting. Climographs tell travelers what kind of weather to expect when they take a trip. Scientists use climographs to predict weather conditions that might increase the chance of such things as forest fires and floods.

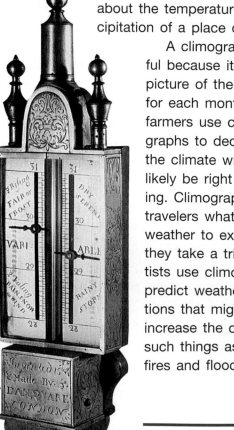

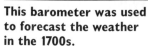

This barometer was used to forecast the weather in the 1700s.

The Granger Collection

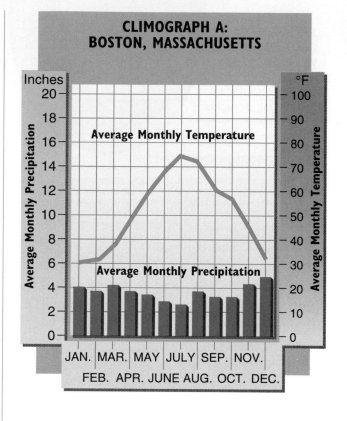

CLIMOGRAPH A: BOSTON, MASSACHUSETTS

USING THE SKILL

Look at Climograph A for Boston, Massachusetts. Notice that it is really two graphs in one—a bar graph and a line graph. To understand a climograph, read it the same way that you would read other kinds of graphs. First look at the title of Climograph A. Then look at the label along the bottom of the climograph.

Now, look at the labels and scales of measurement on the sides of the climograph. The precipitation scale is shown on the left. It is measured in inches. The temperature scale is shown on the right. It is measured in degrees Fahrenheit.

The bar graph uses vertical bars to show Boston's average monthly precipitation. The line graph shows the average monthly temperature. During July, Boston had the highest temperatures and the lowest amount of rainfall.

TRYING THE SKILL

Climographs B and C give temperature and precipitation information for Philadelphia, Pennsylvania, and Charleston, South Carolina. Take a look at the temperature graphs. What is Philadelphia's average temperature in March? Charleston's? How do the temperatures of Philadelphia and Charleston compare in August? In December?

Look at the precipitation graphs in Climographs B and C. Which month has the greatest amount of precipitation for each city? The least?

Now look for connections between the temperature and precipitation in Climograph C. Does warm weather increase or decrease the chance of precipitation? Explain.

Helping yourself

- A **climograph** shows the temperature and precipitation of a place over a period of time.

- Study the information on the side and bottom of the graph. Trace the line graph for temperature. Trace the bar graph to chart precipitation.

REVIEWING THE SKILL

1. What is a climograph?
2. Compare Climograph C to Climograph B. During which month are the temperatures in Philadelphia and Charleston closest? During which month are they farthest apart?
3. Look at climographs A, B, and C. Which city has the wettest climate? The driest? Which city would you expect to have the most snow? Explain how you answered each question.
4. Suppose you are moving to a new city. How would you use climographs to help decide where to move? What would you look for in the climographs?
5. How would a climograph be useful to you?

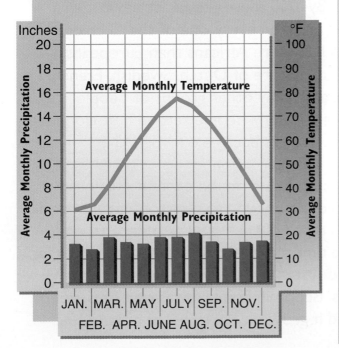

CLIMOGRAPH B: PHILADELPHIA, PENNSYLVANIA

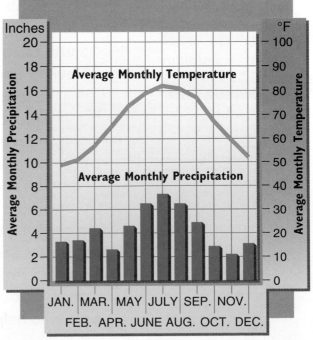

CLIMOGRAPH C: CHARLESTON, SOUTH CAROLINA

243

Cigna Museum and Art Collection

1640 1670 **1700** **1760**

The Colonial Way of Life

Focus Activity

What were some of Benjamin Franklin's contributions to Philadelphia?

VOCABULARY

- frontier
- almanac
- backcountry

PEOPLE

- Benjamin Franklin

PLACES

- Philadelphia
- Shenandoah Valley

Read Aloud

"No gains without pains." Do you recognize this saying? Thousands of people in the 1700s read the writings of Benjamin Franklin in his newspaper, the Pennsylvania Gazette. Franklin is still known today for the many witty sayings he wrote. The one above is often used today by people to describe what they think about exercising.

THE BIG PICTURE

Benjamin Franklin grew up at a time when the English colonies were changing rapidly. Before 1700 eight out of ten colonists were English or had English parents. Then in the 1700s people from Germany, Ireland, France, Scotland, and Africa arrived in the colonies in large numbers. By 1750 these groups of newcomers had made their mark on every one of the 13 colonies. South Carolina had more Africans than Europeans. New York was a mixture of Dutch, Swedish, French, English, Jewish, and many other groups of people.

In almost every colony, people settled first along the coastline. As these areas became crowded, the **frontier** began to move westward. *Frontier* was a word used by colonists to describe land on the edge of European settlement. As colonists moved to the frontier, they took over more and more of the Native Americans' lands.

At the same time, colonial cities were growing larger. By 1775 **Philadelphia** had become the largest city in the 13 colonies. Benjamin Franklin was one of the people who helped it grow.

BENJAMIN FRANKLIN

Ben Franklin, the grandson of an indentured servant, grew up to become the most famous person in the colonies. Born in 1706 into a large Boston family, Franklin learned at a young age that reading was a key to success. He read everything he could get his hands on.

At age 16 he wrote funny stories for his brother's newspaper under the name "Mrs. Silence Dogood." The stories were so good that his brother published them, not knowing that Ben had written them. This was the beginning of Franklin's work as a writer.

Franklin the Writer

In 1729 Franklin founded Philadelphia's first newspaper, the *Pennsylvania Gazette*. As a writer, one of Franklin's greatest successes was *Poor Richard's Almanack*. An almanac is a reference book that contains information about the stars and the weather. Franklin added jokes and sayings to his almanac. From 1732 to 1757 Franklin's almanac sold more copies than any other book in the colonies except for the Bible.

Franklin also wrote clever sayings to fill the blank spaces in his newspaper. The colonists loved the sayings, many of which are still popular today. Read some of Franklin's sayings on this page. What is Franklin trying to teach us?

MANY VOICES
PRIMARY SOURCE

Excerpts from
Poor Richard's Almanack
by Benjamin Franklin, published
from 1732 to 1757.

Early to bed, early to rise, makes a man healthy, wealthy and wise.

Little strokes fell great oaks.

Glass, china, reputation, are easily cracked, and never well mended.

An open foe may prove a curse; but a pretended friend is worse.

One today is worth two tomorrows.

Haste makes waste.

Beware of little expenses. A small leak will sink a great ship.

The sleeping fox catches no poultry.

---

poultry: chicken
foe: enemy

Franklin the Scientist

As a scientist Franklin is best known for his experiments with electricity and his invention of the lightning rod. His other inventions still used today are bifocal eyeglasses and a wood-burning stove called the Franklin Stove.

Franklin's experiments caused excitement in the colonies and in Europe. He received many honors and prizes. His writings and experiments made him the best-known North American in Europe. When he visited Europe, people crowded in the streets to get a glimpse of him.

The Draw Bridge 7 John Wilpain
2 Buds Building 8 Capt Anthony
3 Edw Shipen 9 George Painte
4 Ant. Morris Brew Ho 10 Jos. Shipen
5 Capt Vineing 11 W. Fisburn S
6 Jonathan Dickinson 12 The Scales

Czech Republic, also established a church in Philadelphia.

Franklin Helps Philadelphia

In addition to founding Philadelphia's first newspaper, Franklin did many other things to help Philadelphia grow. He started the city's first public library and its first hospital. He also started the world's first volunteer fire department, called the Union Fire Company.

Franklin also played a role in the government. He served as Postmaster General and as Philadelphia's official printer. The postmaster is an official in charge of a post office.

A University in the City

During much of the 1700s not every person could receive an education. Schooling was mainly for the wealthy. Women and African Americans were not allowed to attend. Franklin wanted to help more people get an education. He himself had gone to school only until the age of ten. "It would be well," he wrote, if students "could be taught everything that is useful."

FRANKLIN'S PHILADELPHIA

When 17-year-old Franklin first came to Philadelphia in 1723, it was a small city of about 10,000 people. By 1775 its population had grown to 35,000. Find Philadelphia on the map on page 248.

Philadelphia was a city of great ethnic and religious diversity. By the end of the 1700s, doctors, lawyers, business owners, silversmiths, and craftspersons from many different backgrounds lived in Philadelphia.

Many different religious groups from Europe found tolerance in Philadelphia. It was home to the English colonies' few Roman Catholic churches. The Moravians (maw RAH vee unz), a Protestant religious group from what is now the

246

The City of
per *Painter*

In *Abm Bickly*
Thomas Masters
Saml Perry
Bank Meeting Hou
Tho. Chakey
Penny Pott House

Philadelphia (above) was growing in 1730. The College of Philadelphia (left) became the University of Pennsylvania in 1791. Deborah Franklin (right) ran a business and a home.

American Philosophical Society

In 1740 Franklin founded Pennsylvania's first college, in Philadelphia, which later became the University of Pennsylvania. It is one of the oldest colleges in the United States. Only three other colleges are older. Harvard University in Cambridge, Massachusetts, was founded in 1636, and the College of William and Mary in Williamsburg, Virginia, was founded in 1693. Yale University in New Haven, Connecticut, was founded in 1701. Franklin also helped start a school for African Americans at the end of the 1700s.

During the middle 1700s a religious movement known as the Great Awakening spread through the colonies. The Great Awakening, begun by Protestants, led to the founding of many other new colleges in the colonies.

Women in the Colonies

The wives of wealthy colonial men lived comfortable lives. Yet they, also, had many responsibilities. Franklin had little time to give to his printing shop because of his many other activities. So Deborah Franklin, his wife, ran much of the business. She also ran the busy Franklin household and took care of their three children. Poorer women worked hard raising families and helping on the farms.

Although the work of colonial women helped to keep farms and businesses running, they had few rights except for those allowed by their husbands. To improve their lives, some women began to start their own shops and businesses. A number of colonial women became highly successful.

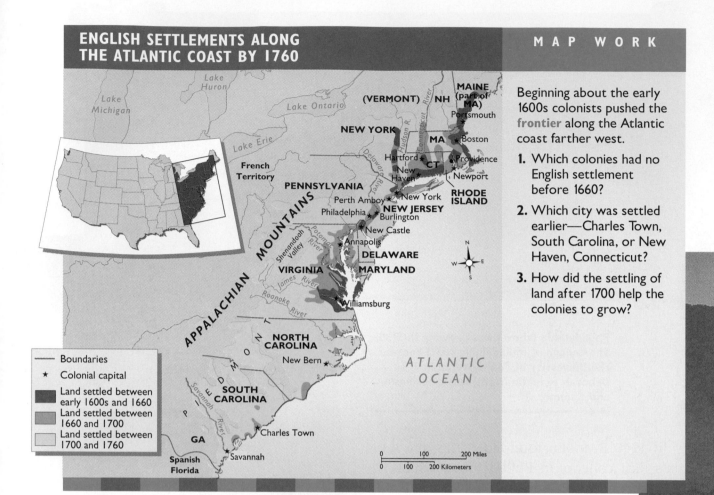

Lake Huron

Lake Michigan

Lake Ontario

Lake Erie

Connecticut River

Hudson R.

(VERMONT) NH

MAINE (part of MA)

Portsmouth

NEW YORK

MA • Boston

Hartford ★

New Haven

CT

★ Providence

Newport

French Territory

PENNSYLVANIA

Delaware River

Perth Amboy ★ New York

Philadelphia ★

Burlington

NEW JERSEY

RHODE ISLAND

★ New Castle

APPALACHIAN MOUNTAINS

Shenandoah Valley

Potomac River

★ Annapolis

DELAWARE

VIRGINIA

MARYLAND

James River

Roanoke River

★ Williamsburg

PIEDMONT

NORTH CAROLINA

New Bern ★

ATLANTIC OCEAN

Savannah River

SOUTH CAROLINA

GA

★ Charles Town

Spanish Florida

★ Savannah

Legend

— Boundaries

★ Colonial capital

Land settled between early 1600s and 1660

Land settled between 1660 and 1700

Land settled between 1700 and 1760

0   100   200 Miles
0   100   200 Kilometers

Beginning about the early 1600s colonists pushed the **frontier** along the Atlantic coast farther west.

1. Which colonies had no English settlement before 1660?

2. Which city was settled earlier—Charles Town, South Carolina, or New Haven, Connecticut?

3. How did the settling of land after 1700 help the colonies to grow?

FROM CITY TO FRONTIER

The settling of the colonies followed a geographical pattern. At first most settled on the Atlantic Coastal Plain. These rich lands were good for growing crops. Their location near large waterways made them ideal for trade. Colonists built successful farms, businesses, and cities there. The map on this page shows you that important colonial cities like Boston, Philadelphia, and Charles Town were located on the Coastal Plain.

By the middle of the 1700s, most of the coastal land was owned by wealthy planters. Thus, many colonists could not afford to buy land there. Colonists began to move west to the frontier to an area they called the backcountry.

The backcountry is the name that these colonists gave to the rugged land near the Appalachian Mountains.

Geography of the Backcountry

The backcountry began in the foothills between the Atlantic Coastal Plain and the Appalachians, or the Piedmont. The Piedmont stretches across the Middle Colonies and part of the Southern Colonies.

Farming in the backcountry was difficult. The land was often rocky and uneven with few large rivers and waterways on which to transport goods.

Without large waterways, colonists found it difficult to

reach the Piedmont. To get there, many colonists followed the trails begun by Native Americans long before. One of the most often used trails led to the Shenandoah Valley. Find this valley on the map on page 248.

Settlers of the Backcountry

Most people who settled in the backcountry lived a rugged life. Both men and women had to work hard to survive. Their houses were often made of roughly cut logs. Many backcountry people carried rifles wherever they went and spent most of the day hunting. Still others became wealthy. The families of two United States Presidents were among the first colonists who settled in the backcountry.

What brought these people to the backcountry? Many backcountry people were poor. A Scottish immigrant named Alexander MacAllister described the North Carolina backcountry as "the best poor man's country I have heard in this age." MacAllister told relatives that a person "might make it rich very fast" there. It was a place where people could "breathe the air of liberty."

The beautiful Shenandoah Valley in Virginia is shown at left. Colonists in the backcountry played the handmade dulcimer and fiddle (near left).

249

In 1762 the Cherokee chief, Cunne Shote, posed for this portrait with some belongings that were important to him.

Native Americans in the Backcountry

The colonists who came to the back-country were moving into lands that had long been home to Native Americans. In some cases the colonists and the Native Americans got along well. Trade between these Native Americans and the colonists helped both groups. However, good trading relations did not stop problems from arising.

Some colonists captured and enslaved Native Americans. In the Yamasee War of 1715, fighting broke out between the colonists of North Carolina and the Yamasee, Muscogee, and Cherokee. The Native Americans almost defeated the colonists. However, the Native Americans had to surrender when the Cherokee switched sides and joined the colonists in exchange for trade goods.

WHY IT MATTERS

"Be always employed in something useful," Benjamin Franklin wrote in his autobiography. Franklin lived by these words. Through his hard work and intelligence he became wealthy and was respected throughout the colonies. Franklin's life was one example of the opportunities that were attracting people to the growing colonies.

Not everyone shared equally in these opportunities. Enslaved people had little opportunity. Poor immigrants had hard lives. All of these different people in the colonies were working to build a new country. Although England still ruled the colonies, the colonists were slowly but surely becoming Americans.

✔️ Reviewing Facts and Ideas

MAIN IDEAS

- People from many different lands lived throughout the English colonies in the 1700s.

- Benjamin Franklin arrived in Philadelphia in 1723. He helped the city of Philadelphia in many ways.

- As a result of high land prices on the Atlantic Coastal Plain, many colonists settled in the backcountry near the Appalachian Mountains.

THINK ABOUT IT

1. What were some of the major achievements of Ben Franklin?

2. Where was the backcountry? On what landforms was it located?

3. **FOCUS** How did the city of Philadelphia change over the lifetime of Ben Franklin?

4. **THINKING SKILL** From Ben Franklin's _point of view_, what was the most important thing in life? Why do you believe he had this view?

5. **WRITE** Choose one of the sayings from _Poor Richard's Almanack_ on page 245 and write a paragraph about the meaning of the saying.

MAKING A DIFFERENCE

Getting Out the News

NEW YORK, NEW YORK—Meet 16-year-old Scarlett Arias and 18-year-old Osiris Adorno. When these two teenagers talk, people listen—about 3 million of them.

Scarlett and Osiris work for the New York office of Children's Express. You have read about Ben Franklin's newspaper, the *Pennsylvania Gazette*. Instead of writing stories for one newspaper, the students at Children's Express gather and write news stories that appear weekly in newspapers across the country.

Children's Express reporters are 8 to 13 years old. The editors range in age from 14 to 18. Teenagers at news offices in Indianapolis, Indiana, Washington, D.C., and New York City work without pay to research and write news stories for a variety of news sources.

Children's Express calls itself the "news service by children for everybody." Explains Scarlett, "Our stories give a young person's point of view on issues from government to life in homeless shelters. Stories spotlight whatever affects children." The Children's Express news teams know that citizens need to be informed about many issues. Their readers have followed Children's Express stories on elections for President of the United States since 1976. News teams have also interviewed people running for other offices, local voters, and such elected officials as senators and mayors.

"We also talk to kids about the issues that concern them directly," says Osiris. "We cover the things that kids hear about or see around them everyday. We try to find out what kids are thinking about—that includes school dropouts and gang members." In 1997, Children's Express editors traveled to Dhaka, Bangladesh, to report on children in the work force. Scarlett believes her years of working on the news stories have helped her in another way. "What I've gained the most is confidence that my voice can be heard."

" . . . my voice can be heard."

Scarlett Arias

CHAPTER 9 REVIEW

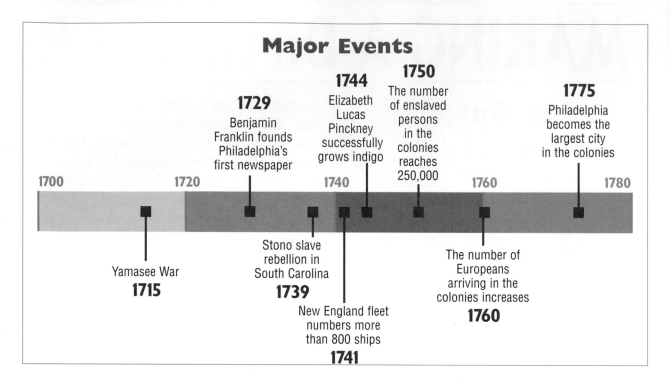

Major Events

1729
Benjamin Franklin founds Philadelphia's first newspaper

1744
Elizabeth Lucas Pinckney successfully grows indigo

1750
The number of enslaved persons in the colonies reaches 250,000

1775
Philadelphia becomes the largest city in the colonies

1700 1720 1740 1760 1780

Yamasee War
1715

Stono slave rebellion in South Carolina
1739

New England fleet numbers more than 800 ships
1741

The number of Europeans arriving in the colonies increases
1760

THINKING ABOUT VOCABULARY

Number a paper from 1 to 10. Beside each number write the word or term from the list below that best completes the sentence.

agriculture   frontier
almanac   Middle Passage
autobiography   overseer
export   plantation
free enterprise   slave codes

1. The _____ were rules that planters made to control enslaved workers.

2. A _____ was a large farm that grew one main crop.

3. The _____ was the second leg of the triangular trade route.

4. In an _____ a person writes about his or her own life.

5. To _____ means to send goods to other countries for sale or trade.

6. Benjamin Franklin wrote a successful reference book called an _____ .

7. In a _____ system, people make their own decisions about business.

8. _____ means the business of farming.

9. The boss of the plantation was called the _____ .

10. Colonists called the land on the edge of settlement the _____ .

THINKING ABOUT FACTS

1. What was the voyage to the American colonies like for both Europeans and African captives?

2. How did England try to control trade in the colonies?

3. How was the family important to enslaved Africans?

4. Why did colonists begin settling in the backcountry?

5. Look at the time line above. Which of the events shown would have been the first item to be covered in Benjamin Franklin's newspaper?

THINK AND WRITE

WRITING A REPORT

Write a report on the triangular trade. Identify the goods and people involved as well as the routes that the trade followed.

WRITING INTERVIEW QUESTIONS

Suppose that you have been assigned by a newspaper to interview one of the people you have read about in this chapter, such as Benjamin Franklin or Olaudah Equiano. Write a series of questions that you would like to ask the person about his or her experiences.

WRITING A JOURNAL ENTRY

Suppose that you and your family have recently moved from a colonial coastal city to a backcountry farm. Write a journal entry describing your new way of life.

APPLYING STUDY SKILLS

READING CLIMOGRAPHS

Answer the questions below to practice the skill of reading climographs.

1. What does a climograph show?

2. What two kinds of graphs are included in a climograph?

3. How would a climograph have helped newcomers to the English colonies?

4. Look at the climograph for Philadelphia on page 243. During which month does the city usually have the highest average precipitation?

5. How are climographs helpful to farmers? How are they useful to scientists?

Summing Up the Chapter

Copy the main idea map on a separate piece of paper. Then review the chapter to complete the main ideas. After you have finished, answer the following question about one region in the colonies: "How did the people in _____ live?"

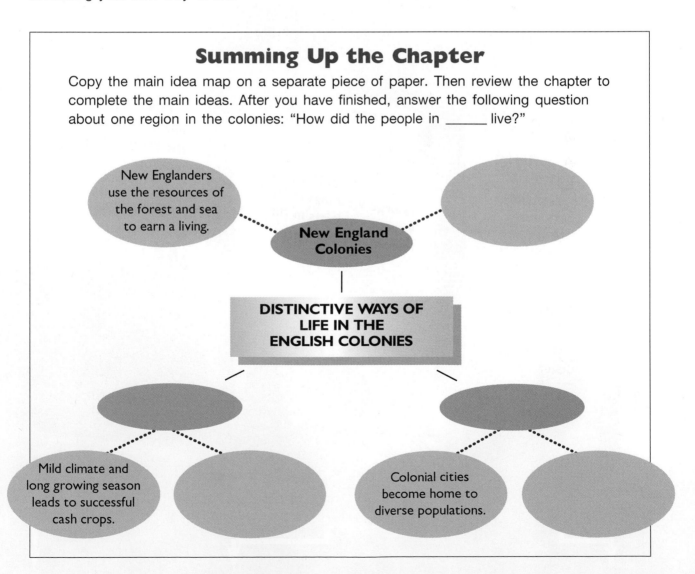

New Englanders use the resources of the forest and sea to earn a living.

New England Colonies

DISTINCTIVE WAYS OF LIFE IN THE ENGLISH COLONIES

Mild climate and long growing season leads to successful cash crops.

Colonial cities become home to diverse populations.

The Struggle for North America

THINKING ABOUT HISTORY AND GEOGRAPHY

Chapter 10 takes place west of the Appalachian Mountains. On the map you can see that the British were not the only Europeans in North America. From the time line and the map you can see how the French and Spanish also claimed lands that had long been home to the Native Americans. In time the British would challenge other European powers for control of North America.

PACIFIC OCEAN

San Diego

1763
OHIO RIVER VALLEY
Pontiac's Rebellion forces the British to defend their territory

1682
MISSISSIPPI RIVER DELTA
Robert La Salle claims Louisiana for France

1754
OHIO RIVER VALLEY
George Washington leads Virginia colonists in the French and Indian War

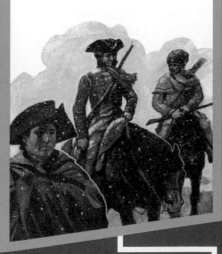

1682

1750

1760

NORTH
AMERICA

Chicago

Ohio River
Valley

THE ENGLISH
COLONIES

Mississippi River
Delta

ATLANTIC
OCEAN

LATE 1700s

SAN DIEGO
The Spanish build missions in California

1770s

CHICAGO
Jean Baptiste Point du Sable establishes a trading post

1770

1780

1600 1609   1769

Spanish Missions

Read Aloud

In the morning when the bell rang, Pueblo people came to church from all around. They came from their homes, from the fields, and from their workshops. When they reached the church, the Spanish priests greeted them. The priests were proud to have brought their religion to the Pueblo. Yet they were also puzzled. Why did the Pueblo continue to practice their traditional religion?

Focus Activity

READ TO LEARN

Why did the Spanish build missions in the West and the Southwest?

VOCABULARY

- mission

PEOPLE

- Don Juan de Oñate
- Antonio de Otermín
- Popé
- Diego de Vargas
- Junípero Serra

PLACES

- St. Augustine
- New Mexico
- Santa Fe
- El Camino Real
- Texas
- San Antonio
- California
- San Diego
- San Francisco

THE BIG PICTURE

As you read in Chapter 6, the Spanish had settled in North America long before the English formed the 13 colonies. You have read about how Francisco Coronado explored the Southwest from 1540 to 1542 in search of the Seven Cities of Gold. By the late 1500s New Spain included most of present-day Mexico, the Caribbean islands, Central America, and the southwestern United States. The Spanish also claimed parts of South America.

In 1565, to protect their sea routes from the English "sea dogs" and their lands from French traders, Spain founded St. Augustine. St. Augustine was Spain's first settlement in what is now the United States. It lay on the Atlantic Coastal Plain in the colony of Florida. St. Augustine was founded 20 years before the English came to Roanoke and over 40 years before the founding of Jamestown.

Later in the 1500s the Spanish began building settlements in the West and the Southwest. Why did they come? What resulted when they met the Pueblo and the other Native Americans who lived there?

THE SPANISH COLONIES

Although Coronado found no gold in the Southwest, other Spanish explorers including **Don Juan de Oñate** (dohn HWAHN DE oh NYAH te) continued the search. A Spanish noble who was born in Mexico, Oñate was one of the last conquistadors to search for gold in the American Southwest. In 1595 Oñate got permission from King Philip III of Spain to build a settlement in the lands the Spanish called **New Mexico**.

In 1598 he built San Gabriel, a settlement where the Rio Grande and Chama River meet. When the Pueblo people in the area resisted Spanish claims to their lands, the colonists left San Gabriel. In 1609 these colonists founded **Santa Fe** and made it the capital of New Mexico.

The Spanish Missions

During the next 20 years, the Spanish built over 100 settlements in New Mexico. Many of them were **missions**. A mission is a religious settlement where missionaries live and work. The Spanish also built towns and set up encomiendas in New Mexico.

The purpose of the Spanish missions was to convert the Pueblo and other Native Americans to the Roman Catholic religion. The center of mission life was the Catholic Church. The missions also had farms, ranches, orchards, workshops, and sleeping quarters. You can see what most Spanish missions in the Southwest looked like in the diagram on page 258.

Spain's Southwestern colonies were connected to Mexico by **El Camino Real** (el kah MEE noh re AHL). *El Camino Real* means "the royal road" in Spanish. Part of El Camino Real began as several Native American trails. Oñate turned it into a major route between New Mexico and Mexico to the south. Many Spanish missions were built along this road.

Today Santa Fe is the capital of New Mexico. It is also a well-known art center, famous for its mix of Native American and Spanish cultures.

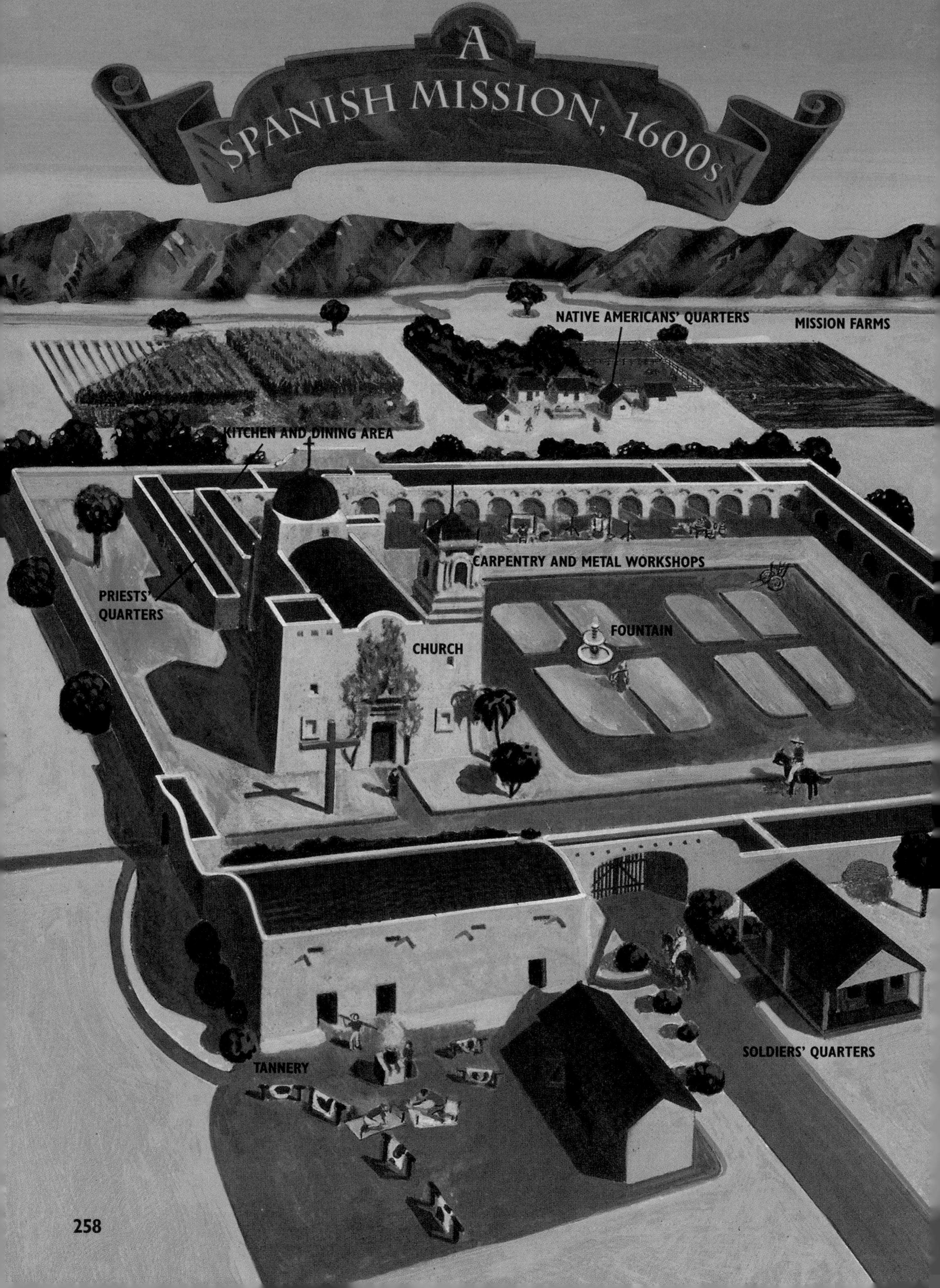

A SPANISH MISSION, 1600s

NATIVE AMERICANS' QUARTERS

MISSION FARMS

KITCHEN AND DINING AREA

PRIESTS' QUARTERS

CARPENTRY AND METAL WORKSHOPS

CHURCH

FOUNTAIN

TANNERY

SOLDIERS' QUARTERS

258

POPÉ AND THE PUEBLO REVOLT

As you have read in Chapter 4, the Pueblo had been living in the Southwest for hundreds of years. How did they respond to the Spanish newcomers?

The Spanish and the Pueblo

As Oñate traveled through the Southwest, he asked Pueblo leaders to meet with him in their kivas. Read the account of one of these meetings. How do you think the Pueblo might have reacted to Oñate's speech?

The Granger Collection

MANY VOICES
PRIMARY SOURCE

Account of a speech
by Don Juan de Oñate
to the Pueblo in about 1598,
recorded by Juan Perez de Donis,
a member of Oñate's expedition.

*He told them that he had been sent by the most powerful king and ruler in the world, Don Philip, king of Spain, who desired especially to serve God our Lord and to bring about the **salvation** of their souls, but wished also to . . . protect and bring justice to them, as he was doing for other natives of the East and West Indies. To this end he sent the Spaniards from such distant lands to theirs, at enormous expense and great effort. . . . By [agreeing to be ruled by Spain] they would live in peace, justice, and orderliness, protected from their enemies.*

salvation: saving

At first many Pueblo accepted the food, clothing, and shelter the Spanish missions provided. Even so, under Spanish rule, more people than ever went hungry. For centuries Pueblo farmers had been giving part of their crops to help the needy in their own communities. Now they also had to give a portion to the Spanish. They were often forced to work for the Spanish without pay. The Spanish also punished the Pueblo for practicing their traditional religion.

The Pueblo Revolt of 1680

By the 1670s thousands of Pueblo people had become Catholics. At the same time, most of them also continued to practice their traditional religion, which angered the Spanish governor, Antonio de Otermín (ahn TOH nee oh DE oh ter MEEN). In 1675 he put 47 Pueblo religious leaders in jail. One of them was named Popé (poh PAY). When the Pueblo threatened to leave the missions, the religious leaders were set free. Immediately after Popé was released, he began planning a rebellion.

Popé convinced Pueblo leaders that they had to force the Spanish to leave. He got them to agree to work together with the Apache who were living in the countryside. By 1680 the Pueblo were united as never before.

Before the revolt was to take place, runners brought knotted cords to each Pueblo village. The knots showed how many days were left before the revolt. On August 10, 1680, the Pueblo attacked "with shamelessness and daring," Otermín wrote. The Spanish were forced to flee New Mexico.

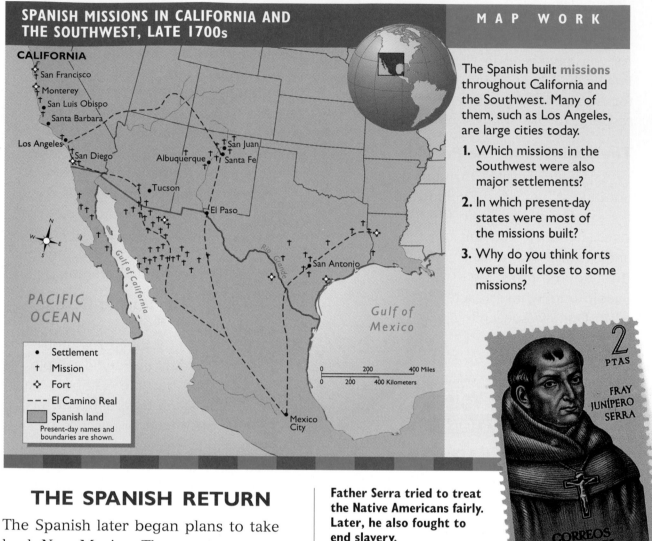

SPANISH MISSIONS IN CALIFORNIA AND THE SOUTHWEST, LATE 1700s

CALIFORNIA

- San Francisco
- Monterey
- San Luis Obispo
- Santa Barbara
- Los Angeles
- San Diego
- Albuquerque
- San Juan
- Santa Fe
- Tucson
- El Paso
- San Antonio
- Mexico City

PACIFIC OCEAN

Gulf of California

Rio Grande

Gulf of Mexico

0   200   400 Miles
0   200   400 Kilometers

- • Settlement
- † Mission
- ◇ Fort
- - - El Camino Real
- Spanish land

Present-day names and boundaries are shown.

MAP WORK

The Spanish built **missions** throughout California and the Southwest. Many of them, such as Los Angeles, are large cities today.

1. Which missions in the Southwest were also major settlements?

2. In which present-day states were most of the missions built?

3. Why do you think forts were built close to some missions?

Father Serra tried to treat the Native Americans fairly. Later, he also fought to end slavery.

2 PTAS
FRAY JUNÍPERO SERRA
CORREOS ESPAÑA
F.N.M.T.

The Granger Collection

THE SPANISH RETURN

The Spanish later began plans to take back New Mexico. They sent an army there in 1692. Diego de Vargas (dee EH goh DE VAHR gahs) led this force of about 200. Without firing a shot, Vargas convinced 23 Pueblo villages to return to Spanish rule.

How did Vargas do it? In 12 years, much had changed. Popé and other Pueblo leaders had died. The Pueblo were no longer united. Yet the Pueblo of New Mexico had still won an important victory. In return for peace, Vargas agreed to allow them to live apart from the Spanish. He also promised to let the Pueblo practice their own religion.

Texas and California Missions

In the 1680s the Spanish also began building settlements in the part of New

Spain that is now the state of Texas. These settlements were built to keep the French explorers and traders out of the area. The missions the Spanish built around what is today the city of San Antonio became known as "the Alamo chain."

260

The area along the Pacific Coast was the last part of New Spain to be settled by the Spanish. In 1769 a Spanish missionary named Father Junípero Serra (hoo NEE pair roh SEH rah) walked from Mexico to the land the Spanish called California. That same year Father Serra founded San Diego, the first mission in California. By 1823 there were 21 missions in California. As you can see from the map on page 260, these missions stretched as far north as present-day San Francisco.

Father Serra believed that the Native Americans should "have their own lands and crops so that poverty will not make them [leave the mission]." Despite his crippled leg, Father Serra visited each of his missions regularly.

WHY IT MATTERS

The Pueblo revolt was only one event in the struggle between Europeans and Native Americans. Although the Pueblo

regained some of the rights they had lost, their victory did not stop the growth of Spanish settlements. By 1800 the Spanish controlled much of the land in what is now the United States.

Both Native American and Spanish influences can still be seen in many parts of the United States. Many cities, like Taos, New Mexico, have Pueblo names. Others, like San Antonio, Texas, have Spanish names.

Today many Navajo raise sheep, an animal that the Spanish introduced in what is now the American Southwest.

✓ Reviewing Facts and Ideas

MAIN IDEAS

- From the late 1500s to the early 1800s the Spanish built many missions in what is today the United States.

- A Pueblo religious leader named Popé organized a successful revolt against Spanish rule in 1680. But in 1692 the Spanish returned and regained control of New Mexico.

- In 1769 the Spanish priest Father Junípero Serra began to build a series of missions throughout California.

THINK ABOUT IT

1. Where in our present-day country did the Spanish build missions?

2. What reasons did Oñate give the Pueblo for agreeing to Spanish rule?

3. **FOCUS** How did the building of missions change the lives of Native Americans in New Mexico?

4. **THINKING SKILL** What alternatives could the Pueblo or the Spanish have chosen to prevent the Pueblo revolt of 1680? _Decide_ which alternative you think would have worked best. Why did you make the choice you did?

5. **WRITE** Write a diary entry about working in a mission from the point of view of a Pueblo person. Include details shown in the diagram on page 258.

261

VAQUEROS AND COWBOYS

The Granger Collection

When the Spanish came to what is now the United States, they brought some of their most valuable animals with them—the horse and the cow. They also brought the skill, developed over many generations in Spain and Mexico, of herding cattle on horseback.

Spanish-speaking and Native American vaqueros (vah KAIR ohz) soon worked the ranches and rode the plains of the West and Southwest. In Spanish the word *vaquero* means "a person who works with cows." The English word for vaquero—cowboy—is probably one you know well. As you look at the photographs on these pages, you will see examples of how the vaqueros' legacy lives on today.

A vaquero (top left) shows his roping skills. Frederic Remington painted *Turn Him Loose, Bill* (above) in the late 1800s. Remington is known for his paintings of cowboys and Native Americans. Today women also work as cowhands (right).

Vaqueros caught cattle by using a braided rope called *la reata* (lah ray AH tah). This rope came to be called a lariat in the United States. Vaqueros wore wide-brimmed hats to keep out the sun and the rain.

1600 1608   1701   1720   1760

The French in North America

Read Aloud

They first arrived on fishing ships. Yet they soon "threw up their old [jobs] . . . for bear skins and beaver skins," wrote historian Francis Parkman. They "followed the Indians . . ., lived with them, [and] grew familiar with their language. . . ." Who were these Europeans who chose to live deep in the forests of North America?

Focus Activity

READ TO LEARN

Why did France build colonies in North America?

VOCABULARY

- portage
- voyageur
- coureur de bois

PEOPLE

- Samuel de Champlain
- Jacques Marquette
- Louis Jolliet
- Robert La Salle
- Jean Baptiste Point du Sable

PLACES

- St. Lawrence River
- Canada
- New France
- Quebec
- Louisiana
- St. Louis
- Detroit
- Chicago

THE BIG PICTURE

While Spain was busy building colonies in Mexico and the Caribbean islands in the early 1500s, France was claiming land farther north in North America. As you read in the Infographic on pages 176–177, French explorers such as Jacques Cartier (kahr TYAY) first came to North America in search of a Northwest Passage to Asia. Then in 1534 the French reached what is now Newfoundland and claimed the land along the **St. Lawrence River**. The French called it **Canada**, after the Huron word *kanata*, which means "village." Later the name of **New France** was given to France's lands along the St. Lawrence River and the Great Lakes.

For over 60 years, few French people settled in New France. Religious wars in Europe between Catholics and Protestants took up much of France's attention. However, some of the French did begin fishing off the coast of New France. They also began a fur trade with the Native Americans. This fur trade would soon bring wealth and power to France.

National Archives of Canada

THE FRENCH COLONIES

Furs were in great demand in France. New France's forests were filled with fur-skinned animals. So in the early 1600s France began to think about starting a colony there to help their fur-trading business. A colony would also make it easier to continue their search for a Northwest Passage, which you read about in Chapter 7.

In 1608 a French geographer and explorer named **Samuel de Champlain** (duh sham PLAYN) founded a trading post called **Quebec** (kwih BEK) on the St. Lawrence River. Quebec was the first permanent French settlement in North America.

The Huron and the French

Champlain knew that France's success in the fur trade depended on its Native American trading partners. Champlain made friends with the Huron near Quebec. He learned their language and respected their ways.

The French also sent missionaries to New France. Unlike most of the Spanish, the French did not, for the most part, force Native Americans to work for them or to live in French missions. Instead, the black-robed French missionaries lived in Huron villages in order to convert them to the Roman Catholic religion.

In 1609 the Huron agreed to supply Champlain with furs if he would help them defeat their rivals in the fur trade, the Iroquois. The French agreed. In return, the Huron helped the French increase their fur-trading business and remained their allies for many years. However, the Iroquois never forgot their defeat at the hands of the Huron and the French.

Champlain (above) is called "the Father of New France." The Huron tray (below) was stitched with moosehair.

National Museum of the American Indian

NEW FRANCE

France's attempts to encourage settlement in New France during the 1600s were not successful. French colonists were not allowed to own land, and farming in Canada's cold climate was difficult. In addition, only Catholics were allowed to settle in New France. As a result, the French who did come to New France were mainly fur traders and missionaries. By 1660 there were fewer than 3,000 French colonists living in Canada.

Marquette and Jolliet

Although Champlain made many explorations into Canada, he failed to find a Northwest Passage. Many other French explorers had also tried. One of them was Jacques Marquette (ZHAHK mahr KET). While working as a missionary in what is today the state of Michigan, Marquette heard Native Americans tell of a mighty river to the west. Could this river be the long-sought-for Northwest Passage?

In 1673 Marquette and a former fur trader named Louis Jolliet (LOO ee JOH LEE et), set out together to find the river Marquette had heard about—the Mississippi River. Marquette told of entering its waters "with a joy I cannot express." You can trace the route of Marquette and Jolliet on the map below. After a long while, when they had reached the Arkansas River, they saw that the Mississippi flowed south. Since the river did not flow west toward the Pacific Ocean, Marquette and Jolliet realized it could not be a Northwest Passage. They decided to return to Lake Michigan.

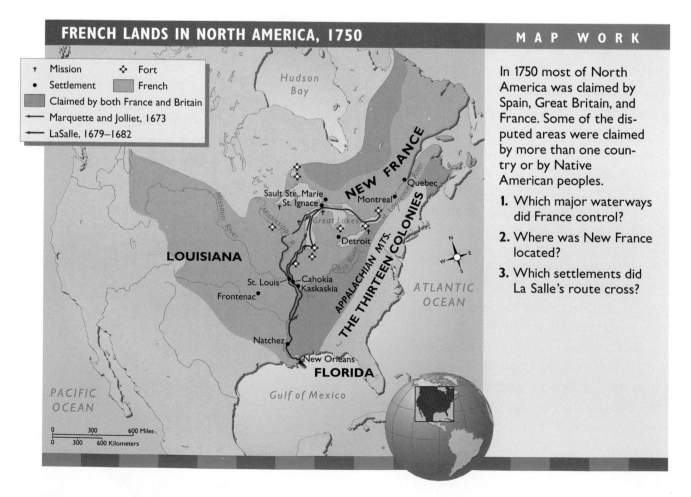

FRENCH LANDS IN NORTH AMERICA, 1750

MAP WORK

Legend:
- † Mission
- ◆ Fort
- • Settlement
- French
- Claimed by both France and Britain
- ← Marquette and Jolliet, 1673
- ← LaSalle, 1679–1682

Map labels: Hudson Bay, NEW FRANCE, Quebec, Montreal, Sault Ste. Marie, St. Ignace, Great Lakes, Detroit, Missouri River, Mississippi, Ohio River, St. Lawrence River, APPALACHIAN MTS., THE THIRTEEN COLONIES, LOUISIANA, St. Louis, Cahokia, Kaskaskia, Frontenac, Natchez, New Orleans, FLORIDA, ATLANTIC OCEAN, PACIFIC OCEAN, Gulf of Mexico

Scale: 0 300 600 Miles / 0 300 600 Kilometers

In 1750 most of North America was claimed by Spain, Great Britain, and France. Some of the disputed areas were claimed by more than one country or by Native American peoples.

1. Which major waterways did France control?

2. Where was New France located?

3. Which settlements did La Salle's route cross?

The Granger Collection

National Postal Museum

Jean Baptiste
Pointe Du Sable
22

Black Heritage USA

Because of its easy access to the Mississippi River and the Great Lakes, Chicago (left and below), founded by Du Sable, grew to become a major transportation center.

Robert La Salle

The French explorer Robert La Salle (lah SAHL) learned of Marquette and Jolliet's journey. In 1682 he set out to find the mouth of the Mississippi River. Near the Arkansas River, La Salle met the Quapaw (KWAH pah). With their help he reached the Gulf of Mexico. La Salle became the first European to see the mouth of the Mississippi River. La Salle claimed the Mississippi River valley for France. He named it Louisiana after King Louis XIV of France. Find Louisiana on the map on page 266.

Settlements in New France

During the late 1600s and early 1700s, the French built forts, missions, and other settlements in New France. Some were built to keep the English from moving into French lands. Some settlements later became major cities.

In 1700 French priests built a mission along the Mississippi River in what is today Missouri. A trading post was soon added. Over the years it grew into the city of St. Louis. In 1701 the French built a trading post along the Detroit River between Lake Huron and Lake Erie. This trading post later became the city of Detroit.

On their return trip, Marquette and Jolliet had used a portage that connected the Mississippi River to the Great Lakes. A portage is a land route from one body of water to another. In the 1770s a Haitian fur trader named Jean Baptiste Point du Sable (ZHAHN bap TEEST PWAN doo SAH bluh) built a trading post along this portage. He became friendly with the Potawatomi who lived around the Great Lakes. The trading post Du Sable built grew to become the city of Chicago.

Buffalo Bill Historical Center

THE FUR TRADE

The fur trade was important to New France. In Europe, the forests had been overhunted for many years, which made fur-skinned animals rare. In addition, beaver hats had become very popular. The money to be made from furs such as beaver fur attracted many trappers and traders to North America.

Trading Posts

By the early 1700s there was a vast network of forts and trading posts in New France. Trappers who often lived in the forests for months at a time to sell or trade furs came to the trading posts for other goods as well.

Fur traders went to the forests and bought furs from French and Native American trappers. The furs were then transported to Quebec by voyageurs (vwah yah ZHURZ). The voyageurs were people who carried furs and other goods from post to post by canoe. From Quebec the furs were shipped to France.

The Coureurs de Bois

France granted only a few people the right to trap and trade in its American colonies. As a result, many trappers became coureurs de bois (KUR rer duh BWAH), which means "woods runners" in French. The coureur de bois trapped furs without permission from the French government. Because colonists could not own land, becoming a coureur de bois was the only way many of them could earn a living.

Many French trappers learned their trade from people such as the Huron, Chippewa, and Ottawa. They taught the French to use lightweight birchbark canoes that traveled quickly along rivers and lakes.

The furs traded by the voyageurs (above) were made into hats like this one worn by Franklin (left).

The Granger Collection

They also taught the French trappers how to survive in the forests.

An adventurous life attracted many voyageurs and coureurs de bois. According to one voyageur:

> There is no life so happy as a voyageur's life; none so independent; no place where a man enjoys so much variety and freedom.

WHY IT MATTERS

By building settlements throughout New France, the French surrounded English lands in North America. As a result, the 13 English colonies had no way to expand. By the middle of the 1700s, the French had won many Native American allies. The voyageurs and coureurs de bois helped to form strong partnerships with them. In the next lesson you will see how the French, English, and Native Americans fought to control much of North America.

Parlez-vous français?

Parlez-vous français? (PAHR lay VOO frahn SAY) means "Do you speak French?" You may know more French words than you think. As you learned in Chapter 4, the Iroquois call themselves the Hodenosaunee. The French called them the Iroquois, and that name stuck. The Wyandot are also generally known by their French name—Huron. Until recently, most people called the Lakota by their French name—the Sioux.

Bonjour! I'm a prairie dog!

Other French words are now part of the English language. Among them are *glacier, plateau, lacrosse,* and *prairie.*

✓// Reviewing Facts and Ideas

MAIN IDEAS

- Samuel Champlain built the first permanent French settlement in North America, called Quebec, in 1608.

- Explorations by Marquette and Jolliet in 1673, and by La Salle in 1682, led to French control of the entire Mississippi River valley.

- By the early 1700s France had a vast network of forts and trading posts throughout North America.

- The fur trade became a source of wealth for the French, who developed good relations with their Native American trading partners.

THINK ABOUT IT

1. Who were some of the French explorers who came to North America? Why did they come?

2. How did Native Americans such as the Huron help the French?

3. **FOCUS** How did the fur trade shape the growth of New France?

4. **THINKING SKILL** *Compare* and *contrast* the French and the English colonies of North America.

5. **GEOGRAPHY** Look at the map of New France on page 266. Plot a route that a voyageur might have taken from St. Louis to Quebec. Then list the trading posts where a fur trapper might have stopped.

Thinking Skills

The Granger Collection

Making Conclusions

VOCABULARY
conclusion

WHY THE SKILL MATTERS

As you read in the previous lesson, in 1682 the French explorer Robert La Salle reached the mouth of the Mississippi River. He was able to do this with the help of the Quapaw people. What did the Quapaw think when they first saw him? They needed to know if he was friendly or not. They looked at La Salle's face, which did not look angry. They saw that he did not reach for a weapon. They also noticed a peace pipe in his hand. From what they saw, the Quapaw made a conclusion that La Salle was friendly.

When you make a conclusion you are acting like a judge in a court. You consider all the pieces of information and add them up to determine what they mean.

Suppose you have to buy a birthday gift for a friend. You know that your friend likes to read. You also know that your friend enjoys learning about science. From this information, you might conclude that a book about robots would be a good gift.

USING THE SKILL

You have also read about two other French explorers, Marquette and Jolliet, who searched for a Northwest Passage to the Pacific Ocean. They had heard about a river that the Native Americans called "big river," or "Mississippi." Marquette and Jolliet thought that this big river might flow into the Pacific Ocean. The explorers paddled down the Mississippi and soon realized that it flowed south. They concluded that the river was probably not the Northwest Passage. Marquette and Jolliet turned back at the mouth of the Arkansas River and headed north.

To make a conclusion, first identify the subject of all the information. In this instance the subject is the Mississippi River. Next, look for connections between the pieces of information and what the connections might tell you. Marquette knew the Mississippi was a wide river. However, he later found that the Mississippi flowed south. From all of this information he was able to conclude that he had, indeed, not found the Northwest Passage.

TRYING THE SKILL

Now that you have seen how to make a conclusion, try to make a conclusion on your own. Marquette and Jolliet paddled down the Mississippi for two months. Finally the speed of the water slowed. They tasted the water and found it salty.

Helping yourself

- **A conclusion** is a final statement based on information about something.
- First gather different pieces of information about a topic.
- Next, look for a common idea behind all the pieces of information considered.

What conclusion do you think they made at this point? Explain how and why they might have made this conclusion. For help, refer to the Helping Yourself box on this page.

REVIEWING THE SKILL

1. What is a conclusion?
2. What do you need to do before you can state a conclusion?
3. Was La Salle expecting to meet Native Americans on his journey? What information did you use to draw your conclusion?
4. Marquette and Jolliet concluded that the Mississippi River was not a Northwest Passage. How did they arrive at this conclusion?
5. What are some examples of how making a conclusion can help people make sense out of a lot of information?

Marquette and Jolliet (right) were the first Europeans to reach the Mississippi. In the painting by George Catlin on page 270, La Salle feasts with Native Americans in what is now Illinois.

1600   1640   1680   1720   1754   1763

The French and Indian War

Focus Activity

READ TO LEARN

What were the results of the French and Indian War?

VOCABULARY

- French and Indian War
- Treaty of Paris
- Proclamation of 1763

PEOPLE

- George Washington
- Edward Braddock
- Pontiac
- King George III

PLACES

- Ohio River valley
- Fort Duquesne
- Fort Necessity
- New Orleans

Read Aloud

George Washington, a 21-year-old lieutenant, looked out over his troops. British and Virginian soldiers marched stiffly in neat rows in red and blue coats. Washington was worried. The troops were an awesome sight. However, they also made an easy target for the enemy. The enemy was not marching in neat rows or wearing bright uniforms. Scattered throughout the forests, the enemy was hard to find.

THE BIG PICTURE

The enemy George Washington worried about was the French. During the 1700s, England, now known as Great Britain, fought several wars with France over control of Europe. By the middle 1700s this struggle had spread to North America.

As you read in Chapter 9, the British colonies in North America were thriving. By the 1750s there were nearly 2 million colonists living there. Yet France had difficulty getting colonists to come to North America. Only about 60,000 French colonists lived in New France.

Trouble began when British colonists started moving into lands claimed by the French. In 1754 this conflict led to what the British called the French and Indian War. The war got its name from the people the British colonists were fighting—the French and their Native American allies.

THE OHIO RIVER VALLEY

The Ohio River valley lies mostly in what is now the Middle Western region of the United States. Both Britain and France claimed the land in the Ohio River valley. Until the middle of the 1700s, the Native Americans who lived there had kept both groups of colonists from settling in the valley. Then disputes among themselves and with the colonists led some Native Americans in the valley to sell their land to the British colonists. Fearing the loss of the fur trade, the French began building a series of forts in the valley to keep the British out.

Fort Duquesne and Fort Necessity

In 1754 young George Washington was sent by the British to force the French to leave the Ohio River valley. There the French had built Fort Duquesne (doo KAIN) where the city of Pittsburgh, Pennsylvania, stands today. The British colony of Virginia also claimed this land in the valley.

When Washington arrived, his troops attacked and defeated a small force of French soldiers in the woods near the fort. This short battle marked the beginning of the French and Indian War. An excited Washington wrote home, "I heard the bullets whistle; and believe me, there is something charming in the sound."

Washington's troops quickly built a temporary fort out of logs and called it Fort Necessity. Soon a larger French army attacked the fort, and Washington's men were defeated.

General Braddock's Defeat

In 1755 the British tried again to capture Fort Duquesne. This time General Edward Braddock led the troops. Braddock's soldiers were well trained. He felt they would easily win the battle. Yet as the British neared the fort, the bullets seemed to come from out of nowhere. Braddock's troops "broke and ran as sheep pursued by dogs," Washington wrote. Braddock himself died four days later from wounds he had received.

Washington learned an important lesson from Braddock's defeat. The French were using Native American methods of warfare. They made surprise attacks on the British from behind trees, large rocks—anywhere they could hide. The British and colonial soldiers' brightly colored jackets only made it easier for the French to take aim.

A young lieutenant in 1754, George Washington later would become one of our country's greatest generals.

THE TIDE TURNS

Because British colonists greatly out-numbered them, French colonists had welcomed the help of the Huron. Washington had seen what valuable allies Native Americans could be. The British decided to ask the Iroquois for help.

The Iroquois were not eager to side with the British. While French settlements were few and scattered, British colonists had taken over much Iroquois land. "You have disregarded us, thrown us behind your back," said Tiyanoga (tih an OH guh), a Mohawk leader. Still, the Iroquois decided to join the British against their old enemies, the Huron and the French. In return the British promised to keep colonists away from Iroquois lands.

Britain Wins the War

The French won victory after victory over the British until 1758. Then Britain began to pour money into winning the war. It bought new equipment and sent more troops and its best generals to the colonies. These resources helped Britain to win the war.

In 1762, as the war was ending, France gave Spain much of Louisiana to keep it out of Britain's hands. This

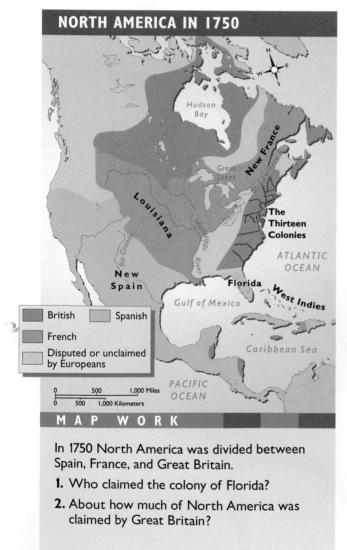

NORTH AMERICA IN 1750

Legend:
- British
- French
- Spanish
- Disputed or unclaimed by Europeans

MAP WORK

In 1750 North America was divided between Spain, France, and Great Britain.

1. Who claimed the colony of Florida?
2. About how much of North America was claimed by Great Britain?

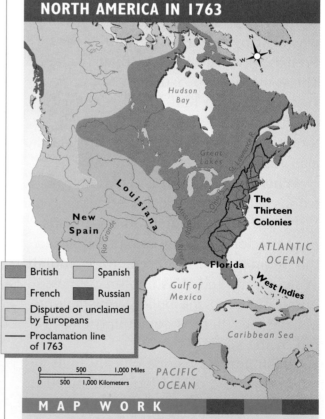

NORTH AMERICA IN 1763

Legend:
- British
- French
- Disputed or unclaimed by Europeans
- Spanish
- Russian
- Proclamation line of 1763

MAP WORK

After the French and Indian War, France lost almost all of its land in North America.

1. What parts of North America did Great Britain gain at the end of the war?
2. Which country claimed Louisiana?

Pontiac's request of his followers to "bury their hatchets" helped to end Pontiac's Rebellion in 1763.

the Proclamation of 1763. This proclamation, or official announcement, gave all land east of the Appalachians to the colonists. Lands west of the mountains would be set aside for Native Americans "as their hunting grounds." This would give control of the fur trade there to Britain.

The colonists did not like being closed off from the western lands and the fur trade. They were also beginning to dislike British rule.

agreement included the city of New Orleans, an important port in the French fur trade.

In 1763 Britain and France signed the Treaty of Paris, which officially ended the French and Indian War. As you can see from the maps on page 274, Great Britain gained almost all of France's lands in North America. Because Spain had been an ally of France in the war, Britain also gained the Spanish colony of Florida.

Pontiac's Rebellion

When the war ended, British colonists again began moving west into the Ohio River valley. An Ottawa chief named Pontiac (PAHN tee ak) urged the Native Americans there to "drive off your land those . . . who will do you nothing but harm."

Pontiac asked the Native Americans of the Ohio Valley to unite in order to fight the British. In 1763 they captured and burned British settlements but were soon defeated by the British army.

WHY IT MATTERS

Pontiac's Rebellion made King George III realize that protecting the colonists from conflict with Native Americans would be costly. As a result, he issued

Reviewing Facts and Ideas

MAIN IDEAS

- In 1754 Britain and France began fighting for control of the Ohio River valley in the French and Indian War.

- By winning the war in 1763, Britain gained control of Florida, Canada, and almost all of New France.

- In response to Pontiac's Rebellion, George III issued the Proclamation of 1763, which granted the rights to lands in the Ohio River valley to the Native Americans who lived there.

THINK ABOUT IT

1. Why were the British soldiers easy targets at Fort Duquesne?

2. Why did Native Americans unite under Pontiac to fight the British?

3. **FOCUS** How did North America change as a result of the French and Indian War?

4. **THINKING SKILL** Based upon the maps shown on page 274, what _conclusions_ can you make about France's influence in North America?

5. **WRITE** Write a letter to a relative from the point of view of a British colonist in 1754. Explain how the French and Indian War is affecting your life.

CHAPTER 10 REVIEW

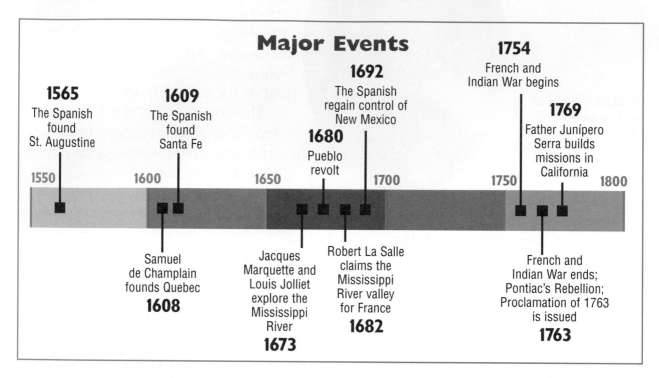

Major Events

1565 The Spanish found St. Augustine

1609 The Spanish found Santa Fe

1692 The Spanish regain control of New Mexico

1680 Pueblo revolt

1754 French and Indian War begins

1769 Father Junípero Serra builds missions in California

1550   1600   1650   1700   1750   1800

Samuel de Champlain founds Quebec **1608**

Jacques Marquette and Louis Jolliet explore the Mississippi River **1673**

Robert La Salle claims the Mississippi River valley for France **1682**

French and Indian War ends; Pontiac's Rebellion; Proclamation of 1763 is issued **1763**

THINKING ABOUT VOCABULARY

Number a paper from 1 to 5. Beside each number write the word or term from the list below that matches the description.

mission   Proclamation of 1763
Pontiac's Rebellion   voyageurs
portage

1. A settlement where missionaries lived and worked

2. An official announcement that gave all the land east of the Appalachian Mountains to the colonists and set aside the land west of the mountains for the Native Americans

3. People who transported furs by canoe for shipment to France

4. An attempt by united Native Americans to drive British colonists out of the Ohio River valley

5. A land route from one body of water to another

THINKING ABOUT FACTS

1. What was the purpose of the Spanish missions?

2. What route connected Spain's colonies in the Southwest to Mexico?

3. What agreement did Diego de Vargas make with the Pueblo people?

4. Why were French colonists slow to settle in New France in the 1600s?

5. What was the most important economic activity of the French in New France? What role did Native Americans play in this activity?

6. Who were the coureurs de bois?

7. What were the causes of the French and Indian War?

8. What did the British gain by the Treaty of Paris in 1763?

9. How was Louisiana claimed at the end of the French and Indian War?

10. Look at the time line above. What events happened in 1763? How were they related?

WRITING A LIST

Using an atlas, write a list of places in the United States that have Native American and Spanish names. Then find out what these names mean in English.

WRITING A TRAVEL LOG

Suppose that you are joining Marquette and Jolliet on their explorations. Write a log entry about what you might expect to find in your travels. Then write a log entry about what you actually find.

WRITING A LETTER

Suppose that you are a soldier defending either Fort Duquesne or Fort Necessity during the French and Indian War in 1754. Write a letter to someone at home describing the actions taking place.

APPLYING THINKING SKILLS

MAKING CONCLUSIONS

Answer the questions below to practice the skill of making conclusions.

1. What is a conclusion?

2. After identifying the subject of the information, what should your next step be in making a conclusion?

3. Suppose that you have not heard the weather report for the day, but you see everyone on your street is carrying umbrellas. What conclusion would you make about the weather forecast?

4. From the information about the Pueblo revolt in this chapter, what conclusion can you make about the importance of unity during a conflict? What evidence leads you to this conclusion?

5. Why is it important to make conclusions about the information you read?

Summing Up the Chapter

Copy the conclusion chart on a separate piece of paper. Then review the chapter to complete the chart. After you have finished, use the information in the chart to answer the question "What are the differences and similarities between how the Spanish, French, and English settled in North America?"

TOPIC	CONCLUSION	EVIDENCE
The Spanish and the Pueblo	The Spanish and the Pueblo are often in conflict.	
French relations with Native Americans	The French usually relate to the Native Americans , in ways different from most Europeans.	
The French and Indian War	The French and Indian War has a major influence on the history of North America.	

UNIT 4 REVIEW

THINKING ABOUT VOCABULARY

Number a paper from 1 to 10. Beside each number write the word or term from the list below that best completes the sentence.

almanac
Conestoga
coureurs de bois
covenant
fall line

import
King Philip's War
overseer
Pontiac's Rebellion
Treaty of Paris

1. The _____ officially ended the French and Indian War in 1763.

2. Each Puritan "free man" signed a _____, or special promise or agreement, to follow Puritan rules.

3. To _____ means to bring goods from another country for sale or use.

4. The _____ trapped furs in New France without the permission of the French government.

5. The people called the Pennsylvania Dutch built a large covered wagon called a _____ to carry their farm goods to market.

6. In 1675 a conflict called _____ began between Native Americans and the New England colonists.

7. The boss of a plantation was called an _____ .

8. During _____, Native Americans of the Ohio River valley united to try to force the British out of western lands.

9. The drop in elevation from the foothills of the Appalachian Mountains to the flatter land along the coast is called the _____ .

10. Benjamin Franklin wrote an _____, a reference book containing facts, figures, and witty stories.

THINK AND WRITE

WRITING A DESCRIPTION

Suppose you are a visitor to Philadelphia in 1775. Write a description of some of the things you find there.

WRITING A JOURNAL

Suppose you are traveling to one of the British colonies in the 1700s. Write a journal entry in which you describe the voyage. Then write an entry about what you find when you arrive. Include the name and description of the colony to which you have come in the entry.

WRITING ABOUT PERSPECTIVES

Reread the Making a Difference feature on page 251. Then think about how a person your age who lived in the 1700s would have viewed the events you read about in this chapter. Write a diary entry in which you describe one of the chapter events from a young person's point of view.

BUILDING SKILLS

1. **Elevation and relief** Look at the map on page 214. At what elevation is the city of Rochester?

2. **Elevation and relief** Look at the same map. What happens to the elevation as you travel west of the Hudson River?

3. **Climographs** Identify three purposes for which climographs are used.

4. **Climographs** Look at the climographs on pages 242–243. Which city has the coldest winters? Which city has the wettest summers?

5. **Conclusions** If you have many pieces of information about a topic, what do you look for before making a conclusion?

YESTERDAY, TODAY & TOMORROW

In this unit you learned about people who moved to new lands for a variety of reasons. Why did the Puritans sail for North America? Why did some colonists move from the coast to the backcountry? What are some reasons that people move today? Will there be different reasons for people to move to new homes in the future?

READING ON YOUR OWN

Here are some books you might find at the library to help you learn more.

ANNE HUTCHINSON: RELIGIOUS LEADER
by Elizabeth Ilgenfritz

The biography describes a leader who raised the question of religious tolerance.

COLONIAL LIFE
by Bobbie Kalman

The photos and text about the colonial time period make you feel as though you are there.

BENJAMIN FRANKLIN: PRINTER, INVENTOR, STATESMAN
by David A. Adler

This fascinating biography is filled with stories and other accounts of Franklin's many outstanding accomplishments.

UNIT 4 REVIEW PROJECT

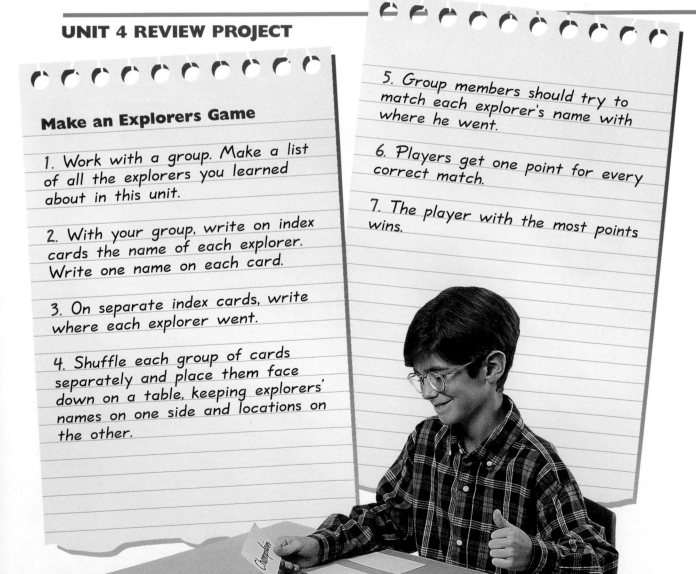

Make an Explorers Game

1. Work with a group. Make a list of all the explorers you learned about in this unit.

2. With your group, write on index cards the name of each explorer. Write one name on each card.

3. On separate index cards, write where each explorer went.

4. Shuffle each group of cards separately and place them face down on a table, keeping explorers' names on one side and locations on the other.

5. Group members should try to match each explorer's name with where he went.

6. Players get one point for every correct match.

7. The player with the most points wins.

279

PATRIOT DRUM

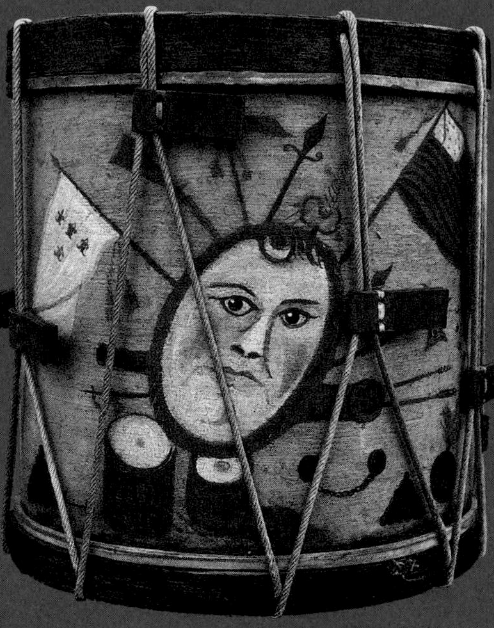

GEORGE WASHINGTON

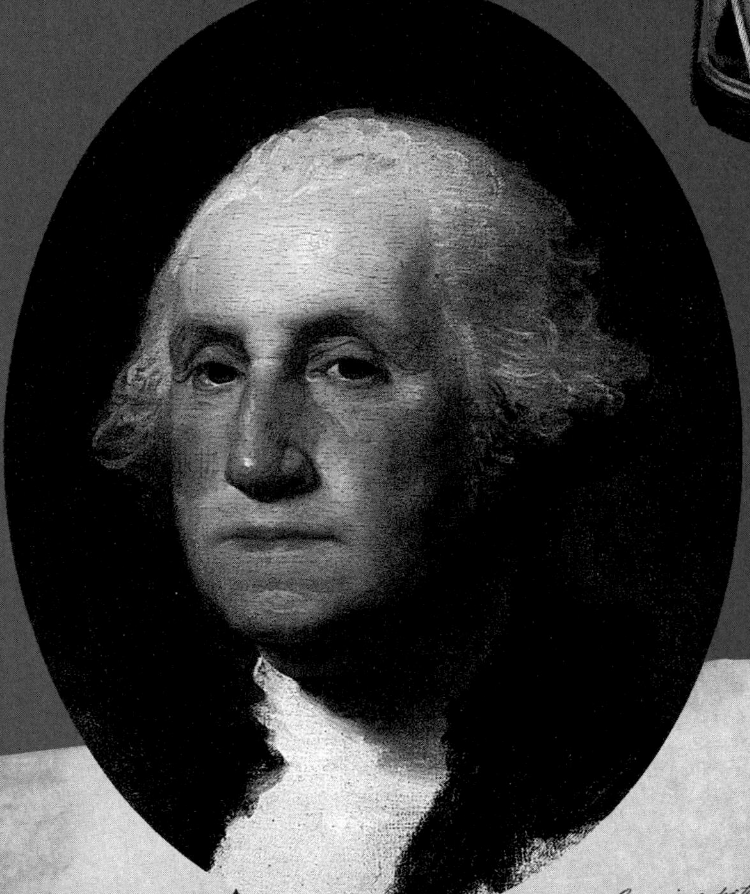

Museum of Fine Arts, Boston

MINUTEMAN OF CONCORD; UNITED STATES CONSTITUTION

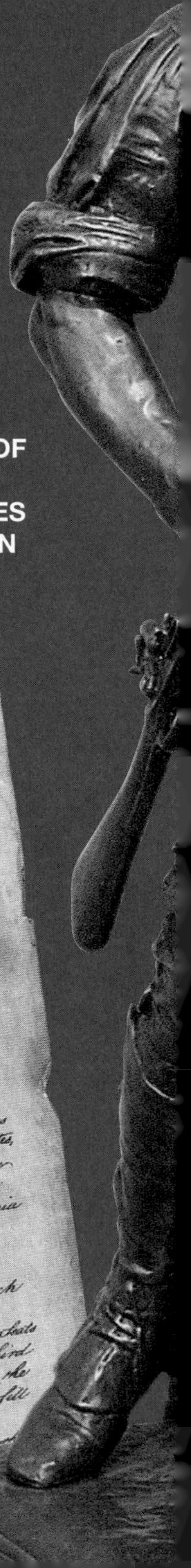

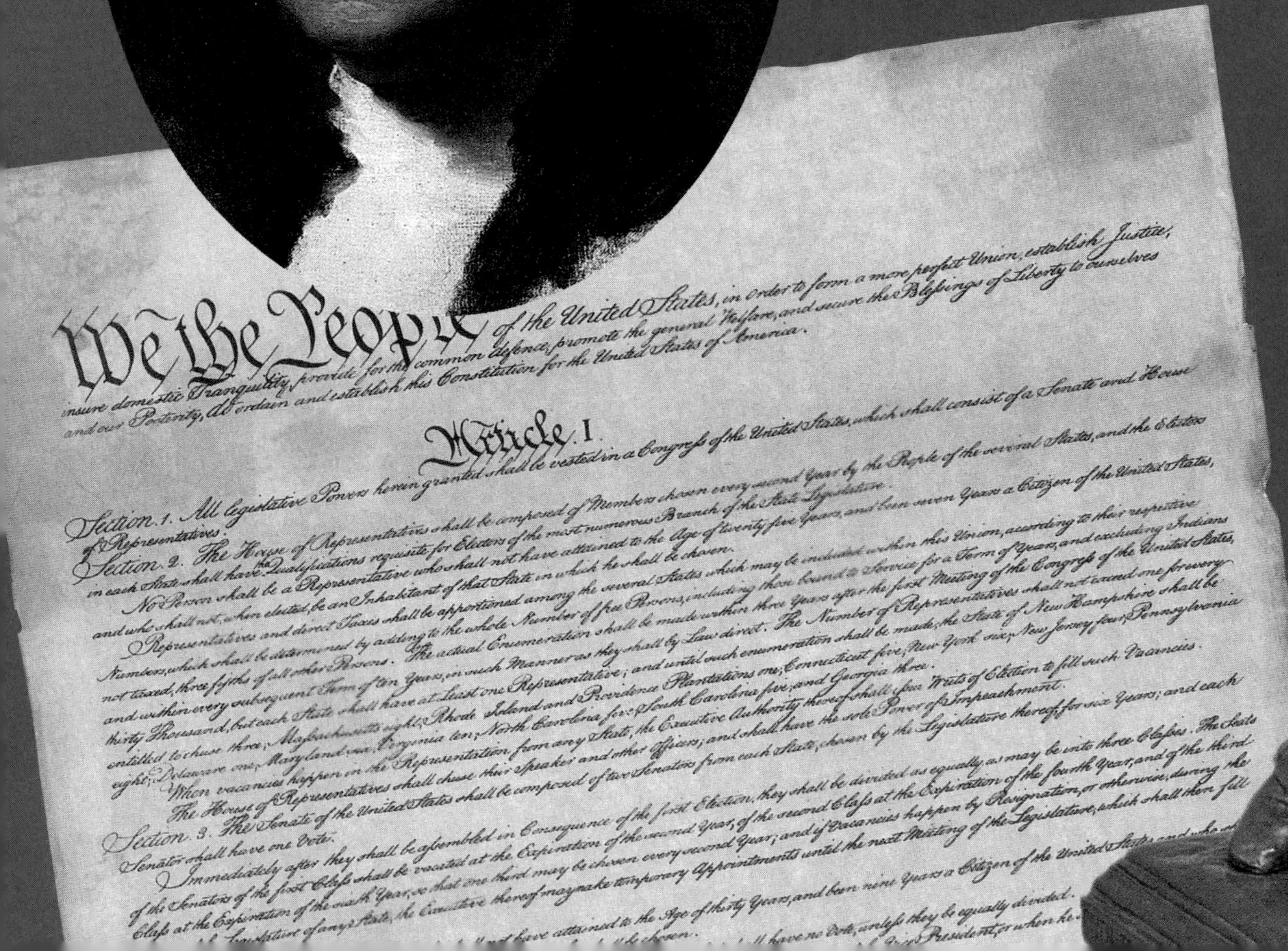

We the People of the United States, in Order to form a more perfect Union, establish Justice, insure domestic Tranquility, provide for the common defence, promote the general Welfare, and secure the Blessings of Liberty to ourselves and our Posterity, do ordain and establish this Constitution for the United States of America.

Article. I

Section. 1. All legislative Powers herein granted shall be vested in a Congress of the United States, which shall consist of a Senate and House of Representatives.

Section. 2. The House of Representatives shall be composed of Members chosen every second Year by the People of the several States, and the Electors in each State shall have the Qualifications requisite for Electors of the most numerous Branch of the State Legislature.

No Person shall be a Representative who shall not have attained to the Age of twenty five Years, and been seven Years a Citizen of the United States, and who shall not, when elected, be an Inhabitant of that State in which he shall be chosen.

Representatives and direct Taxes shall be apportioned among the several States which may be included within this Union, according to their respective Numbers, which shall be determined by adding to the whole Number of free Persons, including those bound to Service for a Term of Years, and excluding Indians not taxed, three fifths of all other Persons. The actual Enumeration shall be made within three Years after the first Meeting of the Congress of the United States, and within every subsequent Term of ten Years, in such Manner as they shall by Law direct. The Number of Representatives shall not exceed one for every thirty Thousand, but each State shall have at Least one Representative; and until such enumeration shall be made, the State of New Hampshire shall be entitled to chuse three, Massachusetts eight, Rhode Island and Providence Plantations one, Connecticut five, New York six, New Jersey four, Pennsylvania eight, Delaware one, Maryland six, Virginia ten, North Carolina five, South Carolina five, and Georgia three.

When vacancies happen in the Representation from any State, the Executive Authority thereof shall issue Writs of Election to fill such Vacancies.

The House of Representatives shall chuse their Speaker and other Officers; and shall have the sole Power of Impeachment.

Section. 3. The Senate of the United States shall be composed of two Senators from each State, chosen by the Legislature thereof for six Years; and each Senator shall have one Vote.

Immediately after they shall be assembled in Consequence of the first Election, they shall be divided as equally as may be into three Classes. The Seats of the Senators of the first Class shall be vacated at the Expiration of the second Year, of the second Class at the Expiration of the fourth Year, and of the third Class at the Expiration of the sixth Year, so that one third may be chosen every second Year; and if Vacancies happen by Resignation, or otherwise, during the Recess of the Legislature of any State, the Executive thereof may make temporary Appointments until the next Meeting of the Legislature, which shall then fill

... attained to the Age of thirty Years, and been nine Years a Citizen of the United States ...

... shall be chosen. ... have no Vote, unless they be equally divided. ... President, or when he ...

Independence and New Government

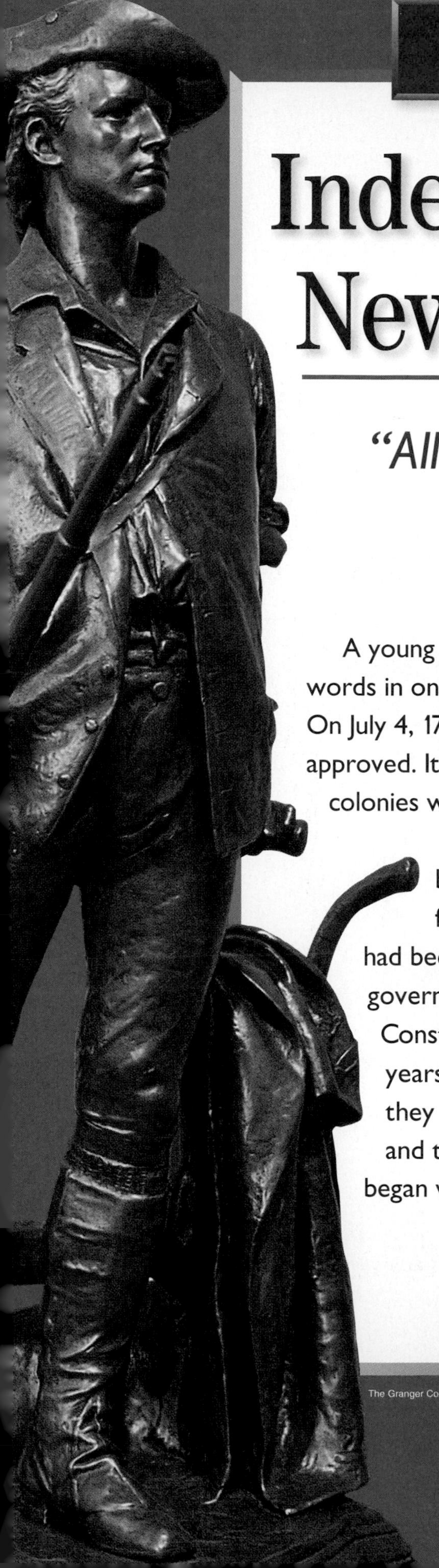

"All men are created equal"

from the Declaration of Independence
See page 316.

Why Does it Matter?

A young Virginian named Thomas Jefferson wrote these words in one of our country's most important documents. On July 4, 1776, the Declaration of Independence was approved. It explained to the world why the American colonies were breaking away from Great Britain.

In 1776 the war for independence had already begun. After six long years the British were finally defeated. The newly independent colonies had become states and needed to create their own government. It was no easy task. In 1789 the Constitution of the United States was accepted. Two years later, the Bill of Rights was added. Together they set down the responsibilities of the government and the rights of the people. A new government began working to build the young United States.

The Granger Collection

FIND OUT MORE!
Visit our website:
www.mhschool.com

*inter*NET
CONNECTION

TOUGH Times

"**I** lay here two nights ... and had not a morsel of anything to eat." Keep that sad sentence in mind as you look over Valley Forge, where General George Washington and some 12,000 soldiers shivered through the winter of 1777–1778. Today, history buffs come to march across these fields. Even when the place is blanketed with snow, it's hard to picture that terrible winter. But imagine you're a soldier whose shoes wore out weeks ago. An officer whose men grow thinner each day. A commander in chief— sitting at a desk in a stranger's house— wondering how your ragtag army can survive, let alone battle the mighty British.

GEO JOURNAL

Imagine getting a letter from that young soldier who hadn't eaten. How would you reply?

Breaking Ties with Great Britain

THINKING ABOUT HISTORY AND GEOGRAPHY

The story of Chapter 11 begins in New York City in 1735. John Peter Zenger, a printer, was one of the first colonists to help establish freedom of the press. For the next 50 years colonists in North America moved toward independence from Great Britain. The time line shows some of the events that led to the birth of the United States of America.

1735

1770

1773

NEW YORK CITY
The trial of printer John Peter Zenger establishes freedom of the press

BOSTON
Protests by Crispus Attucks and other colonists lead to the Boston Massacre

BOSTON HARBOR
Colonists dressed as the Mohawk take part in the Boston Tea Party

1735

1770

1772

NORTH
AMERICA

THE BRITISH
COLONIES

ATLANTIC
OCEAN

Boston
Harbor

Lexington

Boston

New York City

Williamsburg

1775

WILLIAMSBURG
Patrick Henry urges the
House of Burgesses to
vote for war with Britain

1775

LEXINGTON
Paul Revere warns
colonists of a British
attack

1774

1776

1700   1725   **1730**   **1770**   1775   1800

The Road to Self-Government

Focus Activity

READ TO LEARN

How did the colonists begin to govern themselves?

VOCABULARY

- assembly
- town meeting
- militia
- delegate

PEOPLE

- Thomas Jefferson
- Richard Henry Lee
- John Adams
- John Peter Zenger
- Phillis Wheatley

PLACES

- Williamsburg

Read Aloud

In 1741 angry members of the Massachusetts assembly tried to remove Governor Jonathan Belcher from office. The king of England had appointed Belcher, but the assembly members did not like him. The governor, in turn, complained about the members. They think, he said, "that they are as big as the Parliament of Great Britain."

THE BIG PICTURE

As you read in Chapter 9, the population of the colonies grew dramatically in the 1700s. As the colonies grew they gained experience in governing themselves. The colonists had been creating their own governing bodies and laws since the early 1600s. Some followed their own written laws, such as the Mayflower Compact. Most used English laws, such as "innocent until proven guilty," to govern themselves. They modeled their colonial **assemblies**, or law-making bodies, on Parliament. Parliament is Britain's law-making body.

As you read in Chapter 7, the first meeting of Virginia's assembly, the House of Burgesses, took place at the church in Jamestown in 1619. This first colonial assembly served as a model for other colonial assemblies. In this lesson you will read about the colonists' growing desire for self-government. You will also read about how this desire led to the founding of some of the important rights that we enjoy in our country today.

COLONIAL GOVERNMENT

Laws affecting each colony were made by the colonial assemblies. In the New England Colonies, the town meeting was the earliest form of self-government. The town meeting was a group of male colonists who got together to solve local problems.

In other colonies men created written plans for government. These plans spelled out important rights that the colonists would have. The chart on this page lists some of these plans for government in the colonies.

Royal Governors

Eight of the 13 colonies were ruled by royal governors. A royal governor was not elected by the colonists. Instead he was chosen by the king of England. Royal governors saw that the colony obeyed British laws. Sometimes the governor and the assembly disagreed on which laws had to be obeyed. If the governor found the assembly unwilling to support him, he could dissolve, or shut down, the assembly.

Assembly members could, in return, refuse to vote for money for the governor's plans. "Let us keep the dogs poor and we'll make them do what we please," one New Jersey assembly member said of the governors. The royal governors did not always have the same view as the assembly members.

PLANS FOR GOVERNMENT IN THE COLONIES, 1600s

Year	Plan	Description
1620	*Mayflower Compact*	A written agreement to make laws for the Plymouth colony
1639	*Fundamental Orders of Connecticut*	A written plan for government that gave the right to vote to free men who owned property in Connecticut
1649	*Maryland Toleration Act*	A law giving religious freedom to all Christians in Maryland
1682	*Pennsylvania Frame of Government*	A written plan for government that granted religious freedom to colonists in Pennsylvania

City of Norfolk, VA/The Chrysler Museum

CHART WORK

At right is a 1753 mace from Norfolk, Virginia. The mace, a club-shaped staff, has been used by law-making bodies since the 1300s to call an assembly to order. A mace is still used today in the United States House of Representatives.

1. Which plans for government granted Christian colonists freedom of religion?
2. Which plans for government were written for two of New England's colonies?

THE VIRGINIA HOUSE OF BURGESSES

In 1624 King James of Britain had made Virginia a royal colony and appointed a royal governor to rule the colony. The House of Burgesses still had some power. It could, for example, decide whether to divide large counties into smaller ones. It could also make laws about the sale of tobacco. By the middle of the 1700s, the colonial burgesses had gained much valuable experience in self-government.

The Talented Burgesses

On a spring day in 1769, Thomas Jefferson traveled to Williamsburg, Virginia's capital. Only 26 years old, the young planter and lawyer had just been elected burgess. Jefferson judged the House of Burgesses to be "the most dignified body of men ever assembled to [make laws]."

Most of the burgesses were wealthy planters. George Washington and Richard Henry Lee served as burgesses. They felt it was their duty to help govern the colony. But sometimes the assembly could try their patience. Lee, who served from 1758 to 1776, admitted to his brother his disappointment about not getting much work done:

> *I find the attendance on Assemblies so expensive, and the power of doing good so rarely occurring, that I am determined to quit.*

Many burgesses also tired of the many procedures connected to government. Formal ceremonies took up most of Jefferson's first day in office.

Members of the Virginia House of Burgesses met in this room (left) in the 1700s. They wore wigs while there.

The House of Burgesses did make some important laws for the colony. The burgesses had the power to print money, call for taxes, build roads, and make land laws. They also had the power to prepare for war and raise money to support the colony's militia. A colonial militia was a military force made up of volunteers. The militia was similar to today's National Guard, which is made up of citizen soldiers.

A Model for the Colonies

By 1760 Virginia's assembly was the model for colonial government. Every colony had elected an assembly like the House of Burgesses. To be elected, a delegate, or member of the assembly, had to meet several requirements. A delegate had to be an adult white male. In most colonies he also had to own a certain amount of land and follow the Protestant faith. Thus in most colonies women, African Americans, Catholics, Jews, and Native Americans could not be elected.

Most of the delegates were wealthy merchants or lawyers. In 1770 a lawyer named John Adams was elected to the Massachusetts assembly. Benjamin Franklin was pleased to serve in the Pennsylvania assembly. Franklin wrote that he was "flattered."

Early Colonial Elections

Elections in the 1600s and 1700s were noisy, social occasions. An election "causes a Hubbub for a week or so," wrote one Virginia colonist. He explained that to Virginians used to "dull barbecues and yet duller dances," an election was quite an event.

Thomas Jefferson (left) was painted by the artist C. W. Peale. Richard Henry Lee (below) was also a strong supporter of the colonies' rights.

On election day men from all over the county gathered at the court house or village common. Voters looked forward to the punch, cookies, and cakes given by the candidates. George Washington provided similar food and drink during his first election to the Virginia House of Burgesses in 1758.

Unlike today's secret voting, each voter spoke his choice in front of a large crowd. Loud cheers or boos followed each vote. The candidates often personally thanked a voter for his vote.

289

ESTABLISHING FREEDOMS

In their assemblies colonial delegates spoke up for the freedom to rule themselves. The growing spirit of freedom also influenced the press, or news publications in the colonies.

John Peter Zenger

In 1733 a few members of the New York assembly started a newspaper called the *New York Weekly Journal*. They hired John Peter Zenger, a German immigrant, as its printer. Zenger printed stories that criticized New York's royal governor, William Cosby. One story in the newspaper accused Cosby of being dishonest.

In 1734 the New York sheriff, who supported the governor, burned copies of the paper and put Zenger in jail. The governor accused Zenger of publishing remarks attacking the government.

A lawyer named Andrew Hamilton defended Zenger at his trial in 1735. He argued that Zenger could not be punished for printing stories that were true, even if they were about the governor. Every person had a right, Hamilton said, "publicly to

Phillis Wheatley (above) urged colonists to end slavery. Zenger's trial (left) established freedom of speech.

THE·TRIAL·OF·JOHN·PETER·ZENGER·FOR·LIBEL RESULTING·IN·THE·VICTORY·FOR·FREE·PRESS·AUG·4·1735 [oppose] the abuses of power . . . of men in authority."

The jury agreed with Hamilton and found Zenger not guilty. Zenger's victory helped establish an important right, freedom of speech. This right meant that colonists could speak or print the truth without fear of being put in jail.

African Americans Speak Out

Enslaved African Americans took special note of the growing calls for freedom. Alone and in groups, they had long fought to be free from slavery.

One African American who wrote of liberty was Phillis Wheatley. Born in what is now the country of Senegal in West Africa, she was kidnapped and brought to the colonies at the age of eight. Wheatley was then sold as a slave to John Wheatley in Boston. It was common for enslaved people to be given the last name of their owner.

Mr. and Mrs. Wheatley taught young Phillis to read and write English. In 1773 she published a book of poetry while she was still enslaved. Wheatley urged the colonists to free their slaves. "In every human . . . God has implanted a principle, which we call love of freedom," she wrote. "The same principle lives in us."

WHY IT MATTERS

Since their earliest beginnings the 13 colonies practiced some form of self-government. Far from the king of England, the colonists formed town meetings and assemblies and created laws to govern themselves. These laws showed the colonists' desire to be free to live as they chose. These strong beliefs in freedom and self-government would later shape the new government of the United States.

Links to **LANGUAGE ARTS**

The Power of Poetry

Why are Phillis Wheatley's poems remembered today?

People who are not free to do or say what they want sometimes write down their feelings to make them known. Phillis Wheatley was enslaved, and she could not vote. She used poetry to express her opinions about slavery. Find a poem at home or in your library that you think has a message. Share the poems aloud in class and talk about their meanings.

✓ Reviewing Facts and Ideas

MAIN IDEAS

- The early colonial assemblies helped to establish self-government in the 13 colonies.

- Assemblies such as the House of Burgesses made laws to print money, collect taxes, build roads, make land laws, and organize colonial militias.

- John Peter Zenger's trial in 1735 won support for the right to freedom of speech in the colonies.

THINK ABOUT IT

1. What were some of the colonies' earliest written plans for government?

2. Who could be elected to serve in the colonial assemblies?

3. **FOCUS** What were the major duties of the colonial assemblies?

4. **THINKING SKILL** How would the jury have determined which parts of John Peter Zenger's stories contained *facts* and which contained *opinions?*

5. **WRITE** Write a short speech that a British colonist might have written in support of self-government.

1700   1725   1750   1760   1780   1800

The 13 Colonies Rebel

Read Aloud

Hanging from the Liberty Tree, a tall elm in the center of Boston, was a straw puppet of a British tax collector. The colonists were furious about a new tax the British government wanted them to pay. This disagreement was only one of many conflicts between Britain and the 13 colonies that began after the French and Indian War.

Focus Activity

READ TO LEARN

What led the colonies to rebel against Great Britain?

VOCABULARY

- liberty
- rebel
- Stamp Act
- treason
- Sons of Liberty
- repeal
- Townshend Acts
- boycott
- Committees of Correspondence
- Boston Tea Party
- Intolerable Acts

PEOPLE

- Patrick Henry
- Samuel Adams
- Mercy Otis Warren
- Crispus Attucks
- Abigail Adams

THE BIG PICTURE

What is liberty? The word liberty means "freedom." To the colonists liberty came to mean the freedom to govern themselves.

As you read in Chapter 10, the British government did not allow colonists to move onto lands west of the Appalachian Mountains after the French and Indian War. This angered some colonists. A new tax angered them even more. The British government was deeply in debt and needed to pay for the royal governors and British troops it had sent to North America.

The colonists angrily told the British that Parliament had no right to tax them without the vote of the delegates in their own assemblies. Cries of "Taxation without representation is tyranny" filled the streets. Tyranny is the cruel and unfair use of force or power.

These and other conflicts would soon lead the 13 colonies to rebel against the British government. To rebel is to refuse to obey those in charge because of different ideas about what is right.

ENGLAND TIGHTENS ITS GRIP

After the French and Indian War, the British found that governing and defending its new larger empire was difficult. Taxing the colonists seemed like an easy solution to one problem.

The Stamp Act

The Stamp Act of 1765 was one of the first British laws placing taxes on the colonies. The colonists had to pay a tax every time they bought a newspaper or pamphlet or signed a legal document. These items had to have a stamp on them to show that the tax had been paid.

In Virginia a burgess from the back-country named Patrick Henry spoke to the assembly. He said that anyone who paid the stamp tax was an enemy of Virginia. Another burgess accused Henry of treason. Treason is the betrayal of one's country by giving help to one of its enemies. "If this be treason," Henry replied, "make the most of it." Henry's speeches against the Stamp Act were later published in colonial newspapers. His words inspired many colonists to protest against the Stamp Act.

The Colonists Fight Back

To fight the hated Stamp Act, some colonists formed the Sons of Liberty. The Sons of Liberty were groups of colonists who organized protests against the British government. One member, Samuel Adams, wrote news articles for the Boston newspapers attacking the Stamp Act. Sam Adams was a cousin of John Adams.

In other cities the "liberty boys," as they were called, attacked British tax agents. These protests forced some stamp-tax agents to quit their jobs.

In October 1765 delegates from nine colonies attended a Stamp Act Congress. They decided that Parliament could not tax the colonies without their consent. They demanded that the Stamp Act be repealed, or canceled. A year later, Parliament repealed the Stamp Act.

The Sons of Liberty set up a rally (below) to protest the use of tax stamps like this one (right).

The Granger Collection

TROUBLES IN BOSTON

The repeal of the Stamp Act did not end the troubles between Britain and the 13 colonies. Barely a year after the Stamp Act was repealed, Parliament passed another law taxing the colonies. The city of Boston became the center of protest against the new tax.

The Townshend Acts

Charles Townshend (TOWN shund), the treasurer of the British government, called for new taxes in 1767. Parliament then passed the Townshend Acts, which said the colonists had to pay taxes on all the tea, paper, glass, lead, and paint that they imported from Britain.

In Boston the colonists held a town meeting to protest the new taxes. The

Colonists opposing the British often met in Mercy Otis Warren's home. She later wrote a history of how the colonies rebelled.

Museum of Fine Arts, Boston

colonists decided to make a list of all the British goods they would boycott, or refuse to buy. To boycott means to refuse to do business or have contact with a person, group, or country.

Women formed groups called the Daughters of Liberty to support the boycott. The Daughters of Liberty held "spinning bees" to spin thread so that they would not have to import clothes from Britain. The women, wrote one colonial newspaper, act "with the men in contributing to . . . their country and equally share in the honor of it."

Poet and playwright Mercy Otis Warren encouraged women to give up tea and the other goods from Britain. We should make "a small sacrifice," she wrote. "We'll quit the useless vanities [luxuries] of life."

The Boston Massacre

Boston soon faced even bigger conflicts. Warren and other Bostonians expected trouble when British troops marched into town in October 1768. That was the first time soldiers had been sent to control the colonists.

Boston residents grew angry as soldiers began their noisy drills and set up guard posts around the city. Some colonists picked fights with the soldiers. Young boys called the soldiers "lobsters" because of their red uniforms and threw snowballs at them.

The growing anger finally boiled over on March 5, 1770. Church bells rang as a large group of colonists met outside the Customs House. Crispus Attucks, a former slave, yelled to the crowd, "The way to get rid of these soldiers is to attack the main guard." In the confusion that followed, the British soldiers fired. Five men were killed, including Attucks.

The BLOODY MASSACRE perpetrated in King——Street BOSTON on March 5th 1770 by a party of the 29th REGT.

Engrav'd Printed & Sold by PAUL REVERE BOSTON

Unhappy Boston! see thy Sons deplore,
Thy hallow'd Walks besmear'd with guiltless Gore
While faithless P——n and his savage Bands,
With murdrous Rancour stretch their bloody
Like fierce Barbarians grinning o'er their
Approve the Carnage, and enjoy the

The unhappy Sufferers were
Killed Six wou

If scalding drops from Rage from Anguish Wrung
Sorrows lab'ring for a Tongue
World can ought appease
fts of Victims such as these:
'Tears for each are shed,
hich embalms the Dead

But know, Fate summons to that awful Goal,
where Justice strips the Murd'rer of his Soul.
Should venal C——ts the scandal of the Land,
Snatch the relentless Villain from her Hand,
Keen Execrations on this Plate inscrib'd,
Shall reach a Judge who never can be brib'd.

MAVERICK, JAMS CALDWELL, CRISPUS ATTUCKS & PATK CARR
ST. MONK & JOHN CLARK) Mortally

The Granger Collection

Sam Adams (left) and John Adams (above right) led the colonists' early struggles. The Boston Massacre (above), engraved by Paul Revere, horrified many colonists.

The people of Boston were horrified at the killings. The soldiers were arrested. John Adams agreed to defend them. Although he did not want British soldiers in Boston, Adams believed the soldiers should have a fair trial.

The Committees of Correspondence

A major step toward uniting the colonies came through the Committees of Correspondence. In October 1772 Sam Adams asked the members of a Boston town meeting to form a committee "to state the rights of the colonists." By 1774 all of the colonies except Pennsylvania had formed their own Committees of Correspondence. The committees of each colony wrote to each other to inform colonists about important political events in the colonies.

John Adams was also a founder of the Committees of Correspondence. Adams believed that keeping people informed was a very important goal of the committees. He wrote:

Liberty cannot be preserved without a general knowledge among the people, who have a right . . . and a desire to know . . . the characters and conduct of their rulers.

COLONISTS REBEL

After the Boston Massacre some colonists wondered whether they would have to defend their liberty in battle. Although Parliament agreed to repeal the Townshend Acts, it kept the tax on tea. The colonies began to unite in order to fight this hated tax.

The Boston Tea Party

In 1773 British ships carrying thousands of pounds of tea sailed across the Atlantic Ocean to Boston and other colonial ports. In early December, Abigail Adams, the wife of John Adams, reported that the colonists were preparing a protest:

> The Tea . . . is arrived. . . . I hope [effective] opposition had been made to the landing of it. . . . The flame is kindled [lit] and like Lightning it catches from Soul to Soul.

In fact, on a quiet December night, a group of colonists disguised as Mohawks crept toward Boston Harbor. "Boston Harbor will be a teapot tonight!" they shouted. They then boarded a ship and dumped 342 chests of valuable tea into the harbor.

John Adams wrote about the Boston Tea Party in his diary.

A VIEW OF PART OF THE TOWN OF BOSTON

American Nathaniel Currier later painted the Boston Tea Party in his work *The Destruction of Tea at Boston Harbor* (above). The Boston Tea Party led King George III (above right) to blockade Boston Harbor (right).

296

The people should never rise without doing something to be remembered—something notable and striking. This destruction of the tea is so bold, so daring . . . that I can't but consider it as a [new and important period] in history.

Because the men were disguised, the governor did not know whom to charge for destroying the tea. When King George III learned of the "tea party" he demanded that Boston be punished.

In early 1774 Parliament decided to close the port of Boston until the colonists paid for the tea. Town meetings were banned. Parliament also ordered colonists to feed and house British soldiers in the colonies. The colonists called Parliament's actions the Intolerable Acts.

Unknown to the British, the Committees of Correspondence sent food and money to Boston. "Don't pay for an ounce of the . . . tea," they wrote. The committees then worked to decide on a united response to the Intolerable Acts.

WHY IT MATTERS

The colonists learned about the power of writing and organizing in the Committees of Correspondence, which helped them become more united. The committees saw that they could make Britain repeal some of its taxes. John Adams felt that the Committees of Correspondence had become "a great political engine" that would move the colonies closer toward liberty.

Reviewing Facts and Ideas

MAIN IDEAS

- To raise money after the French and Indian War, Parliament passed the Stamp Act in 1765 to collect taxes from the colonies.

- The Townshend Acts of 1767 made colonists pay taxes on many everyday products. After the Boston Massacre in 1770, the Committees of Correspondence were formed to tell colonists of important events.

- The Boston Tea Party led to Britain's strongest actions against the colonies, the Intolerable Acts of 1774.

THINK ABOUT IT

1. Why did many colonists oppose the Stamp Act?

2. How did the Sons and Daughters of Liberty oppose the Stamp Act and the Townshend Acts?

3. **FOCUS** What acts of the British Parliament caused the colonists to rebel?

4. **THINKING SKILL** What *effects* did the Committees of Correspondence have? Explain your answer.

5. **WRITE** Suppose you were a member of the Massachusetts Committee of Correspondence. Describe the Boston Tea Party and Intolerable Acts.

297

The Granger Collection

CARTOON A

Reading Political Cartoons

VOCABULARY
political cartoon
symbol

WHY THE SKILL MATTERS

The trial of John Peter Zenger helped to establish freedom of speech. One way that people in the 13 colonies expressed their opinions was through political cartoons that were printed in newspapers and pamphlets. A political cartoon is a drawing that expresses a cartoonist's opinion about people, political events, or newsworthy issues.

Have you ever drawn a picture to express how you feel about someone or some event? That is what a political cartoon does. Political cartoons deal with very serious issues, such as taxes and elections. Yet cartoonists often treat these issues in a humorous way.

Reading political cartoons can help you learn about the most important issues of a particular time, or in a particular city or country. Political cartoons give readers something to think about, or sometimes something to laugh about.

USING THE SKILL

Political cartoons often contain symbols that help get their message across to readers. A symbol is something that stands for something else. You know, for example, that the 50 stars of the United States flag stand for the 50 states.

Symbols can be hard to understand. Look at Cartoon A about the repeal of the Stamp Act in 1766. The small coffin one man is carrying is a symbol for the Stamp Act that has just been repealed, or "killed." The skulls are symbols for other taxes that the colonies had repealed. The men who are sad are British leaders who supported the Stamp Act. In the background, the ships stand for the trade that will begin again between Great Britain and America.

To help readers understand their drawings, some cartoonists use captions. Or they may use dialogue (DI uh lahg) in order to express their opinions in words. Dialogue is conversation. The caption of Cartoon A is the Repeal, Or the Funeral of Miss Ame-Stamp. It does not have any dialogue, but Cartoon B on this page does.

Helping yourself

- **A political cartoon** shows a cartoonist's opinion about a person, an event, or an issue.

- **To understand a political cartoon, look for symbols** and other clues. If there is dialogue, determine who is speaking.

TRYING THE SKILL

Look at Cartoon B. It was drawn in 1994. What is this cartoon about? It is like many cartoons that find fault with or praise people or events. What point is this cartoonist trying to make? Is this cartoon finding fault with or praising something?

REVIEWING THE SKILL

1. What is a political cartoon?
2. How does a political cartoon express its meaning?
3. What kinds of issues does a political cartoon cover?
4. Do you think political cartoons influence people? Explain your answer.
5. If you had to draw a political cartoon, what issue or person would you picture? What symbols would you use to express your opinion? Why?

Today, **political cartoons appear in a wide variety of magazines and newspapers.**

CARTOON B

1700   1725   1750   1770   1780   1800

The Revolution Begins

Focus Activity

READ TO LEARN

What happened in the first battles of the American Revolution?

VOCABULARY

- First Continental Congress
- petition
- minutemen
- American Revolution
- Battle of Bunker Hill

PEOPLE

- John Hancock
- Paul Revere
- William Dawes
- John Parker
- Ethan Allen
- Israel Putnam
- Peter Salem

PLACES

- Lexington
- Concord
- Fort Ticonderoga
- Charlestown

Read Aloud

"The colonies must either submit or triumph," spoke King George III. The King was sure that the colonies would "submit," or surrender, to the authority of the British government. However, many colonists agreed that now was the time to stand up to Britain and to unite the colonies.

THE BIG PICTURE

On September 5, 1774, delegates from every colony except Georgia met at Carpenter's Hall in Philadelphia. At this **First Continental Congress**, delegates wrote a petition to send to King George III asking for repeal of the Intolerable Acts. A petition is a written request signed by many people. The delegates argued that the Intolerable Acts were illegal and unfair. They also claimed that they had the right to make their own laws without Britain's approval.

To fight the Intolerable Acts, the delegates agreed to stop trade with Britain. They also asked the colonists to gather **minutemen** to defend the cities. Minutemen had to be ready for battle at a minute's notice. They were usually the best trained or most experienced soldiers.

The colonists felt that they needed the minutemen because the conflicts between the colonies and Britain might explode into war at any time. They were right. Within a year the colonists and the British would be fighting a war called the **American Revolution**. A revolution is a sudden, violent, or very great change.

PREPARING FOR WAR

By 1775 every able-bodied man in every colonial town was required to join the militia. Most of the militia members were farmers, craftsworkers, business owners, and wealthy men. Early in the Revolution some militias allowed both free and enslaved African Americans to join. Later most colonial militias refused to accept any African Americans.

The militias near Lexington were given orders "to be ready at the beat of the drum." The rumor was that the British were going to arrest Sam Adams and John Hancock, a leading Boston patriot. Then the British would march to Concord to capture weapons the militia had stored there.

Paul Revere

On the night of April 18, a silver-smith named Paul Revere learned that the British were leaving Boston and heading for Concord. Revere mounted his horse and rode to Lexington to warn Adams and Hancock. Revere's friend, William Dawes, a shoemaker, joined him on the way to Concord. Trace the routes of Revere and Dawes on the map below.

They were joined by a doctor named Samuel Prescott, who was returning home to Concord. A British patrol caught up with the men. The patrol took Revere's horse, but Dawes escaped into the woods. Prescott was the only one to reach Concord.

Revere's cry, "The British are coming!" is remembered today because of the opening lines from the poem "Paul Revere's Ride." Henry Wadsworth Longfellow wrote it in 1863:

*Listen, my children, and you shall hear
Of the midnight ride of Paul Revere.*

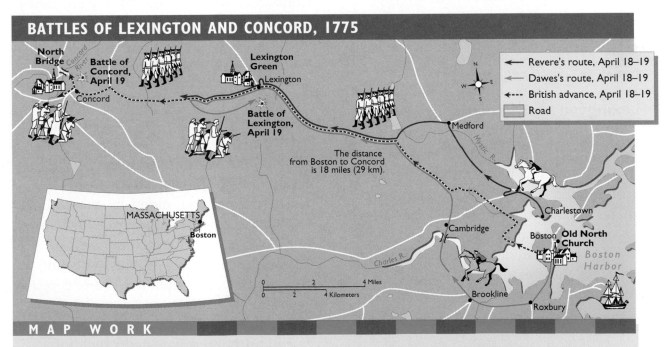

BATTLES OF LEXINGTON AND CONCORD, 1775

North Bridge • Battle of Concord, April 19 • Concord • Lexington Green • Lexington • Battle of Lexington, April 19

The distance from Boston to Concord is 18 miles (29 km).

Revere's route, April 18–19
Dawes's route, April 18–19
British advance, April 18–19
Road

Medford • Charlestown • Cambridge • Boston • Old North Church • Boston Harbor • Brookline • Roxbury

Mystic R. • Charles R.

MASSACHUSETTS • Boston

0   2   4 Miles
0   2   4 Kilometers

MAP WORK

Lexington and Concord were the first major battles of the American Revolution. Because of the warnings provided by Revere and Dawes, the colonists were able to move the weapons they had stored at Concord.

1. Through which cities did Revere ride? Dawes?
2. In which direction did the British travel?
3. Approximately how far is the city of Lexington from Concord?

A farmer at the Battle of Lexington (above) said, "We always had governed ourselves, and we always meant to."

THE FIRST SHOTS ARE FIRED

The night buzzed with activity after Paul Revere's ride. Minutemen galloped from their farms to Lexington. About 700 British redcoats marched toward the town. In the early morning hours of April 19, the first shots of the American Revolution were fired.

Lexington and Concord

With the British troops in view, the militia captain John Parker assembled about 70 men in Lexington. "Stand your ground!" he ordered them. "Don't fire unless fired upon, but if they mean to have a war, let it begin here."

The British advanced, and someone fired. As the Boston poet Ralph Waldo Emerson wrote years later:

> Here once the embattled farmers
>   stood,
> And fired the shot heard round
>   the world.

In the battle that followed, 8 militia men were killed, and 10 were wounded. Only one British soldier was hurt.

The British then marched 5 miles to Concord. Knowing that they were badly outnumbered, the 250 militia men waited for reinforcements as the British searched the town. The British only managed to destroy a cannon and a small amount of ammunition. The women of Concord kept the soldiers from finding most of the supplies. They had hidden them under straw in barns and in freshly plowed fields.

The minutemen, aided by the militias from other towns, came upon British soldiers blocking the bridge west of Concord. With musket balls whistling around them, the militia were ordered to fire "and not kill our own men." The colonists forced the British to retreat.

Hiding behind trees and buildings, the minutemen shot at the weary British soldiers who were retreating back toward Boston. More than 90 British soldiers were killed, and 174 were wounded.

"Liberty or Death"

Muskets were not the only weapons used against the British. In Virginia the fiery speeches of Patrick Henry convinced many in the House of Burgesses that a final break with Great Britain was near.

On March 23, 1775, Henry gave one of the most famous speeches in our country's history. He argued that the British troops were in Boston to take away the colonists' rights. "And what have we to oppose them?" he asked. Read the following excerpt from Henry's speech. What course of action did he suggest the colonies take?

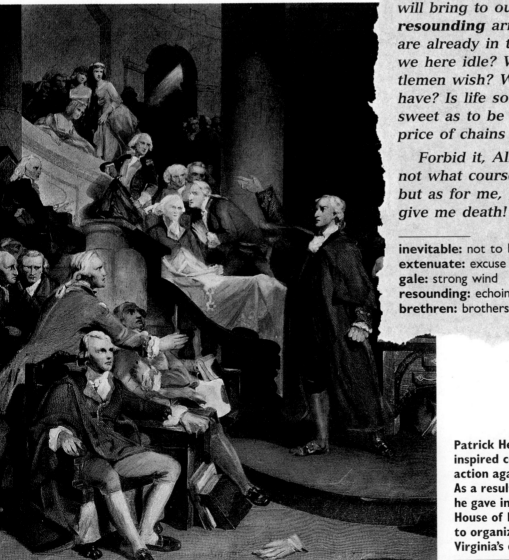

The Granger Collection

MANY VOICES
PRIMARY SOURCE

Excerpt from a speech by Patrick Henry before a meeting at St. John's Church, Richmond, Virginia, 1775.

There is no retreat but in submission and slavery! Our chains are forged. Their clanking may be heard on the plains of Boston! The war is **inevitable**—and let it come!! I repeat it, sir, let it come!!!

It is vain, sir, to **extenuate** the matter. Gentlemen may cry, peace, peace; but there is no peace. The war is actually begun! The next **gale** that sweeps from the north will bring to our ears the clash of **resounding** arms! Our **brethren** are already in the field! Why stand we here idle? What is it that gentlemen wish? What would they have? Is life so dear or peace so sweet as to be purchased at the price of chains and slavery?

Forbid it, Almighty God—I know not what course others may take; but as for me, give me liberty, or give me death!

---

inevitable: not to be avoided
extenuate: excuse
gale: strong wind
resounding: echoing
brethren: brothers

Patrick Henry's speeches inspired colonists to take action against the British. As a result of the speech he gave in 1775, the Virginia House of Burgesses voted to organize a militia for Virginia's defense.

CANNONS ROAR

Henry's powerful speech predicted the battles of the coming war. After Lexington and Concord, the Massachusetts minutemen kept up their attack on the British around Boston.

"Let the cannon roar," said an English lord. Then the colonists will run away "as fast as their feet will carry them." He was wrong.

The Fall of Fort Ticonderoga

While the minutemen surrounded Boston, a militia leader from Vermont named Ethan Allen set his sights on Fort Ticonderoga. This fort on Lake Champlain was one of the main supply posts for the British army.

The Green Mountain Boys served in the militia under Allen. The band of farmers who mostly made up this group included both blacks and whites.

Near dawn on May 10, 1775, the Green Mountain Boys crept past the

fort's light defenses. Allen woke the commander and demanded his surrender. "Come out of there, you old rat," he shouted. Without any bloodshed, the Americans had captured British cannons and cut off British support from Canada.

The Battle of Bunker Hill

In June some 1,200 militia around Boston were sent across the bay to Charlestown. Whoever controlled the

This painting, *Battle of Bunker Hill*, is by John Trumbull. Most of the fighting took place on Breed's Hill.

Yale University Art Gallery

Items carried by men in the colonial militia (left) included a flask, spoon, and plate for meals. They also used a lantern (center) for sending messages.

The Granger Collection

hills surrounding Charlestown would be able to fire cannons on Boston.

Through the night the colonists dug out a rough fort near Breed's Hill. By dawn the soldiers "began to be almost beat out," remembered one colonist, "being tired by our labor and having no sleep the night before." Then a British ship in the harbor began to fire its cannons at the exhausted men.

British troops marched on the fort after noon. "Don't fire till you see the whites of their eyes," ordered the colonial General Israel Putnam. The colonists bravely fought off two charges. But they ran out of ammunition, and a third charge forced them to retreat to nearby Bunker Hill. The British commander Colonel Pitcairn, who had fought the colonists at Lexington, leaped upon a wall of the fort to declare victory. Peter Salem, a former slave, killed him with a single shot.

In what was later called the Battle of Bunker Hill, the British "victory" cost them the lives of more than 1,000 soldiers. Although more than 400 colonists were also killed, they had proven their willingness to put up a hard fight.

WHY IT MATTERS

In the first battles between colonists and British troops, the colonial militias learned some of the skills they would need in the American Revolution. In the First Continental Congress the colonists gained experience in forming a government for a new country.

By 1775 the final break between Britain and its colonies had not yet come. Some colonists still hoped the British would repeal the Intolerable Acts and restore peace. Already colonial unity and military readiness showed the beginning of a new country—a country separate from Britain.

Reviewing Facts and Ideas

MAIN IDEAS

- The First Continental Congress met in 1774 to discuss the colonies' response to the Intolerable Acts.
- The first battles of the American Revolution were fought in Lexington and Concord on April 19, 1775.
- The capture of Fort Ticonderoga and the Battle of Bunker Hill in 1775 proved that the colonists were serious in their struggle against the British.

THINK ABOUT IT

1. What actions did the First Continental Congress decide to take?

2. What forces did the colonists have to defend themselves?

3. **FOCUS** What happened at the battles of Lexington and Concord?

4. **THINKING SKILL** List in *sequence* the events leading to the "shot heard round the world."

5. **GEOGRAPHY** Look at the map on page 301. What waterways did Revere and Dawes cross?

CHAPTER 11 REVIEW

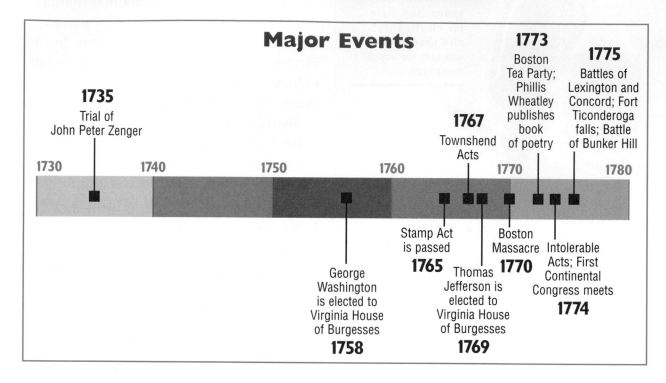

Major Events

1730 — **1740** — **1750** — **1760** — **1770** — **1780**

1735
Trial of John Peter Zenger

1773
Boston Tea Party; Phillis Wheatley publishes book of poetry

1775
Battles of Lexington and Concord; Fort Ticonderoga falls; Battle of Bunker Hill

1767
Townshend Acts

1758
George Washington is elected to Virginia House of Burgesses

1765
Stamp Act is passed

1769
Thomas Jefferson is elected to Virginia House of Burgesses

1770
Boston Massacre

1774
Intolerable Acts; First Continental Congress meets

THINKING ABOUT VOCABULARY

Number a paper from 1 to 5. Next to each number write the two words or terms from the list below that best completes the sentence.

American Revolution	militia
assembly	minutemen
Battle of Bunker Hill	rebel
boycott	Stamp Act
delegate	treason

1. The male colonists elected a _____ to represent them in the _____ .

2. The _____ was one of the first battles of the _____ .

3. The _____ volunteered to serve in the colonial _____ .

4. The _____ was one reason that the colonists decided to _____ British goods.

5. The British thought it was _____ when the colonists decided to _____ against Great Britain's authority.

THINKING ABOUT FACTS

1. Give an example of self-government in the colonies.

2. How did the trial of John Peter Zenger become important to the colonists?

3. Why did the colonies rebel against the British government?

4. Describe the role Samuel Adams played during the conflict between Parliament and the English colonies.

5. Who was Mercy Otis Warren?

6. Who was Crispus Attucks? In which event did he play a key role?

7. How did the Committees of Correspondence help to unify the colonies?

8. What was unusual about the capture of Fort Ticonderoga?

9. What did the Battle of Bunker Hill accomplish?

10. In the time line above, study the dates for the Boston Tea Party and the Intolerable Acts. Which was a cause for the other? Which was an effect?

THINK AND WRITE ◄⬛⬛⬛)

WRITING A POEM
Reread the section on Phillis Wheatley and the power of poetry on page 291. Think about what freedom meant to Wheatley. Then write a poem in which you express what freedom means to you.

WRITING A SPEECH
Reread the excerpt of Patrick Henry's speech to the House of Burgesses on page 303. Suppose that you are a Son or Daughter of Liberty. Write a speech trying to convince others to join your cause.

WRITING A BATTLE REPORT
Suppose that you are assigned to report on the activities of the Patriot forces. Describe the battles of Lexington and Concord and Bunker Hill. Include the basic facts and conclusions about the outcome.

APPLYING STUDY SKILLS

READING POLITICAL CARTOONS
Answer the questions below to practice the skill of reading political cartoons.

1. What is a political cartoon?
2. Look at the political cartoon from 1766 on page 298. What symbols does the cartoonist use? What do they mean?
3. What is the caption of the cartoon on page 298? How does this help you to understand the drawing?
4. How do you think this cartoon might have influenced a colonial reader?
5. Do political cartoons express facts or opinions?

Summing Up the Chapter

Copy the cause-and-effect chart on a separate piece of paper. Then review the chapter to complete the chart. After you have finished, use the chart to answer the question "How can an effect sometimes become the cause of other effects?"

CAUSE	EFFECT
Colonists have a strong belief in freedom and self-government.	
	Colonists protest; Sons of Liberty is formed.
	Colonists boycott British goods.
Boston Tea Party takes place.	
	Colonists stop trading with Britain; minutemen begin defending the colonies.
	Colonists prove the seriousness of their beliefs.

The American Revolution

THINKING ABOUT
HISTORY AND GEOGRAPHY

Chapter 12 begins with the signing of the Declaration of Independence on July 4, 1776. For the next several years the British colonists fought to win independence from Great Britain. Read the time line to follow some of the events of the American Revolution. Almost 300 years after Columbus first reached the Americas, the English colonists began forming their own country, free from European control.

1778

VALLEY FORGE
Martha Washington helps wounded soldiers through a terrible winter

1776

PHILADELPHIA
Thomas Jefferson writes the Declaration of Independence

1776

TRENTON
George Washington crosses the Delaware River to attack the British

1774

1776

1778

NORTH
AMERICA

Fort
Vincennes

Valley Forge
Philadelphia

Trenton

Yorktown

THE BRITISH
COLONIES

ATLANTIC
OCEAN

1779

FORT VINCENNES
George Rogers Clark
captures British forts in
the Ohio River valley

1781

YORKTOWN
The British surrender to
George Washington

1780

1782

1775 1776 1777 1779 1781 1783

The Declaration of Independence

Read Aloud

Benjamin Franklin had hoped that Britain and the colonies would make peace. Yet after the Battle of Bunker Hill, Franklin gave up this hope. He wrote to a friend who was a member of Parliament, "You have begun to burn our Towns, and murder our People. Look upon your Hands! They are stained with the Blood of your Relations! You and I were long Friends: You are now my Enemy, and I am, Yours."

Focus Activity

READ TO LEARN

What was the purpose of the Declaration of Independence?

VOCABULARY

- Second Continental Congress
- Continental Army
- traitor
- Declaration of Independence

PEOPLE

- Thomas Paine
- William Howe
- Henry Knox
- Thomas Jefferson
- John Locke

PLACES

- Monticello

THE BIG PICTURE

News of the Battle of Bunker Hill had made Franklin break with a good friend. Yet not all Americans were ready to break completely from Britain in 1775. Many still wanted Britain and the colonies to compromise. Some felt that the colonies were not strong enough to govern themselves. Most colonists spoke English, shared English customs and laws, and had relatives in Britain. The British were the colonists' major trading partner. British ships protected colonial trade routes.

One fact, however, could not be forgotten. Colonists had lost their lives at Lexington, Concord, and Bunker Hill. The fight for liberty had begun.

King George III did not think much of the colonists' will to fight. He was sure that once they "have felt a small blow, they will submit." In this lesson you will see how the colonists proved the king's prediction wrong.

THE REBELLION CONTINUES

By 1776 more and more colonists wanted to declare independence immediately. "We must be content to wait till the fruit is ripe," Sam Adams told them, "before we gather it."

Common Sense

A talented writer helped to ripen the "fruit" of independence. He was Thomas Paine, an Englishman who had settled in Pennsylvania in 1774.

In January 1776 Paine published a pamphlet entitled *Common Sense*. In it Paine argued that the colonists owed no loyalty to an unjust ruler. It made no sense, Paine wrote, for "a continent to be perpetually *[forever]* ruled by an island . . . Tis time to part."

Paine used language most people could easily understand. In three months, more than 100,000 copies of his pamphlet were sold. "I find *Common Sense* is working a powerful change in the minds of many men," observed George Washington.

The British Leave Boston

Meanwhile, 15,000 American soldiers surrounded the British troops in Boston. When British General William Howe showed no signs of leaving Boston, Washington sent Henry Knox, a former bookseller, to Fort Ticonderoga. Knox and his men dragged cannons from the New York fort more than 250 miles over frozen rivers and snowy hills to Boston. When the British awoke on March 5, 1776, they saw the cannons staring down at them.

The showdown was over. As George Washington told his brother, the British soldiers, along with some 1,000 colonists loyal to Britain, retreated "in a shameful and precipitate *[hurried]* manner." The colonists had retaken Boston.

Ticonderoga Museum

Common Sense (left) inspired support for independence. Cannons from Fort Ticonderoga (above) helped the Patriots retake Boston.

SECOND CONTINENTAL CONGRESS

In May 1775, soon after the battles of Lexington and Concord, the Second Continental Congress had begun to meet. Colonists cheered the delegates as they arrived in Philadelphia. However, the delegates faced troubling new issues. When they had met the year before, the delegates had decided on a peaceful protest. Now British and American soldiers were fighting in New England. The Congress had to decide how to respond.

Preparing for Defense

The delegates did not agree on what path to take. They knew that any actions they took must help protect the colonies against future attacks. John Adams suggested that the Congress form a "Grand American Army," with troops from every colony.

Adams nominated Virginian George Washington to be commander-in-chief of the new Continental Army. He praised Washington as "a gentleman whose skill as an officer . . . would command the respect of America." Washington accepted and promised to use "every power I possess . . . for the support of the glorious cause."

The Second Continental Congress, headed by John Hancock (below right), met in Independence Hall (right) in Philadelphia. Today, thousands visit the site of our country's beginnings (below).

The Congress also started a post office so that all the colonies could share news. Benjamin Franklin, a new delegate to the Congress, was appointed Postmaster General. Afraid that Native Americans would side with the British, the Congress set up a committee to make peace with them. The Congress also began to ask foreign countries to support the colonies against Britain. By taking all of these steps, the Second Continental Congress had begun to act like the central government for a new country.

Franklin's cartoon (left) urged the colonies to unite. It was first used to support Britain in the French and Indian War.

A Last Chance for Peace

"The war is now heartily entered into," wrote Thomas Jefferson of Virginia, a new delegate to the Congress. Many agreed with him, including John Hancock. Hancock, a new delegate from Massachusetts, was serving as president of the Congress.

In July 1775 the Congress agreed to try one last time to make peace with Britain. The delegates sent what they called the "Olive Branch Petition" to King George. The olive branch is a symbol of peace. The petition assured Britain of the loyalty of the Americans. The Olive Branch Petition also asked for the repeal of the Intolerable Acts and an end to the fighting.

Declaring Independence

The king refused to even read the petition from what he called an "illegal congress." He threatened to "bring the traitors to justice." A traitor is someone who turns against his or her country. Many colonists were shocked at the king's angry words.

The delegates then took their biggest step. Early in June 1776 Virginia delegate Richard Henry Lee proposed "that these United colonies are, and of right ought to be, free and independent States." Many agreed. The Congress named a committee to write a statement of independence.

The new committee then asked John Adams, Benjamin Franklin, Thomas Jefferson, Roger Sherman, and Robert Livingston to write the Declaration of Independence. Adams convinced Jefferson to draft the document. "You can write ten times better than I can," Adams argued. Jefferson was only 33 years old at the time.

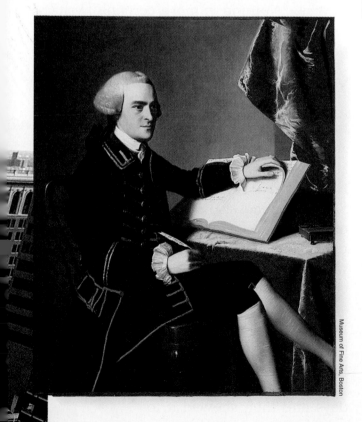

Museum of Fine Arts, Boston

Jefferson's love of architecture and European culture can be seen in his design for Monticello, his home near Charlottesville.

JEFFERSON WRITES THE DECLARATION

Despite his youth, Jefferson was a perfect choice to write the Declaration. The quiet redheaded man, who had served in the Virginia House of Burgesses, rarely took part in debates. However, he worked hard writing articles, laws, and speeches.

A Man of Many Talents

Jefferson was born in 1743 on his family's plantation in what is now Albemarle County, Virginia. He went to school at the College of William and Mary in Williamsburg. Later he practiced law. In his free time Jefferson played the violin and studied history, science, and architecture.

Jefferson's appreciation of European culture can be seen in Monticello (mahn tih SEL oh), the beautiful home he designed and had built near Charlottesville, Virginia. *Monticello* means "little mountain" in Italian. Jefferson also designed the Virginia Capitol building and the University of Virginia, which he founded.

Jefferson owned several slaves in his lifetime and lived in a slave-owning colony. Yet he often spoke out against slavery. "Nothing is more certainly written in the book of fate than that these people are to be free," he wrote.

Writing the Declaration

When Jefferson sat down to write the Declaration, he was well-prepared. As a law student he had heard Patrick Henry speak against the Stamp Act. He had read Thomas Paine's *Common Sense*. He had also studied the ideas of John Locke, an English philosopher from the late 1600s. Locke wrote that all people are born with certain rights, including life, liberty, and the right to own property. Locke believed that it was the responsibility of governments to protect these rights.

Jefferson wrote his draft in two days and then showed it to

The Granger Collection

Franklin and Adams. They made a few changes, but agreed the Declaration was ready to be shown to the Congress. Jefferson was proud of his work. He felt that it was "an expression of the American mind."

Debating the Declaration

On a hot July day the Congress began debating the content of the Declaration. For three days Jefferson sat silently fuming as the delegates made changes in his work. Adams defended the Declaration. Franklin whispered reassuring words to Jefferson.

The delegates toned down some of Jefferson's attacks against King George and Parliament. Because some of the colonies opposed a passage in which Jefferson described slavery as a "cruel war against human nature," the Congress cut it out of the document. After the Declaration was approved, Richard Henry Lee told Jefferson that the delegates had mangled his draft. "However," he added, "the [Declaration] in its nature is so good that no cookery can spoil the dish."

On July 4, 1776, the Declaration of Independence was approved. John Hancock was the first delegate to sign it. He wrote his name in large letters, "so the king doesn't have to put on his glasses," he is supposed to have said. Today a person's signature is sometimes called a "John Hancock."

Signing the document took courage. Each person who signed it knew that he would now be considered a traitor by the British. "We must all hang together," half-joked Benjamin Franklin, "or [else] we shall all hang separately."

In the painting (above) Jefferson, right, works with John Adams, center, and Ben Franklin, left, on a draft of the Declaration of Independence (left).

THE DECLARATION OF INDEPENDENCE

What did the Declaration say that made it so powerful? The purpose of the document was to explain to the world why the colonies had to separate from Great Britain. The colonies took a bold step. No other colony had declared independence from its ruling country in writing before. As one President said many years later, the Declaration gave "hope to the world, for all future time."

Basic Principles of the Declaration

When Jefferson wrote, "We hold these truths to be self-evident," he meant that there are truths that should be clear to everyone. The first is that "all men are created equal." Men have the right given by God to "Life, Liberty, and the pursuit of Happiness."

The second truth is that people establish governments in order to "secure these rights." As you have read in Chapter 1, these governments get their power, or authority, from "the consent of the governed."

Jefferson then listed the colonists' grievances, or complaints, against King George. The king had, for example, dissolved the colonial assemblies, kept soldiers in the colonies, and taxed the colonies without their consent. King George, in short, was "unfit to be the ruler of a free people."

To conclude the Declaration, Jefferson echoed the words of Richard Henry Lee. It was time, he argued, for the colonists to declare "that these United Colonies are, and of Right ought to be, Free and Independent States."

Read the following excerpt from the Declaration. Can you predict what its impact might have been on colonists remaining loyal to Britain?

MANY VOICES
PRIMARY SOURCE

Excerpt from
The Declaration of Independence, 1776.

*When in the Course of human events, it becomes necessary for one people to dissolve the political bands which have connected them with another, and to assume, among the powers of the earth, the separate and equal station to which the Laws of Nature and of Nature's God **entitle** them, a decent respect to the opinions of mankind requires that they should declare the causes which **impel** them to the separation.*

*We hold these truths to be self-evident, that all men are created equal, that they are **endowed** by their Creator with certain **unalienable** Rights, that among these are Life, Liberty, and the pursuit of Happiness.*

*That to secure these rights, Governments are **instituted** among Men, deriving their just powers from the consent of the governed.*

That whenever any Form of Government becomes destructive of these ends, it is the Right of the People to alter or to abolish it. . . .

---

entitle: have as a right
impel: inspire
endowed: given
unalienable: cannot be taken away
instituted: set up

WHY IT MATTERS

After the Declaration was approved, copies were sent immediately to the Continental Army and to cities and towns throughout the colonies. Bells rang, cannons roared, and colonists cheered when the Declaration was read. Today we celebrate Independence Day, July 4th, as the birth of our country. Abigail Adams wrote to her husband John about the celebration that was held in Boston in 1776:

> After dinner the King's [coat of] Arms were taken down from the State House and every [symbol] of him from every place in which it appeared [was] burnt. . . . Thus ends royal Authority in this State.

The Declaration of Independence was one of the most important documents in human history. It was the first to set out the rights and responsibilities of people in a democracy. Although in 1776 only white male property owners were allowed to vote, over time the phrase "all men are created equal" has been expanded to include all people.

People of other countries have also looked to the Declaration of Independence to express their desire for self-government and freedom. Over the years peoples of Europe, Asia, Africa, Central America, and South America have used it as a model for their own statements of independence.

✓ Reviewing Facts and Ideas

MAIN IDEAS

- Published in January 1776, Thomas Paine's *Common Sense* inspired many colonists to break with Britain.

- In 1775 the Second Continental Congress established the Continental Army and chose George Washington as its commander. The Congress also sent the Olive Branch Petition to King George of Britain.

- Thomas Jefferson wrote the Declaration of Independence, which explained why the colonies were breaking away from Britain. The Second Continental Congress approved it July 4, 1776.

THINK ABOUT IT

1. How did Henry Knox help to force the British to leave Boston?

2. What act did the Second Continental Congress make in 1775? In 1776?

3. **FOCUS** What was Thomas Jefferson's purpose in writing the Declaration of Independence?

4. **THINKING SKILL** Read the excerpt from the Declaration of Independence on page 316. Are the statements *facts* or *opinions*? How do you know?

5. **WRITE** Write a pamphlet like *Common Sense* on a subject you would like to inspire others about.

Yale University Art Gallery

Thomas Jefferson presented the Declaration of Independence to the Second Continental Congress.

The Fourth of July

When the colonists celebrated the signing of the Declaration of Independence in July, 1776, a new legacy was created. Today, Independence Day, or the Fourth of July, remains one of our country's most important holidays.

Like the colonists, today we celebrate with parades, picnics, barbecues, bell ringing, patriotic music, cannon salutes, speeches, fireworks, and games. In the photos on these pages, you can see some of the different ways that some Americans celebrate Independence Day. How does your community honor the legacy of independence on the Fourth of July?

Watching fireworks over the Capitol Building (above) is one way Americans celebrate the Fourth.

The Independence Day Parade (top), by Jane Wooster Scott, portrays people enjoying the day in the 1800s. Today, paraders in Revolutionary War uniforms (left) get into the spirit of 1776. This greeting card (above) shows Uncle Sam, who is always dressed for the Fourth.

319

1775   **1776**   **1778**   1779   1781   1783

The Continental Army

Read Aloud

In August 1776 Nathan Hale slipped into New York City. George Washington had asked the 21-year-old teacher from Connecticut to spy on British soldiers. In September the British arrested Hale. They found maps he had drawn of British troop positions. On the morning of September 22, Captain Hale calmly walked to the gallows and said "I only regret that I have but one life to lose for my country."

Focus Activity

READ TO LEARN

How did the leadership of George Washington help the Continental Army?

VOCABULARY

- mercenary
- Loyalist
- Patriot

PEOPLE

- Nathan Hale
- Martha Washington
- John Burgoyne
- Thaddeus Kosciuszko
- Marquis de Lafayette
- Friedrich von Steuben

PLACES

- Mount Vernon
- Trenton
- Saratoga
- Valley Forge

THE BIG PICTURE

The dying words of Nathan Hale proved his loyalty to the new United States of America. At the time things had not been going well for George Washington and the Continental Army. The British had hired German mercenaries to fight the Americans. A mercenary is a soldier paid to fight for another country. In August 1776 these mercenaries, called Hessians after their home in the German state of Hesse, helped the British capture Long Island near New York City.

The British continued to gain territory in New York. In December Washington and his last 3,000 men retreated to Pennsylvania. "I think the game is pretty near up," the tired commander wrote.

Only a few thousand poorly-equipped soldiers stood between the British and the home of the Continental Congress in Philadelphia. How would the Americans keep the British from crushing their revolution, once and for all?

THE CONTINENTAL ARMY

The winter of 1776 was a sad time for the soldiers of the Continental Army. The winter winds chilled them to the bone. Some fought in their own clothes because uniforms were in short supply. Food and ammunition were running low. Most soldiers joined the army for a certain amount of time only and looked forward to leaving as soon as their time was up. As Thomas Paine wrote:

These are the times that try men's souls. The summer soldier and the sunshine patriot will, in this crisis, shrink from the service of their country; but he that stands it now, deserves the love and thanks of man and woman.

Redcoats and Continentals

In contrast, the British soldiers in their fancy red uniforms were well-trained and well-supplied. Britain had the strongest navy in the world and the money to hire mercenaries. The Americans, however, had some strengths. They were defending their homes. Unlike the British, the Americans knew the land well.

Another advantage the Americans had was that it was slow and very costly for Britain to ship troops and supplies across the Atlantic Ocean. As the war dragged on, many British people began to wonder whether the war was worth it.

Patriots and Loyalists

Not all Americans supported the American Revolution. About one out of three of the colonists were Loyalists.

Rhode Island Historical Society

Washington takes command of the Continental Army. (below) The Patriot flag of Rhode Island (left) has 13 stars.

Loyalists were people who remained loyal to Britain.

Another third supported the fight for independence. These Americans were known as Patriots. The remaining one-third of Americans did not take sides. This group included many Quakers, who oppose all wars.

321

GEORGE WASHINGTON TAKES COMMAND

Another advantage the Patriots had was strong leadership. George Washington had been commander of the Virginia militia during the French and Indian War. Now he faced a much greater responsibility. Who was this man who was charged with getting an untrained army ready to fight against a major world power?

The Life of a Leader

George Washington was born in 1732 in Westmoreland County, Virginia. Although his parents were landowners, they were not one of Virginia's wealthiest families. Washington was good at mathematics, but never went to college.

Washington's first job, at the age of 16, was as a surveyor. A surveyor is a person who measures land. In the middle of the 1700s many colonists were moving west and needed his services. His work paid well, and he was able to use his money to buy land.

In 1752 the young Washington joined the Virginia militia. Washington hoped a military career would bring him honor.

He became angry when he learned that soldiers from the colonies were paid less to fight for the British than soldiers in the regular British army. Then, during the French and Indian War, the British lowered Colonel Washington's rank because they did not want colonists to rise above captain. Washington left the militia in protest. He later returned when the governor of Virginia restored his original rank.

In 1758, while still in the military, Washington was elected to the Virginia House of Burgesses. There he met Thomas Jefferson and Patrick Henry, and later joined colonial protests against the British.

In 1759 Washington retired from military life to manage his lands. By then he had become the most famous American in the military. That same year he married a wealthy widow named Martha Custis. George and Martha Washington moved to Mount Vernon, the plantation he owned on the Potomac River in Virginia. Martha

George Washington married Martha Custis in 1759 (left). The young couple went to live on Washington's Virginia plantation, Mount Vernon (below).

Washington also supported the Patriots. During the American Revolution, she helped her husband with his paperwork. She also sewed socks and cooked soup for the soldiers.

Victory in Trenton

Martha Washington often joined George Washington in the field, where things were going badly for the Continental Army at the end of 1776. Washington was discouraged. He wrote, "Such is my situation that if I were to wish the bitterest curse to an enemy on this side of the grave, I should put him in my [place] with my feelings."

Certain of future victories, General Howe decided to rest for the winter in New York City. Washington knew that the British would not try to advance again until the spring. So he planned a surprise attack on the close to 1,400 Hessian troops in Trenton, New Jersey. The password Washington gave his soldiers was "Victory or Death!" After nightfall on Christmas Day, December 25, 1776, Washington and his troops crossed the Delaware River into New Jersey. The next morning, they surprised the Hessians, who quickly surrendered. "This is a glorious day for our country," said Washington.

The Continental Army and Slavery

Among the troops that crossed the Delaware with Washington were Prince Whipple and Oliver Cromwell. They were two of the many African Americans who fought with the Patriots.

In 1775 the Americans had debated whether to allow enslaved men to be soldiers. Many were afraid that enslaved African Americans might rebel if given guns. Washington agreed not to allow any more African Americans to join the army. He himself owned slaves, which his wife's family had given him.

In 1776, however, Washington changed his mind. Britain had won the support of many enslaved people by promising them their freedom.

How could the colonies continue to enslave African Americans when they were willing to fight and die for the freedom of all Americans? Some states began to answer that question. In 1780 Pennsylvania adopted a plan for abolishing, or ending, slavery. Many northern states soon followed. In other states, such as Virginia, enslaved African Americans who fought with the Patriots were freed. One of the plantation owners who freed his slaves after the war ended was George Washington.

TURNING POINTS

In June 1777 a British general named John Burgoyne (bur GOYN) decided to capture the Hudson River valley. This would cut New England and New York off from the rest of the colonies.

The Battle of Saratoga

Starting from Canada, Burgoyne's troops headed south toward Albany, New York. Along the way, groups of Patriots attacked from the woods. Burgoyne's troops were forced to cut roads through thick forests and swamps. It took them all day to travel one mile.

The Americans had time to prepare. Thaddeus Kosciuszko (THA dee us kahs ee US koh), a Polish engineer serving with the Americans, had placed cannons on a high cliff overlooking the road to Albany. Local farmers, many with excellent shooting skills, poured in to the area to help the Patriots. By the time Burgoyne reached Saratoga, New York, the Americans vastly outnumbered the British. After two months of fighting, Burgoyne surrendered on October 17, 1777.

Marquis de Lafayette

Kosciuszko was not the only European who helped the American Patriots. The Marquis de Lafayette (mahr KEE de laf ee ET) was a wealthy French nobleman. His father had died fighting the British when Lafayette was a child.

In July 1777, when he was 19, Lafayette wrote to John Hancock. He asked for two things. The first was to serve at his own expense. The second was to begin his service as a volunteer. Hancock made Lafayette a major general on George Washington's staff. He and Washington became like father and son.

The Winter at Valley Forge

While General Burgoyne was marching to Saratoga, General Howe had captured Philadelphia. The Continental Congress fled to York, Pennsylvania. Washington and his

At Valley Forge (above) Lafayette, left, joins Washington, right. Von Steuben trains the troops (right).

troops set up camp at Valley Forge, near Philadelphia.

Supplies were dangerously low. Most survived by eating firecakes, a thin bread of flour and water cooked over an open fire. Many soldiers left and went home. At least 2,500 died of disease. Martha Washington helped comfort and nurse the sick. One out of three soldiers had no shoes at all. Washington noted bitterly that "you might have tracked the army . . . by the blood of their feet" upon the snow.

Friedrich von Steuben (FREED rihk vahn STOO bun), an energetic soldier from the German state of Prussia, helped train the ragged troops. Von Steuben expected them to be on time. Even rags, he told them, could be kept clean. Von Steuben taught the troops the latest European fighting methods. Under his watchful eyes, a group of storekeepers, farmers, and other citizens was turned into a powerful army.

WHY IT MATTERS

George Washington's strong leadership helped the Continental Army survive the winter at Valley Forge. His men did not know how Washington begged the Continental Congress for food, supplies, and money. By the end of that winter, however, the troops at Valley Forge were willing to follow George Washington anywhere.

The Battle of Saratoga was also a turning point. It proved to Europeans that the Patriots could beat the British. Early in 1778 France joined the war against their longtime enemy, Britain. They sent gunpowder, soldiers, and ships. French support would make a big difference in the outcome of the war.

✓ Reviewing Facts and Ideas

MAIN IDEAS

- Britain had a strong navy and troops who were well-trained and well-supplied. The American soldiers had little training, but they were fighting on their home ground.

- The Patriot victory at the Battle of Saratoga in June 1777 helped the Americans win European support.

- American troops survived a difficult winter at Valley Forge in 1777 and trained to become a strong army.

THINK ABOUT IT

1. What were the strengths and weaknesses of the British and American forces at the start of the Revolution?

2. How did the Patriots and Loyalists feel about the war for independence?

3. **FOCUS** How did George Washington help the Continental Army?

4. **THINKING SKILL** Based on the events in this lesson, what _predictions_ would you make about the rest of the war? Explain your answer.

5. **GEOGRAPHY** What role did climate play in the American victories discussed in this lesson?

CITIZENSHIP
VIEWPOINTS

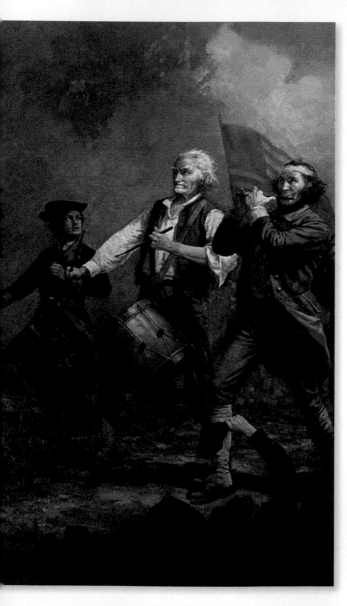

Spirit of '76, the famous painting by Archibald M. Willard, was unveiled at our country's Centennial Exposition in Philadelphia in 1876.

1776: What did colonists think about separating from Great Britain?

By 1776 many Patriots believed independence was the only answer to their conflicts with Great Britain. As Sarah Morris Mifflin expressed in her viewpoint, the Patriots were ready to make sacrifices to be free of British control.

The Loyalists were against separating from Great Britain. Many of them agreed that the colonists had not always been treated fairly. Still, they believed that strong advantages remained in being connected to Britain. According to William Franklin, they did not feel the colonies' economy and military could stand on their own.

Many African Americans refused to take sides. As the unsigned newspaper letter in the third Viewpoint explained, slavery was an exception to the Patriots' call for liberty. Some African Americans joined the Patriot cause hoping that the Revolution would result in the end of slavery. Others supported the British because of the British promise to free any enslaved African Americans who joined their side. Many wondered if either side would end slavery when the war was over.

Read and consider the three viewpoints on the issue of separating from Great Britain. Then answer the questions that follow.

Three DIFFERENT Viewpoints

1 WILLIAM FRANKLIN
Governor of the New Jersey Colony
Excerpt from Letter to the New Jersey Legislature, 1776

Depend upon it, you can never place yourselves in a happier situation than in your dependence on Great Britain. Independence has not even a chance of being gained, without the loss of the lives and properties of many thousands of the honest people of this country—yet *these*, it seems, are as nothing in the eyes of the patriots! But remember, Gentlemen, that I now tell you, that should they by chance achieve their purpose, yet their government will not be lasting.

". . . their government will not be lasting."

2 SARAH MORRIS MIFFLIN
Wife of General Thomas Mifflin of the Continental Army
Excerpt from a letter to a friend in Boston, 1776

I know this, that as free I can die but once; but as a slave I shall not be worthy of life. I have the pleasure to assure you that these are the [feelings] of my sister Americans. They have sacrificed [gatherings], parties of pleasure, teadrinkings and finery, to that great spirit of patriotism which [moves] . . . people throughout this . . . country.

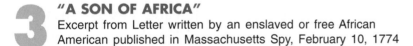

". . . as free I can die but once. . ."

3 "A SON OF AFRICA"
Excerpt from Letter written by an enslaved or free African American published in Massachusetts Spy, February 10, 1774

You are taxed without your consent, (I grant that a grievance,) and have petitioned for relief, and cannot get any. Are not your hearts also hard, when you hold men in slavery who are entitled to liberty by the law of nature, equal as yourselves? When the eyes of your understanding are opened, then will you see clearly between your case and Great Britain, and that of the Africans. If so, is it lawful for one nation to enslave another?

". . . is it lawful for one nation to enslave another?"

BUILDING CITIZENSHIP

1. What was the viewpoint of each person? How did each person support his view?

2. In what ways were some of the viewpoints alike? In what ways were they different?

3. What other viewpoints might people have on this issue? What are some ways in which the issue of colonies separating from their ruling country might be discussed today?

SHARING VIEWPOINTS

Suppose you were a colonist during the American Revolution. Why might you have expected the speakers to have the viewpoints they did? As a class discuss which viewpoints you would have agreed or disagreed with. Are there any statements you could make about the separation from Great Britain with which all speakers could agree?

1775　1777　1783

Independence at Last

Read Aloud

The minutemen had left Groton, Massachusetts, for the battlefield. Yet the town was still protected. "Armed with muskets, pitchforks, and such other weapons as they could find," Prudence Wright, Sarah Shattuck, and some 30 other women guarded the town bridge.

Focus Activity

READ TO LEARN

Who helped the Patriots win the Revolution?

VOCABULARY

• Treaty of Paris

PEOPLE

• George Rogers Clark
• John Paul Jones
• Benedict Arnold
• Mary Ludwig Hays
• Haym Salomon
• Francis Marion
• Nathanael Greene
• Charles Cornwallis
• Bernardo de Gálvez
• James Armistead
• Joseph Brant

PLACES

• Fort Vincennes
• Yorktown

THE BIG PICTURE

You have read about the hardships endured by the Continental Army and about such leaders as Thomas Jefferson and George Washington. Yet the war could not have been won without the help of ordinary citizens like the women of Groton, Massachusetts.

Farmers, craftworkers, and merchants left their families to join the army. Women like Abigail Adams kept the farms and businesses running in addition to raising their families. She wrote to her husband that she was "sometimes thrown into an agony of distress" trying to get everything done.

Some colonists joined the army as cooks and servants. Others raised money, sewed clothes for the soldiers, and nursed the wounded. It was this quiet work that often made the difference between victory and defeat in the Revolution.

Both the Americans and the British had expected the struggle for independence to end quickly. Instead it was eight years before a peace treaty would be signed. In this lesson, you will read about some of the men and women who helped to bring the war to an end.

PATRIOTS IN THE WEST AND ON THE SEAS

In the early days of the American Revolution, much of the fighting took place in the Northeast. However, brave Patriots in the Middle West and on the high seas also fought the British.

Patriots Fight in the West

George Rogers Clark was a surveyor living in Kentucky when the Revolution began. In 1778 he set out to drive the British out of the Ohio River valley, which was then called "the West."

One of the forts Clark captured, Fort Vincennes (vihn SENZ), was soon retaken by the British. Clark refused to give up. He knew that the British would not expect an attack in the winter. So in February 1779, Clark's men marched to the fort again, wading waist-deep through icy, flooded swampland. At night the soldiers slept in mud, covering themselves with wet blankets. "Our suffering is too terrible for any person to believe," Clark said.

By having his men yell and scream as they attacked the fort, Clark tricked the British into believing that he had a large army. The British quickly surrendered. As Clark wrote, "great things" have been done "by a few men." Americans now controlled the Ohio River valley. Clark became known as the "Washington of the West."

Patriots Fight on the Seas

Like the Continental Army, the American navy was also poorly equipped in comparison to the British. However, an American sea captain, John Paul Jones, proved that a strong fighting spirit can make a difference. Some historians have called Jones our country's first naval hero.

In the battle between the *Bonhomme Richard* and the *Serapis*, the United States defeated the great British navy.

In September 1779 Captain Jones's battleship, the *Bonhomme Richard*, faced the British battleship *Serapis*. Jones had named his ship, which means "Poor Richard" in the French language, after Benjamin Franklin's *Poor Richard's Almanac*. The British pounded the *Bonhomme Richard* with cannon fire, leaving it in ruins. When the British captain asked Jones if he was ready to surrender, Jones yelled back, "I have not yet begun to fight."

After three hours of close fighting, it was the *Serapis* that surrendered. One of Jones's men called the battle "the most bloody, the hardest fought . . . between two ships of war of any nation under heaven."

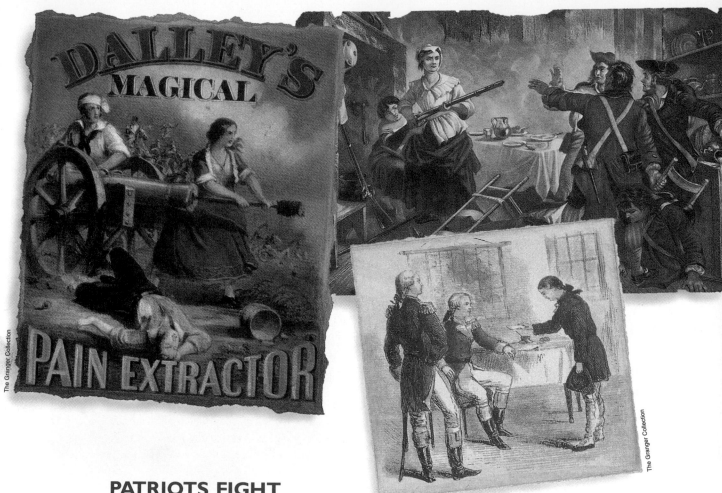

Patriot women who fought the British included Mary Ludwig Hays (left), Nancy Hart (top), and Deborah Sampson (above), who is disguised as a man.

PATRIOTS FIGHT IN THE COLONIES

Patriots like George Rogers Clark and John Paul Jones led the Americans to victories over the British. Other men and women also played important roles in the fight for independence.

Benedict Arnold Turns Traitor

As a Patriot commander, Benedict Arnold had helped the Americans win at Fort Ticonderoga and Saratoga. In 1778, however, Arnold married a woman from a Loyalist family. He lived a life of luxury and was soon in debt.

In 1780 Washington gave Arnold command of West Point, a key fort on New York's Hudson River. In exchange for money, Arnold planned to tell the British about West Point's defenses. When the Americans found out, Arnold escaped and became an officer in the British army. Many British soldiers, however, never fully trusted him. Today, a "Benedict Arnold" has come to mean a traitor to one's country.

Supporting the Soldiers

Fortunately there were many Americans who helped the Continental Army. Mary Ludwig Hays went with her husband to the battlefield. Because she brought pitchers of water to the thirsty soldiers during battles, she was called "Molly Pitcher." She also helped load cannons and even took up her husband's gun when he was wounded.

Some women like Deborah Sampson disguised themselves as men and fought as soldiers. Others like Dicey Langston of South Carolina served as spies. The 16-year-old Langston crossed a river at night to bring news of enemy troop positions to her brother's Patriot camp.

The businessman **Haym Salomon** (HI am SAL uh mun) spied for the Patriots when the British captured New York City. A Jew who had fled Poland when it was invaded by Russia, he believed strongly in the cause of independence and freedom. He also raised money for the Continental Army. Salomon gave so much of his own money to the Patriots that when he died in 1785, he was penniless.

Patriots Fight in the South

The British headed south after the Patriot victories at Saratoga and Vincennes kept them from advancing in the north and the west. You can see some of the major battles fought in the South on the map on pages 332–333. In South Carolina, however, the British were stopped by Captain **Francis Marion**.

Marion's small band of soldiers made lightning-quick attacks on the British before fading back into the Carolina swamps. Because of this, Marion became known as the "Swamp Fox." Years later the poet William Cullen Bryant wrote:

Our band is few, but true and tried,
Our leader frank and bold;
The British soldier trembles
When Marion's name is told.

Marion's men also fought in North Carolina under General **Nathanael Greene**. Greene's approach was simple: "We fight, we get beat, rise, and fight again." By the spring of 1781, British commander **Charles Cornwallis** declared he was "quite tired of marching about the country" chasing Greene.

Instead, Cornwallis decided to head north to Virginia.

The Spanish Help the Patriots

A year after France joined the war, Spain followed suit. Many Spanish soldiers, like Jorge Ferragut (HOHR he fer rah GOOT), fought with the Patriots. Women in Cuba sold their jewelry to raise money for the American cause.

In 1777 **Bernardo de Gálvez** (ber NAHR doh DE GAHL ves) became Governor of Spanish Louisiana. He opened up the port of New Orleans to American ships and ended British trade with Louisiana. Gálvez also sent money and supplies to George Rogers Clark. As a commander of Spain's troops in America, Gálvez won control of several key cities along the Gulf Coast including Pensacola, Florida.

Valentine Museum, Richmond

James Armistead spied for the Patriots and was one of many enslaved African Americans who aided the Revolution.

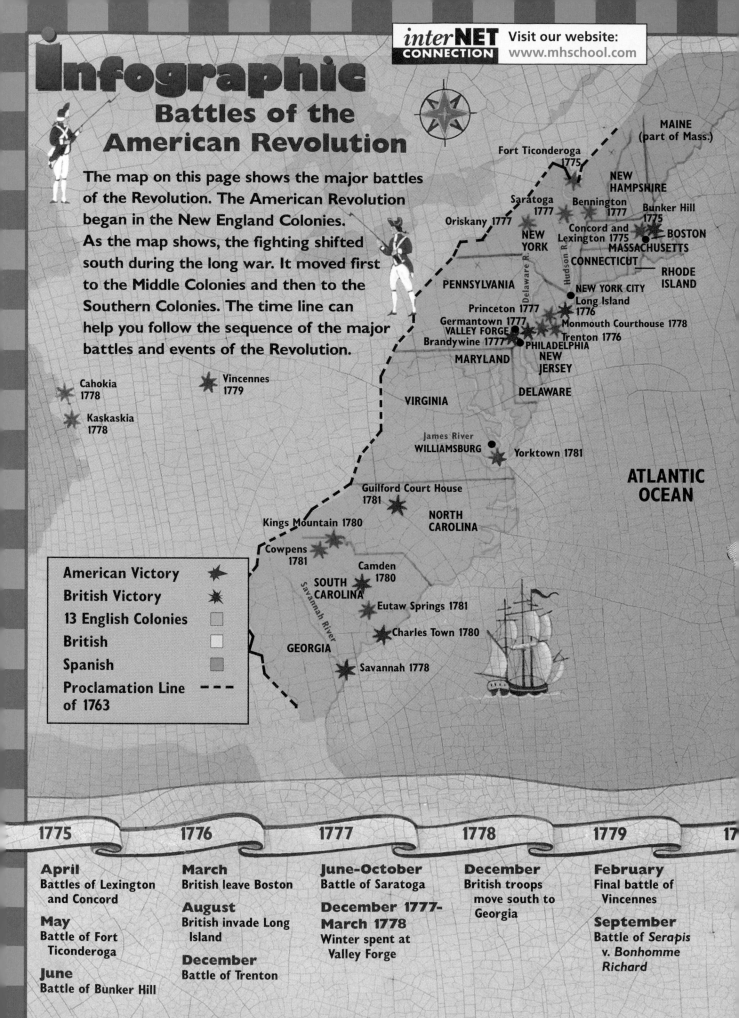

Infographic
Battles of the American Revolution

interNET CONNECTION Visit our website: www.mhschool.com

The map on this page shows the major battles of the Revolution. The American Revolution began in the New England Colonies. As the map shows, the fighting shifted south during the long war. It moved first to the Middle Colonies and then to the Southern Colonies. The time line can help you follow the sequence of the major battles and events of the Revolution.

Map labels:

MAINE (part of Mass.)

Fort Ticonderoga 1775

NEW HAMPSHIRE

Saratoga 1777

Bennington 1777

Bunker Hill 1775

Oriskany 1777

Concord and Lexington 1775 — BOSTON

NEW YORK

MASSACHUSETTS

CONNECTICUT

RHODE ISLAND

PENNSYLVANIA

Hudson R.

Delaware R.

NEW YORK CITY

Long Island 1776

Princeton 1777

Monmouth Courthouse 1778

Germantown 1777

VALLEY FORGE

Trenton 1776

Brandywine 1777

PHILADELPHIA

NEW JERSEY

MARYLAND

DELAWARE

VIRGINIA

Cahokia 1778

Vincennes 1779

Kaskaskia 1778

James River

WILLIAMSBURG

Yorktown 1781

ATLANTIC OCEAN

Guilford Court House 1781

NORTH CAROLINA

Kings Mountain 1780

Cowpens 1781

Camden 1780

SOUTH CAROLINA

Savannah River

Eutaw Springs 1781

Charles Town 1780

GEORGIA

Savannah 1778

Legend:

- American Victory
- British Victory
- 13 English Colonies
- British
- Spanish
- Proclamation Line of 1763

Time line:

1775	1776	1777	1778	1779	17

April Battles of Lexington and Concord

May Battle of Fort Ticonderoga

June Battle of Bunker Hill

March British leave Boston

August British invade Long Island

December Battle of Trenton

June–October Battle of Saratoga

December 1777–March 1778 Winter spent at Valley Forge

December British troops move south to Georgia

February Final battle of Vincennes

September Battle of *Serapis* v. *Bonhomme Richard*

The three-cornered hat worn by American soldiers during the Revolution came to be seen by Europeans as a symbol of liberty.

The first United States military medal was created by George Washington. Known as the Purple Heart, it is still given to soldiers who are wounded in battle.

1781

October
Battle of Yorktown

1783

November
Treaty of Paris

BATTLES IN THE SOUTHERN COLONIES

As the Infographic on these pages shows, the fighting of the Revolution moved to the South. Before heading north to Virginia, General Cornwallis had taken his forces to the Carolinas where he won a series of battles. Cornwallis counted on support from the southern Loyalists. But although some Loyalists joined British troops, they were a small part of the British force.

The vast number of southerners supported the Patriots. They fed and clothed the American troops that marched through the countryside. Still from 1778 to 1781, the outnumbered and poorly equipped Patriots were defeated at Savannah, Charles Town, and Camden. At King's Mountain, North Carolina, in October 1780 the Patriots achieved one of their few victories in the south.

The Battle of Guilford Court House

As you have read, the British Army marched its men shoulder to shoulder toward the enemy's fire, which made the soldiers easy targets. Cornwallis continued to use this traditional European style of fighting despite warnings from his men.

In March 1781 at Guilford Court House, North Carolina, the strategy proved costly once again. Cornwallis lost one-fourth of his men during the fierce battle. The British were able to claim victory only because the Patriot forces led by Nathanael Greene had retreated.

"Another such victory," one British officer said, "would destroy the British army." Although Cornwallis won most of the battles in the south, he left the Carolinas with his forces greatly weakened and in need of supplies.

THE END OF THE WAR

When Nathanael Greene forced the British to retreat north, General Cornwallis went as far as Yorktown, Virginia. This was to be the last stand for the British troops.

Victory at Yorktown

When General Cornwallis asked his servant James Armistead to spy *on* the Americans, he did not realize that Armistead was already spying *for* them. Armistead alerted Lafayette to Cornwallis's plans. He also gave Cornwallis false information about the Americans.

Washington was therefore able to trick Cornwallis into thinking he was going to attack New York. Instead more than 17,000 American and French soldiers surrounded Yorktown. French warships blocked the harbor and prevented the British from retreating. The map on page 337 shows the routes each side took and the positions of their troops. Realizing that he was outgunned and outnumbered, Cornwallis surrendered on October 19, 1781. The Battle of Yorktown was the last major battle of the Revolution.

After the Battle of Yorktown, a disappointed King George III wanted to continue the fight. The British House of Commons, however, was tired of the war. It wanted to make peace.

In the Treaty of Paris of 1783, Britain finally recognized the independence of the United States. The land west of the Appalachian Mountains that had been won by George Rogers Clark became part of the United States. Florida, which had come under British control, was returned to Spain, an ally of the Patriots.

The Iroquois Confederacy

At the end of the war, many Loyalists left the United States for good. Among them were members of the Iroquois Confederacy.

During the Revolution, both the Americans and the British tried to win

The painting by artist John Trumbull shows the British surrendering to the Americans at Yorktown in 1781.

Yale University Art Gallery

the support of Native Americans. In the Iroquois Confederacy, the Tuscarora and Oneida chose not to take sides. The Mohawk, Cayuga, Seneca, and Ononda-ga fought with the British. Their leader, Joseph Brant, had hoped that the British would protect Iroquois lands from settlement by the colonists. When the British lost the war, many Iroquois moved north to Canada.

WHY IT MATTERS

The United States was now independent. Some years later, John Adams was asked about the meaning of the American Revolution. He replied that there had been two revolutions. One was the war itself. The other "was in the minds and hearts of the people." Indeed, by the end of the war many Americans like John Adams wanted more than independence. They wanted the chance to form a new kind of government. In the next chapter, you will read about how this was done.

DID YOU KNOW?

How did the colonists celebrate their victory?

After the Battle of Yorktown, bells all across the country rang out to announce the victory. When the Treaty of Paris became final, weary Continental Army officers cheered and sang the song "Independence." The jubilant Patriots held dances and drank toasts to General Washington. They also honored the heroes who died in the war. Everywhere Washington went, crowds lined the roads to see him. "With a heart full of love and gratitude, I now take my leave of you," Washington told his troops at a farewell dinner in Fraunces Tavern in New York City. Tears were streaming down his cheeks as he hugged each soldier and said goodbye. As one soldier wrote, "such a scene of sorrow and weeping I have never before seen."

✓ Reviewing Facts and Ideas

MAIN IDEAS

- In 1779 George Rogers Clark won control of the Ohio River valley. Later that year John Paul Jones won a victory over the mighty British navy.

- Americans supported the Patriots by running farms and businesses, serving as spies and nurses, and raising money for the cause.

- Francis Marion, Nathanael Greene, and Bernardo de Gálvez helped stop the British advance in the South.

- The Battle of Yorktown in 1781 was the last major battle of the war. The Treaty of Paris of 1783 recognized American independence and set new boundaries for the United States.

THINK ABOUT IT

1. How did the capture of Fort Vincennes help the Americans?

2. How did colonists who stayed home support the Patriot cause?

3. **FOCUS** Name some of the people who helped win the Revolution and list their contributions.

4. **THINKING SKILL** What were the goals of France and Spain in *deciding* to help the Patriots? Explain your answer.

5. **GEOGRAPHY** Look at the map of the Battle of Yorktown on page 337. Why was it a good location for the Patriots and their allies to trap Cornwallis?

Comparing Maps at Different Scales

VOCABULARY

map scale

large-scale map

small-scale map

WHY THE SKILL MATTERS

As you have read, the battles of the American Revolution were fought in different parts of the United States. A map, such as the one on page 332, can give you a great deal of information about the major battles of the Revolution. By looking at that map you can find out the state in which a particular battle was fought.

Most of the time you only need one map to give you all the information you need about a topic. Yet sometimes you may want to find more detailed information. The map of major battles, for example, does not give you information about the route George Washington took to reach Trenton. If you were writing a report on the Battle of Trenton, you would need a map that showed a smaller area—Trenton—in greater detail.

USING THE SKILL

No map can be as large as the part of Earth it shows. So all maps are drawn to scale. A map scale uses a unit of measure, such as an inch, to represent a real distance on Earth. Each map has its own scale depending on the size of the area and the amount of information that needs to be shown. A large-scale map, like the one you would need to show the Battle of Trenton, shows a smaller area in greater detail. A small-scale map,

BATTLES IN THE SOUTHERN COLONIES, 1778–1781

like the map of major battles, shows a large area but not much detail.

Look at the map of the Southern Colonies on page 336. Note the scale. It shows the entire South and the major battles that were fought there during the American Revolution. In order for you to locate each of the battles, the map has to show almost the entire geographical area of the present-day South. On this map, 1 inch stands for about 200 miles. Using the map scale, you can determine the distance Cornwallis had to cover between the Battle of Charles Town and the Battle of Camden that followed it.

Now find the location of the Battle of Yorktown on the same map. Can you see the exact route General Cornwallis took after

Helping yourself

- **Large-scale maps** show more detail.
- **Small-scale maps** show less detail.
- **Compare the map scales** and other information to decide which map to use.

Yorktown? No, because this is a small-scale map. It is not detailed enough to give you this information. You would need a large-scale map that focuses on the area around Yorktown to show Cornwallis's exact route. A large-scale map helps make some information easier to read and interpret.

TRYING THE SKILL

Look at the map of the Battle of Yorktown on this page and find the map scale. Now, look again at the map of the Southern Colonies on page 336. How many miles does 1 inch represent on the map of the Battle of Yorktown? Which map scale is larger? How can you tell?

As you can see from the Helping Yourself box on this page, different map scales give you different types of information. First you have to determine which map scale would best give you the information you are looking for. Which map would you use if you want to find out the distance between Yorktown and Savannah? The areas in the Southern Colonies the British probably controlled? The positions of the troops around Yorktown? Why?

REVIEWING THE SKILL

1. What is a map scale? How is it used?

2. When would it be better to use a small-scale map? A large-scale map?

3. What information can you find on the Southern Colonies map that you cannot find on the Yorktown map?

4. Which map would help you understand the plan of the Americans at the Battle of Yorktown? How do you know?

5. When might you need to compare maps of different scales in your own life?

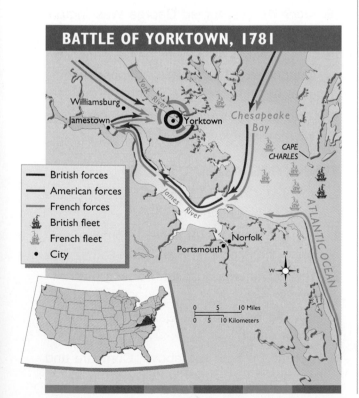

BATTLE OF YORKTOWN, 1781

British forces
American forces
French forces
British fleet
French fleet
City

Williamsburg
Jamestown
York River
Yorktown
Chesapeake Bay
CAPE CHARLES
James River
ATLANTIC OCEAN
Norfolk
Portsmouth

0 5 10 Miles
0 5 10 Kilometers

CHAPTER 12 REVIEW

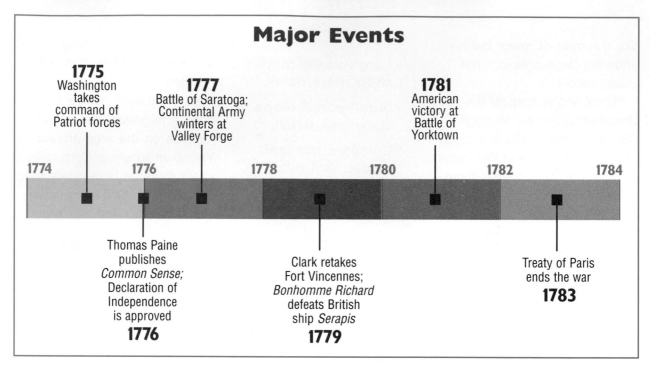

Major Events

1775
Washington takes command of Patriot forces

1777
Battle of Saratoga; Continental Army winters at Valley Forge

1781
American victory at Battle of Yorktown

1774　1776　1778　1780　1782　1784

Thomas Paine publishes *Common Sense;* Declaration of Independence is approved
1776

Clark retakes Fort Vincennes; *Bonhomme Richard* defeats British ship *Serapis*
1779

Treaty of Paris ends the war
1783

THINKING ABOUT VOCABULARY

Number a paper from 1 to 10. Beside each number write the word or term from the list below that best completes the sentence.

Continental Army

Declaration of Independence

large-scale map

Loyalist

map scale

mercenary

Patriot

Second Continental Congress

traitor

Treaty of Paris

1. Colonists cheered the delegates of the _____ when they met in May 1775.

2. A _____ was someone who supported the fight for independence.

3. A _____ is a soldier paid to fight for another country.

4. If your map shows great detail of a small area, it is a _____ .

5. Thomas Jefferson wrote the _____ in Philadelphia in 1776.

6. Britain agreed to the colonies' independence in the _____ in 1783.

7. You must look at the _____ to calculate real distances on a map.

8. John Adams named George Washington as commander-in-chief of the _____ .

9. King George III thought that anyone who supported the colonies' independence was a _____ .

10. One out of three colonists was a _____, or remained loyal to Britain.

THINKING ABOUT FACTS

1. Why was *Common Sense* important to the cause of independence?

2. Why did the issue of slavery come up during the American Revolution?

3. What advantages did the Patriots have in the war?

4. How did Bernardo de Gálvez help the Patriot cause?

5. Look at the time line above. Compare and contrast the events that occurred in 1777.

THINK AND WRITE

WRITING A DIALOGUE
Write a dialogue in which a Loyalist and a Patriot discuss their opinions about the American Revolution.

WRITING A SPEECH
Suppose that George Washington has asked you to help him inspire his troops during their bitter winter at Valley Forge. Write a speech for him to make to his soldiers.

WRITING A NEWSPAPER ARTICLE
Write an article in which you describe one of the battles you have read about in this chapter. Include dates, events, and people who played a key role in the battle. Write a headline for your article.

APPLYING GEOGRAPHY SKILLS

COMPARING MAPS AT DIFFERENT SCALES
Answer the questions below to practice the skill of comparing maps at different scales.

1. What is a map scale?

2. What is the difference between large-scale and small-scale maps?

3. How do you decide whether to use a large-scale map or a small-scale map?

4. Look at the map of the Southern Colonies on page 336. What is the distance between Yorktown and Savannah, Georgia?

5. What kind of information could you see on a large-scale map of Savannah that is not on this map?

Summing Up the Chapter

Copy the main idea map on a separate piece of paper. Then review the chapter to complete the map. After you have finished, choose two of the events shown on the map and answer the question "How are these events related?" For example, how did the approval of the Declaration of Independence lead to the debate over slavery?

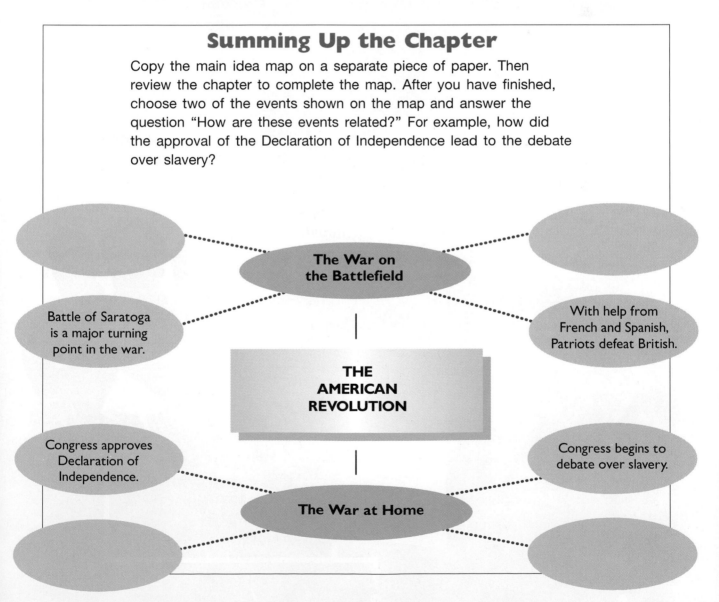

The War on the Battlefield

Battle of Saratoga is a major turning point in the war.

With help from French and Spanish, Patriots defeat British.

THE AMERICAN REVOLUTION

Congress approves Declaration of Independence.

Congress begins to debate over slavery.

The War at Home

The Constitution of the United States

THINKING ABOUT
HISTORY AND GEOGRAPHY

As you can see on the time line, Chapter 13 tells the story of the United States government. The Articles of Confederation, our first central government, did not succeed in uniting the country. In 1787 the Constitution presented a new system of government. Later the Bill of Rights was added to the Constitution and was accepted by the 13 states.

1780s

CINCINNATI
Americans begin moving west into the Northwest Territory

1787

PHILADELPHIA
Delegates sign the United States Constitution

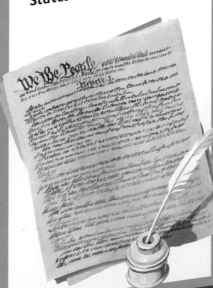

1787

PHILADELPHIA
Richard Allen begins first movement for equal rights by African Americans

1780   1787   1788

NORTH
AMERICA

New York
City

Cincinnati

Philadelphia

UNITED
STATES

ATLANTIC
OCEAN

1789

NEW YORK CITY
George Washington takes
oath as first President of
the United States

1791

NEW YORK CITY
Congress approves the Bill
of Rights

1789

1790

341

Focus Activity

READ TO LEARN

What kind of government did the Articles of Confederation create?

VOCABULARY

- Articles of Confederation
- Shays's Rebellion
- Northwest Ordinance
- territory
- statehood

PEOPLE

- Richard Allen
- Daniel Shays

PLACES

- Northwest Territory
- Indiana
- Wisconsin
- Ohio
- Michigan
- Illinois

LESSON 1

The Articles of Confederation

Read Aloud

The colonists' ragged army had defeated the mighty British. What did that mean for the men and women who had risked their lives for independence? Abigail Adams wrote to her husband, John Adams, and told him what she wanted in the new government. "I desire that you would remember the ladies," she said. "We will not hold ourselves bound to obey laws in which we have no voice or representation."

THE BIG PICTURE

Abigail Adams was not the only American thinking about the changes that independence from Great Britain might bring. Encouraged by their victory over a great European power, people in the 13 states believed that anything was possible. Many of the enslaved African Americans who had fought against the British in the American Revolution asked for their freedom and got it. **Richard Allen**, a former slave, started the Free African Society in 1787. Some historians have called this the first organized movement for rights by African Americans in North America.

Everyone was thinking about change. The states, too, began to explore their independence. First they set up their own governments. By 1777, 10 of the 13 states had adopted constitutions. Soon, however, there were conflicts between the states. In 1783 George Washington wrote, "It is yet to be decided whether the Revolution [was] a blessing or a curse." The states were independent, but they were not fully united.

THE FIRST CENTRAL GOVERNMENT

The Second Continental Congress adopted the Articles of Confederation in 1781. The Articles set up our country's first central government. Years of living under British rule made many Americans distrust government with a strong central power. The Articles of Confederation gave most powers to the governments of the states.

A Weak Government

Under the Articles of Confederation, each state made its own laws, collected its own taxes, and printed its own money. Money printed by one state was not always accepted in another state. Most people thought of themselves only as citizens of the state in which they lived and not as citizens of the United States.

The Congress could do little to settle conflicts between the states. It had no power to enforce the laws it passed.

Congress did not even have money to pay soldiers who had fought in the Revolution. Lack of money caused serious problems in Massachusetts. Massachusetts charged heavy taxes on land. Its courts began jailing farmers and taking their land when they could not pay the taxes. Many of the farmers were owed money by Congress.

In 1786 a Massachusetts farmer named Daniel Shays organized a group of farmers to protest against the courts. The protest soon turned bloody. Over 1,000 farmers battled against the local militia. Eight men were killed before the uprising called Shays's Rebellion was stopped.

Shays's Rebellion led Patrick Henry to conclude, "Our body politic is dangerously sick." Other leaders agreed. Things would never improve, said George Washington, under the "half-starved, limping government" of the Articles of Confederation.

Shays's Rebellion (left) showed that the central government was weak. Neither paper money from Massachusetts nor coins from New Jersey could buy goods in other states.

THE NORTHWEST ORDINANCE

In spite of its weaknesses Congress did pass some very important laws under the Articles of Confederation. One of the most important was the Northwest Ordinance, passed in 1787. This law provided a way for new territories to become states. A territory is an area of land that belongs to a government.

The Northwest Territory

After the American Revolution the United States claimed all land from the Atlantic Ocean to the Mississippi River. This land included a region called the Northwest Territory. Use the map on this page to locate this area. It is now part of the Middle West of the United States. The Northwest Territory included the future states of Indiana, Ohio, Wisconsin, Michigan, and Illinois.

Before Congress passed the Northwest Ordinance, the states quarreled over control of the Northwest Territory. Some states, like Virginia, claimed large parts of the territory. The Northwest Ordinance divided this huge territory into smaller territories. The people who lived in a territory could apply for statehood when its population reached 60,000. Statehood means to become a state. The ordinance did not allow an existing state to claim any part of the new territories.

The Nation Grows

Under the British, the Northwest Territory had been set aside for Native Americans. Now thousands of United States citizens began moving into the area. Many arrived in covered wagons with all their belongings. They were coming for the promise of land.

To control settlement of the Northwest Territory, Congress divided the land into townships of six square miles each. Each township became a self-governing part of the territory.

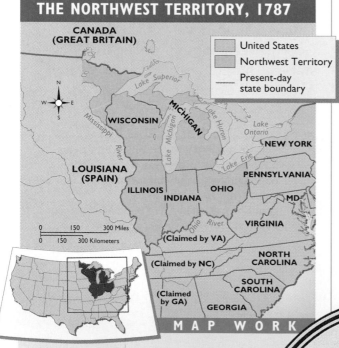

THE NORTHWEST TERRITORY, 1787

CANADA (GREAT BRITAIN)

United States
Northwest Territory
Present-day state boundary

Lake Superior
WISCONSIN
MICHIGAN
Lake Michigan
Lake Huron
Lake Ontario
NEW YORK
Mississippi River
LOUISIANA (SPAIN)
ILLINOIS
INDIANA
OHIO
Lake Erie
PENNSYLVANIA
MD
0   150   300 Miles
0   150   300 Kilometers
Ohio River
VIRGINIA
(Claimed by VA)
(Claimed by NC)
NORTH CAROLINA
(Claimed by GA)
SOUTH CAROLINA
GEORGIA

MAP WORK

Ohio was the first territory to join the United States under the Northwest Ordinance.

1. Which territories do you think would become states after Ohio?

2. What effects do you think settlement of the Northwest Territory had on Virginia and Pennsylvania?

This is a later version of the Great Seal of the United States.

344

The Northwest Ordinance gave new settlers in the territories the same rights that citizens had in the 13 states. The Northwest Ordinance also outlawed slavery and the hiring of indentured servants. In addition the ordinance required that each township set aside land for public schools. Members of Congress believed that if people were going to govern themselves, they had to be educated.

WHY IT MATTERS

One important legacy of the Articles of Confederation was the Northwest Ordinance. It would serve as a model for creating new territories for over 100 years. However, the weaknesses of the Articles of Confederation created problems for the new country. Many Americans concluded that the United States needed a stronger central government.

DID YOU KNOW?

How was the Great Seal of the United States chosen?

In the 1700s most countries had a seal that they used to stamp official documents. When our country won its independence, our leaders decided to create a Great Seal to represent the new country. Benjamin Franklin suggested a picture of a wild turkey on the seal. It was not a bad choice—turkeys are one of the few large birds that are native to North America. However, in 1782 Franklin, Thomas Jefferson, and John Adams settled on a seal that showed an eagle with a ribbon in its mouth. On the ribbon is the Latin phrase *E pluribus unum*. This motto, as you read in Chapter 1, means "Out of many, one."

✓ Reviewing Facts and Ideas

MAIN IDEAS
- The Articles of Confederation, adopted in 1781, set up the first central government for the 13 states.
- The weaknesses of the central government under the Articles of Confederation made it hard to resolve conflicts between the states.
- The Northwest Ordinance was passed under the Articles of Confederation in 1787. It provided a way for territories to become states.

THINK ABOUT IT

1. Why did the Articles of Confederation give most powers to the states?

2. Under the Northwest Ordinance, when could a territory ask for statehood?

3. **FOCUS** How did the Articles of Confederation change the colonists' minds about the role of a central government?

4. **THINKING SKILL** Was Patrick Henry stating a _fact_ or an _opinion_ when he said that the government was "dangerously sick?"

5. **GEOGRAPHY** You read that part of today's Middle West was known as the Northwest Territory. Why do you think this was so?

The Granger Collection

1775　1780　1786 1787　1790　1795

The Constitutional Convention

Read Aloud

In 1786 George Washington opened a letter from Congress asking him to attend a meeting. It said, "Commissioners to meet at Philadelphia on the second Monday in May next, to take into consideration the situation of the United States." Four years before, Washington had said he had "retired forever" from public life. Yet his country needed him again.

Focus Activity

READ TO LEARN

What was the result of the Great Compromise?

VOCABULARY

- Constitutional Convention
- Virginia Plan
- legislative branch
- executive branch
- judicial branch
- Supreme Court
- New Jersey Plan
- Great Compromise
- House of Representatives
- Senate

PEOPLE

- Alexander Hamilton
- James Madison
- George Mason
- Roger Sherman

THE BIG PICTURE

In September 1786 the lawyers **Alexander Hamilton** from New York and **James Madison** from Virginia attended a meeting of the Congress held in Annapolis, Maryland. The purpose of the meeting was to discuss problems between the states. The longer the meeting went on, the more everyone agreed that a second meeting was needed.

The delegates asked Hamilton to write a letter inviting delegates from all 13 states to this second meeting. As you have read in the Read Aloud above, George Washington was invited to this meeting, which became known as the **Constitutional Convention**.

Hamilton had to be careful about what he said in the letter. The government under the Articles of Confederation was not working. Still many leaders were not ready to get rid of the Articles. So the letter talked about changing the Articles of Confederation. What actually happened, as you shall see, was very different.

346

THE DELEGATES MEET

In May 1787 the delegates began arriving in Philadelphia for the meeting. Newspapers called it "The Grand Convention." Fifty-five delegates came. They represented the "wisdom of the continent," wrote one newspaper.

The Constitutional Convention

The meeting could not begin until delegates from at least seven states arrived. The meeting finally began, almost two weeks late, on May 25, 1787, in the Philadelphia State House.

The delegates included Hamilton and Madison. At age 81, Benjamin Franklin of Pennsylvania was the oldest delegate. Other delegates included George Mason, who had helped to write Virginia's constitution, and Gouverneur Morris, who was from New York.

Absent from the convention were Thomas Jefferson, John Adams, and Patrick Henry. Jefferson and Adams were abroad, serving as ambassadors. An ambassador is an official representative sent to another country. Henry refused to attend the convention. "I smell a rat," he declared, believing the delegates would try to take power away from the states.

The delegates had many things in common. All 55 were white men who owned property. More than half of them were lawyers. Most of the delegates had fought beside Washington in the Continental Army. Many had also helped write the constitutions of their own states.

The delegates elected George Washington president of the convention. He insisted that what went on in the meeting be kept secret. It would be easier to work out problems if there were no pressure from the public. So they nailed the windows shut and closed the doors. Not even the terrible summer heat made them open the windows.

Washington Addressing the Constitutional Convention, by Junius B. Stearns, includes portraits of 1. Gouverneur Morris, 2. Benjamin Franklin, 3. James Madison, 4. John Rutledge, 5. Alexander Hamilton, and 6. George Washington.

MADISON AT THE CONVENTION

James Madison came to the convention 11 days early. This was not surprising to those who knew him. Madison liked to be prepared. Long before the meeting, he had asked his friend Thomas Jefferson for books about the governments of other countries. Jefferson sent back trunk loads of books from his library in Paris, France.

Madison spent all of his daylight hours reading what he called his "literary cargo." Delegate William Pierce of Georgia wrote that Madison was "the best informed man on any point in a debate."

Today we know a great deal about what happened at the Constitutional Convention because of the notes kept by James Madison. He chose a seat in front so he could hear and write down everything that was said. "I was not

This portrait of James Madison, made at age 23 or 24, is set in a brooch that is now kept in the Library of Congress in Washington, D.C.

The Library of Congress

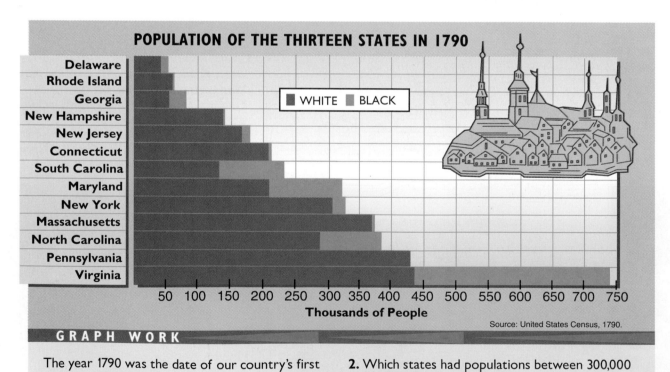

POPULATION OF THE THIRTEEN STATES IN 1790

WHITE ■ BLACK

Delaware
Rhode Island
Georgia
New Hampshire
New Jersey
Connecticut
South Carolina
Maryland
New York
Massachusetts
North Carolina
Pennsylvania
Virginia

50 100 150 200 250 300 350 400 450 500 550 600 650 700 750
Thousands of People

Source: United States Census, 1790.

GRAPH WORK

The year 1790 was the date of our country's first census.

1. In which states were black and white populations almost the same?

2. Which states had populations between 300,000 and 450,000?

3. Why do you think Virginia had the largest population and Delaware the smallest?

absent a single day," wrote Madison, "nor more than a fraction of an hour in any day."

The Virginia Plan

Madison left nothing to chance. He arrived at the meeting with a plan of government already written. He made sure his plan was discussed first. Presented by Virginia's popular governor, Edmund Randolph, it came to be called the Virginia Plan. The plan would establish a republic. One part of the plan said "that a national government ought to be established."

The Virginia Plan said that the central government should have three branches, or parts. A legislative (LEJ ihs lay tihv) branch, or law-making body, called the Congress, would make laws for the country and raise money for the central government. The executive (eg ZEK yuh tihv) branch would be headed by one President. The role of the President would be to carry out the laws made by Congress. The third was a judicial (joo DIHSH ul) branch that would decide the meaning of laws. It would be headed by a body of judges called the Supreme Court. Most states had already adopted this three-part model of government. It was based on the British government.

On May 30 the delegates voted to accept part of the Virginia Plan. This decision was important to Madison because it meant that the delegates were not going to spend time trying to change the Articles of Confederation. Instead, they were going to form a new central government. From that point on, the meeting in Philadelphia was a Constitutional Convention. James Madison later became known as the "Father of the Constitution."

The New Jersey Plan

Two weeks later, delegates from large states and small states were locked in a heated debate. The Virginia Plan called for one house of Congress that would be based on population. The large states liked this plan, because it would give them more representatives than the smaller states. The small states did not like this plan. If they had fewer representatives than the large states, they would have less power and little influence in the Congress.

Under the Articles, all of the states had equal power. The small states wanted to keep it that way. They presented the New Jersey Plan, which gave all states the same number of representatives. As the graph on page 348 shows, Virginia, with a population of over 700,000, would have the same number of representatives as the state of Delaware, which had a population of about 59,000.

Eliza Powel, wife of a former mayor of Philadelphia, was among those who greeted the convention delegates.

Pennsylvania Academy of the Fine Arts

MANY COMPROMISES

The debate between large states and small states threatened to end the convention. Some delegates talked of going home. So the delegates set up a committee to work out a compromise. In a compromise, as you have read in Chapter 4, each side gives up something it wants in order to reach an agreement. It took the delegates two months to find a solution.

The Great Compromise

Roger Sherman from Connecticut proposed what became known as the Great Compromise. Sherman, a judge, was known for his clear thinking. Jefferson claimed Sherman had "never said a foolish thing in his life." In the Great Compromise the new Congress would have two separate houses. In the House of Representatives, the number of each state's representatives would be based on population, which favored the large states. In the Senate, each state would have two representatives, which favored the small states.

This picture of the signing of the Constitution was painted by Howard Chandler Christy in 1940. It hangs in the Capitol Building in Washington, D.C.

Other Compromises

Soon another compromise was needed. Some delegates did not want the people to vote directly for the President. They were afraid that people could too easily be fooled into voting for an unacceptable candidate. Finally, the delegates decided that the people would vote for members of an Electoral College. The Electoral College would then vote for a President. However, as in most European countries at that time, only white men who owned property could vote.

Slavery and the Constitution

Once the delegates started discussing population, the issue of slavery came up. Should enslaved people be counted in a state's population? Many northern states wanted to end slavery. Most southern states, which had many slaves, wanted slavery to continue.

Finally, a compromise was reached. Every five slaves, or people "bound to service," would be counted as three. In addition, the delegates agreed to end slave trading with other countries in 1808.

Many delegates were unhappy with this compromise. Without it, however, the southern states might have left the convention. There would have been no Constitution.

On September 17, 1787, the delegates finally signed the Constitution of the United States. Now they could open the doors and the windows. They would carry the Constitution back to their states for approval. Yet before the Constitution was approved, the states would debate yet another compromise, one that added protection for individual rights.

WHY IT MATTERS

When Ben Franklin came out of the convention hall for the last time, Eliza Powel stopped him. She asked him what kind of government the country would have. "A republic if you can keep it," he told her.

The delegates used this silver inkstand and quill set to sign the Constitution.

The hard job of keeping the republic alive still lay ahead, and it continues today. Writing the Constitution was a struggle that involved many compromises. People with different points of view often have to compromise in order to reach an agreement.

Franklin, Madison, and the other delegates had done something few had done before. They had created a complex written plan of government. You can read the Constitution on pages R22–R45 in the back of this book.

✓✓ Reviewing Facts and Ideas

MAIN IDEAS

- Delegates gathered in Philadelphia in May 1787 for a meeting of the states, which turned into a Constitutional Convention. The writing of the United States Constitution involved many compromises.

- The Constitution set up a central government with three main branches— legislative, executive, and judicial.

- The delegates signed the Constitution of the United States of America on September 17, 1787.

THINK ABOUT IT

1. How did James Madison prepare for the Constitutional Convention?

2. What did the delegates to the Constitutional Convention have in common?

3. **FOCUS** On what issues did the delegates need to compromise in order to get the Constitution signed?

4. **THINKING SKILL** _Compare_ the Virginia Plan to the New Jersey Plan. Who favored each plan? Why?

5. **WRITE** Write a script for a film about the Constitutional Convention. Focus on the debate that took place to make the Great Compromise.

Thinking Skills

Recognizing Point of View

Delegates William Paterson (left) and James Wilson (above) debated how many representatives the states should have.

VOCABULARY

point of view

WHY THE SKILL MATTERS

In the last lesson you read about the Constitutional Convention. The delegates from each state had disagreed about how representatives should be chosen for the United States Congress. They had different points of view. A point of view is the position from which a person looks at something.

The delegates' opinions were shaped by the positions or points of view from which they viewed certain issues. Delegates from small states were concerned about protecting their states from large states. From their point of view, it was important for small states to have representation equal to the states with large populations. Delegates from large states were concerned about losing their power. From their point of view, it was important for representation in Congress to be based on population.

Recognizing a person's point of view is a useful skill. It will help you determine the accuracy of what he or she is writing about.

USING THE SKILL

Read the following statement by William Paterson. He presented the New Jersey Plan to the Constitutional Convention.

There is no more reason that a large state should have more votes than a small one, than that a rich individual citizen should have more votes than a [poor] one. . . . Give the large states an influence in proportion to their

352

[size], and what will be the consequence? Their ambition will be . . . increased, and the small states will have everything to fear.

Paterson's statement reflects the point of view of the small states. There are several ways you can tell what a person's point of view is. First, identify that person's position. Paterson was against basing a state's representation on population.

Next, think about the information a person gives. Identify which statements are facts and which are opinions. Paterson used the word *should*, which is a clue that he was expressing an opinion. He was giving his view of what was the "right" thing to do. He also used the words *rich* and *poor* when he compared the number of votes a citizen should have. These words let you know that Paterson is using an example to describe less wealthy people as small states.

TRYING THE SKILL

Now try identifying the point of view of another delegate from the Constitutional Convention. James Wilson of Pennsylvania said:

As all authority is derived from the people, equal numbers of people ought to have an equal number of representatives, and different numbers of people different numbers of representatives.

In other words, representation should be based on population, which would give large states more votes than small states.

Helping yourself

- **A point of view** is the position from which a person looks at something.

- To recognize a point of view, identify statements of fact and opinion.

- Next, identify words or phrases that tell how the person feels about the subject.

What position did Wilson support in his statement? Is Wilson expressing a fact or an opinion? How do you know? What words or phrases tell you about Wilson's point of view? Why did Wilson have the point of view he had on this topic?

REVIEWING THE SKILL

1. What is a person's point of view?
2. What kinds of clues tell you about a person's point of view?
3. Why is it important to try to be able to recognize a person's point of view?
4. Georgia, then a small southern state, depended on the large southern states for trade. It voted with the large states. What shaped Georgia's point of view? Why do you think it voted with the large states?
5. Historians often present different versions of the same event. How can knowing their points of view help you to understand their accounts of what happened in the past?

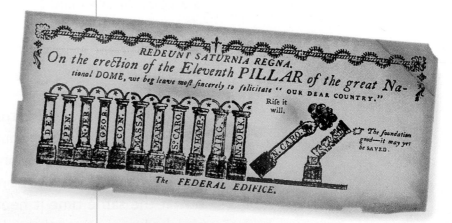

This political cartoon shows that North Carolina and Rhode Island had not yet adopted the Constitution.

Independence National Historical Park

1775   1780   **1786 1787**   1790   1795

How the Constitution Works

Focus Activity

READ TO LEARN

What kind of government did the United States Constitution create?

VOCABULARY

- amendment
- Preamble
- federal system
- checks and balances
- veto

Read Aloud

Tears streamed down Ben Franklin's face as he signed the Constitution. He looked once again at the carving of the sun on the back of George Washington's chair. "I have often looked at that sun behind the president of the convention without being able to tell whether it was rising or setting," he said, "but now, I have the happiness to know that it is a rising and not a setting sun." The rising sun that Franklin spoke of was the new central government of a very young country, the United States of America.

THE BIG PICTURE

The Constitution of the United States is many things. It is a code of laws and a framework for government. It is also a piece of history—the world's oldest written plan of government still in use. How is it that a document written over 200 years ago remains meaningful today?

The Constitution still works because the people who wrote it made sure that it could change with the needs of a growing country. They provided for **amendments**, or additions, to the Constitution. They knew that the Constitution needed to be permanent, but at the same time it needed to allow for change. It also had to protect the rights of both individuals and states. In this lesson you will learn why the Constitution has been able to work for over 200 years.

THE UNITED STATES CONSTITUTION

As the delegates wrote the Constitution, they chose every word carefully. Their struggle with Great Britain had made them distrust living under a powerful central government. Yet they agreed that government under the Articles of Confederation had not been strong enough. They worked for a balance. As James Madison wrote, "Every word [of the Constitution] decides a question between power and liberty."

The Preamble

The introduction, or the Preamble (PREE am bul), to the Constitution begins with the words "We the People." The authors of the Constitution wanted to show that the people held the power in this country. The three main branches of government—legislative, executive, and judicial—had to answer to the people and no one else. Read the Preamble to the Constitution on this page. What other goals does the Preamble list?

Preamble to the Constitution of the United States, approved by the states in 1789.

We the People of the United States, in Order to form a more perfect Union, establish Justice, insure domestic Tranquility, provide for the common Defense, promote the general Welfare, and secure the blessings of Liberty to ourselves and our Posterity, do ordain and establish this Constitution for the United States of America.

domestic tranquility: peace within the country
posterity: future generations
ordain: make legal

A Federal System of Government

The Constitution set up a federal system of government. In a federal system, the states and the central government share power. Some powers are given only to the states. Others are given only to the central government, which is also known as the federal government. For example, only the federal government has the power to declare war, coin money, make treaties with other countries, run the post office, and settle disputes between states.

The states have power to set up public schools and local governments and run elections. Both state and federal governments have the right to collect taxes and pass laws.

CHECKS AND BALANCES

After years of living under British rule, the authors of the Constitution had seen what happened when one branch of government gained too much power. They did not want any branch of the federal government to become too powerful. So they set up a system of **checks and balances**. In this system, the powers of one branch of government are balanced by the powers of another. Each branch can check, or stop, another branch. If one branch tried to use its powers wrongly, the other two could keep it under control. The flow chart below shows how the system of checks and balances works.

How It Works

The system of checks and balances makes it impossible for one branch of the federal government to act without the cooperation of another branch. For example, under the Constitution, the President is allowed to order the army into battle. Yet only Congress can

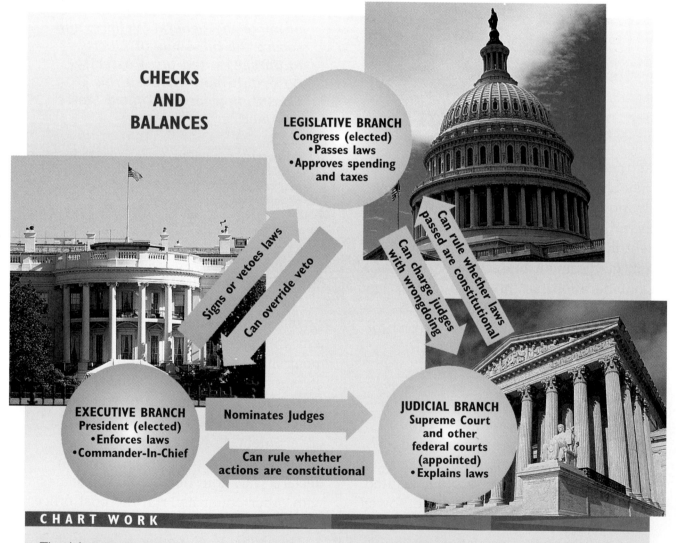

CHECKS AND BALANCES

LEGISLATIVE BRANCH
Congress (elected)
• Passes laws
• Approves spending and taxes

Signs or vetoes laws

Can override veto

Can rule whether laws passed are constitutional

Can charge judges with wrongdoing

EXECUTIVE BRANCH
President (elected)
• Enforces laws
• Commander-In-Chief

Nominates Judges

Can rule whether actions are constitutional

JUDICIAL BRANCH
Supreme Court and other federal courts (appointed)
• Explains laws

CHART WORK

The delegates also debated how many people should head the executive branch. By compromise, the delegates decided on one President.

1. What are the powers of the executive branch?

2. How can Congress check the powers of the executive branch?

3. How can the judicial branch check the powers of both the executive and legislative branches?

declare war. So Congress has a check on the President's powers.

Although the Congress may pass any law, the President can veto, or refuse to approve, that law. The system of checks and balances does not end there. If two-thirds of the members of both houses of Congress agree, Congress can override, or cancel, a veto. In this way, Congress can still pass a law even if the President has vetoed it.

The Supreme Court can check the powers of both the Congress and the President. It can put a stop to any law passed by Congress or signed by the President. To do this, the Supreme Court must decide whether such a law is allowed by the Constitution.

WHY IT MATTERS

The Constitution balances freedom and power by creating a federal system of government. That government unites the states while sharing power with them. The people of each state elect representatives to run the state and federal governments. When times change and new needs arise, the people can amend, or change, the Constitution. The Constitution has been able to work for over 200 years because of the system of checks and balances and its rules for adding amendments.

✓✓ **Reviewing Facts and Ideas**

MAIN IDEAS

- The government set up by the Constitution is a federal system in which the states and the central government share power. The Constitution is the "supreme law of the land," as stated in the Constitution.

- The Constitution may be amended by the people.

- The system of checks and balances prevents any one branch of government from gaining too much power.

THINK ABOUT IT

1. What is a federal system?

2. What are some of the powers that the federal government and the states have under the Constitution?

3. **FOCUS** How does the system of checks and balances keep one branch of the government from gaining too much power?

4. **THINKING SKILL** What was Benjamin Franklin's *point of view* on the carving of the sun on Washington's chair? Explain how you identified Franklin's point of view.

5. **WRITE** Write a description of how a law vetoed by the President can still become a law. Include the role of the judicial branch in your answer.

Washington, D.C., has many more government buildings today than it did in 1790.

1775   1780   1787   1797

Ratifying the Constitution

Read Aloud

In 1787 feelings were running high as the states decided whether or not to approve the new Constitution. Some state leaders, like Amos Singletary of Massachusetts, were against it. "If anybody had proposed such a Constitution as this in 1775," said Singletary, "it would have been thrown away at once." Robert Livingston of New York had a different view. "A vote against the Constitution is a vote for mystery and nonsense," Livingston said. "A vote for it is a vote for clarity and sense."

Focus Activity

READ TO LEARN

How was the Constitution adopted by the states?

VOCABULARY

- ratify
- Federalist
- Antifederalist
- Bill of Rights
- secretary
- Cabinet
- political party

PEOPLE

- George Washington

PLACES

- New York City

THE BIG PICTURE

In the autumn of 1787, the Constitutional Convention closed its doors. Yet the debate over the Constitution was not over. In fact, it had only started.

The approval of nine states—two-thirds of the 13 states—was needed before the Constitution could go into effect. Each of the states held a convention to decide whether or not to **ratify**, or officially approve, the Constitution.

The responses of the citizens varied. The idea of a central government troubled some people. Many, like Amos Singletary, worried that the states would lose their rights. Others, like Robert Livingston, felt that the new country's problems could be solved only by a strong central government. The debates over the Constitution had begun.

358

THE NEW GOVERNMENT

Two days after the Constitutional Convention ended, a Philadelphia newspaper called the *Pennsylvania Packet* published a complete copy of the Constitution. Many other newspapers soon did the same. Within weeks, leaders in the 13 states had taken sides in the debate about the Constitution. They gave speeches, published pamphlets, and wrote newspaper articles supporting their cause.

Federalists and Antifederalists

Supporters of the Constitution were called Federalists because the Constitution called for a federal system of government. Opponents, like Virginia's Patrick Henry, were called Antifederalists. Henry was afraid the states would lose their freedom under the Constitution. "Liberty," Henry said, "give us that precious jewel, and you may take everything else!"

The Federalists included such people as Edmund Pendleton of Virginia, James Madison, and Alexander Hamilton. "There is no quarrel between government and liberty," Pendleton said. Yet Antifederalists, like the Massachusetts writer Mercy Otis Warren, were not convinced. Warren saw efforts to ratify the Constitution as "dark, secret" plots of men who were "growing rich" while "lovers of freedom" suffered.

In a series of 85 articles published in New York newspapers, Madison, Hamilton, and John Jay, a lawyer from New York, built a strong case for the Constitution. These articles became known as *The Federalist Papers*. They argued that a weak government actually threatened people's freedoms. Only the strong government provided by the Constitution could protect the rights of all.

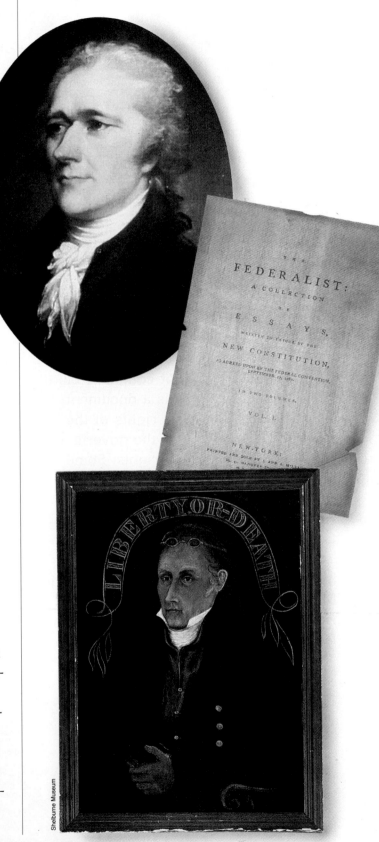

Alexander Hamilton (top) wrote articles in *The Federalist Papers* (center) supporting the Constitution. Patrick Henry (bottom) was a leading Antifederalist.

Shelburne Museum

DELAWARE

2 Senators 1 Representative
64.273 Inhabitants

PENSYLVANIA

2 Senators 14 Representatives
602365 Inhabitants

NEW JERSEY

2 Senators 5 Representative
11.114 Inhabitants

THE BILL OF RIGHTS

By January 9, 1788, five states—Delaware, Pennsylvania, New Jersey, Georgia, and Connecticut—had already ratified the Constitution. Only four more states were needed to approve it. Then, as the debate heated up, the process slowed down.

"There Is No Declaration of Rights!"

The Antifederalists complained that the Constitution did not contain a bill of rights. A bill of rights is a document that describes the basic rights of the people. It also says that the government cannot take away these rights. Some people called this document a "declaration of rights" because it contained rights that were listed in the Declaration of Independence.

Almost every state constitution included a bill of rights. In 1776 George Mason wrote this country's first bill of rights as part of Virginia's constitution. He based it partly on an English bill of rights that had been written almost 100 years earlier.

Mason felt strongly that the United States Constitution should also have a bill of rights. When it was his turn to sign the United States Constitution, Mason refused, saying, "There is no declaration of rights!"

Conflict in Massachusetts

As the delegates gathered in Boston to debate ratifying the Constitution, many in Massachusetts took up Mason's cry. The Federalists said that the Massachusetts constitution already had a bill of rights. The Antifederalists felt this was not enough. They also wanted a bill of rights added to the United States Constitution.

John Hancock, who had become governor of Massachusetts, told the delegates that a bill of rights could be added to the United States Constitution as amendments. This promise persuaded the Massachusetts delegates to ratify the Constitution.

MARYLAND

2 Senators 9 Representatives
300.635 Inhabitants

SOUTH CAROLINA

2 Senators 9 Representatives
343.591 Inhabitants

NEW HAMPSHIRE

2 Senators 4 Representatives
183.858 Inhabitants

Other states followed Massachusetts. On June 21, 1789, New Hampshire became the ninth state to ratify the document. Now the Constitution was law. By 1790, all 13 states had ratified it. A year later Congress added the ten amendments to the Constitution that are known as the Bill of Rights. You can read the Bill of Rights on pages R35–R37.

Amendments to the Constitution

Adding the Bill of Rights to the Constitution was possible because the Constitution included rules for adding amendments. George Mason had realized that people might want to change the Constitution. "It will be better to provide for [amendments] . . . than to trust to chance and violence," he said.

However, the writers of the Constitution did not want people to be able to change it without serious debate. They made changing the Constitution a long, slow process. Before the states can vote on an amendment, it must be approved by two-thirds of both the Senate and the House of Representatives. Or two-thirds of the states can request that Congress call a special convention. Then, three-quarters of all the states must ratify an amendment before it becomes part of the Constitution. Since the Bill of Rights was added in 1791, some 10,000 amendments to the Constitution have been proposed. Only 17 have been added. You can read them on pages R37–R45. You will learn about some of them in chapters to come.

Starting at the top of pages 360–361 with Delaware and ending at the bottom with Rhode Island (below), the seals of the original 13 states appear in the order in which the states ratified the Constitution.

WASHINGTON AS PRESIDENT

Every member of the Electoral College voted for George Washington as President. The Electoral College never again reached a decision so easily.

On April 14, 1789, Washington set out from Mount Vernon for the country's capital, New York City. Parades and cheering crowds greeted him all along the way.

Eight days later, he arrived in New York City. Dressed in a plain brown suit made of American cloth, Washington placed his left hand on an open Bible and took the President's oath of office on April 30, 1789. He swore to "preserve, protect, and defend the Constitution of the United States."

The President's Cabinet

To help the President run the government, Congress set up three government departments. Each was headed by an official called a secretary.

The Secretary of the Treasury, Alexander Hamilton, made decisions about how the federal government spent money. Thomas Jefferson, the Secretary of State, handled the country's dealings with other countries. The Secretary of War, Henry Knox, took charge of the country's defense. The Attorney General made sure that the country's laws were obeyed. Together these officials were called the Cabinet.

Political Parties

Disagreements arose within Washington's Cabinet. Alexander Hamilton believed the country's future lay in trade and industry. He argued for a strong federal government. Thomas Jefferson saw a country of self-sufficient farmers. He argued that the best government was one that governed the least.

Washington (above) arrived in New York City to be sworn in as President at Federal Hall. This statue of Washington (left) is part of a monument in Boston, Massachusetts.

This watercolor shows President Washington and the First Lady, Martha Washington.

These opposing views led to the first political parties. A political party is a group of people who share similar ideas about government. Followers of Hamilton later organized the Federalist Party. Jefferson's followers formed the Democratic-Republican Party.

First in War and Peace

George Washington served two terms, or eight years, as President. In 1797, he retired from office. In his farewell speech, Washington praised the "influence of good laws under a free government." He then returned to Mount Vernon. The country was greatly saddened by Washington's death in 1799. Virginia's United States Representative Henry Lee expressed the feelings of many people in the United States. During a meeting of Congress he said that Washington was "first in war, first in peace, and first in the hearts of his countrymen."

WHY IT MATTERS

The debate over ratifying the Constitution helped establish the tradition of fighting with words rather than with weapons. Each side presented its views in pamphlets, newspapers, and speeches.

The Constitution has become one of the world's most important documents. The United States was the first nation to have a constitution written by the people. The United States seemed to be a great experiment. Most people now agree the experiment succeeded.

✓// Reviewing Facts and Ideas

MAIN IDEAS

- In 1787 the debate over the Constitution began when the states voted whether or not to ratify it. By 1789, nine of the 13 states, or two-thirds, had ratified the Constitution.
- The Bill of Rights was ratified by the states in 1791.
- George Washington was elected the first President of the United States.

THINK ABOUT IT

1. Describe the Federalist's and the Antifederalist's points of view about ratifying the Constitution.

2. How did the views of Thomas Jefferson and Alexander Hamilton on the future of the United States differ?

3. **FOCUS** What compromise did the Federalists make to get enough states to ratify the Constitution?

4. **THINKING SKILL** Why do you think the authors of the Constitution _decided_ to make amending the Constitution a slow and difficult process?

5. **WRITE** Write a short speech an Antifederalist might have given in support of adding the Bill of Rights.

CHAPTER 13 REVIEW

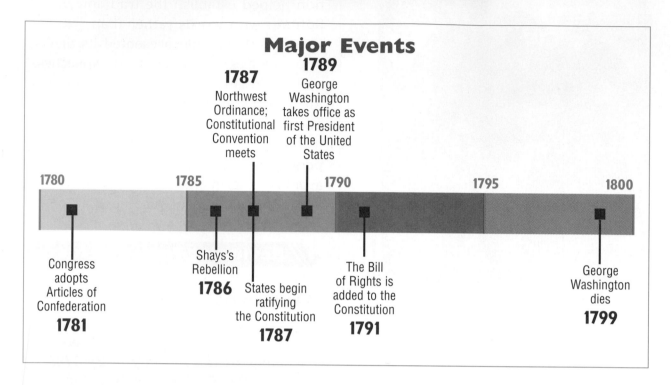

Major Events

1787
Northwest Ordinance; Constitutional Convention meets

1789
George Washington takes office as first President of the United States

1780   1785   1790   1795   1800

Congress adopts Articles of Confederation
1781

Shays's Rebellion
1786

States begin ratifying the Constitution
1787

The Bill of Rights is added to the Constitution
1791

George Washington dies
1799

THINKING ABOUT VOCABULARY

Number a paper from 1 to 5. Beside each number write the word or term from the list below that matches the description.

judicial branch   territory
preamble   veto
ratify

1. Refuse to approve
2. An area of land that belongs to a government
3. Introduction to the Constitution of the United States
4. The branch of government that decides on the meaning of laws
5. Officially approve

THINKING ABOUT FACTS

1. What were the weaknesses of the Articles of Confederation?
2. What was the Northwest Ordinance? What states did it help to create?
3. What was the original purpose of the Constitutional Convention?
4. What three branches of government does the Constitution set up? What does each one do?
5. What was the Great Compromise of the Constitutional Convention? What was decided in the compromise?
6. How did the issue of slavery enter into the Constitutional Convention? What did the delegates vote to do on this issue?
7. What is an amendment? Why is it important that the Constitutional Convention provided for amendments?
8. What is the purpose of the system of checks and balances?
9. What is the Bill of Rights? What role did the Bill of Rights play in convincing the states to ratify the Constitution?
10. Look at the time line above. What events in the chapter could you add to the time period?

THINK AND WRITE

WRITING A DIALOGUE
Write a dialogue between two members of the Constitutional Convention with opposing views about ratifying the Constitution.

WRITING ABOUT COMPROMISE
Write a paragraph about the compromises made in the Constitutional Convention and why compromise was needed to help the delegates reach an agreement. Then write another paragraph explaining how compromise might be useful in your own life.

WRITING A REPORT
Choose one branch of the United States government and write a report on it. Describe the responsibilities of this branch. Include, if possible, the names of government officials who now serve in this branch.

APPLYING THINKING SKILLS

RECOGNIZING POINT OF VIEW
To apply the skill of recognizing point of view, answer the questions below.

1. What is *point of view*?
2. What are some steps you can take to recognize a point of view?
3. Look at page 343. What was Patrick Henry's point of view about the government under the Articles of Confederation?
4. What words did Patrick Henry use that helped you to identify his point of view?
5. Why is recognizing point of view especially important when studying history?

Summing Up the Chapter

Copy the main idea pyramid on a separate piece of paper. Then review the chapter to complete the pyramid. After you have finished, use the information in the pyramid to write a paragraph explaining "How did the Articles of Confederation compare to the Constitution?"

The weaknesses of the Articles of Confederation lead to the writing of a new constitution for the United States.

The new Constitution creates a strong central government and protects people's rights.

• Cannot tax people
• Cannot raise army
• No power to carry out or enforce laws

UNIT 5 REVIEW

THINKING ABOUT VOCABULARY

Number a paper from 1 to 10. Beside each number write the word or term from the list below that best completes the sentence.

amendments
Constitutional Convention
Continental Army
federal system
liberty
mercenaries
Northwest Ordinance
repealed
symbol
town meeting

1. Many _____, or soldiers paid to fight for another country, fought on the side of the British.

2. The colonists demanded that the Stamp Act be _____, or canceled.

3. The _____ was a group of male colonists who met to solve local problems.

4. _____ is another word for freedom.

5. The _____ was the meeting at which delegates debated and wrote a new plan of government for the United States.

6. The Constitution provides for _____, or additions.

7. Under a _____, the states and the central government share power.

8. A _____ is something that stands for something else.

9. The _____ was a 1787 law that provided a way for new territories to become part of the United States.

10. Washington was the commander of the _____, the troops who fought on the side of the Patriots.

THINK AND WRITE

WRITING A BIOGRAPHY
Choose one of the individuals you read about in this unit and, after doing further research, write a short biography about the person. Include facts about the individual's personality, if possible.

WRITING A NEWSPAPER ARTICLE
Suppose that you have been assigned to report on the Constitutional Convention. Write an article about one of the events that takes place there. Include a headline for your article.

WRITING ABOUT PERSPECTIVES
Although the colonists named them the Intolerable Acts, these laws had different names in the British Parliament. Suppose that you are a British government official. Write a speech to your fellow citizens explaining why it is necessary to pass these tax laws.

BUILDING SKILLS

1. **Political cartoons** How is a political cartoon different from other cartoons?

2. **Political cartoons** What is dialogue? What is the purpose of dialogue in some political cartoons?

3. **Map scale** Which kind of map shows more detail, large-scale maps or small-scale maps?

4. **Map scale** Look at the maps on pages 336–337. What kinds of information would each map help you to find?

5. **Point of view** How can recognizing point of view help you to understand historical topics such as the debate over ratifying the Constitution?

YESTERDAY, TODAY &
TOMORROW

Although the Constitution was written over 200 years ago, it remains the law of our country today. How does the amendment process help keep the Constitution useful in the present? What main ideas of the Constitution do you think will continue to make it an important document in the future?

READING ON YOUR OWN

Here are some books you might find at the library to help you learn more.

A MORE PERFECT UNION: THE STORY OF OUR CONSTITUTION
by Betsy and Giulio Maestro

This illustrated story explains how the Constitution was drafted.

THE RIDDLE OF PENCROFT FARM
by Dorothea Jensen

This modern-day mystery can only be solved with the help of a young boy who lived in Valley Forge, Pennsylvania, during the American Revolution.

THE BOSTON TEA PARTY
by Walter Olesky

The events that led up to the Boston Tea Party are traced.

UNIT 5 REVIEW PROJECT

Organize a Living Time Line

1. Have each group member choose an event from this unit to research, such as the Boston Tea Party or Paul Revere's ride.
2. List several facts about each event.
3. Write the name and date of your event on a large piece of oak tag. Decorate it with glitter, colorful markers, and colored tissue paper.
4. On another piece of oak tag, write several facts about your event. Make a border for your facts with ribbon and paint.
5. Tie together the left sides of the oak tag with a piece of string. Then tie together the right sides.
6. Place the pieces of oak tag over your head so that you are wearing one piece in front of you and one piece behind you.
7. Participate in a living time line with your group.

367

THE ALAMO

THOMAS JEFFERSON

WAGON TRAIN
HEADED WEST

Expansion and Change

"The home of the brave"

from the "Star-Spangled Banner" by Francis Scott Key
See page 389.

Why Does it Matter?

The United States, as a new country, had many challenges to meet. Francis Scott Key wrote the words above during one of these challenges—the War of 1812.

After this war Americans continued moving west. New roads, canals, and railroads crossed the land. New technology and inventions changed life on the farm and in the cities. These changes made it an exciting time for our country. By the middle of the 1800s, the United States stretched from the Atlantic to the Pacific oceans.

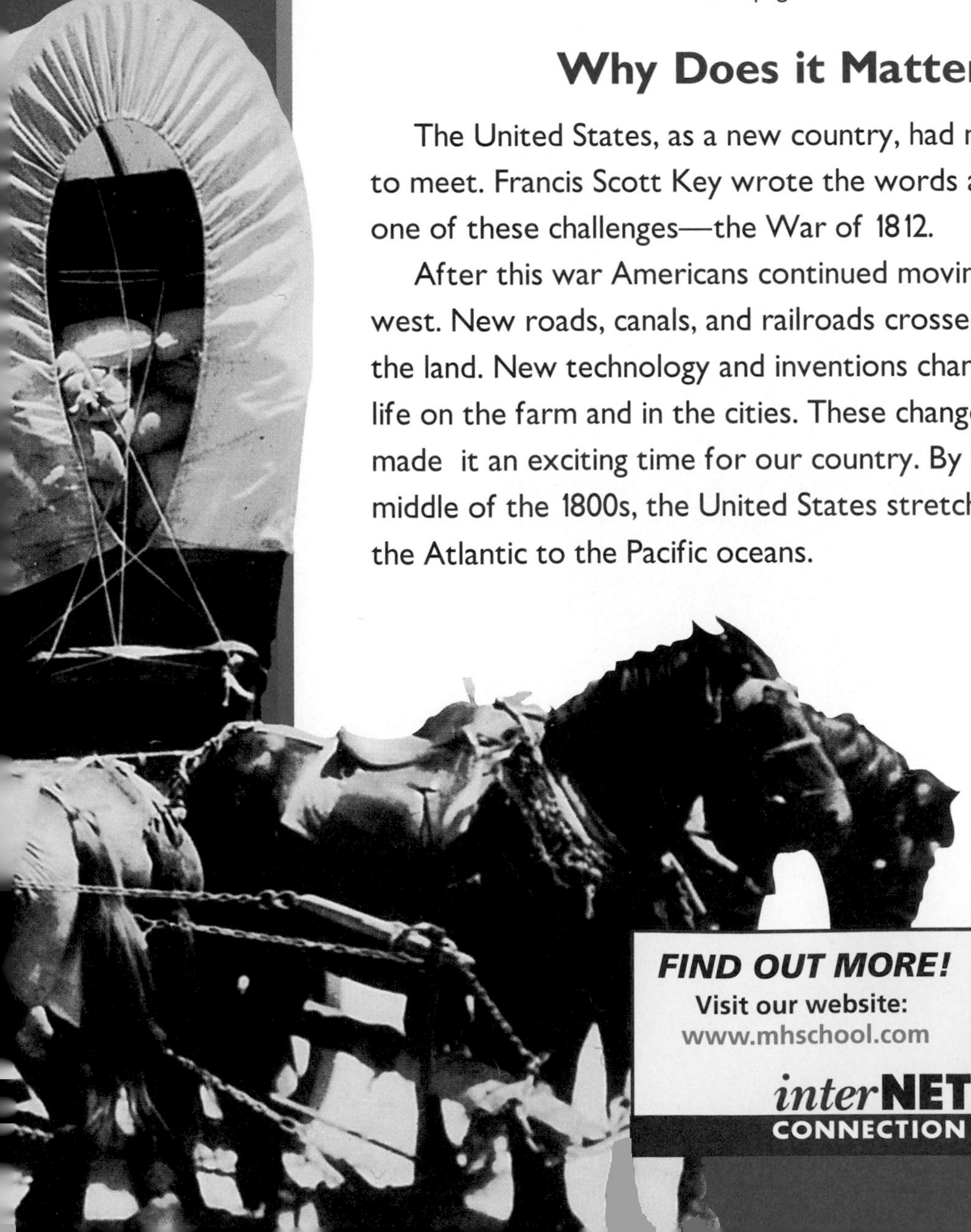

GOLD NUGGETS

FIND OUT MORE!
Visit our website:
www.mhschool.com

*inter***NET**
CONNECTION

Adventures with NATIONAL GEOGRAPHIC

Going for the GOLD

It isn't much to look at, is it? Some trees, some snow, a modest river. Yet this California creek was the setting for the start of a great American drama: the Gold Rush. A few golden flakes showed up here in 1848. A year and a half later, 80,000 people had headed west. In large wooden troughs and small metal pans, they carefully sorted through muck. Even today, the dream of a golden nugget draws Americans of all ages. Children learn old techniques, and grown-ups cherish young hopes. In the words of one miner, "I could be rich tomorrow."

GEO JOURNAL

Would you want to be a gold miner? Why or why not?

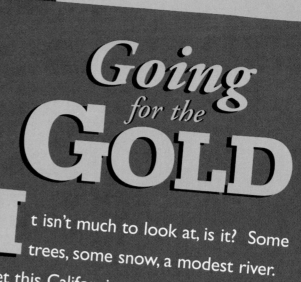

371

CHAPTER 14

A Young United States

THINKING ABOUT HISTORY AND GEOGRAPHY

Chapter 14 describes a time of both growth and change in the United States. In the East, the new capital—Washington, D.C.—became a symbol of the growing country. Follow the time line below to learn more about the young country and the people who helped it to develop.

PACIFIC OCEAN

1775
KENTUCKY
Daniel Boone cuts the Wilderness Road from Native American trails

1791
WASHINGTON, D.C.
Benjamin Banneker helps survey and plan the country's new capital

1804
ST. LOUIS
Lewis and Clark begin their exploration of the Louisiana Territory

1775   1795   1815

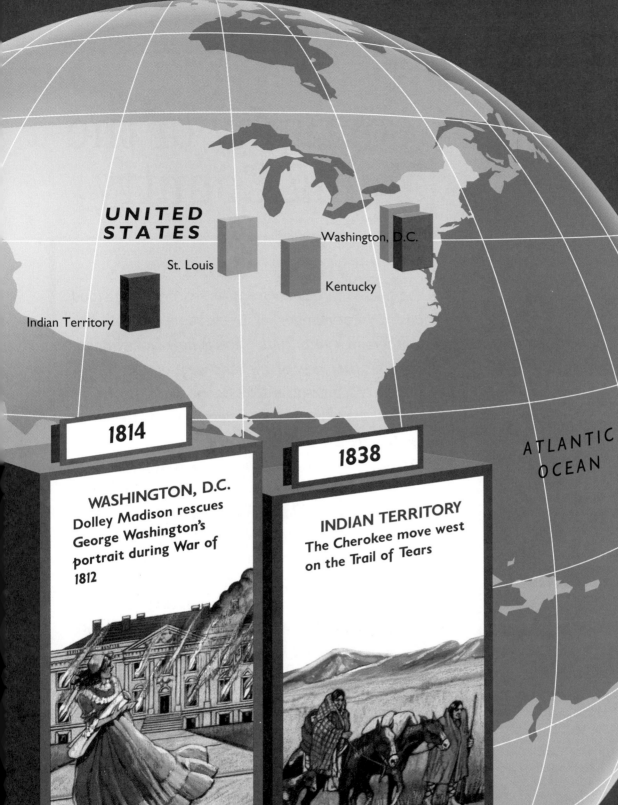

UNITED
STATES

St. Louis

Washington, D.C.

Kentucky

Indian Territory

ATLANTIC
OCEAN

1814

WASHINGTON, D.C.
Dolley Madison rescues
George Washington's
portrait during War of
1812

1838

INDIAN TERRITORY
The Cherokee move west
on the Trail of Tears

1835

1855

1760   1769   1792   1800   1820   1840

Geography of the Young Country

Read Aloud

We had passed through a great forest, on which stood myriads [a great number] of trees, some gay with blossoms, others rich with fruits." This is how Daniel Boone described his first view of the land west of the Appalachian Mountains in 1769. Boone was one of the people who helped new settlers to enter the area that is now the state of Kentucky.

Focus Activity

READ TO LEARN

How did people begin moving west of the Appalachians?

VOCABULARY

- pioneer

PEOPLE

- Daniel Boone
- John Findley
- Abraham Lincoln

PLACES

- Kentucky
- Cumberland Gap
- Wilderness Road
- Boonesborough

THE BIG PICTURE

After the American Revolution, thousands of people flocked to the lands west of the Appalachians. In 1770 the 13 colonies had a population of a little over 2 million. By 1790 the population of the United States had nearly doubled to almost 4 million. As the population grew, cheap farmland in the original 13 states became scarce. It cost up to $50 per acre, too high a price for many. Moving west seemed more attractive to people who could not afford land in the states.

These new settlers were called pioneers. The word pioneer means "a person who leads the way into new areas." To the pioneers the West was a frontier, a land available for settlement. To the Native Americans, the West was home.

Who were the pioneers? Many had come from England. Others were Scots-Irish or German. In this lesson you will read about two famous pioneers who settled west of the Appalachians.

GEOGRAPHY OF A GROWING NATION

As you can see on the map on this page, the young country in 1800 stretched from the 13 original states along the Atlantic Coast to the Mississippi River. The United States was bordered by British Canada to the north and Spanish Louisiana and Florida to the south. To the west, across the Mississippi, also lay Louisiana.

Beyond the Appalachians

Few Americans had settled near the Mississippi River. Most people were still trying to find a safe route beyond the Appalachians.

The Appalachians were rugged and difficult to farm. Beyond the mountains, however, was rich soil ideal for farming. As you can see on the map, the Central Plains lay west of the Appalachians. The woodlands and prairies provided shelter for deer and gophers. South of the Central Plains was the Gulf Coastal Plain. Its dense forests, grassy marshes, and tree-shaded swamps were filled with such wildlife as opossums and muskrats.

Native Americans had long farmed these lands. The Miami had been growing corn in the fertile Ohio River valley for hundreds of years. Along the Gulf Coast were many Choctaw villages and farms. The Shawnee and Cherokee lived in what would become the state of **Kentucky**. This land of plentiful wildlife was an important hunting ground.

Trail blazers marked their path with an ax.

THE UNITED STATES, 1800

200 400 Miles
200 400 Kilometers

Lake Superior
Lake Michigan
Lake Huron
Lake Ontario
Lake Erie
Susquehanna River
Hudson R.

ME (part of Mass.)
VT 1791
NH
MA
NY
RI
CT
NJ
PA
DE
MD

CENTRAL PLAINS
Indiana Territory
Terr. NW of Ohio R.
Missouri River
Ohio River

MOUNTAINS
APPALACHIAN

KY 1792
VA
NC
SC
GA

Potomac River

ATLANTIC OCEAN

Arkansas River
TN 1796
ATLANTIC COASTAL PLAIN
Savannah River

Terr. South of Ohio R.
Mississippi Territory
GULF COASTAL PLAIN
Gulf of Mexico

States
Territories

MAP WORK

After the original 13 states, Vermont, Kentucky, and Tennessee, were the first three states to join the United States once the Constitution was ratified.

1. In which years did Vermont, Kentucky, and Tennessee become states?

2. Which lands were part of the United States but were not yet states?

3. Which was the only state that lay along both the Gulf and Atlantic coastal plains?

THE ROAD TO KENTUCKY

The trails that the pioneers followed to the West began as Native American paths. Men called trailblazers cut their way through the forests. They made paths such as the Natchez Trail larger and easier for people to use.

"The Pathfinder"

Daniel Boone, who explored, hunted, and trapped in the Appalachians, was the most famous trailblazer of all. Asked if he had ever been lost, Boone replied, "No, but I was bewildered [confused] once for three days." Because of his skill at finding trails, Boone earned the nickname "the pathfinder."

Boone first heard about Kentucky from a trader named John Findley in 1755. In 1767 Boone tried to find the way to Kentucky. Findley said that he knew of a "gap," or narrow valley, that Native Americans used. Findley thought they could find it.

Daniel Boone in Kentucky

Locate the gap that Findley described on the map on this page. It is now

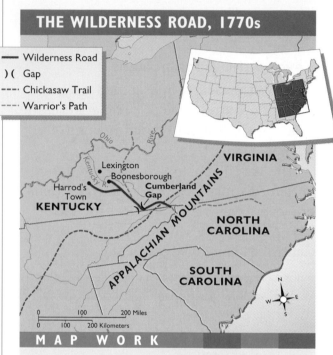

THE WILDERNESS ROAD, 1770s

— Wilderness Road
)(Gap
--- Chickasaw Trail
--- Warrior's Path

Ohio River
Kentucky R.
Lexington
Boonesborough
Harrod's Town
KENTUCKY
Cumberland Gap
VIRGINIA
APPALACHIAN MOUNTAINS
NORTH CAROLINA
SOUTH CAROLINA

0   100   200 Miles
0   100   200 Kilometers

MAP WORK

The Cumberland Gap led to central Kentucky with its fertile meadows.

1. How far is the gap from Boonesborough?
2. Why might the distance traveled be greater than shown on the map?

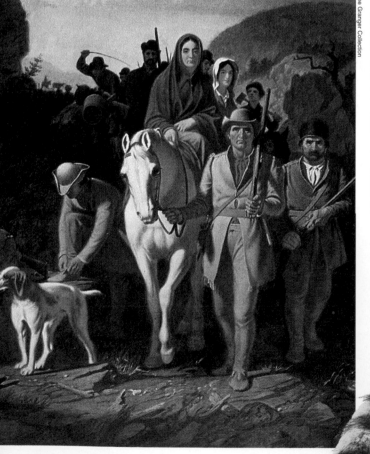

The Granger Collection

Daniel Boone (far left) led settlers through the Cumberland Gap. Although he never wore a coonskin cap, many American children (left) did later.

The painting *Boyhood of Lincoln* shows how much Lincoln enjoyed reading. On the frontier, books were precious.

known as the Cumberland Gap. In 1773 Boone led five families across the gap to settle in Kentucky. That October, a group of Delaware, Shawnee, and Cherokee were returning from a meeting about white settlement on their land. When they spied some of Boone's group, they attacked. Boone's son James and three others were killed. Boone's group decided to leave Kentucky.

In 1775 Boone helped persuade the Cherokee to sell much of their land in Kentucky to a businessman. The businessman then hired Boone to expand other Native American trails that led to the Cumberland Gap. The new trail created by Boone became known as the Wilderness Road.

By 1776 about 200 people were living in Boonesborough, a settlement founded by Boone and his men. By 1792 enough people were living in Kentucky for it to become our fifteenth state.

A Pioneer Childhood

One young pioneer child who would later become famous was born in Kentucky. His grandfather had been a friend of Daniel Boone. At an early age, Abraham weeded crops, collected nuts and berries, and fed animals. Later his family moved to another frontier, the Indiana Territory. Young Abraham grew up to become our country's sixteenth President, Abraham Lincoln.

WHY IT MATTERS

Daniel Boone and other pioneers played a key part in opening up new settlements in the West. Throughout the 1800s people from the United States continued to push the frontier farther west.

✔ Reviewing Facts and Ideas

MAIN IDEAS

- Many new settlers moved west of the Appalachians in the late 1700s.
- Daniel Boone led pioneers west on trails such as the Wilderness Road, which he created in 1775.

THINK ABOUT IT

1. What lands were new settlers moving to in the 1790s? What Native American peoples lived on these lands?

2. What was life like on the frontier for a young boy like Abraham Lincoln?

3. **FOCUS** Why did the pioneers move west in the late 1700s and early 1800s?

4. **THINKING SKILL** What different *points of view* might pioneers and Native Americans in Kentucky have had about the Wilderness Road? Explain.

5. **GEOGRAPHY** Use the map on page 375 to list the original 13 states and new states that joined the country by 1800.

1760   1780   1820   1840
     1791   1809

Jefferson Plans for Growth

Read Aloud

In 1800 John Adams spent his first night in the newly built President's house. "May none but wise and honest men ever rule under this roof," he said. One day the building would be known as the White House, the home of the President and the President's family.

Focus Activity

READ TO LEARN

What was the Louisiana Purchase?

VOCABULARY

- Louisiana Purchase

PEOPLE

- Benjamin Banneker
- Pierre L'Enfant
- Thomas Jefferson
- Napoleon Bonaparte
- Meriwether Lewis
- William Clark
- York
- Sacajawea

PLACES

- District of Columbia
- Missouri River
- Snake River
- Columbia River

THE BIG PICTURE

By 1790 many new settlers were building homes in the West. At the same time the federal government was making plans for its new home. Each state wanted to be the site of the country's new capital. The country's leaders decided to compromise. They agreed to build the capital on land that would not be part of any state.

In 1791 President Washington began making plans for the **District of Columbia**. The district is named after Christopher Columbus. The city within the District of Columbia is called Washington, after George Washington. Washington hired **Benjamin Banneker** to help lay out the city. Banneker was a writer, inventor, and scientist. He was also one of the first African Americans appointed by a President to work for the federal government. Banneker began with plans for the capital already created by a French architect named **Pierre L'Enfant** (pee AIR LAHN fahn).

The capital city was still unfinished when **Thomas Jefferson** became President in 1801. Jefferson also influenced the design of many buildings in the District of Columbia. As you will see, Jefferson would affect far more than the new capital while he was President.

THOMAS JEFFERSON BECOMES PRESIDENT

Thomas Jefferson became the third President of the United States after defeating President John Adams in a bitter election. John Adams belonged to the Federalist Party. As you have read in Chapter 13, the Federalists believed in a strong central government. Jefferson and his supporters belonged to the Democratic-Republican Party. This party's followers believed that the best government was one that governed the least.

Jefferson wanted citizens to feel that Washington, D.C., and the new government belonged to them. Each morning Jefferson opened the White House to visitors and warmly shook their hands.

A Threat from France

In 1801 the United States had 16 states. New settlers were pouring into the Ohio and Indiana territories. Louisiana, the land west of the Mississippi, had been changing hands for almost 40 years. In 1682, Robert La Salle had claimed it for France. In 1762 France gave it to Spain. In 1800 Spain returned the land to France in a secret treaty.

Since 1797 a general named Napoleon Bonaparte (nuh POH lee un BOH nuh pahrt) had ruled France. In the early 1800s Napoleon began fighting with Great Britain and other European countries. He had won many wars and taken over much of Europe. Jefferson feared that Napoleon wanted to expand the French empire in the Americas.

President Thomas Jefferson shown in Gilbert Stuart's painting (above), presided over great changes in our country, including completion of Washington, D.C., which Benjamin Bannecker (far left) helped to lay out.

THE LOUISIANA PURCHASE

President Jefferson was especially worried that France might close Louisiana's main port, New Orleans, to the United States. Farmers from Kentucky, Tennessee, and the territories shipped their goods down the Mississippi River to be sold in that busy port city. Whoever blocked the mouth of the Mississippi, Jefferson declared, was "our natural enemy." Jefferson was also worried that France might stop American settlers from moving west. Rather than start a costly war, Jefferson decided to look into buying New Orleans from France.

James Monroe Goes to France

In 1803 Jefferson sent his friend James Monroe to Paris with an offer to buy New Orleans. Monroe was surprised when a French official asked,

The French beginnings of New Orleans shown in 1803 (bottom) can be seen today in the old French Quarter (below) and in the city's many French customs.

UNDER MY WINGS EVERY THING PROSPERS

Chicago Historical Society

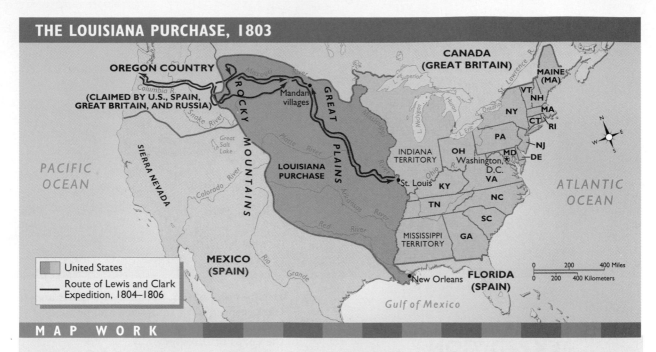

THE LOUISIANA PURCHASE, 1803

CANADA (GREAT BRITAIN)

OREGON COUNTRY
(CLAIMED BY U.S., SPAIN, GREAT BRITAIN, AND RUSSIA)

Mandan villages

ROCKY MOUNTAINS

GREAT PLAINS

LOUISIANA PURCHASE

SIERRA NEVADA

PACIFIC OCEAN

Great Salt Lake

Snake River

Columbia R.

Colorado River

Platte River

Arkansas River

Red River

Rio Grande

MEXICO (SPAIN)

MISSISSIPPI TERRITORY

INDIANA TERRITORY

OH

Washington, D.C.

St. Louis

KY

TN

VA

NC

SC

GA

MAINE (MA)

VT NH MA CT RI

NY

PA

NJ DE MD

ATLANTIC OCEAN

New Orleans

FLORIDA (SPAIN)

Gulf of Mexico

United States

Route of Lewis and Clark Expedition, 1804–1806

0 200 400 Miles
0 200 400 Kilometers

MAP WORK

Like other early explorers, Lewis and Clark found no direct water route to the Pacific Ocean. However, they did answer many questions Americans had about the West.

1. Which rivers did Lewis and Clark travel?

2. During which years did they explore?

3. Which European countries claimed areas that eventually became the United States?

4. What were these areas called?

"How much will you give for the whole of Louisiana?" France badly needed money for its war with Britain.

An agreement was soon reached. For $15 million, the United States bought a huge piece of land stretching west from New Orleans to the border of what is now Idaho and north to Canada. The Louisiana Purchase, as shown on the map on this page, doubled the size of the United States at a very low price—about four cents per acre.

Jefferson Looks to the West

Jefferson knew very little about this huge territory. However, he was excited to find out. In 1804 Jefferson sent an expedition to explore Louisiana and all the land to the Pacific Ocean. He chose his assistant Meriwether Lewis to lead the trip. Lewis had served as an army officer in the Northwest Territory.

Jefferson told Lewis to write down everything he saw—people, landforms, plants, and animals. Lewis sent a letter to his friend, an army officer named William Clark, asking him to help lead the expedition. "My friend," Clark wrote back, "I join you with hand and heart."

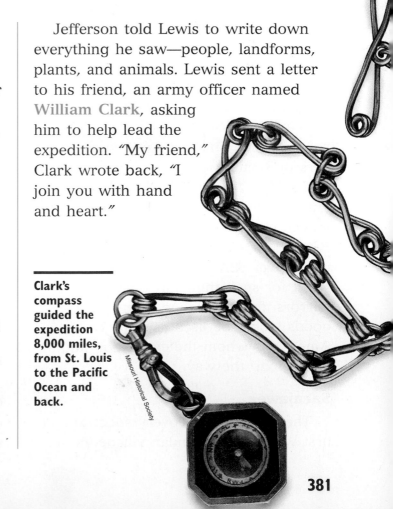

Clark's compass guided the expedition 8,000 miles, from St. Louis to the Pacific Ocean and back.

Missouri Historical Society

Montana Historical Society

This painting by E.S. Paxon shows Lewis and Clark, center, with Sacajawea and possibly York on the left, along with other members of the Corps of Discovery.

THE LEWIS AND CLARK EXPEDITION

Lewis and Clark were given another important job. "Your mission," Jefferson told them, "[is] to explore the Missouri River" and find a safe route to the Pacific. Follow the route that Lewis and Clark took on the map on page 381.

The group called itself the "Corps of Discovery." A corps is a group of people working together toward a common goal. Of the 42 men, about half were soldiers. At least one was an enslaved African American—Clark's servant, named York. The rest were either trappers or scouts.

On May 14, 1804, the explorers set out from St. Louis in three boats. They moved slowly west along the Missouri River. Lewis had spent $2,500 for supplies. Over $2,100 of this amount was spent for such things as eyeglasses, mirrors, fishhooks, and shirts. These goods would be used as gifts for Native Americans whom the expedition might meet along the way.

Sacajawea

The Corps of Discovery spent its first winter in a Mandan village in present-day North Dakota. There they met a French fur trapper named Toussaint Charbonneau (too SAHN SHAHR buh noh). He and his Shoshone wife, Sacajawea (sah kah jah WEE uh), were asked to join the expedition. Lewis and Clark needed Sacajawea to translate for them when they reached the Shoshone lands.

By August the group could see the snowy peaks of the Rocky Mountains. Soon after, a group of Shoshone approached the expedition. Clark wrote that Sacajawea began "to dance and show every mark of joy." The Shoshone chief was her brother Cameauhwait (KAH moh wayt), whom she had not seen since childhood. He gave the expedition the horses it needed to cross the Rocky Mountains.

Reaching the Pacific Ocean

From the Rockies, Lewis and Clark followed the Snake River and then took the Columbia River to the Pacific Ocean. In November

1805, Lewis and Clark arrived at what a Shoshone chief had called the "great shining lake." It had taken them 18 months to reach the Pacific Ocean. You can read an excerpt from William Clark's journal below. How do you think Clark felt when he finally reached the Pacific Ocean?

MANY VOICES
PRIMARY SOURCE

Excerpt from the Journal of William Clark, written on November 7, 1805.

The morning was rainy, and the fog so thick that we could not see across the river.

*We had not gone far from . . . [a small] village when the fog cleared off, and we enjoyed the delightful **prospect** of the ocean—that ocean, the object of all our labors, the reward of all our anxieties. This cheering view **exhilarated** the spirits of all the party, who were still more delighted on hearing the distant roar of the **breakers**.*

prospect: view
exhilarated: excited
breakers: waves that break on a shore

WHY IT MATTERS

Lewis and Clark returned to Washington, D.C., in 1806. They had mapped and explored over 3,000 miles of land. The maps that Lewis and Clark drew made it easier for new settlers to follow the way west. The United States, President Jefferson said, was "a rising nation, spread over a wide and fruitful land." In the next lesson you will see how the United States continued to grow.

Reviewing Facts and Ideas

MAIN IDEAS

- In 1791 work began on plans for the new capital of the United States, called the District of Columbia.

- Thomas Jefferson became President in 1801. For $15 million the United States purchased Louisiana from France in 1803.

- From 1804 to about 1806 Lewis and Clark explored the Louisiana Purchase. With help from Sacajawea and others, they found a route over the Rocky Mountains to the Pacific Ocean.

THINK ABOUT IT

1. What concerns did Jefferson have about French control of Louisiana?

2. What goals did Lewis and Clark have for their expedition?

3. **FOCUS** Describe the lands that became part of the United States under the Louisiana Purchase.

4. **THINKING SKILL** What could you _conclude_ about the history of the United States if the Louisiana Purchase had not been made? Explain how you arrived at this conclusion.

5. **GEOGRAPHY** In 1801 Washington, D.C., was located in the center of the country. Where is the center now?

AMERICAN *Wildlife* ARTISTS

Throughout our country's history people have used artwork to celebrate the variety and abundance of wildlife. Early explorers made drawings of the animals they saw. When Lewis and Clark returned from their expedition they brought with them drawings of animals that most people in the United States had never seen.

Today, as in the past, artists travel from the hottest deserts to the coldest reaches of our country. They take photographs—and now videos, too—of animals most people would never get to see.

Whether they draw, paint, photograph, or create sculptures, wildlife artists provide a lasting legacy of the natural beauty of the United States.

John James Audubon is known for his skill in portraying the birds of our country. The work above is titled *Bald Eagle*.

Wildlife such as the owl (right) have long been the subject of Native American art. The trout (far right) was one of the fish that William Clark drew during his expedition.

Smithsonian Institution

The New York Historical Society

This mountain lion, also called a cougar or puma (PYOO muh), was photographed by Renee Lynn.

The Granger Collection

1760   1780   1800   1809   1824   1840

The War of 1812

Read Aloud

In 1811 talk of war was in the air. In Congress, Senator John Calhoun of South Carolina spoke out against the British: "Which shall we do," he asked, "abandon or defend our rights?" As you will see, President James Madison agreed that it was time to fight Great Britain once again.

Focus Activity

READ TO LEARN

What were the results of the War of 1812?

VOCABULARY

- neutral
- War Hawks
- War of 1812
- national anthem
- Battle of New Orleans
- Era of Good Feelings
- Monroe Doctrine

PEOPLE

- James Madison
- Henry Clay
- Oliver Hazard Perry
- Tecumseh
- Andrew Jackson
- Dolley Madison
- Francis Scott Key
- James Monroe
- Absalom Jones

PLACES

- Washington, D.C.
- Baltimore
- Fort McHenry

THE BIG PICTURE

When **James Madison** became President of the United States in 1809, Great Britain and France had been fighting a long, costly war. Like earlier Presidents, Madison tried to keep the United States **neutral** (NOO trul). Neutral means not taking sides. Both Great Britain and France did not respect the decision of the United States. They both began taking American ships by force. The British also kidnapped American sailors and forced them to serve in the British navy.

People in the United States were angered over Great Britain's actions. "Free trade and seamen's rights!" cried a senator from Kentucky named **Henry Clay**. Clay was the leader of the **War Hawks**, or members of Congress from the South and the West who wanted to declare war against Great Britain. Many War Hawks hoped to drive the British out of Canada and the Spanish out of Florida. They wanted these rich lands for American farmers. Senator Clay urged the United States to "take the whole continent."

The USS *Constitution*, far left, is still a symbol of American might on the seas. Commodore Perry (below) led the United States to one of the greatest victories in the Navy's history.

THE WAR AT SEA

The War Hawks pressed Congress to declare war on Great Britain in June 1812. In the United States the fighting became known as the War of 1812. Former President Thomas Jefferson claimed that the capture of Canada would be "just a matter of marching." He and the War Hawks were mistaken. The United States was not prepared for war.

"Old Ironsides"

Even the War Hawks feared the mighty British navy. Yet it was the war at sea that brought the United States its early victories. One of the most famous battles in United States Navy history took place on August 19, 1812. Off the coast of Nova Scotia in Canada, the USS *Constitution* sank the *Guerrière* (ger ee YAIR), one of Britain's finest warships. After the fierce battle, sailors nicknamed the *Constitution* "Old Ironsides" because cannonballs seemed to bounce off its tough oak sides.

In 1813 United States Commodore Oliver Hazard Perry fought the British navy on Lake Erie. His ship flew a flag that read, "Don't give up the ship." These were the dying words of Captain James Lawrence of the USS *Chesapeake*. The *Chesapeake* had been sunk by the British earlier that year.

Perry kept fighting until most of his crew lay wounded or dead. Perry and a few men then rowed out under heavy fire to a second ship and went on to defeat the British. After the victory, Perry said, "We have met the enemy and they are ours."

387

The Granger Collection

A British view of the invasion incorrectly shows the White House on a hill. First Lady Dolley Madison (below) barely escaped.

The New York Historical Society

THE WAR ON LAND

For the United States, the war was more difficult on land than at sea. On land, the American army faced many Native Americans who sided with the British. Native Americans feared the growing United States would take more of their land.

In the North and Middle West, the United States Army battled Native American forces led by Tecumseh, a Shawnee chief. Tecumseh had begun forming a confederacy of Native Americans in the Ohio River valley. He urged them not to sell their land to new settlers. "Why not sell the air, the clouds, and the great sea?" Tecumseh asked. Tecumseh and the British won several victories near the Great Lakes. In 1813 he was killed in a battle near Detroit.

In Tennessee an American commander named Andrew Jackson defeated the Muscogee (Creek). The United States then took their land. Many fled to Florida and joined Native Americans who later became known as the Seminole.

The War Nears the Capital

By 1814, British troops landed at Chesapeake Bay and began moving west toward Washington, D.C. The capital had few troops to defend it.

Dolley Madison, the First Lady, wrote, "Will you believe it? Here I am within sound of the cannon!" Madison raced through the White House, saving important state papers and a famous painting of George Washington.

"Our Flag was Still There"

After burning Washington, D.C., the British moved on to Baltimore. There they attacked Fort McHenry. A lawyer named Francis Scott Key watched as British cannon fire lit up the sky.

The battle continued throughout the night. As dawn broke he saw that "our flag was still there." You can read the words Key wrote for "The Star-Spangled Banner" on the next page. In 1931 Key's song became our country's national anthem. A national anthem is a song of praise for a country. How do you think Key felt when he saw that our country's flag was still flying?

THE
STAR-SPANGLED BANNER

Music attributed to J. S. Smith   Words by Francis Scott Key

THE ERA OF GOOD FEELINGS

In 1815 Andrew Jackson, now a general, led Americans to a great victory. In the Battle of New Orleans, the British had lost over 2,000 men. The Americans had lost 50. Jackson learned later that the battle could have been avoided. A peace treaty ending the War of 1812 had already been signed in Europe.

After the war, the United States began a time of peace and prosperity. Prosperity is success, wealth, or good fortune. This time period, or era, became known as the Era of Good Feelings. The people were "one great family with a common interest," said James Monroe, the new President.

The Presidency of James Monroe (left) was a time when many Americans, such as Richard Allen (below), felt hopeful about the country.

National Portrait Gallery/Smithsonian Institution

The Monroe Doctrine

Elected in 1816, Monroe believed the President should direct the country in world affairs. In his second term, he became concerned about Latin America where new independent republics had been established after 1821.

It seemed that Europe might try again to take control of Latin America. Worried about this, Monroe issued an historic statement called the Monroe Doctrine in 1823. In it he said that the United States opposed "future colonization by any European powers" in the area. He also

Black, white, and Native American troops cheered Andrew Jackson in his historic victory at the Battle of New Orleans (below).

Historic New Orleans Collection

said that the United States would not take part in any European wars.

The A.M.E. Church

After the War of 1812, free African Americans also enjoyed better times. In 1816 in Philadalphia Richard Allen and another minister named Absalom Jones founded the first official church for African Americans, the African Methodist Episcopal (A.M.E.) Church. Although *African* is part of the church's name, it welcomed all people.

WHY IT MATTERS

Although neither side really won the War of 1812, the United States had become stronger and more successful. Great Britain and France had been forced to respect America's independence. Today we celebrate our country's hard-won freedom each time we sing our national anthem.

Links to **LANGUAGE ARTS**

Spell It in American

Who wrote the first dictionary of American English?

Noah Webster was a young teacher in 1782 when he began to write a spelling book for students. He thought the English way of spelling words was too complicated. He changed words such as *plough* and *colour* to *plow* and *color*. Webster also changed the pronunciations of some words. In 1806 Webster started work on his dictionary. He hoped it would preserve the American-English language "for the glory of [the] country." Choose five words to look up in a dictionary. Write down their meanings. Then find out if these words have different spellings in England.

✔/ **Reviewing Facts and Ideas**

MAIN IDEAS

- Britain's taking of American ships and sailors led Congress to declare war on Great Britain in 1812.

- In the War of 1812, armies from the United States tried to invade Canada but failed. Meanwhile the United States navy won many victories.

- In 1814 the British burned much of Washington, D.C. but were stopped at Fort McHenry. Francis Scott Key wrote "The Star-Spangled Banner" about this battle.

- An Era of Good Feelings followed the end of the War of 1812 as Americans felt great pride in their country and hope for its future.

THINK ABOUT IT

1. What reasons did the United States have for entering the War of 1812?

2. Name some of the major American victories in the War of 1812.

3. **FOCUS** What did the United States gain from the War of 1812?

4. **THINKING SKILL** What was Tecumseh's *point of view* on the War of 1812? What might have led him to look at the war in this way?

5. **GEOGRAPHY** In 1815 news of the peace treaty reached Andrew Jackson too late to stop the Battle of New Orleans. Using the map on page 381, plot a route showing how news of the treaty might have reached Jackson and his troops.

Geography Skills

Comparing Maps

VOCABULARY

political map

WHY THE SKILL MATTERS

In this chapter you have used maps to find out historical information. The maps you used are called historical maps. In this lesson you will learn about maps that communicate other kinds of information. For example,

a **political map** shows the boundaries of states or countries. Relief and elevation maps show what the land is like and how high it is. Sometimes you need information that cannot be obtained from one map alone. In this case you need to compare different kinds of maps.

USING THE SKILL

The map on the left of this page is an historical map. It shows the location of several towns and some of the Native American peoples that Tecumseh visited between 1811 and 1813. The map on the right is a political map. It shows state boundaries for a section

TOWNS TECUMSEH VISITED, 1811-1813

CANADA (British)

Great Lakes

WINNEBAGO
OJIBWA
FOX
SAUK
OTTAWA
POTAWATOMI
WYANDOT
LENAPE
Tippecanoe
KICKAPOO
SHAWNEE
MIAMI
Tanwakanwakaghe
UNITED STATES
OSAGE
Missouri River
Wabash
Ohio River
Tennessee River
CHICKASAW
CHEROKEE
Colbert's Ferry
MUSCOGEE
Mokalusha
Tuckabatchee
MEXICO (Spanish)
CHOCTAW
Mississippi River
Gulf of Mexico
FLORIDA (Spanish)

- Old Piqua — Tecumseh's birthplace
- ✳ Battle of the Thames — Tecumseh is killed
- Towns Tecumseh visited
- Tecumseh's journeys

0   150   300 Miles
0   150   300 Kilometers

THE EASTERN UNITED STATES

CANADA

Great Lakes

MN
WI
MI
NY
IA
OH
PA
NE
IL
IN
Missouri River
Ohio River
WV
VA
KS
MO
KY
Tennessee River
TN
NC
OK
AR
SC
MS
AL
GA
80°W
TX
LA
30°N
Mississippi River
FL
Gulf of Mexico
90°W

0   150   300 Miles
0   150   300 Kilometers

of the United States today. Suppose you wanted to identify the present-day state where the Native American town of Tanwakanwakaghe was located. What would you do?

Alone, neither of the two maps will give you the answer. Using both maps together, however, you can find the state in which Tanwakanwakaghe is located. On the historical map, use landmarks such as the Missouri and Mississippi rivers. Now find the same location on the political map. Use the map scale to make sure your location is about the same distance from these rivers. You will find that Tanwakanwakaghe was located in present-day Missouri.

TRYING THE SKILL

The towns shown on the historical map are just a few of those that were visited by Tecumseh as he tried to form a confederacy of Native American nations. In what present-day state was the town of Tuckabatchee located?

Now find the state of Mississippi on the political map. What Native Americans lived in this area? What landmarks did you use to help you find out?

REVIEWING THE SKILL

1. What does a political map show?

2. How can you locate the same position on two maps?

3. Tecumseh founded a huge community called Tippecanoe as the center of his operations. In what present-day state does the land that Tippecanoe occupied lie?

Helping yourself

- When comparing two or more maps, locate the position you need on the first map. Note the landmarks.

- Use the landmarks to locate the same position on the second map.

- Look at both maps together to find the information you need.

4. Why do people often need more than one map to obtain information?

5. Suppose you wanted to find out which people lived in the different mountain ranges of the world in 1776. Which two kinds of maps would you use? Explain.

This portrait is believed by historians to be of Tecumseh.

1760   1780   1800   1824   1840

The Times of Andrew Jackson

Focus Activity

READ TO LEARN

How did the United States change under President Andrew Jackson?

VOCABULARY

- Indian Removal Act
- Trail of Tears

PEOPLE

- Andrew Jackson
- John Quincy Adams
- Sequoyah
- John Ross
- Osceola

PLACES

- Indian Territory

Read Aloud

When Andrew Jackson won the election for President in 1828, some people were worried. Jackson was the first President who was not born into a wealthy family. He had also grown up on the frontier and was a self-made man. As Senator Daniel Webster of Massachusetts said, "Nobody knows what he will do."

THE BIG PICTURE

During the Era of Good Feelings the country grew in many ways. From 1812 to 1821 six new states joined the United States. The people in these new frontier states had their own way of doing things. They passed laws allowing all white men over the age of 21 to vote. In the original 13 states, only those who owned property could vote.

The older states soon changed their voting laws as well. As a result, almost three times more men voted in 1828 than voted in 1824. Candidates from less wealthy families now had a better chance of being elected. Andrew Jackson, who had led the United States to victory in the Battle of New Orleans, was an example of this new type of elected official.

John Quincy Adams, who was President from 1825–1829, described Jackson as a man "who can scarcely spell his own name." Adams opposed including people in government who were not wealthy.

In this lesson you will read about other ways in which Jackson's election changed our country.

In the 1828 election for President, Jackson's supporters put up this poster (below). On inauguration day crowds of citizens went to meet Jackson in the White House.

The New York Historical Society

A GROWING DEMOCRACY

One of 11 children, Andrew Jackson had been raised in a log cabin. Although he had very little education, he taught himself law and later became a judge.

Jackson was already well known when he ran for President. His victory in the Battle of New Orleans had made him a national hero. In 1813 his troops were marching from Tennessee to New Orleans when Jackson received an order to disband his army immediately. His troops, all volunteers, were tired and sick. It seemed they had just marched a long way for nothing. Jackson refused to obey the order. He gave his horse to a wounded soldier and later had to walk much of the 500 miles home. "He's tough," one soldier said, "tough as hickory." Hickory is a tree that has very hard wood. From this time on Jackson was called "Old Hickory."

The Election of Andrew Jackson

When he ran for President in 1828, his supporters planted hickory sticks everywhere they went. "Old Hickory" won by a landslide. A landslide election happens when one candidate wins a large majority of the votes.

Margaret Smith, who lived in Washington, D.C., wrote about Jackson's first day as President. An enormous crowd gathered in the capital to watch Jackson's inauguration on March 4, 1829. Afterward everyone was invited to the White House for a celebration. People stood on chairs to see the man who would become known as "the People's President." President Jackson was nearly "pressed to death" by the crowd. He barely managed to escape from the crowds out a back door. "It was the People's day," Smith wrote.

INDIAN REMOVAL

As a follower of Thomas Jefferson, Jackson believed in a simple government, "protecting all and granting favors to none." During his time as President, Jackson fought any law or court decision that he believed would harm American farmers, new settlers on the frontier, or working people.

Not everyone, however, was protected by President Jackson. Native Americans were among those who lost rather than gained rights during Jackson's time in office.

Native Americans of the Southeast

In the early 1800s, some Native American communities in the Southeast were growing. Among these groups were the Cherokee, Choctaw, Chickasaw, Muscogee, and Seminole.

One of the achievements of the Cherokee during this period was the development of the first written Native American alphabet. Sequoyah, a Cherokee silversmith, worked for 12 years to create his alphabet. He compared the job to "catching a wild animal and taming it." Sequoyah's writing system used Greek, Hebrew, and English symbols for Cherokee sounds.

In 1824 Sequoyah used his writing system to send messages from Arkansas to the Cherokee living farther east. They were impressed by Sequoyah's "talking leaves," as they called his letters. Within months thousands of Cherokee men, women, and children had learned to read and write in their own language.

In 1828 Sequoyah published the first Native American newspaper, the *Cherokee Phoenix*, which is still printed today. Sequoyah remained a respected leader and educator until his death in 1843. The giant California redwood tree is named *Sequoia* in his honor.

Sequoyah (above) holds a sample of the Cherokee alphabet. The Council House (right) in New Echota served as the Cherokee national capital until 1838.

New Echota State Historic Site

This portrait of President Andrew Jackson was painted by Thomas Sully about 1829.

The Indian Removal Act of 1830

One of the most difficult issues facing President Jackson was the conflict over land between white settlers and the Native Americans in the Southeast. Tensions increased in 1830 when gold was discovered on Cherokee lands within Georgia.

Jackson strongly believed that the Native Americans were a threat to the growth and expansion of the United States. To end the fighting, Jackson wanted the Native Americans to move to lands west of the Mississippi.

In 1830 Congress passed the Indian Removal Act. This law allowed the President to remove Native Americans from their homelands. In return for the land they lost, the Native Americans would receive land in Indian Territory, which is now the state of Oklahoma.

Read Jackson's point of view on the Indian Removal Act in the excerpt on this page. How would you describe his attitude toward Native Americans?

PRIMARY SOURCE

**Excerpt from
Andrew Jackson's Farewell Address
given in March 1837.**

*This **unhappy race** are now placed in a situation where we may well hope that they will share in the blessings of civilization and be saved from that **degradation** and destruction to which they were rapidly hastening while they remained in the [eastern] states. . . . Our own citizens will rejoice that the **remnant** of that ill-fated race has been at length placed beyond the reach of injury or **oppression**, and that the paternal care of the General Government will hereafter watch over them and protect them.*

---

unhappy race: Jackson's description of Native Americans
degradation: lowering of character, quality, or rank
remnant: survivors
oppression: rule by cruel, or unjust, means

In 1831 the United States government began forcing Native Americans to leave their homes. The Choctaw left first, then the Chickasaw and the Muscogee. In Alabama, some of the Muscogee who refused to leave were forced into slavery. Finally, the Georgia government held a lottery to see which white settlers would get the Cherokee farms. The Cherokee still refused to leave.

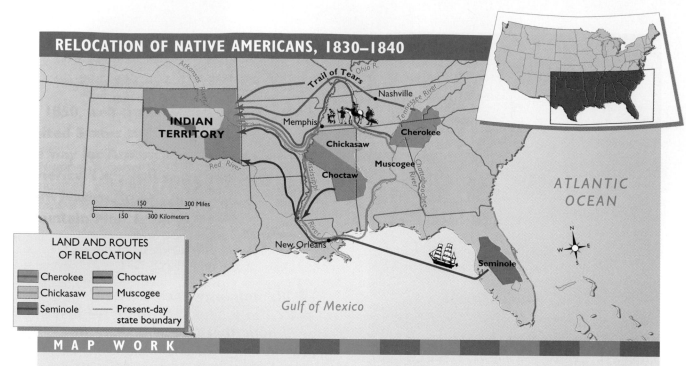

RELOCATION OF NATIVE AMERICANS, 1830–1840

LAND AND ROUTES OF RELOCATION

- Cherokee
- Chickasaw
- Seminole
- Choctaw
- Muscogee
- —— Present-day state boundary

INDIAN TERRITORY

Trail of Tears

Nashville

Memphis

Cherokee

Chickasaw

Muscogee

Choctaw

New Orleans

Seminole

Arkansas River

Ohio R.

Tennessee River

Red River

Mississippi

Chattahoochee River

ATLANTIC OCEAN

Gulf of Mexico

0 150 300 Miles
0 150 300 Kilometers

MAP WORK

The **Trail of Tears** is now a national historic trail. From Georgia, it leads to Tahlequah, Oklahoma, today's Cherokee national capital.

1. Which Native Americans were removed to the Indian Territory?

2. Which Native Americans traveled by water? Describe their route.

3. Which Native Americans were relocated along the Red River?

THE TRAIL OF TEARS

Led by their chief, John Ross, the Cherokee took their case to the Supreme Court. In 1832 the Court ruled that "the laws of Georgia can have no force" on Cherokee lands. The decision meant that Georgia could not force the Cherokee from their land.

Jackson refused to enforce the Court's decision. "Well, [Chief Justice] John Marshall has made his decision, now let him enforce it," Jackson is supposed to have said. In 1838, United States soldiers rounded up the Cherokee and burned their houses. They then forced the Cherokee to march 800 miles to Indian Territory.

"The Place Where They Cried"

The march took over a year. About 4,000 out of 15,000 Cherokee people, or one in four, died along the way. Among them was Quatie, the wife of Chief John Ross. She had given her only blanket to a sick child.

In their own language, the Cherokee called this forced march to the Indian territory "the place where they cried." Over time this bitter journey has come to be known as the Trail of Tears.

On the map above, you can trace the routes that Native Americans of the Southeast followed. Some of the Cherokee fled to North Carolina and Tennessee rather than move to Indian Territory. Cherokee communities continue to exist there today.

A 27-year-old soldier named John Burnett served as an interpreter on the march. Born in Tennessee, Burnett had grown up among the Cherokee. Read the following excerpt from an account Burnett wrote many years later. What was his point of view?

The Granger Collection

MANY VOICES
PRIMARY SOURCE

**Excerpt from an Account,
by John G. Burnett, published in 1890.**

[I**n**] *May 1838, [I] witnessed the* **execution** *of the most brutal order in the History of American Warfare. I saw helpless Cherokees arrested and dragged from their homes . . . I saw them loaded like cattle or sheep into six hundred and forty-five wagons and started toward the west . . . [When] the bugle sounded and the wagons started rolling many of the children rose to their feet and waved their little hands good-by to their mountain homes, knowing they were leaving them forever. Many of these helpless people did not have blankets and many of them had been driven from home barefooted.*

execution: carrying out

The Seminole Resist

In Florida the Seminole also fought against being driven from their homes by the Removal Act. Their chief, Osceola, led his fighters, both men and women, to defend themselves against U.S. soldiers. Osceola was captured in 1837 and died in jail about a year later. Some Seminole ended up in Indian Territory in Florida.

WHY IT MATTERS

In Indian Territory, Native Americans from the Southeast began to rebuild their lives. However, Jackson's treatment of Native Americans cast a cloud over the country. Still, his election represented the growth of democracy in the United States. One of his most important achievements was greater participation in government by the average citizen.

✓✓ Reviewing Facts and Ideas

MAIN IDEAS

- The election of Andrew Jackson in 1828 was the first in which voting was not limited to property owners.
- In 1830 Congress passed the Indian Removal Act, which forced Native Americans to leave their homes in the Southeast to move to Indian Territory in the West.

THINK ABOUT IT

1. How had voting laws changed by 1828? How did this affect elections?

2. Why was Andrew Jackson known as "Old Hickory"?

3. **FOCUS** What events in the United States were affected by President Andrew Jackson?

4. **THINKING SKILL** How did the system of checks and balances apply to the Cherokee struggle to keep their land? Give the reasons for your *conclusion*.

5. **WRITE** Write a letter to President Jackson from your own point of view about the Indian Removal Act.

399

CHAPTER 14 REVIEW

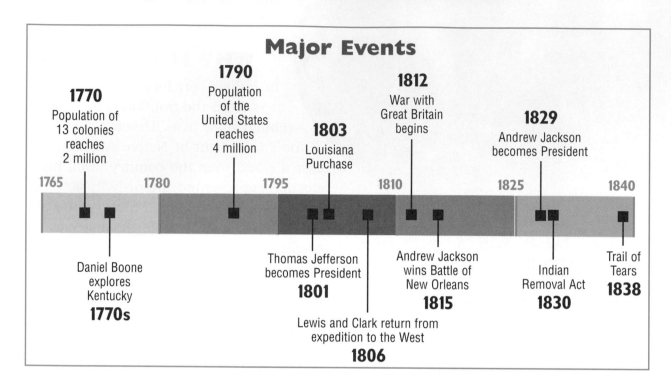

Major Events

1770
Population of 13 colonies reaches 2 million

1790
Population of the United States reaches 4 million

1803
Louisiana Purchase

1812
War with Great Britain begins

1829
Andrew Jackson becomes President

1765   1780   1795   1810   1825   1840

Daniel Boone explores Kentucky
1770s

Thomas Jefferson becomes President
1801

Andrew Jackson wins Battle of New Orleans
1815

Indian Removal Act
1830

Trail of Tears
1838

Lewis and Clark return from expedition to the West
1806

THINKING ABOUT VOCABULARY

Number a paper from 1 to 10. Beside each number, write the word or term from the list below that best completes each sentence.

Era of Good Feelings   pioneer
Indian Removal Act   political map
Louisiana Purchase   Battle of New Orleans
national anthem   War Hawks
neutral   War of 1812

1. The conflict with Great Britain over Canada is known as the _____.

2. A _____ is a map that shows the boundaries of states or countries.

3. The _____ wanted war with Great Britain in 1812.

4. In 1815 Andrew Jackson led American troops to victory in the _____.

5. In 1809 President Madison wanted to keep the United States _____, which means to not take sides.

6. A person who leads the way into areas new to them is a _____.

7. Jefferson paid $15 million in a deal known as the _____.

8. In a law known as the _____ Native Americans in the East were removed from their homelands.

9. A _____ is a song of praise people sing about their country.

10. The peaceful time following the War of 1812 was known as the _____.

THINKING ABOUT FACTS

1. Who was Daniel Boone?

2. What was the goal of Lewis and Clark?

3. Explain the roles of these people in the War of 1812: Oliver Hazard Perry, Tecumseh, Andrew Jackson, Francis Scott Key.

4. What law affecting Native Americans was passed during Andrew Jackson's time as President? What were some of the results of that law?

5. Look at the time line above. What information can you find about the population of the United States?

THINK AND WRITE

WRITING A DIARY ENTRY

Suppose that you are one of the first pioneers to settle in Boonesborough. Write a diary entry describing the first day in your new home on the frontier.

WRITING INSTRUCTIONS

Suppose that you are President Jefferson. Write a letter to Meriwether Lewis in which you give him instructions about what to do on his expedition to explore the Louisiana Purchase.

WRITING A SPEECH

Suppose that you are a member of Congress in 1811. Write a speech that explains your point of view about going to war with Great Britain. Try to persuade other members to support your point of view.

APPLYING STUDY SKILLS

COMPARING MAPS

1. What kind of maps appear on page 392? What other kinds of maps do you know how to read?

2. What are some of the steps involved in comparing maps?

3. Look at the maps on page 392. In what present-day state did the Choctow live?

4. Study the maps again. In what present-day state did the Kickapoo live?

5. Why is it helpful to compare maps?

Summing Up the Chapter

Copy the spider map on a separate piece of paper. Review the chapter to fill in the blank sections in the map. When you have finished, choose one person from the map to write a paragraph about that answers the question "What contributions did _____ make to the United States in the 1800s?"

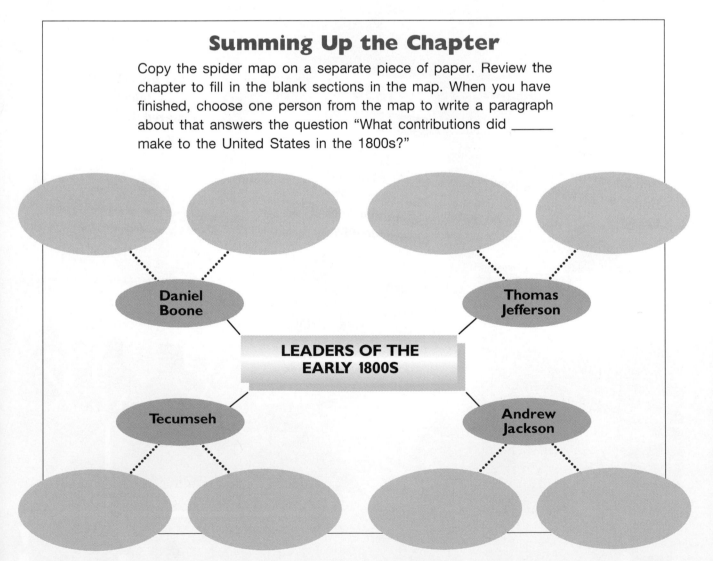

Daniel Boone

Thomas Jefferson

Tecumseh

Andrew Jackson

LEADERS OF THE EARLY 1800S

CHAPTER 15

A Changing Country

THINKING ABOUT
HISTORY AND GEOGRAPHY

The story of Chapter 15 takes place during the first half of the 1800s. In the East large factories manufactured more goods. The new steam engine began speeding people and these goods all over the country. Then, when gold was discovered in California, people raced west in search of fortune and opportunity. Follow the time line below to trace some of the other major events from this period.

Oregon Territory

Sutter's Mill, California

PACIFIC OCEAN

1836

SAN ANTONIO, TEXAS
Alamo defenders are defeated by the Mexican army

1800s

LOWELL, MASSACHUSETTS
The Industrial Revolution brings factory jobs to New England

1830

BALTIMORE, MARYLAND
The steam-powered locomotive races a horse-drawn carriage

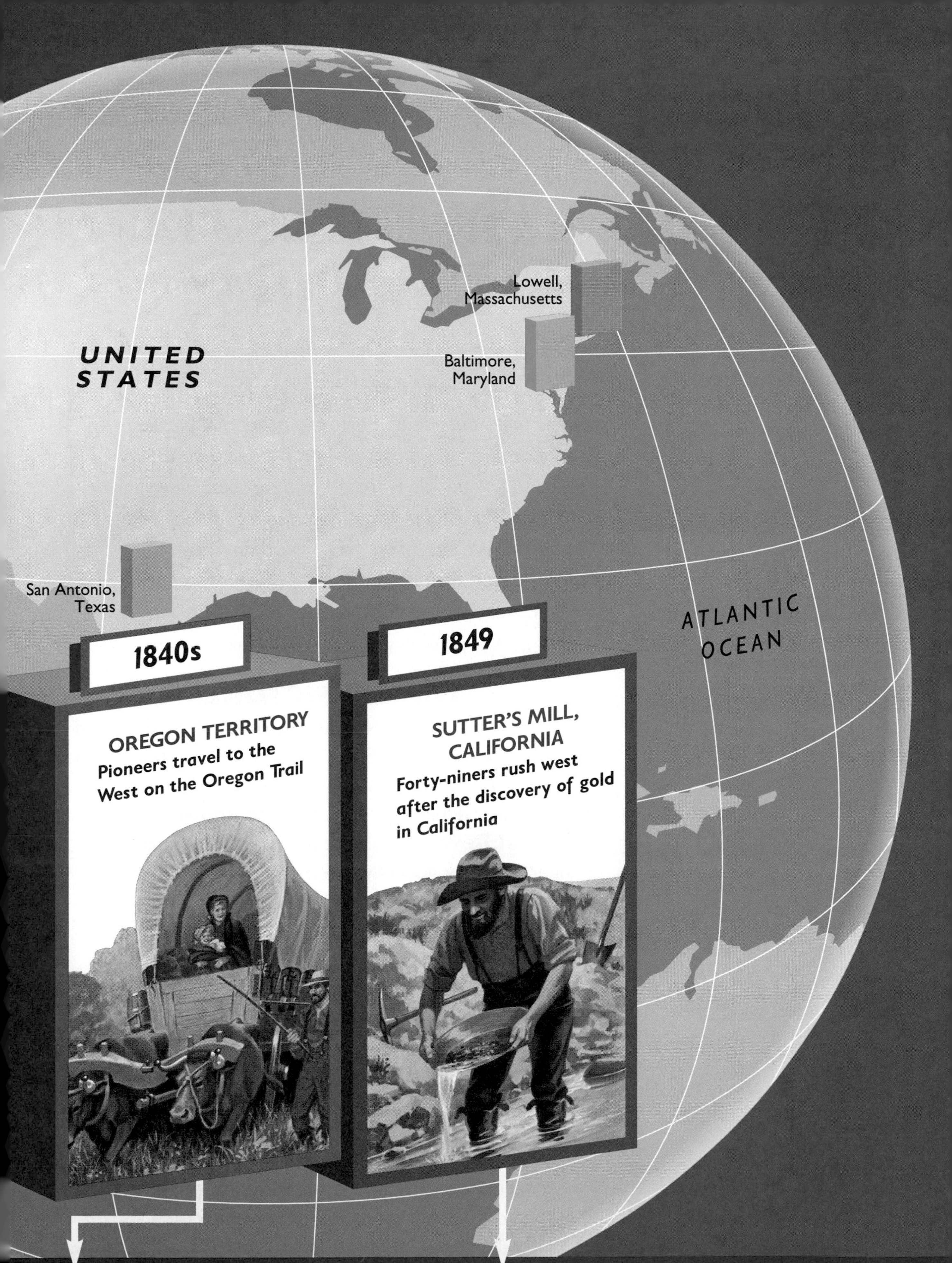
UNITED STATES
Lowell, Massachusetts
Baltimore, Maryland
San Antonio, Texas
ATLANTIC OCEAN
1840s
OREGON TERRITORY
Pioneers travel to the West on the Oregon Trail
1849
SUTTER'S MILL, CALIFORNIA
Forty-niners rush west after the discovery of gold in California

1845

1860

1760   1780   1850   1880

The Industrial Revolution

Read Aloud

A few miles outside of Boston, a new brick building stood beside the Charles River. The year was 1814. Inside, a few people watched as a machine wove yarn into cloth far more swiftly than a person could weave it by hand. "We sat by the hour," Nathan Appleton remembered, "watching the beautiful movement of this new and wonderful machine."

Focus Activity

READ TO LEARN

What were the effects of the Industrial Revolution?

VOCABULARY

- Industrial Revolution
- cotton gin
- interchangeable parts
- reaper

PEOPLE

- Samuel Slater
- Eli Whitney
- Francis Cabot Lowell
- Cyrus McCormick
- John Deere

PLACES

- Lowell, Massachuetts

THE BIG PICTURE

The new machine that Nathan Appleton described had been invented in Great Britain. In the late 1700s British inventors and businesses brought about the changes in industry and technology that became known as the **Industrial Revolution**. The Industrial Revolution changed the way goods were made. Goods that had been made by hand in homes or workshops were now made by machines, often in factories.

Before the Industrial Revolution, women and children slowly spun yarn and wove cloth by hand. The first British factories used water-powered machines to spin cotton yarn and weave cloth. After the Industrial Revolution, production increased and costs decreased.

At the time of Britain's Industrial Revolution, the young United States was still mainly a land of farms. Before long, though, a British mechanic named **Samuel Slater** would bring the Industrial Revolution to the United States. His yarn-spinning machine would come to represent the beginning of a new way of life for our country.

INVENTIONS AND THE FREE MARKET

Because of the Industrial Revolution, no other country in the world could make cloth as cheaply as Great Britain. The British wanted to keep their profitable technology a secret. So they passed laws making it illegal to export machines or machine plans. The people who operated machines in cotton factories were not even allowed to leave the country.

In 1789 Samuel Slater memorized the plans of the British spinning machines. He had heard that, because of the free market in the United States, business owners there would pay for this new technology. In a free market, producers of goods and services freely decide how to use resources in response to demand. People in the United States wanted to start their own business in making cloth.

Slater slipped out of the country and came to the United States. Soon he was hired by a merchant to build spinning machines in Rhode Island. By 1790 Slater had built the first American machines to spin cotton into yarn.

The Cotton Gin

Slater had to pay a high price for the cotton he used in his factory, which limited his profits. In 1793, however, an American inventor built a machine that made cotton cheaper to produce. His name was **Eli Whitney**.

Whitney heard planters talk about how long it took enslaved workers to remove the stubborn seeds stuck to cotton. Whitney invented the cotton gin in ten days. Whitney's gin, which is short for "engine," helped workers clean up to 50 times more cotton than they could by hand.

As you can see from the bar graph below, cotton production boomed after the invention of the cotton gin. Together, slave labor and the cotton gin made growing cotton more profitable. Many planters became more determined to keep slavery alive.

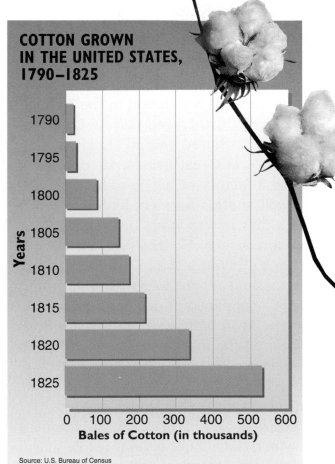

COTTON GROWN IN THE UNITED STATES, 1790–1825

Years (vertical axis): 1790, 1795, 1800, 1805, 1810, 1815, 1820, 1825

Bales of Cotton (in thousands): 0, 100, 200, 300, 400, 500, 600

Source: U.S. Bureau of Census

GRAPH WORK

Cotton was a major cash crop in the 1800s.

1. In which year did the largest increase in cotton production occur?

2. What factors other than the cotton gin might have caused this large increase?

Whitney's original cotton gin is kept today in the National Museum of History in Washington, D.C.

LOWELL, MASSACHUSETTS

The cotton gin helped create a plentiful supply of cotton. However, the United States did not have Great Britain's water-powered machines, called "power looms." The looms wove cloth more quickly and cheaply than Slater's machines.

From Cotton to Cloth

Like Samuel Slater and Eli Whitney, Francis Cabot Lowell helped spread the Industrial Revolution in the United States. In 1810 Lowell, a New England merchant, toured several cloth-making factories in Great Britain. He decided to build a factory of his own. In 1813 Lowell and his partners built our country's first power loom, in Waltham, Massachusetts. For the first time all stages of cloth-making—from spinning cotton into thread to weaving yarn into cloth—happened under one roof.

The swift waters of the Charles River powered the machines. The diagram on the next page shows how the water-wheel spun big leather belts. The belts, in turn, kept the machines moving.

Lowell died in 1817, but his business partners later built several textile mills next to the Merrimack River in Massachusetts. They also built a town, which they called Lowell, around the mills for the workers. It was the first planned town for workers to be built in the United States.

Working at Lowell

Mostly unmarried women between the ages of 15 and 19 worked at the mills in Lowell and other towns. Few jobs were open to women then. Therefore, many were glad to get the work, although they had long and tiring days.

The women from New England who worked at Lowell were called "mill girls." They lived in boarding houses built by the mill owners. In their spare time, the women attended lectures and reading clubs. Some also wrote poetry and stories for the *Lowell Offering*, a magazine published by the mill girls.

A mill girl spent 12 to 14 hours a day working at her machine, six days a week. The noise was often deafening. Lucy Larcom complained of "the buzzing and hissing of pulleys and rollers and spindles." Read the following excerpt from a Lowell mill girl's letter home to her father. What rule did she have to follow? Why do you think that rule was important?

MANY VOICES
PRIMARY SOURCE

Excerpt from a letter written by Mary S. Paul on April 12, 1846.

*I am at work in a spinning room and tending four sides of **warp** which is one girl's work. The overseer tells me that he never had a girl get along better than I do and that he will do the best he can by me. . . . I have a very good boarding place [and] have enough to eat. . . . The girls are all kind and **obliging**. The girls that I room with are all from Vermont and good girls too. Now I will tell you about our rules at the boarding house. We have none in particular except that we have to go to bed about 10 o'clock. At half past 4 in the morning the bell rings for us to get up and at five for us to go into the mill.*

---

warp: lengthwise threads of the spinning machine
obliging: helpful

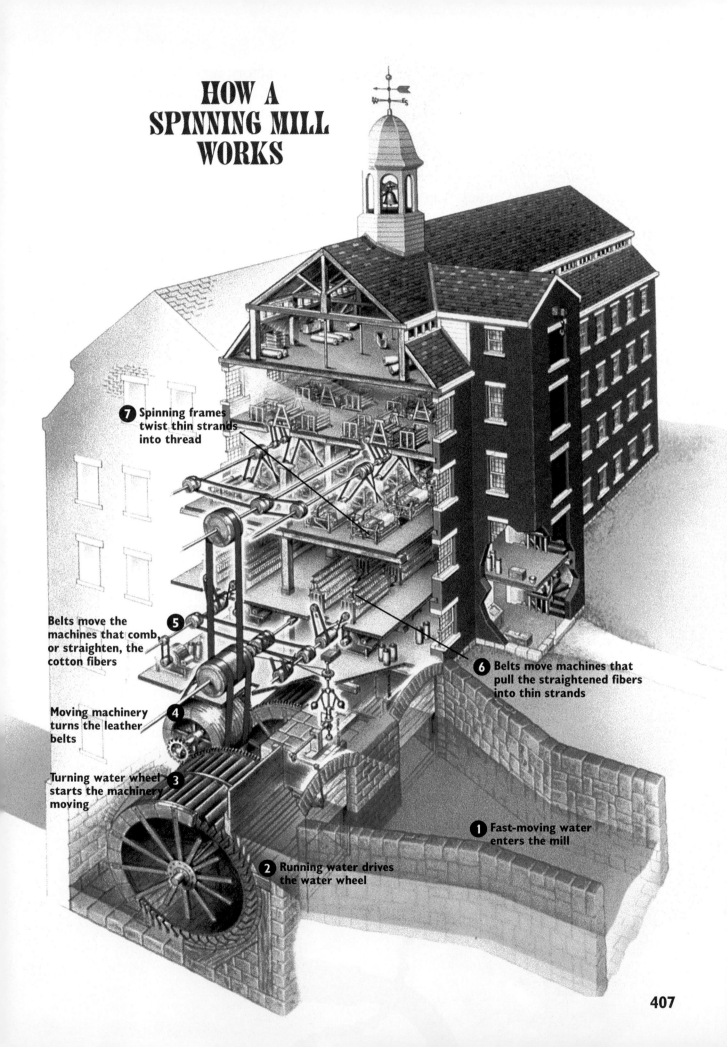

HOW A
SPINNING MILL
WORKS

7 Spinning frames twist thin strands into thread

Belts move the machines that comb, or straighten, the cotton fibers **5**

Moving machinery turns the leather belts **4**

Turning water wheel starts the machinery moving **3**

6 Belts move machines that pull the straightened fibers into thin strands

1 Fast-moving water enters the mill

2 Running water drives the water wheel

407

TOOLS FOR CHANGE

In addition to the cotton gin, Eli Whitney introduced another idea that helped to spread the Industrial Revolution in the United States. The idea came from a French inventor, but Whitney was the first to use it in this country.

In 1798 Whitney got a contract to make 10,000 guns, called muskets for the United States Army. Muskets were among the many items that were still being made by hand. When a musket broke, for example, a gun maker had to make a special part in order to fix it.

Whitney said that he could make the 10,000 muskets in only two years. Many people doubted that Whitney could deliver them in time. Yet Whitney had an idea. He planned to create tools that would make each part of a musket the same, or a standard, size. Each part for his musket would fit in any of his other muskets. In addition, all these same-sized parts for his muskets would be made at once, which also saved time. These standard-sized parts were called interchangeable parts.

At his factory near New Haven, Connecticut, Whitney slowly brought together machines and workers. He did not deliver the muskets in time. However, his efforts cleared the way for new advances in the Industrial Revolution.

Changes on the Farm

In 1832 the Industrial Revolution came to the farm. A Virginia farmer named Cyrus McCormick improved the horse-drawn reaper. A reaper is a machine that uses sharp blades to cut and harvest grain. By hand, farmers cut 2 or 3 acres of wheat a day. Using McCormick's reaper, they could now cut up to 12 acres a day.

In his factory in Chicago, McCormick made reapers with interchangeable parts. The parts allowed farmers to repair broken reapers quickly. McCormick even sent agents to make on-the-spot repairs during the harvest season.

In the Middle West, farmers complained that wooden plows were unable to cut through the tough roots of the prairie grass. In 1837 an Illinois blacksmith named John Deere made a better plow. He took an old steel saw and bent it over a log. The soil fell cleanly off the steel saw. Soon many farmers were using Deere's plow. Later, historians called it "the plow that broke the plains" of the West.

Thanks to interchangeable parts, people can replace brakes, handle bars, tires — practically every part of the bicycle.

The old horse-drawn reaper (top) and the modern gasoline-powered reaper (above) have both been labor-savers for American farmers.

WHY IT MATTERS

The Industrial Revolution brought great wealth to some entrepreneurs (ahn truh pruh NURZ) and improved the lives of many who could buy factory goods. An entrepreneur is a person who starts and owns a business. Yet a price was paid for these gains. Many people worked long hours in difficult conditions. In the South, slavery was strengthened. Differences between the North and South became even greater.

The Industrial Revolution brought other changes. In 1800 most people lived on farms. By the end of the 1800s, workers in the United States were producing more factory goods than in any other country, including Britain.

✓ Reviewing Facts and Ideas

MAIN IDEAS

- The Industrial Revolution came to America in 1790 when Samuel Slater began building spinning machines.

- In 1793 Eli Whitney invented the cotton gin, which increased cotton production and made it more profitable.

- In 1813 Francis Cabot Lowell built the first mill that handled all stages of cloth production under one roof.

- Cyrus McCormick's reaper of 1832 and John Deere's steel plow of 1837 made work on farms easier.

THINK ABOUT IT

1. How were Slater and Lowell important to the Industrial Revolution?

2. In what ways did the Industrial Revolution change farming?

3. **FOCUS** What changes in work did the Industrial Revolution bring?

4. **THINKING SKILL** What were some positive and negative *effects* of Eli Whitney's cotton gin?

5. **WRITE** Suppose you are a mill girl. Write an article for the *Lowell Offering* that explains what you like and dislike about your work.

1760   1790   1808   1830   1850   1880

Roads, Rivers, and Rails

Focus Activity

READ TO LEARN

What inventions led to better transportation across the country?

VOCABULARY

- stagecoach
- steam engine
- canal
- investor
- lock

PEOPLE

- Robert Fulton
- DeWitt Clinton
- Peter Cooper

PLACES

- National Road
- Erie Canal

Read Aloud

In 1788 a French traveler named Brissot de Warville (bree SOH duh vahr VEE yuh) boarded a stagecoach in Fairfield, Connecticut. The coach clattered over the steep and rocky road to New York. Warville could not understand how the driver avoided "dashing the carriage to pieces." Soon there would be better ways for people to travel across the United States.

THE BIG PICTURE

In 1800 the best roads in the United States were paved with rocks or logs. Most roads were narrow dirt trails filled with roots and tree stumps that broke wagon wheels. When it rained, deep puddles and sticky mud slowed the wagons and horses even more. It took a **stagecoach**, for example, four days to cover the 215 miles between Boston and New York. A stagecoach was a large, horse-drawn carriage that carried passengers, baggage, and mail.

In 1811 the federal government started building the **National Road**. When finished, the road would stretch from Cumberland, Maryland, all the way west to Vandalia, Illinois. Made of stone and gravel, the National Road linked the East with what was then the West. It was a big improvement in transportation. "The whole population is in motion," wrote one observer in 1828. Soon, however, the **steam engine** would make travel even easier over both land and water. A steam engine uses the energy from steam to power its engine.

STEAM POWER

Roads were not the only way to travel in the United States. Because river travel was cheap, canoes and flat-bottomed boats also carried many goods and passengers on the country's rivers. Log rafts floated crops and goods downstream on the Mississippi River to the port of New Orleans. As a young man Abraham Lincoln guided a flat-bottomed boat down the river from Indiana. Going upstream, or against the current, was much harder. The steam engine solved this problem.

Full Steam Ahead!

An American artist named **Robert Fulton** learned of a powerful steam engine that had been developed in Scotland. Although he was a successful painter, Fulton had a strong interest in engineering. In 1793 he gave up painting and began to design a steamboat. As its name suggests, a steamboat is a boat powered by a steam engine.

After years of work, Fulton designed a boat that used a steam engine and two large paddle wheels. Fulton called his steamboat the *Clermont*. Others called it "Fulton's Folly." One observer said it looked like "a backwoods sawmill mounted on a scow [flat boat] and set on fire."

In August 1807, the *Clermont* was ready for a run from New York City north to Albany. Crowds lined the banks of the Hudson River and cheered as the steamboat paddled upriver. The 150-mile trip took only 32 hours, a record time for those days. A flat-bottomed boat took from 8 to 11 days for the same trip. Soon tourists looking for pleasure rides, and merchants wanting to ship their goods, began using the steamboat. The *Clermont* proved that steamboats could move people and goods quickly and cheaply.

Robert Fulton (below) and his *Clermont* (bottom) proved that steamboats were an easier way to travel upstream.

INVENTOR OF THE STEAMBOAT. IN 1807 HIS FIRST STEAMBOAT THE CLERMONT APPEARED ON THE HUDSON.

ROBERT FULTON

BORN IN PENNSYLVANIA IN 176[

CLAREMO

411

HIGHER LEVEL

LOCK GATES BEING CLOSED

CANAL TOWPATH

HOW A CANAL LOCK WORKS
What do you think happens as a boat travels through each lock of the canal?

HORSES AND MULES TOW BOATS ALONG CANAL

LOCK GATES BEING OPENED

LOWER LEVEL

STONE WALL OF CANAL

THE ERIE CANAL

The governor of New York, DeWitt Clinton, dreamed of linking the Hudson River with Lake Erie through what he called a "Grand Canal." Such a canal, or human-built waterway, would allow boats to travel from New York City all the way north and west to the Great Lakes.

"Clinton's Ditch"

When people heard about Clinton's idea, they said it was impossible. The distance between Lake Erie and the Hudson River is about 350 miles. "It is little short of madness to think of it!" said Thomas Jefferson.

No one had ever attempted to build such a long canal. Most canals at this time were only a few miles long. It seemed nearly impossible to raise the amount of money—$7 million—needed to dig the canal. Critics began calling the canal "Clinton's Ditch."

Clinton asked investors from Europe to buy a share in the canal. An investor is a person who uses money to buy or make something that will make a profit. By the summer of 1817, Clinton had found enough investors to pay for the cost of digging the canal.

Digging the Canal

In a ceremony on July 4th, Clinton broke ground for the Erie Canal. From the beginning, the digging was tough. One of the biggest problems was finding enough workers. Engineers had hired farmers to build the first stretch of canal, but there were not enough of them. The builders solved the problem by hiring immigrants from Europe.

Another problem was elevation. The land along Lake Erie was 565 feet higher than the land along the Hudson River. To solve this problem, the workers built canal locks. A canal lock is a kind of water elevator that moves boats to higher or lower levels. Review the diagram on page 412 to see how a canal lock works.

The Completed Canal

Finally, after eight years of hard work, the Erie Canal was finished in 1825. Cannons roared and people cheered as Clinton sailed in a canal boat into New York Harbor from Lake Erie. When he reached the Atlantic Ocean, Clinton poured a barrel of Lake Erie water into the ocean to represent the new link. "They have built the longest canal in the world in the least time, with the least experience, for the least money, and to the greatest public benefit," reported one newspaper in Buffalo, New York.

The Erie Canal was an immediate success. Before, shipping goods over land between Buffalo on Lake Erie and New York City took 20 days and cost $100 a ton. The Erie Canal brought the price down to $10 a ton and cut travel time to eight days.

Farmers in Indiana, Illinois, northern Ohio, and the territory of Michigan could ship their crops more easily to cities in the East. Eastern merchants could sell their iron and manufactured goods in the West. With the Erie Canal, trade boomed, and New York City quickly became the country's biggest and most important port and city.

The success of the Erie Canal caused a rush of canal-building in the 1820s. However, a new invention that used a steam engine soon made canals less important. In Great Britain, the railroads carried people and goods faster

than anyone had dreamed. As the maps on this page show, roads and railroads soon began crossing the United States as well.

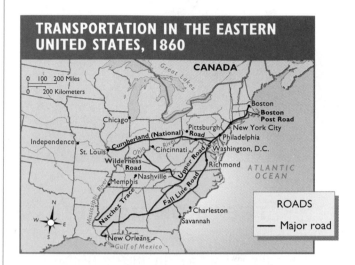

TRANSPORTATION IN THE EASTERN UNITED STATES, 1860

ROADS
— Major road

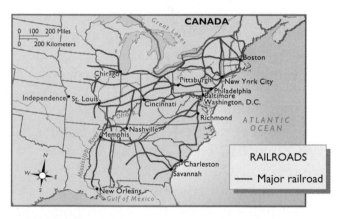

RAILROADS
— Major railroad

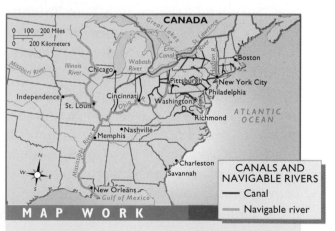

CANALS AND NAVIGABLE RIVERS
— Canal
····· Navigable river

MAP WORK

People in the East could choose between three different forms of transportation.

1. Which cities had road, river, and rail transportation?
2. Which roads crossed the East Coast?

The *Tom Thumb* marked the first use of steam engines on our country's railroads.

THE "IRON HORSE"

The first railroad cars were pulled on iron rails by horses. In 1829 a British inventor replaced the horses with an "iron horse"—a steam locomotive. In 1830 a New York businessman, Peter Cooper, brought the iron horse to this country.

Tom Thumb

Cooper suggested that the Baltimore & Ohio Railroad Company use steam power instead of horses. "I will knock an engine together in six weeks that will pull carriages 10 miles an hour," he said. He named the engine *Tom Thumb,* after a character in a children's story.

People doubted that the *Tom Thumb* could travel fast. A Baltimore stagecoach company decided to challenge the *Tom Thumb* to a race. At first "the race was neck and neck." Then, something went wrong on the *Tom Thumb.* The horse-drawn coach won. Still the *Tom Thumb* proved steam engines could haul large loads long distances.

WHY IT MATTERS

In the early 1800s, new inventions and improvements in roads helped to increase trade and lower the cost of transportation in the United States. The Erie Canal carried thousands of European immigrants from New York City to the West. Swift travel helped to expand and to unify the young country.

✓ Reviewing Facts and Ideas

MAIN IDEAS

- The Erie Canal, completed in 1825, increased trade between East and West.
- Peter Cooper built the *Tom Thumb* in 1830 and showed that a steam locomotive could haul large loads over long distances.

THINK ABOUT IT

1. What were some of the problems of our country's early roads?
2. What did Robert Fulton's steamboat, the *Clermont* prove?
3. **FOCUS** How did the steam engine change travel in America?
4. **THINKING SKILL** What are some different *points of view* about the Erie Canal expressed in the lesson?
5. **GEOGRAPHY** What kinds of maps would a canal builder use? Explain your answer.

MAKING A DIFFERENCE

Cleaning Up Lake Pontchartrain

NEW ORLEANS, LOUISIANNA— Lake Pontchartrain is the largest body of water in Louisiana and a popular place for boating and picnics. But Pontchartrain has a problem—pollution.

Since 1990, teacher Sue Ellen Lyons and the students in Project FUR have been hard at work attacking this problem. FUR stands for Fight Urban Runoff. "Sometimes," says Mrs. Lyons, "city dwellers throw used motor oil, old paint, and other dangerous chemicals down the drains. Water that goes into the drains flows into the drainage canals and then into Lake Pontchartrain. Many people just don't make the connection between dumping trash down the storm drains and lake pollution."

The pollution in Lake Pontchartrain hurts shrimp, crab, fish, and other plant and marine life in the lake. "To fight this problem," says Mrs. Lyons, "FUR members go storm drain stenciling." Several times a year, 20 to 30 students spread out through city neighborhoods with spray paint and stencils. The volunteers stencil the warning "Dump No Waste—Drains to Lake" on drain covers or on the curb near the drain. This helps remind residents that dumping dangerous material into drains hurts Lake Pontchartrain. Charles Childress, age 12, says he became a volunteer because, "I wanted to make people aware of what

we're doing to the earth, how we might be harming it when we could be helping it."

The students encourage people to recycle used motor oil by bringing it back to service station collection centers. "Every time a person sees our spray-painted warning on a storm drain and decides not to throw their trash into the drain, we're making a difference," says Charles. "I think everyone should care about this. The future depends on it. After all, if we abuse our natural resources now, they might not be there when we grow up."

". . . everyone should care about this."

Charles F Childress III

1760   1790   1820   1850   1880

Moving To Texas

Read Aloud

Mary Austin Holley was impressed with the rich lands of Texas. In 1831 she wrote to her friends in the United States, "The newcomer has but to plant his seeds in the ground, and the increase is astonishing." Holley was one of the many people who had left the United States to start a new life in Texas.

Focus Activity

READ TO LEARN

How did Texas become part of the United States?

VOCABULARY

- Stephen F. Austin
- Antonio López de Santa Anna
- Juan Seguín
- David Crockett
- Jim Bowie
- William Travis
- Suzanna Dickenson
- Sam Houston
- Lorenzo de Zavala

PLACES

- Texas
- The Alamo
- Goliad
- San Jacinto River
- Houston

THE BIG PICTURE

The first Europeans to set foot in Texas were Spanish explorers. For many years the Spaniards who colonized Mexico heard stories of "the great kingdom of the Tejas (TAY hahs)." These stories described Native American people, the Caddo, who called themselves tejas, or "friends." Later, Spanish explorers began calling the entire region Texas.

Texas was part of the Spanish territory of Mexico. In 1821 Mexico won its independence from Spain after ten hard years of fighting.

Mexican leaders worried that there were not enough people living in Texas, which was one of Mexico's northern provinces, or states. They believed the United States might take control of Texas if there were too few people to defend it. To attract more settlers, the Mexican government offered land to Mexicans who were willing to move north to Texas. The Mexican government also began looking to Europe and the United States for more settlers.

416

"TEXAS FEVER"

In 1821 Moses Austin, a Missouri merchant, got permission from Spanish officials to start a colony of Americans in Texas. However, Austin became ill and died before he could complete his plan. He asked his son, Stephen F. Austin, to take over for him.

By 1822 Austin had brought about 300 families from the United States to settle in Texas. This group of American settlers came to be known as "The Old 300." Soon "Texas fever" swept through the United States. Americans, mostly from the southern states, rushed to accept Austin's offer of cheap, fertile land.

"Gone to Texas"

All across the South the sign "G.T.T." hung on abandoned cabins and houses. The letters stood for "Gone to Texas." In the 1820s and 1830s, many United States farm families bought land in Texas. During this time, land in the United States cost more than in Texas. In the 1830s land was being offered in Texas for free.

Southern farmers found that the woodlands and coastal plains of Texas were perfect for growing corn and cotton and for raising cattle. Many of the planters who moved into Texas brought enslaved African Americans with them. Slavery was illegal in Mexico. However, Mexican leaders decided to allow slavery in Texas in order to encourage American immigration.

In exchange for the right to settle in Texas, the Mexican government required that Americans become Mexican citizens and join the Roman Catholic Church. The Americans were also expected to speak Spanish, the official language of Texas. Mexico's leaders hoped these rules would make the Americans loyal to Mexico rather than to the United States. Yet most Americans did not learn Spanish or change their religion. They were able to ignore the laws because the newly formed government of Mexico was too weak to enforce them.

This oil painting of Stephen F. Austin (below) hangs in the Texas Capitol in Austin. The longhorn (bottom) was one of the first breeds of cattle to come through Texas.

417

GROWING CONFLICTS

As the number of American immigrants increased, leaders of Mexico's government began to worry that they would lose Texas. By 1830 American settlers in Texas outnumbered Mexican residents, or Tejanos, by three to one. Tejanos were Mexicans who lived in Texas. Mexican leaders decided to stop all immigration from the United States. This decision angered many of the Americans living in Texas.

Some Americans were also upset that Mexico had outlawed slavery in Texas the year before. Many planters began complaining that they would not be able to grow cotton without using slave labor. A planter named John Durst wrote to Stephen F. Austin, "We are ruined forever."

In 1833 the Texans sent Austin to Mexico's capital, Mexico City, to explain why the Texans opposed the new laws and why Texas should be a separate state in Mexico. However, Austin was accused of trying to start a rebellion in Texas and was put in jail for more than a year.

The Texas Rebellion

In 1835 about 1,400 Mexican troops rode north toward Texas. They were sent by Mexico's president Antonio López de Santa Anna (ahn TOH nee oh LOH pes DE SAHN tah AH nah). In 1834 Santa Anna had taken total control of the central Mexican government. He had thrown out Mexico's constitution and made himself president for life. Now Santa Anna planned to take control of Texas.

Texas State Library

Many Texans—Tejanos and Americans—opposed Santa Anna's takeover of the government. Tejanos joined with the Americans to fight the Mexican Army. A Tejano leader, Juan Seguín (HWAHN se GHEEN), organized the volunteers who joined the volunteer Texas Army.

Recent immigrants to Texas, who arrived in 1836, also joined the fight. A former United States congressman from Tennessee named David Crockett was there. Jim Bowie, also from Tennessee, led a volunteer force. William Travis, a lawyer from Alabama, was commander of the Texas Army.

Texas rebels, including David Crockett (left) and Juan Seguín (far left) fought to defend The Alamo. The Texas rebels finally defeated Santa Anna (bottom) at the San Jacinto River.

◇ THE LAST STAND AT THE ALAMO ◇

Thirteen Days at The Alamo

In December 1835 the Texas Army had defeated the Mexican Army and taken control of The Alamo, an old Spanish mission that had been changed into a fort. Texas rebels, along with some of their wives and children, camped inside. Scholars disagree about how many people were inside The Alamo. Estimates range from 187 to 257 people. Over 4,000 of Santa Anna's troops camped outside the fort. On February 23, 1836, the Mexican troops attacked The Alamo. On March 6, after almost two weeks of constant fighting, Mexican soldiers broke through the Texans' defenses. In tough, hand-to-hand fighting, most of The Alamo's defenders were killed. Over 1,000 Mexican soldiers were killed as well.

The Alamo survivors, mostly women and children, met Santa Anna. He ordered Suzanna Dickenson, whose husband had been killed, to tell the news of the Texans' defeat. She carried a letter from Santa Anna to the headquarters of Sam Houston. Houston, born in Virginia, had fought with Andrew Jackson in the War of 1812. He was the general of the Texas Army.

Dickenson learned that while the battle of The Alamo was being fought, 59 Texas delegates had approved a Declaration of Independence on March 2, 1836. The Declaration proclaimed the new Republic of Texas.

On March 19, in another battle, outnumbered Texan troops were defeated. Over 350 Texans were forced to march to the fort at Goliad (GOH lee ad). Against his officers' advice, Santa Anna ordered the Texans be put to death.

The Battle of San Jacinto

As Sam Houston retreated from Santa Anna's army, he worked to train about 750 soldiers. The retreat ended in April when Houston's troops surprised Santa Anna near the San Jacinto (sahn hah SEEN toh) River. Shouting "Remember The Alamo!" and "Remember Goliad!" the Texans defeated the Mexican force on April 21.

The battle took only about 18 minutes, but it ended the war. Santa Anna tried to escape and was caught. His army destroyed, Santa Anna agreed to ask the Mexican government to grant independence to Texas in exchange for his freedom.

419

INDEPENDENCE FOR TEXAS

After their victory at the Battle of San Jacinto, the Texans organized their new government. Sam Houston was elected the first president of the Republic of Texas. Lorenzo de Zavala (loh REN soh DEH sah VAH lah), a Tejano who had fought in the Texas Army, became the republic's first vice president.

A flag with a single white star flew over the republic's capitol at Houston, which was named after Sam Houston. Texas soon became known as the "Lone Star Republic."

"Foreigners in Their Native Land"

At first the Tejanos and the Americans who had fought together for independence shared power in the government. In 1837 all but 1 of the 41 candidates running for elected office in San Antonio were Tejanos.

Then thousands more settlers from the United States began arriving in the Texas republic. Within ten years the Tejanos had lost their political power. By 1847 only five Tejanos ran for office in the government.

Juan Seguín, who had fought for Texas independence, said that the Tejanos felt like "foreigners in their native land." Seguín, like many other Tejanos, eventually left Texas to live in Mexico.

The Lone Star State

After Sam Houston was elected president of Texas, he asked his old friend, President Andrew Jackson, to allow the Republic of Texas to become part of the United States. "I look to you as a friend and patron of my youth to save us," Houston wrote.

Lorenzo de Zavala (top) designed the first flag of the Republic of Texas. Sam Houston (right) became its first President and later the first governor of Texas.

The flags of Texas—a republic (top) and now as a state (bottom)—both share the lone star design created by Lorenzo de Zavala.

President Jackson turned down Houston's request to allow Texas into the United States. Mexico had threatened to go to war if the United States made Texas a state. In addition Jackson knew that Texas would continue to allow slavery if it became a state. Many leaders of the northern states opposed slavery. The President did not want to lose their support in Congress.

WHY IT MATTERS

By 1844 government leaders in the United States had a growing interest in settlement of the West. A presidential candidate named James K. Polk, who had promised the American people "all of Texas," won the election.

In 1845 Congress voted to admit Texas as a slave state. On December 29, 1845, Texas became our country's 28th state. As Mexico had warned, this act would lead to more conflict for the countries.

✔ Reviewing Facts and Ideas

MAIN IDEAS

- In 1821 Mexico won its independence from Spain. By 1822 large numbers of immigrants from the United States began to settle in Texas, which was part of Mexico.
- After Sam Houston's defeat of the Mexican army at the Battle of San Jacinto in 1836, Texas declared independence from Mexico.
- In 1834 Juan Seguín organized the Texas Mexican volunteers. Jim Bowie, David Crockett, and William Travis were among the Texas rebels who died defending The Alamo in 1836.
- Opposition to slavery and fear of war with Mexico delayed statehood for Texas until 1845.

THINK ABOUT IT

1. How did Stephen F. Austin help Texas to grow?

2. What tensions developed between Texans and the Mexican government?

3. **FOCUS** How did Texas become part of the United States?

4. **THINKING SKILL** Explain the Mexican government and the Texan *points of view* about Texas independence. How do you account for any differences between them?

5. **WRITE** Suppose that you are a Texas newspaper reporter. Write an article explaining why so many people joined the rebellion against Mexico.

421

War With Mexico

Read Aloud

On September 13, 1847, cannon balls broke through the stone walls of an old fort called Chapultepec (chah pool te PEK) Castle. Mexican soldiers, some no older than 13, tried to protect Mexico City. In the fierce battle many lost their lives. These young soldiers were later called Los Niños Heroes (lohs NEE nyohs er oh ES), which means "The Young Heroes" in Spanish.

Focus Activity

READ TO LEARN

What were the effects of the war between the United States and Mexico?

VOCABULARY

- Mexican War
- Battle of Buena Vista
- Treaty of Guadalupe Hidalgo

PEOPLE

- James K. Polk
- Zachary Taylor
- Winfield Scott

PLACES

- Rio Grande
- Chapultepec

THE BIG PICTURE

As you have read, Texas became part of the United States in 1845. Yet Mexico and the United States could not agree on where the border between Texas and Mexico should be. The United States claimed that the **Rio Grande** should form the Texas border. Mexico wanted the border to be further north and east, at the Nueces (nyu AY sus) River.

In November 1845 President **James K. Polk** sent a government official to Mexico to settle on a border at the Rio Grande. This official offered $30 million for the Mexican territories of California and New Mexico. At that time these territories included almost all of what is now the Southwest region of the United States.

One newspaper editor in Mexico said that Mexico's President Jose Herrera (hoh SE ehr RER ah) was "vile," or evil, for even considering the deal with the United States. Herrera refused the offer. A war with Mexico was not long in coming.

THE PATH TO WAR

American troops led by General Zachary Taylor waited in Texas. When Mexico refused to sell its northern lands, President Polk ordered the troops south. There they would take control of the disputed border at the Rio Grande. American ships blocked Mexican boats from using the Rio Grande. "If this movement of ours does not lead to . . . bloodshed," worried one American commander, "I am much mistaken."

The United States Declares War

In April 1846 a Mexican force crossed the Rio Grande and attacked American troops. Mexico "has invaded our territory," President Polk announced in a statement to Congress. He said that war had begun "by the act of Mexico

This print of General Zachary Taylor includes a scene of the Battle of Buena Vista in the bottom right corner.

herself." On May 13, 1846, Congress voted by a large majority to officially declare war. The Mexican War lasted from 1846 to 1848.

Opinion about the war was divided in the United States. One opponent was Representative Abraham Lincoln of Illinois. He reminded Congress that the land was not "American soil," but was claimed by Mexico.

General Zachary Taylor

General Zachary Taylor led American troops in Mexico. Because he was always ready for battle, his troops named him "Old Rough and Ready." By the end of 1846 Taylor's troops had marched south past the Rio Grande and captured several Mexican cities. At the Battle of Buena Vista in 1847, Taylor's outnumbered forces defeated Santa Anna's army. Buena Vista is a city near Monterey. In 1849 Zachary Taylor became the twelfth President of the United States.

Western Revolt

In June 1846 Americans in California also rebelled against the government of Mexico. Although California was still officially a part of Mexico, these Americans declared their land an independent republic. The United States Navy soon arrived and claimed California for the United States.

Meanwhile, American commander Stephen Kearny and his troops captured New Mexico's capital at Santa Fe without much fighting. Kearny then marched with his men to California. Californios, or Mexicans living in California, had won control of a United States fort in Los Angeles. After several battles the United States Army forced the Californios to surrender in January 1847.

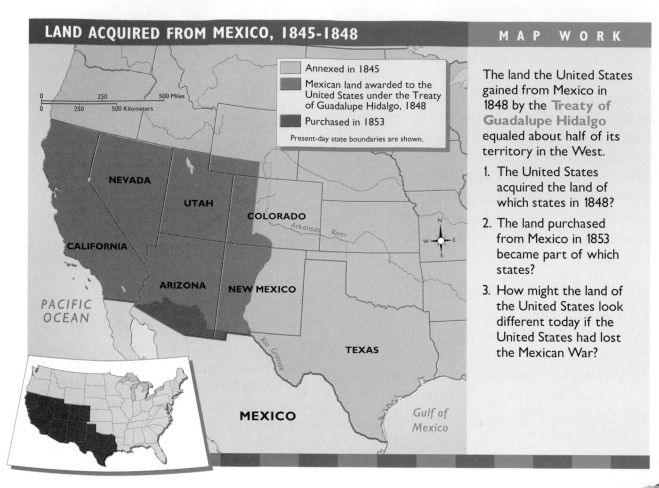

LAND ACQUIRED FROM MEXICO, 1845-1848

MAP WORK

Legend:
- Annexed in 1845
- Mexican land awarded to the United States under the Treaty of Guadalupe Hidalgo, 1848
- Purchased in 1853

Present-day state boundaries are shown.

0 250 500 Miles
0 250 500 Kilometers

NEVADA

UTAH

COLORADO

Colorado River

Arkansas River

CALIFORNIA

PACIFIC OCEAN

ARIZONA

NEW MEXICO

Rio Grande

TEXAS

MEXICO

Gulf of Mexico

The land the United States gained from Mexico in 1848 by the Treaty of Guadalupe Hidalgo equaled about half of its territory in the West.

1. The United States acquired the land of which states in 1848?

2. The land purchased from Mexico in 1853 became part of which states?

3. How might the land of the United States look different today if the United States had lost the Mexican War?

VICTORY AT CHAPULTEPEC

By early 1847 the United States Army held key parts of northern Mexico, including New Mexico and California. Under the command of General Winfield Scott, the army landed on Mexico's coast and fought its way to Mexico City, Mexico's capital.

The castle of Chapultepec guarded the entrance to Mexico City. In September, Scott's troops attacked the walls of the fortress. Fewer than 1,100 Mexican troops, including *Los Niños,* defended Chapultepec. Santa Anna, who again was president of Mexico, did not send more troops to aid the defenders. The fort fell, and United States troops moved into Mexico City.

A Treaty with Mexico

The United States won much of Mexico's northern territory. Mexico surrendered. In 1848 the Treaty of Guadalupe Hidalgo (GWAH dul oo pay hih DAL goh), ended the war. Mexico was forced to accept the Rio Grande as its border with Texas.

As the map on this page shows, Mexico also had to give up half of its territory to the United States. In exchange for this territory, the United States agreed to pay $15 million to Mexico.

This photograph shows Winfield Scott's troops entering Mexico City on the same road Hernando Cortés traveled 300 years earlier.

424

The Treaty of Guadalupe Hidalgo gave the 80,000 Mexicans living in the territory the choice of remaining Mexican citizens or becoming citizens of the United States. All except 2,000 became United States citizens. Mexican Americans were guaranteed the same rights as other Americans, including the right to keep their property. Yet many Mexican Americans, who were unfamiliar with the English language and with American courts of law, lost their lands.

WHY IT MATTERS

After the Mexican War, the borders of the United States stretched to the Pacific Ocean. This pleased many Americans who believed that the United States had a "manifest destiny" to extend its borders from the Atlantic to the Pacific.

This term was first used in an 1845 article about Texas by John O'Sullivan, a New York writer. Manifest destiny was a belief in the right to claim new lands for the United States. This belief continued to play a key role in the United States settlement of western lands, especially in the rush to California.

The successes of the Mexican War helped General Zachary Taylor become President of the United States in 1849. Although the United States Army was outnumbered, it won most of its battles. In addition many officers gained wartime experience. Not even 20 years later, these veterans would be fighting again—this time on United States soil.

✓ Reviewing Facts and Ideas

MAIN IDEAS

- The Mexican War lasted from 1846 to 1848.
- The capture of Mexico City in 1847 ended the war.
- The 1848 Treaty of Guadalupe Hidalgo forced Mexico to give half of its territory to the United States.

THINK ABOUT IT

1. What dispute between the United States and Mexico led to war?

2. What is Chapultepec? What happened there?

3. **FOCUS** What were the results of the Mexican War?

4. **THINKING SKILL** Reread the section titled "The United States Declares War" on page 423. Which statements are *facts*? Which are *opinions*? How can you tell?

5. **GEOGRAPHY** Using the map on page 424, list the states formed from the land gained by the United States in the Mexican War.

Using Reference Sources

VOCABULARY

reference source
encyclopedia
atlas
historical atlas

CD-ROM
card catalog
call number

WHY THE SKILL MATTERS

In the last lesson you read about General Zachary Taylor's leadership during the Mexican War. If you wanted to write a report about the battles that Taylor fought, you could try to find information in a reference source. A reference source is a book or other source that contains facts about many different subjects. Reference sources are mostly found in a special section of the library.

There are many different kinds of reference sources. Not all of them are books. Knowing the different types of reference sources and the

kinds of information each contains will help you to find information quickly and easily.

USING REFERENCE SOURCES

One of the best places to start looking for information about a particular subject is in an encyclopedia. Encyclopedias provide very general information about important people, places, topics, and events. The subjects are arranged in alphabetical order in a series of books.

To learn more about Zachary Taylor, you need the encyclopedia volume that includes

The Library of Congress's reading room (right) is a quiet place to review reference sources. A computer disk (above) is the latest way to store information.

the letter *T*. Often a bibliography at the end of each entry will give you titles of books about related subjects. You might also look in the encyclopedia's main index to see if Taylor is discussed under another subject heading.

If you already know the names of some places where Taylor fought, an atlas will help you locate these places.

An atlas is a reference source that provides maps and other geographical information, such as latitude and longitude. The reference section of your textbook contains an atlas. Historical atlases are especially useful when you are researching a history report. An historical atlas includes maps of important battles and changes over time that affected political boundaries.

A CD-ROM is another kind of reference source. A CD-ROM is a computer disk that can contain as much information as a set of encyclopedias. In fact some encyclopedias are stored on CD-ROMs. Other CD-ROMs contain geographical and historical information, as well as photographs and paintings from museums.

USING THE CARD CATALOG

What if you need more specific information about Taylor's military plans but you do not know the title of a book on this subject? The card catalog will help you find it. A card catalog is a listing of all the books a library contains. The catalog is arranged alphabetically by author, title, and subject.

Helping yourself

- A **reference source** is a book or other source that contains facts about many different subjects.

- Think about which reference sources are most likely to help you find the information you need.

- Search for the information.

Each card has a call number listed on it. The call number is a series of letters and numbers that tells you the exact location of the book on the shelf.

Many libraries now have their card catalogs stored on computers. The computer can help you search for a book more quickly. For example, if you type in Taylor's name as a subject, then biographies and other reference sources about him soon appear on the screen. Which related subjects do you think might help you find other useful books?

TRYING THE SKILL

Historians do not always agree on how to interpret history, so it is always best to look at different sources to compare their points of view.

What do you think would be the best source to find out the major battles of the Mexican War? If you wanted to find biographical details about Juan Seguín, where would you look?

REVIEWING THE SKILL

1. What kinds of reference sources are available in most libraries?

2. Where would you find the most complete information about historical events? Explain your answer.

3. In what ways can you use a card catalog to research a subject?

4. What is a CD-ROM? What kinds of information does it contain?

5. Why would it be helpful for you to know how to use a variety of reference sources?

427

1760   1790   1820   1836   1860   1880

Western Trails

Focus Activity

READ TO LEARN

Who traveled on the western trails?

VOCABULARY

- gold rush
- Forty-Niners

PEOPLE

- Narcissa Whitman
- Brigham Young

PLACES

- Oregon Territory
- Oregon Trail
- Mormon Trail
- Great Salt Lake
- Utah
- Salt Lake City
- California Trail
- Sutter's Mill

Read Aloud

In the middle 1800s thousands of people were traveling to the same place, but they called it by different names. To Native Americans, it was home. United States citizens called it the West—the land of opportunity. Some Americans thought of it as the "Promised Land," where they could find freedom from slavery and religious prejudice. Mexicans living south of the Rio Grande called it el Norte (EL NAWR tay), or "the North." To Chinese immigrants sailing across the Pacific Ocean, the West was called "Gold Mountain." What exactly was this place? Why were so many people going there?

THE BIG PICTURE

Groups of families as well as individuals in the East traveled to the Oregon Territory and other parts of the West in the middle 1800s. Both the United States and Great Britain claimed the Oregon Territory. In 1846 the two countries agreed to divide it.

People made the journey west for many reasons. Some people sought religious freedom. Others wanted to make their fortunes in gold. Many—perhaps most—wanted to find cheap land where they could build new lives as farmers or ranchers.

The Oregon Trail had the largest share of travelers moving west. Between 1840 and 1860, almost 300,000 people traveled on the Oregon Trail. So many wagons made the trip that in some places the deep ruts of the wagon wheels are still visible today.

MIGRATING WEST

In 1836 two missionary couples set out on the Oregon Trail. Marcus and Narcissa Whitman and Henry and Eliza Spalding hoped to teach the Cayuse people in the Oregon Territory about Christianity. After traveling about six months, the Whitmans set up their mission near the Columbia River. The mission also served as a resting place for travelers.

In letters to her family, Narcissa Whitman described the rich farmland, dense woodlands, and mountains. "It is indeed, a lovely situation," Whitman wrote. Her letters were later published and helped encourage Americans to settle in Oregon.

The Mormons

Early in 1847 another group of religious followers headed west. More than 14,000 travelers left from Nauvoo, Illinois, along a route called the Mormon Trail. The trail got its name from the people who traveled it. They were part of a religious group called the Church of Jesus Christ of Latter-day Saints, or Mormons. Because of mistreatment in Nauvoo, the Mormons decided to move west. On the Infographic on pages 430–431, you can see that the Mormon Trail closely follows the Oregon

Brigham Young (left) led the Mormons to Utah in a wagon train (below) after their first leader was killed in Illinois.

Trail through the Great Plains.

The Mormon leader Brigham Young led the long march. The Mormons' wagons crossed ice-covered rivers as they followed the Oregon Trail. Near Fort Bridger the group left the trail and headed south into lands claimed by Mexico. Finally, in July 1847, the first group of Mormons reached a large lake now known as the Great Salt Lake. The region's inhabitants included the Ute (YOOT) and Shoshone peoples. The present-day state of Utah got its name from the Ute.

"Everything looked gloomy, and I felt heartsick," wrote a Mormon traveler named Harriet Young after her first view of the dry land. The Mormons decided to use irrigation to grow crops of potatoes, grain, and apples. Salt Lake City, one of the first Mormon settlements, grew rapidly. By 1850 there were about 5,000 Mormons living in the town.

Infographic

Moving West, 1840-1860

By 1850, well-traveled wagon trails snaked across the United States to the West Coast. These trails paved the way for Americans to move west across North America. They had been developed in the early 1800s from Native American trails by fur trappers called Mountain Men. Look at the map on the next page.

Wyoming Division of Cultural Resources

Fort Bridger

This fort, south of the Mormon and California trails, was a stopping off point for many settlers moving west. There they traded goods and repaired their wagons and tools. The fort was established by a Mountain Man named Jim Bridger in 1843.

Nebraska Game and Parks Division

Chimney Rock

Settlers traveling on the Oregon Trail probably reached this landmark as their supplies began to run low. At this point the oxen that had pulled their heavily loaded wagons would also have grown weak. To lighten the load, settlers tossed out furniture they had planned to use in their new homes in the West.

inter NET CONNECTION Visit our website: www.mhschool.com

Trails to the West

Legend:
- ══ Mountain Pass
- 🏠 Fort
- ● City
- ～ Trail

Ft. Vancouver
Ft. Walla Walla
Whitman's Mission
Ft. Boise
Bozeman Trail
Oregon Trail
Ft. Hall
SODA SPRINGS
South Pass
SACRAMENTO
Beckwourth Pass
California Trail
SALT LAKE CITY
Mormon Trail
Ft. Bridger
Split Rock
Red Buttes
Independence Rock
Ft. Laramie
Castle Rock
Chimney Rock
Mormon Trail
OMAHA
NAUVOO
Donner Pass
Sutter's Fort
SAN FRANCISCO
Oregon Trail
INDEPENDENCE
ST. LOUIS
Old Spanish Trail
Santa Fe Trail
SANTA FE
El Camino Real (from Mexico)
EL PASO
LOS ANGELES

James Beckwourth

A runaway slave, he became a Mountain Man and was hired as a trader by the American Fur Company. In 1850 Beckwourth reached a gap in the northern Sierra Nevada Mountains, now called Beckwourth Pass. Beckwourth, like many Mountain Men, got along with Native Americans. He was made chief of the Crow people and was buried on their land.

431

THE CALIFORNIA GOLD RUSH

One January morning in 1848, a carpenter named James Marshall stood beside the American River in California. The morning sun caught the gleam of something shiny in the water. "I reached my hand down and picked it up," remembered Marshall, "it made my heart thump, for I was certain it was gold."

Marshall was right. By early 1849 people from all over the world raced along yet another western trail, the California Trail to reach the west. This trail led through the Rocky Mountains to California and then to Sutter's Mill.

Sutter's Mill was the name of the sawmill in the Sacramento River valley where Marshall first saw gold. So many people came seeking a fortune in gold that this event became known as the California gold rush.

The Forty-Niners

"Your streams have minnows and ours are paved with gold," wrote the mayor of Monterey, California, to a newspaper in Philadelphia. In response to such accounts and letters, "gold fever" struck thousands of would-be miners. They called themselves Forty-Niners, for the year in which many reached California.

Although a few lucky Forty-Niners struck it rich, most of the miners found only hard work and disappointment. Most lived in wooden huts or canvas tents. They waded all day in streams or bent over gravel beds, but most did not find gold.

As more miners came to California, the price of food and supplies became very high. An ounce of gold, which was worth about $16, could not buy much.

Chinese, Irish, African American, and Native American miners panned for gold in California's many rivers and streams.

For example, a miner had to spend $12 for a blanket and $35 for a barrel of flour. The merchants who sold supplies to the miners were more likely to get rich than the miners themselves. Most miners returned home broke, having spent most of their money on supplies.

California Becomes a State

The gold rush helped California to become a state in a short period of time. In 1847 San Francisco had only 800 people. By December 1849 the population had skyrocketed to 25,000. Many Californians wanted statehood. They believed that California needed courts of law and elected officials to keep order in the fast-growing region.

Some people did not want California to become a state because they did not agree with the California constitution. California's constitution gave married women the right to own property. In the rest of the United States, a wife's property belonged to her husband. In addition, Southerners did not like it that California had already outlawed slavery. Still, in September 1850, California became a state. You will read how this happened in the next chapter.

WHY IT MATTERS

The 1840s to the 1860s was one of the great periods of movement in the history of the United States. People kept moving west, forever changing the lands between the Mississippi River and the Pacific Ocean. However, the time of the wagon trains did not last long. By 1860 a war would interrupt most of the traffic. By 1869 the railroad lines would connect the two coasts, making it easier to cross the country.

Links to ART

Hold That Pose

In 1839 the art of photography was invented. Some hardy photographers packed their bulky cameras and heavy glass plates in wagons and set out to photograph the West. Photographs of the beautiful western landscapes and the towns captured the imaginations of Americans in the East. Look at the photograph on page 428. What features help you identify the place?

✔ Reviewing Facts and Ideas

MAIN IDEAS

- From 1840 to 1860 almost 300,000 people traveled to the West seeking a better life.
- Travelers to the West followed the Oregon Trail, the Mormon Trail, the California Trail, and other trails to the West. These trails were established by the Native Americans and by Mountain Men.
- The 1849 gold rush attracted thousands of people from the United States and all over the world to areas around Sutter's Mill, California.

THINK ABOUT IT

1. What religious group moved to Utah in early 1847?

2. Why did Californians want their territory to become a state?

3. **FOCUS** Why did large numbers of people travel on trails to the West in the middle 1800s?

4. **THINKING SKILL** What were some *effects* of the gold rush on California?

5. **GEOGRAPHY** Name two landforms that the Oregon Trail crossed.

CHAPTER 15 REVIEW

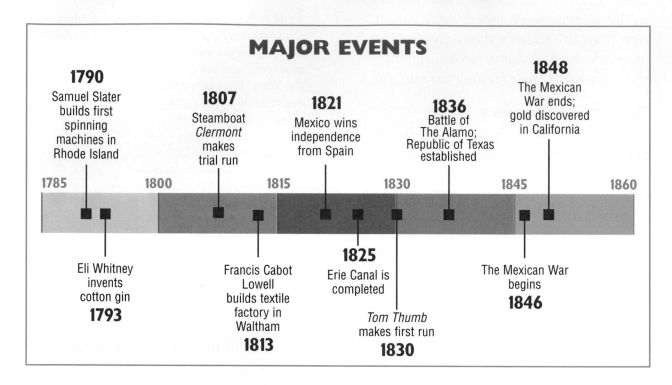

MAJOR EVENTS

1790
Samuel Slater builds first spinning machines in Rhode Island

1807
Steamboat *Clermont* makes trial run

1821
Mexico wins independence from Spain

1836
Battle of The Alamo; Republic of Texas established

1848
The Mexican War ends; gold discovered in California

1785　　1800　　1815　　1830　　1845　　1860

Eli Whitney invents cotton gin
1793

Francis Cabot Lowell builds textile factory in Waltham
1813

1825
Erie Canal is completed

Tom Thumb makes first run
1830

The Mexican War begins
1846

THINKING ABOUT VOCABULARY

Number a paper from 1 to 5. Beside each number, write the word or term from the list below that best matches each description.

atlas   investor
canal   reaper
gold rush

1. A person who uses money to buy or to make something that will make more money

2. A reference source that provides maps and other geographical information such as latitude and longitude

3. A machine that uses sharp blades to cut and harvest grain

4. Term used to describe crowds of people going somewhere to seek gold

5. A human-built waterway

THINKING ABOUT FACTS

1. How did the invention of the cotton gin affect life in the South?

2. What role did interchangeable parts play in the Industrial Revolution?

3. How did the National Road improve transportation in the United States?

4. Why did Peter Cooper race the *Tom Thumb* against a horse-pulled coach?

5. What led to the Mexican War?

6. Why did President Jackson not allow Texas to join the United States?

7. What were some of the reasons people moved to the West in the early to middle 1800s?

8. Why did some people oppose California's becoming a state?

9. Name three trails on which pioneers traveled to the West between 1840 and 1860. Where did these trails lead?

10. Look at the time line above. What event helps explain why canals were important for only a short time? Explain.

THINK AND WRITE

WRITING AN ADVERTISEMENT
Write an advertisement for one of the inventions you read about in the chapter. Be sure to describe how the invention is useful.

WRITING A NEWSPAPER ARTICLE
Suppose you are a newspaper reporter assigned to write an article about the race between *Tom Thumb* and the horse-drawn coach. Include people's reactions to the new steam locomotive in your article.

WRITING COMPARISONS/CONTRASTS
Write several paragraphs in which you compare and contrast how Texas and California joined the United States. Include the dates of important events.

APPLYING STUDY SKILLS

USING REFERENCE SOURCES
1. What is a reference source?
2. What should you think about before using a particular reference source?
3. What kind of information do encyclopedias provide? Why do many researchers use encyclopedias?
4. What is the purpose of a call number?
5. In what form are encyclopedias available other than as books? How is this other form helpful?

Summing Up the Chapter

Copy the matrix chart on a separate piece of paper. Then review the chapter to fill in the blank sections. After you have finished, use the information in the chart to write a paragraph that answers the question "How did the Industrial Revolution change the United States?"

DISCOVERY/ INVENTION	PERSON	LOCATION	RESULT
		Georgia	Cotton production booms
	Cyrus McCormick	Chicago	
Steam-powered trains		Baltimore	
Gold			Forty-niners rush to area, which soon becomes a state

UNIT 6 REVIEW

THINKING ABOUT VOCABULARY

Number a paper from 1 to 10. Beside each number write the word or term from the list below that best completes each sentence.

Battle of New Orleans   steam engine
cotton gin   Trail of Tears
gold rush   Treaty of Guadalupe Hidalgo
Industrial Revolution
Louisiana Purchase   War Hawks
Mexican War

1. Quatie, the wife of a Cherokee chief, died during the _____, which is called "the place where they cried" by the Cherokee.

2. Robert Fulton used a _____ to power his boat the *Clermont*.

3. Eli Whitney invented the _____, a device that made cleaning cotton much faster and easier.

4. President Thomas Jefferson arranged the _____, which doubled the size of the United States at a low price.

5. The _____ was a conflict that began under President James Polk in 1846.

6. Senator Henry Clay was the leader of the _____ who argued for war against Great Britain.

7. James Marshall's discovery at Sutter's Mill led to the California _____ in 1849.

8. Andrew Jackson became famous for winning the _____ in the War of 1812.

9. After General Winfield Scott captured Mexico City, the _____ was signed to end the Mexican War.

10. Samuel Slater brought the _____ to the United States when he built his spinning machines in Rhode Island.

THINK AND WRITE ◄═══▶

WRITING A SKIT

Choose one of the events you have read about in this unit and write a skit about it. For example, you might write a skit about travelers on the Oregon Trail, or about soldiers inside Fort McHenry in the War of 1812. Remember to include several characters in your skit as well as facts.

WRITING A LIST

Suppose you are about to move from one part of the United States to another in the 1800s. Think about where you might be going and what you might need when you get there. Make a list of things to bring with you on your journey. Remember that you might not be able to carry a large amount.

WRITING ABOUT PERSPECTIVES

This unit describes how the United States grew from a small country along the Atlantic Ocean to a large country extending to the Pacific Ocean. How would the perspective of a national leader have changed between the time at the beginning of the unit and at the end of the unit? Write a paragraph to explain your views.

BUILDING SKILLS

1. **Comparing maps** How is an historical map different from a political map?

2. **Comparing maps** Look at the map on page 381. How could you find out in which part of the Louisiana Purchase Native Americans were living?

3. **Using reference sources** Why is it important to know how to use different kinds of reference sources?

4. **Using reference sources** How are bibliographies at the end of encyclopedia articles useful?

5. **Using reference sources** What different reference sources appear in this book?

YESTERDAY, TODAY & *TOMORROW*

Our country did not just grow geographically in the 1800s. New inventions and new ideas led to people changing their ways of life. What were some of these inventions? How did they affect the way we live now? Can you think of discoveries happening today that will change the way we live in the future?

READING ON YOUR OWN

These are some of the books you could find at the library to help you learn more.

PIONEERS
by Martin W. Sandler
Pioneer life is accurately presented with fascinating details, posters, quotes, and art.

SEQUOYAH'S GIFT: A PORTRAIT OF THE CHEROKEE LEADER
by Janet Klausner
This biography of Sequoyah shows how he created a written language for the Cherokee.

GROWING UP IN AMERICA: 1830–1860
by Evelyn Toynton
This book tells what it was really like to grow up in the middle 1800s in such places as New England, the Plains, and the South.

UNIT 6 REVIEW PROJECT

ROLE-PLAY AN INTERVIEW

1. Working in groups of three each member chooses one of the following people from the unit.
   - A pioneer moving west of the Appalachians in 1775.
   - A southerner moving to Texas in the 1830s.
   - A "forty-niner" looking for gold in California in 1849.

2. Write an interview. Be sure to include questions about the individuals, their travels, what each expects to find, and the purpose of the journey.
3. Take turns role playing each interview.

The Granger Collection

GETTYSBURG
ADDRESS

Executive Mansion,

Washington, ..., 186

score and seven years ago our fathers brought

...k, upon this continent, a n.... conceived

liberty, and dedicated to t....

.ll men are created equal"

Now we are engaged in a g....

whether that nation, or an...

and so dedicated, can long....

on a great battle field of....

come to dedicate a portion....

ing place for those who d....

might live. This we may, in....

...ger sense, we can not....

...crate— we can not....

...o men, living....

hallowed it, fa....

... The world will l....

...ay here; while it can ne....

...her....

...living; few be o....

...remember....

forget what th....

it is rather for....

PRESIDENT ABRAHAM LINCOLN

CIVIL WAR BUGLE

Slavery and Emancipation

"this nation . . . shall have a new birth of freedom."

from the Gettysburg Address by President Abraham Lincoln
See pages 484–485.

HARRIET TUBMAN

Why Does it Matter?

President Abraham Lincoln wrote and spoke these words during the Civil War. In this war thousands of lives were lost and deep wounds were felt across the country. Still, Lincoln believed that the war had a purpose—the preservation of the United States.

In keeping the country together, new promises had to be made and old ones had to be renewed. For enslaved African Americans the promises meant the end of slavery. For American women the struggle to win the right to vote was only beginning. Still, with the end of the Civil War, the chance for "a new birth of freedom" was possible for more Americans than ever before.

The Granger Collection

FIND OUT MORE!
Visit our website:
www.mhschool.com

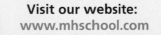

*inter*NET
CONNECTION

Adventures with NATIONAL GEOGRAPHIC

ON A GREAT BATTLEFIELD

T he last bullets flew over Gettysburg more than a hundred years ago. Yet the hills are alive with the sounds of history. Civil War buffs in Union blue and Confederate gray still come to re-create this crucial three-day battle. And more than a million other visitors walk over the green fields each year. They struggle to grasp that some 50,000 Union and Confederate soldiers perished here. A few visitors stop at the nearby house where a wax figure of President Abraham Lincoln sits as if deep in thought. Here, four months after the battle, Lincoln polished the brief speech he would give at a ceremony the next day. His Gettysburg Address called for "a new birth of freedom" for all Americans.

GEOJOURNAL

Imagine you're walking through Gettysburg today. What are your thoughts about what happened here?

The Time of Slavery

THINKING ABOUT HISTORY AND GEOGRAPHY

By the middle of the 1800s, the United States was almost its present size. Yet this country became more and more divided on one issue—slavery. This and other conflicts between the North and the South would cause the Southern states to form their own country. The time line below features some of the people and events of this period.

PACIFIC OCEAN

1848

SENECA FALLS, NEW YORK

The first women's rights convention is held

1850s

BUCKTOWN, MARYLAND

Harriet Tubman leads captives to freedom along the Underground Railroad

1852

ROCHESTER, NEW YORK

Frederick Douglass begins speaking out against slavery

1848   1852   1856

UNITED
STATES

Rochester

Seneca
Falls

Springfield

Harpers Ferry

Bucktown

ATLANTIC
OCEAN

1859

HARPERS FERRY, VIRGINIA

John Brown leads a small rebellion against slavery

1860

SPRINGFIELD, ILLINOIS

Abraham Lincoln wins the Presidential election

1860

1864

1800   1820   1831   1860   1880

Slavery Divides the Country

Focus Activity

READ TO LEARN

What were the major differences between the North and the South in the 1850s?

PEOPLE

- Nat Turner
- Frederick Douglass

PLACES

- Weeksville
- Umbler

Read Aloud

Frederick Douglass's childhood was similar to that of many enslaved African American children. Soon after his birth in about 1817, his mother was sent to another plantation. At times she slipped away at night to visit her young son. If caught, she would have been beaten severely. "I do not recall ever seeing my mother by the light of day," Douglass once said. He saw her only four or five times before she died when he was 7 years old.

THE BIG PICTURE

By the 1850s the question of slavery deeply divided the United States. Slavery, however, was part of a larger issue—the economy. The South had an economy based largely on agriculture. Large plantations using slave labor grew most of the crops sold in the South.

Although most people in both the North and the South were farmers, manufacturing was becoming much more important in the North. The work in the Northern factories was done largely by immigrants. In 1854 the number of immigrants who came to the United States reached a high of over 400,000. The largest number came from Ireland and Germany. These people were fleeing political and economic problems in their homelands. Most immigrants settled in the large cities of the North, where jobs were plentiful.

By 1850 these differences had created two distinct ways of life in the United States—one Northern and one Southern.

NORTH AND SOUTH

The two circle graphs on this page show the different groups that made up the populations of the North and the South in 1860. Differences in the way people in these regions lived and worked affected their views on slavery.

Two Points of View About Slavery

Although some immigrants had enough money to buy land, most found work in the shops and factories in the North. Working conditions were often unhealthy and unsafe. Workdays were long, and wages were low. In many families even the children had to work.

Most Southerners owned small farms but did not own slaves. Still, it was cotton, grown on large plantations, that produced most of the South's wealth. In 1860 about four million enslaved African Americans did the backbreaking work of picking and cleaning cotton. By then the South produced about two-thirds of the world's supply of this valuable crop. "Cotton is king," went the old saying.

The population differences between the North and the South led to differing views on what slavery was like. Supporters of slavery pointed out that cotton made up about half of all goods exported from the United States. Some also argued that enslaved people in the South were better off than immigrants and other workers in the North. In 1857 George Fitzhugh, a Virginia lawyer, compared slavery with working for pay:

The [N]egro slaves are the happiest, and, in some sense, the freest people in the world. . . . [They] have all the comforts and necessaries of life provided for them. . . . The free laborer must work or starve. He is more of a slave than the [N]egro, because he works longer and harder for less allowance [reward] than the slave, and has no holiday.

Many people, however, saw slavery as an unjust and terrible cruelty. In 1842 J. S. Buckingham wrote about the enslaved people he saw on a rice plantation in Georgia:

Absence from work, or neglect of duty, was punished with stinted [reduced] allowance [of food], imprisonment and flogging [beating]. . . . Their lot was one of continued toil, from morning to night, uncheered even by the hope of change, or prospect of improvement in condition.

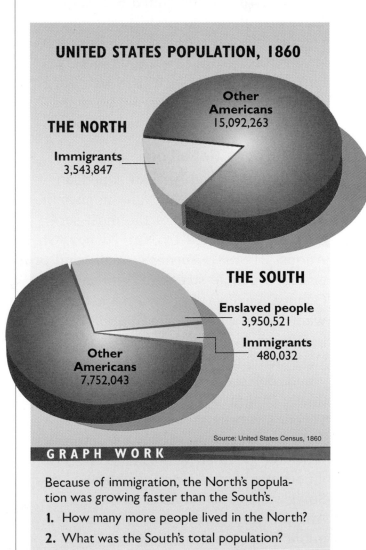

UNITED STATES POPULATION, 1860

THE NORTH

Other Americans
15,092,263

Immigrants
3,543,847

THE SOUTH

Enslaved people
3,950,521

Immigrants
480,032

Other Americans
7,752,043

Source: United States Census, 1860

GRAPH WORK

Because of immigration, the North's population was growing faster than the South's.

1. How many more people lived in the North?

2. What was the South's total population?

The Maryland slave quarters in which Frederick Douglass was raised were similar to these at Carter's Grove plantation in Virginia.

RESISTING SLAVERY

In 1808, Congress made importing slaves from Africa illegal. Still the number of slaves in the United States grew. Slaves continued to be brought into the country illegally. Others were born into slavery because their parents were enslaved. In states such as South Carolina, enslaved people made up more than half of the population by 1860.

Nat Turner's Rebellion

As the enslaved African American population grew, so did the number of slave rebellions. One of the most serious revolts was led by Nat Turner. On August 21, 1831, Turner's small band of enslaved people struck in Southampton County, Virginia. For two days, they went from farm to farm and killed nearly 60 men, women, and children from slave-owning families. Turner hid in the woods for six weeks before he was finally caught. All of the members of Turner's rebellion were hanged.

In the weeks that followed Turner's rebellion, terrified whites killed over 100 innocent enslaved and free blacks. Some states passed laws forbidding African Americans from gathering in public places and holding their own religious services.

Frederick Douglass

Some states, such as Alabama, made it a crime to teach a slave to read or write. When Frederick Douglass was 8 years old, he heard the slave owner's wife reading aloud from the Bible. When he asked her to teach him to read, her husband was furious. "If he learns to read the Bible it will forever unfit him to be a slave," he told her. "He should know nothing but the will of his master, and learn to obey it."

Douglass decided that he wanted to learn. He convinced poor white children to give him reading lessons in exchange for bread. Before long, he could read the newspaper. Later, he learned to write by tracing the letters on the ships in his owner's shipyard.

In 1838, a friend gave the 20-year-old Douglass money for a train ticket to the North. Another friend gave him false papers that identified Douglass as a sailor. On September 4, 1838, Douglass walked down the streets of New York City. "A new world had opened upon me," he wrote.

Speaking Out Against Slavery

Douglass soon moved to New Bedford, Massachusetts. He hoped to find work in the shipyards there. In 1841 he spoke about his experiences as a slave at a meeting of the Massachusetts Anti-Slavery Society. Douglass was quickly hired by the society to give speeches about slavery all over the country. In 1845 he wrote a book about his early years, *Narrative of the Life of Frederick Douglass, An American Slave*. It became an instant bestseller. The details his book provided about his life, however, increased his chances of being recaptured. As a result, Douglass spent the next few years in Europe speaking out against slavery.

Douglass's speeches encouraged many others to attack slavery. Read the excerpt from a speech he gave at an Independence Day picnic. What made Douglass's remarks so powerful?

Read the meeting notice for the Massachusetts Anti-Slavery Society (below). Douglass's moving talks about life under slavery made him (right) one of its key speakers.

Excerpt from a speech by Frederick Douglass in Rochester, New York, July 4, 1852.

*Fellow citizens—Pardon me, and allow me to ask, why am I called upon to speak here today? What have I, or those I represent, to do with your national independence? Are the great principles of political freedom and of natural justice, **embodied** in that Declaration of Independence, extended to us? . . . Your high independence only reveals the immeasurable difference between us. The blessings in which you this day rejoice are not enjoyed **in common**. . . . This Fourth of July is yours, not mine. You may rejoice, I must mourn. . . .*

*[Why should I have] to argue that it is wrong to make men **brutes**, to rob them of their liberty, to work them without wages, to keep them ignorant of their relations to their fellow-men, to beat them with sticks, to **flay** their flesh with the lash, to load their limbs with irons, to hunt them with dogs, to sell them at auction, to **sunder** their families, to knock out their teeth, to burn their flesh, to starve them into obedience and submission to their masters?*

embodied: contained
in common: by all
brutes: animals
flay: strip away
sunder: break apart

447

FREE AFRICAN AMERICANS

Although slavery increased in the South, over 430,000 free African Americans were also living in the United States by 1850. Many had been freed when the northern states ended slavery. Some southern whites, such as George Washington, had freed their slaves after the American Revolution. Other enslaved people purchased their freedom. Some blacks and whites thought that blacks should be sent to Africa to found their own country.

Prejudice in the North

Although Douglass was overjoyed to be free, he quickly learned that life for African Americans was also difficult in the North. "Slave catchers" roamed the cities looking for escaped slaves. Sometimes the slave catchers would kidnap African Americans who had been born free and then sell them into slavery.

Although Douglass was a shipbuilder, he could not get work in his trade. When he first arrived in the North, Douglass had to take such jobs as collecting trash and digging cellars. Because of prejudice, most skilled work was closed to African Americans.

In many places African Americans were barred from lecture halls, hotels, and restaurants. They were forced to sit in separate sections in white churches. And they still could not vote.

Building Communities

To cope with prejudice and other challenges, many free African Ameri-

Weeksville Society

This photograph from the 1800s (left), called a tintype, was found in 1968 during the restoration of Weeksville. By 1850 this community in Brooklyn, New York, had its own school (below).

cans founded communities of their own. Communities like Weeksville in New York City and Umbler in Virginia had existed since the early 1700s.

Free African Americans also set up organizations to meet their needs. Many of these organizations were run by both Baptist and Methodist church groups. For example, by 1846 the African Methodist Episcopal Church had nearly 300 branches throughout the United States. These churches established schools, organized social events, and helped escaping slaves.

WHY IT MATTERS

Mostly because of slavery, the divisions between the North and the South had widened by 1850. "On the subject of slavery," said one South Carolina newspaper, "the North and South . . . are not only two Peoples, but they are rival, hostile Peoples." In 1850 Northern political leaders were still careful about attacking slavery in the South. They feared that a struggle over slavery would destroy the country. It was a struggle, however, that would not be avoided for long.

The Brooklyn, New York, branch of the African Methodist Episcopal Church (above) was founded in 1818. The church remains an important part of African American life today.

✓ Reviewing Facts and Ideas

MAIN IDEAS

- By 1850, the North, with its large cities and immigrant labor, had become a region whose wealth was based more on manufacturing. The South had become a wealthy agricultural region because of the cotton produced by slave labor.

- Some African Americans, such as Frederick Douglass, escaped to freedom in the North and joined the fight against slavery.

- Free African Americans found support by building communities and organizations of their own.

THINK ABOUT IT

1. Describe the different ways in which Frederick Douglass resisted slavery.

2. What were some of the problems free African Americans faced?

3. **FOCUS** Summarize the major differences that had formed between the North and the South by 1860.

4. **THINKING SKILL** *Compare and contrast* the views of slavery given by George Fitzhugh on page 445 and Frederick Douglass on page 447.

5. **WRITE** Write a response to one of the arguments Southerners used to defend slavery.

WORDS OF FREEDOM

The printed word played a key role in convincing people to join the fight against slavery. By 1860 about 17 African American newspapers were printed in the United States. These newspapers were read by both whites and blacks.

The most famous and influential was the *North Star*, started by Frederick Douglass in 1847. There were others, such as *Freeman's Advocate*, *Freedom's Journal*, and *The Mirror of Liberty*. They included news of speeches, reports of meetings, notices of upcoming activities, and articles related to ending slavery. The legacy of these newspapers can be seen in today's many African American publications.

The *North Star* was read by people all over the country. Douglass named the paper after the star that many escaping slaves used to guide themselves to the North.

St. John Fisher College

John Russwurm (left) and Samuel E. Cornish founded *Freedom's Journal*, the first African American-owned newspaper in the United States, in 1827. One of its goals was to "arrest the progress of prejudice." The journalist Ida Wells (below left) was an owner of the Memphis paper *Free Speech* in the early 1900s. Today several publications are owned by African Americans (below).

Ida B. Wells
25
Black Heritage USA

National Postal Museum, Smithstonian Institution

NEW YORK Amsterdam News
Vol. 86 No. 39 Saturday, September 30, 1995
© 1995 The Amsterdam News
New York City Outside N.Y.C.

CELEBRATING OUR 25TH ANNIVERSARY YEAR
ESSENCE
OCTOBER 1995
$2.25

50 YEARS AS THE NO.1 BLACK MAGAZINE
EBONY
OCTOBER 1995 USA $2.25/CANADA $2.6

HARLEM LANDMARK

MILLIO
Jackson, S

BLACK ENTERPRISE
MONEY MANAGEMENT SPECIAL
OCTOBER 1995
25TH ANNIVERSARY
GET MORE FOR YOUR

Can Myrlie ers-Williams Save The NAACP?

Annual undup: Gone? New? Back?

BARBARA McKNIGHT'S MONEY MANAGEMENT STRATEGIES HELP HER MAKE THE MOST OF HER RETIREMENT

STAR.
GOD IS THE FATHER OF US ALL, AND ALL MEN ARE BRETHREN.
JOHN DICK, Printer.
AY, FEBRUARY 22, 1850.
WHOLE NO. 113

WOMAN'S RIGHTS CONVENTION

Focus Activity

Who led the struggles for abolition and women's rights?

- abolitionist
- Underground Railroad
- Seneca Falls Convention

- William Lloyd Garrison
- Angelina Grimké
- Sarah Grimké
- Levi Coffin
- Catherine Coffin
- Harriet Tubman
- Lucretia Mott
- Elizabeth Cady Stanton
- Sojourner Truth

- Seneca Falls

1800　1820　**1831**　**1860**　1880

The Fight for Equality

Read Aloud

"Women ought to feel a special sympathy for the colored man, for, like him, she has been accused of mental inferiority and denied a good education." These words were spoken by Angelina Grimké, who was among the first to see the connection between seeking women's rights and ending slavery.

THE BIG PICTURE

Opposition to slavery began long before the United States became an independent country. Before the American Revolution, many Quakers worked to end slavery. The Quakers were among the first **abolitionists**. An abolitionist was someone who wanted to abolish, or end, slavery in the United States. You have read about one abolitionist, Frederick Douglass. Abolitionists were both black and white, Northern and Southern, and male and female. As the practice of slavery increased during the 1800s, more people began to speak out against it.

As women fought for equal rights for African Americans, they also began to think more about their own rights. Like African Americans, women in the early 1800s had very few legal rights. A married woman could not own property. If she worked, she had to give her wages to her husband. Women could not vote. Most colleges and professions were closed to women. As the abolition movement strengthened, so did the fight for women's rights that grew out of it.

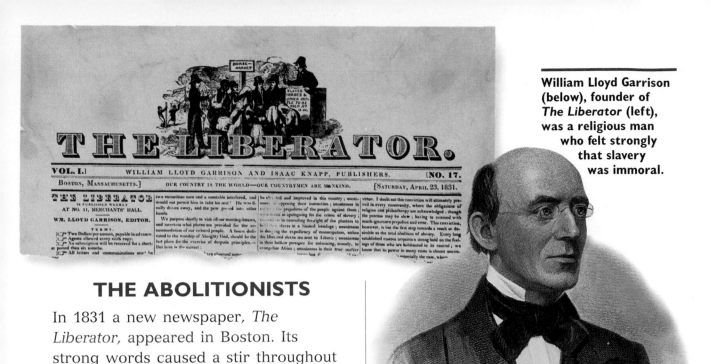

The Granger Collection

William Lloyd Garrison (below), founder of *The Liberator* (left), was a religious man who felt strongly that slavery was immoral.

THE ABOLITIONISTS

In 1831 a new newspaper, *The Liberator,* appeared in Boston. Its strong words caused a stir throughout the United States.

William Lloyd Garrison

An abolitionist named William Lloyd Garrison began *The Liberator.* Garrison believed that no compromises should be made when it came to slavery. Slavery was wrong and should be ended immediately. Black people, he said, should have the same rights as white people. In the first issue of his paper he warned:

> *On this subject I do not wish to think, or speak, or write with moderation. . . . Tell a man whose house is on fire to give a moderate alarm; . . . but urge me not to use moderation in a cause like the present. . . . I will not retreat a single inch—and I will be heard.*

Garrison's message was indeed heard. In some places copies of *The Liberator* were burned and mail carriers refused to deliver it. In Georgia a $5,000 reward was offered for Garrison's arrest. He was often attacked by angry crowds. One newspaper referred to Garrison as "the most mobbed man in the United States." Some Northerners also opposed Garrison. Although these Northerners did not own slaves, they did not support equal rights for blacks and whites.

Southerners Who Opposed Slavery

A number of Southern whites supported Garrison's message. After Nat Turner's rebellion in 1831 it became especially dangerous for Southerners to speak out against slavery. Those who did were often attacked and forced to leave their homes.

Angelina Grimké and Sarah Grimké were daughters of a wealthy South Carolina judge and plantation owner. They had seen the evils of slavery firsthand. "From early childhood," Sarah wrote, "[I] long believed their bondage [slavery] inconsistent with justice and humanity." Eventually, the two sisters decided to move to the North where they could work openly for the end of slavery. There they made history as the first women to speak publicly for the abolitionist cause.

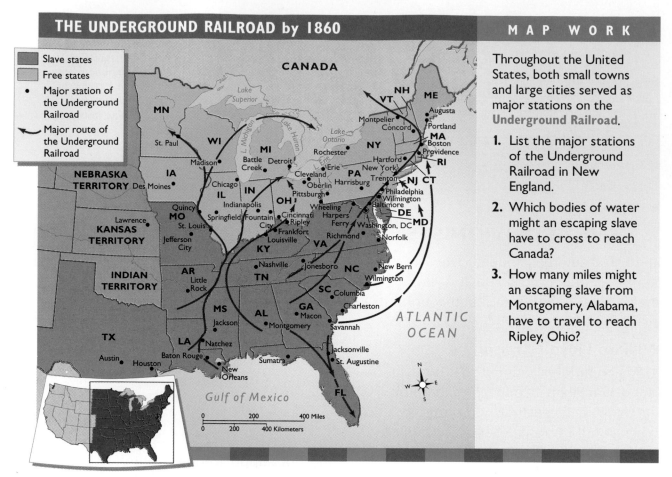

MAP WORK

Throughout the United States, both small towns and large cities served as major stations on the Underground Railroad.

1. List the major stations of the Underground Railroad in New England.

2. Which bodies of water might an escaping slave have to cross to reach Canada?

3. How many miles might an escaping slave from Montgomery, Alabama, have to travel to reach Ripley, Ohio?

THE UNDERGROUND RAILROAD

Meanwhile, enslaved African Americans continued to suffer. For some, like Frederick Douglass, life under slavery was so terrible they risked their lives to escape from it. Slaves often had to travel hundreds of miles before reaching freedom in the North. Slaveowners considered their slaves valuable property. As a result slave catchers were immediately sent out to capture slaves who escaped.

A Different Kind of Railroad

Many slaves who did escape got help on the Underground Railroad. This was not a real railroad, but a system of secret routes that escaping captives followed to freedom. On this "railroad," the slaves were called "passengers." Those who guided and transported them were "conductors." The places where slaves hid along the way were called "stations." People who fed and sheltered them were "stationmasters."

Enslaved people often used songs to signal their plan to escape. One song, "Follow the Drinking Gourd," gave directions for escaping north in code:

> *The river ends between two hills,*
> *Follow the drinking gourd.*
> *There's another river on the other side,*
> *Follow the drinking gourd.*
> *When the great big river meets the*
>   *little river,*
> *Follow the drinking gourd.*
> *For the old man is a-waiting for to*
>   *carry you to freedom*
> *If you follow the drinking gourd.*

Each of the rivers in the song was an actual river. For example, the "great big river" was the Ohio River. The "drinking gourd" was the Little Dipper. One

The Granger Collection

Tubman fled from the plantation in the middle of the night and headed for the house of a white woman known to help escaping slaves. The woman gave her two slips of paper with the names of families on the route north who would help her. These were Tubman's first "railroad tickets."

Tubman traveled at night, mostly through swamps and woodlands. After traveling 90 miles, she reached the free soil of Pennsylvania. She later said:

> I looked at my hands, to see if I was the same person now that I was free. There was such a glory over everything; the sun came like gold through the trees, and over the fields, and I felt like I was in heaven.

of the stars in the Little Dipper is the North Star, which escaping slaves used to guide them north.

Levi Coffin, a Quaker from Indiana, was one of many people who helped slaves to escape. His wife Catherine Coffin fed, clothed, and hid the slaves in their house. What they did took great courage. If caught, they could have been hanged. Because their work was so secret, we will never know how many people actually worked or escaped on the Underground Railroad.

Harriet Tubman

In 1849 Harriet Tubman heard that she and other slaves on her Maryland plantation were to be sold further south. Tubman knew that life was even harder for slaves on the large cotton plantations there. She told her husband, John, "There's two things I've a right to: death or liberty. One or the other I mean to have. No one will take me back alive."

Tubman returned many times to guide her family and many others to freedom. She was given the nickname "Moses," after the Hebrew prophet who led his people out of slavery in Egypt. Thousands of dollars were offered for Tubman's capture. More than 300 slaves owed their freedom to her.

Harriet Tubman (right) and Levi and Catherine Coffin (above) helped slaves escape to freedom in the North.

The Granger Collection

WOMEN SPEAK OUT

When the Grimké sisters first made speeches about abolition, they were criticized for speaking in public because they were women. In 1837 Angelina Grimké wrote: "The discussion of the rights of the slave has opened the way for the discussion of other rights." She meant the rights of women. In 1840 William Lloyd Garrison named a woman for a leadership position in the American Antislavery Society. Many delegates resigned in protest against having a female leader.

That same year, the World Antislavery Convention, which was meeting in London, refused to seat the women delegates. When the women protested, they were invited to sit silently behind a curtain while the men discussed slavery. Angered, the women decided to meet to discuss women's rights.

The Seneca Falls Convention

Two of the women who attended the London convention were the abolitionists Lucretia Mott and Elizabeth Cady Stanton. Lucretia Mott had been a founder of the American Antislavery Society. In 1848 Stanton, Mott, and three other women met in Seneca Falls, New York, where Stanton lived. They decided to hold a convention to discuss "the social, civil, and religious condition and rights of women."

Before the convention, they wrote a statement that they modeled after the Declaration of Independence. Called "A Declaration of Rights and Sentiments," their document listed 18 rights they believed women should have. It began with the statement that "all men and women are created equal."

More than 240 people attended the Seneca Falls Convention, which began on July 19, 1848. After two days of discussion, the convention approved the "Declaration of Rights and Sentiments." Read the excerpt from the Declaration below. In what ways is it like the Declaration of Independence?

MANY VOICES
PRIMARY SOURCE

Excerpt from
the Declaration of Rights and Sentiments, Seneca Falls, New York, 1848.

*The history of mankind is a history of repeated injuries and **usurpations** (yoo sur PAY shunz) on the part of man toward woman, having in direct object the establishment of an absolute **tyranny** over her. To prove this, let facts be submitted to a **candid** world.*

He has never permitted her to exercise her inalienable right to [vote]. . . .

*He has made her, if married, in the eye of the law, **civilly dead**.*

He has taken from her all right in property, even to the wages she earns. . . .

He has denied her the facilities for obtaining a thorough education, all colleges being closed against her.

----
usurpations: taking over by force
tyranny: power
candid: honest
civilly dead: without rights

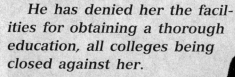

Sojourner Truth

The women's movement continued to grow. In 1851 a women's rights convention was held in Akron, Ohio. Men spoke there about how a woman's place was in the home and how women were weaker than men. Suddenly, a woman mounted the steps to the platform. She rolled up her sleeve and raised her strong and muscular arm in the air. "Look at me!" she said. "I have plowed, and planted, and gathered [crops] into barns, and no man could head [outdo] me! And ain't I a woman?"

The speaker's name was Sojourner Truth. Born into slavery about 1797, she was freed when she was 30 years old. At the age of 46, she began speaking out about the evils of slavery. Throughout the 1840s and the 1850s, Sojourner Truth gave speeches around the country in support of both abolition and women's rights.

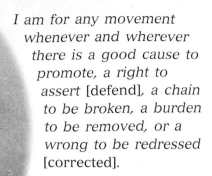

I am for any movement whenever and wherever there is a good cause to promote, a right to assert [defend], a chain to be broken, a burden to be removed, or a wrong to be redressed [corrected].

Like Douglass many people found that the abolition movement and the women's rights movement strengthened each other. Both would result in gains before long.

WHY IT MATTERS

At the Seneca Falls Convention, Frederick Douglass spoke in support of the women's cause. To him, the connection between abolition and women's rights was clear. He later wrote:

Abolitionists Elizabeth Cady Stanton (left) and Sojourner Truth (above) were among the earliest founders of the women's rights movement.

Reviewing Facts and Ideas

MAIN IDEAS

- In 1831 William Lloyd Garrison began publishing *The Liberator,* an abolitionist newspaper.

- Many enslaved African Americans escaped through the Underground Railroad. Harriet Tubman guided hundreds to freedom.

- The women's rights movement began with the Seneca Falls Convention, held in New York in 1848.

THINK ABOUT IT

1. Who supported Garrison's newspaper? Who opposed it? Why?

2. What rights did women lack in the early and middle 1800s?

3. **FOCUS** Who were the leaders of the abolition and women's rights movements? How were these two movements connected?

4. **THINKING SKILL** *Predict* what effects conflicts over slavery would have on the movement for women's rights.

5. **GEOGRAPHY** Look at the map on page 454. Why do you think some slaves escaping from Texas headed south?

Reading a Newspaper

VOCABULARY

news article
headline
dateline
feature article
editorial
editor

WHY THE SKILL MATTERS

In the nineteenth century newspapers were people's main source of information. There was no television or radio. There were no computers. People had to rely on newspapers to find out what was happening in their town, city, or country, as well as in the world. Frederick Douglass and William Lloyd Garrison each started a newspaper, which was the best way, they thought, to inform and inspire their fellow Americans.

Today, people can get news from television or radio. Still, many read newspapers to find out what is going on in the country and in the world. For example, if you follow sports, you read the sports section to find out the previous day's sporting events. If you want to see a film, you look at the entertainment page in your local paper to find out what is playing.

USING THE SKILL

In order to understand a newspaper and to make the best use of it, you need to know about its different parts, or sections. The first part usually contains **news articles**. A news article describes an important event that has recently taken place. News articles can be about local, state, national, or international events.

The County Standard

Thursday, July 20, 1848

Seneca Falls, New York

WOMEN'S CONVENTION HELD

Yesterday, in the Wesleyan Chapel in Seneca Falls, a convention was held. A group of five local women organized the meeting to discuss the rights of women. The convention opened at 11:00 A.M. to an audience of over 100 gentlemen and ladies. The first session, called to order by Mr. James Mott, opened with an address by Mrs. Elizabeth Cady Stanton. Mrs. Stanton declared the goal of the meeting was "to discuss our rights and wrongs, civil and political." She then read a document titled "The Declaration of Rights and Sentiments." A spirited debate followed in which both the ladies and gentlemen present participated.

TURNER TERRIFIES SLAVE OWNERS

A news article always begins with a **headline**, or a sentence or phrase printed in large type across the top of a news article. Headlines, like the one about Turner's Rebellion on page 458, are meant to catch the reader's attention. Usually a news article also has a **dateline**. A dateline tells when and where the story was written. The dateline on the news article in the Legacy on pages 450–451 is Rochester, N.Y., Friday, February 22, 1850.

The first paragraph of a news article is designed to catch the reader's interest and to tell the most important facts in the story. Usually the first paragraph answers the questions *Who? What? When?* and *Where? Who* is the story about? *What* is it about? *When* did the events take place? *Where* did they take place? The rest of the article gives more facts. It generally does not give opinions.

Many newspapers also offer **feature articles**. A feature article is a detailed report on a person, an issue, or an event. For example, the newspaper containing the article shown here might have also included a feature article about other women who have fought for equal rights.

In most newspapers you might also find an **editorial** page. An editorial is an article in which the **editors**, or people who run the newspaper, give their opinions on important issues. The editorial page might also contain letters to the editors which are written by the newspaper's readers to tell how they feel about certain issues. For example, a week after the Seneca Falls Convention, the *County Standard* might have published letters by supporters and opponents of the Convention.

Helping yourself

- **A news article tells about important events. A feature article gives details about a person, issue, or event. The editorial page has opinions written by the editors.**

- **Decide which part of the newspaper you want or need to read.**

TRYING THE SKILL

Newspapers like Douglass's *North Star* or William Lloyd Garrison's *The Liberator* played an important role in the anti-slavery cause. What might the headline for a news article in one of their newspapers say about a slave auction? Do you think the headline would have described the event in a positive, negative, or neutral way? What information would such a news article give in the first paragraph? In the other paragraphs? What kinds of feature articles might be included?

Both Douglass's and Garrison's newspapers contained an editorial page. What opinions do you think they might have written for this section of their newspaper? Suppose you wanted to read an article about Sojourner Truth in either of their newspapers. What type of article would it be?

REVIEWING THE SKILL

1. What is a headline of a news article? A dateline? An editorial?

2. What is the purpose of the first paragraph of a news article?

3. Why might the writer of a newspaper article find it necessary to answer the questions *Who? What? When? Where?* in the first paragraph?

4. What would be some topics for at least three feature articles in an edition of *The County Standard*?

5. How can knowing how to read a newspaper help someone to be a better citizen?

The Granger Collection

The Nation Heads for War

Read Aloud

"A house divided against itself cannot stand. I believe this government cannot endure half slave and half free." This warning was given to the American people by Abraham Lincoln, a candidate for the United States Senate in 1858. Although he lost the election, his prediction proved true. By 1860 the issue of slavery would tear the country apart.

Focus Activity

READ TO LEARN

What caused the country to pull apart in 1860?

VOCABULARY

- Missouri Compromise
- Fugitive Slave Law of 1850
- Compromise of 1850
- Kansas-Nebraska Act
- Dred Scott Decision
- states' rights
- secede
- Confederate States of America

PEOPLE

- John C. Calhoun
- Henry Clay
- Harriet Beecher Stowe
- Abraham Lincoln
- John Brown
- Jefferson Davis

PLACES

- Harpers Ferry

THE BIG PICTURE

By the early 1800s many Americans had begun to refer to the United States as the Union. A union is a group of political bodies, such as states, that have joined together for a common purpose. In 1819 the United States was evenly divided between free states and slave states. Free states did not permit slavery within their borders. Slave states did. That year Missouri asked to join the Union as a slave state.

To maintain a balance between free states and slave states, Congress passed the Missouri Compromise in 1820. This compromise created an imaginary line from east to west through the Louisiana Territory, as you can see on the map on page 461. Slavery would be allowed in all states south of the line. It would be forbidden in all states north of the line except for Missouri. Missouri was admitted to the Union as a slave state, and Maine was admitted as a free state.

In 1850 California asked to join the United States as a free state. California would tip Congress in favor of the free states. Leaders sought another compromise, but compromising over slavery was becoming more difficult.

CONGRESS COMPROMISES

Many members of Congress thought they would never find a solution to the California question. Senator John C. Calhoun of South Carolina had all but given up. "There is little or no prospect of any change for the better," he wrote.

The Compromise of 1850

As you read in Chapter 15, the United States had gained Texas, New Mexico, and California from Mexico in 1848. Both northerners and southerners were worried about the role of slavery in these territories. Northerners and Southerners were also divided on a bill in Congress called the Fugitive Slave Law of 1850. This law would require police in the free states to help capture slaves escaping from slave states.

Senator Henry Clay of Kentucky had worked out the Missouri Compromise many years earlier. Although Clay was a slave owner, he believed strongly in the importance of the Union. "I know no South, no North, no East, no West to which I owe allegiance," he declared. Clay vowed to work out another compromise. His solution became known as the Compromise of 1850. In this compromise, California would be admitted as a free state, which would benefit the North. In return, the North would agree to obey the Fugitive Slave Law. The other territories that had been gained from Mexico in 1848 would decide for themselves whether or not to allow slavery. After six months of debate, Clay's compromise was accepted by Congress. The Union had been saved once again.

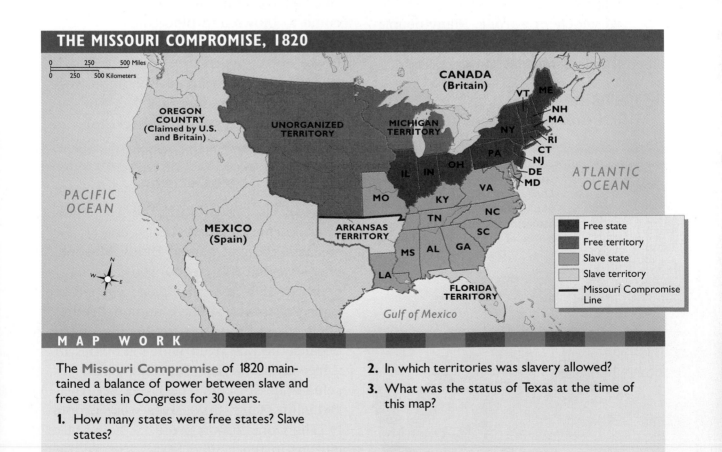

THE MISSOURI COMPROMISE, 1820

OREGON COUNTRY (Claimed by U.S. and Britain)

UNORGANIZED TERRITORY

CANADA (Britain)

MICHIGAN TERRITORY

PACIFIC OCEAN

MEXICO (Spain)

ARKANSAS TERRITORY

FLORIDA TERRITORY

Gulf of Mexico

ATLANTIC OCEAN

VT ME NH MA NY RI CT NJ PA DE MD OH IN IL MO KY VA TN NC SC MS AL GA LA

Legend:
- Free state
- Free territory
- Slave state
- Slave territory
- Missouri Compromise Line

MAP WORK

The Missouri Compromise of 1820 maintained a balance of power between slave and free states in Congress for 30 years.

1. How many states were free states? Slave states?

2. In which territories was slavery allowed?

3. What was the status of Texas at the time of this map?

A HOUSE DIVIDED

Although the Compromise of 1850 was approved, many problems remained. Abolitionists stated that the Fugitive Slave Law clashed with the Bill of Rights. Under the Fugitive Slave Law, a free African American could be captured and sold into slavery.

Uncle Tom's Cabin

In 1852 Harriet Beecher Stowe, the daughter of a Massachusetts minister, wrote a novel called *Uncle Tom's Cabin* to protest the Fugitive Slave Law. Stowe, who was an abolitionist, wrote about how a slave named Eliza Harris escaped to prevent her young son from being sold away from her. Another slave, Uncle Tom, died under the whip of the cruel overseer Simon Legree.

Uncle Tom's Cabin sold more than 300,000 copies within the first year. It was translated into several languages and was read widely in Europe. Many people were deeply moved by Stowe's novel and joined the fight against slavery.

"Bleeding Kansas"

In 1854 Congress passed the Kansas-Nebraska Act. This law allowed the Kansas and Nebraska territories to decide for themselves whether to allow slavery. Both territories were north of the Missouri Compromise Line.

Slave owners were pleased because the new law opened Kansas and Nebraska to slavery. Many Northern farmers and workers who wanted to move west opposed the law. They worried that rich Southern planters would grab the best land in these territories and use slave labor to farm it. They demanded that the western lands be "free soil."

Many "free soilers" joined with abolitionists to form the Republican Party. The Republicans believed that no person should own another and that all new states should be free states. One of the members of the new party was Abraham Lincoln, a lawyer from Illinois. Lincoln opposed the Kansas-Nebraska Act and warned that "the contest will come to blows and bloodshed."

As Lincoln predicted, violence soon broke out between free soilers and slave owners in Kansas. Buildings were burned and people were killed. The newspapers referred to the territory as "Bleeding Kansas."

The Dred Scott Decision

In 1856, after living in the free state of California for three years, an enslaved woman named Biddy Mason was awarded her freedom in a local court. In 1857 a similar case reached the Supreme Court. A slave named Dred Scott asked the Court for his freedom because he had lived with his owner in a free territory. The Supreme Court ruled against Scott. The Dred Scott Decision stated that slaves were property. The Constitution protects the right of citizens in the United States to take their

Uncle Tom's Cabin, by the abolitionist Harriet Beecher Stowe, made many Americans aware of the horrors of slavery.

Temple University

property anywhere. The Supreme Court also said that the Missouri Compromise was unconstitutional. Congress did not have the right to make certain territories "free," since that would keep slave owners from moving their property.

Several Northern state legislatures passed resolutions stating that the Dred Scott Decision "was not binding in law and conscience." Some leaders said that the Dred Scott Decision did not have to be obeyed.

In 1857 the Supreme Court ruled that slaves, such as Dred Scott (left), were property. As such, they had no rights of their own.

The Granger Collection

John Brown's Raid

At dawn on October 16, 1859, a group of men took control of a building in Harpers Ferry, Virginia, where weapons were being stored by the federal government.

The leader of the group was an abolitionist named John Brown. The raiders hoped to start a rebellion by passing out the captured weapons to slaves. Brown and his men, however, were quickly arrested. Brown was found guilty of treason and hanged.

Northerners were divided about the raid. Abolitionist Theodore Parker called Brown "a saint." Yet *The Liberator*, however, called Brown's plan "insane." Many Southerners feared that Northerners would stop at nothing to abolish slavery.

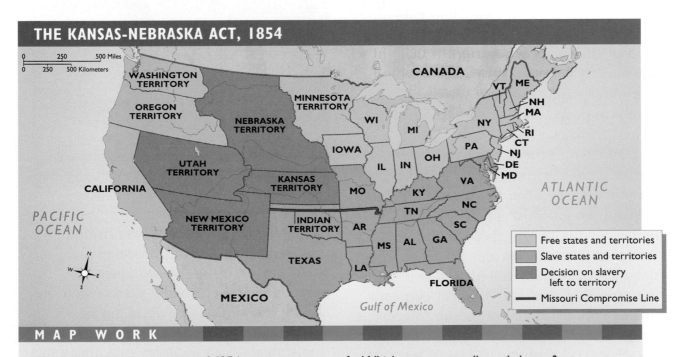

THE KANSAS-NEBRASKA ACT, 1854

Free states and territories
Slave states and territories
Decision on slavery left to territory
— Missouri Compromise Line

MAP WORK

The Kansas-Nebraska Act of 1854 overturned terms of the Missouri Compromise by opening territories north of the Missouri Compromise Line to slavery. Compare the map above to the map on page 461.

1. Which new states allowed slavery?
2. Which territories did not allow slavery?
3. What slave territory is now the state of Oklahoma?

Slavery and states' rights were major issues in the Lincoln-Douglas debates (left). In these debates, Abraham Lincoln (below) took a strong stand against slavery.

The Granger Collection

ABRAHAM LINCOLN

As a young man, Abraham Lincoln had taught himself law and become a lawyer in Illinois. He then served four terms in the state legislature and one term as a representative in Congress.

In 1858 Lincoln ran for senator against Senator Stephen A. Douglas of Illinois. Douglas was known as the "Little Giant" because, although he was very short, he was a powerful speaker. During the campaign, Lincoln challenged Douglas to a series of debates. One of the topics to be debated was slavery. "If slavery is not wrong," Lincoln once said, "nothing is wrong." He firmly opposed slavery spreading to any new territories.

Douglas, on the other hand, supported states' rights. He believed each state should be allowed to make its own decision about most issues. Slavery, he believed, was one of these issues. Although Lincoln lost the election, the debates made him well-known across the country. "Perhaps no local contest in this country ever excited an interest as that now waging in Illinois," wrote the *New York Tribune*.

The Election of 1860

In 1860 Lincoln faced Douglas again. This time they were both running for United States President. Of the four candidates, only Lincoln was firmly opposed to the spread of slavery.

To preserve the Union, Lincoln pledged to leave slavery alone where it already existed. However, if no new slave states were admitted to the Union, free states would soon be a majority in Congress. The South would lose its political power. Some Southern states talked about seceding if Lincoln were elected. To secede meant that the states would leave the Union.

South Carolina Secedes

When Lincoln won the election, people waited anxiously to see whether any states would carry out their threat of seceding from the Union. Lincoln called talk of leaving the Union "humbug." In December 1860, however, the state of South Carolina voted to secede.

By March 1861, Mississippi, Florida, Alabama, Georgia, Louisiana, Texas, and South Carolina had formed a new country, the Confederate States of America. They drafted a constitution and named a president. They chose Jefferson Davis, a United States Senator from Mississippi and a planter who had fought in the Mexican War. The Union was now split.

WHY IT MATTERS

By the late 1850s divisions between North and South became so deep that they could no longer be settled by compromise. For many Southerners, the only course of action left seemed to be to secede. To newly elected President Lincoln, the answer was clear. To secede was illegal and would not be allowed. The conflict between the North and the South was about to become a war.

Jefferson Davis, a former Secretary of War, supported states' rights and believed that slavery was necessary to the South's economy.

DID YOU KNOW?

Why was Lincoln called "Honest Abe"?

As an adult, Lincoln opened a store. When the store failed, he owed a lot of money. It took several years, but he repaid every penny. For this reason, he became known as "Honest Abe."

ILLINOIS

✓ Reviewing Facts and Ideas

MAIN IDEAS

- The Missouri Compromise divided the country into free and slave states. In the Compromise of 1850, California became a free state, and Congress passed the Fugitive Slave Law.

- The *Dred Scott* Decision, *Uncle Tom's Cabin*, the 1854 Kansas-Nebraska Act and John Brown's raid in 1859 deepened conflicts between North and South.

- After Abraham Lincoln was elected President in 1860, seven Southern states seceded to form the Confederate States of America.

THINK ABOUT IT

1. What was the Fugitive Slave Law?

2. What two government actions undid the Missouri Compromise?

3. **FOCUS** What events of the 1850s caused the country to pull apart?

4. **THINKING SKILL** *Compare* the various opinions about John Brown's raid.

5. **GEOGRAPHY** Using the maps on pages 461 and 463, describe how the United States changed between 1820 and 1854.

CITIZENSHIP
VIEWPOINTS

Museum of the Confederacy

The first flag of the Confederacy (right) had a star for each state that had seceded. The flag on the left is a Union flag from 1860.

1860: Do states have the right to secede?

In the debate over whether states had the right to secede, both the North and the South referred to the Constitution. Those in favor of secession argued that the federal government is a union of states. As a part of that union, the states had trusted that their rights would be respected. Interfering with slavery went against the rights of the Southern states and was, therefore, unconstitutional. As you can read in Jefferson Davis's argument, they also believed that the Declaration of Independence gave people the right to change their government when they believed it no longer served them.

Those against secession, such as James Buchanan, argued that the Constitution did not give states the right to secede. Abraham Lincoln had been elected by a democratic process. Anger over his election was not enough of a reason to release any state from the Union. Secession was, they said, unconstitutional. It was an act of rebellion that should be stopped by force.

Abolitionists did not believe that states' rights and secession were the main issues. They believed that the conflict was really a fight over whether slavery should be allowed to continue. Consider the three viewpoints on this issue and answer the questions that follow.

Three DIFFERENT Viewpoints

1 JAMES BUCHANAN
President of the United States, 1857-1861
Excerpt from Message to Congress, January 8, 1861

No state has a right by its own act to secede from the Union, or throw off its Federal obligations at pleasure. . . . Even if that right existed and should be exercised by any state of the confederacy, the executive department of this government [has] no authority under the Constitution to recognize its validity by acknowledging the independence of such State.

"no state has a right . . . to secede"

2 JEFFERSON DAVIS
Senator from Mississippi
Excerpt from Speech to the United States Senate, December 10, 1860

The sacrifices made by Americans during the American Revolution [were to] establish community independence, and the great American idea that all governments rest on the consent of the governed, and that the people may, at their will, alter or abolish their government, however, and by whomsoever instituted.

"the people may . . . abolish their government"

3 FREDERICK DOUGLASS
Abolitionist and Publisher
Excerpt from Speech published in Douglass' Monthly, August 1861

The war is called a section [regional] war; but there is nothing in the sections [regions], in the difference of climate or soil, to produce conflicts between the two sections. . . . The two sections are inhabited by the same people. . . . There is nothing existing between them to prevent . . . peace but the existence of slavery. Everybody knows this, everybody feels this, and yet the great mass of the people refuse to confess it, and the government refuses to recognize it.

"nothing . . . to prevent peace . . . but . . . slavery"

BUILDING CITIZENSHIP

1. What was the viewpoint of each person? How did each person support his view?

2. In what ways were some of the viewpoints alike? In what ways were they different?

3. What other viewpoints might people have had on this issue? What are some ways in which the issue of states' rights might be discussed today?

SHARING VIEWPOINTS

Discuss reasons Southerners believed they should secede and Northerners believed secession was unconstitutional. As a class discuss which viewpoints you agree or disagree with. What are some statements, if any, that all three speakers could have agreed on?

CHAPTER 16 REVIEW

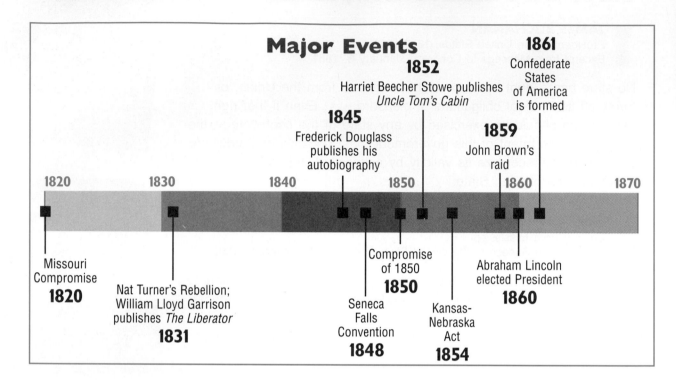

Major Events

1861
Confederate States of America is formed

1852
Harriet Beecher Stowe publishes *Uncle Tom's Cabin*

1845
Frederick Douglass publishes his autobiography

1859
John Brown's raid

1820   1830   1840   1850   1860   1870

Missouri Compromise
1820

Nat Turner's Rebellion; William Lloyd Garrison publishes *The Liberator*
1831

Compromise of 1850
1850

Seneca Falls Convention
1848

Abraham Lincoln elected President
1860

Kansas-Nebraska Act
1854

THINKING ABOUT VOCABULARY

Number a paper from 1 to 5. Beside each number, write the word from the list below that completes the numbered blank in the paragraph.

abolitionist   secede
dateline   Underground Railroad
editorial

The __(1)__ on the newspaper read *Boston, January 7, 1855*. Inside was an article about a local __(2)__ who was a conductor on the __(3)__ and who now was working to bring an end to slavery in the United States. The newspaper's editors, in an __(4)__, expressed an opinion in support of this effort. The article said that it would be better for the United States to fall apart than for slavery to continue. The antislavery cause was just, the newspaper said, even if the Southern states decided to __(5)__, or leave the Union.

THINKING ABOUT FACTS

1. Describe the differences between the North and the South in the 1850s.

2. What did the Missouri Compromise do? For how long was it successful?

3. How did Frederick Douglass and Harriet Tubman fight against slavery?

4. What were some of the reasons for the large increase in immigration to the United States in the middle 1800s? Where did most of the immigrants settle?

5. What happened in Seneca Falls, New York, and why was it important?

6. List the details of the Compromise of 1850. Why was it important?

7. What were the effects of the book *Uncle Tom's Cabin* on its readers?

8. What was Abraham Lincoln's position on slavery during the election of 1860?

9. Who won the election of 1860 and what was the immediate result?

10. How are the events listed on the time line for 1850 and 1852 related?

THINK AND WRITE

WRITING A LETTER
Suppose that you are an observer at the Seneca Falls Convention of 1848. Write a letter home describing the people you meet there and the events taking place.

WRITING A CHARACTER SKETCH
Choose one of the people you read about in this chapter. Make a list of facts about the person and of words that describe him or her. Use your notes to write a short character sketch, or several paragraphs that describe this person.

WRITING AN EDITORIAL
Suppose that you are the editor of a newspaper in 1860 in either the North or the South. Write an editorial in which you react to Abraham Lincoln's election as President.

APPLYING STUDY SKILLS

READING A NEWSPAPER
Answer the following questions to practice the skill of reading a newspaper.

1. What are three different kinds of articles that can be found in a newspaper?
2. What appears on the editorial page of a newspaper?
3. Reread the article from the *County Standard* on page 458. What is the dateline for that article?
4. Using the same article, answer the questions *Who? What? When?* and *Where?*
5. Why is knowing how to read a newspaper an important skill?

Summing Up the Chapter

Copy the cause-and-effect chains on a separate piece of paper. Review the chapter to complete the blank sections. When you have completed the chart, use the information in the chart to help you answer the question "What event appeared to change the balance between slave states and free states? What was the result of this event?"

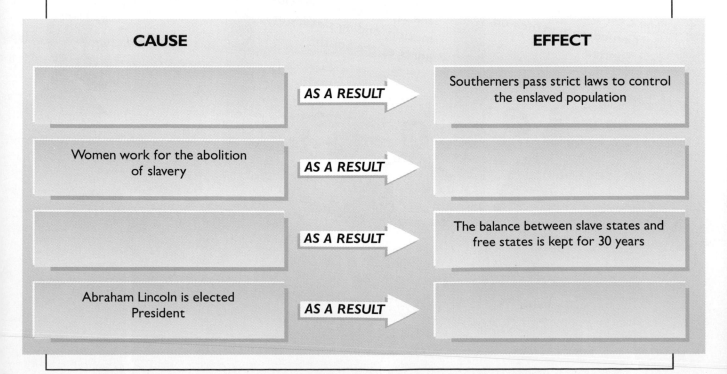

CAUSE		EFFECT
	AS A RESULT	Southerners pass strict laws to control the enslaved population
Women work for the abolition of slavery	AS A RESULT	
	AS A RESULT	The balance between slave states and free states is kept for 30 years
Abraham Lincoln is elected President	AS A RESULT	

The Civil War and Reconstruction

THINKING ABOUT HISTORY AND GEOGRAPHY

The story of Chapter 17 begins when the armies of the Southern states attacked Northern troops at a fort in South Carolina. Study the time line and the map to see other events that occurred during the Civil War—a time when Americans fought Americans within the borders of the United States. After the war, Northerners and Southerners began the work of reuniting the country.

PACIFIC OCEAN

1861

CHARLESTON, SOUTH CAROLINA
The Civil War begins with the Confederate attack on Fort Sumter

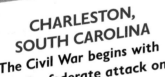

1862

WASHINGTON, D.C.
Lincoln's Cabinet approves the Emancipation Proclamation, ending slavery in parts of the South

1863

GETTYSBURG, PENNSYLVANIA
President Lincoln honors fallen soldiers in the Gettysburg Address

1861   1862   1863

UNITED
STATES

Pennsylvania
Washington, D.C.

Virginia

South
Carolina

Mississippi

ATLANTIC
OCEAN

1865

APPOMATTOX, VIRGINIA
Confederate General Lee surrenders to Union General Grant

1875

MISSISSIPPI
During Reconstruction, Blanche Bruce and Hiram Revels are elected to the United States Senate

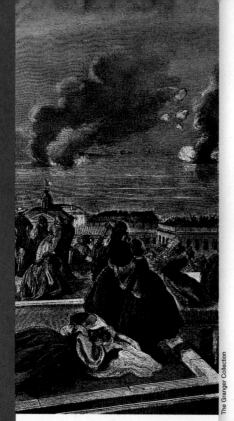

The Granger Collection

1861 1862   1865   1870   1875   1880

The War Between the States

Read Aloud

On April 12, 1861 the people of Charleston, South Carolina, came out to the waterfront to watch the attack on Fort Sumter. "I had a splendid view," wrote Emma Holmes. "I saw the shots as they struck the fort." One Charleston teenager wrote, "A perfect sheet of flame flashed out, a deafening roar, a rumbling, deadening sound, and the war was on."

Focus Activity

READ TO LEARN

How did the Civil War begin?

VOCABULARY

- Civil War
- Anaconda Plan
- blockade

PEOPLE

- Abraham Lincoln
- Winfield Scott
- Robert E. Lee
- Thomas "Stonewall" Jackson
- Rose Greenhow

PLACES

- Fort Sumter
- Richmond
- Bull Run

THE BIG PICTURE

In April 1861 the United States was split apart. Seven Southern states had seceded and were about to join together in battle against the Union.

Newly elected President **Abraham Lincoln** believed that it was unconstitutional for the Southern states to secede. He was determined to hold the country together. When he took office on March 4, 1861, Lincoln promised to "hold, occupy, and possess" all federal property in the Southern states. This property included **Fort Sumter** in Charleston, South Carolina. The people of South Carolina considered themselves citizens of the Confederate States of America. They wanted the United States flag at Fort Sumter taken down and a Confederate flag flown in its place. Within a month Confederate cannons were lined up around the fort. The **Civil War** was about to begin.

The American Civil War lasted over four years. Because the Northern states fought the Southern states in this war, it is also known as the War Between the States.

WAR BREAKS OUT

At 4:30 A.M. on April 12, 1861, Confederate guns opened fire on Fort Sumter as Northern ships neared the port. The crashing cannonballs marked the beginning of the Civil War.

After 34 hours of cannon blasts, the Union troops surrendered. United States Commander Robert Anderson took down the United States flag. He and his men were allowed to return to the North. No one had been killed in this first battle.

North and South Expect to Win

Most leaders, North and South, believed the Civil War would be over in a few short months. Northerners believed they would win because they had a larger population and more resources than the Confederacy. They could build and supply a larger army.

You can see from the graph on this page that most of the country's people and factories were in the North. The factories would be used to make weapons and uniforms for the Union Army. In addition, the North was better able to feed a large army. Although the South was a farming area, the North grew most of the country's food. Finally, the North had most of the country's railroads, which could be used for moving soldiers and supplies.

After the Union troops at Fort Sumter surrendered, four more slave states left the Union—Virginia, North Carolina, Arkansas, and Tennessee. With 11 states in the Confederacy, white Southerners also hoped for a quick victory. The South had many well-trained officers. Also, many Southerners had grown up riding horses and using guns to hunt. Southerners would fight fiercely because they believed they were fighting to protect their homes and their way of life.

Only about one-fourth of the Southerners owned slaves. Yet large numbers of Southerners who did not own slaves volunteered to fight. One such person was 21-year-old Sam Watkins, who was eager to join the war. Like many others he believed the conflict would be over quickly. Said Watkins, "We were all afraid it would be over and we [would] not [be] in the fight." By the war's end, about 1.5 million people fought for the North, and about 1 million people fought for the South.

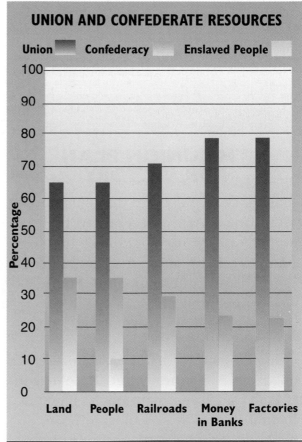

UNION AND CONFEDERATE RESOURCES

Union ▮ Confederacy ▯ Enslaved People ▯

(Bar graph, y-axis: Percentage 0–100; x-axis categories: Land, People, Railroads, Money in Banks, Factories)

GRAPH WORK

The Union and the Confederacy went into the Civil War with unequal resources.

1. Which resources of the North were the strongest compared to the South?

2. In which resource was the South the weakest?

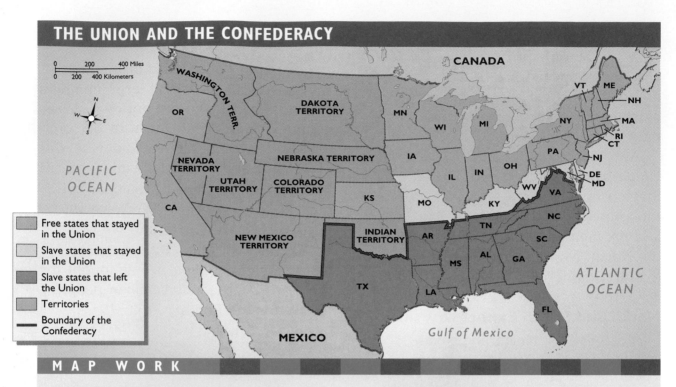

THE UNION AND THE CONFEDERACY

Map legend:
- Free states that stayed in the Union
- Slave states that stayed in the Union
- Slave states that left the Union
- Territories
- Boundary of the Confederacy

Map labels: CANADA, WASHINGTON TERR., OR, DAKOTA TERRITORY, MN, WI, MI, VT, ME, NH, NY, MA, RI, CT, PA, NJ, NEVADA TERRITORY, NEBRASKA TERRITORY, IA, OH, IN, IL, DE, MD, UTAH TERRITORY, COLORADO TERRITORY, KS, MO, KY, WV, VA, PACIFIC OCEAN, CA, NEW MEXICO TERRITORY, INDIAN TERRITORY, AR, TN, NC, SC, MS, AL, GA, TX, LA, FL, ATLANTIC OCEAN, MEXICO, Gulf of Mexico

MAP WORK

After the battle at Fort Sumter, four more states seceded. A total of 11 states were then members of the Confederacy.

1. How many states remained in the Union?

2. Which slave states did not secede?

3. What was the status of Kansas? Nebraska?

THE UNION PLAN FOR VICTORY

General Winfield Scott, the commander of the Union Army, recognized that the Confederate Army would be a tough enemy. To help defeat the South, Scott planned to cut the region off from getting more supplies.

The Anaconda Plan

Scott's plan for a Union victory was called the Anaconda Plan. The Anaconda Plan had three main goals. First, Northern ships would block off, or blockade, Southern seaports. Without trade the South would be unable to buy the weapons and supplies it needed. Second, the North would take control of the Mississippi River. This would cause the South to be split into two parts. Also, the South would not be able to use the river to move supplies. Finally,

The anaconda is a large South American snake that squeezes its prey to death.

Union troops would invade the South from both the east and the west.

Scott hoped that his plan would squeeze the Confederacy in the same way that an anaconda snake squeezes its prey. Looking at the map on this page you can see how the plan would affect the Confederate states.

Scott's plan was not popular at first. Many Northerners thought that if the Union Army could capture the Confederate capital of Richmond, Virginia, the war would be over quickly. Only later would people realize the importance of the Anaconda Plan.

474

THE CONFEDERACY AT WAR

Jefferson Davis, president of the Confederate States of America, had experienced generals and a good army. What he did not have were enough weapons, food, and ships. Davis knew that a Union blockade of major Southern ports could be very damaging to the Confederacy.

However, Davis believed that Great Britain needed Southern cotton so badly that it would send British ships to break the blockade. Davis was mistaken. As it turned out, Britain had a surplus of cotton that year. The British did not want to get involved in a United States war. Help from the mighty British navy never came.

These photos of Confederate generals Robert E. Lee (right) and Thomas "Stonewall" Jackson (below) were taken in about 1862.

Robert E. Lee Takes Command

Robert E. Lee of Virginia was a respected leader in the country's army. He had graduated from the United States Military Academy at West Point, and had served in the military for more than 30 years. When the Civil War began, Lincoln asked Colonel Lee to command the Union Army.

Lee faced a tough choice. He did not like slavery. However, Lee's loyalty to Virginia was more important to him. Lee said, "I cannot fight against my birthplace." He became the commander of the Confederate Army. General Scott told Lee, "You have made the greatest mistake of your life."

The First Battle of Bull Run

"On to Richmond," Northerners cried in the summer of 1861. Union troops were sent to Virginia. On the way, however, they met Confederate troops in battle at a muddy stream called Bull Run, near Washington, D.C.

At first, the Union Army appeared to be winning. As some Confederates began to flee, an officer noticed that Confederate General T.J. Jackson was standing firm with his troops. "There stands Jackson like a stone wall!" he cried. From then on, Jackson was known as Thomas "Stonewall" Jackson.

The Confederates regrouped around Jackson in what came to be known as the First Battle of Bull Run. Soon, frightened Northern troops began the "great skedaddle," which meant running away in panic. The Union troops retreated to Washington, D.C. The war's first major battle thus ended with a victory for the South.

SHIPS AND SOLDIERS

New technology made the Civil War more deadly than earlier wars. Rifles could now shoot farther. The Gatling machine gun could fire 250 bullets in a minute. Iron-covered battle ships, called ironclads, made wooden ships seem outdated overnight.

The *Monitor* and the *Merrimack*

With only 42 ships, the Union could not stop all cargo from entering and leaving the South's ports. Over time, the blockade was strengthened as Northern shipyards began building new ships. By 1864 almost 700 ships were in the Union Navy.

From the beginning Confederate leaders knew they could not compete with the Union Navy. They had few ships and lacked the resources to build new ones. So they decided to improve the ships they already had. The Confederates raised a sunken Union ship named the *Merrimack* and covered it with thick metal plates. It could stand more blasts of cannon fire. On March 8, 1862, the *Merrimack* sank two Northern ships and defeated three others near Hampton Roads, Virginia.

The next day a strange looking Union ship appeared in the harbor near Hampton Roads. "There was a craft such as the eyes of a seaman never looked upon before," said Confederate Lieutenant James H. Rochelle. "No sails, no wheels, no smokestack, no guns. What could it be?" It was the *Monitor*, an ironclad Union ship. For more than four hours the *Monitor* and the *Merrimack* battled in the harbor. In the end, neither one could damage the other. However, they had begun a new age of warfare—the age of ironclad ships.

Troops and Spies

War was not the adventure some had thought it would be. Soldiers often marched all day and slept on the ground. Because of the blockade, Southerners often went hungry and had no shoes. "Tell Ma I think of her beans and collards often and wish for some," wrote one Southern soldier.

On the battlefield, commanders often depended on spies to report on enemy battle positions. During the war Harriet Tubman served the Union as a spy as well as a scout and nurse. You have read how Tubman helped African

This young sailor (far left) carried ammunition to the gunners during sea battles like the one between the *Monitor* and the *Merrimack* (left).

Americans escape slavery on the Underground Railroad.

Rose Greenhow was a Confederate spy. Before she was caught, Greenhow directed a group of spies from her home in Washington, D.C. She got information from friends and sent it in code to the Confederate Army. Greenhow's daring work might have been the key to the Southern victory at Bull Run.

WHY IT MATTERS

After the First Battle of Bull Run many people realized that the war would last years. The Confederate victory at Bull Run showed that victory would depend on the efforts of leaders like Stonewall Jackson as much as on supplies.

New technology in the Civil War made long-range fighting common. Railroads and telegraphs changed how generals made battlefield decisions. At sea the battle of the ironclad ships also changed warfare. Other countries were beginning to realize the growing military power of the United States.

Links to CURRENT EVENTS

Hot Off the Press

The Civil War was said to be the first modern war. For the first time, troops traveled by railroad. Messages were sent by telegraph. Reporters followed the troops to cover battles for their newspapers. Photographers recorded the harsh reality of war.

Unlike today's photographers, Civil War photographers could not take action shots. Instead, subjects had to remain still for a long time. Since soldiers on the battlefield could not stay still, artists made drawings of battle scenes. These drawings were then printed in newspapers and magazines.

Compare photographs from a newspaper or magazine today to those in this chapter. How are they different?

Reviewing Facts and Ideas

MAIN IDEAS

- The Civil War began on April 12, 1861, when Confederates fired on Fort Sumter in Charleston, South Carolina.

- The North had more soldiers, resources, factories, and railroads. Southerners had more experience with horses and guns.

- The battle of the *Merrimack* and the *Monitor* in 1862 showed how new technology could change the way wars were fought.

THINK ABOUT IT

1. How did new technology change how wars were fought?

2. Describe the Anaconda Plan and how it was supposed to work.

3. **FOCUS** How did the Civil War begin?

4. **THINKING SKILL** Choose the *point of view* of either the North or the South. Tell why that side expected to win.

5. **GEOGRAPHY** Using the Atlas map on pages R8–R9, draw your own map showing General Scott's Anaconda Plan. Which Confederate cities were ports? How would these cities be affected by Scott's plan?

1860 1862 1863 1865 1870 1875 1880

The Union Moves Toward Victory

Read Aloud

"Day after day and night after night did we tramp along the rough and dusty roads, 'neath the most broiling sun with which the month of August ever afflicted a soldier," wrote one 16-year-old Confederate soldier. Both Union and Confederate troops were losing heart. When would this war end?

Focus Activity

READ TO LEARN

How did the Union turn the tide of the war in its favor?

VOCABULARY

- Emancipation Proclamation
- Gettysburg Address

PEOPLE

- Charlotte Forten
- Robert Gould Shaw
- Clara Barton
- Sally Tompkins
- Ulysses S. Grant
- George Meade
- George Pickett

PLACES

- Antietam
- Fort Wagner
- Shiloh
- Vicksburg
- Gettysburg

THE BIG PICTURE

In the autumn of 1862 Union troops were making little progress. Northern support for the war was starting to weaken. President Lincoln needed a victory. The victory he found was a costly one, at **Antietam** (an TEE tum), Maryland, on September 17, 1862. Over 23,000 men on both sides were killed or wounded. This was one of the bloodiest battles in United States history.

President Lincoln also found a way to inspire his troops. Five days later, Lincoln issued the **Emancipation Proclamation**. To emancipate means to free someone. The Proclamation said that as of January 1, 1863, "all persons held as slaves within any state . . . in rebellion against the United States, shall be then, thenceforth, and forever free." The Emancipation Proclamation ended slavery in the Confederacy. However, it did not apply to slave states that had stayed in the Union.

The Emancipation Proclamation changed the way people thought of the Civil War. What had been a struggle to preserve the Union was now also a battle to end slavery.

THE EMANCIPATION PROCLAMATION

Opinions about the Emancipation Proclamation varied. Southern slave owners were outraged over the Proclamation. They felt that Lincoln had no right to take away their slaves, which they considered to be property. Northern abolitionists, meanwhile, were overjoyed. Frederick Douglass wrote, "We shout for joy that we live to record this righteous decree."

Others in the North, however, were not overjoyed. Some pointed out that the Proclamation would take effect only in those Confederate areas under control of Union troops. Some Northerners felt Lincoln had gone too far. They were fighting to preserve the Union and did not want to risk their lives to end slavery. Lincoln responded to all, "In giving freedom to the slave, we assure freedom to the free."

This etching shows the first reading of the Emancipation Proclamation by President Lincoln to his cabinet in 1862.

"A Brilliant Dream"

On January 1, 1863, when the Emancipation Proclamation went into effect, African Americans greeted the news with great joy. Former slaves marked the event in different ways. Charlotte Forten, a free African American from Philadelphia, attended a celebration in Port Royal, South Carolina. Forten had traveled South to teach reading and writing to the newly freed people. She described the day of celebration as "a brilliant dream."

For many African Americans in the South, however, the dream came later. It took years for the Union Army to put the Emancipation Proclamation into effect throughout the Confederacy. For example, the news did not reach African Americans in Texas until June 19, 1865—more than two years after the Proclamation was issued. June 19, often called "Juneteenth," is still celebrated in African American communities in Texas and in other parts of the United States as the anniversary of the end of slavery.

AFRICAN AMERICAN TROOPS

The Emancipation Proclamation not only freed African Americans, it also allowed them to serve in the Union Army. To Northerners who opposed sending African Americans to the battlefield, Frederick Douglass responded, "I don't say that they will fight better than other men. All I say is, give them a chance!"

The 54th Massachusetts

One of the first African American troops to fight for the Union Army was the 54th Massachusetts Colored Regiment. A regiment is a group of at least 1,000 soldiers. This all-volunteer regiment included the two sons of Frederick Douglass. Led by a white colonel named Robert Gould Shaw, the 54th attacked Fort Wagner in Charleston, South Carolina, on July 18, 1863. Harriet Tubman, who was working as a nurse for Union soldiers, wrote:

> We heard the thunder, and that was the big guns; and then we heard the rain falling, and that was the drops of blood falling.

The 54th Massachusetts Colored Regiment fought bravely. Almost half of its members were killed, wounded, or captured in the Southern victory at Fort Wagner. Although they were not always treated as well as white soldiers, over 180,000 African Americans served with the Union forces.

Confederate Soldiers

Not all African Americans served on the Union side. On March 13, 1865, General Lee convinced the Confederate Congress to allow African Americans to fight for the South. These African Americans were promised freedom.

On March 19, in Richmond, Virginia, a new Confederate unit, which included African American hospital workers, marched up Main Street. None had uniforms, but they began training on Capitol Square. However, the war ended before they had a chance to fight.

As the war dragged on, all of the soldiers—black and white, Northern and Southern—tried hard to keep their spirits up. Music often helped them. Sometimes the two armies even sang the same song with different words. One example is the song, "The Battle Cry of Freedom," on the next page. How do you think each of the troops felt when they heard it?

The Granger Collection

This print shows the storming of Fort Wagner by African American soldiers of the 54th Massachusetts Colored Regiment in 1863.

Northern version by George F. Root, 1861
Southern version by W.H. Barnes, 1861

THE BATTLE CRY OF FREEDOM

North: Yes we'll ral - ly 'round the flag, boys, we'll
South: Our_____ flag is proud - ly float-ing, On the

ral - ly once a - gain, Shout - ing the bat - tle cry of
land and on the main, Shout, shout the bat - tle cry of

Free - dom, We will ral - ly from the hill - side, we'll
Free - dom; Be - neath it oft we've con-quered, And will

gath - er from the plain, Shout - ing the bat - tle cry of Free - dom.
con - quer oft a - gain, Shout, shout the bat - tle cry of Free - dom.

The Un - ion for - ev - er, Hur - rah boys, Hur - rah!
Our Dix - ie for - ev - er, she's nev - er at a loss;

Down with the trai - tor, Up with the star; While we ral - ly 'round the flag, boys,
Down with the ea - gle, Up with the cross. We'll____ ral - ly 'round the bon - ny flag, we'll

Ral - ly once a - gain. Shout - ing the bat - tle cry of Free - dom.
ral - ly once a - gain. Shout, shout the bat - tle cry of Free - dom.

481

THE WAR RAGES ON

"The suffering of men in battle," wrote one Northern woman, "is nothing next to the agony that women feel sending forth their loved ones to war." Women were not allowed in either the Union or the Confederate Army. Yet they contributed to the war effort in many ways.

Many women worked outside their homes for the first time in their lives. Some worked in factories and stores. Others became schoolteachers and clerks. Many ran their family businesses, farms, and plantations while the men were away. Malinda Blalock of North Carolina was one of hundreds of Northern and Southern women who disguised themselves as men to fight on the battlefield.

Women in the North

Over 3,000 Northern women worked as Army nurses. Mary Ann Bickerdyke served for the Union in 19 battles. She performed medical operations and passed out food and supplies. Clara Barton also began her war work passing out food and supplies to troops. Later she assisted with hundreds of operations, even digging bullets out of soldiers' wounds with her penknife.

Union General George McClellan called Barton "the true heroine of the age, the angel of the battlefield." After the war Barton went on to found the American Red Cross in 1881.

Women in the South

Women of the South filled many roles in the Confederate war effort. They ignored those who called their hard work "unladylike." The mayor of Savannah, Georgia, described some of the work done by the city's women. He wrote:

> They are daily engaged . . . in the preparation of cartridges both for muskets and cannon. . . . Others are cutting out and sewing flannel shirts. Others are still making bandages.

Women in the South also served as nurses. Sally Tompkins ran a private hospital in Richmond, which treated over 1,300 soldiers during the war. Her hospital saved all but 73 of them—the best record of any war hospital North or South. Tompkins was the only woman to hold a military rank in the Confederate Army.

Soldiers Young and Old

In the second year of the war, the number of dead and injured soldiers rose steadily. Men of all ages served. In both the North and the South, boys as young as 14 years of age joined the fighting by pretending to be 18. Those as young as 12 signed up to play instruments in the army bands. In the North, some boys wrote the number *18* on a piece of paper and slipped it inside their shoe. Then, they thought

This photograph of Clara Barton is one of the many that Mathew Brady took during the Civil War.

The Granger Collection

Ulysses S. Grant (below), photographed by Mathew Brady, won the Battle of Vicksburg (left), which cut the Confederacy in two.

they could say, "I'm *over 18*," when they were asked if they were old enough to be in the army.

Men in their 60s and 70s also fought. The oldest man to serve in the war was an 80-year-old grandfather from Iowa.

Grant in the West

In the winter of 1862, Ulysses S. Grant led some important Union campaigns in the West. First he won a major victory at Fort Donelson in Tennessee. When the Confederate Army there asked for terms to end the fighting, Grant demanded "unconditional surrender." This meant that he would not stop fighting until they agreed to surrender on his conditions. People began saying that *U.S. Grant* stood for "Unconditional Surrender" Grant.

Grant won more victories at Shiloh, Tennessee, and elsewhere in the West. "I can't spare this man," Lincoln once said of Grant. "He fights."

The Battle at Vicksburg

As you read in Lesson 1, one of the goals of the Anaconda Plan was for the Union to gain control of the Mississippi River and split the Confederacy. Grant was close to achieving this goal in the spring of 1863. One city—Vicksburg,

Mississippi—stood in his way. A steep hill protected the northern edge of the city. Grant realized that getting over the hill would be too difficult. Instead, the Union Army attacked from the southern side.

Grant trapped the Confederates in the city and pounded them with cannon fire. "We are utterly cut off from the world," said Dora Miller, a resident of Vicksburg. The attack continued for 48 days. On July 3, 1863, lacking supplies, the Confederates surrendered. Later, Grant said, "The fate of the Confederacy was sealed when Vicksburg fell."

GETTYSBURG

Vicksburg was not the only major battle in July 1863. At the same time, General Lee's men faced Union troops under General George Meade in Gettysburg, Pennsylvania. Neither army had planned to fight there. When the paths of the two sides crossed, however, the Battle of Gettysburg began. Bullets were "whizzing so thick that it looked like a man could hold out a hat and catch it full," said one Confederate soldier.

The Battle of Gettysburg

On July 3, the third day of the battle, General George Pickett was ordered to charge the center of the Union lines across a great open field. "The enemy is there," Lee said, "and I am going to strike him."

As the Confederate Army made what came to be known as Pickett's Charge, the Union troops fired. "A moan went up from the field," said one officer. Lee's army had to retreat.

Over 28,000 Confederate soldiers were killed or wounded. The Union victories at both Vicksburg and Gettysburg had changed the course of the war in favor of the North. Months later President Lincoln came to Gettysburg to declare the battlefield a national cemetery for Union soldiers. Read the famous speech he made there, his Gettysburg Address. What purpose did Lincoln see in the Battle of Gettysburg?

Gettysburg (right) was one of the bloodiest battles in the war. During the entire war, though, many more soldiers died of disease than in combat.

The Granger Collection

MANY VOICES
PRIMARY SOURCE

The Gettysburg Address, delivered by President Abraham Lincoln on November 19, 1863.

Fourscore and seven years ago our fathers brought forth, on this continent, a new nation, conceived in Liberty, and dedicated to the proposition that all men are created equal.

Now we are engaged in a great civil war, testing whether that nation, or any nation so conceived, and so dedicated, can long endure. We are met on a great battlefield of that war. We have come to dedicate a portion of that field, as a final resting-place for those who here gave their lives, that that nation might live. It is altogether fitting and proper that we should do this.

But, in a larger sense, we cannot dedicate, we can not consecrate, we can not hallow, this ground. The brave men, living and dead, who struggled here, have consecrated it far above our poor power to add or

detract. The world will little note, nor long remember what we say here, but it can never forget what they did here. It is for us the living, rather, to be dedicated here to the unfinished work which they who fought here have thus so far nobly advanced. It is rather for us to be here dedicated to the great task remaining before us that from these honored dead we take increased devotion to that cause for which they gave the last full measure of devotion; that we here highly resolve that these dead shall not have died in vain; that this nation, under God, shall have a new birth of freedom; and that government of the people, by the people, for the people, shall not perish from the earth.

---

score: times twenty
fathers: forefathers or ancestors
conceived: formed
dedicated: set apart for a special purpose
proposition: intention or plan
consecrate: set apart as holy
hallow: consider holy
detract: take away
devotion: loyalty or deep affection

WHY IT MATTERS

The Gettysburg Address only lasted two minutes. When Lincoln finished speaking, the audience was silent. Lincoln thought his speech was a failure. However, it became known as one of the greatest speeches ever given. Lincoln's words inspired the war-weary Union not to give up on the war. He made it clear that democracy, a united country, and the abolition of slavery were causes worth fighting for to the bitter end.

✓ Reviewing Facts and Ideas

MAIN IDEAS

- In 1862 both North and South suffered great losses at Antietam.
- The Emancipation Proclamation outlawed slavery in the Confederacy. Over 180,000 African Americans joined in the Union Army.
- The Union victories at Vicksburg and Gettysburg changed the course of the war in favor of the North.

THINK ABOUT IT

1. Why did Lincoln announce the Emancipation Proclamation *after* the Battle of Antietam?

2. Explain the role of each of these people in the Civil War: Charlotte Forten, Clara Barton, Sally Tompkins.

3. **FOCUS** What events helped to turn the war in favor of the Union?

4. **THINKING SKILL** Compare reactions to the Emancipation Proclamation from the *point of view* of Southern slave owners, Northern abolitionists, other Northerners, and newly freed slaves.

5. **WRITE** Write a newspaper article about one of the events in the lesson.

Making Generalizations

VOCABULARY

generalization

WHY THE SKILL MATTERS

You have read about a number of Civil War commanders. At first it might seem that men as different as Ulysses S. Grant, Robert E. Lee, George Meade, and Thomas "Stonewall" Jackson had little in common. However, if you look closer, you might see some similarities. From those similarities you might be able to make a broad statement about what made a commander successful in the Civil War. If you made such a statement, you would be making a generalization.

A generalization is a broad statement that tells a way in which all examples or members of a certain group are similar. A statement like "all Civil War commanders were men" is a generalization. A generalization applies to a number of separate cases and not just to one.

Generalizations are useful because they explain many specific examples that may be too numerous to study or remember. Generalizations can also help you to make sense of new information about a topic you will encounter later.

USING THE SKILL

To make a generalization, you must first identify the topic you want to generalize. Next, you need to collect information about that topic. Finally, you must look at the information for common features, trends, and connections. Then, come up with a single statement that applies equally to each of the specific cases you have studied, but which does not mention any specific instance or example.

More powerful weapons increased the number of people killed in battle. Over 26,000 soldiers died at Antietam (below).

Suppose you wanted to discover if there were qualities common to all successful commanders in the Civil War. You might start by reading about some of the most successful commanders, for example, generals Grant and Meade of the Union and generals Lee and Jackson of the Confederacy. You would ignore the surface differences that might stand out at first. Instead, you would focus on what the four commanders had in common. Your reading would tell you that each attended the United States Military Academy at West Point and had fighting experience in the Mexican War. You might also learn that the four leaders were usually decisive, calm under fire, and respected by their soldiers.

What generalization could you draw from these facts? You could say that successful commanders in the Civil War had had previous war experience.

TRYING THE SKILL

Try making your own generalization about the Civil War. You read how new inventions like the rifle and the Gatling gun enabled soldiers to kill or disable more of their enemies faster than ever before. You also read about Pickett's Charge at Gettysburg. Pickett's soldiers attacked heavily armed Union forces. The attack resulted in terrible losses for the Confederacy. At the Battle of Fredericksburg in 1862, Union troops made a similar attack.

Helping yourself

- **A generalization is a statement that applies to many different examples of a group or topic.**

- **First decide on a topic, then collect information showing examples of it.**

- **Study the details of the information to find a single feature that is true of all the examples or instances of the topic.**

They charged against strongly armed Confederate troops. The result was equally bad. Union troops lost over 12,500 men in one day.

Now make a generalization about the Civil War based on these facts. One generalization might be "New inventions enabled Civil War troops to kill more enemies." What themes or ideas do the facts in the paragraph you have just read have in common? How does each fact contribute to this generalization? What other generalizations might be made from these facts?

REVIEWING THE SKILL

1. What is a generalization?

2. What steps do you follow in making a generalization?

3. Is the statement "Civil War commanders preferred to defend well-armed areas against attack" a generalization? Why or why not?

4. Alabama, Kentucky, Maryland, Mississippi, Missouri, North Carolina, and South Carolina were all slave states. Kentucky, Maryland, and Missouri remained in the Union. They had fewer than two slaves for every eight free persons. Alabama, Mississippi, and South Carolina seceded. They had more than four slaves for every six free persons. What generalization can you make about why some slave states seceded from the Union while other slave states did not?

5. Why is making a generalization helpful in learning about history?

1860   1864 1865   1870   1875   1880

The Union Stands

Read Aloud

By 1864 nearly everyone had suffered some kind of loss as a result of the Civil War. No one had thought the war would last so long or cause so much destruction. "Our bleeding, bankrupt, almost dying country," wrote newspaperman Horace Greeley, "longs for peace [and] shudders at the prospect . . . of new rivers of human blood."

Focus Activity

READ TO LEARN

How did the Civil War end?

VOCABULARY

- total war

PEOPLE

- William Tecumseh Sherman

PLACES

- Atlanta
- Petersburg
- Appomattox Court House

THE BIG PICTURE

Northerners were running out of patience with the war. Progress had been made on the battlefield. But each day the need for more soldiers increased. In 1863 President Lincoln announced that all men aged 20 to 45 would be drafted into the Union Army. Being drafted means having to serve in the military. Until that time, soldiers had volunteered to serve. The draft angered many men who did not want to fight to end slavery. Some were angry that rich men could avoid the draft by paying others who wer less fortunate to fight for them. Riots against the draft broke out in New York and other Northern cities. "I am a tired man," Lincoln said about the hardships of the war. "Sometimes I think I am the tiredest man on earth."

By 1864 the Union blockade of the Southern ports had wounded the Confederacy. The South was running out of food and supplies. Prices climbed higher and higher. One Virginia woman complained that she needed a shopping bag full of Confederate money to buy a pocketbook full of groceries. An end to the war, though, was drawing nearer.

GRANT LEADS THE UNION

In Lesson 2 you read of Ulysses S. Grant's successes in the West. In March 1864 Lincoln put Ulysses S. Grant in charge of the entire Union Army. "Grant is my man," Lincoln said, "and I am his for the rest of the war."

Grant began a major series of battles in Virginia. His goal was to capture Richmond. Grant's troops slowly moved south toward the Confederate capital. Lee kept one step ahead of him. In the first month Grant lost an average of almost 2,000 men each day. "I propose to fight it out on this line if it takes all summer," he said.

Sherman's March

Now General William Tecumseh Sherman led Union forces in the West. "We cannot change the hearts of these people of the South," Sherman said, "but we can make them so sick of war that generations [will] pass before they [try it] again." Sherman practiced what has been called total war. Total war is an all-out war to destroy people's ability and will to fight. Sherman's troops seized or destroyed nearly everything in their path.

In September 1864 Sherman captured and burned Atlanta, Georgia, one of the South's largest cities. Then Sherman marched to Savannah, on the Atlantic coast of Georgia. His 60,000 men cut a 300-mile path of destruction across Georgia. Sherman reached the Atlantic Coast in December 1864. He telegraphed Lincoln that he had a "Christmas gift" for him—he had captured the city of Savannah.

From there Sherman marched into South Carolina. Many Northerners blamed South Carolina for starting the war because it had been the first state to secede from the Union. The Union troops destroyed or burned down nearly every building in their path. Many people in the Confederacy sensed that the end of their struggle was approaching. "The deep waters are closing over us," wrote South Carolina resident Mary Chestnut.

William Tecumseh Sherman (right) practiced total war. Sherman's March to the Sea (below) destroyed the Confederacy's last source of supplies for its armies.

The Granger Collection

The Granger Collection

Infographic

inter**NET**
CONNECTION
Visit our website:
www.mhschool.com

The Civil War

Early in the morning on April 12, 1861, Confederate troops attacked Fort Sumter, a Union fort off the coast of South Carolina. With this battle the Civil War between the Union and the Confederacy began. After several defeats in the beginning of the war, the Union Army began a series of victories. Find the location of some major battles on the map on these pages.

NEBRASKA
TERRITORY

COLORADO
TERRITORY

KANSAS

MAJOR BATTLES OF THE CIVIL WAR, 1861-1865

- Union states
- Confederate states
- Union victory
- Confederate victory
- Undecided battle
- Territories
- Union capital
- Confederate capital
- Union blockade
- Sherman's March, 1864

The Civil War cap was worn by a soldier in the Confederate Army. Confederate soldiers were known for wearing mostly gray uniforms. However, each state's troops often wore an item that made them look different from other troops. A bugle, such as the one above used by a Union force, signaled battlefield commands.

This young Confederate officer (right) probably had this photograph taken to send home to his family or perhaps a sweetheart. The photograph of Union troops (far right), was probably taken by Mathew Brady after the Battle of Antietam. Brady's darkroom wagon is in the background.

The Granger Collection

IOWA

ILLINOIS

INDIANA

OHIO

PENNSYLVANIA
Gettysburg
1863

NEW
JERSEY

Antietam 1862

MD

DELAWARE

Cincinnati

Potomac River

Washington, D.C.

Missouri River

St. Louis

Ohio River

MISSOURI

Wilderness 1864
Chancellorsville 1863

Bull Run 186

WEST
VIRGINIA

Fredericksburg
1862

Cold Harbor 1864

Richmond

VIRGINIA

INDIAN
TERRI-
TORY

KENTUCKY

Perryville
1862

Appomattox
Court House

Monitor and Merrimack
1862

ARKANSAS

Mississippi River

Nashville
1864

Tennessee River

NORTH CAROLINA

TENNESSEE

Chattanooga
1863

Shiloh
1862

Chickamauga
1863

Atlanta
1864

SOUTH
CAROLINA

Atlanta

TEXAS

MISSISSIPPI

ALABAMA

GEORGIA

Charleston

Fort Sumter
1861

N
W   E
S

Vicksburg
1863

Savannah

ATLANTIC
OCEAN

LOUISIANA

New Orleans

Mobile Bay
1864

New Orleans
1862

FLORIDA

Gulf of Mexico

THE SOUTH SURRENDERS

Grant was slowly closing in on Lee. He knew that Lee was camped with his men in the city of Petersburg, Virginia, not far from Richmond. Lee was running out of soldiers and supplies. The Union Army waited outside of Petersburg for nine months. By April 1865, Grant's 125,000 men surrounded Lee's starving army of 35,000. Finally, on April 2, 1865, Lee took his army west, hoping to find food and to gather more Confederate troops. In response to Lee's actions, Union forces entered Petersburg and Richmond.

The Surrender at Appomattox

Lee found that his path west was blocked by Union soldiers. "There is nothing left for me to do," Lee said, "but go to General Grant." The Confederate Army was ready to surrender.

On April 9, 1865, Grant and Lee met in Appomattox Court House, Virginia. Lee wore a crisp grey uniform. "I have to look my best," he said. "I may be Grant's prisoner." Grant did not take any prisoners. Instead, Grant said, "Each . . . man will be allowed to return to his home, not to be disturbed by the United States authorities."

After Lee's surrender, Jefferson Davis fled westward, where he hoped to keep the Confederacy alive. On May 10, 1865, he was captured. Davis was later imprisoned for two years at Fort Monroe in Virginia.

The Troops Return Home

When Robert E. Lee returned from Appomattox Court House, he told his men, "I have done the best I could for you. Go home now. . . . I shall always be proud of you." Ulysses S. Grant told the Union troops, "The war is over . . . the rebels are our countrymen again."

The soldiers returned to their homes. One Union soldier, on seeing his family's farm in Indiana, spoke of "a feeling of profound contentment . . . too deep to be expressed by mere words." The next day, he said, he put on old clothes and went to work in his father's cornfields.

Lee's surrender to Grant at Appomattox Court House on April 9, 1865, marked the end of the bloodiest war in United States history.

By the end of the war, the Confederacy's capitol, Richmond, Virginia, lay in ruins (left), as did much of the South.

The Granger Collection

In the South there were few farms left that were in working condition. Property was not the only thing that had been destroyed in the Southern states. A way of life had ended forever. One Confederate soldier, returning home to Richmond, wrote "I shall not attempt to describe my feelings. The city [is] in ruins . . . With a raging hcadache and a swelling heart I reach my home, and here the curtain falls."

WHY IT MATTERS

The Civil War ended in 1865, reuniting the North and South. It would have a lasting effect on the United States. About 620,000 people had died in the war. That was about one out of every 50 people who had lived in the United States in 1860. Almost every family experienced a loss.

In the South one of every four white men had been killed. Two-thirds of its wealth had been lost. It would take many years for the South to recover.

The war had put an end to the debate over slavery. However, it had not made African Americans truly free. In chapters to come you will see how

African Americans continued the struggle for freedom.

The Union had survived, but the cost of the Civil War had been huge. The task of rebuilding the country still lay ahead for both the North and the South, united once again.

✓✓ Reviewing Facts and Ideas

MAIN IDEAS

- The Confederacy was running out of supplies in 1864. The Union was losing patience with the war.

- In 1864 Grant was named commander of the entire Union Army.

- General Sherman waged total war on the South during his march from Atlanta to Savannah. Many buildings and farms in Georgia and South Carolina were destroyed.

- Lee surrendered to Grant on April 9, 1865, at Appomattox Court House in Virginia. The Union and Confederate troops returned home, but both sides were deeply scarred.

THINK ABOUT IT

1. Why had the North lost patience with the war in 1864?

2. How did total war help the Union defeat the Confederacy?

3. FOCUS What key events and battles helped end the Civil War?

4. THINKING SKILL What _generalizations_ can you make about the costs of the Civil War for both the North and the South?

5. WRITE Write a dialogue based on what you think Lee and Grant might have said to each other at Appomattox Court House.

The Granger Collection

Focus Activity

VOCABULARY

- **Reconstruction**
- **Thirteenth Amendment**
- black codes
- **Freedmen's Bureau**
- sharecropping
- **Fourteenth Amendment**
- **Fifteenth Amendment**
- impeach
- **Ku Klux Klan**
- **Jim Crow laws**
- segregation

PEOPLE

- **Andrew Johnson**
- **Blanche K. Bruce**
- **Hiram R. Revels**

1860   1865   1877   1880

Reconstruction

Read Aloud

Less than a week after Lee's surrender, President Lincoln was watching a play at Ford's Theater in Washington, D.C. Suddenly a gunshot rang out. John Wilkes Booth had shot the President. The next morning, April 15, 1865, President Lincoln died. The poet Walt Whitman expressed the country's sadness:

*O Captain! my Captain, our fearful trip is done,
The ship has weather'd every storm, the prize we sought is won.*

THE BIG PICTURE

Whitman's "prize" was many things. It was an end to the war, an end to slavery, and a new beginning for the United States, which was united once again.

Yet many tasks remained. The South was in ruins. Before his death Lincoln had spoken of **Reconstruction**, or rebuilding the South. As he began his second term as President, Lincoln had encouraged Americans to put away their malice, or bad feelings, about the Confederacy. "With malice toward none, with charity for all," he said, asking people to "bind up the nation's wounds and achieve a lasting peace." Now Lincoln was dead. What would happen to the country without his leadership?

REJOINING THE UNION

After Lincoln's death Vice President Andrew Johnson of Tennessee became President. He pushed ahead with Lincoln's plan for Reconstruction. The plan was simple. When one-tenth of a Confederate state's voters swore loyalty to the Union, they could form a new state government. The new government then had to approve the Thirteenth Amendment to the Constitution. This amendment abolished slavery.

Johnson Clashes with Congress

By December of 1865, every Confederate state but Texas had followed these steps to rejoin the Union. President Johnson was ready to declare Reconstruction complete. Many members of Congress did not agree. Some wanted to punish the South. Others objected that many of the South's newly elected officials were the same people who had led the Confederacy.

Members of Congress also pointed out that under the leadership of all-white legislatures, very little was likely to change for blacks. In fact, not one Southern state allowed blacks the same rights as whites.

Across the South the new state governments had passed laws called black codes. The black codes described the rights and duties of the freed African Americans. They made it unlawful for African Americans to live in certain areas and to hold certain jobs. The black codes also said that African Americans without jobs could be arrested, fined, or put in jail.

The members of Congress voted not to admit the newly elected Southern leaders to Congress. Instead, the Congress began to develop its own plan for Reconstruction.

Mourners followed the funeral car bearing Lincoln's body (left) as it traveled down Broadway in New York City (below).

The Freedmen's Bureau founded schools like this one in Charleston, South Carolina (left), to educate former slaves (below).

The Granger Collection

REBUILDING THE SOUTH

While Congress and President Johnson argued over Reconstruction, millions of newly freed African Americans, or "freedmen," faced an uncertain future. For freedmen without jobs or land, emancipation meant hunger and homelessness. In March 1865 Congress created the Freedmen's Bureau. The Bureau provided food, clothing, shelter, medical care, jobs, and legal help to both blacks and whites. The Bureau also set up over 4,000 schools for newly freed people.

African Americans also provided their own schooling. By 1870 they spent over $1 million on education. In time, black colleges and universities were started in the South. Among them were Fisk University in Tennessee and Morehouse and Spelman Colleges in Georgia.

Opportunity and Hardship

By 1868 African Americans had the right to vote, to hold office, and to hold jobs. However, most Southern blacks were poor. "Give us our own land and we [will] take care of ourselves," said one former slave. Yet many whites would not sell land to African Americans in the South.

Most farmland was still owned by the planters, who had little or no money to pay freedmen to work the land for them. Instead, the planters divided up their land and rented it. The landowners usually accepted part of the crop grown on their land as rent. Often the landowner's share was as much as one half of the crop. This system of renting land for a share of the crop raised on it is called sharecropping. The people who rent the land are called sharecroppers.

Many freed blacks and poor whites became sharecroppers. It was a hard life. Sharecroppers often had to borrow money to buy seeds and supplies. Crops were often poor and prices low. Sometimes sharecroppers were cheated by the landowners. Every year most sharecroppers slipped deeper into debt.

New Amendments

In 1866 Congress had said that the Thirteenth Amendment did not go far enough to improve the condition of the former slaves in the South. Congress proposed a Fourteenth Amendment.

This amendment made blacks citizens of the United States and guaranteed them the same legal rights as whites. President Johnson tried to block the Fourteenth Amendment, but it became part of the Constitution in 1868.

In 1870 the **Fifteenth Amendment** became law. It said that states could not deny people the right to vote "on account of race or color." However, the amendment did not give women the right to vote. You can compare the three amendments on the chart that appears on this page. They helped Congress strengthen their control over the southern states.

Congress Takes Control

After two years of struggling with President Johnson over who would control Reconstruction, Congress passed the First Reconstruction Act in 1867. Under this Act the South would be ruled by the Union Army until new state governments were formed.

Along with the troops came many Northerners who planned to start businesses. Southerners often called these Northerners carpetbaggers because many of them carried suitcases made of carpeting. Southerners believed that carpetbaggers were looking to profit from the South's suffering.

Under Reconstruction, more than 600 African American officials were elected to state office. Sixteen African Americans were elected to Congress, including **Blanche K. Bruce** and **Hiram R. Revels** from Mississippi, who were elected to the United States Senate.

The President on Trial

Meanwhile, President Johnson was battling to stay in office. Congress had passed laws limiting the President's powers. In 1868 the House of Representatives voted to impeach the President because he refused to obey these new laws. To impeach means to charge a government official with wrongdoing. Under the Constitution, if two-thirds of the Senate find a President guilty, the President is removed from office.

At the trial the vote was tied. Only one vote remained. "Not a foot moved," wrote Senator Edmund Ross of Kansas, describing how the Senate waited for his vote. "Not guilty," said Ross. Johnson would serve out his term in office.

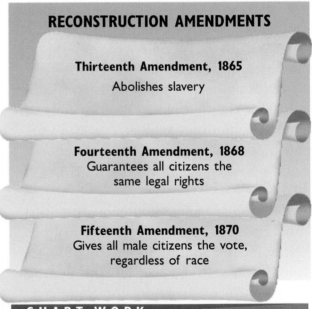

RECONSTRUCTION AMENDMENTS

Thirteenth Amendment, 1865
Abolishes slavery

Fourteenth Amendment, 1868
Guarantees all citizens the same legal rights

Fifteenth Amendment, 1870
Gives all male citizens the vote, regardless of race

CHART WORK

The **Reconstruction** amendments gave Americans some important rights.

1. Which of the amendments affected all African Americans?
2. Which of the amendments applied to all Americans?

Hiram Revels (left), the first African American senator, was a clergyman and an educator.

RECONSTRUCTION ENDS

Most Southern whites were angered by the new state governments. Leaders had raised taxes sharply to pay for new schools and roads. Many whites were also angered by seeing blacks holding public office. They were not ready to accept African Americans as equals.

Violence

Some Southerners turned to violence to frighten African Americans and their white supporters. In 1866 six former Confederate officers formed the **Ku Klux Klan**. Disguised in white robes and hoods, its members terrorized African Americans. "The Ku Klux Klan [is] riding nightly over the country . . . robbing, whipping, . . . and killing our people," said a petition to Congress by black citizens of Kentucky in 1871. The Klan drove people from their homes and destroyed their property.

Blacks working for whites were often told that they would be fired if they voted. Sometimes whites kept the voting places secret from black voters.

Jim Crows Laws

"We have tried this Reconstruction long enough," said a Northern leader. "Now let the South alone." By 1877 the last Union soldiers had left the South.

After Reconstruction, the Southern states quickly passed **Jim Crow laws**. Jim Crow laws made the separation of white and black people legal. Another name for the separation of people by race is **segregation**. Under Jim Crow laws, blacks and whites could not use the same schools, restaurants, trains, hotels, or parks. Frederick Douglass said in 1883, "Thus in all the relations of life and death we are met by the color line."

WHY IT MATTERS

Reconstruction gave African Americans citizenship. Yet sharecropping and segregation had bound African Americans into lives of poverty and unequal rights. Not until the Civil Rights movement of the 1950s and 1960s would African Americans begin to gain the rights guaranteed to all citizens by the Thirteenth, Fourteenth, and Fifteenth amendments to the Constitution.

✓ Reviewing Facts and Ideas

MAIN IDEAS

- After Lincoln was killed in 1865, President Andrew Johnson began a Reconstruction program to rebuild the South. Although Johnson was impeached in 1868, he was not removed from office.

- The Thirteenth, Fourteenth, and Fifteenth amendments extended rights to African American citizens.

- The Freedmen's Bureau helped African Americans. Still, many African Americans became sharecroppers. By 1877 Reconstruction had ended. Laws were soon passed to keep blacks separate from whites.

THINK ABOUT IT

1. What rights did the new amendments grant?

2. How did the Freedmen's Bureau help people in the South?

3. **FOCUS** How did Reconstruction change life in the South?

4. **THINKING SKILL** What *effects* did groups like the Ku Klux Klan have on the progress of Reconstruction?

5. **WRITE** Write a paragraph that explains the words of Frederick Douglass that appear on this page.

MAKING A DIFFERENCE

Solving Conflicts Peacefully

RICHARDSON, TEXAS. As you read, Congress and President Andrew Johnson disagreed over Reconstruction. Their dispute became so heated that Congress finally tried to remove President Johnson from office.

Disagreements in everyday life can also cause problems. At Terrace Elementary, "it used to be that kids in trouble for fighting spent a lot of time in the principal's office. But no more," says Ellen Boehmer (BEEM er). "Now they've found a better way to work out their conflicts."

Mrs. Boehmer, the guidance counselor at Terrace Elementary, started the school's *peer mediation* program in 1990. *Mediate* means "bring about an agreement between opposing sides." In peer mediation the students settle conflicts themselves. The mediators are elected by their classmates and trained by the school counselor.

Peer mediation can be requested by students who are fighting or by a teacher. Fifth-grade mediator Bellor Ngbor (ENG bor) explains what happens next. "We find a quiet hallway and tell the kids arguing they have to agree to certain rules. They have to tell the truth and they cannot call each other names or interrupt. No physical fighting is allowed."

Mediators set a 30-minute time limit for discussing the problem. If all parties agree to a solution, the mediator writes it down and has everyone sign it. If no agreement is reached, the problem is referred to a teacher to resolve.

Sixth grader Antjuan (AN toine) Lawson has been a mediator for three years. The hardest part of the job for him is not taking sides. "You have to know how to control your temper. If the people fighting are your friends, you probably should let somebody else do it." Antjuan explains that he used to be one of the kids who was always getting into fights. Now he has learned to apply the skills he has learned as a mediator to his own life. He said, "I've learned to try to understand how other people are feeling even when I don't agree."

" . . . understand how other people are feeling . . ."

Antjuan Lawson
Bellor Ngbor

CHAPTER 17 REVIEW

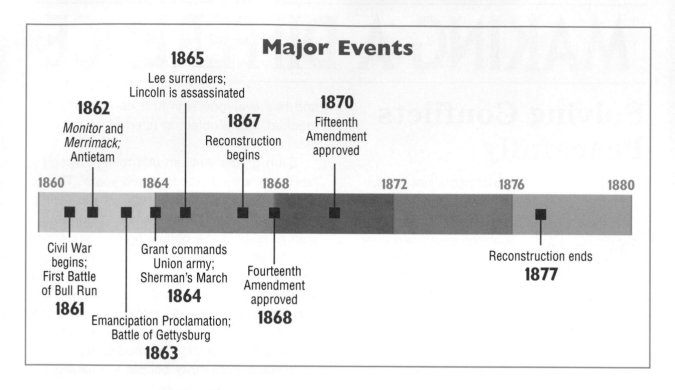

Major Events

1865
Lee surrenders;
Lincoln is assassinated

1862
Monitor and
Merrimack;
Antietam

1867
Reconstruction
begins

1870
Fifteenth
Amendment
approved

1860   1864   1868   1872   1876   1880

Civil War
begins;
First Battle
of Bull Run
1861

Grant commands
Union army;
Sherman's March
1864

Fourteenth
Amendment
approved
1868

Reconstruction ends
1877

Emancipation Proclamation;
Battle of Gettysburg
1863

THINKING ABOUT VOCABULARY

Number a paper from 1 to 10. Beside each number, write the word or term from the list below that best completes each sentence.

Anaconda Plan
blockade
Civil War
generalization
impeach

Jim Crow laws
Reconstruction
segregation
sharecropping
total war

1. A _____ is a broad statement that ties together facts, ideas, or examples.

2. An all-out effort to destroy people's ability to fight is called _____.

3. To _____ means to charge a government official with wrongdoing.

4. Southern governments passed _____ to separate the races.

5. The separation of peoples based on skin color is called _____.

6. Winfield Scott developed the _____ for Union victory in the Civil War.

7. In _____ land is rented for a share of the crop raised on it.

8. Another name for the _____ is the War Between the States.

9. The rebuilding of the South after the war is known as _____.

10. The Union planned to _____ Southern seaports, so that the South would run low on supplies.

THINKING ABOUT FACTS

1. Describe the First Battle of Bull Run.

2. What was the Emancipation Proclamation? How did it change the way people thought of the Civil War?

3. How did the Civil War affect the North? How did it affect the South?

4. What gains did African Americans make during the early years of Reconstruction? Did they last? Why or why not?

5. Look at the time line above. What can you conclude from the date Grant took command and the date the war ended?

THINK AND WRITE ◄══▷

WRITING A DIARY ENTRY
Write a diary entry in which you describe Sherman's March. Write your entry either from the viewpoint of a soldier in Sherman's army or a farmer through whose land the Union forces marched.

WRITING HISTORICAL FICTION
Suppose that Abraham Lincoln had not been killed. Write an historical story in which you describe how Reconstruction might have occurred differently if Lincoln had remained alive as President.

WRITING AN ANALYSIS
Write a paragraph in which you analyze the effects of the Thirteenth, Fourteenth, and Fifteenth amendments on the United States in the 1860s and 1870s.

APPLYING STUDY SKILLS

MAKING GENERALIZATIONS

1. What is the first step in making a generalization?

2. What information do you look for when making generalizations?

3. Based on the battles of Vicksburg and Petersburg, what generalization can you make about the role of supplies in warfare?

4. Suppose that you go to your local grocery store at 7:00 P.M., and it is closed. Another night you try the drugstore at the same time, and it is closed. Finally, the next evening, you walk by the bakery at 7:00 P.M. and notice it is closed. What generalization might you make about your local businesses?

5. Why is making generalizations useful?

Summing Up the Chapter

Copy the main-idea table on a separate piece of paper. Review the chapter to fill in the main idea and the missing names. When you have finished, use the information in the table to write a paragraph that answers the question "How was the Civil War fought differently from other wars you have read about?"

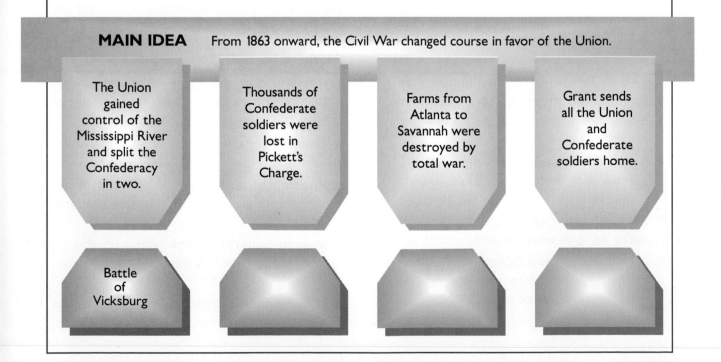

MAIN IDEA   From 1863 onward, the Civil War changed course in favor of the Union.

| The Union gained control of the Mississippi River and split the Confederacy in two. | Thousands of Confederate soldiers were lost in Pickett's Charge. | Farms from Atlanta to Savannah were destroyed by total war. | Grant sends all the Union and Confederate soldiers home. |

Battle of Vicksburg

UNIT 7 REVIEW

THINKING ABOUT VOCABULARY

Number a paper from 1 to 10. Write the word or term from the list below that best matches the description.

Civil War	Gettysburg Address
feature article	Ku Klux Klan
Fifteenth Amendment	states' rights
Fourteenth Amendment	Thirteenth Amendment
Fugitive Slave Law	Underground Railroad

1. Amendment to the Constitution that abolished slavery

2. Hate group formed in 1865 that terrorized African Americans with threats and violence

3. War in the United States in which the troops of the Northern states fought the troops of the Southern states

4. Amendment to the Constitution that made African Americans citizens of the United States and guaranteed them the same legal rights as whites

5. Famous speech given by Abraham Lincoln in 1863 when he set aside a national cemetery for fallen Union soldiers

6. A newspaper's detailed report on a person, an issue, or an event

7. An 1850 law that required police in the free states to help capture escaping slaves

8. A network of people and buildings that guided, fed, sheltered, and hid runaway slaves on their journey to the North

9. Political claim that each state should make its own decision about most issues

10. Amendment to the Constitution that said states could not deny men the right to vote "on account of race or color"

THINK AND WRITE

WRITING A DIALOGUE

Suppose that you have the opportunity to meet one of the people whom you read about in this unit, such as Abraham Lincoln, Frederick Douglass, Harriet Tubman, or Elizabeth Cady Stanton. Think about what questions you would like to ask this person. Write a dialogue between yourself and the person you have chosen.

WRITING WORDS TO A SONG

Reread the *Many Voices* "The Battle Cry of Freedom" and think about how important music was to soldiers on both sides in the Civil War. Write your own words to a song that you think would have helped keep up the spirits of either the Union or Confederate troops.

WRITING ABOUT PERSPECTIVES

You read in this unit how a book like *Uncle Tom's Cabin* can have an important effect on events. Write two reviews of the book, one from the perspective of an abolitionist and the other from the perspective of a Southern supporter of slavery.

BUILDING SKILLS

1. **Reading a newspaper** Where do the editors of a newspaper express their opinions about important issues?

2. **Reading a newspaper** What kinds of events are described in a news article?

3. **Reading a newspaper** Which part of a newspaper is meant to catch the reader's attention?

4. **Making generalizations** What do you need to have before you make a generalization?

5. **Making generalizations** What is the final step involved in making a generalization?

YESTERDAY, TODAY &
TOMORROW

Abraham Lincoln gave the Gettysburg Address when he set aside the site at Gettysburg, Pennsylvania, as a national cemetery for soldiers. Why do you think Lincoln felt honoring the soldiers with a memorial was important? What other memorials do you know of? How do you think people will view them in the future?

READING ON YOUR OWN

These are some of the books you could find at the library to help you learn more.

MINTY: A STORY OF YOUNG HARRIET TUBMAN
by A. Shroeder
This story, based on facts, tells about Harriet Tubman's childhood.

I SPEAK FOR THE WOMEN: A STORY ABOUT LUCY STONE
by Stephanie Sammartino McPherson
This story tells of one woman's determination and courageous fight for women's rights.

THE BOY'S WAR: CONFEDERATE AND UNION SOLDIERS TALK ABOUT THE CIVIL WAR
by Jim Murphy
Read the diary entries and personal letters of boys under sixteen who fought in the Civil War.

UNIT 7 REVIEW PROJECT

Make a Civil War Drum

1. With your group, research different battles of the Civil War. Make a list and write some facts about each one. Include information about where the battle took place, what the outcome was, and how it affected the war.
2. Draw a large circle on a piece of cardboard, cut it out, and make another one of equal size.
3. Then roll a piece of oak tag so that the opening on the top and bottom equals the size of the cardboard pieces. With a pencil, mark where you will tape the ends of the oak tag together.
4. On the oak tag, write about one battle on your list. Be sure to write your information inside your pencil marks. Decorate the oak tag with colored paper, glitter, and markers.
5. Finally, tape the oak tag together and glue the cardboard pieces onto it to create a drum.

EARLY AIRPLANE

ELLIS ISLAND

PRESIDENT
THEODORE ROOSEVELT

UNIT EIGHT

Immigration and Industry

"We are not building this country . . . for a day."

from a speech by President Theodore Roosevelt
See page 564.

Why Does it Matter?

What makes our country great? In the words of President Theodore Roosevelt above, it is the hard work of all Americans that maintains this country for future generations. Roosevelt saw a country whose vast size and wealth of resources attracted newcomers from many parts of the world. He also saw a country filled with talented people who were developing new and amazing technologies.

From the late 1800s to the early 1900s, the United States changed greatly. New towns developed and old cities grew, populated by millions of newly arrived immigrants. The lands of Native Americans in the West also became the home of different people.

The transcontinental railroad was one of the new marvels of technology that Americans were developing. The United States was growing, building, and becoming a world leader.

EARLY CAMERA

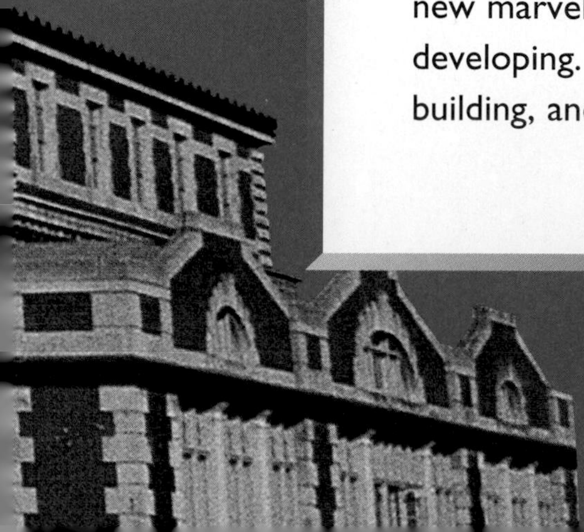

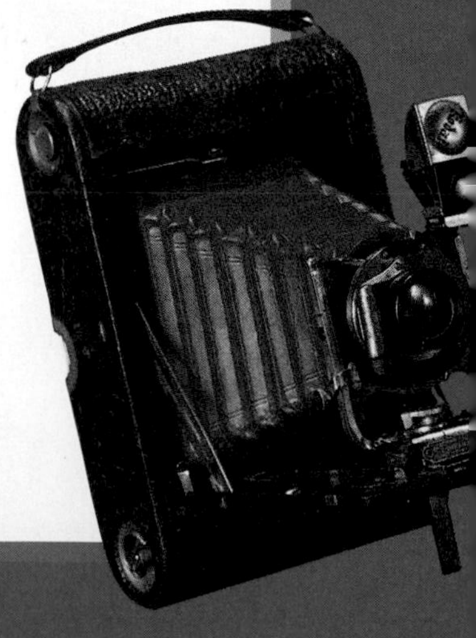

FIND OUT MORE!
Visit our website:
www.mhschool.com
*inter*NET CONNECTION

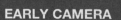

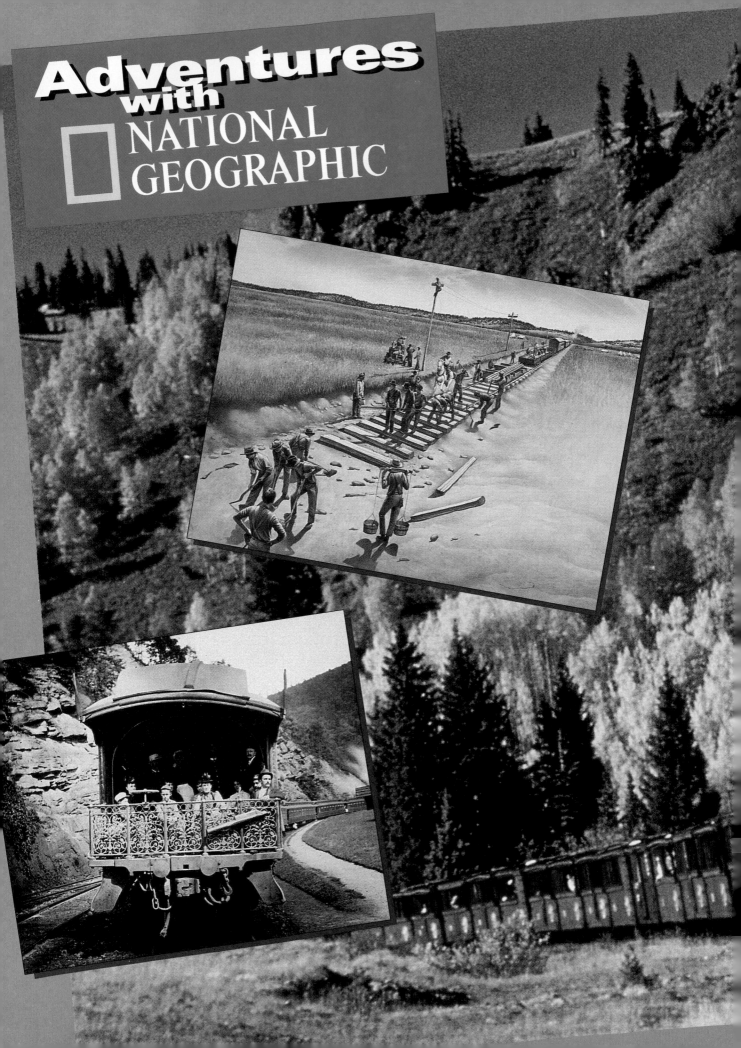

Adventures with
NATIONAL GEOGRAPHIC

Are We There Yet?

"I've been workin' on the rail-road, all the livelong day...." It wasn't just a song. Building the transcontinental railroad meant years of backbreaking labor for thousands of men in the 1860s. Workers laid 1,775 miles of track between Nebraska and California. The last spike—made of gold—went in on May 10, 1869. Joyful officials and witnesses posed for a picture, one of the most famous in American history. Slicing weeks off a cross-country trip, railroads encour-aged new waves of migration.

GEOJOURNAL

Draft a short speech for the ceremony to celebrate the completion of the transconti-nental railroad.

Newcomers Change the West

THINKING ABOUT HISTORY AND GEOGRAPHY

From the time line below you can see that the story of Chapter 18 begins with the completion of the movement of Americans to the West. After the building of the transcontinental railroad, people, goods, and information could be transported East and West faster than ever before. This cross-country railroad helped establish new industries in lands west of the Mississippi River.

PACIFIC OCEAN

1860s

GREAT PLAINS, KANSAS

Homesteaders establish new towns in the West

1869

PROMONTORY POINT, UTAH

The first transcontinental railroad is completed

1870s

CHISHOLM TRAIL, TEXAS

Cowhands begin driving their cattle north

1860   1865   1870

Bearpaw
Mountain

Little Bighorn
River

Promontory
Point

**UNITED
STATES**

Great Plains

Chisholm Trail

ATLANTIC
OCEAN

1876

**LITTLE BIGHORN
RIVER, MONTANA**
Native Americans defeat
General Custer and his
cavalry

1877

**BEAR PAW MOUNTAIN,
MONTANA**
Chief Joseph surrenders to
the United States Army

1875

1880

1850   1869   1880   1890

Rails Across the Country

Read Aloud

In the summer of 1865, a Massachusetts newspaper editor named Samuel Bowles (BOHLZ) went on a trip to the West. Wherever he went, "between the Plains and Pacific, in country and on coast, on the Columbia, on the Colorado," wrote Bowles, "the first question asked of us by every man and woman . . . has been, 'When do you think the Pacific Railroad will be done?'"

Focus Activity

READ TO LEARN

In what ways did the transcontinental railroad help our country grow?

VOCABULARY

- transcontinental railroad
- Pacific Railroad Act

PEOPLE

- Grenville Dodge
- Charles Crocker

PLACES

- Promontory Point

THE BIG PICTURE

Although the Civil War was over and the country was reunited, another division still existed—between the East and the West. People in the East had no quick way to reach the rich farm lands and gold mines of the West.

Wagon trains took four to six months to cross the country. The journey was often dangerous. To travel by boat required sailing around the southern tip of South America, or sailing to Central America, crossing it by land, and then sailing north to California. Both of these water routes also took months.

A transcontinental railroad, some said, was needed. A transcontinental railroad is a railroad that crosses an entire continent. In 1854 most of the country's 14,000 miles of railroad track were east of the Mississippi River. A transcontinental railroad would make the long journey between the Atlantic and the Pacific coasts faster, cheaper, and safer. How would this dream become a reality?

PLANNING THE RAILROAD

In 1838 the people of the Iowa Territory sent a petition to Congress asking for help to build a transcontinental railroad. Congress denied the petition, saying it would be like trying "to build a railroad to the moon."

Obstacles to the Railroad

Disputes about building the transcontinental railroad began almost as soon as the idea was suggested. People from Chicago, St. Louis, and Memphis all argued that their city would be the best starting point for the railroad.

The varied geography of the West discouraged many railroad builders. The railroad would have to cross the vast Great Plains, the snow-covered Rocky Mountains, the deserts of the Great Basin, and the rugged Sierra Nevada Mountains of California.

Some builders worried about possible conflicts with the many Native Americans who lived in the West. The railroad would cut across their lands and bring many new settlers.

The Pacific Railroad Act

The desire for a transcontinental railroad grew after the gold rush in California in 1849. In July 1862 Congress passed the Pacific Railroad Act. This act offered two companies government loans and free land to build the railroad. President Lincoln hoped that a transcontinental railroad would strengthen the Union during the Civil War.

One of the companies chosen to build the transcontinental railroad was the Union Pacific Railroad, headed by Thomas Durant. Under the leadership of a former Union general named Grenville Dodge, the Union Pacific would lay track westward from Omaha, Nebraska. The other company selected was the Central Pacific Railroad, headed by Leland Stanford. Under the direction of a merchant named Charles Crocker, the Central Pacific would build eastward from Sacramento, California.

Among the major costs Crocker (top left) had was blasting through the Sierra Nevadas (far left). Getting supplies was costly for both Crocker and Dodge (above).

BUILDING THE RAILROAD

Building the transcontinental railroad was not easy. During the Civil War supplies were often difficult to get and had become more expensive. The Central Pacific, for example, had to ship iron rails from the East Coast by sea, which was costly and took months. Because railroads did not reach Omaha, the Union Pacific's starting point, the company had to ship rails by steamboat on the Missouri River. Thus, by 1865 neither railroad company had laid more than 50 miles of track.

Workers on the Railroad

Both companies also had trouble finding workers to lay the track. Many men were still serving in the Union and Confederate armies. In addition, the Central Pacific had trouble keeping its workers from taking better paying jobs or quitting to look for gold and silver. To solve his labor problem, Crocker began hiring Chinese immigrants in

1865. By 1867 Chinese workers made up nine out of every ten workers. The Central Pacific saved money by paying the Chinese workers less than other railworkers. The Chinese also had to provide their own food and shelter, unlike the rest of the crew.

Accidents were common on most railroad building jobs, especially for the workers on the Central Pacific. Chinese and Irish workers did some of the most dangerous work. To blast roadbeds through the Sierra Nevada Mountains, they used a method developed in China. By lowering themselves down the mountains in baskets, they were able to drill holes in the the hard granite rock. They then filled the holes with gun powder. Thousands of workers died in blasting accidents and other mishaps.

Work on the Union Pacific was different from that of the Central Pacific, but it had problems as well. At first the Union Pacific hired former Civil War soldiers and free African Americans to work on the railroad. Later, Grenville Dodge hired mostly Irish and German immigrants. These workers were paid low wages for the times—about $2.50 to $4 a day. Yet, their pay was more money than the Chinese workers earned. In addition, Irish and German workers were provided food and housing.

The song on the next page was sung by Irish workers on the Union Pacific. They were often called "tarriers," possibly because they were said to have worked as hard as terrier dogs. How did the workers in the song view working on the railroad?

In 1865 this Central Pacific crew was still west of the mountains.

S12

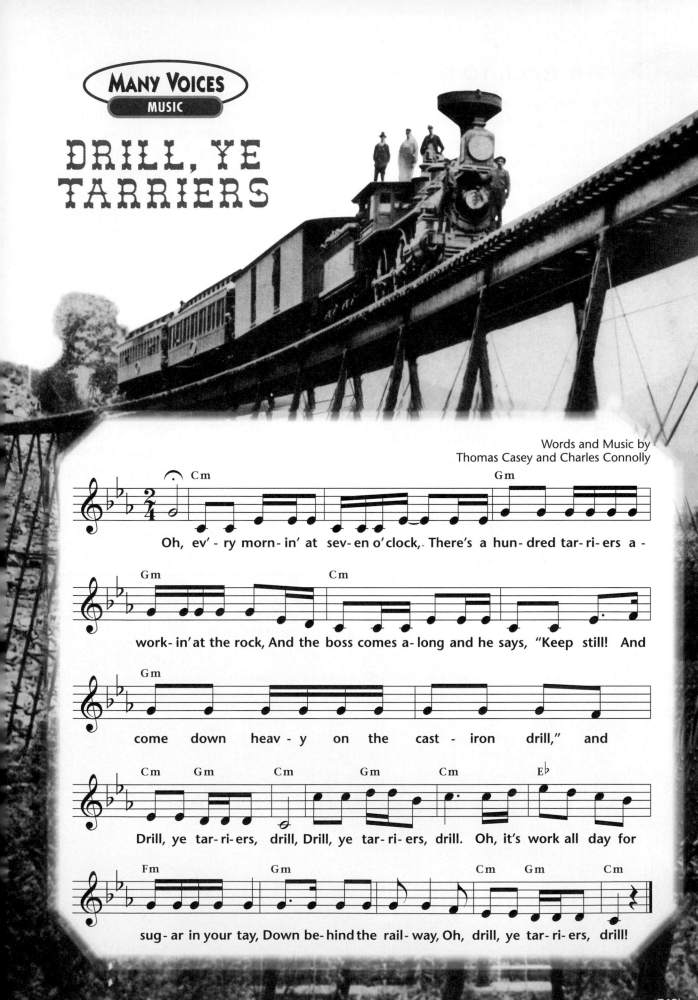

DRILL, YE TARRIERS

MANY VOICES MUSIC

Words and Music by
Thomas Casey and Charles Connolly

Oh, ev'-ry morn-in' at sev-en o'clock, There's a hun-dred tar-ri-ers a-

work-in' at the rock, And the boss comes a-long and he says, "Keep still! And

come down heav-y on the cast-iron drill," and

Drill, ye tar-ri-ers, drill, Drill, ye tar-ri-ers, drill. Oh, it's work all day for

sug-ar in your tay, Down be-hind the rail-way, Oh, drill, ye tar-ri-ers, drill!

Stanford University Museum of Art

THE RACE TO FINISH

The two railroad companies competed for the government loans, land, and bonuses. Amendments to the Pacific Railroad Act offered more money and land for every mile of completed track. The Union Pacific quickly won the lead. Dodge's crew laid track across the Great Plains. Crocker's men had to cross mountains. His workers transported supplies over the mountains ahead of the crew. Then they would not have to wait for the supply train to come to them as they laid new track.

The Ten-Mile Day

The race between the two companies heated up as the transcontinental railroad neared completion. One day Charles Crocker heard that the Union Pacific had finished six miles of track in one day. Crocker made a $10,000 bet with Thomas Durant, head of the Union Pacific, that the Central Pacific could lay ten miles of track in a day.

On April 28, 1869, only 16 miles separated the two companies. Iron rails and wooden ties were piled up along the route. In 12 hours the crew of the Central Pacific finished the 10 miles plus a few feet more. Onlookers were amazed. This feat set an all-time record for many years to come. The Ten-Mile Day came to symbolize the hard work of the thousands of men who worked on the railroad.

The Golden Spike

On May 10, 1869, the two railroads met at Promontory Point, Utah. This point is a peninsula extending into the Great Salt Lake. In six years of constant effort, the workers had laid more than 1,700 miles of track. A crowd of railroad workers, reporters, and soldiers gathered to watch the last spikes being hammered into the tracks.

With the Utah sun shining down upon him, the Central Pacific's Leland

The golden spike (above) was used in the ceremony at Promontory Point. It reads, "May God continue the unity of our Country as the Railroad united two great Oceans of the world."

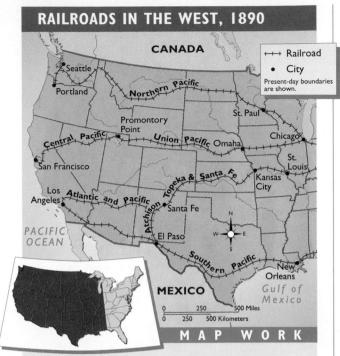

CANADA

Railroad
• City
Present-day boundaries are shown.

Seattle
Portland
Northern Pacific
St. Paul
Promontory Point
Central Pacific
Union Pacific
Omaha
Chicago
San Francisco
St. Louis
Los Angeles
Atlantic and Pacific
Atchison Topeka & Santa Fe
Kansas City
Santa Fe
PACIFIC OCEAN
El Paso
Southern Pacific
New Orleans
MEXICO
Gulf of Mexico

0   250   500 Miles
0   250   500 Kilometers

MAP WORK

Once the **transcontinental railroad** was built, more railroads began to connect cities.

1. Identify the railroads shown on the map.
2. Which cities were connected to the transcontinental railroad?

Stanford held a spike made of gold from California's mines. When the golden spike was hammered in, a simple message was telegraphed throughout the country: "Done."

Cannons roared, bells rang, and fireworks exploded to celebrate the completion of the transcontinental railroad. Crowds paraded down Chicago's streets. New York City's businesses shut down for the day. In Sacramento, 30 trains whistled the city's joy. The famous writer Bret Harte wrote a poem about the meeting of the two engines, the *Jupiter* and the *No. 119*. He wondered:

> *What was it the engines said,*
> *Pilots touching, head to head*
> *Facing on the single track,*
> *Half a world behind each back?*

WHY IT MATTERS

The transcontinental railroad helped our country to grow, but there were serious costs. Many rail workers lost their lives along the way. The Native Americans of the Plains had built their own way of life around the buffalo. The railroads ended this way of life forever.

When the transcontinental railroad was completed, people and products could travel from New York to San Francisco in a little over a week. More people began moving west and more railroads were built. How many railroads are shown on the map on this page? The newcomers made the West grow by building towns, farms, and ranches.

✓ Reviewing Facts and Ideas

MAIN IDEAS

- In 1862 the Union Pacific and Central Pacific railroads began building a transcontinental railroad to link the eastern and western United States.

- The transcontinental railroad was completed on May 10, 1869, when the Union Pacific and Central Pacific met at Promontory Point, Utah.

THINK ABOUT IT

1. What problems did the builders of the transcontinental railroad face?

2. What was the Ten-Mile Day?

3. **FOCUS** How did the transcontinental railroad help our country to grow?

4. **THINKING SKILL** *Predict* the *effects* that the transcontinental railroad would have on Native Americans.

5. **GEOGRAPHY** Use the map on this page and the Atlas map on pages R10–R11 to identify the landforms the transcontinental railroad had to cross. What role did elevation play in the building of the railroad?

STORIES ON STAGE

Do you like telling stories? Telling stories on stage through music and drama has long been a tradition in many cultures around the world.

In the United States, many immigrants have used characters and stories from their home countries to create plays for the American stage. Sometimes these works have described what growing up in the United States was like for these newcomers.

Theater today—whether written in the United States or elsewhere—continues the legacy of inspiring, educating, and entertaining all Americans.

Above is a scene from the Chinese drama *Ching-Shih Mountain*, performed in New York City.

This 1915 poster (left) advertises a play called *The Green Millionaire*, performed in New York's Yiddish theatre.

The Asian American dancer (above) is performing in a traditional Cambodian play in the United States. The lights of Broadway (left) in New York City attract people to its many plays and musicals.

1850   1860   1866   1886 1890

Life on the Range

Read Aloud

A cowboy's life is a dreary, dreary life,
Some say it's free from care;
Rounding up the cattle from morning till night
In the middle of the prairie so bare.

From 1866 to 1886, cowboys herded millions of cattle
from Texas to the railroads in Missouri and Kansas. This
period gave rise to the romantic image of cowboys
seen in films and on television. As you will see, however,
life on the range was hard and often filled with danger.

Focus Activity

READ TO LEARN

How did the cattle industry change the West?

VOCABULARY

- cattle drive
- railhead

PEOPLE

- Nat Love
- Joseph McCoy

PLACES

- Chisholm Trail
- Abilene
- Dodge City

THE BIG PICTURE

Cowboys, or cowhands, have lived and worked in what is now the United States since the Spanish brought cattle and horses to North America in the 1500s. In the colonies English people raised cattle to sell for their hides and fat, or tallow, which was used to make candles.

By the middle 1800s, Texas ranchers raised millions of longhorn cattle. This sturdy breed of cattle thrived on the open ranges of Texas. In 1866 a steer could be sold for about $5 in Texas. In the North, where cattle were scarce, a steer was worth $40. As industry grew in the North after the Civil War, so did the population. The growing population created a great demand for beef.

Texans realized that if they could get their cattle to the railroads, they could ship them east and sell them for more money. Thus began the era of the **cattle drives**. A cattle drive was a long journey taken by cowboys to herd, or drive, cattle from ranches in Texas north on trails leading to the railroads.

THE CATTLE DRIVE

The cowboys of the middle 1800s were a varied group. Most of the white cowboys had fought for the Confederacy during the Civil War. About one-quarter to one-third of all cowboys were African American or Mexican American. Although they faced prejudice, they often earned the respect of other cowboys on the drives because of their skill at handling cattle. As you have read in Chapter 10, Mexican and Native American *vaqueros* started many of the cattle ranching practices that are still used in the United States today.

Many of the African American cowboys were former slaves. Among them was Nat Love, who was once called the "champion roper of the Western cattle country." In his autobiography Love told about what he called the cowboy's code:

> There's a man's work was to be done, and a man's life to be lived, and when death was to be met, he met it like a man.

Life on the Trail

Life on the range, however, was most often one of unending work. A typical cattle drive in the 1860s began in the spring, since it was easier to travel during warm weather. The trail boss and the chuck wagon, which carried the food and supplies, led the way. Behind them was about a two-mile-long herd of 2,000 to 3,000 longhorn cattle, tended by 8 to 20 cowboys. The most dangerous part of the drive was usually controlling the cattle.

Booming thunder or lightning streaking across the sky could frighten a herd and trigger a stampede. In a stampede, the cattle scatter wildly. In their fear, stampeding cattle could trample anything in their path, including cowboys. To keep them calm, cowboys often sang to the cattle. They also sang to ease their own loneliness on the trail.

Nat Love (right) and other cowboys from about the early 1900s (left) spent long days on the dusty range.

319

THE CATTLE INDUSTRY

The millions of longhorns that headed north from Texas carved out many trails on the Great Plains. One of the most famous was the Chisholm Trail. As you can see on the map on page 521, this trail ran from San Antonio, Texas, to Abilene, Kansas.

Railheads and Cowtowns

Towns like Abilene and Dodge City, Kansas, developed along railroad lines. These towns were called railheads. The people of Kansas realized that they could make money from the cattle trade as well as from the railroads.

In 1867 a cattleowner named Joseph McCoy set up stockyards, or cattle pens, in the small town of Abilene. McCoy's stockyards were right next to the railroad tracks. Ranchers paid McCoy a fee to house their longhorns there before they were shipped east. McCoy also built a hotel for the weary cowboys off the trail. Soon stores, restaurants, and other businesses sprang up. Many cowboys were eager to relax and spend their wages after being on the trail for so long.

Soon railheads such as Abilene and Dodge City became centers of the cattle industry. Chicago also grew into a major city as a result of the cattle industry. From the railheads in the Great Plains, longhorns were shipped to meat-packing plants in Chicago. By 1870 Chicago was the world's largest supplier of fresh beef.

Although the railroads helped the cattle industry to grow, they also brought about the end of the era of cattle drives and cowboys. When railroads were built south into Texas, the long

Cattle in many cowtowns like Goldfield, Nevada (below), were herded straight down Main Street.

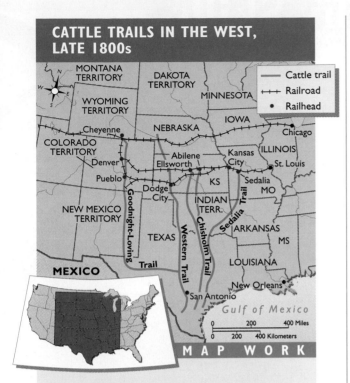

CATTLE TRAILS IN THE WEST, LATE 1800s

Cattle trail
Railroad
Railhead

MAP WORK

Cattle drives began in Texas and headed north to various **railheads**.

1. Which railhead did the Western Trail meet?

2. Which trail led to both Ellsworth and Abilene?

cattle drives became a thing of the past. Melvin Wipple, a modern-day cowboy poet, mourned the end of the old days of the cowboy:

> *Those days are gone forever*
> *Only one place they're still at*
> *Is in some old man's memories*
> *Underneath a greasy hat.*

WHY IT MATTERS

During the long, dangerous, and sometimes boring drives, the cowboys formed traditions that live on today. The old, sad songs the cowboys sang to the herd or to themselves are still heard around campfires across the country today. Many people also continue to enjoy reading stories or watching films and television shows about the "old West."

Wearing cowboy boots and hats—and roping steers—the cowboys continue to work on cattle ranches. Now, however, they ride pick-up trucks, helicopters, and small airplanes as well as horses. Many use computers to help them keep track of how many cattle they have. These modern cowboys help make the cattle industry an important part of the United States economy. In 1997 alone, ranchers sold more than $36 billion worth of cattle.

✓ Reviewing Facts and Ideas

MAIN IDEAS

- Cattle ranching in what is now the United States dates back to the 1500s. After the Civil War ranchers made large profits by selling their cattle in the North.

- On their long cattle drives cowboys worked hard and they faced many dangers.

- Towns called railheads sprang up in the Middle West to serve the ranchers of the cattle industry.

- The era of cattle drives came to an end as railroads were built in Texas.

THINK ABOUT IT

1. When did the cattle industry in the United States begin to make big profits? Why?

2. What were some of the dangers cowboys faced on the cattle drives?

3. **FOCUS** How did the cattle drives and the cattle industry change the country?

4. **THINKING SKILL** What were the _effects_ of the railroad on the cattle industry during the late 1800s?

5. **GEOGRAPHY** Using the map on this page, make a list of the important cattle trails and the railheads where the trails ended.

Geography Skills

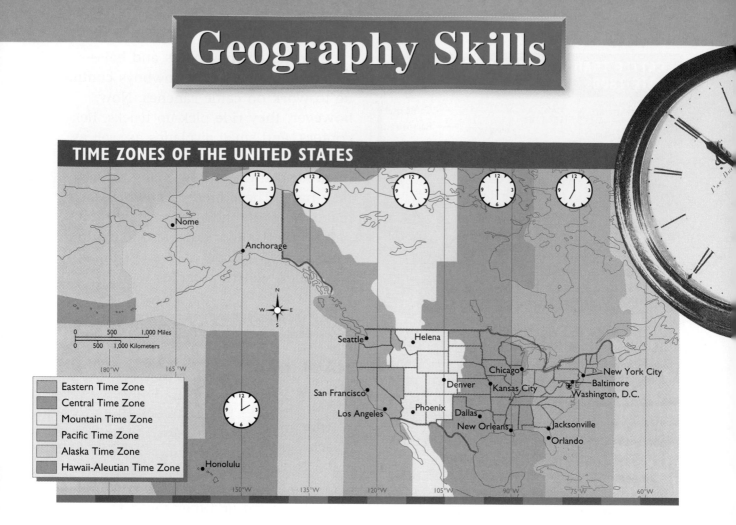

TIME ZONES OF THE UNITED STATES

Eastern Time Zone
Central Time Zone
Mountain Time Zone
Pacific Time Zone
Alaska Time Zone
Hawaii-Aleutian Time Zone

Reading Time Zone Maps

VOCABULARY

time zone

WHY THE SKILL MATTERS

By 1880 over 93,000 miles of railroads crisscrossed the United States. Cattle, wheat, and other farm products filled the railroad cars heading east. Since it became much easier to cross the country, passengers also crowded onto the trains.

The increase in long-distance travel caused a problem. Every town and city across the country set its own time by the location of the sun in the sky. When the sun was directly overhead in Chicago, it was noon. When it was noon in Chicago, the sun had already passed this high point farther east in New York. A person traveling by train from New York to Chicago might be confused about what the time was in each town along the way.

USING THE SKILL

In the late 1800s the fact that every town had a different time troubled the people who set the train schedules. Travelers had to ask, "Is the train going to arrive at 6:00 P.M. our time or their time?" To solve this problem, time zones were set up in 1884. The world was divided into 24 different time zones—one for each hour in a day. Starting from the prime meridian at Greenwich, England, the time zones were laid out at every 15 degrees of longitude. Every town and city in a single time zone would use the same time.

As you can see from the map key on this page, the United States has six time zones. The map shows that the borders of the time zones no longer follow exactly the longitude lines. Today's time zone borders take into account national and state borders.

The time zone map can help you figure out what time it is in different parts of the United States. The time in any zone *east* of you is always *later* than it is in your zone. The time in any zone *west* of you is always *earlier* than it is in your zone. As you move to the east, add one hour to your watch for each time zone that you cross. As you move west, subtract one hour for each time zone that you cross.

Suppose that you are on a cattle drive heading to Abilene, Kansas. You reach Abilene at noon. From Abilene, you can board a train headed to San Francisco, California, or to New York, New York. Before you go, you want to set your watch for the correct time for each city.

To figure out what time it is in New York, count the number of time zones east of Kansas through New York. Because Kansas and New York are one time zone apart, add one hour to 12:00 P.M. Thus, when it is noon in Abilene, it is 1:00 P.M. in New York City.

To figure out what time it is in San Francisco, count the number of time zones west of Abilene through San Francisco. Abilene and San Francisco are two time zones apart. You must subtract two hours from 12:00 P.M. Thus, it will be 10:00 A.M. in San Francisco when it is noon in Abilene.

TRYING THE SKILL

Using the time zone map, find out which time zone Denver, Colorado, is in. Then, using the Helping Yourself box on this page,

Helping yourself

- **A time zone is one of 24 divisions of Earth used to measure standard time.**
- **Find your starting point on the map.**
- **Add an hour for each time zone east of you. Subtract an hour for each time zone west of you.**

figure out the following time zone problems.

What time zone is to the west of Denver? What time zone is to the east? If the President planned to broadcast a live speech from Denver at 5:00 P.M., what time would the broadcast air in Seattle, Washington? How did you calculate the broadcast times?

Suppose that your family is planning a trip from Denver to Orlando, Florida. You plan to call the visitor center in Orlando to find out what kinds of fun things there are to do. The visitor center is open from 9:00 A.M. to 5:00 P.M. You get home from school at 4:00 P.M. Will you be able to call the office before it closes? Why or why not?

Suppose your mother wants to visit a family member in Los Angeles. She leaves Denver on a 6:00 P.M. flight, which takes three hours. At what time will she arrive in Los Angeles? How did you calculate your answer?

REVIEWING THE SKILL

1. What is a time zone?

2. What time zone do you live in?

3. When people in Washington, D.C., are getting up at 7:00 A.M., what time is it in Kansas City? In Anchorage, Alaska? How do you know?

4. Between which two cities could you take a one-hour plane trip and arrive at the same time you left: New Orleans to Dallas or Kansas City to Denver?

5. Why might knowing how to read time zone maps be an important skill to have when planning a trip by airplane?

University of Oklahoma

1850   1862   1879   1890

Homesteading on the Plains

Read Aloud

"Large Discounts for Cash! Better Terms Than Ever!"
promised the advertisement. The ad pictured farmers
plowing lush fields in Nebraska's Big Blue Valley. Such
offers of cheap, fertile land drew a wave of new set-
tlers to the Great Plains after the Civil War.

Focus Activity

READ TO LEARN

Who came to the Great
Plains after the Civil War?

VOCABULARY

- Homestead Act
- homesteader
- sodbuster
- exoduster

PEOPLE

- James Oliver
- Emma Brown
- Joseph Glidden
- Henry Adams
- George Washington

PLACES

- South Bend
- Nicodemus

THE BIG PICTURE

By the end of the Civil War, both coasts of the United
States were populated with cities and farms. Few newcomers, however, had moved to the land between the
Missouri River and the Rocky Mountains. This land,
called the Great Plains, had long been the home and
hunting grounds of Native Americans. People in the East
thought of the Great Plains as the "Great American
Desert." It was not a desert, although as you have read
in Chapter 2, the Great Plains, or simply, the "Plains,"
are on the dry side of the line separating Humid America
and Arid America.

The completion of the transcontinental railroad
opened new possibilities. The same railroads that
shipped cattle back East could also carry farmers'
goods to markets in the East. The United States government and railroad companies offered vast acres of
these lands for sale at low prices.

Many people in the East took advantage of the offer.
African Americans who came from the South hoped to
find good farmland and build new lives as free people.
Immigrants from France, Denmark, Norway, Sweden,
and Russia sought opportunity too. From about 1862
the United States government sold or gave away almost
300 million acres of land to new settlers on the Plains.

HOMESTEADERS

Few Americans believed that they could farm the dry, treeless Great Plains. It would take help from the government for farmers to risk moving there. During the Civil War President Lincoln signed the Homestead Act. This act gave 160 acres (one-quarter of a square mile) of public land to adult men 21 years of age, widows, or heads of a family. All the new settlers had to do was pay a small fee, farm the land, and live on it for five years. The people who claimed land under this act were called homesteaders.

Hopes and Hard Work

Government leaders believed that the Homestead Act would encourage more farmers to move to the Great Plains. They also hoped that the United States economy would grow as the railroads began shipping farm crops to the East and bringing eastern products to the farms of the West.

Homesteaders got a chance to own farmland in the land rush of the 1800s (top). The receipt (above) shows this claim cost $12.

Many homesteaders eagerly sought the free land. They hoped to set up farms and build better lives for themselves and their families. Most of the homesteaders claimed land in Kansas, Nebraska, and the Dakota Territory. By 1895 more than 430,000 new settlers had claimed homesteads. The lack of trees and water and the harsh climate made farming difficult on the Plains. Yet through hard work and with the help of new technology, many homesteaders succeeded in building farms.

SODBUSTERS

In bouncing stagecoaches, chugging railroads, and crowded Conestoga wagons, the homesteaders set out for the prairie. When they arrived, the flat, windy land seemed strange and lonely. It was "just sky and grass and grass and sky," wrote Kansas homesteader Lydia Toothaker.

Sod Houses

The vast acres of tall buffalo grass were both a blessing and a curse to the new settlers. The thickly tangled roots of the grass filled the top 3 inches of the soil. This "sod" was so matted and tough that it broke most iron plows. Because they had to "bust" through the thick sod to plant their crops the new settlers became known as sodbusters.

To turn the sod into farmland, many homesteaders used a new type of steel plow made by James Oliver in South Bend, Indiana. In 1877 Oliver invented a plow that was able to slice cleanly through the sod without getting stuck.

The sodbusters discovered a way to put the tough prairie sod to use. Without trees or stone to build homes, the settlers had to use prairie sod as a building material. They cut thick brick-shaped slabs of sod to make the walls and roofs of their homes. Houses made from sod were called "soddies." The soddies were often dark, uncomfortable, and also contained insects.

This plow by James Oliver is exhibited in a museum in Floyd County, Indiana.

Emma Brown was a Kansas homesteader who lived in a sod house. Read this excerpt from one of her letters. Why might she and other homesteaders have wanted to build wooden houses as soon as they could?

MANY VOICES
PRIMARY SOURCE

Excerpt from the letters of Emma Brown, 1870.

The roof of the new house was of Kansas dirt, and when the rains came proved unsatisfactory indeed. We moved into this house about the first of August, 1870, and I felt as happy as a Queen. But a rainy time set in and continued. ... It was two weeks I was left alone with the children. And the roof leaked!

Finally, when nearly everything in the house was soaked and the fuel gone I went to a neighbor's and found **haven** in their **dugout**. But before morning there was six inches of water in it, so we had to make another move. The next shelter was under some boards stood up against a stone wall, [and we remained] there a day and a night.

___

haven: shelter
dugout: underground house

Life on the Plains

Homesteaders faced many hardships. Among them were prairie fires and unpredictable weather. The dry prairie grass could easily catch fire. Such a fire could destroy everything in its path. The

The soddie belonging to this Nebraska homesteading family allowed them to park their wagon on the roof.

new settlers learned to dig trenches around their homes and fields to slow the spread of the fires.

Weather on the plains was also hard to bear. In winter blizzards began so suddenly that a person could get lost between the house and barn and freeze to death. A Dakota schoolboy described an oncoming blizzard in 1888:

Suddenly we looked up and saw something coming rolling toward us with great fury from the northwest, and making a loud noise. It looked like a long string of big bales of cotton, each one bound tightly with heavy cords of silver.

Grasshoppers and locusts were a hazard of the summer months. In 1874, called the "Great Grasshopper Year," millions of grasshoppers swarmed over the Great Plains. In some places the hungry insects were piled on top of each other 6 inches deep. They could eat 100 acres of corn in a few hours. Many new settlers had to abandon their farms that year.

Farming the Plains

For every homesteader who left the Plains, there were more people who stayed and learned to adapt to the hardships. Technology made life a little easier. Windmills made it possible to get water from deep underground. The windmills, powered by the constant prairie winds, pumped underground water to the surface. Farmers then dug irrigation ditches to water crops.

In 1874 a new kind of wheat was introduced by Russian settlers. It was hardy enough to survive on the Plains.

Without wood, farmers could not build fences to keep cattle out of their fields. Then in 1874 Joseph Glidden invented barbed wire. First, he twisted two wires together. Then he wrapped sharp barbs around the wire. By 1880 he had sold 80 million pounds of wire.

EXODUSTERS

Among the many homesteaders who settled on the Great Plains were thousands of African Americans. They came hoping to find freedom from violence and unfair treatment. The most famous town they settled was Nicodemus, Kansas. It was founded by African Americans from Kentucky. At first many worked as farm hands to earn the money to pay the fee for a homestead. They faced tough years when their supplies ran low and rancher's cattle trampled their crops. Still, Nicodemus thrived.

Leaving the South

In the 1870s Henry Adams, a former Civil War soldier, made speeches encouraging his fellow African Americans to leave the South. "We lost all hopes," reported Adams. "The whole South—every state in the South—had got into the hands of the very men who held us as slaves."

In 1879, thousands of African Americans lined the banks of the Mississippi River, waiting to sail north. They were bound for Kansas in what came to be called the Kansas Fever Exodus. *Exodus* means "a journey to freedom," which describes the exodus led by Moses. According to the Bible, Moses helped the Israelites escape slavery in Egypt to reach the Promised Land.

Many freed slaves believed that Kansas could be the kind of Promised Land that the Israelites had sought. During 1879 alone, 20,000 African Americans from the South went to Kansas. So many left that they were called exodusters.

Many exodusters sang hopeful songs along their journey to Kansas. In the song, "The Land That Gives Birth to Our Freedom," the exodusters sang of what they hoped to find in Kansas:

> We want peaceful homes and quiet
>   firesides;
> No one to disturb us or turn us out.
>
> Marching along, yes we are
>   marching along,
> To Kansas City we are bound.

The Granger Collection

All Colored People
THAT WANT TO
GO TO KANSAS,
On September 5th, 1877,
Can do so for $5.00

These exodusters (below) stopped to rest in Topeka, Kansas, in 1880.

University of Kansas

570

The Granger Collection

Family farms are still a part of the economy and culture of the Great Plains.

The Kansas Fever Exodus did not last for long. Some white Southerners jailed or refused to let black passengers onto boats leaving the South. However, the exodusters left a legacy of successful farming communities in Kansas.

African Americans continued their search for freedom in other places in the West—in California, Oregon, and Washington. A homesteader named George Washington founded the town of Centralia, Washington, in 1875.

WHY IT MATTERS

Despite the hardships of rough winters, droughts, and swarms of insects, the sodbusters and exodusters turned the Great Plains into "America's breadbasket." In 1860 the United States exported 2 million bushels of wheat. In 1890 over 90 million bushels were exported. If you visit the Great Plains today, you will find miles and miles of wheat fields along with fields of corn and other grains. Towns and farmhouses stand shaded by tall trees—many planted by the sodbusters and exodusters over 100 years ago.

Reviewing Facts and Ideas

MAIN IDEAS

- Americans from the East and the South as well as people from Europe moved to the Great Plains to find land and to make better lives for themselves. Many of these people became known as the homesteaders and the exodusters.

- The Homestead Act of 1862 gave free land to people willing to live on and farm the land for five years.

THINK ABOUT IT

1. What was the Homestead Act signed by President Lincoln?

2. Where did the nicknames "sodbuster" and "exoduster" come from?

3. **FOCUS** How did people who settled on the Great Plains after the Civil War survive in their new homes?

4. **THINKING SKILL** *Compare* the reasons that both white and black homesteaders left their homes to settle on the Great Plains.

5. **WRITE** Write a letter as a sodbuster or exoduster to a friend back home. In one paragraph describe the best thing about life on the Great Plains. In another paragraph describe the hardest part of life there.

1850　1860　1870　1874　1881　1890

The Plains Wars

Read Aloud

"As long as I live I will fight you for the last hunting grounds of my people!" said Red Cloud. The Lakota leader knew that the soldiers wanted to build a road through Lakota lands for new settlers and gold seekers. He was tired of what he saw as the government's broken promises. Red Cloud and other Native American leaders were ready to go to war with the army of the United States.

Focus Activity

READ TO LEARN

What events led to the Plains Wars?

VOCABULARY

- property rights
- reservation

PEOPLE

- Crazy Horse
- George Custer
- Sitting Bull
- Chief Joseph
- Helen Hunt Jackson

PLACES

- Black Hills
- Little Bighorn River
- Wallowa River

THE BIG PICTURE

Beginning in the 1860s, the Native Americans on the Great Plains had seen railroads steam through their lands. Millions of longhorn cattle were roaming the prairie. Homesteaders had carved out farms on lands that had once been their hunting grounds.

These events had a great effect on Native Americans. The railroads brought in hunters who shot buffalo by the hundreds. Longhorns ate the prairie grasses that the buffalo needed. Homesteaders plowed under the prairie and fenced off the land. As a result, by 1890 the number of buffalo, which had ranged from more than 15 million to 50 million, shrank to less than 1,000.

With the buffalo dying off, Native Americans lost their main source of food, shelter, and clothing. Yet Native Americans fought back, hoping to keep their lands and their way of life.

NATIVE AMERICAN LANDS

The West offered new settlers a chance to own land and to improve their fortunes. The Homestead Act gave settlers property rights to the land they settled. Property rights are the rights to own or use something—such as land—for gain, profit, or sale. Native Americans who lived on the Plains viewed the land differently. They did not own land in their own names. Instead land was used by all their people. Most Native Americans did not believe that anyone could sell land. "One does not sell the earth upon which the people walk," explained Crazy Horse, a Lakota chief. Still, Native American groups did fight each other over hunting grounds.

Life on the Reservation

Since the early 1800s the government made treaties with the Native Americans of the Plains. In these treaties the government promised not to take over the Native Americans' lands. Yet sometimes the government gave these lands to homesteaders, breaking its promises to the Native Americans.

The government decided to resettle Native Americans on reservations. A reservation is a territory reserved, or set aside, for Native Americans. United States government leaders hoped that the Native Americans would give up hunting buffalo and settle down to become farmers. The government would then be able to make room for more new settlers on the Plains.

Most Native Americans of the Plains did not want to live on a reservation. Riding their swift horses, they were used to tracking buffalo over hundreds of miles of prairie. They had learned to survive the long winters and harsh summers on the Plains by moving their camps. A Comanche (kuh MAN chee) leader named Ten Bears explained why he and many other Native Americans did not want to settle on reservations:

I was born upon the prairie where the wind blew free and there was nothing to break the light of the sun. I was born where there were no enclosures [fences or walls] and where everything drew a free breath. I want to die there and not within walls.

Sitting Bull's granddaughter, Nancy, far left, attended a Native American school (left) in North Dakota in 1914. At this time most Native Americans lived on reservations (above).

Riding with the cavalry (left) was part of the rugged life officers such as George Custer (below) endured.

WARS IN THE WEST

The Native Americans of the Plains had clashed with settlers and soldiers many times during the middle 1800s. This period of conflict is often called the Plains Wars. The Native Americans usually lost these battles. Although the Native Americans of the Plains were skilled warriors known for their excellent horsemanship, they were no match for either the weapons or the growing numbers of new settlers that they faced. In 1850 the white population of the West was less than 200,000. By 1870, the number had grown to nearly 1,400,000.

The Battle of the Little Bighorn

In 1874, on the northern Plains, groups of Lakota, Cheyenne, and Arapaho united to fight. They hoped to protect their territory around the Black Hills in what are today the states of South Dakota and Wyoming. In the Treaty of 1868, the government had agreed that this territory belonged to the Lakota. The treaty promised them the land "so long as the grass grows."

The peace was shattered in 1874. In that year Colonel George Custer led a group of miners, journalists, and photographers into the Black Hills. They found gold near a town that is now called Custer, South Dakota. Word of the gold strike spread throughout the East. Before long, 15,000 miners rushed to Lakota lands to find gold.

The government offered to buy the Black Hills for $6 million. The Lakota refused. The government then ordered the Lakota to leave their land and to settle on reservations. Led by two Lakota chiefs, Sitting Bull and Crazy Horse, many Lakota set up camps on the Little Bighorn River. The neighboring Cheyenne and Arapaho joined them. Together, they had more than 2,000 fighters.

Colonel Custer and 600 of the Seventh Cavalry soldiers camped nearby. Cavalry are soldiers who fight on horseback. Custer did not know that his men were outnumbered. He decided to split them into three forces. Early on June 25, 1876, Custer led one-third against the Native American's camp from the northeast. Major Marcus A. Reno led the second group to attack the camp from the west side of the river, and Captain Fred Benteen led the last third to attack from the south.

Reno's men reached the camp, but almost 1,000 guns quickly defeated the small force. Benteen was unable to reach Custer when his men were attacked from all sides. Colonel Custer died, along with more than 200 soldiers.

The Battle of the Little Bighorn, also known as "Custer's last stand," was to be the last major Native American victory on the Plains. The United States sent even more soldiers to defeat the Native Americans. After years of losing battles, the last Native Americans of the Plains were moved to reservations beside the Missouri River in 1877.

The Nez Percé Leave Their Home

At about the same time that the Lakota, Cheyenne, and Arapaho were defeated, the Nez Percé (nez PURS) were fighting to keep their lands along the Wallowa River in Oregon.

In 1876, to make room for new settlers and miners, the government demanded that the Nez Percé move to a reservation in the Idaho Territory. Chief Joseph of the Nez Percé refused. Fighting between white settlers and young Nez Percé men soon led to war. The chiefs knew that they would soon be forced to leave. In late June 1877 they decided to flee to Canada.

With about 700 men, women, and children, the Nez Percé began a 1,200-mile march. The Nez Percé were only 40 miles from the Canadian border when a large force of soldiers caught up with them. Chief Joseph surrendered on October 5, 1877. In the following speech, Chief Joseph explained why he gave up fighting. What concerns did Chief Joseph have for his people?

MANY VOICES
PRIMARY SOURCE

Excerpt from
Chief Joseph's Speech
as reported
by Lieutenant C.E.S. Wood, 1877.

*Tell General Howard I know his heart. What he told me before I have in my heart. I am tired of fighting. Our chiefs are killed . . . . Looking Glass is dead. **Tu-hul-hil-sote** is dead. The old men are all dead. He who led the young men, Alikut [Joseph's brother], is dead. It is cold and we have no blankets. The little children are freezing to death. My people, some of them, have run away to the hills, and have no blankets, no food; no one knows where they are—perhaps freezing to death. I want to have time to look for my children and see how many of them I can find. Maybe I shall find them among the dead. Hear me, my chiefs. I am tired; my heart is sick and sad. From where the sun now stands I will fight no more forever.*

Tu-hul-hil-sote: a wise elder

Chief Joseph (above left) and his people came very close to escaping the United States cavalry.

A CENTURY OF CHANGE

The Nez Percé were taken to a fort in Kansas after their surrender. Far from their homeland and without their freedom, many died. The Lakota and many other Native Americans faced similar losses. As you can see from the map on this page, today few lands still belong to the Native Americans.

Defending the Native Americans

Many Americans, including religious leaders and writers, criticized the way the United States had treated the Native Americans. A writer from Massachusetts, Helen Hunt Jackson, described in her book *A Century of Dishonor* the feelings of regret shared by many. In 1881 she wrote:

My object . . . has been to simply show our causes for national shame in the matter of our treatment of the Indians . . . for the American people, as a people, are not at heart unjust.

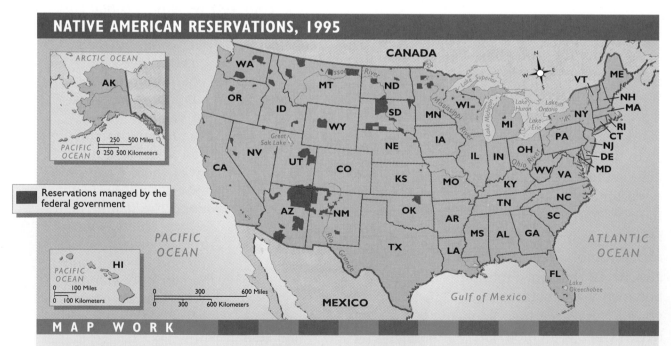

NATIVE AMERICAN RESERVATIONS, 1995

Reservations managed by the federal government

MAP WORK

The Navajo of northeastern Arizona live on the largest reservation in the United States.

1. Which other states have reservations similar in size to those in Arizona?

2. Which states in the Southeast have reservations?

3. Why do you think most reservations are located in the western United States?

Helen Hunt Jackson (far left) helped change people's views about Native Americans. Today Lakota children on reservations (left) learn new skills. Native Americans still enjoy traditions such as the pow wow (below).

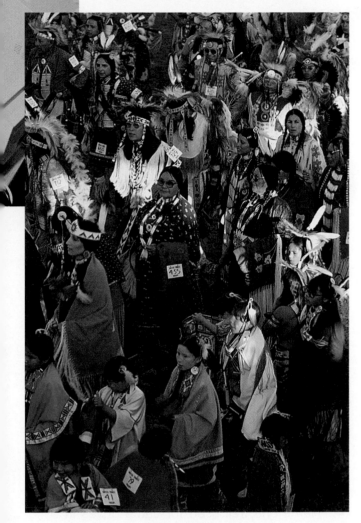

Because of the strong reaction to her book, the government later asked Jackson to report on the treatment of the Native Americans in California.

WHY IT MATTERS

The Plains Wars of the middle and late 1800s marked a low point for Native Americans. Yet through decades of battles and life on reservations, Native Americans have endured. In the 1900s Native Americans began bringing to court cases asking the United States government to honor its earlier treaties.

Native Americans have won greater rights to govern themselves on their reservations and to control their own resources. Some peoples have also won back lands that the government had taken away.

✓ Reviewing Facts and Ideas

MAIN IDEAS

- Many changes on the Plains, including the railroads, cattle drives, and new settlers, caused the buffalo to begin dying out in the middle 1800s.

- In the middle 1800s the United States government began forcing Native Americans of the Plains onto reservations. The government then allowed new settlers to move onto their lands.

- Native Americans led by Sitting Bull and Crazy Horse defeated Colonel George Custer at the Battle of the Little Bighorn in 1876. The following year, the Nez Percé were defeated.

- The treatment of Native Americans in the United States was brought to the country's attention by such people as writers and religious leaders in the late 1800s.

THINK ABOUT IT

1. How did newcomers to the West change the way of life of the Native Americans on the Plains?

2. What was the Native American view of property rights?

3. **FOCUS** What factors led to the Plains Wars of the middle and late 1800s?

4. **THINKING SKILL** *Predict* how things might be different on the Great Plains if there were no railroads.

5. **GEOGRAPHY** Using the map on page 534, identify the regions of the United States with the greatest number of reservations.

CHAPTER 18 REVIEW

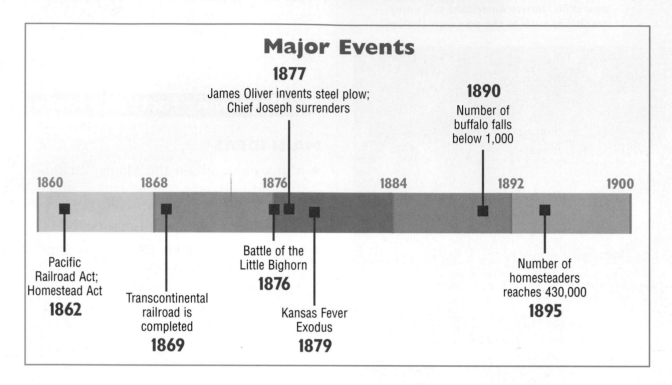

Major Events

1877
James Oliver invents steel plow;
Chief Joseph surrenders

1890
Number of
buffalo falls
below 1,000

1860   1868   1876   1884   1892   1900

Pacific
Railroad Act;
Homestead Act
1862

Transcontinental
railroad is
completed
1869

Battle of the
Little Bighorn
1876

Kansas Fever
Exodus
1879

Number of
homesteaders
reaches 430,000
1895

THINKING ABOUT VOCABULARY

Number a paper from 1 to 5. Beside each number, write the word or term from the list below that completes the sentence.

cattle drive   reservation
homesteaders   sodbusters
railheads

1. People who claimed land under an act of Congress passed in 1862 were called _____.

2. Abilene, Dodge City, and other towns that sprang up along new railroad lines were called _____.

3. A _____ is a territory set aside for Native Americans by the United States government.

4. Homesteaders on the Great Plains also became known as _____, because they had to work hard to make the thick soil suitable for planting their crops.

5. During a _____, cowboys journeyed from ranches in Texas to the railroads.

THINKING ABOUT FACTS

1. List some of the benefits of the transcontinental railroad.

2. Who worked on the transcontinental railroad? What was the work like?

3. In what ways were cowboys in the middle 1800s a diverse group?

4. Name one trail used for cattle drives in the 1800s and describe its route.

5. How did the growth of the railroads change the cowboys' way of life?

6. Name three present-day states in which homesteaders settled after 1862.

7. What hardships did the homesteaders face? How did they meet some of these challenges?

8. How did railroads affect Native Americans of the Great Plains?

9. In what ways did Native Americans resist the end of their way of life? What was the result of their efforts?

10. Look at the time line above. How are the last two events on the line related?

THINK AND WRITE

WRITING A NEWS STORY

Suppose that you are a newspaper reporter. Write a news story about the completion of the transcontinental railroad. Include details about the railroad and the celebrations.

WRITING A POEM

Write a verse of a poem or song that describes an event or issue that you read about in the chapter. Possible subjects for your poem might include what it was like to work on the railroad or the loneliness of life on the range.

WRITING A BROCHURE

Suppose you have been hired to convince African Americans in the South to move to the Great Plains in the 1870s. Write a brochure that describes the benefits of beginning a new life in the West.

APPLYING GEOGRAPHY SKILLS

READING TIME ZONE MAPS

1. What difficulties existed before the introduction of time zones?

2. How many time zones are there across the United States including Alaska and Hawaii?

3. Is the time in a zone *east* of you later or earlier than the time in your zone?

4. If you are in Los Angeles and need to telephone someone in Chicago at 6:00 P.M., at what time in your zone do you need to make the call?

5. Why is it useful to be able to read a time zone map?

Summing Up the Chapter

Copy the main idea pyramid on a separate piece of paper. Review the chapter to complete the blank sections. After you have finished, use the pyramid to answer the question, "How did the environment of the Great Plains change in the 1800s?"

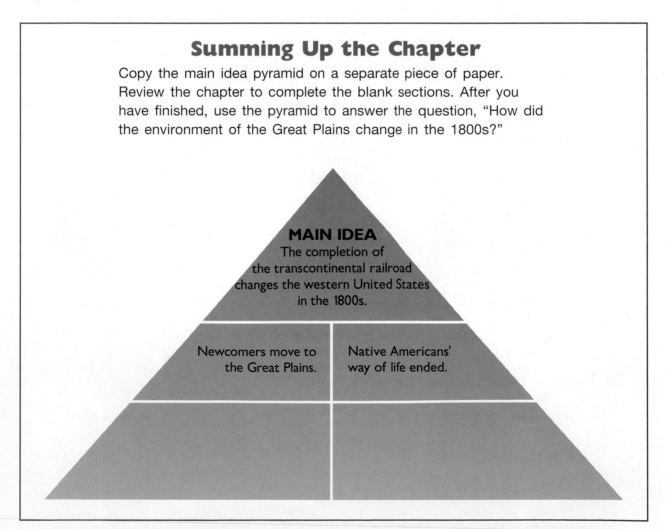

MAIN IDEA
The completion of the transcontinental railroad changes the western United States in the 1800s.

Newcomers move to the Great Plains.

Native Americans' way of life ended.

Industry Changes the Country

THINKING ABOUT HISTORY AND GEOGRAPHY

During the late 1800s and early 1900s, new industries developed more quickly than at any other time in the history of the United States. Read the time line below. During this period, many immigrants also came to the United States in search of freedom and opportunity. They settled in cities in the Middle West and the East. And in such places as Cuba, the United States began participating in world events.

PACIFIC OCEAN

1890s

1873

1889

ELLIS ISLAND, NEW YORK HARBOR
Millions of European immigrants begin entering the United States

PITTSBURGH, PENNSYLVANIA
Andrew Carnegie helps build a new steel mill

CHICAGO, ILLINOIS
Jane Addams opens Hull House to help immigrants

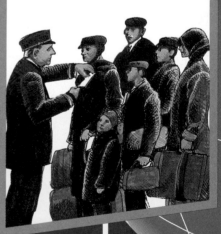

1870   1880   1890

Chicago

Pittsburgh

Ellis Island

Kitty Hawk

UNITED
STATES

ATLANTIC
OCEAN

1898

SAN JUAN HILL, CUBA
Theodore Roosevelt leads
United States troops in
the Spanish-American War

1903

KITTY HAWK,
NORTH CAROLINA
The Wright brothers make
the first engine-powered
airplane flight

San Juan
Hill

1900

1910

1850   1870   1930
1878   1911

The Rise of Big Business

Focus Activity

READ TO LEARN

How did the way people worked change in the late 1800s?

VOCABULARY

- monopoly
- corporation
- shareholder
- sweatshop
- labor union
- strike

PEOPLE

- Thomas Alva Edison
- Alexander Graham Bell
- Lewis Latimer
- Elijah McCoy
- Andrew Carnegie
- John D. Rockefeller
- Mary Harris Jones
- Samuel Gompers

PLACES

- Menlo Park
- Pittsburgh

Read Aloud

One of our country's greatest inventors once said, "There is no substitute for hard work." Thomas Alva Edison was speaking about himself, but he was also describing the achievements of the inventors you will read about in this lesson. Because of their toil and dedication, many amazing inventions were about to change forever the way Americans lived and worked.

THE BIG PICTURE

You have read about how the Industrial Revolution and the transcontinental railroad helped our country to grow. New inventions continued to appear throughout the 1800s. The sewing machine, invented by Elias Howe of Massachusetts in the 1850s, is one example. Between 1891 and 1895, over 108,420 new inventions were created in the United States. The United States soon became known as the "invention capital of the world."

The new technologies of the late 1800s made many people's lives easier. New inventions created great wealth for some people. These inventions also created major changes in the way work was done in the United States. For example, they led to the development of new businesses and new jobs. In this lesson you will read about some of the most important inventions of this time period and the changes they helped bring about.

INVENTIONS CHANGE THE WORLD

Two inventors were especially responsible for helping to move our country into the modern age. They were Thomas Alva Edison and Alexander Graham Bell.

Thomas Alva Edison

The young Thomas Alva Edison was fascinated by how things worked. By the time he was 11 years old, he had built his own telegraph set. A year later he became partly deaf. As an adult Edison once claimed that this helped him pay better attention to his work.

At his workshop in Menlo Park, New Jersey, he produced over 1,000 inventions, including motion pictures and the phonograph. The Menlo Park workshop was one of the world's first research laboratories.

In 1878 Edison began working on the problem of how to change electric current into light. "The electric light has caused me the greatest amount of study," he wrote. For two years Edison searched for the right material to use for the wire in his light bulb. Finally, he settled on a cotton thread. Later, Lewis Latimer found a way to make this wire, or filament, out of carbon, which lasted longer. By 1900 many cities in the United States were using electric lights.

Alexander Graham Bell

The man chiefly responsible for inventing the first telephone was Alexander Graham Bell, a teacher of the deaf. In order to help his students, Bell set out to invent a machine that could transmit the human voice. The plans were drawn by Lewis Latimer.

On the morning of March 10, 1876, Bell set up one part of his machine in one room and the other part in a room far away. The two parts were connected by wires. While tinkering with his part of the machine, Bell called to his assistant in the other room, "Mr. Watson—Come here—I want to see you." Having spoken softly, he had not expected to be heard. To his amazement Watson appeared. Watson had heard Bell through the machine. By 1900 over 1.5 million telephones were in use.

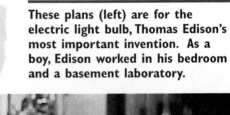

These plans (left) are for the electric light bulb, Thomas Edison's most important invention. As a boy, Edison worked in his bedroom and a basement laboratory.

The Granger Collection

Statens Museum, Copenhagen

INDUSTRIAL GIANTS

In 1872 Elijah McCoy invented an "oil cup" that allowed locomotives and other machines to oil their parts while they were running. McCoy's product was so good that people insisted on buying only the "real McCoy."

McCoy organized McCoy Manufacturing Company to make and distribute his product. Edison's invention led to the formation of the General Electric Company, and Bell's to the Bell Telephone Company. Companies such as these that made use of new technologies would make the United States an industrial giant by the end of the 1800s.

The Steel Industry

One of the largest and most important new industries in the late 1800s was steel making. Although people had known how to make steel for centuries, producing it was costly. As a result, iron was used to make most machines

Andrew Carnegie (right) built steel mills like the one in this painting (above). These mills provided work for many immigrants.

in the United States, even though steel was stronger.

Then in the 1850s a method of making steel more cheaply was discovered. A young businessman named Andrew Carnegie saw how important this new money-saving method could be. In 1873 he built a steel mill near Pittsburgh, Pennsylvania, to put this new technology to work.

In 1870, before the introduction of the new steel-making process, the United States produced 68,000 tons of steel a year. By 1900 it produced more than 10 million tons a year. Much of that steel was produced by the Carnegie Steel Company.

By 1900 Carnegie, who had come to the United States as a poor immigrant from Scotland, was one of the richest men in the world. Carnegie never forgot what it was like to be poor. After retiring in 1901 Carnegie spent the rest of his life using his money to build universities, hospitals, libraries, parks, museums, and concert halls throughout the United States. These were places most poor people could not otherwise afford to visit. Indeed, Carnegie is often remembered for having said, "The man who dies rich dies disgraced."

The Oil Industry

Like Carnegie, John D. Rockefeller had come from a poor family. In the 1860s Americans were beginning to drill for petroleum (pih TROH lee um), a fossil fuel found in the earth. Rockefeller learned that a way had been found to make kerosene (KER uh seen), a type of fuel oil, from petroleum. He believed that because kerosene was cheap to produce, it would soon replace animal fat as a source of fuel. So in 1865 Rockefeller went into the oil-refining business.

Because competition was fierce, Rockefeller set out to make his refineries the most productive in the industry. By 1879 his company, Standard Oil, controlled about nine-tenths of the oil business in the United States. It had become a monopoly, or a company that controls an entire industry. A monopoly can charge higher prices for its goods or services because there is little or no competition. Customers must choose whether to buy these goods at such prices or to do without them.

The Rise of Corporations

At this time, many businesses became corporations. A corporation is a large business that is owned by people who invest their money in that company. Investors are called shareholders because they own a share of the company. Some corporations, such as Standard Oil, became large and powerful.

The development of new technology and the rise of large corporations changed the lives of workers. Some workers continued to work in small businesses. Others worked in sweatshops. These small factories are often unsafe buildings with unhealthy working conditions. However, by the late 1800s, more people worked in large factories or mines run by corporations.

DID YOU KNOW?

What other "big businesses" began in the late 1800s?

Many of the big businesses of today began in the late 1800s. In 1888 the Box Camera, the first Kodak, was introduced by George Eastman. Customers mailed the unopened camera to the manufacturer after they had taken 100 photographs. There, the film was taken out and developed.

The first version of the modern typewriter was manufactured by E. Remington and Sons in 1874. Because this model did not allow the user to see what was being typed, it did not sell very well. By 1880, however, the inventors had corrected this problem.

Many products still used by children were invented in this era. These include animal crackers, Jell-O, cones for ice cream, and Crayola crayons.

THE LABOR MOVEMENT

Many of the industrial workers during this time period were immigrants. People had come from other countries eager to work in the United States' growing industries. Many immigrants were used to a lower standard of living in their homeland. As a result, they were often willing to work for lower wages than native-born Americans.

Long Hours, Low Pay

Still, both immigrants and native-born laborers often worked 12 to 14 hours a day, 6 days a week. Holidays and vacations were rare. Many workplaces were hot in summer and cold in winter. The air was often full of harmful fumes. Workers were often injured on the job. In 1911 a fire in the Triangle Shirtwaist factory in New York City took the lives of 146 women and girls. The sweatshop owners had refused the workers' demands for fire escapes and unlocked doors.

Thousands of children, some ten years old or younger, worked long hours in coal mines and in other businesses. Many never went to school. Boys who worked in cotton mills had only half the chance of reaching the age of 20 compared to boys outside the mills.

Women who worked outside the home made only about half as much as men. One female worker wrote, "It took me months and months to save up money to buy a dress or a pair of shoes."

Workers Organize Unions

To help solve these problems, workers formed organizations called labor unions. By uniting to fight for better wages and working conditions, labor union members had a greater chance of being heard.

Most business owners fought against unions. People who joined unions were often fired. Sometimes labor unions called a strike. In a strike, all the workers in a business refuse to work until the owners meet their demands. In response, owners often hired men called strikebreakers to beat up strikers. Owners also hired nonunion workers to replace those on strike.

One of the most famous labor union leaders was Mary Harris Jones, known as "Mother" Jones. When the coal

In the late 1800s, many workers put in long hours for low pay at large factories like this one in Michigan.

"Mother" Jones organized coal miners and helped end child labor in the United States.

miners went on strike in Pennsylvania in 1900, "Mother" Jones organized a group of women to drive away strikebreakers. In 1903 she led a march of children who worked in mines to protest child labor. As a result of her efforts, the Pennsylvania legislature passed a law in 1905 forbidding children under 14 years of age from working.

American Federation of Labor

In 1886 a cigar maker named Samuel Gompers founded the American Federation of Labor, or AFL. A federation is an organization made up of several groups that have a common goal. Gompers believed that the strike was an important weapon in the struggle for workers' rights:

> I regard the strikes as the sign that the people are not yet willing to surrender every spark of their manhood and their honor and their independence. It is the protest of the workers against unjust conditions.

The AFL won many victories for workers. It helped to get laws passed that shortened work hours, ended child labor, and required employers to pay workers for injuries received on the job.

WHY IT MATTERS

We do not often think about how the inventions of the 1800s were created. Imagine what life would be like without the automobile, the telephone, and the electric light. The growth of new technologies—aided by our free enterprise system—has continued up to the present day. The twentieth century has seen the invention of the airplane and the computer. Industry has continued to grow and change in response to new technology.

Industry has also changed in response to the struggles of the labor unions. Workers in most industries today work eight hours a day, five days a week. Many also receive paid vacations and other benefits.

Reviewing Facts and Ideas

MAIN IDEAS

- In the late 1800s inventions such as the electric light bulb and the telephone changed how Americans lived.
- New technologies also resulted in the growth of large and powerful new industries and corporations.
- Workers organized unions to fight for better wages and working conditions.

THINK ABOUT IT

1. Why were Thomas Edison's inventions so important?

2. How did John D. Rockefeller gain a monopoly in the oil refining industry?

3. **FOCUS** Beginning in the late 1800s how did the way people work change?

4. **THINKING SKILL** What *generalizations* can you make about the development of big business in the late 1800s and early 1900s?

5. **WRITE** Describe something you think ought to be invented. Explain why it would be useful.

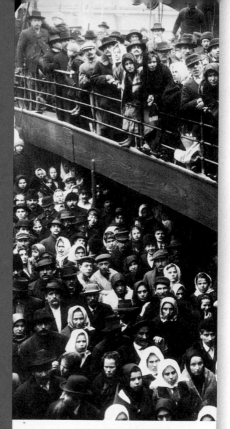

1850   1870   1880   1924 1930

The Growing Cities

Focus Activity

READ TO LEARN

What was life like for immigrants in cities?

VOCABULARY

- slum
- tenement
- Great Chicago Fire
- settlement house

PEOPLE

- Jane Addams

PLACES

- Ellis Island
- Angel Island

Read Aloud

Give me your tired, your poor,
Your huddled masses yearning to breathe free,
The wretched refuse of your teeming shore.
Send these, the homeless, tempest-tost to me,
I lift my lamp beside the golden door!

This poem, written by Emma Lazarus, is engraved on a tablet inside the building on which the Statue of Liberty stands. Lazarus's ancestors were Jews who had come to the colonies in the 1600s. They were fleeing persecution in Portugal. Today the Statue of Liberty remains a symbol of the freedom that millions of immigrants have found in our country.

THE BIG PICTURE

Between 1870 and 1924 nearly 26 million immigrants entered the United States. By 1920 about 1 out of every 4 people in the United States was an immigrant. The new immigrants were different from those who had come earlier. First, there were far more of them. Second, most were from southern and eastern Europe. Italians were fleeing drought, disease, and economic problems at home. Jews from eastern Europe were fleeing religious persecution and poverty.

Some immigrants spent their life savings to come to the United States on dirty, overcrowded ships. Once they arrived they were examined at such places as **Ellis Island** in New York Harbor or **Angel Island** in San Francisco Bay before being allowed into the country. What challenges did they face in the United States?

IMMIGRANTS IN THE CITIES

American cities grew rapidly after the Civil War. In 1860 about 15 million people lived in cities. By 1900 over 30 million Americans were city-dwellers. This increase was partly due to the large numbers of immigrants.

Most immigrants headed directly for cities in the Northeast, where jobs were plentiful. In these cities they formed their own communities where they could live with others who spoke their language and followed their traditions.

How They Lived

In America is a home for everybody. . . . An end to the worry for bread. . . . Everybody can do what he wants with his life in America. . . . plenty for all. Learning flows free like milk and honey.

This is what writer Anzia Yezierska (ahn ZEE uh yez YAIR skah) wrote of her new country before she came here from Russia. What she found in New York was very different. "Where are the green fields and open spaces in America? Where is the golden country of my dreams?" she asked.

Many immigrants faced lives of great hardship in the United States. Still, they hoped for a better life, especially for their children. The vast number of immigrants arriving created a housing shortage. As a result, immigrants often wound up living in slums. A slum is a poor, crowded section of a city with run-down and unsafe housing. Often immigrants lived crowded together in tenements. A tenement is a building that is carved up into small apartments. Some tenements lacked heat and hot water. Bathrooms were often in the hallway and shared by several families.

New York's Lower East Side was an important immigrant community by 1900.

Often families of six or seven people lived together in one or two rooms. Under these crowded conditions diseases spread rapidly.

To house the large numbers of immigrants in Chicago, small wooden buildings had been built quickly without regard for fire safety. In 1871 a terrible fire broke out. One story says that a Mrs. O'Leary's cow had knocked over a kerosene lamp, but no one knows for sure how the fire started. With all of its wooden buildings, the fire spread quickly. By the time it was finally put out 24 hours later, the Great Chicago Fire had killed hundreds of people. Nearly 100,000 people were left homeless. A third of the city of Chicago had been destroyed.

infographic

interNET CONNECTION Visit our website: www.mhschool.com

The Immigrants, 1870-1924

Between 1870 and 1924 about 25,763,000 immigrants came to the United States from Europe and Asia. The bar graph below shows the year of the greatest number of immigrants to the United States during this time period. From what country did most people come during that year?

IMMIGRATION TO THE UNITED STATES, 1907

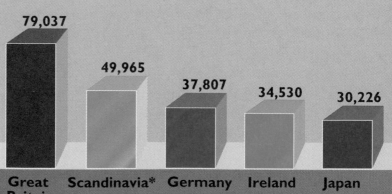

Austria-Hungary	Italy	Russia	Great Britain	Scandinavia*	Germany	Ireland	Japan
338,452	285,731	258,943	79,037	49,965	37,807	34,530	30,226

SOURCE: U.S. BUREAU OF THE CENSUS

*Includes Norway, Sweden, Denmark, and Iceland Note: Between 1899 and 1919, Poland was included with Austria-Hungary, Germany, and Russia.

Asia
790,455

Eastern Europe
3,707,833

Central Europe
8,063,654

Southern Europe
5,345,545

Northwestern Europe
7,855,522

SOURCE: U.S. BUREAU OF THE CENSUS

**IMMIGRATION,
1870-1924**

The photograph (above), taken about 1900, shows European immigrants arriving in the United States at Ellis Island, New York. Some had family members waiting for them. Some were arriving on their own. Many immigrants also had to learn a new language—English. The "McGuffy Reader" (below), as this textbook was called, was one way that they taught themselves.

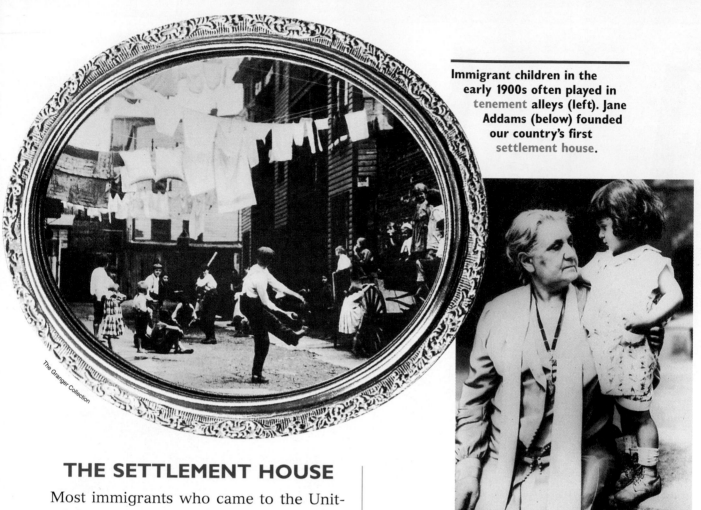

The Granger Collection

Immigrant children in the early 1900s often played in tenement alleys (left). Jane Addams (below) founded our country's first settlement house.

THE SETTLEMENT HOUSE

Most immigrants who came to the United States before the Civil War had an easier time of fitting in. The immigrants from Ireland already spoke English. Many Germans had money to buy land or start businesses. In contrast, nearly all of the new immigrants were poor. Few spoke English. Their languages, religions, and other traditions seemed foreign to many Americans.

Jane Addams Founds Hull House

In the 1900s the Thorek family fled Hungary to escape the killing of Jewish people there. In their new home in Chicago, they had a hard time making ends meet. Young Max Thorek dreamed of going to medical school. Many immigrants shared his despair:

> Only the greatest resolution enabled me to hide from my parents the despair in my heart. . . . Medical education—I might just as well hope for the moon!

In the late 1880s, a young Chicago woman named Jane Addams decided to share her knowledge of art and literature with the poor. In 1889 she and a friend moved into an old house once owned by Charles Hull. At Hull House they held readings, slide shows, and teas for the neighborhood women. They soon realized that their neighbors had more important needs.

Help with Basic Needs

Hull House was the country's first settlement house. A settlement house is a community center that provides child care, education, and other services to the poor. Soon Hull House was offering classes in a variety of subjects. It helped immigrants learn English, find jobs, and become American citizens.

Hull House sponsored lending libraries, summer camps, and playgrounds. By 1900 there were over 100 settlement houses in cities throughout the country.

Many immigrants also founded organizations for people who had come from the same community in their homeland. They provided help to members in times of hardship.

WHY IT MATTERS

As the number of immigrants increased, a growing number of Americans wanted the flood of newcomers stopped. Some Americans believed that immigrants were taking jobs away from native-born citizens. From 1882 to 1943, a law kept Chinese immigrants from entering the United States. In 1924 Congress passed a law limiting the number of immigrants from Europe. This law ended 300 years of free immigration from Europe. The number of immigrants dropped to a trickle.

Most immigrants today come from Asia, Latin America, and the Caribbean islands. They face many of the same challenges as earlier immigrants.

Today many immigrants come from such Asian countries as China and Korea.

Immigrants to the United States came from many different cultures, bringing new traditions and skills. They helped our country to meet the growing demand for labor created by the Industrial Revolution. They worked hard on the railroads and in the factories and mines. The contributions made by immigrants have helped our country to grow even stronger.

✓ Reviewing Facts and Ideas

MAIN IDEAS

- In the late 1800s the number of immigrants to the United States increased greatly. Many of the newcomers were from southern and eastern Europe.

- Most of the immigrants settled in cities because of job opportunities. As a result, the cities grew rapidly in the late 1800s.

- Jane Addams founded the first settlement house in 1889. Settlement houses helped immigrants meet their basic needs and improve their lives.

THINK ABOUT IT

1. Why did immigrants from southern and eastern Europe come to the United States?

2. What opportunities did immigrants find in the United States?

3. **FOCUS** What was life like for immigrants in cities in the late 1800s?

4. **THINKING SKILL** *Compare* and *contrast* the immigrants who came in the middle 1800s with those who came during the early 1900s.

5. **GEOGRAPHY** Look at the Infographic on pages 548–549. List the five countries with the most immigrants. Using the Atlas map on pages R14–R15 create a map to illustrate your list.

PLAY BALL!

GEORGE HERMAN (BABE) RUTH

BIG LEAGUE CHEWING GUM

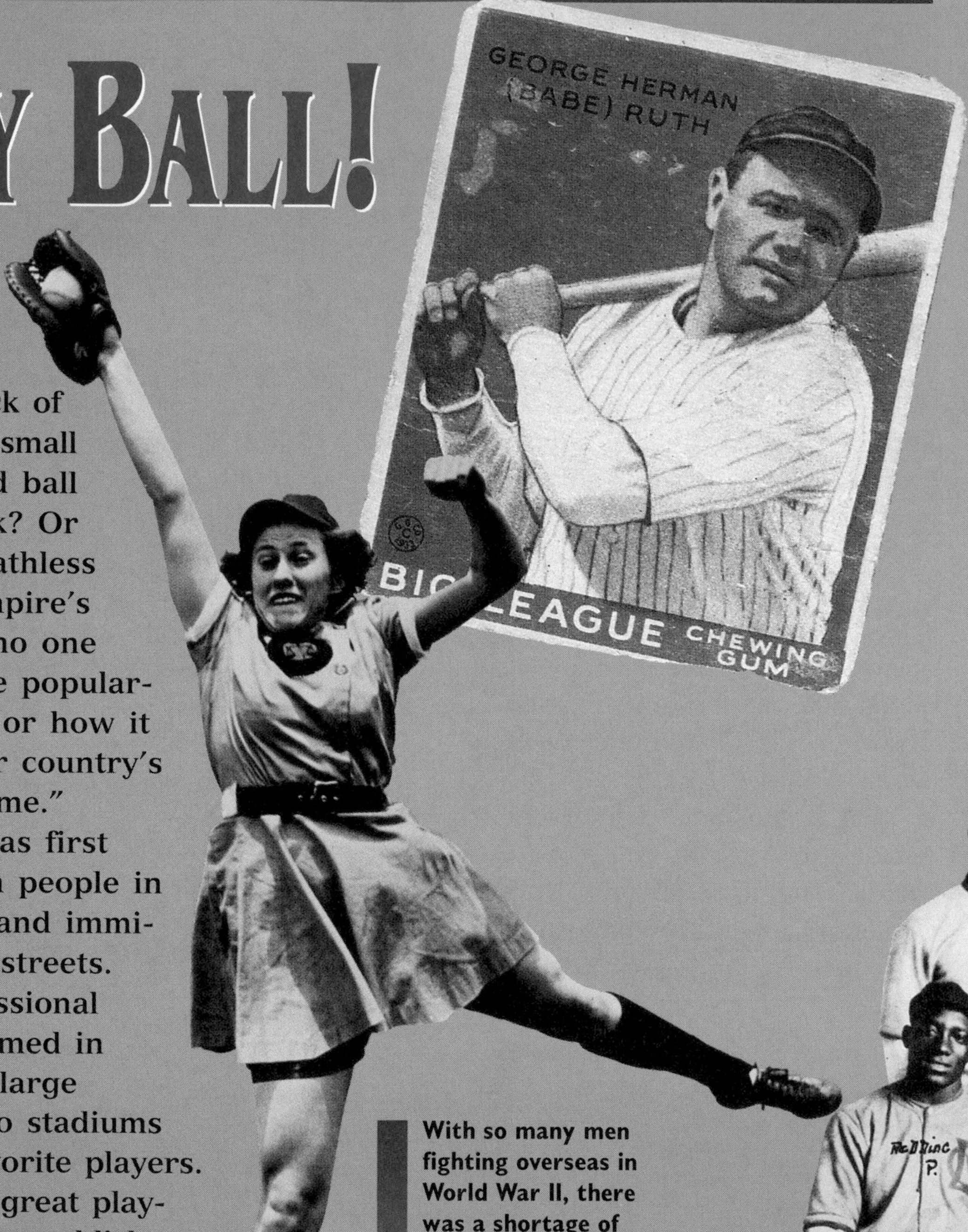

Was it the crack of a bat hitting a small leather-covered ball out of the park? Or was it the breathless wait for an umpire's call? Perhaps no one can explain the popularity of baseball or how it came to be our country's "national pastime."

The game was first played by farm people in country fields and immigrants on city streets. The first professional league was formed in 1871. By 1900 large crowds came to stadiums to see their favorite players.

Some of the great players who helped establish the legacy of baseball appear on these pages. Yet it is the fan who lives to see the next pitch, the next run around the bases, and the next great player that keeps the game alive today.

With so many men fighting overseas in World War II, there was a shortage of male baseball players. In response, in 1943, baseball team owners formed the All-American Girls Baseball League. A female player (above) catches a fly ball.

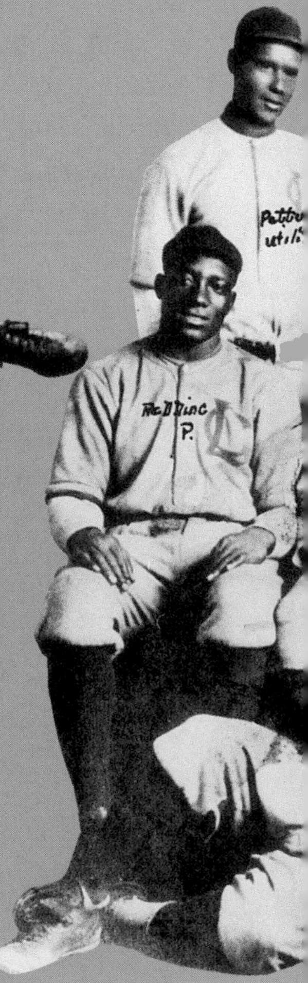

552

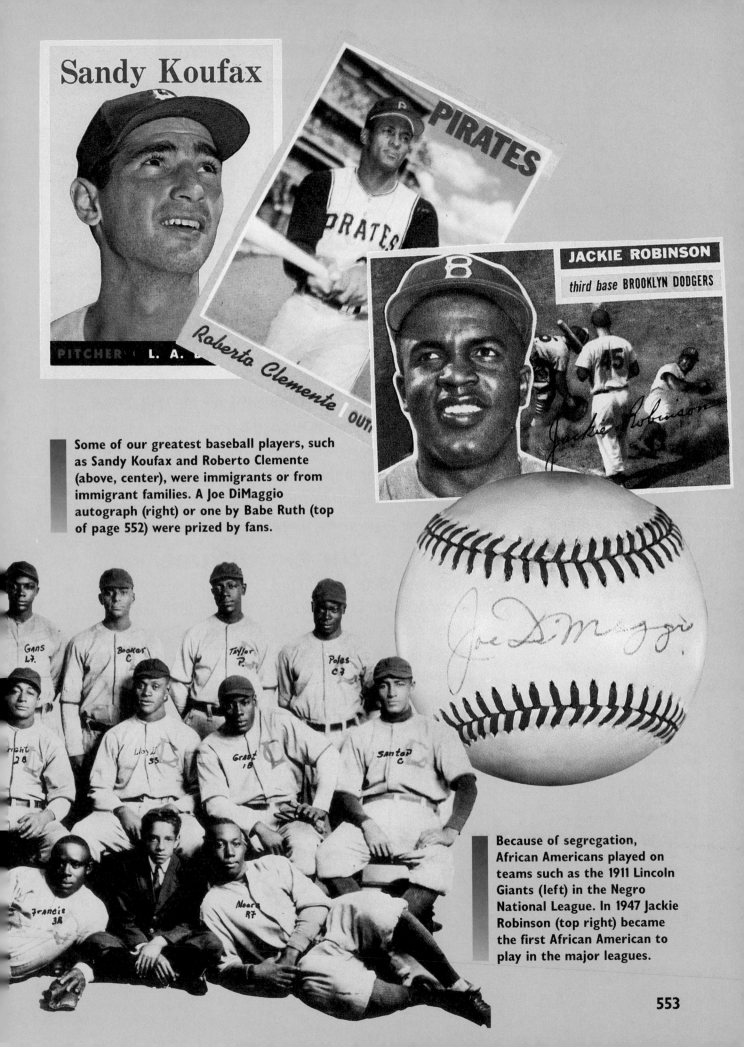

Sandy Koufax

PITCHER L. A. D...

Roberto Clemente | OUT...

PIRATES

JACKIE ROBINSON

third base BROOKLYN DODGERS

Some of our greatest baseball players, such as Sandy Koufax and Roberto Clemente (above, center), were immigrants or from immigrant families. A Joe DiMaggio autograph (right) or one by Babe Ruth (top of page 552) were prized by fans.

Because of segregation, African Americans played on teams such as the 1911 Lincoln Giants (left) in the Negro National League. In 1947 Jackie Robinson (top right) became the first African American to play in the major leagues.

1850   1867   1901 1910   1930

The United States Expands

Focus Activity

READ TO LEARN

Which new territories did the United States gain in the late 1800s?

VOCABULARY

- Spanish-American War

PEOPLE

- James Cook
- Queen Liliuokalani
- William McKinley
- George Dewey
- Theodore Roosevelt

PLACES

- Alaska
- Hawaii
- Juneau
- Honolulu
- Puerto Rico
- Cuba
- Philippines
- Guam

Read Aloud

"We need Hawaii just as much and a good deal more than we did California. It is Manifest Destiny." In 1898, President William McKinley's statement about "manifest destiny" had a new meaning for the United States. Americans wanted to expand beyond North America. The desire for new territories and colonies abroad grew stronger in the United States on the eve of the Spanish-American War.

THE BIG PICTURE

In the late 1800s the United States was busy with events within its own borders. From 1889 to 1896, for example, seven states joined the United States. Only five more states remained to complete the 50 states that make up our country today.

European leaders did not yet see the United States as a major power. The United States did not have a strong military or receive much respect abroad. In the late 1800s, however, the rise of industry created greater strength and prosperity in the United States. The country began to take a leading role in world events.

"As one of the great nations of the world," remarked Senator Henry Cabot Lodge of Massachusetts, "the United States must not fall out of the line of march." Senator Lodge's goal was expansion. He felt the country should seek new territories abroad. By 1900 United States power and influence had reached beyond its own borders.

TWO NEW TERRITORIES

In the late 1800s the United States gained the territories of Alaska and Hawaii. In 1959 Alaska became the 49th state and Hawaii became the 50th state.

Alaska

Alaska is a vast land of over 500,000 square miles. The modern-day native peoples of Alaska such as the Inuit have lived there for thousands of years.

In 1867 Russia offered to sell its colony of Alaska to the United States. American Secretary of State William Seward offered $7.2 million for Alaska, or about 2 cents an acre. Some Americans thought the deal was foolish and referred to Alaska as "Seward's ice box" or "Seward's folly."

People soon saw how valuable Seward's purchase was. In the 1880s gold was discovered in the area that is now the city of Juneau, Alaska's state capital. Today Alaska's plentiful resources include fish, lumber, and oil.

Hawaii

Most scholars believe that people first reached the Hawaiian Islands, located in the Pacific Ocean, between A.D. 600 and A.D. 1000. In 1778 an English sea captain named James Cook opened the way for Christian missionaries, who arrived in Hawaii in the 1820s.

By the 1890s American owners of pineapple and sugar cane plantations had become powerful. Queen Liliuokalani (lee lee oo woh kah LAH nee), Hawaii's ruler, wanted to restore power to native-born Hawaiians. In 1893 the American planters led a revolt against her. They then asked to join the United States. Five years later Hawaii became a United States possession.

Today most Hawaiians live in cities, especially the capital city of Honolulu, which has a population of more than 300,000. Thousands of tourists visit the islands every year to enjoy the warm climate and beautiful beaches.

Queen Liliuokalani (right) composed the state song of Hawaii, *Aloha Oe* (uh LOH uh OY). Hawaii became a republic after she was overthrown.

The Granger Collection

555

THE SPANISH-AMERICAN WAR

By the 1890s Spain had only two colonies in the Western Hemisphere—the Caribbean islands of Puerto Rico and Cuba. In 1895 the people of Cuba began a revolt against their colonial government. Thousands of Cubans were jailed or killed by Spanish troops.

"Remember the *Maine*"

In January 1898 President William McKinley sent the battleship *USS Maine* to Havana, Cuba, to protect Americans there. On February 15, an explosion sunk the *Maine* and killed 260 United States sailors.

At that time, two newspapers in New York City were competing for readers. Their news stories made the Spanish seem cruel and unjust. One paper, *The Journal,* said that the *Maine* was destroyed by Spain. There was no proof that Spain had set the explosion. Still, "Remember the *Maine*" became the country's battle cry. On April 25, 1898, Congress declared war.

United States battleships under Admiral George Dewey sailed to the Spanish colony of the Philippines in the Pacific. Dewey told his ship's captain, "You may fire when you are ready, Gridley." The Spanish fleet in the Pacific was destroyed. The United States Navy also defeated Spain's ships near Cuba. These first battles of the Spanish-American War proved that the United States had become a world power.

Roosevelt Leads the Charge

Theodore Roosevelt, the Assistant Secretary of the Navy, was eager to join the fighting. He quit his job and called on friends and volunteers to go

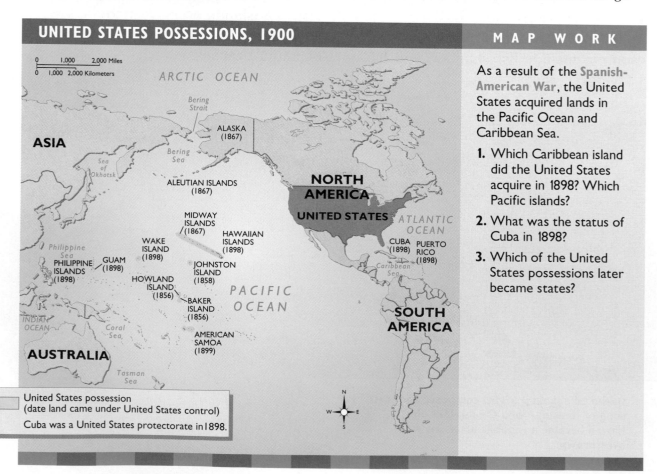

UNITED STATES POSSESSIONS, 1900

0 1,000 2,000 Miles
0 1,000 2,000 Kilometers

ARCTIC OCEAN

Bering Strait

ALASKA (1867)

ASIA

Bering Sea

Sea of Okhotsk

ALEUTIAN ISLANDS (1867)

NORTH AMERICA

UNITED STATES

MIDWAY ISLANDS (1867)

HAWAIIAN ISLANDS (1898)

WAKE ISLAND (1898)

Philippine Sea

PHILIPPINE ISLANDS (1898)

GUAM (1898)

JOHNSTON ISLAND (1858)

HOWLAND ISLAND (1856)

BAKER ISLAND (1856)

PACIFIC OCEAN

ATLANTIC OCEAN

CUBA (1898)

PUERTO RICO (1898)

Caribbean Sea

INDIAN OCEAN

Coral Sea

AMERICAN SAMOA (1899)

SOUTH AMERICA

AUSTRALIA

Tasman Sea

N
W E
S

☐ United States possession (date land came under United States control)

Cuba was a United States protectorate in 1898.

MAP WORK

As a result of the Spanish-American War, the United States acquired lands in the Pacific Ocean and Caribbean Sea.

1. Which Caribbean island did the United States acquire in 1898? Which Pacific islands?

2. What was the status of Cuba in 1898?

3. Which of the United States possessions later became states?

Roosevelt's Rough Riders (above) and the Buffalo Soldiers (left) fought together during the Spanish-American War.

with him to Cuba. This group of volunteers, which included cowhands from the West and former Civil War soldiers, was known as the Rough Riders.

On July 1, 1898, Roosevelt led a charge against the Spanish in the Battle of San Juan Hill. They were joined by African American cavalries known as the "Buffalo Soldiers," who had defended new settlers during the Plains Wars. The Americans were victorious.

In August 1898 the Spanish-American War was over. The treaty that ended the war gave Cuba independence from Spain. As you can see on the map on page 556, the United States gained

control of Puerto Rico, Guam, and the Philippines.

Rebels in the Philippines had been battling for independence from Spain. When the United States took control of the Philippines, Filipinos continued to fight for independence until 1901.

WHY IT MATTERS

The Spanish-American War helped show that the United States had become a world power. It is a role that has lasted throughout the twentieth century. The last new states of Alaska and Hawaii have also contributed to our country's power. In 1946, the Philippines gained independence from the United States. However, both Guam and Puerto Rico still belong to the United States and their people are citizens of the United States.

✔ Reviewing Facts and Ideas

MAIN IDEAS

- During the 1890s Americans became interested in gaining new territory abroad, including Alaska and Hawaii.
- In the Spanish-American War of 1898 the United States gained Puerto Rico, Guam, and the Philippines.

THINK ABOUT IT

1. How did Hawaii become a United States territory?

2. What resources are found in Alaska?

3. **FOCUS** What were the results of the Spanish-American War?

4. **THINKING SKILL** What _effects_ did the sinking of the _Maine_ have in the United States and elsewhere?

5. **GEOGRAPHY** Look at the map on page 556. Which lands did the United States control by 1900?

Remington Art Museum

Using Primary and Secondary Sources

Frederic Remington painted *Charge of the Rough Riders at San Juan Hill* in 1898. Sent by a newspaper to cover the war, he witnessed the battle firsthand.

VOCABULARY

primary source
secondary source

WHY THE SKILL MATTERS

When you become particularly interested in something that happened in the past, you probably want to learn all you can about it. Where do you look? There are two kinds of sources you need to check.

The first kind is called a **primary source**. Primary sources are accounts by people involved in the events being written about. They provide important, firsthand details that give you an idea of how people of the time thought and felt. Most of the "Many Voices" features in this book are from primary sources. Items such as letters, diaries, newspaper stories, speeches, and official documents are primary sources, as well. Photographs and paintings can also be primary sources too, since they also tell us about the time during which they were created.

The second kind is called a **secondary source**. Secondary sources are written by people who were not there themselves. Secondary sources are usually based on many primary sources. Thus, they often provide useful summaries of historical events. They can also help you see how an event is part of larger trends or developments. This textbook is an example of a secondary source. Encyclopedias, atlases, and history books on particular topics are also secondary sources.

In order to get the most complete information, you will want to use both primary and secondary sources. Primary sources are best for giving you an understanding of what a past event was like. Primary sources express the view of only one person. Secondary sources often compare and analyze different points of view. They provide a broader view of an event. Together, primary and secondary sources can help you to form a more complete picture of an event.

USING PRIMARY SOURCES

The following passage is a primary source. It is taken from the *Autobiography of Theodore Roosevelt*. It gives an "insider's" view of the United States forces at the Battle of San Juan Hill.

I had come to the conclusion that it was silly to stay in the valley firing at the hills, . . . I waved my hat, and we went up the hill with a rush. . . . I was never more pleased than to see the way in which the hungry, tired, shabby men all jumped up and ran forward to the hill crest, so as to be ready for the attack.

Roosevelt's account tells you what it was like to be in the middle of the fighting. It lets you know what Roosevelt thought at the time about the battle.

USING SECONDARY SOURCES

Now read this excerpt about the Battle of San Juan Hill from *The Spanish-American War* written by a historian named Deborah Bachrach in 1991.

The Spanish were outnumbered . . . on San Juan Hill 16 to 1. But before the day was over, it was clear that the American army had underestimated the military skill of the Spanish soldiers.

Helping yourself

- **A primary source is a personal or eyewitness account of an event or situation.**

- **A secondary source is an account of a past event written by someone who did not actually witness the event.**

. . . [It] was Theodore Roosevelt's recklessly brave antics that captured the imagination of the American public. . . . Despite these heroics, General Shafter [an American general] was horrified by the casualties among the American soldiers.

Notice that the writer of this passage does not limit her account to the actions of Theodore Roosevelt. Bachrach gives you information about both of the armies that took part in the battle.

TRYING THE SKILL

Now reread each of the preceding passages. Which source would you use to learn about the United States troops in general during the Battle of San Juan Hill? Which source tells you how some soldiers might have felt about the battle?

Finally, look at Frederic Remington's painting *Charge of the Rough Riders* on page 558. Remington was in Cuba in 1898 during the Spanish-American War. Do you think this painting is a primary or a secondary source? Explain your answer.

REVIEWING THE SKILL

1. What is a primary source? What is a secondary source?

2. Which passage on this page expresses the opinion of one person?

3. Which passage discusses the opinions of many people?

4. Which passage do you think gives a more balanced account of the battle of San Juan Hill? Explain.

5. How do both primary and secondary sources help you to understand history?

1850   1870   1890   1901   1914   1930

The World of Theodore Roosevelt

Read Aloud

President Theodore Roosevelt is famous for his sayings. He often responded with "Bully," when he came upon something he liked. He is also known for saying "Speak softly and carry a big stick; you will go far." Under President Roosevelt the United States did go far. It underwent great change and showed a new strength among the countries of the world.

Focus Activity

READ TO LEARN

What happened in the United States while Theodore Roosevelt was President?

VOCABULARY

- reform
- assembly line
- Model T
- national park

PEOPLE

- Theodore Roosevelt
- Upton Sinclair
- Ida Tarbell
- William Gorgas
- Orville Wright
- Wilbur Wright
- Henry Ford
- John Muir

PLACES

- Isthmus of Panama
- Panama Canal
- Kitty Hawk
- Yosemite National Park

THE BIG PICTURE

By the end of the 1800s, the United States had become a wealthy country and a world power. For example, by 1870 it already produced more steel than any other country in the world.

The growth of large corporations had made some people rich. Others, however, were living in poverty and working under difficult conditions. Reform, or changes designed to make things better, became an important common goal. Reformers wanted the government to control the unfair practices of some big businesses.

Among the reformers was Theodore Roosevelt, who had been elected Vice President in 1900. When President William McKinley was shot and killed in 1901, Theodore Roosevelt became President. Roosevelt was only 42 years old, the youngest person to take the office of President at that time. Roosevelt and the reformers helped the United States enter a new century as a major world power.

THEODORE ROOSEVELT

Born in 1858, Theodore Roosevelt was often sick as a child. Determined to become stronger, he began a program of physical exercise. By the time he was an adult, he claimed "I am as strong as a bull moose." Throughout his life Roosevelt continued his habit of working hard at everything he did.

Roosevelt gained political fame through his role as a Rough Rider in the Spanish-American War. After finishing President McKinley's term, Roosevelt campaigned for a second term as President in 1904. He said he would "see to it that every man has a square deal, no less and no more." By a "square deal," Roosevelt meant that the government and businesses would deal fairly with people.

Because of muckrakers like Ida Tarbell (left) and Upton Sinclair, supermarkets today (below) must follow safety standards for packaging meat.

Muckrakers and Trust Busters

President Roosevelt was not the only person pushing for reform. Writers known as "muckrakers" helped to focus the country's attention on unfair business practices. One of the muckrakers, novelist Upton Sinclair, wrote about problems in the meat packing industry. His novel *The Jungle* described how unhealthy and dirty food was sold to unknowing customers. "There was never the least attention paid to what was cut up for sausage," he wrote. In 1906 Roosevelt pushed Congress to pass the Pure Food & Drug Act and the Meat Inspection Act. These acts helped make sure that medicines did what their makers claimed and that food was safe.

In 1903 a muckraking reporter named Ida Tarbell published a series of magazine articles. Her articles described the unfair business practices of the Standard Oil Company. Standard Oil, a monopoly, controlled almost the entire oil industry. Another word for *monopoly* used at that time was *trust*. Tarbell wrote about Standard Oil:

> I was willing that they should . . . grow as big and rich as they could, but only by legitimate [fair] means. But they had never played fair, and that ruined their greatness for me. I am convinced that . . . [they] contributed not only to a weakening of the country's moral standards but to its economic unsoundness.

Roosevelt agreed. He believed that although big business was important to the economy, the government should have the power to break up "bad" trusts. By the time he left office, Roosevelt had forced 25 trusts, including Standard Oil Company, to be divided into smaller companies. This earned Roosevelt the nickname of "the trust buster."

THE UNITED STATES UNDER ROOSEVELT

President Roosevelt believed that the country should "dare mighty things." In the early 1900s, this daring was shown through new technology that would change the way Americans lived forever.

The Panama Canal

The Spanish-American War had shown Roosevelt the need for a canal across the **Isthmus** (IS mus) **of Panama**. An isthmus is a narrow strip of land that connects two larger landmasses—in this case, North and South America. When the Spanish-American War began, the battleship *Oregon* left San Francisco for Cuba. By the time it had arrived, more than a month had passed since the war began. A canal would have cut the distance of the voyage by 7,000 miles.

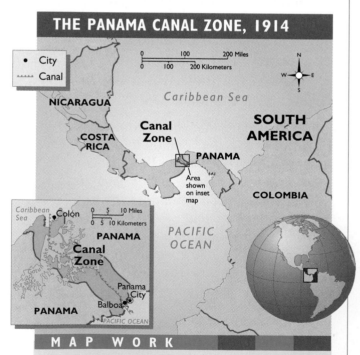

THE PANAMA CANAL ZONE, 1914

MAP WORK

After years of construction, the Panama Canal opened in 1914.

1. Which countries border Panama?
2. Which major bodies of water does the Panama Canal join?

After helping it gain independence from the South American country of Colombia in 1903, the United States purchased a 10-mile wide strip of land from Panama. Known as the Canal Zone, this strip provided the land needed to build the **Panama Canal**. Roosevelt gave orders to "make the dirt fly in Panama."

From 1881 to 1887 a French company had tried to dig the canal. However, the job of cutting through thick rain forests and draining wetlands had proved too difficult. Diseases such as malaria and yellow fever, both carried by mosquitoes, were another problem.

When the United States took over, the task of battling the mosquitoes fell to Colonel **William Gorgas**. Gorgas was a doctor who had successfully fought yellow fever in Cuba after the Spanish-American War. In Panama he tried to limit the mosquitoes by spreading oil over the pools of water where the insects laid their eggs. By 1906 the area was safe for digging to begin.

Over 40,000 men worked on the Panama Canal for seven years. Thanks to Dr. Gorgas the death rate among the workers was not as high as it might have been. Still, 5,609 lives were lost due to disease and accidents. The work was hard and dangerous. The digging of the canal was made possible by the railroads, steam shovels, and other new American technology.

The Wright Brothers Take Off

Another triumph was made by two American brothers, **Orville** and **Wilbur Wright**. For centuries, people had been fascinated with the idea of building flying machines. The Wrights began by reading everything they could find about flight. Then, in the fall of 1900,

The Granger Collection

The first airplane flight at Kitty Hawk (left) and the development of the Model T (below) took place while Roosevelt was President.

they selected the beach at Kitty Hawk, North Carolina, to begin their own experiments with gliders. By 1902 their glider could stay in the air over a distance of about 600 feet. In 1903 they added an engine to their aircraft.

On the morning of December 17, the brothers moved their airplane out onto the track, and Orville climbed aboard. They started the engine. The airplane ran along the sand for about 40 feet—and then lifted up into the sky. It flew about 100 feet before landing again. Orville wrote later that the flght was a "first in the history of the world." A flying "machine carrying a man had raised itself by its own power into the air in full flight." A man who had seen the flight ran to the local post office shouting, "They have done it!"

Henry Ford's Model T

The first automobiles were made in Europe in the late 1800s. By the 1890s, Americans were making automobiles of their own. The early cars took a long time to build and were quite costly.

In 1913 Henry Ford, an early automobile manufacturer, invented a way to build more cars quickly and cheaply. Ford built his cars on an assembly line. This method of producing manufactured goods took the automobile parts to the workers instead of the workers to the automobile parts. Partially built cars were carried on a moving belt from one work area to the next. At each area, a worker fitted one part to the car as it moved past. Ford focused on building only one type, or model, of car. He also made sure the parts for the car were interchangeable and manufactured in huge numbers.

The assembly line method cut the price of Ford's most popular car, the Model T, from $850 in 1908 to $300 in 1925. By 1923 one out of every two cars sold in the country was a Model T.

CONSERVATION

All his life Theodore Roosevelt loved nature and the outdoors. As a result, he believed that the country needed to practice conservation.

National Parks and Forests

In 1903 Roosevelt visited Yosemite National Park with John Muir. Muir was one of the country's first conservationists, or people who work to preserve the wilderness. Read the excerpt from Roosevelt's speech about visiting Yosemite. What did he think about preserving natural resources?

MANY VOICES
PRIMARY SOURCE

Excerpt from Speech in Sacramento, California, by President Theodore Roosevelt, 1903.

*Lying out at night under those giant Sequoias [trees] was like lying in a temple built by no hand of man, a temple grander than any human architect could by any possibility build, and I hope for the preservation of the groves of giant trees simply because it would be a shame to our civilization to let them disappear. They are monuments in themselves. . . . In California I am impressed by how great your state is, but I am even more impressed by the immensely greater greatness that lies in the future, and I ask that your marvelous natural resources be handed on **unimpaired** to your **posterity**. We are not building this country of ours for a day. It is to last through the ages.*

unimpaired: undamaged
posterity: future generations

While President, Roosevelt created new national parks. A national park is an area set aside for its natural beauty. No one is allowed to settle or farm the land. Roosevelt established many of the country's natural wonders, such as the Grand Canyon, as national monuments. He also had about 150 million acres of land declared national forests.

Roosevelt showed his concern for animals by creating many wildlife refuges. A wildlife refuge is a natural environment where animals and birds are protected from hunters and trappers. Roosevelt once saved a small bear that was being chased for sport. A newspaper cartoonist heard this story and did a cartoon drawing of the bear. Soon toy bears known as "teddy bears" were being manufactured and sold. Teddy bears are still sold today.

Roosevelt is shown at Yosemite National Park with John Muir in 1903.

Today many people visit California's Muir Woods, named after John Muir, which is home to giant redwood trees.

WHY IT MATTERS

The early years of the century saw the start of many things that shape the way Americans live today. Theodore Roosevelt played a part in many of these developments.

To many, Roosevelt reflected the energetic character of the United States as it entered the 1900s. The government began to take on a new role on behalf of the people. Reformers such as the muckrakers helped bring unfair practices to the public's attention. At the same time, the United States had become powerful enough to put down revolts in foreign countries. To protect United States citizens and businesses

overseas, Roosevelt sent troops to Haiti, Panama, Nicaragua, Mexico, and the Dominican Republic. The Panama Canal was known as the greatest engineering project of its time. Building it showed how the United States could use its power in other lands. In 1977 the United States agreed to return ownership of the Canal to Panama in the year 2000.

Reviewing Facts and Ideas

MAIN IDEAS

- Theodore Roosevelt became President in 1901. He promised a "square deal" for all Americans. With the help of reformers, he broke up trusts that used unfair business practices.

- In 1903 the United States began building the Panama Canal, and the Wright Brothers made the first airplane flight. Henry Ford's invention of the assembly line in 1913 lowered the cost of automobiles. The lower price made it possible for many Americans to buy them.

- Roosevelt created new national parks and worked to preserve the country's natural beauty for the future.

THINK ABOUT IT

1. What did Roosevelt mean when he promised Americans a "square deal"?

2. What role did technology play in the building of the Panama Canal?

3. **FOCUS** What are some of the events that took place in the United States while Roosevelt was President?

4. **THINKING SKILL** What have been some of the *effects* of the automobile on the American way of life?

5. **WRITE** Look at the map on page 562. Why was the Isthmus of Panama a good location for building a canal?

CITIZENSHIP
VIEWPOINTS

Millions of acres of forest land in the United States have been damaged by fires like this one in Yellowstone National Park.

2000: How should we manage forest fires?

In 1988 huge fires swept through Yellowstone National Park in Wyoming. One-third of the park's 2.2 million acres was burned. After the fire, the National Park Service issued new fire guidelines. In Yellowstone forest fires are allowed to burn only if the fire does not affect the safety of people or damage property. Fires caused by natural events such as lightning are also allowed to burn.

Most people agree that when a fire threatens life and property, it should be put out. Those who favor putting out fires also think that trees should be cut down rather than allowed to catch fire and burn naturally. Those who favor allowing fires to burn in national parks, however, believe that trees need the heat of fire to regenerate, or produce new trees. Natural fires also create a variety of shelters for plants and wildlife. If forests are not allowed to burn, large amounts of dry underbrush build up that could result in stronger fires.

Read and consider the viewpoints on this issue. Then answer the questions that follow.

Three DIFFERENT Viewpoints

1 KRISTIN HAYES
Student, Pollock, Louisiana
Excerpt from Interview, 1997

There are some fires we should put out at once because they ruin the land by destroying all the timber and by leaving the ground so bare that the rain carries away the soil, causing erosion. Other forest fires can be nature's helpers. It depends on how big the fire is. If it is a small wild fire, let it burn for a little while. That's called prescribed burning. It clears the land and allows berries and grasses to sprout that animals like deer and rabbits feed on.

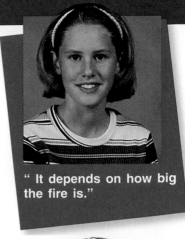

" It depends on how big the fire is."

2 STEVE MEALEY
United States Forest Service, Boise, Idaho
Excerpt from Interview, 1997

It depends on what the Congress and the American people want to do with their public land. What we do with fires depends on how a forest is used. We have a specific policy for wilderness; a different policy for multiple-use forests where logging and grazing are allowed. If the intent of policy is to make the best use of the products of the land, then allowing high intensity fires to burn over large areas may not be good policy.

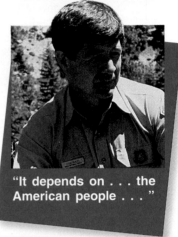

"It depends on . . . the American people . . . "

3 FELICE PACE
Teacher, Etna, California
Excerpt from Interview, 1997

In the national forests, we've suppressed [put out] every single fire, since the early 1900s. . . . It is like our western public forests have become a fireplace. When a fire hits, there is so much fuel it becomes almost impossible to control. The western forests are going to burn. They are either going to burn more often at a lower intensity and clean out the forests or they are going to burn very hot . . . , go out of forest areas, and threaten life and property.

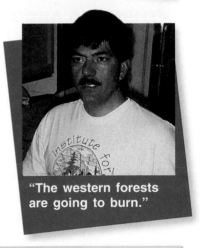

"The western forests are going to burn."

BUILDING CITIZENSHIP

1. What is the viewpoint of each person? How does each person support his or her view?

2. In what ways do some of the viewpoints agree? In what ways do they disagree?

3. What other viewpoints might people have on this issue? How might viewpoints on this issue have changed since the first national parks were built?

SHARING VIEWPOINTS

Discuss why some people favor allowing forest fires to burn and others oppose it. Consider what other opinions people might have if the question included forest fires on private land. Identify two or three issues related to our national parks that everyone in your class could agree on.

567

CHAPTER 19 REVIEW

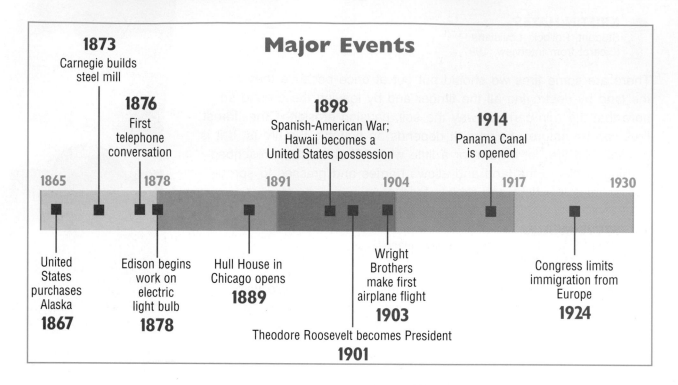

Major Events

1873
Carnegie builds steel mill

1876
First telephone conversation

1898
Spanish-American War; Hawaii becomes a United States possession

1914
Panama Canal is opened

1865   1878   1891   1904   1917   1930

United States purchases Alaska
1867

Edison begins work on electric light bulb
1878

Hull House in Chicago opens
1889

Wright Brothers make first airplane flight
1903

Congress limits immigration from Europe
1924

Theodore Roosevelt becomes President
1901

THINKING ABOUT VOCABULARY

Number a paper from 1 to 5. Beside each number, write the letter of the phrase that correctly completes the sentence.

1. A monopoly is _____.
   a. a company that controls an industry
   b. a small company with little business
   c. a company that charges low prices

2. Many immigrants were forced to live in slums, which are _____.
   a. large farm areas
   b. clean areas next to small towns
   c. rundown sections of cities

3. Reform, or _____, became a goal of many Americans by the end of the 1800s.
   a. the idea that everything should remain the same
   b. changes to make things better
   c. expanding to gain land overseas

4. A labor union is _____.
   a. an organization in which workers unite to fight for better wages and working conditions

   b. an organization of people who own different kinds of businesses
   c. a way of building such things as cars more easily and quickly

5. After the Civil War, many businesses became corporations, or _____.
   a. small, hometown businesses
   b. large businesses that are owned by shareholders
   c. large businesses that operate without permission from the government

THINKING ABOUT FACTS

1. How did the borders of the United States change by 1900?

2. From which countries did many of the immigrants who entered the United States between 1870 and 1924 come? How did immigrants affect American cities?

3. Why was the *USS Maine* important?

4. What is a trustbuster? A muckraker?

5. Look at the time line above. What new technologies were developed?

WRITING AN EDITORIAL

Write an editorial that might have appeared in a newspaper in the late 1800s about changes in industry. You may choose to support big businesses or the labor unions or both. Include facts to support your point of view.

WRITING A SCHEDULE

Suppose that you are the director of a settlement house. Write a daily schedule of events, listing the activities and services that you have planned for one day.

WRITING AN INTRODUCTION

Suppose that President Theodore Roosevelt is coming to speak to your government club. Write some short remarks that you will give to introduce the President before he speaks.

APPLYING STUDY SKILLS

USING PRIMARY AND SECONDARY SOURCES

1. What is the difference between a primary source and a secondary source?

2. Name three examples of primary sources.

3. What kind of source is this textbook?

4. Reread the sources on page 559. What information did you find in the secondary source that you did not find in the primary source?

5. Why is it important to use both primary sources and secondary sources?

Summing Up the Chapter

Copy the flow chart on a separate piece of paper. Review the chapter to complete the missing events. After you have finished, use the chart to answer the question, "How did the Industrial Revolution change American cities in the 1800s?"

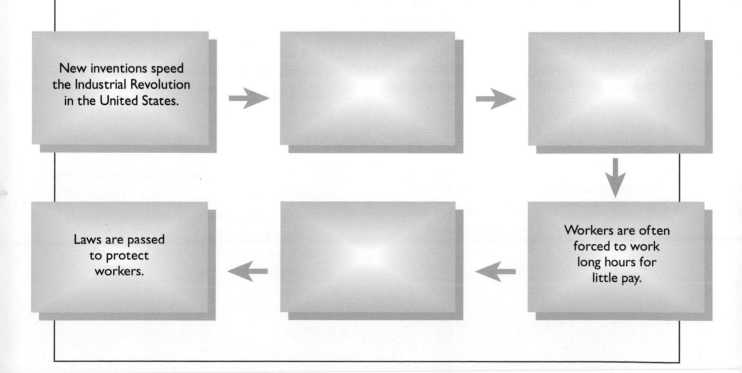

New inventions speed the Industrial Revolution in the United States.

Workers are often forced to work long hours for little pay.

Laws are passed to protect workers.

UNIT 8 REVIEW

THINKING ABOUT VOCABULARY

Number a paper from 1 to 10. Beside each number, write the word or term from the list below that matches the description.

assembly line   settlement house
exoduster   shareholder
Model T   strike
primary source   sweatshop
property rights   tenement

1. A building carved up into small, low-cost apartments

2. A person who invests money in a corporation

3. Most popular car built by Henry Ford until 1925

4. Name given to African Americans who left the South to settle on the Great Plains

5. A community center that provides child care, education, and social services to the poor

6. A personal or eyewitness account of an event or situation

7. Method of building cars invented by Henry Ford in which workers fit the parts to the car as it is carried past on a moving belt

8. Rights to own or use something—such as land—for gain, profit, or sale

9. A small, dirty, often airless factory that is sometimes run out of people's homes

10. The refusal of all the workers in a business to work until the owners meet their demands

THINK AND WRITE

WRITING A PLAY

Choose one of the events you read about in this unit and write a scene or dialogue for a play about it. Use the primary sources in the unit or others that you find through your own research to help you write the dialogue for the characters.

WRITING A SPEECH

Suppose that "Mother" Jones has asked you to help her convince businesses to stop using child labor. As a young person, think about what you would say to the business leaders, and then write a speech in which you present your ideas.

WRITING ABOUT PERSPECTIVES

Write several paragraphs in which you explain the different perspectives Native Americans and white settlers had on the idea of property rights. What primary source material can you include in your writing?

BUILDING SKILLS

1. **Time zone maps** Why were time zones set up in 1884?

2. **Time zone maps** How many time zones are there around the world?

3. **Time zone maps** If it is 7:00 P.M. in Boston, what time is it in Minneapolis?

4. **Primary and secondary sources** Is the speech given by President Roosevelt on page 564 a primary source or a secondary source?

5. **Primary and secondary sources** Is an encyclopedia a primary source or a secondary source? Which kind of source is a photograph?

YESTERDAY, TODAY & *TOMORROW*

How did the immigrants you read about in this unit experience the United States differently from the way earlier immigrants had? In what ways were their experiences similar? What do you know about immigrants to the United States today? How do you think immigrants in the future might experience this country?

READING ON YOUR OWN

These are some of the books you could find at the library to help you learn more.

TEN MILE DAY AND THE BUILDING OF THE TRANSCONTINENTAL RAILROAD
by Mary Ann Fraser
The author describes how transcontinental railroad workers laid ten miles of track in a day.

THE NEZ PERCÉ
by Virginia Driving Hawk Sneve
This account of the way of life of the Nez Percé is accompanied by dramatic paintings.

THE REAL McCOY: THE LIFE OF AN AFRICAN AMERICAN INVENTOR
by Wendy Towle
This biography tells the story of Elijah McCoy, a pioneer in engineering.

UNIT 8 REVIEW PROJECT

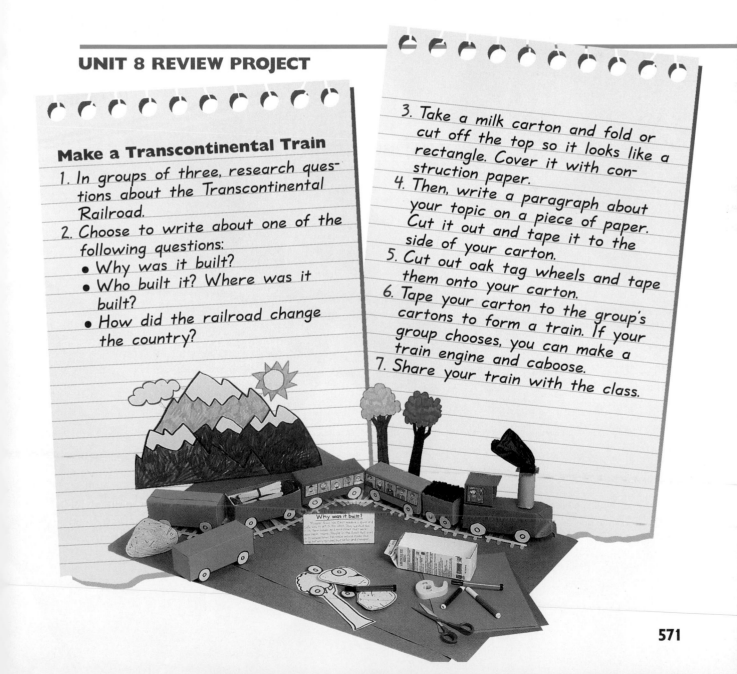

Make a Transcontinental Train

1. In groups of three, research questions about the Transcontinental Railroad.
2. Choose to write about one of the following questions:
   • Why was it built?
   • Who built it? Where was it built?
   • How did the railroad change the country?
3. Take a milk carton and fold or cut off the top so it looks like a rectangle. Cover it with construction paper.
4. Then, write a paragraph about your topic on a piece of paper. Cut it out and tape it to the side of your carton.
5. Cut out oak tag wheels and tape them onto your carton.
6. Tape your carton to the group's cartons to form a train. If your group chooses, you can make a train engine and caboose.
7. Share your train with the class.

I WANT YOU
FOR U.S. ARMY
NEAREST RECRUITING STATION

UNCLE SAM RECRUITING POSTER;
THE MOON;
NEIL ARMSTRONG, JR.

SANDRA DAY O'CONNOR;
MARTIN LUTHER KING, JR.,
LEADING A MARCH

Hopes for Peace and Prosperity

"I have a dream."

From a speech by Martin Luther King, Jr.
See page 619.

Why Does it Matter?

The dream that Martin Luther King, Jr., spoke of is a dream shared by many in the United States. Yet the American dream has many forms. It is the dream of freedom, equality, peace, and prosperity. It can be as grand as exploring the moon and as simple as buying a family home.

In the second half of the twentieth century, the United States has become the leading power in the world. From far and wide, people in other countries look to the United States as a symbol of liberty, economic opportunity, and hope for world peace. The future of liberty, equality, and democracy lies in the hands of the people of the United States.

FIND OUT MORE!
Visit our website:
www.mhschool.com

*inter*NET
CONNECTION

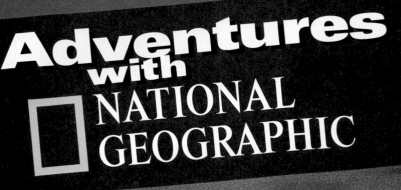

Adventures
with
NATIONAL
GEOGRAPHIC

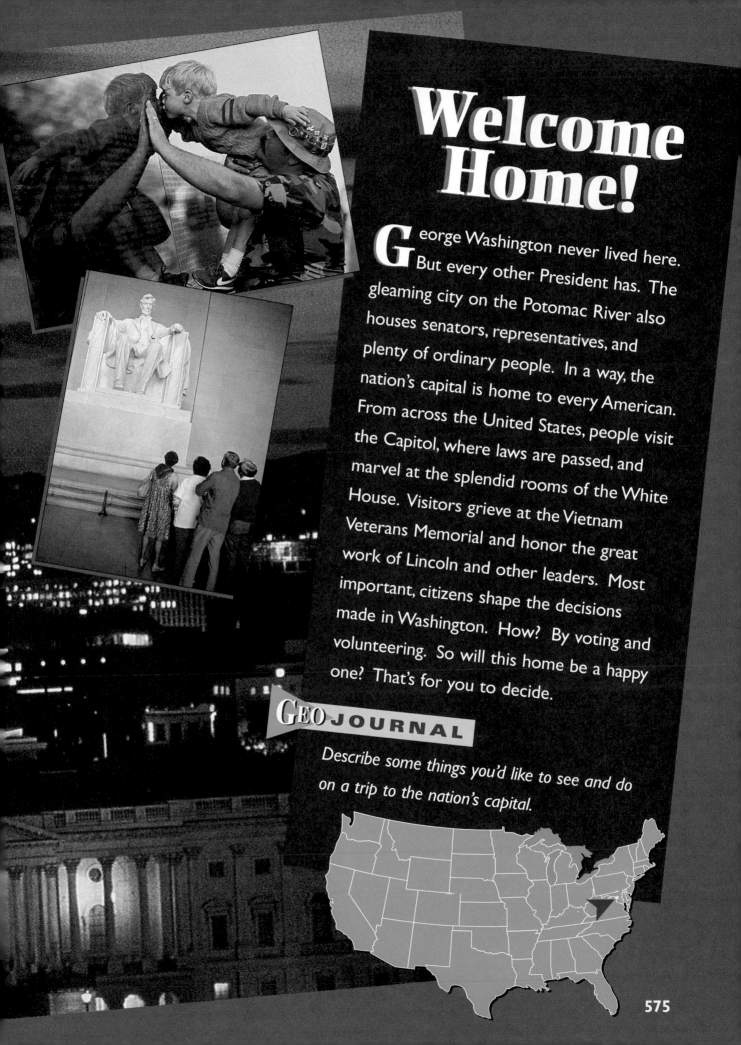

Welcome Home!

George Washington never lived here. But every other President has. The gleaming city on the Potomac River also houses senators, representatives, and plenty of ordinary people. In a way, the nation's capital is home to every American. From across the United States, people visit the Capitol, where laws are passed, and marvel at the splendid rooms of the White House. Visitors grieve at the Vietnam Veterans Memorial and honor the great work of Lincoln and other leaders. Most important, citizens shape the decisions made in Washington. How? By voting and volunteering. So will this home be a happy one? That's for you to decide.

GEO JOURNAL

Describe some things you'd like to see and do on a trip to the nation's capital.

Good Times, Hard Times, and World War

THINKING ABOUT HISTORY AND GEOGRAPHY

The story of Chapter 20 takes place during the first half of the 1900s. Look at the time line below. Through these years the United States faced conflict overseas as well as economic hardships at home. With the end of World War II, the country faced yet another great challenge. The Cold War, as it became known, would last for over 40 years and affect the lives of people throughout the United States and the world.

PACIFIC OCEAN

Pearl Harbor

1915

ATLANTIC OCEAN

The sinking of the Lusitania draws the United States into World War I

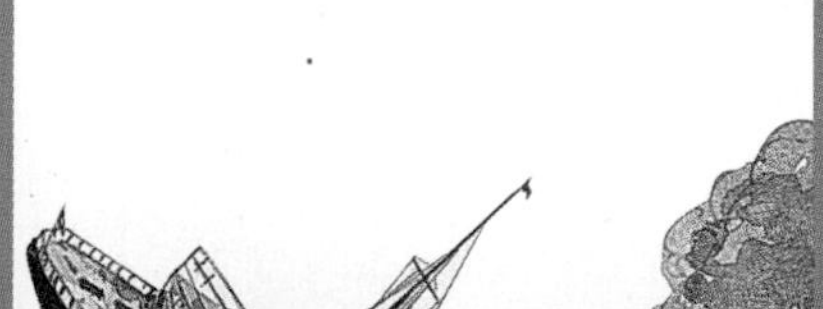

1930s

DUST BOWL

A long drought forces families to move West during the Depression

1915

1925

1935

UNITED
STATES

New York
City

Atlantic
Ocean

Washington, D.C.

ATLANTIC
OCEAN

1933

Dust Bowl

WASHINGTON, D.C.
Franklin Delano Roosevelt
becomes President

1941

PEARL HARBOR,
HAWAII

Japan makes a surprise
attack on the United
States naval base

1945

TIMES SQUARE,
NEW YORK CITY

Americans celebrate the
end of World War II

1940

1945

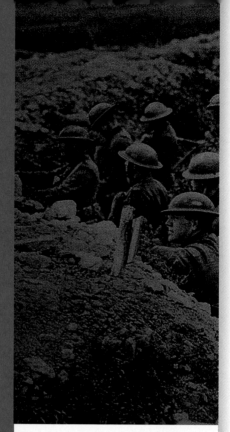

1910　**1914**　**1919**　　1930　　1940　　1950

World War I

Read Aloud

"Send the word, send the word, over there, that the Yanks are coming, the Yanks are coming."

In a George M. Cohan song of 1917, "over there" meant "Europe," where a war was raging. Soon "the Yanks," or Americans, also would be fighting "over there."

Focus Activity

READ TO LEARN

How did World War I change the United States?

VOCABULARY

- World War I
- Allied Powers
- Central Powers
- Treaty of Versailles
- League of Nations
- Great Migration
- discrimination
- NAACP

PEOPLE

- Woodrow Wilson
- Booker T. Washington
- W.E.B. Du Bois
- Ida Wells-Barnett

PLACES

- Virgin Islands
- Versailles

THE BIG PICTURE

In August 1914 World War I broke out in Europe. On one side were the Allied Powers, which included the countries of Britain, France, Italy, Belgium, and Russia. On the other side were the Central Powers, led by Germany, Austria-Hungary, and Turkey. The bloody struggle among these countries would drag on for more than four years.

Few Americans were eager to involve the United States in a distant conflict. In fact, when President Woodrow Wilson was reelected in 1916, one of his campaign slogans was "He kept us out of war." Still, the country would soon be drawn into a world war.

DANGERS AT SEA

In addition to fighting on land, Germany and Great Britain fought over control of the seas. Each country hoped to prevent supplies from being shipped to the other. In the Atlantic Ocean the Germans used their new and deadly submarines known as U-boats. These underwater boats could sneak up on ships, rise to the surface, and sink them without warning.

On May 1, 1915, a British passenger ship called the *Lusitania* set sail from New York. Its cargo also included weapons for the British. On May 7 a German U-boat sank the *Lusitania*. Among the 1,198 people who died, 128 were United States citizens. People throughout the country were angered by the German attack.

Going to War

To protect American shipping and the Panama Canal from attack, the United States bought the Virgin Islands from Denmark for $25 million in 1917. Engineers then began building a naval base on these islands in the Caribbean.

From January to March 1917, the Germans sank eight American ships. In response, President Wilson asked Congress to declare war on the Central Powers. Four days later the United States was at war. Read the excerpt from Wilson's speech. What reasons does he give for going to war?

The Granger Collection

**Excerpt from
Address to Congress
by President Woodrow Wilson
on April 12, 1917.**

*It is a fearful thing to lead this great peaceful people into war, into the most terrible and disastrous of all wars, civilization itself seeming to be in the balance. But the right is more precious than peace, and we shall fight for the things which we have always carried nearest to our hearts—for democracy, . . . the rights and liberties of small nations, [and] for a universal **dominion** of right by such a **concert** of free peoples as shall bring peace and safety to all nations.*

dominion: rule
concert: alliance

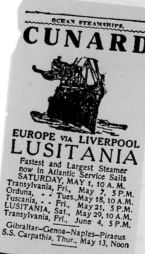

Newspapers warned passengers on the *Lusitania* about the dangers of traveling on the Atlantic.

"OVER THERE"

The United States declared war on Germany on April 16, 1917. Thousands of American troops were rushed overseas in groups of ships that traveled together for safety. In May 1918, the number of American soldiers crossing the Atlantic reached almost 250,000.

The War Front

As the soldiers soon discovered, the war being fought in Europe was a new kind of war. Advances in technology had made combat more destructive than ever before. Bullets from machine guns hit dozens of soldiers at a time. Airplanes attacked from above. Armor-covered vehicles called tanks rumbled across the battlefield.

Another new and terrifying weapon was poison gas. If a soldier failed to wear a gas mask, he could be burned or blinded. An American named Jeremiah Evarts later recalled a German poison gas attack:

> They fired so many mustard gas shells one night that an actual gas pond formed in a gully [ditch]. And that mustard stuff was horrible. Many times you wouldn't even know it was there until it had burned . . . you.

Airplanes (top) and machine guns (above) were among the new weapons used in World War I. A United States poster (right) asked young men to sign up for the war.

These weapons took a terrible toll on human lives. During the Battle of Meuse-Argonne (MYOOZ ahr GUN) in 1918 almost 30,000 Americans lost their lives. About 896,000 United States troops fought in this battle, which helped the Allied Powers win the war.

By the end of the war, about two million Americans had served in the military. The soldiers had come from every part of our country. One army division included men from 26 different states. It was nicknamed the "Rainbow Division." Blacks, however, were not permitted to fight alongside whites. The military would remain segregated for years to come.

The "Home Front"

Americans on the "home front" also made contributions to the war effort. The army needed weapons, food, clothing, and fuel. To speed production, the government took over the railroads and telegraphs. Many factories worked overtime. Almost ten million Americans worked in the war industries. With so many men fighting in the war, jobs that had been closed to women and African Americans became available to them for the first time. Over 100,000 women went to work in weapons factories.

People also helped the war effort by saving scarce products or doing without them. Many people responded to the government's request for "Wheatless Mondays" and "Meatless Tuesdays" so more would be available for troops.

The war effort even affected the way people set their clocks. In 1918 Congress adopted daylight saving time. By setting their clocks an hour earlier, Americans gained an extra hour of daylight and saved tons of fuel needed for the war.

Newspapers worldwide announced the war's end.

Making Peace

The continuing arrival of American troops, money, and supplies weakened the Central Powers. On November 11, 1918, they finally surrendered. In the United States we celebrate this day as Veterans Day.

The "war to end all wars" had come to an end. The costs had been terrible for both sides. At least 10 million soldiers were killed on the battlefield. Over 100,000 were American soldiers.

In 1919 representatives of the Allied Powers met at Versailles (vair SĪ), near Paris, France. There they created a peace agreement that placed responsibility for the war on Germany. The Treaty of Versailles took away Germany's colonies, redrew its national borders, and demanded that Germany pay heavy fines to the Allied Powers.

At the same time President Wilson persuaded the Allied Powers to create the League of Nations, the first organization of countries designed to prevent future wars. According to Wilson, the League of Nations would ensure "political independence and territorial integrity [wholeness] to great and small" countries alike.

Many Americans, however, were concerned that membership in the League of Nations would draw the United States into other wars. Congress rejected Wilson's plans to join the League.

The artist Jacob Lawrence painted many scenes of the Great Migration (left). Booker T. Washington (below) stressed education as a way to fight discrimination.

CHICAGO   NEW YORK   ST. LOUIS

The Phillips Collection

THE GREAT MIGRATION

In the 1890s many African Americans from rural areas in the Southeast had begun moving to urban areas in the Northeast and Middle West. Historians call this the Great Migration. Most African Americans moved north to escape discrimination and poverty. Discrimination is an unfair difference in the treatment of people.

As more jobs became available during World War I, the number of African Americans migrating north increased greatly. In Chicago the African American population climbed from 44,000 to 110,000 in the years 1910 to 1920. About 500,000 African Americans went north during the war years.

For many African Americans factory jobs were a great improvement over farm work. A popular African American newspaper called the *Chicago Defender* encouraged African Americans to move north with the slogan *"The Defender* Says Come."

Struggles for Justice

Although African Americans still faced problems in both the North and South, they were making progress. In 1881 a former slave named Booker T. Washington founded the Tuskegee Institute in Alabama. At Tuskegee, African Americans were taught skills such as printing, bricklaying, and teaching, which would help them rise out of poverty.

To fight discrimination, the National Association for the Advancement of Colored People, or NAACP, was founded in 1909 by both blacks and whites. By 1920 the NAACP had 90,000 members. W.E.B. Du Bois (doo BOYS), one of its founders, wrote that an African American wished to keep from "having the doors of opportunity closed roughly in his face." Du Bois, an educator and historian, was one of the first leaders to urge African Americans to join together to fight prejudice. His books are still used today.

Another founder of the NAACP was Ida Wells-Barnett. A former slave, Wells-Barnett became a reporter and part owner of *Free Speech,* a newspaper in Memphis, Tennessee. Her articles about violence toward African Americans inspired others to work to end it. "Can you remain silent," she wrote ". . . when [African Americans are being killed] in our own community and country?"

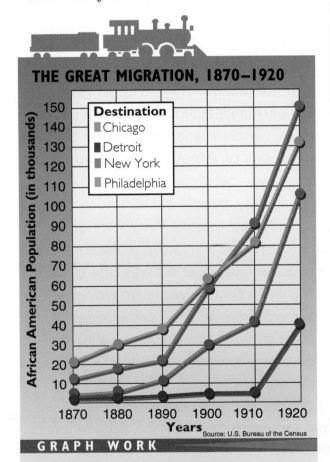

THE GREAT MIGRATION, 1870–1920

Destination
- Chicago
- Detroit
- New York
- Philadelphia

African American Population (in thousands)

Years

Source: U.S. Bureau of the Census

GRAPH WORK

The railroad was the common way for African Americans from the South to travel north.

1. How many decades does the line graph show?

2. Which city had received the greatest number of African Americans by 1920?

WHY IT MATTERS

World War I strengthened the role of the United States in international events. The war also produced much suffering and sadness. Once the "war to end all wars" was over, Americans looked forward to happier times.

World War I also helped make the Great Migration possible. Some African Americans who moved north were able to make better lives for themselves and their children. Today many African Americans are returning to the South because of new economic opportunities there. Organizations like the NAACP continue to fight for equal rights.

✔️ Reviewing Facts and Ideas

MAIN IDEAS

- The United States entered World War I in 1917 and helped the Allied Powers win the war. President Wilson helped create the League of Nations in 1919, although the United States did not join.

- The Great Migration of African Americans from the Southeast to cities of the Northeast and Middle West increased during World War I.

THINK ABOUT IT

1. Why did the United States enter World War I?

2. Why was World War I so much more destructive than earlier wars?

3. **FOCUS** How did World War I change the United States?

4. **THINKING SKILL** Name one *cause* and one *effect* of the Great Migration. Give reasons for your choice.

5. **WRITE** Write a newspaper editorial supporting or opposing membership in the League of Nations.

The Granger Collection

"The Diamond as Big as the Ritz"
By F. Scott Fitzgerald

Focus Activity

READ TO LEARN

Why are the 1920s known as "the Roaring Twenties"?

VOCABULARY

- Roaring Twenties
- jazz
- media
- suffrage
- Nineteenth Amendment
- League of Women Voters

PEOPLE

- Duke Ellington
- F. Scott Fitzgerald
- Langston Hughes
- Charles Lindbergh
- Amelia Earhart
- Susan B. Anthony
- Carrie Chapman Catt

1910   1919 1928   1940   1950

The Roaring Twenties

Read Aloud

Calvin Coolidge, the President from 1923 to 1929, called the 1920s "a new era of prosperity." For many Americans this description was "right on the money."

THE BIG PICTURE

For about ten years after World War I, the United States enjoyed a time of prosperity. Although many people struggled to earn a living, incomes were rising. A growing number of people made fortunes by buying and selling stocks. Millions of Americans enjoyed better living conditions than ever before.

Along with more money, people gained more free time in which to spend their money. Why? For one thing, labor unions fought for a shorter workday. In 1923 United States Steel Corporation was one of the first companies to change to an eight-hour workday. Soon the eight-hour workday became widespread. At the same time industries were producing new products. They included new electrical appliances—such as washing machines, irons, and vacuum cleaners—that made household chores easier to perform.

The prosperity and excitement of the decade led to the nickname, the Roaring Twenties, for these years. In the following pages you will learn more about this exciting period.

GOOD TIMES

After the hardships of the war, Americans were eager to enjoy themselves. During the 1920s people also began listening to a new kind of music called jazz. Rooted in African American culture, jazz is full of striking rhythms and sounds. One of the composers who brought this new music to audiences across the country was Duke Ellington. Ellington helped to give the decade yet another nickname, "the Jazz Age."

An Inspiring Decade

Many American writers tried to capture the special feeling of the Roaring Twenties. One such writer, F. Scott Fitzgerald, once described the 1920s as "the greatest, gaudiest spree [liveliest party] in history." His full name, Francis Scott Key Fitzgerald, was given in honor of a famous ancestor. Today Fitzgerald is remembered for writing stories and novels that described life in the 1920s. Other writers who became known during this period were Ernest Hemingway, William Faulkner, and Dorothy Parker.

A cultural movement called the Harlem Renaissance reflected African American life during the 1920s. Harlem is a neighborhood in New York City. The writer Langston Hughes used rhythms of African American music in his poetry. In "Harlem Night Song," Hughes wrote about his own sense of the decade:

> Night-sky is blue.
> Stars are great drops
> Of golden dew.
> In the cabaret [nightclub]
> The jazz-band's playing . . .

Other writers of the Harlem Renaissance were Countee Cullen and Zora Neale Hurston.

Duke Ellington (below) composed jazz music tunes that many young people (left) enjoyed.

Charlie Chaplin (hanging upside down) was a popular comic actor in the silent films.

NEW TECHNOLOGY

New technology helped shape the Roaring Twenties. The automobile brought people closer together, and electricity put entertainment at their fingertips. The widespread use of the automobile, indeed, changed life in the United States and the world.

A Revolution on Four Wheels

During the 1920s many people with moderate incomes owned automobiles for the first time. By the end of the 1920s, there was one car on the road for every five people. The automobile linked the city and country more closely. Children in rural areas could travel to school without difficulty. Farmers could bring their crops to market quickly in reliable trucks. In addition, people could shop more easily. The first shopping center with a parking lot opened in Kansas City, Missouri, in 1924.

The automobile also encouraged tourism. Many people—whose jobs allowed for vacations for the first time—explored the country by car. In fact, the word *motel*—meaning a hotel for motorists—first appeared in 1925.

Radios and "Talkies"

Electricity brought a greater variety of entertainment into the homes of anyone who could buy a radio. The first radio station started broadcasting in 1920. Within 20 years people were listening to the radio on an average of four and a half hours every day. People gathered around radios of all shapes and sizes to listen to music, news, sporting events, comedy shows, and the first "soap operas."

At the same time Thomas Edison's invention, the "talking picture," was sweeping the country. People in the United States had been enjoying silent films since the early 1900s. When Al Jolson's *The Jazz Singer* appeared in 1927, this first "talkie" won a whole new audience. By 1930 more than 80 million Americans went to movie theaters every week. They cheered at westerns and laughed at comedians like Charlie Chaplin.

The Media Explosion

Radio and film were only part of the rapid growth of media in the United States. We use the word *media* to describe methods of communication that reach large numbers of people. The media includes radio, newspapers, and magazines. During the Roaring Twenties, all these forms of media began to boom like never before. Of course, there was no television yet. Many magazines you see today—such as *Reader's Digest* and *Time*—started during the decade of the 1920s.

The media explosion gave birth to the advertising industry. Manufacturers saw an opportunity to reach the public through newspapers, magazines, and radio. Soon people were humming tunes from commercials and using advertising slogans in their conversations.

Media Celebrities

The 1920s also saw the rise of media celebrities. The fame of some people was spread to even the most remote places by newspapers, radio, and newsreels, or short films about current events.

One of the most famous people of the decade was Charles Lindbergh. In May 1927 the young pilot made the first non-stop, solo airplane flight across the Atlantic Ocean. In 33 hours and 29 minutes, he flew from New York to Paris, France. Six other pilots had died trying to accomplish this feat.

In any era people would have admired Lindbergh's skill and bravery. In this decade, however, "Lucky Lindy" instantly became a national hero. People waited by their radios to hear news of his flight. The papers were brimming with photographs, articles, and poems about the 25-year-old pilot.

Similar fame awaited another pilot, Amelia Earhart. In 1928, on the 25th anniversary of the Wright Brothers' flight, Earhart became the first woman to cross the Atlantic. Like Lindbergh, she caught the spirit of the age with her adventurousness. Thanks to the media, she too became famous to Americans.

Ideals A heating plant sightly and shining, with the swiftest response to her slightest touch. So clean that the loveliest gown is not blemished, so economical that it is OF THE FUEL... it owns a proud right to its name. ...see it for your own sake, but even more for her. For all ...ly fulfilled in this new IDEAL Type "A" Heat Machine.

RADIATOR COMPANY NEW YORK and CHICAGO

The radio (left) and the home heater (above) brought new entertainment and comfort to many American homes.

The Granger Collection

After years of protest (below), the Nineteenth Amendment gave women the vote. This magazine celebrates the victory (left).

WOMEN FIGHT FOR SUFFRAGE

Amelia Earhart was only one of millions of women who were reaching new goals in the 1920s. After more than 50 years of struggle and hard work, women had finally won the right to vote in national elections.

The fight for suffrage, or the right to vote, began with the Seneca Falls Convention in 1848, which you have read about in Chapter 16. Leaders of the convention believed that women could use the vote to gain other rights for themselves. As Susan B. Anthony argued, suffrage was "the pivotal [crucial] right, the one that underlies all other rights."

The suffrage movement gained strength in 1870 when the Fifteenth Amendment granted African American men the right to vote. In 1872 Anthony and a group of women marched into a polling place in Rochester, New York, and cast their votes in a presidential election. The women were arrested and fined. Six years later, in 1878, a women's suffrage amendment was introduced in Congress.

The Nineteenth Amendment

The women's suffrage amendment did not pass the first year that it was introduced. The women did not give up. The amendment was reintroduced in every session of Congress for the next 40 years.

Many suffrage leaders like Carrie Chapman Catt crisscrossed the country giving speeches, writing articles, and organizing workers. Catt led a "suffrage army" of one million volunteers. She made expert use of the media to spread her arguments.

In 1919 these efforts finally paid off. Congress passed the Nineteenth Amendment, which gave women the right to vote. On August 26, 1920, the states approved this amendment, which guaranteed every adult woman the right to a voice in the government of the country.

For Carrie Chapman Catt and her supporters, however, other battles still remained. In 1920 Catt helped to found the League of Women Voters. Since the 1920s this organization has helped to inform both women and men about political issues.

Women in the Workplace

Although women had won the right to vote, they made little progress in the workplace during the 1920s. During World War I with most men serving as soldiers, many women went to work in factories and other businesses. After the war, however, many women returned to their homes. By 1920 fewer women worked outside the home than had done so a decade earlier. Most women worked at home as homemakers.

Even so the U.S. Census of 1930 listed women in jobs ranging from lawyers to house painters. There was also a woman governor in 1924—Nellie Tayloe Ross of Wyoming. Yet most employed women worked in important but low-paying jobs such as nursing, teaching, housekeeping, and office work.

WHY IT MATTERS

The Roaring Twenties did not bring good times for everyone. Many people who returned from fighting in World War I believed that jobs should go to people born in the United States. Immigrants had a hard time finding jobs. African Americans also faced difficult times. They struggled even more as hate groups such as the Ku Klux Klan gained new strength.

The Roaring Twenties would not last forever. As you will read in the next lesson, hard times were ahead for practically all Americans.

Could women vote before the Nineteenth Amendment?

The Nineteenth Amendment granted women the right to vote in 1920. Yet 15 states and territories had already granted full voting rights to women decades earlier. The Wyoming Territory was the first to grant women suffrage, in 1869. A year later the women of the Utah Territory also won the vote. Colorado was next, in 1893. Idaho followed in 1896.

VOTING BOOTH

✓ Reviewing Facts and Ideas

MAIN IDEAS

- The 1920s were a decade of prosperity and excitement.
- The automobile and other technology dramatically changed life during the 1920s.
- In 1919 women in the United States won the right to vote with the passage of the Nineteenth Amendment.

THINK ABOUT IT

1. How did the automobile change life in our country?

2. What differences did the Nineteenth Amendment make?

3. **FOCUS** How did the Roaring Twenties earn this nickname?

4. **THINKING SKILL** Put these events in the proper *sequence*: Lindbergh's Atlantic flight, the first commercial radio station, the Nineteenth Amendment, the appearance of motels.

5. **WRITING** Suppose you were writing a newspaper article in favor of women's suffrage. What would your arguments be?

Citizens Helping Citizens

Do you belong to a soccer or baseball league? Take dance classes? Help to feed homeless people? Activities such as these are often run by organizations in your community. How did these organizations get started?

Many Americans who prospered during the early 1900s had come from poor families. Often they had learned valuable skills or received help from organizations such as those shown on these pages. They wanted to extend this chance to others. The organizations they founded are a living legacy of the tradition of citizens helping citizens in the United States.

Girls Scouts of the U.S.A.

Juliet Low (above, center) founded the Girl Scouts of America in Savannah, Georgia, in 1912. Girl Scouts today (left) continue to serve their communities through volunteer activities.

Mary McLeod Bethune (center) founded Bethune-Cookman College for African Americans in Florida in 1904. She later helped found the National Association for Colored Women to work for equal rights.

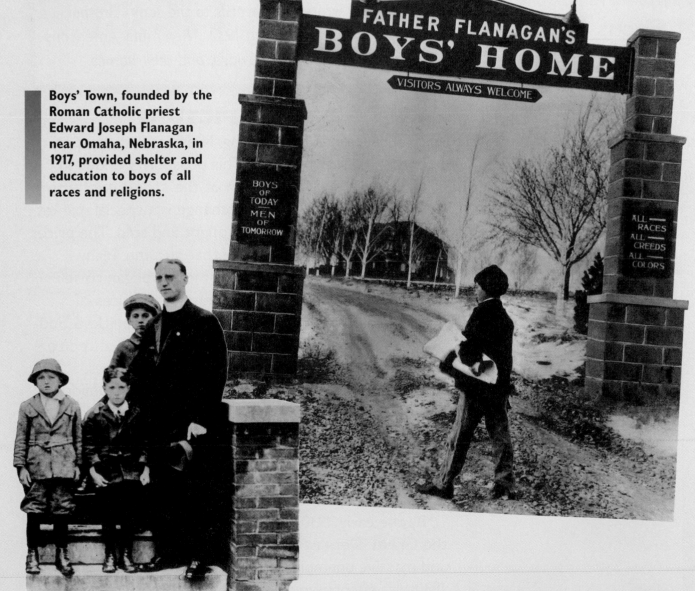

Boys' Town, founded by the Roman Catholic priest Edward Joseph Flanagan near Omaha, Nebraska, in 1917, provided shelter and education to boys of all races and religions.

1910   1920   1940   1950
        1929   1938

The Great Depression

Read Aloud

They used to tell me I was building a dream
With peace and glory ahead.
Why should I be standing in line
Just waiting for bread?

Yip Harburg wrote these words to the song "Brother,
Can You Spare a Dime?" in 1932. Then many Americans
had lost their jobs, their savings, and their homes.

Focus Activity

READ TO LEARN

What happened during the Great Depression?

VOCABULARY

- stock exchange
- Great Depression
- New Deal
- unemployment
- hydroelectricity

PEOPLE

- Herbert Hoover
- Franklin Delano Roosevelt
- Eleanor Roosevelt

PLACES

- Dust Bowl
- Hoover Dam

THE BIG PICTURE

As you have read, the Roaring Twenties brought prosperity to many Americans. This prosperity ended in 1929, however, with the crash of the **stock exchange** in New York City. A stock exchange is a special market where shares of stocks are bought and sold. The prices of stocks began to drop early that autumn. Many investors, afraid of losing more money, began to sell their stocks. The sudden sale caused the prices of stocks to fall even more. Investors were panicked. Suddenly, everyone wanted to sell and no one wanted to buy. As a result, many stocks became worthless.

The stock market crash shook Americans' confidence in the economy. In the years after 1929, many banks and businesses failed. Thousands of Americans lost their savings and their jobs. Some people no longer had the money to buy goods. With fewer customers, still more companies and factories had to shut down.

By the early 1930s, the United States was undergoing the **Great Depression**. This period of failed businesses and massive unemployment would last throughout the 1930s. Its effects would be felt for years.

Many farm houses, barns, and other buildings in the Dust Bowl were covered above the windows by eroded soil in the 1930s.

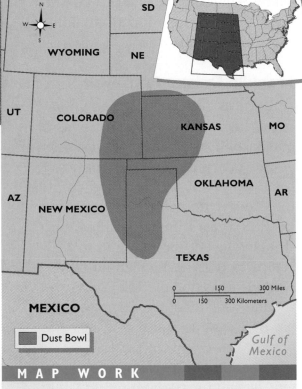

THE DUST BOWL, 1935–1940

Dust Bowl

SD
WYOMING
NE
UT
COLORADO
KANSAS
MO
AZ
NEW MEXICO
OKLAHOMA
AR
TEXAS
MEXICO
Gulf of Mexico

0   150   300 Miles
0   150   300 Kilometers

MAP WORK

The droughts that caused the Dust Bowl ruined farms in six states.

1. Which states were affected by the Dust Bowl?
2. Which parts of these states received little or no rain?

HARD TIMES

The effects of the Great Depression were widespread. By 1932 more than 5,000 banks had failed, and 32,000 companies and stores had closed. More than 12 million Americans—one out of every four adults—were out of work.

The shortage of jobs created other problems. Many families lost their homes since they lacked the money to pay for them. With many people unable to pay taxes, some communities had to close their schools.

The Dust Bowl

Nature added its own disaster to the Great Depression. Years of drought during the 1930s turned more than 150,000 square miles of the Great Plains into dust. Use the map on this page to locate the "Dust Bowl." Many farmers in the Dust Bowl watched as their fields dried up and their crops died.

"Black blizzards," or giant dust storms, blew across the entire region. They blotted out the sun and buried farmhouses up to the windowsills. "When they would hit," a woman named Mary Owsley recalled, "you had to clean house from attic to ground. Everything was covered in sand." Thousands of farmers went broke. More than half of the population of the Dust Bowl left the region. Many hoped to find work picking crops in California. Yet jobs were scarce there, too, at this time.

FRANKLIN ROOSEVELT BECOMES PRESIDENT

At first the federal government did little to try to ease the Depression. President Herbert Hoover, like many, believed that the economy would soon recover. He promised Americans that better times were "just around the corner." Instead the hard times got harder. Many Americans turned to another leader whom they hoped would guide the United States through this crisis.

Franklin Delano Roosevelt

Born in 1882, widely known as FDR, Franklin Delano Roosevelt was a cousin of Theodore Roosevelt. As a young man FDR entered politics. In 1921, however, a disease called polio took away the use of his legs. Over the next few years, his wife, Eleanor Roosevelt, encouraged him to return to politics. In 1928 he was elected governor of New York.

One year after the Depression hit, Roosevelt spoke of new solutions. "The country," he said, "demands bold, persistent [steady] experimentation." Statements like this raised people's hopes. In 1932 FDR was elected President.

The newly elected President faced a difficult job. The country's spirit seemed to have fallen along with the economy. In his Inaugural Address FDR promised to fight the Depression with all the powers of the federal government. Read the excerpt from this address. What did Roosevelt mean by "the only thing we have to fear is fear itself"?

MANY VOICES
PRIMARY SOURCE

Excerpt from Inaugural Address, by President Franklin Delano Roosevelt, March 4, 1933.

*This is **pre-eminently** the time to speak the truth, the whole truth, frankly and boldly. Nor need we shrink from honestly facing conditions in our country today. This great nation will endure as it has endured, will revive and will prosper. So, first of all, let me **assert** my firm belief that the only thing we have to fear is fear itself. . . . We do not distrust the future of **essential** democracy. The people of the United States have not failed. In their need they have registered a **mandate** that they want direct, **vigorous** action. They have asked for discipline and direction under leadership. They have made me the instrument of their wishes. In the spirit of the gift I take it.*

pre-eminently: above all
assert: state directly
essential: basic
mandate: vote
vigorous: forceful

By selling apples or whatever else they could find, many Americans tried to soften the blow of **unemployment**.

The New Deal

Roosevelt believed that the government had to change the way the economy worked in order to end the Great Depression. The program he developed to bring about this change was called the New Deal.

Under the New Deal, banks were closed and then reopened under government supervision. Loans were given to farmers and to businesses in danger of closing. A system was developed to control the sale of stocks.

A key law of the New Deal was the Social Security Act of 1935. It gave financial help to retired Americans and the disabled. Yet it was mainly designed to help the jobless. By 1940 the government had provided $16 billion to help the jobless. The New Deal also helped people who did have jobs. Congress passed a law that recognized the right of workers to form labor unions. Years later another law set a minimum wage for all Americans and made the standard work week 40 hours long.

UNEMPLOYMENT IN THE UNITED STATES, 1920–1940

Unemployed People (in millions) — Years

Source: U.S. Bureau of the Census

GRAPH WORK

So many Americans were out of work during the Great Depression that large numbers became homeless and lived in places known as tent cities.

1. In what year did unemployment reach its highest point?

2. About how many people were without jobs during that year?

3. During which two years did the greatest number of people become unemployed?

595

The Granger Collection

PUTTING PEOPLE TO WORK

The New Deal helped save existing jobs. It also helped people without jobs. As the graph on page 595 shows, unemployment—the number of workers without jobs—remained a major problem. To put Americans back to work, Roosevelt created various programs funded by taxes paid to the government.

The "Alphabet Administration"

Many of these programs were identified by their initials. Over time Roosevelt's government became known as the "Alphabet Administration." The Works Progress Administration, or WPA, was a program that put jobless people to work building schools, libraries, playgrounds, and hospitals. The WPA also employed artists, teachers, and musicians. The Civilian Conservation Corps, or the CCC, hired more than 250,000 young men to maintain the forests.

Another important program President Roosevelt created was the Tennessee Valley Authority, or TVA. The TVA built bridges, roads, and dams. Other dams, such as the giant Hoover Dam on the Colorado River, were completed in 1936. These dams helped irrigate the soil, which allowed more land to be farmed. They also prevented flooding and generated hydroelectricity for people in rural areas. Hydroelectricity is electricity generated by the force of running water.

Eleanor, Everywhere

Helping the United States recover from the Depression was a huge job. Eleanor Roosevelt played a key role in helping FDR meet this challenge. Traveling throughout the country, she became an extra set of "eyes and ears" for FDR. In 1933 alone she traveled 40,000 miles. This earned her a nickname, "Eleanor, everywhere."

The mural (left) was painted in 1934 for the WPA. Young men who worked for the Civilian Conservation Corps (below), known as CCC boys, built and maintained parks.

In 1936 Eleanor Roosevelt began writing a newspaper column called "My Day." For millions of her readers, she became a symbol of the link between the federal government and its citizens.

Eleanor Roosevelt also fought hard for issues that concerned her, such as civil rights and equality for women. As she said years later in a speech in 1958:

> *Where, after all, do universal rights begin? In small places, close to home . . . where every man, woman, and child seeks equal justice, equal opportunity, equal dignity without discrimination.*

WHY IT MATTERS

Although the New Deal did not end the Great Depression, it helped millions of people to survive until the economy recovered. The ideas behind the New

Deal continued to shape our government for many years to come. Many of the laws passed, such as the Social Security Act and the Wagner Act, are still in place today.

Under the New Deal the role government played in people's lives increased greatly. The low-cost electricity provided by the TVA projects still exist. However, people are now debating the role of the federal government. Often these debates are over the programs that began under the New Deal.

✓ Reviewing Facts and Ideas

MAIN IDEAS

- The stock market crash of 1929 signaled the beginning of the Great Depression. Banks and businesses failed, putting millions of Americans out of work.

- Franklin Roosevelt was elected President in 1932. He fought the Great Depression with a wide variety of New Deal programs.

- Although the New Deal did not end the Great Depression, it made many Americans more hopeful and helped them to survive the hard times.

THINK ABOUT IT

1. What was the Dust Bowl?

2. Name two New Deal programs and explain what they did.

3. **FOCUS** What were some of the effects of the Great Depression?

4. **THINKING SKILL** What can you <u>conclude</u> about how the role of the federal government changed under Franklin Roosevelt? Give evidence to support your conclusion.

5. **WRITE** Write an editorial about the Great Depression and suggest some solutions for ending it.

The Granger Collection

World War II

Focus Activity

READ TO LEARN

What was the role of the United States in World War II?

VOCABULARY

- dictator
- Axis
- Allies
- World War II
- communism
- relocation camp
- concentration camp
- Holocaust
- atomic bomb

PEOPLE

- Adolf Hitler
- Josef Stalin
- Dwight D. Eisenhower
- Harry S Truman
- Albert Einstein

PLACES

- Pearl Harbor
- Hiroshima
- Nagasaki

Read Aloud

"It's the only war I can think of that I would have volunteered for," said Bill Mauldin a United States soldier. Like millions of Americans, he viewed World War II as a tragic struggle—but a necessary one.

THE BIG PICTURE

As you have read, Americans spent the 1930s surviving the Great Depression. Many other countries around the world were also experiencing great difficulties and changes at this time. In several countries, power-hungry **dictators** were taking control. A dictator is a leader with complete authority over the government.

Who were these power-hungry dictators? Benito Mussolini (be NEE toh mus oh LEE nee) made himself dictator of Italy. In Germany, **Adolf Hitler** and his Nazi (NAH tsee) Party took control of the government. In Japan a group of military officers made most of the important decisions for their people. In 1936 these three countries signed a treaty of friendship. They called themselves the **Axis** countries.

Throughout the 1930s the Axis leaders expanded their power by invading neighboring countries. Japan conquered a region of China called Manchuria. Italy invaded Ethiopia in East Africa. Germany took over Austria and Czechoslovakia.

As Americans listened to war reports on their radios, most hoped the United States would not get involved in the fighting. Soon, however, the United States itself would come under attack.

598

THREATS TO PEACE

At first most countries in Europe and Asia tried to tolerate Axis invasions into nearby countries. After the damage caused by World War I, many were afraid of starting another large-scale conflict. On September 1, 1939, however, Hitler invaded Poland. Both Great Britain and France, who called themselves the Allies, declared war on the Axis. World War II had begun.

Hitler then advanced into Denmark and Norway. In May 1940 his armies invaded the Netherlands, Belgium, and France. In all of western Europe, only Great Britain remained free of Axis rule.

The Bombing of Pearl Harbor

Many Americans hoped to stay out of the conflict in Europe. President Roosevelt promised them, "We will not send our army, naval or air forces to fight in foreign lands . . . except in case of attack."

A surprise attack by Japan drew the United States into the war. By 1941 the Japanese were taking over islands in the Pacific Ocean. Part of their plan was to force the United States out of this region.

On December 7, 1941, the Japanese struck the American base in Pearl Harbor, Hawaii, without warning. The Japanese bombs destroyed ships, planes, and military supplies. They also killed 2,403 Americans. John Garcia, a Hawaiian civilian who was then only 16 years old, helped rescue American sailors:

Some were unconscious, some were dead. So I spent the rest of the day swimming inside the harbor along with some other Hawaiians. I brought out I don't know how many bodies. . . Another man would put them in ambulances and they'd be gone.

The next day President Roosevelt asked Congress to declare war on Japan. He called the Japanese attack "a date which will live in infamy," or be remembered for evil. Three days later Germany and Italy declared war on the United States.

Japan's attack on battle ships (left) at Pearl Harbor drew our country into World War II. Adolf Hitler (below) symbolized the threats the Allies were fighting.

The Granger Collection

Both men and women built war planes (left) in the United States. "Rosie the Riveter" (below) represented the contribution of women.

The Granger Collection

JOINING THE ALLIES

To defeat the Axis, the United States joined the Allies, which now included the Soviet Union. The largest part of the Soviet Union was Russia, a country which had been controlled by a communist government since a revolution in 1917. Communism is an economic and political system in which all property is owned by the government.

Since the 1920s the Soviet Union had been ruled by a dictator named Josef Stalin. In 1939 Stalin had made a deal with Hitler to keep the two countries from fighting each other. In June 1941, however, Hitler's army attacked the Soviet Union. From that point on, the Soviet Union fought with the Allies against Germany.

A War on Two Fronts

The United States had entered a worldwide conflict and had to fight a war on two fronts, or areas of battle. On the Pacific front the Allies fought the Japanese. On the other front, which stretched through Africa and Europe, it faced Germany and Italy.

This two-front war required a giant army. Over the next four years, more than 15 million Americans served in the military. As in World War I, the army

was still segregated. Yet for the first time women were allowed to join the military services. By 1943 every branch of the United States military had created units for women. More than 270,000 signed up for such units as the Women's Army Corps, or WAC. Women pilots also flew supply planes across the Atlantic.

Working Overtime

Earlier in this chapter, you studied the home-front activities of World War I. Similar efforts also took place during World War II, but on a greater scale. President Roosevelt declared that the United States must become "the arsenal of democracy." An arsenal is a place where weapons are made or stored. Across the country, factories worked overtime to produce goods for the war. By the end of the war, more than 70,000 ships and 3 million machine guns had rolled off the production lines. A German general had said that "the Americans can't build planes, only electric iceboxes and razor blades." He was wrong. By 1944 American factories produced an average of 263 planes a day!

Many of these war goods were made by women. The employment of women nearly doubled during World War II. By the end of 1943, more than 300,000 women had worked in the aircraft industry alone.

As in World War I, Americans were asked to conserve products. Children collected scrap metal, bottle caps, and rubber bands, which were recycled into military products. People cut down on their use of gasoline, aluminum foil, meat, and other items.

American Relocation Camps

In the days following Pearl Harbor, some people on the home front began to worry that the large number of Japanese Americans living on the West Coast might be loyal to the enemy. These fears proved to be groundless. No Japanese Americans were found guilty of treason.

In 1942, the government made more than 100,000 Japanese Americans leave their homes on the West Coast. Many of their rights were taken away, including freedom of speech and the right to vote. These Americans were also deprived of their homes, businesses, and property and were moved to hastily built relocation camps farther inland. Yuri Tateishi (UR ee ta TAY shee) described the Manzanar camp where she was taken:

> The floors [of our barrack] were boarded, but they were about a quarter to a half inch apart, and the next morning you could see the ground below. . . . Our family was large enough that we didn't have to share our barrack with another family but all seven of us were in one room.

Even while living in relocation camps, about 330,000 Japanese Americans volunteered to serve in the United States military. During the war and long afterward, people protested against relocation camps. Finally, in 1988, the United States government issued an official apology for its actions.

New York City children (left) show tin cans they collected for the war effort. A ration coupon (above) helped conserve food.

601

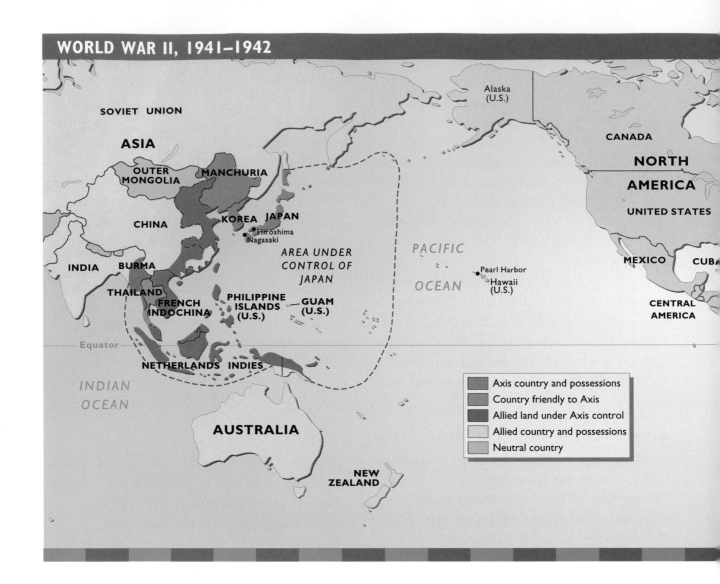

SOVIET UNION

ASIA

OUTER MONGOLIA

MANCHURIA

CHINA

KOREA   JAPAN

• Hiroshima
Nagasaki

AREA UNDER
CONTROL OF
JAPAN

INDIA   BURMA

THAILAND

FRENCH
INDOCHINA

PHILIPPINE
ISLANDS
(U.S.)   GUAM
(U.S.)

Equator

NETHERLANDS INDIES

INDIAN
OCEAN

AUSTRALIA

NEW
ZEALAND

Alaska
(U.S.)

CANADA

NORTH
AMERICA

UNITED STATES

MEXICO   CUBA

CENTRAL
AMERICA

PACIFIC

OCEAN

• Pearl Harbor
Hawaii
(U.S.)

	Axis country and possessions
	Country friendly to Axis
	Allied land under Axis control
	Allied country and possessions
	Neutral country

BATTLES AROUND THE WORLD

Unlike previous wars, World War II was truly a world war. Its battles were fought around the globe. Widely sepa-rated as they were, these clashes marked a turning point. Throughout 1943 and 1944, the Allies pushed back their enemies. The Axis had stopped expanding and was on the defensive.

Victory in Europe

By 1944 most of Europe was still under Axis control. The leader of the Allies' military forces in Europe, General Dwight D. Eisenhower, began planning for a massive invasion. This invasion took place on June 6, or "D-Day." Several hundred thousand Allied

General Eisenhower (left) met with United States troops on June 6, 1944, before the invasion of Normandy.

MAP WORK

The fighting of World War II involved every inhabited continent on Earth.

1. Which country in Asia was friendly to the Axis?

2. Which countries on the European continent remained neutral during the war?

3. Which countries in Asia formed the Axis?

4. Which Allied countries under Axis control were west of Germany?

troops landed at Normandy, France. Find Normandy on the map above.

The fighting at Normandy was fierce. Many Allied soldiers lost their lives. Still, the Normandy invasion was an Allied military success. By September 11, the Allies had freed France, Belgium, and Luxembourg from the Axis. Allied troops soon began pushing east toward Germany.

At the same time the Soviet army was moving west. At Stalingrad, it began driving Hitler's forces back to Germany.

Berlin, the German capital, fell on April 16, 1945. Germany surrendered on May 7. The war in Europe was over.

United States troops marched through Germany in December 1944.

FINAL VICTORY AND ITS COSTS

Much of Europe had been reduced to rubble by large-scale bombing. Some of the worst slaughter of the war, however, took place off the battlefield.

The Holocaust

As the Allies advanced toward Germany in 1944, they came across several concentration camps. Here the Germans enslaved and murdered those people they considered their enemies.

As many as 12 million men, women, and children died at the hands of Nazi Germany. About half of the victims were Jews. In a 1939 speech Hitler had promised to destroy the Jews in Europe. Unfairly blaming Jews for Germany's loss in World War I, as well as for other problems, Hitler singled them out for destruction. By the end of the war six million Jews had been murdered, many in gas chambers built for that purpose. This attempt to destroy the Jewish people is known as the Holocaust (HAHL uh kawst). The word *holocaust* means "destruction by fire."

The Soviet Army freed several concentration camps as it advanced from the east. The rest of the Allies freed prisoners from other camps.

The Americans were shocked by what they discovered. Leon Bass, a soldier in an African American unit described the scene at one camp:

> I saw human beings. . . standing there, skin and bones, dressed in striped pajamas. They had skeletal faces with deep-set eyes.

Japan Surrenders

Nonmilitary groups, or civilians, suffered in Asia as well as in Europe. Millions of Asians continued to live under Japanese control. In China, for example, over 200,000 civilians were massacred in Nanjing in 1937.

In 1945 Americans struck against Japan and captured two of Japan's islands, Iwo Jima and Okinawa. Thousands of Americans died in these two battles.

President Roosevelt himself died suddenly in April 1945. Harry S Truman became President and soon faced a difficult decision. Should he invade Japan? Or should he use the atomic bomb? The atomic bomb was a new weapon based on the latest advances in science. As yet unused in war, it was thought to be more destructive than any bomb ever created.

German troops rounded up Jewish men, women, and children (left) and took them to concentration camps.

The mushroom-shaped cloud of the atomic bomb rose over Nagasaki after it exploded.

Truman decided that the United States should drop the bomb to end the war and to spare the lives of those who would die in continued fighting. On August 6, 1945, a single airplane, the *Enola Gay,* flew over the Japanese city of Hiroshima and dropped its deadly cargo. The city was reduced to ashes, and at least 100,000 people died. Japan did not surrender completely. Three days later a second bomb was dropped on Nagasaki and caused another 70,000 deaths. On August 14, 1945, the Japanese government surrendered. World War II had finally ended.

WHY IT MATTERS

The atomic bomb brought the war against Japan to a quick close. Anton Bilek, who fought there, remembered:

If we'd landed there with a force, we'd have killed off more people than were killed by the bomb.

A new, powerfully destructive weapon, which few people knew much about, had been created. Albert Einstein, the scientist whose ideas had helped develop the bomb, said:

The unleashed power of the atom has changed everything . . . and we thus drift toward unparalleled catastrophes [unequaled disasters].

World War II was a terrible war. Over 50 million soldiers and civilians died. As a result of the war the United States became the most powerful country in the world. It would be up to the United States to help the world rebuild.

✔ Reviewing Facts and Ideas

MAIN IDEAS

- Invasions by the Axis in the 1930s set the stage for World War II.

- As a member of the Allies, the United States fought the war on two fronts—in Europe and Asia. The Axis was defeated in 1945.

- Over 50 million soldiers and civilians died in World War II.

THINK ABOUT IT

1. What is a dictator?

2. In what ways did Americans at home and abroad support the war?

3. **FOCUS** What was the Holocaust?

4. **THINKING SKILL** Was World War II a cause or an effect of the Axis invasions of the 1930s? Explain how you reached your *conclusion*.

5. **GEOGRAPHY** Look at the map on pages 602–603. Why did the United States fight the war on two fronts?

The Granger Collection

Determining the Credibility of a Source

VOCABULARY
credibility

WHY THE SKILL MATTERS

In Chapter 19 you learned about primary and secondary sources. We use information for understanding history. In this chapter, on page 594, for example, you read information in a primary source from President Franklin Delano Roosevelt.

This newspaper from Hawaii (left) gave the details of Japan's surprise attack on Pearl Harbor.

When learning about a new topic, however, how can you tell whether you should believe the source you are using? Asking a few key questions will help you to determine the credibility, or believability, of a source and the information in it.

USING THE SKILL

To determine if a source is credible, it is important to consider information about the source's author. You can use the steps in the Helping Yourself box on the next page to make this evaluation.

Reread the excerpt from Lesson 4 below. The quote, as you remember, comes from John Garcia, who was at Pearl Harbor when the Japanese attacked. He actually did the things he describes:

> *Some were unconscious, some were dead. So I spent the rest of the day swimming inside the harbor along with some other Hawaiians. I brought out I don't know how many bodies. . . . Another man would put them in ambulances and they'd be gone.*

Is Garcia's account a credible source? Ask yourself about the author. Was he in a position to describe the subject accurately? Since Garcia was present at the event and saw what happened, the answer is yes. Did Garcia have anything to gain by giving an untruthful account of the event? In this case the answer would seem to be no. After asking yourself these questions, you can conclude that the source is credible.

There is another way to check the source's credibility. If possible, you could locate another account of the same event and compare the two to see if the facts agree.

TRYING THE SKILL

Now look at this source. This is a quote that you read in the last lesson from a German general during World War II. Use the Helping Yourself to evaluate the credibility of this source.

The Americans can't build planes, only electric ice boxes and razor blades.

Based on your evaluation, is this a credible source about American technology in World War II? Remember, you should also consider comparing this source with other sources on the same subject.

Helping yourself

- Determining a source's **credibility** means deciding if the source can be believed.

- Determine whether the author has expert knowledge of the subject.

- Determine if the author has any reason to describe events a certain way.

- Find out if the author has a reputation for being accurate.

REVIEWING THE SKILL

1. What does *credibility* mean?

2. What questions should you ask to help you determine if a source is credible?

3. How can a second source be useful in establishing a document's credibility?

4. Given the following two choices, which would be a more credible source about World War II? Why?

a. The autobiography of an American Air Force pilot who kept a diary as he served in Europe between 1942 and 1944

b. A work of historical fiction about the events of D-Day written by an American author who was born in 1950

5. Why is it important to establish the credibility of any source when studying history?

This Pearl Harbor memorial was built to honor fallen sailors on the *U.S.S. Arizona.*

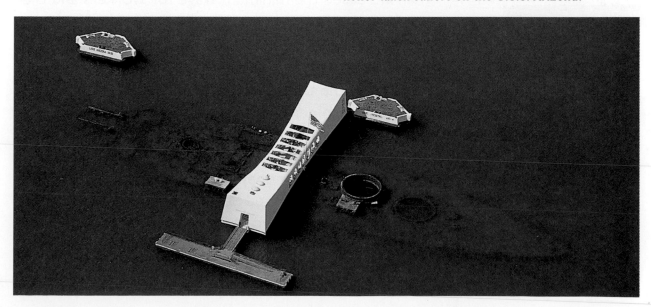

1910　1920　1930　1940　1945　1959

The Cold War

Read Aloud

In April 1945 delegates from 50 countries met in San Francisco to set up a new organization, the United Nations. Their meeting was to be the largest gathering of government representatives in history. Their goal was to maintain world peace. Yet in 1950 the United States would be fighting again.

Focus Activity

READ TO LEARN

How did the Cold War affect the United States?

VOCABULARY

- Cold War
- Iron Curtain
- Korean War
- United Nations
- arms race

PEOPLE

- Harry S Truman
- Dwight D. Eisenhower
- Joseph McCarthy

PLACES

- South Korea
- North Korea

THE BIG PICTURE

After World War II much of the world lay in ruins. The United States, however, stood largely untouched. The country's factories soon began turning out refrigerators, cars, and other peacetime products. By the 1950s American workers were producing and using over one third of all the world's goods.

The new President, **Harry S Truman**, carried on many of Franklin Roosevelt's New Deal programs. Truman also added his own called the "Fair Deal." Truman increased the minimum wage for workers and created housing for poor people. Veterans from the war were provided money for housing and education. Truman also supported equal rights. In 1948 he ended segregation in the United States armed forces and the federal government.

Truman's main concern, however, was the **Cold War** with the Soviet Union. The Cold War was a war fought with ideas, words, money, and sometimes force. After World War II the United States and the Soviet Union became the world's two most powerful countries. They had been allies during World War II, but the two "superpowers" became bitter enemies when the war ended. Read to discover why.

THE COLD WAR IN EUROPE, 1946

Communist countries
Non-communist countries
— "Iron Curtain"

ARCTIC OCEAN

250   500 Miles
250   500 Kilometers

ICELAND

ASIA

NORWAY

FINLAND

SWEDEN

North Sea

Baltic Sea

GREAT BRITAIN

DENMARK

IRELAND

SOVIET UNION

NETHERLANDS

POLAND

BELGIUM

EAST GERMANY

LUXEMBOURG

WEST GERMANY

CZECHOSLOVAKIA

ATLANTIC OCEAN

FRANCE

AUSTRIA

HUNGARY

Caspian Sea

SWITZERLAND

ROMANIA

Black Sea

YUGOSLAVIA

PORTUGAL

ITALY

BULGARIA

SPAIN

ALBANIA

GREECE

Mediterranean Sea

AFRICA

MAP WORK

Over the years the Iron Curtain had been the source of much tension between the United States and the Soviet Union.

1. Which countries bordered the Iron Curtain?

2. How many countries were under communist control?

3. Which noncommunist countries were north of the Iron Curtain dividing Germany?

THE "IRON CURTAIN"

Important differences had long divided the United States and the Soviet Union. Although these differences had been set aside during World War II, they caused tensions again after the war was over.

The Cold War Begins

After the war, the Soviet Union sent troops into Eastern Europe and put these countries under Soviet rule. Stalin did not let the countries hold free elections as he promised he would. The map on this page shows which countries became communist after World War II.

Stalin's actions concerned many world leaders. Winston Churchill, Great Britain's prime minister during World War II, declared in a 1946 speech, "An Iron Curtain has descended across the Continent." As the map above shows,

President Truman helped rebuild Western Europe after World War II.

the Iron Curtain was the imaginary line separating Europe's communist countries from its noncommunist ones.

In 1949 the United States and the countries of Western Europe formed an alliance called the North Atlantic Treaty Organization (NATO). NATO's goal was to fight the spread of communism.

President Truman then sponsored a program to provide $13 billion in food and goods to help Western Europe recover from the damage caused by the war. Called the Marshall Plan, the program helped prevent the spread of communism in Western Europe.

609

THE UNITED STATES IN THE COLD WAR

In June 1950 the Korean War began in Asia when a communist country invaded a noncommunist country. The Korean peninsula had been divided into two countries. After elections South Korea became a republic. North Korea had a communist government. On June 25, 1950, North Korean troops led a surprise attack on South Korea to unite the two countries by force under communist rule.

The Korean War

On July 5 United States troops rushed to aid South Korea. Under the leadership of the United Nations, or UN, 16 countries sent soldiers to South Korea. The United Nations is the world organization founded at the end of World War II to

Among the events and people that are often associated with the 1950s are the Korean War (top), President Eisenhower and his campaign slogan (right), and the popularity of large automobiles (far right).

keep world peace, promote justice, and protect human rights.

United Nations forces, most of which came from the United States, turned back the North Koreans and freed Seoul (SOHL), the capital city of South Korea. The UN troops then moved north into North Korea. China, which had been a communist country since 1949, then sent its armed forces to the aid of North Korea. After two more years of fighting, the war ended when a settlement was reached in July 1953.

Eisenhower Becomes President

In 1953 Dwight D. Eisenhower became President. Like Truman, President Eisenhower was determined to stop the spread of communism.

In the early 1950s, the United States and the Soviet Union became locked in a costly race to build the world's most powerful weapons. This competition became known as the arms race. Many people feared that a war involving nuclear weapons might end all life on Earth. Some families built bomb shelters in their backyards. Fear of the Soviet Union also grew.

A United States senator named Joseph McCarthy started a campaign

to rid the country of communists. Between 1950 and 1954 many people were called before McCarthy's Senate committee. Some lost their jobs and were sent to jail, whether or not they were communists. The word *McCarthyism* is used today to describe false accusations made to damage people because of their political beliefs.

Americans Prosper

The 1950s were also a time of prosperity for many Americans. Many people could also afford new cars and travel from place to place by airplane. With special loans from the federal government, millions of war veterans and their families built new homes in the suburbs.

WHY IT MATTERS

The Cold War conflicts between the United States and the Soviet Union affected the world for over 40 years. The Korean War was one example of how this conflict led to war.

DID YOU KNOW?

W*hen did television begin?*

The first public showing of television programs in the United States took place as early as 1939. World War II, however, delayed further development of television while the electronics industry shifted to war work. By 1950, however, one out of ten American families owned a television set. By the early 1960s ownership had jumped to nine out of ten.

Television programs in the early 1950s were different from today's shows. News programs lasted only 15 minutes. Comedy shows and plays were broadcast live, directly to viewers—mistakes and all. In 1956 the invention of videotape made it easier to tape shows ahead of time.

✓ Reviewing Facts and Ideas

MAIN IDEAS

- When World War II ended, an "Iron Curtain" created by Josef Stalin divided the communist and noncommunist countries of Europe. The Cold War between the United States and the Soviet Union, the world's two superpowers, would last over 40 years.

- The Korean War lasted from 1950 until 1953. The United States and other United Nations countries supported South Korea. China supported communist North Korea.

- Fear of communism and greater prosperity both had a major effect on the country.

THINK ABOUT IT

1. What were the goals of the United Nations?

2. What caused the Korean War?

3. **FOCUS** What effects did the Cold War have on the United States?

4. **THINKING SKILL** Which leaders mentioned in this lesson would be *credible* *sources* on the spread of communism? Why?

5. **GEOGRAPHY** Look at the map on page 609. Give two reasons, other than military strength, why the Soviet Union could place such a vast area of Europe under communist control.

CHAPTER 20 REVIEW

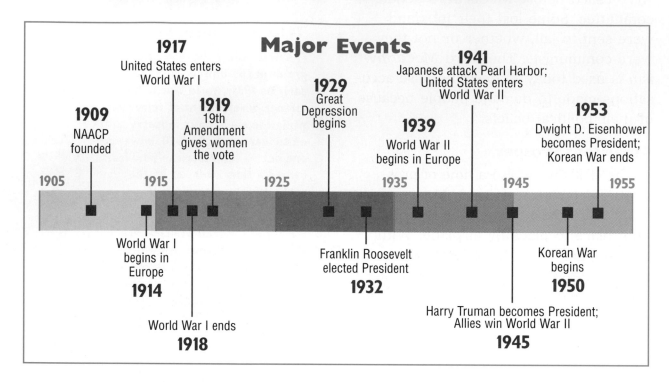

Major Events

1909 NAACP founded

1917 United States enters World War I

1919 19th Amendment gives women the vote

1929 Great Depression begins

1939 World War II begins in Europe

1941 Japanese attack Pearl Harbor; United States enters World War II

1953 Dwight D. Eisenhower becomes President; Korean War ends

1905   1915   1925   1935   1945   1955

World War I begins in Europe **1914**

World War I ends **1918**

Franklin Roosevelt elected President **1932**

Harry Truman becomes President; Allies win World War II **1945**

Korean War begins **1950**

THINKING ABOUT VOCABULARY

Number a paper from 1 to 10. Beside each number, write the word or term from the list below that best matches the description.

Allied Powers   jazz
arms race   media
dictator   stock exchange
discrimination   suffrage
Great Migration   unemployment

1. An unfair difference in the treatment of people

2. Special market where shares of stock are bought and sold

3. A leader with complete authority over the government

4. Music rooted in African American culture, full of striking rhythms and sounds

5. In World War I, the union of Britain, France, Italy, Belgium, and Russia

6. The number of workers without jobs

7. Competition between the superpowers to build the most powerful weapons

8. Methods of communication that reach large numbers of people, such as radio, newspapers, and magazines

9. The movement of many African Americans from rural areas in the Southeast to urban areas in the Northeast and Middle West beginning in the 1890s

10. The right to vote

THINKING ABOUT FACTS

1. How did life change for American women during and after World War I?

2. Name two American writers of the 1920s.

3. Why was Eleanor Roosevelt known as "Eleanor, everywhere"?

4. What decision did President Truman have to make about ending the war with Japan? What were its results?

5. Look at the time line above. How is the event of 1950 related to the beginning of the Cold War?

THINK AND WRITE

WRITING A MAGAZINE STORY
Suppose that you are a writer for one of the many new magazines that began in the 1920s. Write a story about one of the developments of that time, such as radio programs, "talkie" movies, or the way in which automobiles changed the country.

WRITING A LIST
Write a list of ways that the United States changed during World War II. Include changes on the job, in the home, and in the government.

WRITING A TRAVEL LOG
Suppose that you are Charles Lindbergh or Amelia Earheart flying across the Atlantic Ocean for the first time. Write a description of what you see looking down at the world from the air.

APPLYING THINKING SKILLS

DETERMINING THE CREDIBILITY OF A SOURCE

1. What does determining the credibility of a source mean?

2. If the author of a source had something to gain by describing events in a particular way, is it likely that the source would be a credible one? Explain.

3. Is a work of fiction the most credible source to use for a history report? Why or why not?

4. Read Yuri Tateishi's description of a relocation camp on page 601. How credible do you think this source is? Why?

5. Do you think that determining the credibility of a source would be helpful in the study of subjects other than history? Why or why not?

Summing Up the Chapter

Copy the semantic map on a separate piece of paper. Review the chapter to complete the blank sections. After you have finished, use the map to answer the question "How did each time period on the map come to an end?"

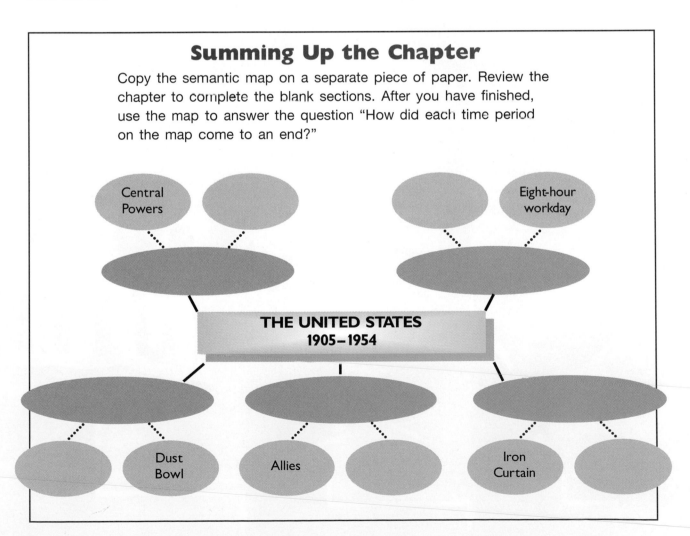

Central Powers

Eight-hour workday

THE UNITED STATES 1905–1954

Dust Bowl

Allies

Iron Curtain

The United States Looks to a New Century

THINKING ABOUT HISTORY AND GEOGRAPHY

The events of Chapter 21 take place during the last half of the 1900s. Look at the time line to learn about some of the events that have occurred as the United States moved closer to the year 2000. As you can see, more Americans began speaking out for fair and equal treatment. After the end of the Cold War, the United States continues to hold a leadership position among the countries of the world.

PACIFIC OCEAN

1955

MONTGOMERY, ALABAMA
Martin Luther King, Jr., leads the boycott against segregation on city buses

1961

WASHINGTON, D.C.
President Kennedy orders a blockade of communist Cuba

1970

NEW YORK CITY, NEW YORK
The women's movement begins calling for equal rights

1955   1965   1975

Seattle

New York City

Washington, D.C.

UNITED STATES

Montgomery

ATLANTIC OCEAN

1987

WASHINGTON, D.C.
President Reagan and Soviet President Gorbachev limit the building of nuclear weapons

1990s

SEATTLE, WASHINGTON
Companies develop computer technology for home and office use

1985

1995

1950 1954 1965 1970 1980 1990

The Civil Rights Movement

Read Aloud

Oh, deep in my heart I do believe
We shall overcome some day.

Many Americans sang these words during the early 1960s. What they wanted to overcome were prejudice and discrimination. These Americans were working for equal rights for all our country's citizens.

Focus Activity

READ TO LEARN

What has the civil rights movement achieved?

VOCABULARY

- **Thurgood Marshall**
- **Jo Ann Robinson**
- **Rosa Parks**
- **Martin Luther King, Jr.**
- **John F. Kennedy**
- **Lyndon Baines Johnson**

PLACES

- **Montgomery**
- **Greensboro**

THE BIG PICTURE

You have read that African Americans gained many of the rights they have today after the Civil War. By the 1950s, however, some rights were still being denied to them, including voting. Segregation was also widespread, particularly in the South. Because of segregation, blacks were not permitted to live in the same neighborhoods or to eat in the same restaurants as whites.

According to the Supreme Court, segregation was legal. In 1892 an African American named Homer Plessy refused to sit in a segregated railroad car. When the Court heard his case, it upheld the idea of "separate but equal" services for blacks and whites. This Supreme Court decision in 1896, called *Plessy* versus *Ferguson*, meant that separate railcars and other segregated facilities were legal if they were of equal quality. In reality, the facilities reserved for African Americans were rarely equal. As you have read, civil rights are a citizen's right to equal treatment under the law. As you will read, civil rights for African Americans finally started becoming a reality in the 1950s.

SEPARATE BUT NOT EQUAL

After the Plessy Decision, segregation became more widespread. Every part of American life was seriously affected.

For example, the schools that black children attended were often run-down and of lesser quality than those attended by white children. Why? Many state governments spent much less money on schools for African Americans. This lack of money often meant that black students had to study with no books, or discarded books no longer used by white students. This same lack of quality affected the hospitals, restaurants, and even cemeteries set aside for African Americans.

The Brown Decision

During the 1940s the NAACP began working to have the Plessy Decision overturned. A lawyer named Thurgood Marshall led the organization's team of lawyers. Marshall won several court cases proving that states had to provide more money to black schools. Marshall said that he was impatient to "go for the whole hog"—to attack segregation itself.

The opportunity came in the early 1950s. The parents of an African American girl named Linda Brown insisted that their daughter was receiving a second-rate education in a segregated school. The Browns took their case, *Brown* versus *Board of Education of Topeka, Kansas*, to court.

Marshall argued the case before the Supreme Court. On May 17, 1954, the Court ruled that segregation in public schools was unconstitutional. Overturning the Plessy Decision, Chief Justice Earl Warren declared that "in the field of public education the doctrine [*practice*] of 'separate but equal' has no place." With this success, the struggle for equal rights focused on other areas of life.

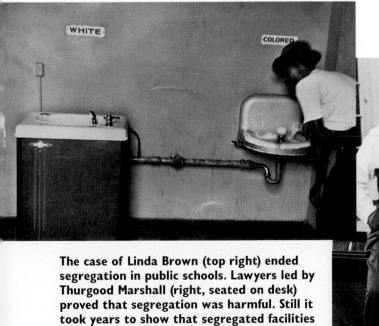

The case of Linda Brown (top right) ended segregation in public schools. Lawyers led by Thurgood Marshall (right, seated on desk) proved that segregation was harmful. Still it took years to show that segregated facilities (above) were unconstitutional.

THE MONTGOMERY BUS BOYCOTT

In the 1950s and earlier, transportation systems in the United States, especially in the South, were often segregated. When a bus carried both black and white passengers, a black passenger was expected to give his or her seat to a white passenger. Blacks and whites often had to use separate entrances—whites boarded in the front and blacks boarded in the back.

The NAACP and other groups worked to end segregation on the buses. In Montgomery, Alabama, Jo Ann Robinson led an organization called the Women's Political Council, or WPC. In late 1955 the WPC brought this issue to the attention of the entire country.

Rosa Parks Says "No"

On December 1, 1955, Rosa Parks boarded a bus in Montgomery. The "white section" of the bus soon filled up, and the driver ordered Parks to give up her seat. Parks stayed where she was. This was not the first time Parks had resisted the bus company's rules. In 1943 a driver had put her off the bus for refusing to board at the back.

In her autobiography, Parks wrote about what happened next. "Look, woman," the driver said, "I told you I wanted the seat. Are you going to stand up?"

"No, I am not," Parks answered. The driver threatened to have her arrested. Parks told him to go right ahead. Parks was arrested, fined, fingerprinted, and put in jail.

The Boycott Begins

News of Parks's arrest spread quickly. Jo Ann Robinson wrote and distributed a pamphlet addressed to Montgomery's African Americans. She urged people to stay off the buses in support of Parks.

The Montgomery bus boycott had begun. For almost a year hundreds of African Americans in Montgomery refused to ride the buses. Some people organized car pools. Others walked. Some leaders of the boycott were arrested.

Many whites were angry about the boycott. A few tried to fight it by bombing the homes and churches of African Americans. The Supreme Court finally heard the case of Rosa Parks. In December 1956 it ordered Montgomery to end segregation on its buses. The court decision was a triumph for civil rights. It also focused attention on one organizer of the boycott—Martin Luther King, Jr.

As a leader in the boycott arising from Rosa Parks's arrest (top), Martin Luther King, Jr., was arrested along with his wife, Coretta Scott King (left).

King is known for giving many speeches, but the one he gave in Washington, D.C., in 1963 is his most famous.

MARTIN LUTHER KING, JR.

Martin Luther King, Jr., was born in Atlanta in 1929. As a young man he attended Atlanta's Morehouse College, where he planned to study medicine. He later decided to study religion. In 1955 King became the pastor of an African American church in Montgomery.

King's success in the Montgomery bus boycott made him a national civil rights leader. His sermons and speeches won both black and white followers. King always stressed the importance of nonviolence. King based his ideas of nonviolence on the Bible's teaching "love your enemies." When his house was bombed in 1956, he refused to give in to hatred. "I want you to love our enemies," he told one audience. "We must meet hate with love."

The March on Washington

In June 1963 King and other leaders called for a march on Washington, D.C., to persuade the federal government to pass a new civil rights law. The March on Washington was a great success. More than 250,000 Americans gathered on August 28, 1963, to hear speeches, songs, and prayers. King gave a now well-known speech. You may recognize the words from the Declaration of Independence. What was King's dream?

MANY VOICES
PRIMARY SOURCE

Excerpt from a Speech by Martin Luther King, Jr., in Washington, D.C., on the steps of the Lincoln Memorial.

*I have a dream that one day this nation will rise up and live out the true meaning of its **creed**: "We hold these truths to be self-evident, that all men are created equal. . . ."*

I have a dream that my four little children will one day live in a nation where they will not be judged by the color of their skin but by the content of their character. . . .

This will be the day when all of God's children will be able to sing with a new meaning, "My country, 'tis of thee, sweet land of liberty, of thee I sing. Land where my fathers died, land of the pilgrim's pride, from every mountainside, let freedom ring."

*When we let freedom ring, when we let it ring from every village and every **hamlet**, from every state and every city, we will be able to speed up that day when all of God's children, black men and white men, Jews and Gentiles, Protestants and Catholics, will be able to join hands and sing in the words of the old **Negro spiritual**, "Free at last! free at last! thank God Almighty, we are free at last!"*

creed: stated belief
hamlet: small town
Negro spiritual: African American religious song

The Greensboro sit-ins at Woolworth's lunch counter helped spark protests by college students across the country.

THE MOVEMENT GROWS

After the March on Washington, the civil rights movement continued to grow. In 1963 more than 1,000 protests took place, and thousands of protesters were arrested. President John F. Kennedy increased efforts to get a new civil rights law passed by the Congress.

At the same time the response to the struggle grew more violent. On June 12, 1963, a civil rights worker in Mississippi named Medgar Evers was shot and killed as he returned home from work. Much of this violence was broadcast on television sets across the United States. Millions of Americans were shocked by what they saw.

Freedom Summer

In 1960 African American college students from Greensboro, North Carolina, began protesting the segregated lunch counters in the city's coffee shops and restaurants. They held sit-ins at the lunch counters, which led to the birth of the Student Nonviolent Coordinating Committee, or SNCC. In 1964 SNCC set up a project known as "Freedom Summer." During their summer vacation, hundreds of college students went to Mississippi to help register African American voters.

One of the SNCC members from Mississippi was Fannie Lou Hamer, an African American woman. She joined the civil rights movement in 1962 after trying to register to vote. When her employer found out that she had tried to register, she was fired.

People who worked to register African American voters in Mississippi during Freedom Summer were beaten or arrested. Three were killed. For these young Americans, the cause of civil rights came at a high price.

A Civil Rights Law

In 1964 President Lyndon Baines Johnson promised to support a new civil rights law. "We have talked for 100 years or more," President Johnson told the country. "Yes, it is time now to write the next chapter—and to write it in books of law."

Johnson worked hard to convince members of Congress to vote for the bill. Within months he signed the Civil Rights Act of 1964. This law made segregation illegal in public places, including such places as hotels, theaters, playgrounds, and libraries.

A year later Johnson signed a second law. The Voting Rights Act of 1965 outlawed many actions that had been used to keep some people from voting. In some parts of the country some whites had blocked the entrance to voting places or threatened blacks who tried to vote. The Voting Rights Act of 1965 protected the right of African Americans to vote. By 1968 African Americans began being elected to government offices. Read the graph on this page to trace how the number of black elected officials has grown since then.

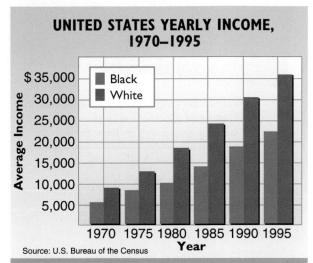

UNITED STATES YEARLY INCOME, 1970–1995

Average Income

Legend: Black / White

Years: 1970, 1975, 1980, 1985, 1990, 1995

Source: U.S. Bureau of the Census

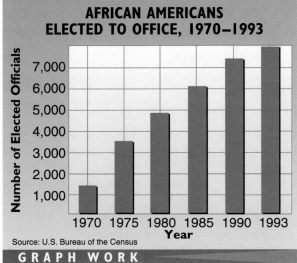

AFRICAN AMERICANS ELECTED TO OFFICE, 1970–1993

Number of Elected Officials

Years: 1970, 1975, 1980, 1985, 1990, 1993

Source: U.S. Bureau of the Census

GRAPH WORK

Although African Americans have made gains, much work remains.

1. Which year shows the smallest difference in black and white incomes?
2. Which year shows the greatest increase in elected officials?

WHY IT MATTERS

Much has changed since the civil rights movement began in the 1950s. Segregation is illegal in all public and most private places. Discrimination still exists, but our country has come closer to the ideal of "liberty and justice for all." Leaders such as Jesse Jackson and Coretta Scott King, King's widow, have carried the legacy of the movement into the 1990s. As you will read, the nonviolent ideas and methods of Martin Luther King, Jr., have inspired other groups to struggle for their rights.

✓ Reviewing Facts and Ideas

MAIN IDEAS

- In 1954 the Supreme Court ruled segregation in public schools illegal.
- In 1955 a boycott led by Martin Luther King, Jr., ended segregation on buses in Montgomery, Alabama.
- The Civil Rights Act of 1964 outlawed segregation in all public places. The Voting Rights Act of 1965 struck down illegal ways of keeping people from voting.

THINK ABOUT IT

1. What was meant by the phrase "separate but equal?" When was it first used?
2. Explain how the Montgomery bus boycott began.
3. **FOCUS** What did the Civil Rights Act of 1964 accomplish?
4. **THINKING SKILL** Make a _generalization_ about the leaders of the civil rights movement. Explain how you made your determination.
5. **WRITE** Write a short essay describing the nonviolent ideas followed by Martin Luther King, Jr.

Writing an Outline

VOCABULARY
outline

WHY THE SKILL MATTERS

In the last lesson you learned about the history of the civil rights movement. You read about many events, people, and dates. If you were asked to write a report on this subject, it might seem difficult at first to organize the information. Making an outline helps you to group facts into broad categories and to see how facts are related. An outline is a plan that presents ideas about a subject in an organized way.

USING THE SKILL

A good way to start an outline would be to state clearly the topic of your report. The next step would be to choose two or three main ideas about your topic. As you complete your research, you could add details that relate to each of these main ideas.

When you write an outline start with Roman numerals to show the sequence of the main ideas. Then, under each Roman numeral, order the related details by placing a capital letter next to each one.

Suppose that you were asked to write a report on the life of Thurgood Marshall. Since Marshall had many achievements throughout his long life, an outline can help you to organize the information you find.

You might begin your outline with three main ideas: "Marshall's Early Life," "The NAACP Years," and "The Supreme Court Years." During your research you could determine which details would go under each

Before serving on the Supreme Court, Thurgood Marshall was sworn in (above) as a judge in New York.

of these main categories. Eventually, your outline might look like this one:

I. Marshall's Early Life
   A. Born in Baltimore in 1908
   B. Attended segregated public schools
   C. Earned law degree at Howard University

II. The NAACP Years
   A. Worked for NAACP from 1938 to 1961
   B. Argued *Brown* versus *Board of Education* before Supreme Court in 1954
   C. Became known as "Mr. Civil Rights"

III. The Supreme Court Years
   A. First African American appointed to the Court in 1967
   B. Strong voice for civil rights on the Court for 24 years
   C. Retired in 1991 and died in 1993

How does the outline make it easier to understand Marshall's life? What other main ideas could you have included?

TRYING THE SKILL

Now suppose that you have been asked to write an outline about how the Brown

622

Decision was put into practice in Little Rock, Arkansas. First read the paragraphs below from a history of Arkansas.

The Supreme Court's Brown Decision caused a great deal of disagreement in our state. Orval Faubus, who was elected governor of Arkansas in 1954, favored the "separate but equal" policy in the schools. The state legislature passed a law opposing the Supreme Court's decision.

On September 4, 1957, nine African American students tried to enter Central High School for the first time. Angry crowds surrounded the school, and members of the Arkansas National Guard blocked the students' way.

On September 24, President Dwight D. Eisenhower decided that the Little Rock crisis had gone on long enough. He sent United States Army troops to restore order. Under the army's supervision, the "Little Rock Nine" were finally allowed to

Helping yourself

- **To write an outline, first choose several main ideas.**

- **As you collect facts, place each one beneath the related main idea.**

- **Organize your outline by using roman numerals and capital letters.**

begin the school year at Central High.

What steps would you take to create an outline? List two or three main ideas. How would they help you to organize this information?

REVIEWING THE SKILL

1. What is an outline?

2. Which are the main ideas in the Marshall outline? How do you know?

3. Where would you place this fact in your outline? *Marshall Named Supreme Court Justice by President Johnson.*

4. How would you sort the details about admitting African American students to Little Rock's Central High School in your outline? Could your outline be organized in more than one way? Explain.

5. How can writing an outline help you to understand historical information?

The Little Rock Nine (below) had to be escorted to and from Central High School by United States troops.

1950   1959   1973   1980   1990

A Decade of Change

Read Aloud

"Ask not what your country can do for you: Ask what you can do for your country." In his inaugural address in 1961, President John F. Kennedy challenged all Americans to defend freedom and to help people in need both at home and throughout the world.

Focus Activity

READ TO LEARN

How did the United States change after 1960?

VOCABULARY

- Cuban Missile Crisis
- Vietnam War

PEOPLE

- John F. Kennedy
- Fidel Castro
- Lyndon Baines Johnson
- Malcolm X
- César Chávez
- Dolores Huerta
- Richard Nixon

PLACES

- Watts
- North Vietnam
- South Vietnam
- Cambodia

THE BIG PICTURE

In 1961 John F. Kennedy became the country's first Roman Catholic President. At the age of 43 he was also the first President to be born in the 1900s, and the youngest president ever elected. "The torch [of leadership] has been passed to a new generation of Americans," Kennedy declared.

The Cold War was still going on. Kennedy faced tough decisions about our country's arms race with the Soviet Union. The problems of discrimination and poverty in the United States also remained. Kennedy's programs, called the "New Frontier," tried to address some of these problems. Like Presidents Roosevelt, Truman, and Eisenhower before him, Kennedy increased aid to the elderly and the poor. Another of Kennedy's most successful programs was the Peace Corps. It sent Americans abroad to help provide health care and education to people in poor countries. Many young Americans were inspired to participate. Before it was over the decade of the 1960s would involve Americans in sweeping changes around the world.

The wife and two children of slain President Kennedy leave the funeral service held for him in Washington, D.C.

AN UNEASY PEACE

In 1959 Fidel Castro led a revolution in Cuba. Under Castro, Cuba became the first communist country in the Western Hemisphere. His new government alarmed many people in the United States, because Cuba is only 90 miles from the southern tip of Florida.

The Cuban Missile Crisis

In 1961 a group of anticommunist Cubans supported by the United States government tried to overthrow Castro. This attempt failed. It also led to much worse relations between the United States and Cuba. In October 1962 the United States learned that the Soviet Union was setting up nuclear missiles in Cuba. The missles were aimed at the United States.

Kennedy responded by ordering the United States Navy to blockade Cuba. He also demanded that the Soviet Union remove its missiles. For over a week the possibility of nuclear war between the United States and the Soviet Union became more real. People around the world waited in fear to find out how the Cuban Missile Crisis would end.

Finally, the Soviet Union backed down and agreed to remove the nuclear missiles from Cuba. In return, the United States promised not to invade Cuba. After the threat of war had passed, Kennedy spoke of the importance of working for peace:

Some say it is useless to speak of world peace . . . but we have no more urgent task. . . . We all inhabit this small planet. We all cherish our children's future.

Kennedy Is Assassinated

Only a year later, on November 22, 1963, the United States suffered a sudden and great blow. On that day the President was traveling with the First Lady Jacqueline Kennedy in Dallas, Texas. The top had been taken down on the President's car so that the crowds could see him. Then shots were fired, and President Kennedy was dead.

Americans were shocked. Many wondered how such a violent act could have been made against a United States President. Within only a few hours, the Vice President, Lyndon Baines Johnson, was sworn in as the new President.

President Johnson (below) led the "War on Poverty." During his Presidency Americans became more active in the government's business (left).

FIGHTING POVERTY

In 1964 President Johnson declared a "War on Poverty." His programs were aimed at building what he called the "Great Society." This society, he said, "rests on abundance [*plenty*] and liberty for all. It demands an end to poverty and racial injustice."

President Johnson wanted to provide education and health care to all Americans. One Great Society program was Medicare. It was intended to help people over the age of 65 pay for their medical care.

A "Long, Hot Summer"

Although the 1950s had been a time of increased wealth for our country, this wealth did not reach all Americans. Many African Americans still suffered from discrimination and poverty. In 1965 almost 5 out of every 10 nonwhite Americans were officially considered poor by the government. About 2 out of every 10 white Americans were this poor.

On August 11, 1965, white police officers pulled over the car of two young African Americans in Watts, a neighborhood of Los Angeles. Many African Americans had long believed that they were treated unfairly by the police. Soon a crowd began to gather and a riot broke out. A riot is a large-scale, violent outbreak in which property is damaged and people may be hurt or killed. The riot in Watts lasted for six days. By the time it ended, 34 people had been killed, almost 1,000 people had been injured, and over $46 million worth of damage had occurred. However, this was not the only riot of the decade. During the "long, hot summers" from 1965 to 1968, riots broke out in many cities across the country.

The "Poor People's Campaign"

Poverty and discrimination in the cities drew the attention of many leaders, including Martin Luther King, Jr. King began a new program, which he called "The Poor People's Campaign." Its goal was to end poverty for both blacks and whites.

Some people felt that an end to the problems of poverty and discrimination was not coming fast enough. Malcolm X, for example, believed that change would be made faster if African Americans took control of their own lives. For many years Malcolm X did not believe in working together with whites to achieve equal rights for blacks. "You'll get freedom by letting your enemy know that you'll do anything to get your freedom," he said in 1964. Later, however, Malcolm X began saying that whites and blacks could work together for "the cause of brotherhood."

Neither Malcolm X nor Martin Luther King, Jr., would live to see the results of their struggles. Malcolm X was shot to death while he was speaking in New York City in February 1965. Three years later King was shot and killed in Memphis, Tennessee.

"La Causa"

Migrant farmworkers also suffered poverty and discrimination. Migrant workers are people who move from farm to farm picking different crops. These workers often labor under harsh conditions for little pay.

In March 1962 two Mexican Americans decided they needed to form a labor union for the migrant workers. Working day and night, César Chávez (SE sahr CHAH ves) and Dolores Huerta (WER tah) founded the National Farm Workers Association. Chavez, the president, and Huerta, the vice president, traveled to farms and organized workers to fight for better, safer working conditions.

The farm workers' struggle for a better life came to be called *La Causa*—"the cause" or "the struggle." Chávez explained the labor union's goals:

> *Our struggle is not easy. . . . [I]t is how we use our lives that determines what kind of men we are. . . . I am convinced that the truest act of courage is to sacrifice for others in a totally nonviolent struggle for justice.*

Like Martin Luther King, Jr., Chávez and Huerta believed in nonviolence. They protested through labor strikes, boycotts, and marches. These efforts won better treatment for migrant farm workers from California to Florida.

Chávez, center, and Huerta, far right, held many protests for migrant farm workers' rights.

THE VIETNAM WAR

Throughout the 1960s a war was fought in Asia that had a huge effect on the United States. The country of Vietnam had been divided in two in 1954. North Vietnam had a communist government supported by the Soviet Union and China. South Vietnam was a republic backed by the United States. A war between the two Vietnams alarmed leaders in the United States. They feared that a North Vietnamese victory would lead to the spread of communism throughout Asia.

"Hawks" and "Doves"

In 1964 the United States became involved in fighting with North Vietnam. Over the next three years, over 500,000 American soldiers fought in the Vietnam War.

Americans could watch the war on television newscasts. They saw American soldiers being killed. They saw no sign that the enemy was being defeated.

People in the United States became deeply divided over the Vietnam War. "Hawks" believed the United States had to fight North Vietnam to stop communism from spreading. Barry Goldwater, a United States Senator from Arizona, wrote in 1964 that Vietnam was "a major battlefield of the free-world struggle against the Communist threat to engulf [swallow up] all of free Asia."

"Doves," on the other hand, believed that the United States should not fight in a war where its own safety was not threatened. In 1968 Robert Kennedy, a United States Senator from New York and the brother of President Kennedy, said, "How much more destruction will be asked to provide the military victory that is always just around the corner?"

The United States Pulls Out

In 1968 Richard Nixon was elected President. He promised to achieve "peace with honor" in Vietnam. In 1969

NORTH VIETNAM AND SOUTH VIETNAM, 1961–1975

0   200   400 Miles
0   200   400 Kilometers

Red River

CHINA

BURMA

Hanoi

LAOS

Gulf of Tonkin

NORTH VIETNAM

Mekong River

THAILAND

CAMBODIA

SOUTH VIETNAM

Saigon

South China Sea

MAP WORK

South Vietnam and North Vietnam are located within a region called Southeast Asia.

1. What countries bordered the two Vietnams?
2. What were the capitals of the two Vietnams?

In the Vietnam War sometimes the soldiers' only link to headquarters was a radio.

Both their families and the returning prisoners of war from Vietnam were glad to be reunited.

he began withdrawing United States troops. However, Nixon continued the bombing of North Vietnam. United States planes also began bombing communist targets in Cambodia, a country west of Vietnam. In 1970 the United States sent soldiers there as well.

Nixon's expansion of the United States role in the war angered the country's "doves." Over one million college students across the country protested against the war. Many colleges were shut down because of protests. At Kent State University in Ohio, four unarmed student protesters were shot to death by National Guard troops who were called in to maintain order. The troops feared they would be attacked.

The country remained badly divided over the war. Finally in 1973, the United States signed a treaty to end the fighting with North Vietnam. Almost two million people died in the war, including over 56,000 Americans. Over 1,000 Americans were still missing in action.

WHY IT MATTERS

Fighting continued in Vietnam after the United States troops withdrew. In 1975 North Vietnam conquered South Vietnam. The two parts of Vietnam were reunited under a communist government. As a result, thousands of South Vietnamese fleeing mistreatment by the communist government, came to the United States.

The fate of American soldiers still missing in action continues to be a source of conflict between the United States and Vietnam. In the early 1990s, however, the Vietnamese government began releasing information on the missing soldiers. In 1995 the United States reopened trade and other relations with Vietnam.

✔ Reviewing Facts and Ideas

MAIN IDEAS

- During the Cuban Missile Crisis of 1962, Soviet nuclear missiles were finally withdrawn from Cuba.

- From 1963 to 1968, the United States increased its involvement in the Vietnam War.

- In 1973 the United States stopped fighting with North Vietnam.

THINK ABOUT IT

1. What is the Peace Corps?

2. What was Johnson's "Great Society"?

3. **FOCUS** How did world events affect life in the United States in the 1960s?

4. **THINKING SKILL** Find two _facts_ about the Vietnam War that appear in this lesson. Then find two _opinions_ about the same subject.

5. **GEOGRAPHY** How did Cuba's location affect its role in the Cold War?

1950   1960   **1972**   **1995**

The Cold War Ends

Focus Activity

READ TO LEARN

What major events affected the United States at the end of the twentieth century?

VOCABULARY

- Watergate Scandal
- Persian Gulf War

PEOPLE

- Richard Nixon
- Gerald Ford
- Shirley Chisholm
- Sandra Day O'Connor
- Jimmy Carter
- Ronald Reagan
- Mikhail Gorbachev
- George Bush
- Bill Clinton

PLACES

- Berlin Wall
- Iraq
- Kuwait

Read Aloud

In 1972 Richard Nixon became the first United States President to visit China. He remarked to Mao Zedong (MOU DZE DUNG), the Chinese communist leader, "I know that you are one who sees when an opportunity comes." In the 1950s and 1960s, the United States had clashed with China over Korea, then Vietnam. Now the United States was entering a new era when old conflicts would be put to rest.

THE BIG PICTURE

In the 1970s the United States was still in the process of ending its involvement in the Vietnam War. President Richard Nixon faced many other challenges as well. Billions of tax dollars were being spent on the Vietnam War and on the arms race with the Soviet Union. As new and more powerful weapons were developed, the world was becoming a more dangerous place.

In 1972 Nixon opened talks between the United States and several communist countries. After his historic visit to China, Nixon became the first President to visit the Soviet Union since World War II.

The 1970s was also the beginning of many changes within the United States. Women, older Americans, and Americans with disabilities were working to achieve equal rights. New leaders were elected to bring the United States beyond the Cold War era into the future.

NEW CHALLENGES

The easing of Cold War tensions was an important achievement for President Nixon. In 1972 he was reelected by a large majority. Two years later, however, he was forced to leave office because of the Watergate Scandal. A scandal is any action that brings disgrace.

The Watergate Scandal

On June 17, 1972, five men were arrested for breaking into an office in the Watergate building in Washington, D.C. The men, who were connected to the President's reelection campaign, had been spying on the headquarters of Nixon's political opponent.

Nixon said he knew nothing about the break-in. Later, White House recordings showed that he was involved in the Watergate Scandal and the efforts to cover it up. Congress prepared to impeach President Nixon for breaking the law. Instead of risking impeachment, Nixon resigned from office on August 9, 1974. He was the first President ever to resign.

New Leaders

Gerald Ford of Michigan then took office as President. He had been named Vice President by Nixon in 1973. Ford was the first person to serve as Vice President and President without having been elected to either office.

Early in his presidency, Ford gave Nixon a pardon. This meant that Nixon would not be punished for any crimes. Ford said that the Watergate Scandal was "an American tragedy . . . which . . . could go on and on and on, or someone must write the end to it."

Many people disagreed with Ford's decision to pardon Nixon. They believed that if there was evidence of wrongdoing, Nixon should have been brought to trial.

After the Watergate Scandal many people lost confidence in the government and their elected leaders. In 1974 many new leaders were elected to Congress. The 1974 election year was also known as "the year of the woman in politics" because more women ran for office than ever before. Ella Grasso, for example, was elected governor of Connecticut. She became the first woman governor in United States history who had not replaced or filled in for her husband. As you will read, government was not the only place where women were making gains.

After the Watergate Scandal, members of Congress met to discuss whether to impeach President Nixon.

Shirley Chisholm was one of the leaders in the changing roles of women.

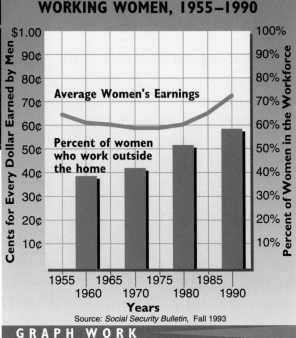

WORKING WOMEN, 1955–1990

Cents for Every Dollar Earned by Men

Percent of Women in the Workforce

Average Women's Earnings

Percent of women who work outside the home

Years

Source: *Social Security Bulletin,* Fall 1993

GRAPH WORK

Information about the line graph is found on the left side and for the bar graph, the right side.

1. In which years did both earnings and the size of the work force increase?

2. In which two years were women's earnings the same?

EQUAL RIGHTS FOR ALL

In addition to the civil rights and *La Causa* movements of the 1950s and 1960s, other groups began protesting for equal rights in the 1970s.

The Women's Movement

Although women won the right to vote in 1919, they were often discouraged from seeking careers. Many women felt they could make a contribution outside the home. One of these was Betty Friedan. In 1963 she published a widely read book called *The Feminine Mystique.* It raised questions about women's traditional roles. "Who knows what women's intelligence will contribute when it can be nourished?" Friedan asked. In 1966 Friedan helped to found the National Organization for Women, or NOW. Many women disagreed with NOW. They believed that the most important job a woman could have was in the home.

Phyllis Schlafly became a major spokeswoman in support of women's traditional roles. According to Schlafly, "Marriage and motherhood give a woman a new identity and the opportunity for all-round fulfillment."

During the last 30 years, more women have begun working outside the home. In 1968 Shirley Chisholm became the first African American woman to win election to the House of Representatives. In 1981 Sandra Day O'Connor became the first woman named to the Supreme Court. Look at the graph to see how many women started to work outside the home after 1955.

The Gray Panthers

In 1970 a woman named Maggie Kuhn became concerned about the older Americans in our country. Kuhn's employers had forced her to retire from her job when she became 65 years old. Kuhn felt that this was unfair, since she still wanted to work. "The first myth is that old age is a disease," Kuhn said. "Well, it's not a disease—it's a triumph. Because you've survived." Kuhn helped to found the Gray Panthers. This organization, which today has a membership of 40,000 people, changed many Americans' ideas about getting older. In 1978, 78-year-old Claude Pepper, a Congressman from Florida, helped pass a law to protect people over 65 years of age from being forced to retire.

Americans with Disabilities

Another struggle for rights took place at Gallaudet (gawl uh DET) University in Washington, D.C., in 1988. In that year a new president was hired at this school for the deaf. The school officials refused to appoint a deaf person to the job. Gallaudet students fought back with boycotts, petitions, and marches. In time the position went to I. King Jordan, an educator who was partly deaf.

The Gallaudet protest was part of a larger fight for the rights of people with disabilities. A major gain was made in 1990 when the Americans with Disabilities Act, or ADA, became law. This law made it illegal for employers to discriminate against people with disabilities. It also guaranteed them access to public facilities.

Links to HEALTH

Mom Gets MADD

While some organizations are formed to fight discrimination, others are formed to teach about health and safety in the community. Mothers Against Drunk Driving, or MADD, was started in 1980 by Candy Lightner, whose teenage daughter was killed by a drunk driver. Since it began, MADD has helped to prevent countless traffic deaths by teaching young people and adults about the dangers of drinking alcohol and driving an automobile. With your classmates, discuss another health concern important to your community.

DON'T DRINK AND DRIVE

The appointments of Sandra Day O'Connor, Clarence Thomas, and Ruth Bader Ginsburg helped to make the Supreme Court more representative of the American population.

Carter attended the signing of the Middle East peace agreement in 1979 (left). Reagan and Gorbachev (below) began to warm relations beween their countries.

ENDING THE COLD WAR

The United States continued to play a major role in world events. In 1976 Jimmy Carter, a former governor of Georgia, was elected President. Carter was interested in strengthening human rights around the world.

World Tensions

Carter helped bring peace to two long-time enemies in Southwest Asia, or the Middle East. In 1979 Egypt's leader Anwar Sadat (AHN wahr sah DAHT) and Israel's leader Menachem Begin (men AH hem BAY gin) signed a peace treaty in Washington, D.C. That same year Carter also signed a treaty with Soviet leaders to limit the building of certain nuclear weapons.

In 1980 Ronald Reagan, a former California governor, was elected President. Reagan, a leader of the growing conservative movement, believed it was important to strengthen the United States against the Soviet Union, which he called an "evil empire." Reagan also wanted to reduce the role of government in people's lives.

During the 1980s the United States greatly increased spending on nuclear weapons and continued to pay for many other government programs. From 1981 to 1988 the national debt almost tripled. The national debt is the amount of money the government owes. In 1995 the national debt was almost $5 trillion. That amount was equal to $20 thousand for every person in the United States!

The Iron Curtain Is Lifted

Like the United States, the Soviet Union was also spending large amounts of money on the arms race. The great cost of weapons was one factor that helped to bring an end to the Cold War.

Another factor in the Cold War's end was the reform policy of a Soviet leader named Mikhail Gorbachev (MIHK il GAWR buh chahv), who took office in March 1985. He gave more freedoms to the Soviet people. He also worked to improve relations with the United States. In 1987 Reagan and Gorbachev signed the first arms treaty that called for both superpowers to destroy some nuclear missiles.

People in other communist countries responded to Gorbachev's changes by demanding more freedom for themselves. In 1989 the people of East Germany tore down the Berlin Wall, a structure that symbolized the Iron Curtain. It had divided the city of Berlin into East Berlin, which was communist, and West Berlin, which was democratic and had a free enterprise system.

Soon communist governments in East Germany, Poland, Hungary, Czechoslovakia, and Romania were overthrown. The Iron Curtain of communism was lifted completely in 1991, when the Soviet Union broke up into 15 independent republics. The Cold War was over at last. The United States and its allies had won. The new republics, however, had to begin searching for ways to make their economies stronger and more stable.

In the Persian Gulf War, General Colin Powell (above) helped prepare United States troops (left) for on-the-ground fighting which lasted only 100 hours.

Bill Clinton (left) began his second term as President of the United States in 1997.

A NEW HOPE FOR PEACE

The end of the Cold War brought new challenges. For example, the United States became the world's only superpower. How would it fulfill its new role?

In 1989 Reagan's Vice President, George Bush of Texas, became President. He soon faced a major challenge in the Middle East. In 1990 Iraq invaded the oil-rich country of Kuwait. In response Bush sent almost 500,000 American troops to the region. The Persian Gulf War of 1991 involved forces from dozens of other countries as well. The war lasted only six weeks.

WHY IT MATTERS

After the Persian Gulf War, the United States continued to play a role in the Middle East. In 1992 Arkansas governor Bill Clinton was elected President. Clinton urged an end to fighting between Israelis and Palestinians. Leaders of the two peoples signed peace agreements in 1993 and 1995.

In addition to his foreign policy successes, Clinton could boast of good economic times during his Presidency. However, Clinton also spent much of his two terms under investigation for possible illegal actions. In 1998, as a result of this investigation, Clinton became the first elected President to be impeached by the House of Representatives.

✓✓ Reviewing Facts and Ideas

MAIN IDEAS

- Richard Nixon's visits to China and the Soviet Union in 1972 began to ease tensions in the Cold War. In 1974 Nixon resigned from office because of the Watergate Scandal.

- In the 1970s great gains in equal rights were made by women, senior citizens, and people with disabilities.

- In the 1980s Ronald Reagan and Mikhail Gorbachev ended the arms race, which helped bring the Cold War to a close by 1991.

- After 1991 George Bush and Bill Clinton directed the new role of the United States in the world.

THINK ABOUT IT

1. What was the Watergate Scandal?

2. What was the purpose of the Americans with Disabilities Act?

3. **FOCUS** What issues did the United States deal with in the late 1900s?

4. **THINKING SKILL** Which of these two sources would most likely provide a more _credible_ account of the Soviet Union under Gorbachev? Explain.

   a. an article written by a former Soviet official who lost his job because of reforms

   b. an editorial in a British newspaper by a British writer who lived in Moscow at the time

5. **WRITE** Write a newspaper article about one event at the end of the Cold War. Give reasons why this event is important.

MAKING A DIFFERENCE

Taking Another View

CHARLOTTE, NORTH CAROLINA. What is it like always to be seated in a world where everyone else can stand? Laura Stinson and Sharaye (shah RAY) LaMothe can answer that question. Both girls have depended on wheelchairs for many years.

When the two girls were in the sixth grade at Lebanon Elementary School, they decided to share their outlook on the world with other students. In April 1993 the two girls created "Chairs 'R Us," a show-and-tell program for younger students at their school. Laura and Sharaye begin their sessions by explaining how uncomfortable they feel when people stare at them. "We would prefer them to come to us and ask us questions if they like," Sharaye says.

"The only thing wrong with me," says Sharaye, "is I can't use my legs. I can think, talk, cook, draw, and even dance." The "Chairs 'R Us" team told the students about the challenges that people with disabilities face at amusement parks and shopping malls. "We can't really go on the rides because of the steps," Sharaye says. Laura points out, "I can't ride the Ferris wheel because they don't stop the ride long enough for me to get out of my wheelchair and into the seat."

After each session the girls give two students a chance to use a wheelchair. "At first they thought it was fun," said Laura, "but then they'd get tired. It showed them how hard it was for us to get around sometimes." Both girls agreed that "Chairs 'R Us" had made a difference. Laura said, "We helped some kids understand that people with disabilities have feelings. They want people to treat them normally. They want a fair chance and they don't want obstacles." Sharaye added, "I learned something too. I learned that when people stare, they're not trying to be mean. They are just wondering what it's like to be in a wheelchair."

" . . . come to us and ask us questions . . ."

Sharaye LaMothe

Laura Stinson

1950 1959 2000

Preparing for a New Century

Read Aloud

During the early 1990s President Bill Clinton introduced the White House to new ways of using resources and technology. The White House now uses recycled paper. Electronic mail, or Email, on computers link the White House offices to people around the world. The President even has a new address in addition to "1600 Pennsylvania Avenue." People can send E-mail to "president@whitehouse.gov."

Focus Activity

READ TO LEARN

How can advances in technology help us in the future?

VOCABULARY

- space race
- satellite
- Internet

PEOPLE

- John Glenn
- Neil Armstrong

PLACES

- Cape Canaveral

THE BIG PICTURE

Developments in technology during the 1900s have dramatically changed the way Americans live. The discoveries made by Albert Einstein in the early 1900s laid the foundation for many of these changes. Since World War II, however, the speed with which technology changes has continued to increase. Whole new industries, providing thousands of jobs, were created to market new inventions to consumers. Today it is difficult to imagine life without televisions, pocket-sized radios, fax machines, videotapes, video games, computers, or even check-out "scanners" in supermarkets.

Many changes in technology grew out of the competition between the United States and the Soviet Union. As each country tried to outdo the other, technology advanced in leaps and bounds. In the exploration of outer space, the rivalry between the superpowers was quite dramatic. By the 1950s, the space race—the competition to gain control of outer space—had begun.

Neil Armstrong's moon landing actually left human footprints on the moon's surface.

THE SPACE RACE

In 1957 the Soviet Union stunned the world by sending the first satellite, *Sputnik,* into space. A satellite is an object that circles a larger object, such as Earth. Four years later a Soviet cosmonaut—the Soviet term for an astronaut—became the first human being in outer space.

Americans in Space

Despite the Soviet Union's head start, the United States soon pushed ahead in the space race. In 1962 the *Mercury* project made astronaut John Glenn the first American to orbit Earth. The *Apollo* project followed *Mercury.* It sought to put a man on the moon before 1970. Almost 500,000 people worked on the *Apollo* project. On July 16, 1969, three astronauts blasted off from what is now Cape Canaveral in Florida toward the moon. Their spacecraft was directed by "mission control" in Houston, Texas. Neil Armstrong, the flight's commander, looked outside as they hurtled through space. Read this excerpt about his historic mission. What did Armstrong notice about the moon?

MANY VOICES
PRIMARY SOURCE

Interview with Neil Armstrong, 1970.

*We were still thousands of miles away, but close enough so that the moon almost filled our circular window. It was **eclipsing** the sun, from our position, and the **corona** of the sun was visible . . . as a gigantic . . . saucer-shaped light. . . . I was really aware . . . that the moon was in fact a sphere, not a disc. It seemed almost as if it were showing us its roundness, its similarity in shape to our Earth, in a sort of welcome. I was sure that it would be a **hospitable** host. It had been awaiting its first visitors for a long time.*

eclipsing: hiding
corona: outer ring
hospitable: friendly

On July 20, 1969, Armstrong became the first human being to set foot on the moon. "That's one small step for man, one giant leap for mankind," Armstrong said. About 600 million people back on Earth followed his steps on television and radio.

Since Armstrong's historic moon landing, our country has made more explorations into outer space. Sally Ride, the first American woman astronaut, and other astronauts, have used space shuttles to put satellites into outer space. A space shuttle blasts off like a rocket and returns to Earth like an airplane.

Infographic

interNET CONNECTION Visit our website: www.mhschool.com

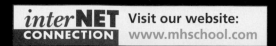

The United States Explores Outer Space

On these pages appear the different planets that make up our solar system and the achievements of various spacecrafts that the United States has built to explore them.

The Space Shuttle

First sent into outer space in 1981, the space shuttle is the first spacecraft that can be reused. Astronauts have used it for repairing satellites and conducting scientific experiments.

PLUTO
NEPTUNE
MERCURY
SUN
EARTH
JUPITER

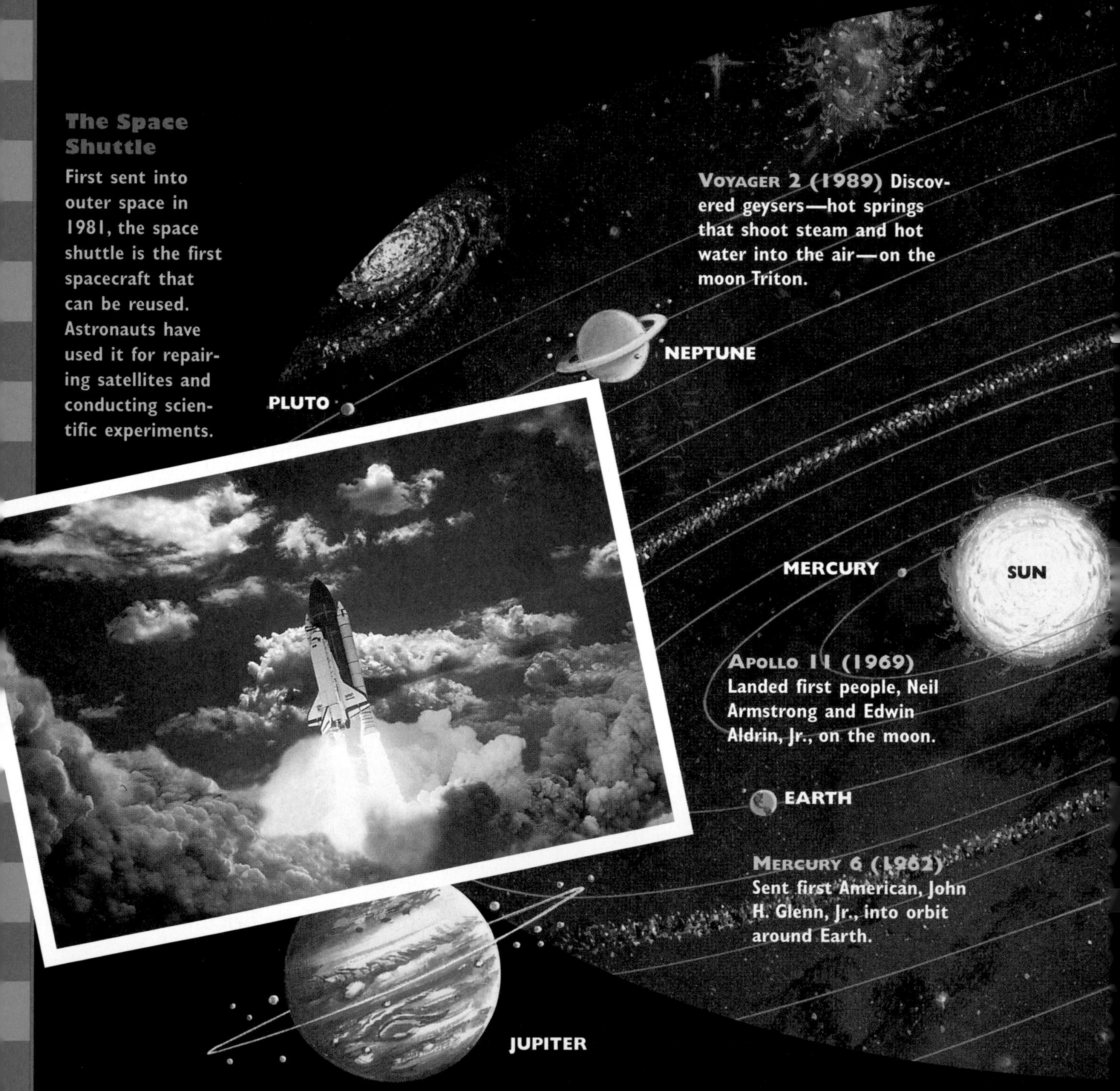

Voyager 2 (1989) Discovered geysers—hot springs that shoot steam and hot water into the air—on the moon Triton.

Apollo 11 (1969) Landed first people, Neil Armstrong and Edwin Aldrin, Jr., on the moon.

Mercury 6 (1962) Sent first American, John H. Glenn, Jr., into orbit around Earth.

Voyager 2 (1979) Provided information about Jupiter's Great Red Spot and found active volcanoes on Io, one of Jupiter's moons.

Galileo

First launched in 1989, Space Probe Galileo began sending us photos and information about Jupiter's weather and landforms in 1995. From this, scientists hope to learn more about Earth.

VIKING 1 & 2 (1975) Studied Mars' weather and searched for life forms.

MARS

VOYAGER 2 (1981) Photographed Saturn's enormous rings.

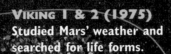

MAGELLAN (1990) Mapped the surface of Venus.

VENUS

SATURN

The Hubble Space Telescope

The Hubble Telescope was sent into orbit around Earth in 1990 to help scientists observe space. Astronauts had to repair the lens on the telescope in 1993.

URANUS

VOYAGER 2 (1986) Discovered Uranus has at least 11 rings and 15 moons.

ADVANCES IN SCIENCE AND TECHNOLOGY

The space race has inspired developments in science and technology. Those developments, in turn, have also shaped your own life at home and at school.

A Better World

More than ever, doctors use advances in science and technology to help them search for cures for diseases such as cancer and AIDS. Lasers, for example, help doctors to perform complex operations on many parts of the human body, even the eye and heart. Lasers are devices that produce powerful beams of light.

New technologies have helped scientists in other areas as well. Researchers in agriculture at Indiana's Purdue University, for example, developed a new type of corn that has more protein.

Wildlife scientists use electronic devices to gather information about animals of all kinds. In 1995 Chessie the Manatee made news. Scientists tracked her movements as she swam from Florida to New England—farther north than it was thought her species could travel. With new technology wildlife scientists hope to keep endangered animals, such as the American buffalo, from becoming extinct.

The Computer Age

Computers also have undergone rapid change and improvement. The earliest computer, built in the 1940s, filled a whole room. It had to be rewired whenever it was used to perform a new task. By the 1970s American inventors such as An Wang had shrunk the size of computers and made them more powerful. Still, only big businesses could afford computers. In 1976 two young Californians, Steve Wozniak and Steve Jobs, built a model for an easy-to-use personal computer, or "PC." By the 1980s their company succeeded in making personal computers affordable for many Americans. Soon thousands of homes, schools, and businesses were using PCs.

By the 1990s a Seattle businessman, Bill Gates, had created a

At one of NASA's research centers, an astronaut uses virtual reality, computer technology which copies an actual experience, to learn new skills.

software program to make PCs work even better. Software contains instructions that tell a computer how to perform specific tasks. So many individuals and corporations used Gates's software that his business became one of the largest companies in the world.

PCs today allow people to use the "information superhighway" and communicate directly with other people across the globe. Computer networks such as the Internet make information from faraway libraries, government offices, businesses, and other sources easily available. Together with pagers and cellular telephones, these new technologies have made instant worldwide communication possible.

WHY IT MATTERS

Since the 1950s technology has greatly changed the way Americans live. As we approach the new century, we can look forward to still more changes. What new inventions will make today's spaceships and computers arti-

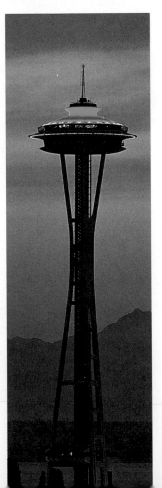

Seattle's famous building, the Space Needle, is a symbol of the high-tech industries that have developed in the Western region.

facts of the past? Who will find the cure for diseases? Will you become the future scientist, doctor, or inventor who unlocks such secrets? You and your classmates will be the leaders who take our country into the future.

✓ Reviewing Facts and Ideas

MAIN IDEAS

- The space race between the United States and the Soviet Union began in the 1950s during the Cold War. It helped lead to Americans landing on the moon and exploring other regions of outer space.

- Advances in technology have helped Americans to produce better crops, improve medical care, and communicate more efficiently.

- The computer has been a major invention of the late 1900s.

THINK ABOUT IT

1. What was the space race?

2. What changes have made computers easier to use?

3. **FOCUS** How have science and technology helped people in the United States and other countries?

4. **THINKING SKILL** *Evaluate* the primary source on page 639 for *credibility*. Why might you think Neil Armstrong is a credible source for information on space travel? Give reasons to support your evaluation.

5. **WRITE** Research one of the uses of science or technology discussed in this lesson. Ask a librarian or seek another source of information about how you can use technology yourself to learn about your subject. Use at least one of these sources to write a paragraph on your topic.

CHAPTER 21 REVIEW

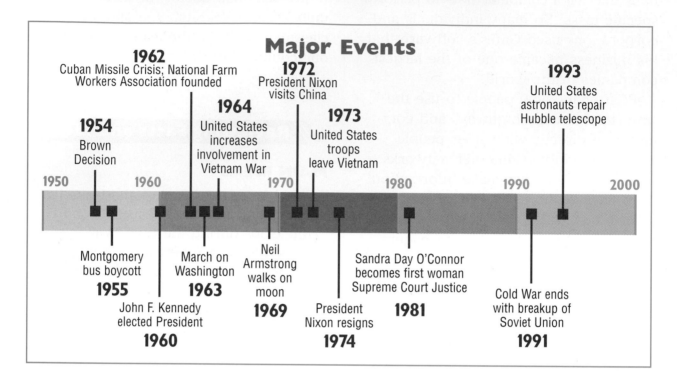

Major Events

1962
Cuban Missile Crisis; National Farm Workers Association founded

1972
President Nixon visits China

1993
United States astronauts repair Hubble telescope

1954
Brown Decision

1964
United States increases involvement in Vietnam War

1973
United States troops leave Vietnam

1950   1960   1970   1980   1990   2000

Montgomery bus boycott
1955

March on Washington
1963

Neil Armstrong walks on moon
1969

Sandra Day O'Connor becomes first woman Supreme Court Justice
1981

Cold War ends with breakup of Soviet Union
1991

John F. Kennedy elected President
1960

President Nixon resigns
1974

THINKING ABOUT VOCABULARY

Number a paper from 1 to 5. Beside each number, write the word or term from the list below that best completes the numbered blank in the paragraph.

Cuban Missile Crisis   outline
Internet   Vietnam War
Persian Gulf War

One way to organize information about the decades that followed the Korean War is to write an ___(1)___ . Under the heading of "Fighting Overseas" one of the first entries would be the ___(2)___ , the war which deeply divided Americans. Another entry from more recent times would be the ___(3)___ , which was fought in the Middle East. "World Events" would be another important heading. The first entry might be the ___(4)___ , the tense standoff in which the United States demanded that the Soviet Union remove its missiles. There would be other sections as well. Under what heading would you place an entry about the ___(5)___ , the computer information and communication network?

THINKING ABOUT FACTS

1. What was the importance of the Supreme Court's decision in the *Brown* case?

2. What role did Jo Ann Robinson play in the Montgomery bus boycott?

3. What was *La Causa*? What conditions were its leaders trying to change?

4. Why did the Cuban Missile Crisis cause great fear all over the world?

5. What events occurred during the "long, hot summers" of 1965 to 1968? Where did these events take place?

6. Describe the views of "hawks" and "doves" during the Vietnam War.

7. What was the importance of President Nixon's visit to China?

8. How was the 1987 treaty signed by Ronald Reagan and Mikhail Gorbachev different from all arms treaties before it?

9. What technologies changed life in recent years?

10. Look at the time line above. How are the events of 1969 and 1993 related?

WRITING A NEWS STORY

Write a news story in which you describe the 1963 March on Washington. Include in your report quotes from the speech by Martin Luther King, Jr.

WRITING A JOURNAL ENTRY

Choose one of the following people and write a journal entry describing his or her feelings on the given day: Rosa Parks after refusing to give up her seat, Neil Armstrong after walking on the moon, President Reagan after signing the 1987 treaty to reduce nuclear missiles.

WRITING AN E-MAIL MESSAGE

What would you like to ask the President of the United States? Write a message to the President that you would send over the Internet to the White House.

APPLYING STUDY SKILLS

WRITING STUDY SKILLS

1. What is the purpose of an outline?
2. What are the three parts of an outline?
3. How are the different parts of an outline identified?
4. Under which main idea of the outline on page 622 would you place a detail about a decision Marshall wrote for the Supreme Court?
5. What three headings might you choose if you were writing an outline about the year 1974?

Summing Up the Chapter

Copy the cause-and-effect chart on a separate piece of paper. Review the chapter to complete the blank sections. When you have finished, use the chart to answer the question "What effects did technology have in the United States in the twentieth century?"

CAUSES	EFFECTS
Civil Rights Act of 1964	
	Cuban Missile Crisis
North Vietnam invades South Vietnam.	
	Many women join the workforce.
Mikhail Gorbachev introduces reforms in the Soviet Union.	
	Many people use the Internet to get information from faraway sources.

UNIT 9 REVIEW

THINKING ABOUT VOCABULARY

Number a paper from 1 to 10. Beside each number, write the word or term from the list below that best completes the sentence.

communism
concentration camps
credibility
hydroelectricity
League of Nations

League of Women Voters
Persian Gulf War
satellite
space race
Watergate Scandal

1. The _____, formed in the 1920s, helps inform both men and women about political issues.

2. Dams such as the Hoover Dam used the force of running water to provide _____ to people in rural areas.

3. In 1991 the United States and Iraq fought the _____ over Iraq's invasion of Kuwait.

4. President Ford pardoned President Nixon for any crimes he may have committed during the _____ .

5. Asking questions helps to determine the _____, or believability, of a source.

6. President Wilson wanted the United States to join the _____, an organization of countries designed to prevent future wars.

7. Beginning in the late 1950s, the United States and the Soviet Union began a _____, which was a competition to gain control of outer space.

8. During World War II, the Germans imprisoned and murdered those they considered enemies in places called _____.

9. A social and political system in which all property is owned by the government is called _____ .

10. A _____ is an object that circles a larger object, such as Earth.

THINK AND WRITE

WRITING A RADIO ANNOUNCEMENT
Suppose that you are a radio announcer on one of the first radios. Write a news item about an event in that time period to read over the radio to your listeners.

WRITING A DESCRIPTION
Look again at section on the Vietnam War on pages 628-629. Why do you think many Americans have such a strong response to this war ? If you have ever visited the Vietnam Veterans Memorial by Maya Lin, write several paragraphs describing that experience. If you have not seen it, write several paragraphs describing what you think the experience might be like.

WRITING ABOUT PERSPECTIVES
Since the United States began sending astronauts into outer space in 1962, Americans have had different opinions about the importance of our country's space program. Some feel that learning about other planets is necessary for the future. Others feel that the space program costs too much money. Write a short essay explaining each of these points of view.

BUILDING SKILLS

1. **Credibility of a source** What is one clue that a source is not credible?

2. **Credibility of a source** How can an author's reputation help you to determine his or her credibility?

3. **Credibility of a source** Who might be a more credible source for information on the space race: an official in the United States space program or a reporter for a local newspaper?

4. **Outline** What is a good first step in preparing an outline?

5. **Outline** What part of an outline is identified by capital letters?

YESTERDAY, TODAY &
TOMORROW

In this unit, you read about the different relationships between the United States and other countries. How did the role of the United States as a world leader change over the last 50 years? What is the role of the United States in the world today? Do you think our country will play the same role in the world 50 years from now? Why or why not?

READING ON YOUR OWN

Here are some books you might find at the library to help you learn more.

THE BREAD WINNER
by Arvella Whitmore

A young girl helps her family during the Great Depression by selling her homemade bread.

BASEBALL SAVED US
by Ken Mochizuki

Playing baseball helps a young boy survive life in a Japanese American relocation camp.

DEAR MRS. PARKS: A DIALOGUE WITH TODAY'S YOUTH
by Rosa Parks

The woman known as the "Mother of the civil rights movement" answers letters that she has received from young people.

UNIT 9 REVIEW PROJECT

Conduct a Get-Out-the-Vote Campaign

1. Review the unit to see how women and African Americans won the right to vote.
2. With your group, write a list of reasons why it is important for people to vote. Include reasons from the unit as well as your own opinion.

3. Think of ways you can get your message across. You might want to start with a poster. Use a large piece of oak tag, write a slogan, and decorate it with colored paper, glitter, and paints. Be sure to list reasons to vote.
4. You may also want to create pamphlets, a banner, or make stickers and buttons.
5. Have your group present your get-out-the-vote poster and campaign to the class.

647

Canada and Latin America

THINKING ABOUT HISTORY AND GEOGRAPHY

The Special Section begins by visiting two countries that border the United States—Canada and Mexico. Next, you will travel south to Central America, a strip of land that narrows as it nears South America. Then, to the east, you will explore the island countries of the Caribbean. Finally, you will reach South America, which, like its northern neighbors, has a variety of people and geographical features.

CANADA

Rocky Mountains

NORTH AMERICA

UNITED STATES

THE CARIBBEAN

ATLANTIC OCEAN

Uxmal

Belize

San Blas Islands

MEXICO

CENTRAL AMERICA

SOUTH AMERICA

São Paulo

PACIFIC OCEAN

Rocky Mountains
WESTERN CANADA

Western Canada has deep lakes covered by glaciers, hot springs, and snow-capped mountains.

Uxmal
SOUTHERN MEXICO

Like other Maya ruins you have read about, Uxmal (oosh MAHL) is known for its architecture.

San Blas Islands
CARIBBEAN SEA

The San Blas Islands are a chain of islands off Panama's northern coast.

Rain forest
BELIZE

In the highlands of Belize, near the Maya Mountains, it rains more than 200 inches a year.

São Paulo
BRAZIL

São Paulo, with skyscrapers and large parks, is one of the world's largest cities.

Countries of the Western Hemisphere

NORTH AMERICA

CANADA

CAPITAL ★ Ottawa
POPULATION 28,800,000
MAJOR LANGUAGES English and French

UNITED STATES

CAPITAL ★ Washington, D.C.
POPULATION 265,500,000
MAJOR LANGUAGE English

BERMUDA
Dependency of the United Kingdom

CAPITAL ★ Hamilton
POPULATION 62,100
MAJOR LANGUAGE English

MEXICO

CAPITAL ★ Mexico City
POPULATION 95,772,000
MAJOR LANGUAGE Spanish

CENTRAL AMERICA

BELIZE

CAPITAL ★ Belmopan
POPULATION 219,000
MAJOR LANGUAGES English and Spanish

COSTA RICA

CAPITAL ★ San José
POPULATION 3,463,000
MAJOR LANGUAGES Spanish and English

EL SALVADOR

CAPITAL ★ San Salvador
POPULATION 5,829,000
MAJOR LANGUAGES Spanish and Nahua

GUATEMALA

CAPITAL ★ Guatemala City
POPULATION 11,278,000
MAJOR LANGUAGES Spanish and Maya dialects

HONDURAS

CAPITAL ★ Tegucigalpa
POPULATION 5,605,000
MAJOR LANGUAGE Spanish

NICARAGUA

CAPITAL ★ Managua
POPULATION 4,272,352
MAJOR LANGUAGE Spanish

PANAMA

CAPITAL ★ Panama City
POPULATION 2,655,000
MAJOR LANGUAGES Spanish and English

THE CARIBBEAN

ANTIGUA AND BARBUDA

CAPITAL ★ St. John's
POPULATION 65,000
MAJOR LANGUAGE English

BAHAMAS

CAPITAL ★ Nassau
POPULATION 259,000
MAJOR LANGUAGES English and Creole

BARBADOS

CAPITAL ★ Bridgetown
POPULATION 257,000
MAJOR LANGUAGE English

CUBA

CAPITAL ★ Havana
POPULATION 11,000,000
MAJOR LANGUAGE Spanish

DOMINICA

CAPITAL ★ Roseau
POPULATION 83,000
MAJOR LANGUAGES English and French patois

DOMINICAN REPUBLIC

CAPITAL ★ Santo Domingo
POPULATION 8,000,000
MAJOR LANGUAGE Spanish

GRENADA

CAPITAL ★ St. George's
POPULATION 95,000
MAJOR LANGUAGES English and French patois

HAITI

CAPITAL ★ Port-au-Prince
POPULATION 6,732,000
MAJOR LANGUAGES French and French Creole

JAMAICA

CAPITAL ★ Kingston
POPULATION 2,595,000
MAJOR LANGUAGES English and Jamaican Creole

PUERTO RICO
Commonwealth of the United States

CAPITAL ★ San Juan
POPULATION 3,802,000
MAJOR LANGUAGES Spanish and English

ST. KITTS AND NEVIS

CAPITAL ★ Basseterre
POPULATION 41,369
MAJOR LANGUAGE English

ST. LUCIA

CAPITAL ★ Castries
POPULATION 158,000
MAJOR LANGUAGES English and French patois

ST. VINCENT AND THE GRENADINES

CAPITAL ★ Kingstown
POPULATION 118,000
MAJOR LANGUAGE English

TRINIDAD AND TOBAGO

CAPITAL ★ Port-of-Spain
POPULATION 1,300,000
MAJOR LANGUAGES English, Hindi, and French

SOUTH AMERICA

ARGENTINA

CAPITAL ★ Buenos Aires
POPULATION 34,672,997
MAJOR LANGUAGES Spanish, English, and Italian

BOLIVIA

CAPITAL ★ Sucre (judicial) and La Paz (administrative)
POPULATION 7,165,000
MAJOR LANGUAGES Spanish, Quechua, and Aymará

BRAZIL

CAPITAL ★ Brasília
POPULATION 162,661,000
MAJOR LANGUAGES Portuguese, Spanish, French, and English

CHILE

CAPITAL ★ Santiago
POPULATION 14,333,000
MAJOR LANGUAGE Spanish

COLOMBIA

CAPITAL ★ Bogotá
POPULATION 36,813,000
MAJOR LANGUAGE Spanish

ECUADOR

CAPITAL ★ Quito
POPULATION 11,466,291
MAJOR LANGUAGES Spanish and Quechua

FRENCH GUIANA
Overseas Department of France

CAPITAL ★ Cayenne
POPULATION 151,000
MAJOR LANGUAGE French

GUYANA

CAPITAL ★ Georgetown
POPULATION 712,091
MAJOR LANGUAGES English, Hindi, and Urdu

PARAGUAY

CAPITAL ★ Asunción
POPULATION 5,504,000
MAJOR LANGUAGES Spanish and Guarani

PERU

CAPITAL ★ Lima
POPULATION 24,523,000
MAJOR LANGUAGES Spanish, Quechua, and Aymará

SURINAME

CAPITAL ★ Paramaribo
POPULATION 436,000
MAJOR LANGUAGES Dutch, English, and Hindi

URUGUAY

CAPITAL ★ Montevideo
POPULATION 3,238,952
MAJOR LANGUAGES Spanish and Brazilero

VENEZUELA

CAPITAL ★ Caracas
POPULATION 21,983,000
MAJOR LANGUAGES Spanish and Indian dialects

PART I

Canada

Read Aloud

The True North strong and free;
From far and wide,
O Canada, we stand on guard for thee.

If you went to a baseball game in Toronto, Canada, fans would sing these words. These are lines from "O Canada," the Canadian national anthem. If you went to a game in Montreal, Canada, you would hear the same tune with different words—in French.

Focus Activity

READ TO LEARN

Who are the people of Canada?

VOCABULARY

- bilingual
- province
- North American Free Trade Agreement

PEOPLE

- Jacques Cartier
- Samuel de Champlain

PLACES

- Canada
- Great Lakes-St. Lawrence Lowlands
- Canadian Shield
- Nunavut
- Vancouver
- Toronto
- Quebec
- Nova Scotia

THE BIG PICTURE

As you read in Chapter 7, the explorers Jacques Cartier and Samuel de Champlain claimed Canada, our neighbor to the north, for France. As a result of the French and Indian War, the British won control of Canada in 1763. Now Canada is a bilingual country. The word *bilingual* means "two languages." Canada has two official languages—English and French.

Canada shares the continent of North America with the United States, Mexico, and Central America.

Although Canada and the United States share some geographical features, the two countries differ in many ways. Canada has a colder climate because it lies farther north. Unlike the United States, Canada became independent from Britain gradually, without fighting a war. The Canadian people have their own unique customs, traditions, and culture.

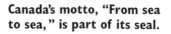

Canada's motto, "From sea to sea," is part of its seal.

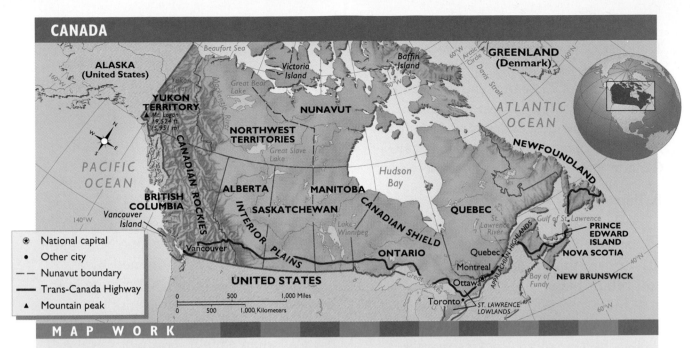

ALASKA (United States)

Beaufort Sea

Victoria Island

Great Bear Lake

Baffin Island

GREENLAND (Denmark)

ATLANTIC OCEAN

YUKON TERRITORY
Mt. Logan 19,524 ft. (5,951 m)

NUNAVUT

NORTHWEST TERRITORIES

Great Slave Lake

Hudson Bay

NEWFOUNDLAND

PACIFIC OCEAN

CANADIAN ROCKIES

ALBERTA

MANITOBA

CANADIAN SHIELD

QUEBEC

St. Lawrence River

Gulf of St. Lawrence

PRINCE EDWARD ISLAND

BRITISH COLUMBIA

Vancouver Island

SASKATCHEWAN

INTERIOR PLAINS

Lake Winnipeg

ONTARIO

APPALACHIAN HIGHLANDS

NOVA SCOTIA

Vancouver

Quebec

Montreal

NEW BRUNSWICK

Bay of Fundy

UNITED STATES

Ottawa

Toronto

ST. LAWRENCE LOWLANDS

Legend:
- ⊛ National capital
- • Other city
- – – Nunavut boundary
- — Trans-Canada Highway
- ▲ Mountain peak

0   500   1,000 Miles
0   500   1,000 Kilometers

M A P   W O R K

Not only do they share a border and are part of the same land mass, the United States and Canada share some geographical features.

1. Name three landforms or waterways that the United States and Canada have in common.

2. What is the capital of Canada? In which province is it located?

THE GEOGRAPHY OF CANADA

Canada is the world's second largest country, after Russia. It stretches across North America from the Atlantic Ocean to the Pacific Ocean. It is bordered on the north by the ice-filled Arctic Ocean and on the south by the United States. Canada is divided into ten provinces and two territories. A province is a territory that has its own government, like the states in the United States.

Canada's population is quite small—over 29 million—for such a large country. Most Canadians live in the southeastern part of the country, within 100 miles of the United States border. Why? The answer lies with Canada's geography. As you can see on the map, most of Canada's major cities are located in the Great Lakes-St. Lawrence Lowlands area, close to the United

States. Because this area has fertile soil, good transportation, and a mild climate, nine out of ten Canadians live here.

The largest region is the Canadian Shield in central Canada. Carved out by glaciers long ago, it divides the eastern and western parts of the country. "I have called [it] the Stoney Region," wrote an early explorer. "It is little else than rocks with innumerable [many] lakes and rivers." Although it is rich in lumber, oil, and natural gas, few people other than the Inuit live there because of its poor soil and harsh climate.

The Canadian government has agreed to return a vast area of the Canadian Shield to the Inuit, which they call Nunavut, in 1999. This area is now part of the Northwest Territories. The Inuit, whom you have read about in Chapter 19, have lived in Nunavut for hundreds of years. They also live in Alaska.

THE PEOPLE OF CANADA

The first Canadians were native American peoples such as the Inuit and the Cree. Many of their descendants live in Canada today. The largest group of Canadians are descendants of British and French colonists. Like the United States, Canada also has many immigrants.

A Trip Across Canada

In order to meet some of the people of Canada, you might travel across the country on the Trans-Canada Highway. You might begin your trip in the west, in Vancouver. Until the Canadian Pacific Railroad was built in the late 1800s, the Canadian Rockies were a barrier to colonial settlement of the west. Today, Vancouver is Canada's third largest city. Located near the Pacific Ocean, it has strong trade ties to the countries of Asia. Locate Vancouver and trace the rest of your journey by using the map on page 653.

Next, cross the majestic Rockies to the vast wheat fields of the Interior Plains. Many of the farms and ranches on the plains here are owned by descendants of Irish, Polish, Russian, German, and Scandinavian immigrants. You might spend a night in an inn owned by a métis (MAY tees) family, who have both European and Indian ancestors.

After a long drive across the stony, flat Canadian Shield, you will see the

Canada's diverse heritage includes French signs in Quebec (below), a British-style Parliament (below center), Inuit traders (right), and a fishing village in Nova Scotia (below right).

skyscrapers of Toronto, one of Canada's largest cities. Living in this city are descendants of the Mohawk who moved here after the American Revolution. You will also find newcomers from the Caribbean, Central America, Africa, and South America. Many Jews who fled from the Nazis during World War II also made their home in Toronto.

License plates in Quebec declare: *Je me souviens* (JUH MUH soo VYEN), which is French for "I remember." The many French-speaking Canadians in Quebec proudly preserve their cultural heritage. Some of them believe that Quebec should become an independent country. Others believe Quebec should remain part of Canada. In 1995, Canadians in Quebec narrowly voted to remain part of Canada.

End your journey through Canada by strolling through the fishing villages of Nova Scotia on the rocky Atlantic Coast. *Nova Scotia* means "New Scotland" in Latin. Many people from Scotland and Ireland settled in this province in the 1700s and 1800s.

Back home you might tell friends how Canada is truly a country of many lands and peoples. You might also describe how Canadians work in an often harsh environment to turn their country's many resources into wealth.

WHY IT MATTERS

"Geography has made us neighbors," President John F. Kennedy of the United States once told Canadians, "History has made us friends. Economics has made us partners."

Canada and the United States share the world's longest undefended border. Canada is also the largest trading partner of the United States. In 1992 Canada, Mexico, and the United States signed the North American Free Trade Agreement (NAFTA) to boost trade among the three neighbors.

✓ Reviewing Facts and Ideas

MAIN IDEAS

- Canada's varied geography has affected where people live and work.
- Canada is a land of diverse peoples, including descendants of Native Americans, British, and French colonists, and immigrants.

THINK ABOUT IT

1. List the provinces and territories of Canada.

2. Who lives in Canada today?

3. **FOCUS** What are some of the cities and regions of Canada? What are some activities in these places?

4. **THINKING SKILL** *Compare* and *contrast* the geography of the United States and Canada.

5. **GEOGRAPHY** Name some of the advantages and disadvantages of Canada's geography.

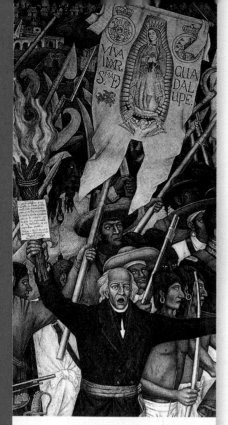

PART 2

Mexico

Read Aloud

Each year, at eleven o'clock on the night of September 15, shouts fill the air of every Mexican city and town. Mexicans are celebrating the "Call of Dolores," a speech made by a Roman Catholic priest named Miguel Hidalgo (mee GEL ee DAHL goh). This speech inspired Mexicans to fight for independence from Spain.

Focus Activity

READ TO LEARN

Who are the people of Mexico?

VOCABULARY

- rain forest
- mestizo

PEOPLE

- Miguel Hidalgo
- Benito Juárez

PLACES

- Mexico
- Mexico City
- Acapulco
- Guadalajara

THE BIG PICTURE

Although Mexico is in North America, it is also part of Latin America. The name Latin America is given to the lands in the Western Hemisphere that were settled by the Spanish and Portuguese. Latin America includes Mexico, Central America, South America, and much of the Caribbean. Mexico's almost 90 million people make it the largest Spanish-speaking country in the world.

Long before the Spanish reached the Americas, the Maya, Aztec, and other peoples had built complex civilizations in what is now Mexico. As you read in Chapter 3, Mexico became a Spanish colony in 1521 after Hernando Cortés defeated the Aztec. Then in 1810 Miguel Hidalgo, inspired by the American Revolution, asked the Mexicans, "Will you make the effort to recover from the hated Spaniards the lands stolen from your forefathers 300 years ago?" After years of struggle with Spain, Mexico became independent in 1821. Today Mexico is a federal republic with 31 states.

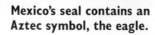

Mexico's seal contains an Aztec symbol, the eagle.

THE GEOGRAPHY OF MEXICO

Mexico and the United States share a nearly 1,900-mile border. As you can see on the map on this page, about half of that border is formed by the Rio Grande. The Gulf of Mexico and the Caribbean Sea lie to the east and the Pacific Ocean to the west.

Mexico is a mostly dry country with limited land suitable for farming. Much of Mexico is covered by mountains and deserts. In northern Mexico is the Sonora Desert. As the Atlas map on pages R10-R11 shows, the Sonora Desert also covers parts of the United States.

As you follow the Rocky Mountains south you can see that they split into two. In Mexico, this split forms the Western Sierra Madre (see ER rah MAH dre) and the Eastern Sierra Madre. *Sierra Madre* means "mother mountains" in the Spanish language.

Many of Mexico's mountains, such as Mount Popocatépetl (poh poh kah TE pe tul), are active volcanoes.

Find the high Central Plateau on the map below. This is where most of Mexico's people live and where Mexico's capital, Mexico City, is located. Although Mexico lies in the tropics, Mexico City has a moderate climate because it is so high above sea level.

In contrast, Mexico's lowland coastal plains have a tropical climate. Oil has been discovered along the lowlands and in the waters of the Gulf of Mexico. Rain forests cover parts of the Yucatán peninsula. A rain forest is a forest that receives lots of rain year round.

Mexico's geography poses many challenges for its people. Tropical storms, volcanic eruptions, and earthquakes cause a great deal of damage. In 1985 about 10,000 people died in the worst earthquake in Mexico's history.

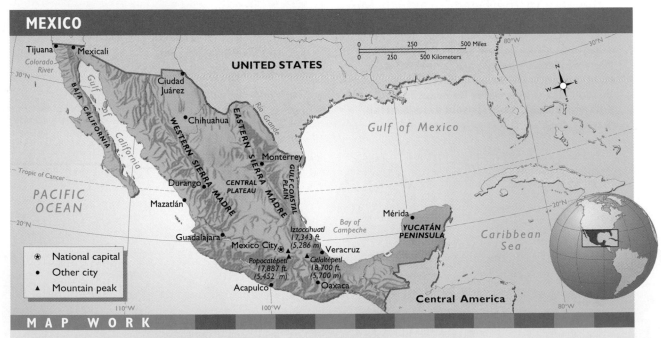

MEXICO

MAP WORK

Mexico shares part of its northern border with the southwestern United States. Lying farther south than the United States, much of Mexico has a tropical climate.

1. What is Mexico's highest mountain peak?
2. What geographical features does Mexico share with the United States?

THE PEOPLE OF MEXICO

Some Mexicans are descendants of Indian ancestors and some are descendants of Spanish colonists. About seven out of every ten Mexicans, however, are mestizos (mes TEE sohs). Mestizos have both Indian and Spanish ancestors. A small number of Mexicans are the descendants of Africans who were enslaved there in the 1500s and 1600s.

A Blending of Cultures

Today Mexico is a blend of both Indian and Spanish cultures. Although Spanish is the national language, the Aztec language of Nahuatl is still spoken by many Mexicans. More than 15 other Indian languages are also spoken.

As you have read, the Spanish brought Christianity to the Indians throughout their colonies in the Americas. Today, most Mexicans are Roman Catholics. However, many still observe Indian holidays and customs. For example, the Day of the Dead, in which Mex-icans honor their dead relatives, was an important Aztec holiday.

For centuries, the Indians living under Spanish rule were denied basic rights. In the middle 1800s, a Zapotec Indian, Benito Juárez (be NEE toh HWAHR es), became president. He set out to improve life for all Mexicans. Despite his reforms, many Indians continue to face prejudice and discrimination. In the 1990s, Indians in the

Many of Mexico's people are farmers (below right) or factory workers (above right). Guadalajara is known for its beautiful pottery (below), which is sold in its central market area.

Benito Juárez was painted by the artist José Orozco. Juárez's motto was, "Nothing by force. Everything through law and reason."

southern Mexican state of Chiapas began a movement for equal rights.

A Land of Many Resources

Today tourists flock to Mexico to see its ancient Indian cities and Spanish architecture. Many come to lie on the beautiful beaches of resort cities such as Acapulco on the Pacific Ocean. Many tourists also visit Guadalajara (gwah dah lah HAH rah), Mexico's second largest city. Located in a rich farming region, Guadalajara is known for its fine pottery and glassware.

Mexico also has other important industries. In the 1980s Mexico became the world's fourth largest exporter of oil. It is also one of the world's leading producers of silver and other minerals.

In recent years, large companies from other countries have opened factories called *maquiladoras* (mah kee lah DOHR ahs) in Mexico. Thousands of Mexicans now work in maquiladoras, making cars, textiles, computers, and other products.

Today Mexico City is the fastest growing city in the world. With over 24 million people in Mexico City and the surrounding area, it is the world's second largest city after Tokyo.

WHY IT MATTERS

Many people who live in California and the southwestern United States have roots in Mexico. As you have read, these lands became part of the United States after the Mexican War in 1848. Today, Mexico and the United States maintain close economic ties. NAFTA, which you read about in Part 1, has opened the way for more trade between the two neighbors.

✔ Reviewing Facts and Ideas

MAIN IDEAS

● Much of Mexico is covered by deserts and mountains, including many active volcanoes. Most people live on the Central Plateau.

● Mexican culture is a blend of Indian and Spanish traditions.

THINK ABOUT IT

1. Summarize the geography of Mexico.

2. What challenges does climate pose for Mexicans?

3. FOCUS How is modern Mexico a blend of Indian and Spanish cultures?

4. THINKING SKILL Based on what you have read in this and other lessons, make a *conclusion* about why the Mexicans wanted independence from Spain. Explain the reasons for your answer.

5. GEOGRAPHY How has geography affected the economy of Mexico?

PART 3

Central America and the Caribbean

Focus Activity

READ TO LEARN

Who are the people of Central America and the Caribbean?

VOCABULARY

- hurricane

PEOPLE

- Toussaint L'Ouverture
- Rigoberta Menchú

PLACES

- Haiti
- Guatemala

Read Aloud

I have crossed an ocean
I have lost my tongue
from the root of the old one
a new one has sprung.

In this poem Grace Nichols talks about the many people whose ancestors were brought to the Caribbean by force from their African homelands. They helped create the culture of the Caribbean today—a blend of African, Asian, Indian, and European traditions.

THE BIG PICTURE

Central America and the Caribbean islands are part of the Western Hemisphere. Before 1492 both were home to different Indian cultures. After Columbus's voyage, the Spanish and later the French, British, and Dutch set up colonies here. In the 1790s, **Toussaint L'Ouverture** (too SAN loo ver TYUR) led a revolution that ended slavery and won **Haiti** independence from France. In 1821 five Central American countries became independent from Spain. In time other countries in Central America and the Caribbean won independence, too.

Even after they became independent, small groups of landowners continued to control most of these countries' wealth and power. These wealthy landowners often backed dictators whose armies helped them maintain their power. In the 1980s longtime dictators in Haiti, Panama, El Salvador, and Nicaragua were overthrown.

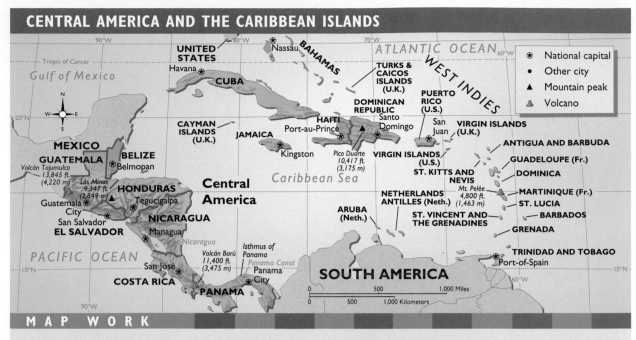

Although most of the countries in Central America and the Caribbean have a tropical climate, somewhat cooler temperatures can be found in the mountainous areas.

1. Which two countries share the same island?
2. Name the largest lake in Central America.
3. Which Caribbean island chains are closest to the United States?

CENTRAL AMERICAN AND CARIBBEAN LANDS

Locate the Caribbean islands on the map on this page. Columbus called these islands "the Indies" because he thought that he had reached India, a country in Asia. To the west is Central America, an isthmus connecting Mexico with South America.

Rugged mountains run through Central America like a prickly backbone. Many of these mountains are active volcanoes. Large parts of Belize, Guatemala, and Honduras in Central America are covered with dense rain forests. Along the Pacific and Caribbean coasts are steamy lowlands.

Many of the Caribbean islands are made of coral reefs. Others are the tops of undersea volcanoes that reach above sea level. Most of these volcanoes are inactive. The largest islands in the Caribbean are Hispaniola, Cuba, Puerto Rico, and Jamaica.

"O dread wind of the sea," the Taino people prayed, "stay away from our shores." The Taino, whom you read about in Chapter 6, respected a powerful god called Hurakan (HOO ruh kahn). It was Hurakan, they believed, who hurled terrible rain storms at the islands. Europeans named these storms hurricanes, after the Taino god. Volcanic eruptions and earthquakes also cause great damage in this region.

Most of the countries of Central America and the Caribbean islands have a tropical climate. Over 500 years ago, Columbus described Hispaniola as "a land to be desired, and once seen, never to be left." The beautiful beaches of the Caribbean islands have made them popular with tourists from Europe and North America.

A BLENDING OF PEOPLES

Have you ever heard calypso or reggae music? These musical styles of the Caribbean are a blend of African, Indian, and European sounds and instruments. They are one example of the blending of cultures in the Caribbean.

Most of the people of the Caribbean are the descendants of Europeans and Africans. In the late 1800s workers from India, China, and Southeast Asia came to work on Caribbean plantations. The languages and customs of all of these countries are found in the Caribbean. For example, the people of Haiti speak Haitian Creole, a mix of French and African languages.

Many descendants of the Maya and other Indians live in Central America. A majority of the population of Guatemala is Indian. Many people in Belize have African roots, while people in Costa Rica have mainly European roots. In Nicaragua and El Salvador, most people are mestizo.

Struggles and Triumphs

In many Central American and Caribbean countries, Indians are fighting for equal rights. In the 1970s and 1980s, thousands of Indians were killed during a civil war in Guatemala. The victims included the brother, father, and mother of a Quiche (KEE che) Indian woman named Rigoberta Menchú (ree goh BER tah men CHOO). This led Menchú to dedicate her life to

A volcano erupts over Costa Rica (left). Ports in the Caribbean Islands include Curaçao (far left). Rigoberta Menchú (below left) of Guatemala has led struggles for democratic rights. In 1995 René Préval (below) was elected president of Haiti.

helping Indians fight for their rights. For her efforts Menchú won the Nobel Prize for Peace in 1992.

Despite the money earned from tourism, most countries in the region are poor. Geography limits the amount of land that is suitable for farming. Still the economy of the region is based on agriculture. In some countries most crops are grown at the foot of volcanoes, where the soil is made fertile by ash from the volcanoes. Crops such as sugar, coffee, and bananas are grown for export.

WHY IT MATTERS

Ever since the Monroe Doctrine became a United States policy in 1823, our country has played a major role in Central America and the Caribbean. After the Spanish-American War, as you read in Chapter 19, the United States occupied Cuba briefly and gained control of Puerto Rico. Today Puerto Rico is a commonwealth closely linked to the United States. A commonwealth is a country or state governed by its people. Because of this relationship, many Puerto Ricans now live in the continental United States. Many people from other Caribbean islands and Central America have also moved here, fleeing persecution or poverty.

The United States has many economic interests in the region. The Panama Canal, under United States control until the year 2000, has been an important trade route for the United States.

✓ **Reviewing Facts and Ideas**

MAIN IDEAS

- Central America and the Caribbean islands contain many mountains, some of which are active volcanoes. Most of the countries have a tropical climate.

- The people in these regions have mainly Indian, African, Asian, and European ancestors.

THINK ABOUT IT

1. Why did the Taino have such respect for their god Hurakan?

2. What role has the United States played in the region?

3. **FOCUS** Who are the peoples that make up Central America and the Caribbean islands?

4. **THINKING SKILL** What *effects* did European colonization have on the peoples of Central America and the Caribbean? How can you tell?

5. **GEOGRAPHY** What difficulties does geography pose to the peoples in the region?

PART 4

South America

Read Aloud

"I swear before God and by my honor never to allow my hands to be idle nor my soul to rest until I have broken the chains that bind us to Spain."

Simón Bolívar (see MOHN boh LEE var) made this vow in the early 1800s. Bolívar would become a hero to the people of South America.

Focus Activity

READ TO LEARN

Who are the peoples of South America?

VOCABULARY

- favela

PEOPLE

- Simón Bolívar
- José de San Martín

PLACES

- Brazil
- Andes Mountains
- Amazon River
- São Paulo

THE BIG PICTURE

South America lies in the southern part of the Western Hemisphere. As you can see from the map on page 665, South America stretches from the tropical Caribbean Sea to the cold, stormy waters off Cape Horn. As you read in Chapter 6, Spain claimed much of South America in the 1500s, while Portugal set up a colony in **Brazil**. Later, Britain, France, and the Netherlands colonized other parts of the continent.

By the early 1800s the American Revolution had inspired the people of South America to fight for independence. In 1810 **Simón Bolívar** of Venezuela began the fight to free South America from Spanish control.

After years of struggle, Bolívar helped win independence for much of northern South America. Many South Americans called him "The Liberator." He then helped **José de San Martín** of Argentina free colonies in the south. To defeat the Spanish, both leaders had to cross the rugged **Andes Mountains**, losing many soldiers along the way. By 1830 the Spanish had given up control of all of their colonies in South America. In 1822 Brazil won its independence from Portugal.

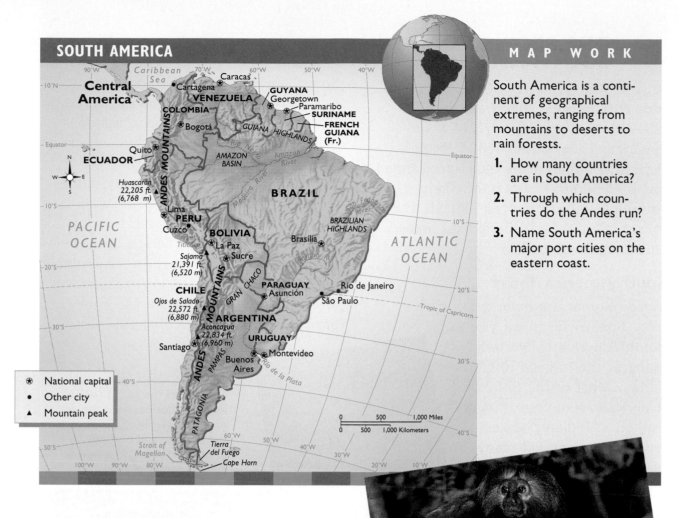

SOUTH AMERICA

Caribbean Sea

Central America

Cartagena • • Caracas

VENEZUELA
Georgetown
GUYANA
• Paramaribo
COLOMBIA
SURINAME
• Bogotá
FRENCH GUIANA (Fr.)

GUIANA HIGHLANDS

Rio Negro

Amazon River

Equator

Quito
ECUADOR

ANDES MOUNTAINS

AMAZON BASIN

Madeira River

BRAZIL

São Francisco River

Huascarán 22,205 ft. (6,768 m)

Lima
PERU
Cuzco •

BRAZILIAN HIGHLANDS

ATLANTIC OCEAN

PACIFIC OCEAN

Titicaca

BOLIVIA
La Paz
• Sucre

Brasília

Sajama 21,391 ft. (6,520 m)

CHILE

GRAN CHACO

ANDES MOUNTAINS

PARAGUAY
Asunción

Tropic of Capricorn

Rio de Janeiro
São Paulo

Ojos de Salado 22,572 ft. (6,880 m)

ARGENTINA

Aconcagua 22,834 ft. (6,960 m)

URUGUAY

Santiago

PAMPAS
Buenos Aires
Montevideo

Río de la Plata

National capital
• Other city
▲ Mountain peak

PATAGONIA

ANDES

Strait of Magellan
Tierra del Fuego
Cape Horn

0   500   1,000 Miles
0   500   1,000 Kilometers

South America is a continent of geographical extremes, ranging from mountains to deserts to rain forests.

1. How many countries are in South America?
2. Through which countries do the Andes run?
3. Name South America's major port cities on the eastern coast.

THE GEOGRAPHY OF SOUTH AMERICA

If you went to Chile (CHEE le) in July, you might find cold winter weather. If you arrived in February, you would find the schools closed for summer vacation. Because Chile lies south of the equator, its seasons are the reverse of ours.

Much of South America lies in the tropics. Yet temperatures can vary greatly. In lowland areas, it is often hot. In the mountains, it can be bitterly cold. Most countries near the equator have wet and dry seasons.

Find the Amazon River on the map. The world's second longest river, it snakes east more than 4,000 miles from the Andes Mountains through Brazil to the Atlantic Ocean. Also, the world's largest tropical rain forest is in Brazil's Amazon Basin. In contrast, the world's

The tamarin is one of the many animals in the Amazon rain forest.

driest desert is also in South America, on the west coast. Parts of the Atacama Desert have had no rainfall for 100 years. Much of Argentina is a wide plain, known as the pampas.

The soaring, snowcapped Andes Mountains form the world's longest unbroken mountain range. They stretch more than 4,000 miles along the western coast of South America.

665

THE PEOPLES OF SOUTH AMERICA

As you will recall from Chapter 3, the Inca empire once stretched for 2,500 miles along the west coast of South America. Then, in the 1530s, Francisco Pizarro conquered the Inca and claimed much of South America for Spain. Although the Inca empire ended, today tourists flock to see the sturdy roads, cities, and forts built by the Inca.

South America Today

The Roman Catholic missionaries from Spain who first came to South America converted many of the Indians to Christianity. Most of the South Americans today are Roman Catholics. Indian peoples have also continued many of their traditional religious practices.

As elsewhere in Latin America, a new population of mestizos was born in South America. In many countries, Europeans brought Africans by force to work on plantations. African religious beliefs, music, and dance have enriched the culture of all of South America.

In the 1800s and 1900s many immigrants from Europe and Asia came to South America for the same reasons they came to North America. A large number of Italians settled in Argentina and Brazil. President Alberto Fujimoro of Peru is the son of Japanese immigrants. Brazil has one of the largest

The Inca in the Andes (below left) and businesses in Buenos Aires (below right) reflect a mix of past and present. Brazil's Pelé (left) is a world-famous soccer player.

Scientists study plants and animals in rain forests such as the Amazon. They hope to find new ways to improve peoples' lives.

Japanese communities to exist outside of Japan.

Today, the mix of cultures has given booming cities like São Paulo (SOW POW loh) in Brazil an international flavor. Every year thousands of people move to São Paulo, the world's third largest city, seeking better opportunities. The rich live alongside millions of poor people struggling to survive in the favelas (fah VAY lahz), or slums.

The economy of many countries is based on South America's plentiful mineral resources. In the 1500s Spain gained wealth from the gold and silver it found in South America. Today oil has helped Venezuela prosper. The Amazon rain forest is rich in mineral, timber, and other resources as well.

Agriculture is also a major part of the economy of South America. Colombia, for example, grows sugar, coffee, cacao, and bananas for export. In the Andes, hundreds of different kinds of potatoes are grown. The cattle industry thrives on the pampas of Argentina. Today, manufacturing and trade are important to the economies of many countries. For example, Buenos Aires (BWAY nohs Ī rus) in Argentina, is a major port city.

WHY IT MATTERS

The United States imports products from South America such as coffee and sugar. United States businesses also purchase many raw materials for industry from South America. In the future, trade might increase if NAFTA is expanded to include South America.

The vast Amazon rain forest is home to thousands of plants and animals. Some of them play an important role in medical research. Rain forests also supply much of the world's oxygen. Brazil's challenge is to develop its rain forest resources without damaging the rain forest itself.

✓ Reviewing Facts and Ideas

MAIN IDEAS

- South America has varied climates and landforms, including the Andes Mountains and Amazon River.
- The population of South America is a mix of mainly Indian, European, African, and Asian cultures.

THINK ABOUT IT

1. Name some of the major landforms of South America.

2. How do many people in South America earn a living?

3. **FOCUS** How did colonial rule affect the population of South America?

4. **THINKING SKILL** What _generalizations_ can you make about the impact of geography on South America?

5. **WRITE** Write a short travel brochure that encourages people from the United States to visit South America.

SPECIAL SECTION REVIEW

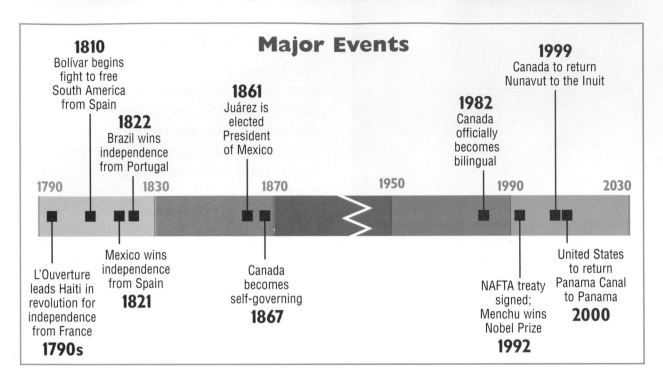

Major Events

1810
Bolívar begins fight to free South America from Spain

1822
Brazil wins independence from Portugal

1861
Juárez is elected President of Mexico

1982
Canada officially becomes bilingual

1999
Canada to return Nunavut to the Inuit

1790   1830   1870   1950   1990   2030

L'Ouverture leads Haiti in revolution for independence from France
1790s

Mexico wins independence from Spain
1821

Canada becomes self-governing
1867

NAFTA treaty signed; Menchu wins Nobel Prize
1992

United States to return Panama Canal to Panama
2000

THINKING ABOUT VOCABULARY

Number a paper from 1 to 5. Beside each number, write the word or term from the list below that best matches the description.

bilingual   mestizo
favela   province
hurricane

1. This word means "two languages," which in Quebec refers to English and French.

2. This European name for a terrible rain storm comes from the name of a powerful Taino god.

3. This South American word means "slum", or a very poor neighborhood in a big city.

4. This word describes seven out of every ten Mexicans, meaning a Mexican who has both Indian and Spanish ancestors.

5. This name for any of Canada's ten divisions means "an area that has its own government."

THINKING ABOUT FACTS

1. How has the geography of Canada affected where Canadians live?

2. What is the largest geographical region of Canada? Describe this region.

3. What issue is under debate in Quebec?

4. What is the capital of Mexico? In what geographical region is it located?

5. What are some of Mexico's most important industries?

6. What three countries signed the North American Free Trade Agreement in 1992? What is the purpose of NAFTA?

7. Why was Rigoberta Menchú awarded the Nobel Prize for Peace in 1992?

8. What are the largest islands in the Caribbean? What kind of climate do most Caribbean countries have?

9. What challenges face countries rich in rain forests, such as Brazil?

10. What events on the time line reflect our country's relations with Canada and Mexico?

THINK AND WRITE ◀▭▭▶

WRITING AN ITINERARY

An itinerary is a list and brief description of all the places a person is going to visit. Choose an area or city you have read about in this section and write an itinerary including locations you would like to visit.

WRITING A LETTER

Suppose that you are a pen pal with someone in a country described in this section. Write a letter in which you describe your life. Ask your new pen pal questions about life in his or her country.

WRITING ABOUT PERSPECTIVES

The people of Canada have differing opinions about the future of Quebec. Write several paragraphs from the point of view of a French-speaking resident of Quebec and an English-speaking Canadian.

IDENTIFYING PEOPLE AND PLACES

Number a paper from 1 to 5. Beside each number write the letter that correctly identifies the person or place.

1. Belize
2. Nova Scotia
3. Simón Bolívar
4. Mexico City
5. Benito Juárez

a. A country in Central America covered largely by dense rain forests

b. This Zapotec leader sought to improve the lives of Indians in Mexico.

c. The province of Canada whose name means "New Scotland"

d. Many South Americans call him "The Liberator"

e. Mexico's capital, and the fastest growing city in the world

---

Summing Up the Section

Copy the matrix chart on a separate piece of paper. Review the Special Section to complete the chart. When you have finished, use the chart to answer the question "How does the geography of each region affect the people who live there?"

COUNTRY REGION	GEOGRAPHY/CLIMATE	PEOPLE
	World's second largest country; varied geography including fertile plains, rugged mountains, and icy stretches to the north	
	Mountainous, mostly dry; limited farming land; tropical conditions along the coastal plains	
	Rugged mountains with volcanoes; dense rain forests; islands of coral with beautiful beaches	
	A varied area; high mountains with bitter cold, tropical lowland areas as well as dense rain forests and deserts	

REFERENCE SECTION

The Reference Section has many parts,
each with a different type of information.
Use this section to look up people,
places, and events as you study.

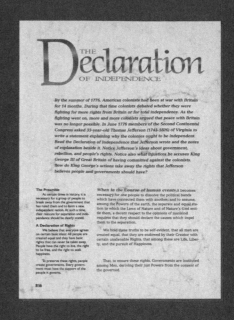

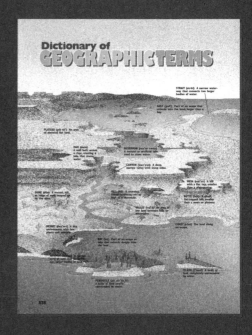

Atlas

An atlas is a collection of maps. An atlas can be a book or a separate section within a book. This Atlas is a separate section with maps to help you study the history and geography presented in this book.

MAP BUILDER
The Growth of the United States

The map on the facing page is a special kind of map. Each transparent overlay shows the United States in a different year. You can see how our country has grown since it first became independent. Start by lifting all of the transparent overlays and studying the base map, which shows the United States in 1790. Then cover the base map with the first overlay and compare how the United States looked in 1820 with how it looked in 1790. Add the overlays for 1860 and the United States today in the same way.

Each overlay shows when certain areas were added to the United States. Also shown are the names of the individual states and the year in which each became a state. Look near the title of each overlay to see the national flag that was used in the year shown by that overlay. Which overlay shows the most new states?

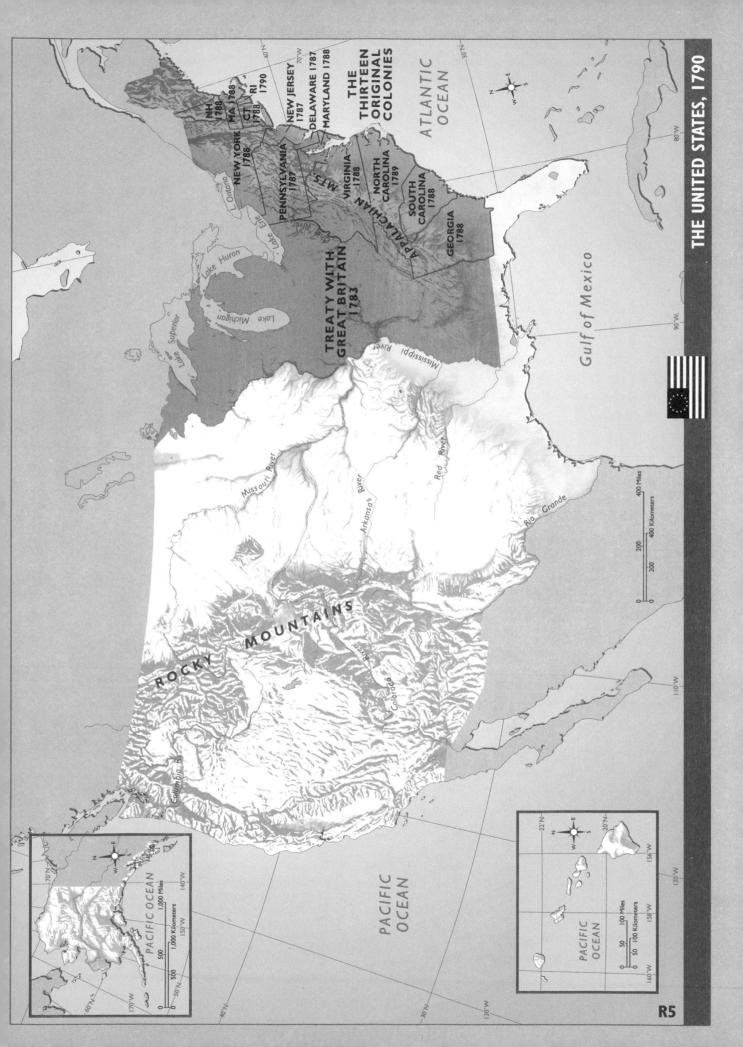

THE
THIRTEEN
ORIGINAL
COLONIES

NH
1788
MA 1788
CT
1788
RI
1790
NEW JERSEY
1787
DELAWARE 1787
MARYLAND 1788
NEW YORK
1788
PENNSYLVANIA
1787
VIRGINIA
1788
NORTH
CAROLINA
1789
SOUTH
CAROLINA
1788
GEORGIA
1788

APPALACHIAN MTS.

ATLANTIC
OCEAN

TREATY WITH
GREAT BRITAIN
1783

L. Ontario
Lake Erie
Lake Huron
Lake Michigan
Lake Superior

Ohio River

Mississippi River
Missouri River
Arkansas River
Red River
Rio Grande
Colorado River
Columbia R.

Gulf of Mexico

ROCKY MOUNTAINS

PACIFIC OCEAN

PACIFIC
OCEAN

400 Miles
200   400 Kilometers
0   200

N
W   E
S

PACIFIC OCEAN
500   1,000 Miles
500   1,000 Kilometers
0

PACIFIC OCEAN
50   100 Miles
50   100 Kilometers
0

40°N
70°W
30°N
80°W
90°W
110°W
120°W
130°W
160°W

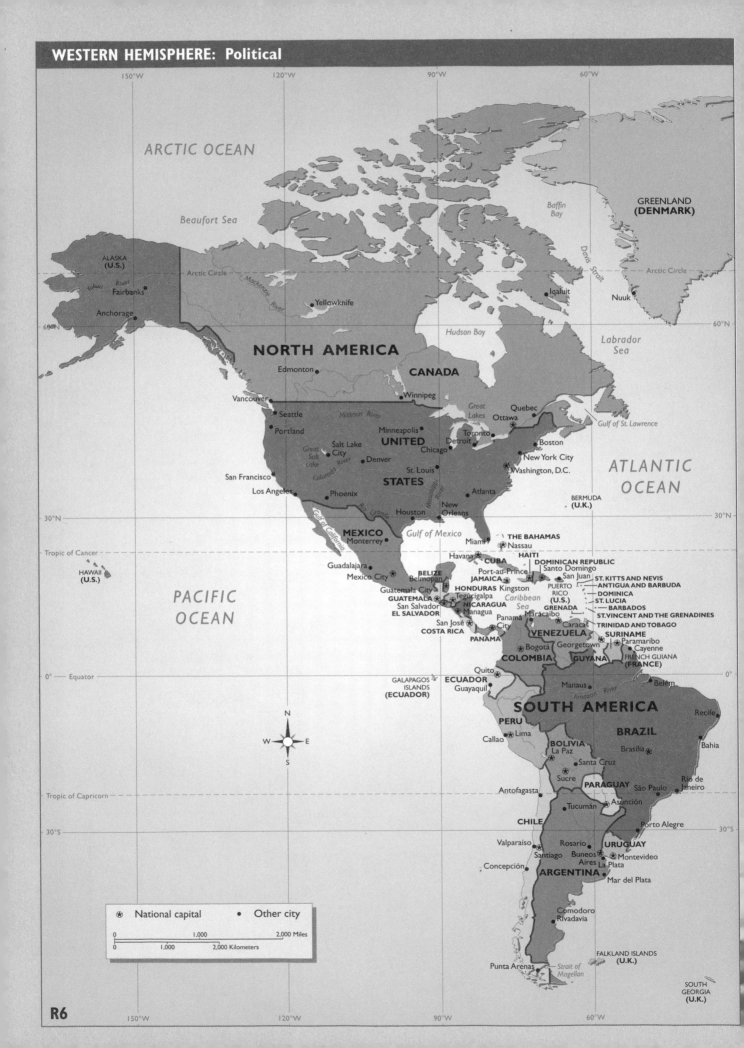

WESTERN HEMISPHERE: Political

ARCTIC OCEAN

GREENLAND
(DENMARK)

Beaufort Sea

ALASKA
(U.S.)

Yukon River
Fairbanks

Anchorage

60°N

Arctic Circle

Mackenzie River

Yellowknife

Baffin
Bay

Davis Strait

Iqaluit

Nuuk

Arctic Circle

60°N

Hudson Bay

NORTH AMERICA

Labrador
Sea

CANADA

Edmonton

Vancouver

Winnipeg

Quebec

Ottawa

Gulf of St. Lawrence

Seattle

Portland

Missouri River

Minneapolis

UNITED

Great
Lakes

Toronto

Detroit

Boston

ATLANTIC
OCEAN

Great
Salt
Lake

Salt Lake
City

Denver

Chicago

New York City

Washington, D.C.

San Francisco

Colorado River

STATES

St. Louis

Mississippi River

Atlanta

BERMUDA
(U.K.)

Los Angeles

Phoenix

Rio Grande

Houston

New
Orleans

30°N

30°N

Gulf of California

MEXICO

Monterrey

Gulf of Mexico

Miami

THE BAHAMAS

Nassau

Tropic of Cancer

HAWAII
(U.S.)

Guadalajara

Mexico City

Havana

CUBA

HAITI

DOMINICAN REPUBLIC

Santo Domingo

ST. KITTS AND NEVIS

PACIFIC
OCEAN

BELIZE

Belmopan

JAMAICA

Port-au-Prince

PUERTO
RICO
(U.S.)

San Juan

ANTIGUA AND BARBUDA

DOMINICA

Guatemala City

HONDURAS

Kingston

Caribbean

ST. LUCIA

GUATEMALA

Tegucigalpa

Sea

BARBADOS

San Salvador

NICARAGUA

GRENADA

ST. VINCENT AND THE GRENADINES

EL SALVADOR

Managua

TRINIDAD AND TOBAGO

San José

Panama
City

Maracaibo

Caracas

SURINAME

COSTA RICA

VENEZUELA

Georgetown

Paramaribo

Cayenne

PANAMA

Bogotá

GUYANA

FRENCH GUIANA
(FRANCE)

COLOMBIA

GALAPAGOS
ISLANDS
(ECUADOR)

Quito

ECUADOR

Manaus

Amazon River

Belém

0°

Equator

0°

Guayaquil

SOUTH AMERICA

Recife

PERU

BRAZIL

Callao

Lima

BOLIVIA

Brasília

Bahia

La Paz

Santa Cruz

Sucre

PARAGUAY

São Paulo

Rio de
Janeiro

Tropic of Capricorn

Antofagasta

Tucumán

Asunción

Porto Alegre

30°S

30°S

CHILE

Valparaíso

Rosario

URUGUAY

Santiago

Buneos
Aires

Montevideo

Concepción

La Plata

ARGENTINA

Mar del Plata

Comodoro
Rivadavia

⊛ National capital   • Other city

0   1,000   2,000 Miles

0   1,000   2,000 Kilometers

FALKLAND ISLANDS
(U.K.)

Punta Arenas

Strait of
Magellan

SOUTH
GEORGIA
(U.K.)

R6

150°W   120°W   90°W   60°W

N
W E
S

ARCTIC OCEAN

Queen Elizabeth Islands

Greenland

Banks Island

Baffin Bay

Point Barrow

Beaufort Sea

Victoria Island

Baffin Island

BROOKS RANGE

Mt. McKinley 20,320 ft. (6,194 m)

Yukon River

Mackenzie River

Great Bear Lake

Great Slave Lake

Arctic Circle

Davis Strait

Cape Farewell

60°N

ALASKA RANGE

Alaska Peninsula

Gulf of Alaska

COAST MOUNTAINS

NORTH AMERICA

Hudson Bay

Labrador Sea

LABRADOR

Saskatchewan River

CANADIAN SHIELD

Newfoundland

Vancouver Island

ROCKY MOUNTAINS

GREAT PLAINS

Lake Winnipeg

Great Lakes

St. Lawrence River

Gulf of St. Lawrence

Nova Scotia

ATLANTIC OCEAN

CASCADE RANGE

Snake River

Missouri River

Cape Mendocino

COAST RANGES

SIERRA NEVADA

GREAT BASIN

Great Salt Lake

Colorado River

Mississippi River

Ohio River

APPALACHIAN MOUNTAINS

Cape Cod

Long Island

COASTAL PLAINS

30°N

30°N

Baja California

SIERRA MADRE OCCIDENTAL

SIERRA MADRE ORIENTAL

Rio Grande

Gulf of Mexico

Florida Peninsula

Tropic of Cancer

Hawaiian Islands

Gulf of California

Straits of Florida

Yucatán Peninsula

Cuba

WEST

Greater Antilles

Hispaniola

INDIES

Lesser Antilles

PACIFIC OCEAN

Gulf of Honduras

Caribbean Sea

CENTRAL

Lake Nicaragua

Isthmus of Panama

Gulf of Panama

AMERICA

Lake Maracaibo

Magdalena River

LLANOS

Orinoco River

GUIANA HIGHLANDS

0°

Equator

Galápagos Islands

Rio Negro

River

Amazon River

Cape São Roque

0°

AMAZON BASIN

ANDES MOUNTAINS

Madeira River

SOUTH AMERICA

Tocantins River

São Francisco River

N

W E

S

MATO GRASSO PLATEAU

BRAZILIAN HIGHLANDS

Lake Titicaca

Paraguay River

GRAN CHACO

Tropic of Capricorn

Paraná River

Uruguay River

30°S

30°S

Mt. Aconcagua 22,834 ft. (6,960 m)

PAMPAS

PATAGONIA

0 1,000 2,000 Miles

0 1,000 2,000 Kilometers

Strait of Magellan

Falkland Islands

South Georgia

Tierra del Fuego

Cape Horn

THE UNITED STATES: Political

RUSSIA

ARCTIC OCEAN

70°N

ALASKA

CANADA

•Nome

Yukon

•Fairbanks

60°N

•Anchorage

Juneau★

PACIFIC OCEAN

180°

170°W

160°W

150°W

140°W

0   250   500 Miles

0   250   500 Kilometers

CANADA

River

Seattle•

Spokane•

WASHINGTON

★Olympia

Great Falls•

Helena ★

MONTANA

Columbia

•Portland

Missouri River

•Billings

★Salem

IDAHO

•Eugene

OREGON

40°N

Boise★

WYOMING

Snake River

•Pocatello

Casper•

NEVADA

Great Salt Lake

•Ogden

Cheyenne★

•Reno

★Carson City

★Salt Lake City

COLORADO

San Francisco•

★Sacramento

•Provo

Denver★

•Oakland

UTAH

Colorado Springs•

•San Jose

Pueblo•

PACIFIC OCEAN

CALIFORNIA

Las Vegas•

•Los Angeles

Santa Fe★

•Long Beach

Colorado

ARIZONA

Albuquerque•

30°N

San Diego•

NEW MEXICO

★Phoenix

30°W

Tucson•

El Paso•

Rio Grande

160°W

PACIFIC OCEAN

155°W

Kauai

N

Oahu

Niihau

W   E

Honolulu★

Molokai

S

Lanai   Maui

HAWAII   Kahoolawe

20°N

Hawaii   Hilo

MEXICO

0   100   200 Miles

0   100   200 Kilometers

20°W

120°W

110°W

CANADA

MAINE
★ Augusta

NORTH
DAKOTA
Grand
Forks
★ Bismarck Fargo

MINNESOTA
Duluth

Lake Superior

MICHIGAN

Lake Huron

Burlington ★ Montpelier
VERMONT NEW ★ Portland
HAMPSHIRE ★ Concord

SOUTH
DAKOTA
★ Pierre
• Sioux
Falls

WISCONSIN
Minneapolis • ★ St. Paul

Green
Bay

Lake Michigan

Grand
Rapids • Lansing
Detroit

Lake Ontario

NEW
YORK
Buffalo • Albany ★

MASSACHUSETTS
Boston ★
Providence

Madison Milwaukee
★

Lake Erie

PENNSYLVANIA

Hartford ★
CONNECTICUT

RHODE
ISLAND

NEBRASKA

Missouri
River

IOWA
Cedar
Rapids Rockford •
Davenport •
★ Des
Moines

Chicago
•

Gary •
Fort
Wayne

Toledo

Cleveland

Newark • ★ New York
Trenton ★
NEW JERSEY
• Philadelphia

Omaha •

Peoria
•

Pittsburgh • Harrisburg ★

Platte River
• Lincoln

OHIO
Wheeling

Dover ★

★ Springfield
INDIANA
★ Indianapolis

Columbus •

Baltimore •
Annapolis ★
DELAWARE
Washington, MARYLAND
D.C.

Cincinnati

Ohio
River

KANSAS

Arkansas

Kansas
City
Topeka ★

MISSOURI
Kansas
City

St.
Louis

ILLINOIS

Evansville •

Frankfort ★

WEST
VIRGINIA
★ Charleston

VIRGINIA
Richmond ★

• Norfolk

Louisville •

• Wichita

★ Jefferson
City

KENTUCKY

River

TENNESSEE

Nashville
★

• Knoxville

NORTH
CAROLINA
★ Raleigh

• Tulsa

ARKANSAS

Memphis
•

Tennessee
River

• Charlotte

OKLAHOMA

Oklahoma ★
City

Fort
Smith •

Little ★
Rock

SOUTH
CAROLINA
★ Columbia

• Atlanta

• Charleston

Red River

MISSISSIPPI
Birmingham
•

GEORGIA

Mississippi River

★ Jackson

ALABAMA
★ Montgomery

• Columbus

• Savannah

TEXAS

Fort
Worth • • Dallas

Shreveport •

LOUISIANA

Biloxi • • Mobile

★ Tallahassee • Jacksonville

• Austin

Houston
•

Baton Rouge ★

New Orleans •

FLORIDA

• San
Antonio

Gulf of Mexico

Tampa
•

ATLANTIC OCEAN

• Laredo • Corpus
Christi

THE
BAHAMAS

• Miami

⊛ National capital ★ State capital • Other city

0   150   300 Miles
0   150   300 Kilometers

CUBA

50°N

40°N

70°W

30°N

100°W   90°W   80°W   R9

RUSSIA

ARCTIC OCEAN

BROOKS RANGE

ALASKA

ALASKA RANGE

Yukon River

CANADA

▲ Mt. McKinley
20,320 ft.
(6,194 m)

Bering Strait

Bering Sea

0   250   500 Miles

0   250   500 Kilometers

170°W   160°W   150°W   140°W

70°N
60°N

CANADA

Puget Sound

Mt. Rainier
14,410 ft.
(4,391 m)

▲ Mt. St. Helens
8,366 ft.
(2,550 m)

Columbia River

COAST RANGES

CASCADE RANGE

▲ Mt. Hood
11,235 ft.
(3,424 m)

COLUMBIA PLATEAU

Missouri   River

Yellowstone River

ROCKY MOUNTAINS

▲ Granite Peak
12,799 ft.
(3,900 m)

TETON RANGE

BLACK HILLS

Snake   River

40°N

130°W

Cape Mendocino

▲ Mt. Shasta
14,162 ft.
(4,316 m)

Great Salt Lake

GREAT SALT LAKE DESERT

RANGE

GREAT PLAINS

COAST

Sacramento River

SIERRA NEVADA

CENTRAL VALLEY

Lake Tahoe

GREAT BASIN

▲ Kings Peak
13,528 ft.
(4,123 m)

WASATCH

Mt. Elbert ▲
14,433 ft.
(4,398 m)

Pikes Peak
▲ 14,107 ft.
(4,301 m)

San Francisco Bay

San Joaquin   River

RANGES

▲ Mt. Whitney
14,491 ft.
(4,418 m)

DEATH VALLEY

Lake Mead

COLORADO PLATEAU

PACIFIC OCEAN

MOJAVE DESERT

River

Colorado

Wheeler Peak
13,065 ft.
(3,982 m)

▲ Humphreys Peak
12,633 ft.
(3,850 m)

30°N

Salton Sea

SONORA DESERT

Gila   River

Pecos   River

Guadalupe Peak
8,751 ft.
(2,667 m)

EDWARDS PLATEAU

Rio Grande

Gulf of California

MEXICO

120°W   110°W

160°W   155°W

PACIFIC OCEAN

Kauai

Oahu

N
W   E
S

Maui

HAWAII

Hawaii

Mauna Kea
13,796 ft.
(4,205 m)

20°N

0   100   200 Miles

0   100   200 Kilometers

CANADA

Lake of
the Woods

Lake Superior

GREAT

LAKES

MESABI RANGE

Mississippi

St. Lawrence River

WHITE MTS.

GREEN MTS.

Mt. Washington
6,288 ft.
(1,917 m)

ADIRONDACK
MTS.

Lake Ontario

Hudson River

Cape Cod

CENTRAL PLAINS

Lake Michigan

Lake Huron

Lake Erie

ALLEGHENY
PLATEAU

APPALACHIAN MOUNTAINS

Long Island

40°N

70°W

Platte River

Missouri

River

Wabash River

Ohio River

River

ALLEGHENY MOUNTAINS

Potomac River

Susquehanna River

Delaware Bay

ATLANTIC COASTAL PLAIN

Chesapeake Bay

Arkansas

River

INTERIOR PLAINS

OZARK
PLATEAU

OUACHITA
MOUNTAINS

Red

River

Mississippi

River

Tennessee

River

River

Alabama

River

Chattahoochee

River

Mt. Mitchell
6,684 ft.
(2,037 m)

PIEDMONT

Savannah River

Cape Hatteras

ATLANTIC OCEAN

30°N

Brazos

River

Colorado River

GULF COASTAL PLAIN

Mobile Bay

Mississippi Delta

Galveston Bay

Gulf of Mexico

Lake
Okeechobee

Bahama Islands

Florida Keys

Straits of Florida

80°W

90°W

N
W E
S

0   150   300 Miles

0   150   300 Kilometers

CUBA

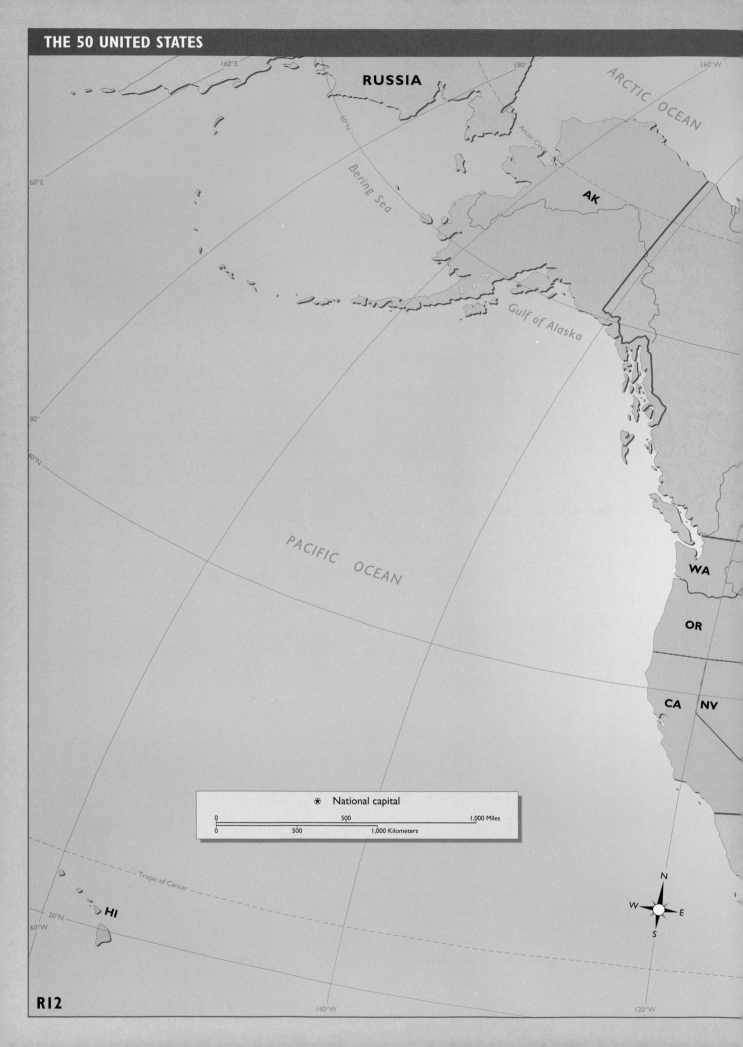

RUSSIA

ARCTIC OCEAN

160°E

180°

160°W

60°N

Bering Sea

Arctic Circle

AK

60°E

Gulf of Alaska

80°

40°N

PACIFIC OCEAN

WA

OR

CA   NV

⊛   National capital

| 0 | 500 | 1,000 Miles |
| 0 | 500 | 1,000 Kilometers |

Tropic of Cancer

HI

N

20°N   W   E

60°W   S

140°W

120°W

Greenland
(DENMARK)

CANADA

Hudson Bay

Great Lakes

MT
ND
MN
MI
ID
WI
MI
ME
VT
NH
NY
MA
CT
RI
SD
WY
IA
PA
NJ
UT
NE
IL
IN
OH
WV
Washington, D.C.
MD
DE
CO
KS
MO
KY
VA
AZ
NM
OK
AR
TN
NC
TX
MS
AL
GA
SC
LA
FL

ATLANTIC OCEAN

Gulf of Mexico

MEXICO

CUBA

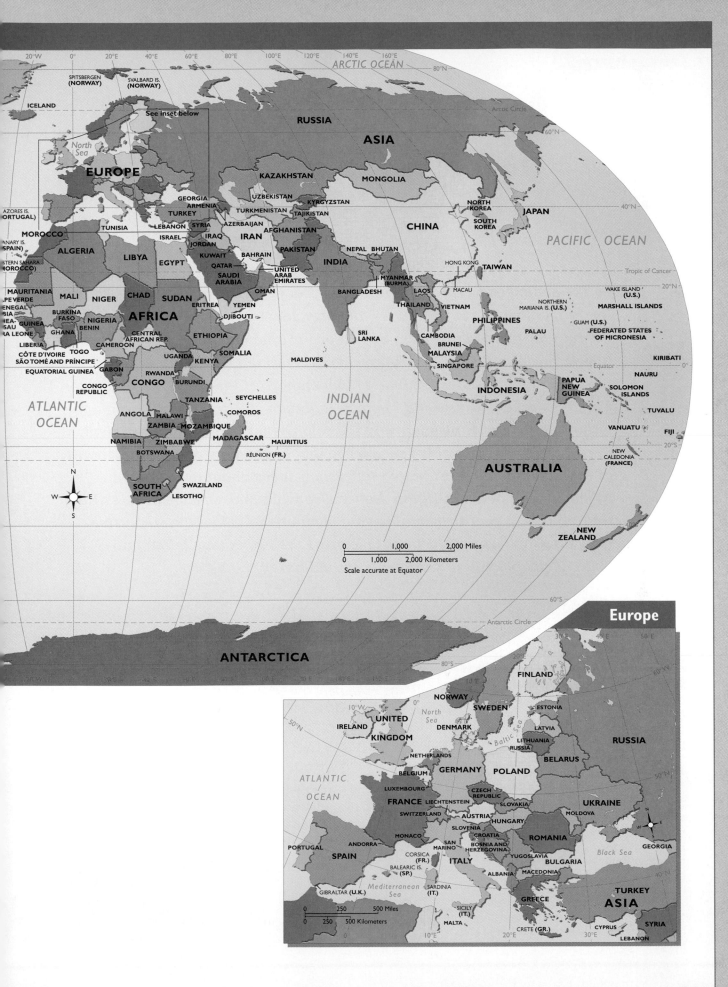

ARCTIC OCEAN

RUSSIA

ASIA

EUROPE

See inset below

North Sea

ICELAND

SPITSBERGEN (NORWAY)

SVALBARD IS. (NORWAY)

AZORES IS. (PORTUGAL)

MOROCCO

ANARY IS. SPAIN)

TUNISIA

ALGERIA

LIBYA

EGYPT

GEORGIA
ARMENIA
TURKEY

LEBANON
ISRAEL
JORDAN
SYRIA

AZERBAIJAN

IRAQ

IRAN

AFGHANISTAN

KUWAIT
BAHRAIN
QATAR
UNITED
ARAB
EMIRATES
OMAN

SAUDI
ARABIA

YEMEN

KAZAKHSTAN

UZBEKISTAN

TURKMENISTAN

KYRGYZSTAN

TAJIKISTAN

PAKISTAN

MONGOLIA

CHINA

NORTH
KOREA

SOUTH
KOREA

JAPAN

PACIFIC OCEAN

NEPAL BHUTAN

INDIA

HONG KONG

TAIWAN

Tropic of Cancer

WAKE ISLAND
(U.S.)

BANGLADESH

MYANMAR
(BURMA)

LAOS

MACAU

NORTHERN
MARIANA IS. (U.S.)

MARSHALL ISLANDS

GUAM (U.S.)

THAILAND

VIETNAM

PHILIPPINES

FEDERATED STATES
OF MICRONESIA

PALAU

KIRIBATI

MAURITANIA
PE VERDE
ENEGAL
BIA
NEA-
SAU
RA LEONE

MALI

NIGER

CHAD

SUDAN

ERITREA

DJIBOUTI

AFRICA

BURKINA
FASO

NIGERIA

BENIN

GHANA

CENTRAL
AFRICAN REP.

ETHIOPIA

LIBERIA
CÔTE D'IVOIRE
SÃO TOMÉ AND PRÍNCIPE

TOGO

CAMEROON

UGANDA

SOMALIA

KENYA

EQUATORIAL GUINEA

GABON

CONGO
REPUBLIC

CONGO

RWANDA

BURUNDI

MALDIVES

SRI
LANKA

CAMBODIA

BRUNEI

MALAYSIA

SINGAPORE

INDONESIA

PAPUA
NEW
GUINEA

NAURU

SOLOMON
ISLANDS

Equator

TUVALU

ATLANTIC
OCEAN

ANGOLA

MALAWI

ZAMBIA

MOZAMBIQUE

TANZANIA

SEYCHELLES

COMOROS

INDIAN
OCEAN

NAMIBIA

ZIMBABWE

BOTSWANA

MADAGASCAR

MAURITIUS

RÉUNION (FR.)

VANUATU

FIJI

NEW
CALEDONIA
(FRANCE)

AUSTRALIA

SOUTH
AFRICA

SWAZILAND

LESOTHO

N
W   E
S

1,000   2,000 Miles

1,000   2,000 Kilometers

Scale accurate at Equator

NEW
ZEALAND

ANTARCTICA

Arctic Circle

Antarctic Circle

Europe

FINLAND

NORWAY

UNITED
KINGDOM

SWEDEN

ESTONIA

IRELAND

DENMARK

North
Sea

LATVIA

Baltic
Sea

LITHUANIA

RUSSIA

ATLANTIC
OCEAN

NETHERLANDS

BELGIUM

GERMANY

POLAND

BELARUS

LUXEMBOURG

CZECH
REPUBLIC

FRANCE

LIECHTENSTEIN

SLOVAKIA

UKRAINE

SWITZERLAND

AUSTRIA

HUNGARY

MOLDOVA

MONACO

SLOVENIA

CROATIA

ROMANIA

GEORGIA

PORTUGAL

ANDORRA

SAN
MARINO

BOSNIA AND
HERZEGOVINA

YUGOSLAVIA

BULGARIA

SPAIN

CORSICA
(FR.)

ITALY

ALBANIA

MACEDONIA

Black Sea

BALEARIC IS.
(SP.)

GIBRALTAR (U.K.)

Mediterranean
Sea

SARDINIA
(IT.)

GREECE

TURKEY

ASIA

SICILY
(IT.)

MALTA

CRETE (GR.)

CYPRUS

SYRIA

LEBANON

THE Declaration OF INDEPENDENCE

By the summer of 1776, American colonists had been at war with Britain for 14 months. During that time colonists debated whether they were fighting for more rights from Britain or for total independence. As the fighting went on, more and more colonists argued that peace with Britain was no longer possible. In June 1776 members of the Second Continental Congress asked 33-year-old Thomas Jefferson (1743-1826) of Virginia to write a statement explaining why the colonies ought to be independent. Read the Declaration of Independence that Jefferson wrote and the notes of explanation beside it. Notice Jefferson's ideas about government, rebellion, and people's rights. Notice also what injustices he accuses King George III of Great Britain of having committed against the colonists. How do King George's actions take away the rights that Jefferson believes people and governments should have?

The Preamble

At certain times in history, it is necessary for a group of people to break away from the government that has ruled them and to form a new, independent nation. At such a time, their reasons for separation and independence should be clearly stated.

A Declaration of Rights

We believe that everyone agrees on certain basic ideas: All people are created equal and they have basic rights that can never be taken away. People have the right to live, the right to be free, and the right to seek happiness.

To preserve these rights, people create governments. Every government must have the support of the people it governs.

When in the Course of human events, it becomes necessary for one people to dissolve the political bands which have connected them with another, and to assume, among the Powers of the earth, the separate and equal station to which the Laws of Nature and of Nature's God entitle them, a decent respect to the opinions of mankind requires that they should declare the causes which impel them to the separation.

We hold these truths to be self-evident, that all men are created equal, that they are endowed by their Creator with certain unalienable Rights, that among these are Life, Liberty, and the pursuit of Happiness.

That, to ensure these rights, Governments are instituted among Men, deriving their just Powers from the consent of the governed.

That, whenever any Form of Government becomes destructive of these ends, it is the Right of the People to alter or to abolish it, and to institute new Government, laying its foundation on such Principles, and organizing its powers in such form, as to them shall seem most likely to effect their Safety and Happiness.

Prudence, indeed, will dictate that Governments long established should not be changed for light and transient causes; and, accordingly all experience hath shown, that mankind are more disposed to suffer, while evils are sufferable, than to right themselves by abolishing the forms to which they are accustomed. But, when a long train of abuses and usurpations, pursuing invariably the same Object, evinces a design to reduce them under absolute Despotism, it is their right, it is their duty, to throw off such Government, and to provide new Guards for their future security.

Such has been the patient sufferance of these Colonies; and such is now the necessity which constrains them to alter their former Systems of Government. The history of the present King of Great Britain is a history of repeated injuries and usurpations, all having in direct object the establishment of an absolute Tyranny over these States.

To prove this, let Facts be submitted to a candid world.

He has refused his Assent to Laws the most wholesome and necessary for the public good.

He has forbidden his Governors to pass Laws of immediate and pressing importance, unless suspended in their operation till his Assent should be obtained; and when so suspended, he has utterly neglected to attend to them.

He has refused to pass other Laws for the accommodation of large districts of People, unless those People would relinquish the right of Representation in the Legislature, a right inestimable to them and formidable to tyrants only.

He has called together legislative bodies at places unusual, uncomfortable, and distant from the depository of their Public Records, for the sole purpose of fatiguing them into compliance with his measures.

If a government loses this support or tries to take away basic freedoms, people have the right to change their government or to get rid of it and form a new government that will protect their rights.

However, people should not change governments that have long been in power for minor or temporary problems. We have learned from history that people are usually more willing to put up with a bad government than to get rid of it. But when people see their government misusing its power and mistreating its people time after time, it is the right and duty of the people to get rid of their government and to form a new one.

A List of Abuses

The colonies have suffered patiently long enough, and it is now time to change our government. King George III of Great Britain has ruled badly for many years. His main goal has been to establish total control over the colonies.

These statements are proven by the following facts:

King George III has rejected much-needed laws passed by the colonists.

He has not permitted important laws to be passed by his governors in America.

He has refused to redraw the borders of large voting districts unless the people living there agreed to give up their right to be represented in the legislature.

He has ordered lawmakers in the colonies to meet far from their homes and offices in places that are unusual and difficult to get to. His only reason for doing this has been to tire out the lawmakers so that they will accept his rule.

When lawmakers have criticized the king for attacking their rights, he has broken up the legislature's meetings.

After breaking up their meetings, the king has refused to allow new elections. As a result, colonists have been living in danger, unable to protect themselves or pass new laws.

He has tried to stop colonists from moving west and settling in new lands. He has also tried to prevent people from foreign countries from settling in America by making it hard for newcomers to become citizens.

In some places, he has not let colonists set up a system of courts.

He has forced colonial judges to obey him by deciding how long they can serve and how much they are paid.

He has sent officials from Britain to fill new government offices in the colonies. These officials have mistreated people and demanded unfair taxes.

In times of peace, he has kept soldiers in the colonies even though Americans did not want them.

He has tried to give soldiers power over colonial legislatures.

He and other leaders in Great Britain have passed laws for the colonies that Americans did not want. In these laws the British government has:

forced colonists to house and feed British soldiers;

protected these soldiers by giving them phony trials and not punishing them for murdering colonists;

cut off trade between Americans and people in other parts of the world;

demanded taxes that colonists never agreed to;

prevented colonists accused of crimes from having their trials decided fairly by a jury;

He has dissolved Representative Houses repeatedly, for opposing, with manly firmness, his invasions on the rights of the people.

He has refused for a long time, after such dissolutions, to cause others to be elected; whereby the Legislative Powers, incapable of Annihilation, have returned to the People at large for their exercise; the State remaining in the mean time exposed to all the dangers of invasion from without, and convulsions within.

He has endeavoured to prevent the Population of these States; for that purpose obstructing the Laws of Naturalization of Foreigners; refusing to pass others to encourage their migration hither, and raising the conditions of new Appropriations of Lands.

He has obstructed the Administration of Justice by refusing his Assent to Laws for establishing judiciary Powers.

He has made judges dependent on his Will alone, for the tenure of their offices, and the amount and payment of their salaries.

He has erected a multitude of New Offices, and sent hither swarms of Officers to harass our People, and eat out their substance.

He has kept among us, in times of Peace, Standing Armies, without the Consent of our legislature.

He has affected to render the Military independent of and superior to the Civil Power.

He has combined with others to subject us to a jurisdiction foreign to our constitution, and unacknowledged by our laws; giving his Assent to their Acts of pretended Legislation:

For quartering large bodies of armed troops among us:

For protecting them, by a mock Trial, from Punishment for any Murders which they should commit on the Inhabitants of these States:

For cutting off our Trade with all parts of the world:

For imposing Taxes on us without our Consent:

For depriving us, in many cases, of the benefits of Trial by jury:

For transporting us beyond Seas to be tried for pretended offences:

For abolishing the free System of English Laws in a neighbouring Province, establishing therein an Arbitrary government, and enlarging its Boundaries, so as to render it at once an example and fit instrument for introducing the same absolute rule into these Colonies:

For taking away our Charters, abolishing our most valuable Laws, and altering fundamentally the Forms of our Governments:

For suspending our own Legislatures, and declaring themselves invested with Power to legislate for us in all cases whatsoever.

He has abdicated Government here, by declaring us out of his Protection and waging War against us.

He has plundered our seas, ravaged our Coasts, burnt our towns, and destroyed the Lives of our People.

He is at this time transporting large Armies of foreign Mercenaries to compleat the works of death, desolation and tyranny, already begun with circumstances of Cruelty & perfidy scarcely paralleled in the most barbarous ages, and totally unworthy the Head of a civilized nation.

He has constrained our fellow Citizens taken Captive on the high Seas to bear Arms against their Country, to become the executioners of their friends and Brethren, or to fall themselves by their Hands.

He has excited domestic insurrections amongst us, and has endeavoured to bring on the inhabitants of our frontiers, the merciless Indian Savages, whose known rule of warfare, is an undistinguished destruction of all ages, sexes and conditions.

In every stage of these Oppressions We have Petitioned for Redress in the most humble terms: Our repeated Petitions have been answered only by repeated injury. A Prince, whose character is thus marked by every act which may define a Tyrant, is unfit to be the ruler of a free People.

brought colonists falsely accused of crimes to Great Britain to be put on trial;

extended the borders of the neighboring province of Quebec to include lands stretching to the Ohio River, thus forcing colonists in this region to obey harsh French laws rather than English laws. The goal of the British government is to force all colonists to obey these harsh laws;

taken away our charters, or documents that make governments legal, canceled important laws, and completely changed our forms of government;

broken up our legislatures and claimed that Great Britain has the right to pass all laws for the colonies.

King George III has ended government in the colonies by waging war against us and not protecting us.

He has robbed American ships at sea, burned down our towns, and ruined people's lives.

He is right now bringing foreign soldiers to the colonies to commit horrible and brutal deeds. These actions by the king are some of the cruelest ever committed in the history of the world.

He has forced colonists captured at sea to join the British navy and to fight and kill Americans.

He has urged enslaved people in the colonies to rebel, and he has tried to get Native Americans to fight against colonists.

Statement of Independence

For years we have asked King George III to correct these probems and safe-guard our rights. Unfortunately, the king has refused to listen to our complaints and he continues to treat us badly. The king is such an unfair ruler that he is not fit to rule the free people of America.

We have also asked the British people for help. We have told them many times of our problems and pointed out the unfair laws passed by their government. We hoped they would listen to us because they believed in reason and justice. We hoped they would listen to us because we are related to each other and have much in common. But we were wrong: The British people have not listened to us at all. They have ignored our pleas for justice. We must, therefore, break away from Great Britain and become a separate nation.

Nor have We been wanting in attention to our British brethren. We have warned them from time to time of attempts by their legislature to extend an unwarrantable jurisdiction over us. We have reminded them of the circumstances of our emigration and settlement here. We have appealed to their native justice and magnanimity, and we have conjured them by the ties of our common kindred to disavow these usurpations, which, would inevitably interrupt our connections and correspondence. They too have been deaf to the voice of justice and of consanguinity. We must, therefore, acquiesce in the necessity, which denounces our Separation, and hold them, as we hold the rest of mankind, Enemies in War, in Peace Friends.

Signers

Button Gwinnett (Ga.)
Lyman Hall (Ga.)
George Walton (Ga.)

William Hooper (N.C.)
Joseph Hewes (N.C.)
John Penn (N.C.)
Edward Rutledge (S.C.)
Thomas Heyward, Jr. (S.C.)
Thomas Lynch, Jr. (S.C.)
Arthur Middleton (S.C.)

John Hancock (Mass.)
Samuel Chase (Md.)
William Paca (Md.)
Thomas Stone (Md.)
Charles Carroll of Carrollton (Md.)
George Wythe (Va.)
Richard Henry Lee (Va.)
Thomas Jefferson (Va.)
Benjamin Harrison (Va.)
Thomas Nelson, Jr. (Va.)
Francis Lightfoot Lee (Va.)
Carter Braxton (Va.)

We, therefore, the Representatives of the United States of America, in General Congress Assembled, appealing to the Supreme judge of the world for the rectitude of our intentions, do, in the Name, and by Authority of the good People of these Colonies, solemnly publish and declare, That these United Colonies are, and of Right ought to be Free and Independent States; that they are Absolved from all Allegiance to the British Crown, and that all political connection between them and the State of Great Britain, is and ought to be totally dissolved; and that as Free and Independent States, they have full Power to levy War, conclude Peace, contract Alliances, establish Commerce, and to do all other Acts and Things which Independent States may of right do. And for the support of this Declaration, with a firm reliance on the protection of divine Providence, we mutually pledge to each other our Lives, our Fortunes and our sacred Honour.

In the name of the American people, we members of the Continental Congress declare that the United States of America is no longer a colony of Great Britain but is, instead, a free and independent nation. The United States now cuts all its relations with Great Britain. As a free nation, the United States has the right and power to make war and peace, make agreements with other nations, conduct trade, and do all the things that independent nations have the right to do. To support this Declaration of Independence, we promise to each other our lives, our fortunes, and our personal honor.

Robert Morris (Pa.)
Benjamin Rush (Pa.)
Benjamin Franklin (Pa.)
John Morton (Pa.)
George Clymer (Pa.)
James Smith (Pa.)
George Taylor (Pa.)
James Wilson (Pa.)
George Ross (Pa.)
Cæsar Rodney (Del.)
George Read (Del.)
Thomas McKean (Del.)

William Floyd (N.Y.)
Philip Livingston (N.Y.)
Francis Lewis (N.Y.)
Lewis Morris (N.Y.)
Richard Stockton (N.J.)
John Witherspoon (N.J.)
Francis Hopkinson (R.I.)
John Hart (N.J.)
Abraham Clark (N.J.)

Josiah Bartlett (N.H.)
William Whipple (N.H.)
Samuel Adams (Mass.)
John Adams (Mass.)
Robert Treat Paine (Mass.)
Elbridge Gerry (Mass.)
Stephen Hopkins (R.I.)
William Ellery (R.I.)
Roger Sherman (Conn.)
Samuel Huntington (Conn.)
William Williams (Conn.)
Oliver Wolcott (Conn.)
Matthew Thornton (N.H.)

THE Constitution
OF THE UNITED STATES

PREAMBLE

We the People of the United States, in Order to form a more perfect Union, establish Justice, insure domestic Tranquility, provide for the common defense, promote the general Welfare, and secure the Blessings of Liberty to ourselves and our Posterity, do ordain and establish this Constitution for the United States of America.

Article 1. THE LEGISLATIVE BRANCH

Section 1. The Congress

All legislative powers herein granted shall be vested in a Congress of the United States, which shall consist of a Senate and House of Representatives.

Section 2. The House of Representatives

1. The House of Representatives shall be composed of members chosen every second year by the people of the several states, and the electors in each state shall have the qualifications requisite for electors of the most numerous branch of the state legislature.

2. No person shall be a Representative who shall not have attained to the age of twenty-five years, and been seven years a citizen of the United States, and who shall not, when elected, be an inhabitant of that state in which he shall be chosen.

3. Representatives ~~and direct taxes~~ shall be apportioned among the several states which may be included within this Union, according to their respective numbers, ~~which shall be determined by adding to the whole number of free persons, including those bound to service for a term of years, and excluding Indians not taxed, three-fifths of all other persons~~. The actual enumeration shall be made within three years after the first meeting of the Congress of the United

Explanation and Summary

The following text explains the meaning of the Constitution and its Amendments. Crossed out sentences are no longer in effect.

The people of the United States make this Constitution for several reasons: to form a stronger and more united nation; to ensure peace, justice, and liberty; to defend its citizens; and to improve the lives of its people.

Congress has the power to make laws. Congress is made up of two houses: the Senate and the House of Representatives.

1. Members of the House of Representatives are elected every two years by qualified voters in each state.

2. To be a member of the House of Representatives, a person must be at least 25 years old, a United States citizen for at least seven years, and live in the state he or she represents.

3. The number of Representatives for each state is based on the population, or number of people, who live in that state. Every ten years a census, or count, must be taken to determine the population of each state. At first, this census of the population included indentured servants but not most Native Americans. Each enslaved

States, and within every subsequent term of ten years, in such manner as they shall by law direct. The number of Representatives shall not exceed one for every 30,000, but each state shall have at least one Representative; ~~and until such enumeration shall be made, the state of New Hampshire shall be entitled to choose three, Massachusetts, eight, Rhode Island and Providence Plantations, one, Connecticut, five, New York, six, New Jersey, four, Pennsylvania, eight, Delaware, one, Maryland, six, Virginia, ten, North Carolina, five, South Carolina, five, and Georgia, three.~~

person was counted as three-fifths of a free person. Today all people are counted equally. (The crossed-out sections of the Constitution are no longer in effect.)

4. When vacancies happen in the representation from any state, the executive authority thereof shall issue writs of election to fill such vacancies.

4. Special elections called by the state's governor must be held to fill any empty seat in the House of Representatives.

5. The House of Representatives shall choose their Speaker and other officers; and shall have the sole power of impeachment.

5. Members of the House of Representatives choose their own leaders. House members alone have the power to impeach, or accuse, government officials of crimes in office.

Section 3. The Senate

1. The Senate of the United States shall be composed of two Senators from each state, ~~chosen by the legislature thereof,~~ for six years; and each Senator shall have one vote.

1. Each state has two Senators. Each Senator serves a term of six years and has one vote in the Senate. At first, state legislatures elected Senators, but the 17th Amendment changed the way Senators are chosen. Senators are now elected directly by the people.

2. ~~Immediately after they shall be assembled in consequence of the first election, they shall be divided as equally as may be into three classes. The seats of the Senators of the first class shall be vacated at the expiration of the second year, of the second class at the expiration of the fourth year, and of the third class at the expiration of the sixth year, so that one-third may be chosen every second year; and if vacancies happen by resignation, or otherwise, during the recess of the legislature of any state, the executive thereof may make temporary appointments until the next meeting of the legislature, which shall then fill such vacancies.~~

2. One-third of the Senate seats are up for election every two years. The 17th Amendment changed the way empty seats are filled.

3. No person shall be a Senator who shall not have attained to the age of thirty years, and been nine years a citizen of the United States, and who shall not, when elected, be an inhabitant of that state for which he shall be chosen.

3. To be a Senator, a person must be at least 30 years old, a citizens of the United States for at least nine years, and live in the state he or she represents.

4. The Vice President of the United States shall be president of the Senate, but shall have no vote, unless they be equally divided.

4. The Vice President of the United States is the officer in charge of the Senate but votes only to break a tie.

5. The Senate shall choose their other officers, and also a president pro tempore, in the absence of the Vice President,

5. Senators choose their own leaders. When the Vice President is absent, the Senate leader is called the

President *pro tempore* (prō tem′pə rē), or temporary President.

6. The Senate holds all impeachment trials. When the President of the United States is impeached, the Chief Justice of the Supreme Court is the judge for the trial. Conviction, or judgment of guilt, is decided by a two-thirds vote.

7. Impeached officials convicted by the Senate can be removed from office and barred from serving again in government. Regular courts of law can decide other punishments.

1. State lawmakers set rules for Congressional elections. Congress can change some of these rules.

2. Congress meets at least once a year, beginning in December. The 20th Amendment changed this date to January 3.

1. The Senate and House of Representatives decide if their members were elected fairly and are qualified to take their seats. At least half the members of each house of Congress must be present for Congress to do most business. Absent members can be required to attend sessions of Congress.

2. Each house of Congress may set its own rules and punish members for breaking them. A two-thirds vote is needed to expel, or force out, a member.

3. Each house of Congress keeps and publishes a record of its activities. Secret matters may be left out of the published record. If one-fifth of the members demand it, a vote on any matter will be published.

or when he shall exercise the office of the President of the United States.

6. The Senate shall have the sole power to try all impeachments. When sitting for that purpose, they shall be on oath or affirmation. When the President of the United States is tried, the Chief Justice shall preside; and no person shall be convicted without the concurrence of two-thirds of the members present.

7. Judgment in cases of impeachment shall not extend further than to removal from office, and disqualification to hold and enjoy any office of honor, trust or profit under the United States; but the party convicted shall nevertheless be liable and subject to indictment, trial, judgment and punishment, according to law.

Section 4. Elections and Meetings of Congress

1. The times, places and manner of holding elections for Senators and Representatives shall be prescribed in each state by the legislature thereof; but the Congress may at any time by law make or alter such regulations, except as to the places of choosing Senators.

2. The Congress shall assemble at least once in every year and such meeting shall be on the first Monday in December, unless they shall by law appoint a different day.

Section 5. Rules of Procedure for Congress

1. Each house shall be the judge of the elections, returns and qualifications of its own members, and a majority of each shall constitute a quorum to do business; but a smaller number may adjourn from day to day, and may be authorized to compel the attendance of absent members, in such manner, and under such penalties as each house may provide.

2. Each house may determine the rules of its proceedings, punish its members for disorderly behavior, and with the concurrence of two-thirds, expel a member.

3. Each house shall keep a journal of its proceedings, and from time to time publish the same, excepting such parts as may in their judgment require secrecy; and the yeas and nays of the members of either house on any question shall, at the desire of one-fifth of those present, be entered on the journal.

4. Neither house, during the session of Congress, shall, without the consent of the other, adjourn for more than three days, nor to any other place than that in which the two houses shall be sitting.

4. During a session of Congress, neither house can stop meeting for more than three days or decide to meet somewhere else unless the other house agrees.

Section 6. Privileges and Restrictions of Members of Congress

1. The Senators and Representatives shall receive a compensation for their services, to be ascertained by law, and paid out of the Treasury of the United States. They shall in all cases, except treason, felony and breach of the peace, be privileged from arrest during their attendance at the session of their respective houses, and in going to and returning from the same; and for any speech or debate in either house, they shall not be questioned in any other place.

1. Each member of Congress receives a salary from the United States government. Except for very serious crimes, no member can be arrested in the place where Congress is meeting while in session. Members cannot be arrested for anything they say in Congress.

2. No Senator or Representative shall, during the time for which he was elected, be appointed to any civil office under the authority of the United States, which shall have been created, or the emoluments whereof shall have been increased during such time; and no person holding any office under the United States, shall be a member of either house during his continuance in office.

2. Senators and Representatives may not hold any other job in the federal government while they serve in Congress.

Section 7. How Laws Are Made

1. All bills for raising revenue shall originate in the House of Representatives; but the Senate may propose or concur with amendments as on other bills.

1. All money and tax bills must begin in the House of Representatives. The Senate can later pass or change these bills.

2. Every bill which shall have passed the House of Representatives and the Senate, shall, before it become a law, be presented to the President of the United States. If he approve he shall sign it, but if not he shall return it, with his objections to that house in which it shall have originated, who shall enter the objections at large on their journal, and proceed to reconsider it. If after such reconsideration two-thirds of that house shall agree to pass the bill, it shall be sent, together with the objections, to the other house, by which it shall likewise be reconsidered, and if approved by two-thirds of that house, it shall become a law. But in all such cases the votes of both houses shall be determined by yeas and nays, and the names of the persons voting for and against the bill shall be entered on the journal of each house respectively. If any bill shall not be returned by the President within ten days (Sundays excepted) after it shall have been presented to him, the same shall be a law, in like manner as if he had signed it, unless the Congress by their adjournment prevent its return, in which case it shall not be a law.

2. After a bill, or suggested law, passes both the House of Representatives and the Senate, it goes to the President. If the President signs the bill, it becomes a law. If the President vetoes, or rejects, the bill, it goes back to Congress. A President's veto can be overridden, or upset, if Congress votes again and two-thirds of the members of each house vote in favor of the bill. The bill then becomes a law. If the President neither signs nor vetoes a bill within 10 days (not counting Sundays) of first receiving it, the bill becomes a law. If Congress stops meeting *before* 10 days have passed, however, the bill does *not* become a law. This last type of action is called a "pocket veto."

3. Every act passed by Congress must be presented to the President either to be signed or vetoed. The only exception is when Congress votes to adjourn, or stop meeting.

Congress has the power to:

1. raise and collect taxes to both pay debts and to protect and serve the nation, but taxes must be the same everywhere in the United States;

2. borrow money;

3. control trade with foreign nations, between states, and with Native Americans;

4. decide how people from foreign countries can become citizens of the United States and to make laws dealing with people and businesses unable to pay their debts;

5. print money, set its value, and set the standards of weights and measures used throughout the nation;

6. punish people who make counterfeit, or fake, money and bonds;

7. set up post offices and roads for mail delivery;

8. protect the rights and creations of scientists, artists, authors, and inventors;

9. create federal, or national, courts lower than the Supreme Court;

10. punish crimes committed at sea;

11. declare war;

12. establish and support an army, but no amount of money set aside for this purpose can be for a term longer than two years;

13. establish and support a navy;

3. Every order, resolution, or vote to which the concurrence of the Senate and House of Representatives may be necessary (except on a question of adjournment) shall be presented to the President of the United States; and before the same shall take effect, shall be approved by him, or being disapproved by him, shall be repassed by two-thirds of the Senate and House of Representatives, according to the rules and limitations prescribed in the case of a bill.

Section 8. Powers Granted to Congress

1. The Congress shall have power to lay and collect taxes, duties, imposts and excises, to pay the debts and provide for the common defense and general welfare of the United States; but all duties, imposts and excises shall be uniform throughout the United States;

2. To borrow money on the credit of the United States;

3. To regulate commerce with foreign nations, and among the several states, and with the Indian tribes;

4. To establish a uniform rule of naturalization, and uniform laws on the subject of bankruptcies throughout the United States;

5. To coin money, regulate the value thereof, and of foreign coin, and fix the standard of weights and measures;

6. To provide for the punishment of counterfeiting the securities and current coin of the United States;

7. To establish post offices and post roads;

8. To promote the progress of science and useful arts, by securing for limited times to authors and inventors the exclusive right to their respective writings and discoveries;

9. To constitute tribunals inferior to the Supreme Court;

10. To define and punish piracies and felonies committed on the high seas and offenses against the law of nations;

11. To declare war, ~~grant letters of marque and reprisal~~, and make rules concerning captures on land and water;

12. To raise and support armies, but no appropriation of money to that use shall be for a longer term than two years;

13. To provide and maintain a navy;

14. To make rules for the government and regulation of the land and naval forces;

15. To provide for calling forth the militia to execute the laws of the Union, suppress insurrections and repel invasions;

16. To provide for organizing, arming, and disciplining, the militia, and for governing such part of them as may be employed in the service of the United States, reserving to the states respectively, the appointment of the officers, and the authority of training the militia according to the discipline prescribed by Congress;

17. To exercise exclusive legislation in all cases whatsoever, over such district (not exceeding ten miles square) as may, by cession of particular states, and the acceptance of Congress, become the seat of the government of the United States, and to exercise like authority over all places purchased by the consent of the legislature of the state in which the same shall be, for the erection of forts, magazines, arsenals, dockyards, and other needful buildings;—and

18. To make all laws which shall be necessary and proper for carrying into execution the foregoing powers, and all other powers vested by this Constitution in the government of the United States, or in any department or officer thereof.

Section 9. Powers Denied to Congress

1. ~~The migration or importation of such persons as any of the states now existing shall think proper to admit, shall not be prohibited by the Congress prior to the year one thousand eight hundred and eight, but a tax or duty may be imposed on such importation, not exceeding ten dollars for each person.~~

2. The privilege of the writ of habeas corpus shall not be suspended, unless when in cases of rebellion or invasion the public safety may require it.

3. No bill of attainder or ex post facto law shall be passed.

4. No capitation, or other direct, tax shall be laid, unless in proportion to the census or enumeration herein before directed to be taken.

5. No tax or duty shall be laid on articles exported from any state.

14. make rules for the armed forces;

15. call the militia (today called the National Guard) to enforce federal laws, put down rebellions, and fight invasions;

16. organize, train, and discipline the National Guard. States have the power to name officers and train soldiers in the National Guard under rules set by Congress;

17. govern the capital and military sites of the United States; and

18. make all laws necessary to carry out the powers of Congress. This is called the "elastic clause" because it stretches the powers of Congress.

Congress does *not* have the power to:

1. stop enslaved people from being brought into the United States before 1808. In 1808, the first year allowed, Congress passed a law banning the slave trade;

2. arrest and jail people without charging them with a crime. The only exception is during a rebellion or emergency;

3. punish a person without a trial in a court of law; nor punish a person for doing something wrong that was not against the law when the person did it;

4. pass a direct tax (such as an income tax) unless it is in proportion to the population. The 16th Amendment allowed an income tax;

5. tax goods sent out of a state;

6. give ports of one state an advantage over ports of another state; nor can one state tax the ships of another state that enter its borders;

7. spend money without both passing a law and keeping a record of all its accounts;

8. grant any title of nobility (such as king or queen); nor may any worker in the federal government accept any gift or title from a foreign government.

State governments do *not* have the power to:

1. make treaties, print money, or do anything forbidden to the federal government outlined in Section 9 of the Constitution, above;

2. tax goods sent into and out of a state unless Congress agrees;

3. keep armed forces, go to war, or make agreements with others states or foreign countries unless Congress agrees.

1. The President has the power to execute, or carry out, the laws of the United States. The President and Vice President together serve a term of four years.

2. The President is chosen by electors from each state. Today these electors are chosen by the voters and called the *Electoral College*. The number of

6. No preference shall be given any regulation of commerce or revenue to the ports of one state over those of another; nor shall vessels bound to, or from, one state, be obliged to enter, clear, or pay duties in another.

7. No money shall be drawn from the Treasury, but in consequence of appropriations made by law; and a regular statement and account of the receipts and expenditures of all public money shall be published from time to time.

8. No title of nobility shall be granted by the United States; and no person holding any office of profit or trust under them, shall, without the consent of the Congress, accept of any present, emolument, office, or title, of any kind whatever, from any king, prince, or foreign state.

Section 10. Powers Denied to the States

1. No state shall enter into any treaty, alliance, or confederation; grant letters of marque and reprisal; coin money; emit bills of credit; make anything but gold and silver coin a tender in payment of debts; pass any bill of attainder, ex post facto law, or law impairing the obligation of contracts, or grant any title of nobility.

2. No state shall, without the consent of the Congress, lay any imposts or duties on imports or exports, except what may be absolutely necessary for executing its inspection laws; and the net produce of all duties and imposts, laid by any state on imports or exports, shall be for the use of the Treasury of the United States; and all such laws shall be subject to the revision and control of the Congress.

3. No state shall, without the consent of Congress, lay any duty of tonnage, keep troops, or ships of war in time of peace, enter into any agreement or compact with another state, or with a foreign power, or engage in war, unless actually invaded, or in such imminent danger as will not admit of delay.

Article 2. THE EXECUTIVE BRANCH

Section 1. Office of President and Vice President

1. The executive power shall be vested in a President of the United States of America. He shall hold his office during the term of four years, and, together with the Vice President, chosen for the same term, be elected, as follows:

2. Each state shall appoint, in such manner as the legislature thereof may direct, a number of electors, equal to the whole number of Senators and Representatives to which the

state may be entitled in the Congress; but no Senator or Representative, or person holding an office or trust or profit under the United States, shall be appointed an elector.

3. ~~The electors shall meet in their respective states, and vote by ballot for two persons, of whom one at least shall not be an inhabitant of the same state with themselves. And they shall make a list of all the persons voted for, and of the number of votes for each; which list they shall sign and certify, and transmit sealed to the seat of the government of the United States, directed to the president of the Senate. The president of the Senate shall, in the presence of the Senate and House of Representatives, open all the certificates, and the votes shall then be counted. The person having the greatest number of votes shall be the President, if such number be a majority of the whole number of electors appointed; and if there be more than one who have such majority, and have an equal number of votes, then the House of Representatives shall immediately choose by ballot one of them for President; and if no person have a majority, then from the five highest on the list the said House shall in like manner choose the President. But in choosing the President, the votes shall be taken by states, the representation from each state having one vote; a quorum for this purpose shall consist of a member or members from two-thirds of the states, and a majority of all the states shall be necessary to a choice. In every case, after the choice of the President, the person having the greatest number of votes of the electors shall be the Vice President. But if there should remain two or more who have equal votes, the Senate shall choose from them by ballot the Vice President.~~

4. The Congress may determine the time of choosing the electors, and the day on which they shall give their votes; which day shall be the same throughout the United States.

5. No person except a natural born citizen, ~~or a citizen of the United States, at the time of the adoption of this Constitution,~~ shall be eligible to the office of the President; neither shall any person be eligible to that office who shall not have attained to the age of thirty-five years, and been fourteen years a resident within the United States.

6. In case of the removal of the President from office, or of his death, resignation, or inability to discharge the powers and duties of the said office, the same shall devolve on the Vice President, and the Congress may by law provide for

electoral votes for each state is determined by adding up the number of the state's Senators and Representatives.

3. This part of the Constitution describes an early method of electing the President and Vice President. The 12th Amendment changed this method. Originally, the person who received the most electoral votes became President and the person who received the next highest number became Vice President.

4. Congress decides when Presidential electors are chosen and when they vote. The electors vote on the same day throughout the United States. Today people vote for the electors on the Tuesday after the first Monday of November. Presidential elections take place every four years.

5. To be President, a person must be a citizen born in the United States, at least 35 years old, and have lived in the United States for at least 14 years.

6. If the President leaves office for any reason or can no longer serve as President, the Vice President becomes President. If there is no Vice

President, Congress may decide who becomes President. The 25th Amendment changed the method of filling these vacancies, or empty offices.

the case of removal, death, resignation, or inability, both of the President and Vice President, declaring what officer shall then act as President, and such officer shall act accordingly, until the disability be removed, or a President shall be elected.

7. The President receives a set salary that can neither be raised nor lowered during the President's term of office. The President can receive no other gift or salary from the United States or any of the states while in office.

7. The President shall, at stated times receive for his services, a compensation, which shall neither be increased nor diminished during the period for which he shall have been elected, and he shall not receive within that period any other emolument from the United States, or any of them.

8. Before taking office, the person elected President takes an oath. In this oath, the person promises to carry out the laws of the United States and defend the Constitution.

8. Before he enter on the execution of his office, he shall take the following oath or affirmation:—"I do solemnly swear (or affirm) that I will faithfully execute the office of President of the United States, and will to the best of my ability, preserve, protect and defend the Constitution of the United States."

Section 2. Powers Granted to the President

1. The President is in charge of the armed forces and state militias (today the National Guard) of the United States. The President can demand advice and opinions, in writing, of the people in charge of each executive department. These advisers are called the President's Cabinet. The President also has the power to pardon, or free, people convicted of federal crimes, except in cases of impeachment.

1. The President shall be Commander in Chief of the Army and Navy of the United States, and of the militia of the several states, when called into the actual service of the United States; he may require the opinion, in writing, of the principal officer in each of the executive departments, upon any subject relating to the duties of their respective offices, and he shall have power to grant reprieves and pardons for offenses against the United States, except in cases of impeachment.

2. The President has the power to make treaties, but they must be approved by two-thirds of the Senate. The President also has the power to name ambassadors, important government officials, and judges of the Supreme Court and other federal courts, with the approval of the Senate.

2. He shall have power, by and with the advice and consent of the Senate, to make treaties, provided two-thirds of the Senators present concur; and he shall nominate, and by and with the advice and consent of the Senate, shall appoint ambassadors, other public ministers and consuls, judges of the Supreme Court, and all other officers of the United States, whose appointments are not herein otherwise provided for, and which shall be established by law; but the Congress may by law vest the appointment of such inferior officers, as they think proper, in the President alone, in the courts of law, or in the heads of departments.

3. The President has the power to fill empty offices for a short time when the Senate is not meeting.

3. The President shall have power to fill up all vacancies that may happen during the recess of the Senate, by granting commissions which shall expire at the end of their next session.

Section 3. Duties of the President

The President must inform Congress from time to time on the condition of

He shall from time to time give to the Congress information of the state of the Union, and recommend to their consideration such measures as he shall judge necessary and expedient; he may, on extraordinary occasions, convene both houses, or either of them, and in case of disagreement between them, with respect to the time of adjournment, he may adjourn them to such time as he shall think proper; he shall receive ambassadors and other public ministers; he shall take care that the laws be faithfully executed, and shall commission all the officers of the United States.

the nation. Today, this speech is called the State of the Union address and is given once a year, usually in late January. In this message, the President recommends laws to improve the nation. The President can also, in time of emergency, call Congress to meet. If, in other situations, Congress cannot decide whether or not to adjourn, the President can make this decision. The President receives foreign officials, makes sure the nation's laws are carried out, and signs orders naming officers in the armed forces.

Section 4. Removal from Office

The President, Vice President and all civil officers of the United States, shall be removed from office on impeachment for, and conviction of, treason, bribery, or other high crimes and misdemeanors.

The President, Vice President, and other non-military officers of the United States may be impeached, or accused of committing crimes, and removed from office if found guilty.

Article 3. THE JUDICIAL BRANCH

Section 1. Federal Courts

The judicial power of the United States shall be vested in one Supreme Court, and in such inferior courts as the Congress may from time to time ordain and establish. The judges, both of the Supreme and inferior courts, shall hold their offices during good behavior, and shall, at stated times, receive for their services, a compensation, which shall not be diminished during their continuance in office.

The judicial power, or the power to make decisions in courts of law, is held by the Supreme Court and other lower federal, or national, courts that Congress may set up. Supreme Court and other federal judges hold office for life if they act properly. Judges receive a set salary that cannot be lowered.

Section 2. Powers of Federal Courts

1. The judicial power shall extend to all cases, in law and equity, arising under this Constitution, the laws of the United States, and treaties made, or which shall be made, under their authority; to all cases affecting ambassadors, other public ministers and consuls; to all cases of admiralty and maritime jurisdiction; to controversies to which the United States shall be a party; to controversies between two or more states; between a state and citizens of another state; between citizens of different states, between citizens of the same state claiming lands under grants of different states, and between a state, or the citizens thereof, and foreign states, citizens or subjects.

1. Federal courts have legal authority over:

a) all laws made under the Constitution;

b) treaties made with foreign governments;

c) cases involving matters occurring at sea;

d) cases involving the federal government;

e) cases involving different states or citizens of different states; and

f) cases involving foreign citizens or governments.

The 11th Amendment partly limits which cases federal courts can hear.

2. In all cases affecting ambassadors, other public ministers and consuls, and those in which a state shall be party, the

2. In cases involving either states or ambassadors and government officials, the Supreme Court is the first and only court that makes a judgment. All other cases begin in lower courts but may later be appealed to, or reviewed by, the Supreme Court.

3. All criminal cases, except those of impeachment, are judged by trial and jury in the state where the supposed crime took place. If a crime occurs outside of any state, Congress decides where the trial takes place.

1. Treason is the crime of making war against the United States or helping its enemies. To be found guilty of treason, a person must confess to the crime or two witnesses must swear to having seen the crime committed.

2. Congress decides the punishment for treason. Relatives of people convicted of treason cannot also be punished for the crime.

Supreme Court shall have original jurisdiction. In all the other cases before mentioned, the Supreme Court shall have appellate jurisdiction, both as to law and fact, with such exceptions, and under such regulations as the Congress shall make.

3. The trial of all crimes, except in cases of impeachment, shall be by jury; and such trial shall be held in the state where the said crimes shall have been committed; but when not committed within any state, the trial shall be at such place or places as the Congress may by law have directed.

Section 3. The Crime of Treason

1. Treason against the United States shall consist only in levying war against them, or in adhering to their enemies, giving them aid and comfort. No person shall be convicted of treason unless on the testimony of two witnesses to the same overt act, or on confession in open court.

2. The Congress shall have power to declare the punishment of treason, but no attainder of treason shall work corruption of blood, or forfeiture except during the life of the person attainted.

Article 4. RELATIONS AMONG THE STATES

Section 1. Recognition by Each State of Acts of Other States

Each state must respect the laws, records, and court decisions of every other state in the United States. Congress may pass laws to help carry out these matters.

Full faith and credit shall be given in each state to the public acts, records, and judicial proceedings of every other state. And the Congress may by general laws prescribe the manner in which such acts, records and proceedings shall be proved, and the effect thereof.

Section 2. Rights of Citizens in Other States

1. Citizens are guaranteed all their basic rights when visiting other states.

1. The citizens of each state shall be entitled to all privileges and immunities of citizens in the several states.

2. A person charged with a crime, who flees to another state, must be returned to the state where the crime took place if the governor of the state demands.

2. A person charged in any state with treason, felony, or other crime, who shall flee from justice, and be found in another state, shall on demand of the executive authority of the state from which he fled, be delivered up, to be removed to the state having jurisdiction of the crime.

3. A person enslaved in one state, who escapes to another state, is still considered enslaved and must be returned to the person's owner. The 13th Amendment, which outlawed slavery, nullified, or overturned, this section of the Constitution.

3. No person held to service or labor in one state, under the laws thereof, escaping into another, shall, in consequence of any law or regulation therein, be discharged from such service or labor, but shall be delivered up on claim of the party to whom such service or labor may be due.

Section 3. Treatment of New States and Territories

1. New states may be admitted by the Congress into this Union; but no new state shall be formed or erected within the jurisdiction of any other state; nor any state be formed by the junction of two or more states, or parts of states, without the consent of the legislatures of the states concerned as well as of the Congress.

2. The Congress shall have power to dispose of and make all needful rules and regulations respecting the territory or other property belonging to the United States; and nothing in this Constitution shall be so construed as to prejudice any claims of the United States, or of any particular state.

Section 4. Guarantees to the States

The United States shall guarantee to every state in this Union a republican form of government, and shall protect each of them against invasion; and on application of the legislature, or of the executive (when the legislature cannot be convened) against domestic violence.

Article 5. AMENDING THE CONSTITUTION

The Congress, whenever two-thirds of both houses shall deem it necessary, shall propose amendments to this Constitution, or, on the application of the legislatures of two-thirds of the several states, shall call a convention for proposing amendments, which, in either case, shall be valid to all intents and purposes, as part of this Constitution, when ratified by the legislatures of three-fourths of the several states, or by conventions in three-fourths thereof, as the one or the other mode of ratification may be proposed by the Congress; provided that no amendment which may be made prior to the year one thousand eight hundred and eight shall in any manner affect the first and fourth clauses in the Ninth Section of the First Article; and that no state, without its consent, shall be deprived of its equal suffrage in the Senate.

Article 6. DEBTS, FEDERAL SUPREMACY, OATHS OF OFFICE

Section 1. Prior Debts of the United States

All debts contracted and engagements entered into, before the adoption of this Constitution, shall be as valid against the United States under this Constitution, as under the Confederation.

1. Congress may let new states become part of the United States. No new state can be formed from another state or by joining parts of other states, unless Congress and the legislatures of the states involved approve.

2. Congress has the power to make all laws and rules over territories and government properties of the United States.

The federal government guarantees that the people of each state have the right to elect their leaders. The federal government also promises to protect each state from invasion, rebellion, and violent disorders.

There are two ways to make amendments, or changes, to the Constitution: two-thirds of each branch of Congress can suggest an amendment; or, two-thirds of the state legislatures can call a convention to suggest an amendment. Once the amendment has been suggested, three-fourths of the state legislatures or three-fourths of special state conventions must approve the amendment for it to become part of the Constitution. No state can be denied its equal vote in the Senate without its approval. No amendment could be made before 1808 that affected either the slave trade or certain direct taxes.

The United States government promises to pay back all debts and honor all agreements made by the government under the Articles of Confederation.

The Constitution and all the laws and treaties made under it are the supreme, or highest, law in the United States. If state or local laws disagree with federal law, the federal law must be obeyed. All judges must follow this rule.

Section 2. The Supreme Law of the Land

This Constitution, and the laws of the United States which shall be made in pursuance thereof; and all treaties made, or which shall be made, under the authority of the United States, shall be the supreme law of the land; and the judges in every state shall be bound thereby, anything in the constitution or laws of any state to the contrary notwithstanding.

All officials of the federal and state governments must promise to support the Constitution. A person's religion may never be used to qualify or disqualify a person from holding federal office.

Section 3. Oaths of Office

The Senators and Representatives before mentioned, and the members of the several state legislatures, and all executive and judicial officers, both of the United States and of the several states, shall be bound by oath or affirmation, to support this Constitution; but no religious test shall ever be required as a qualification to any office or public trust under the United States.

Article 7. RATIFICATION OF THE CONSTITUTION

The Constitution will become law when special conventions in 9 (of the 13 original) states approve it.

The ratification of the conventions of nine states, shall be sufficient for the establishment of this Constitution between the states so ratifying the same.

This Constitution is completed by the agreement of everyone at this convention on September 17, 1787, in the 12th year of the independence of the United States of America.

Done in convention by the unanimous consent of the States present the Seventeenth day of September in the year of our Lord one thousand seven hundred and eighty seven, and of the Independence of the United States of America the Twelfth.

The people present have signed their names below.

In witness whereof we have hereunto subscribed our names.

George Washington, President and deputy from Virginia

DELAWARE
George Read
Gunning Bedford, Jr.
John Dickinson
Richard Bassett
Jacob Broom

MARYLAND
James McHenry
Daniel of St. Thomas
  Jenifer
Daniel Carroll

VIRGINIA
John Blair
James Madison, Jr.

NORTH CAROLINA
William Blount
Richard Dobbs Spaight
Hugh Williamson

SOUTH CAROLINA
John Rutledge
Charles Cotesworth
  Pinckney
Charles Pinckney
Pierce Butler

GEORGIA
William Few
Abraham Baldwin

NEW HAMPSHIRE
John Langdon
Nicholas Gilman

MASSACHUSETTS
Nathaniel Gorham
Rufus King

CONNECTICUT
William Samuel Johnson
Roger Sherman

NEW YORK
Alexander Hamilton

NEW JERSEY
William Livingston
David Brearley
William Paterson
Jonathan Dayton

PENNSYLVANIA
Benjamin Franklin
Thomas Mifflin
Robert Morris
George Clymer
Thomas FitzSimons
Jared Ingersoll
James Wilson
Gouverneur Morris

Attest: William Jackson,
  Secretary.

AMENDMENTS TO THE CONSTITUTION

Amendment 1. *Freedom of Religion, Speech, Press, Assembly, and Petition (1791)*

Congress shall make no law respecting an establishment of religion, or prohibiting the free exercise thereof; or abridging the freedom of speech, or of the press; or the right of the people peaceably to assemble, and to petition the government for a redress of grievances.

Amendment 2. *Right to Keep Weapons (1791)*

A well-regulated militia, being necessary to the security of a free state, the right of the people to keep and bear arms shall not be infringed.

Amendment 3. *Protection Against Quartering Soldiers (1791)*

No soldier shall, in time of peace, be quartered in any house, without the consent of the owner, nor in time of war, but in a manner to be prescribed by law.

The first ten amendments to the Constitution ensure basic freedoms and are known as the Bill of Rights. Under the First Amendment, Congress cannot make laws:

1) setting up an official religion;

2) preventing people from practicing their religion;

3) stopping people or the press from saying what they want;

4) preventing people from gathering peacefully and asking the government to listen to their complaints and to correct problems.

People have the right to keep weapons and be part of the state militia (today the National Guard).

During peacetime, people cannot be forced to quarter, or house and feed, soldiers in their homes. During time of war, Congress may set other rules.

People are protected against unreasonable arrests and searches of their homes and property. To search a person's home or property, the government must get a search warrant, or special approval, describing exactly what place is to be searched and what items are expected to be found.

A person cannot be charged with a serious crime unless a grand jury, or a group of citizens appointed to study criminal evidence, decides that a good reason exists to put the person on trial. (The only exceptions are cases involving people in the armed forces.) A person judged innocent by a court of law cannot be put on trial again for the same crime. People on trial cannot be forced to testify, or speak in court, against themselves. A person cannot have life, liberty, or property taken away unless fairly decided by a court of law. If the government takes away property for public use, a fair price must be paid the owner.

In all criminal cases, a person accused of a crime has the right to a fast, public trial by a fair jury in the place where the crime took place. All persons accused of a crime have the right to:

1) know the charges against them;

2) hear the evidence and witnesses against them;

3) call witnesses in their defense;

4) have a lawyer.

A person has the right to a trial by jury in civil, or noncriminal, cases involving more than $20.

The government cannot require very high bail, or deposit of money, from a

Amendment 4. *Freedom from Unreasonable Search and Seizure (1791)*

The right of the people to be secure in their persons, houses, papers, and effects, against unreasonable searches and seizures, shall not be violated, and no warrants shall issue, but upon probable cause, supported by oath or affirmation, and particularly describing the place to be searched, and the persons or things to be seized.

Amendment 5. *Rights of Persons Accused of a Crime (1791)*

No person shall be held to answer for a capital, or otherwise infamous, crime, unless on a presentment or indictment of a grand jury, except in cases arising in the land or naval forces, or in the militia, when in actual service in time of war or public danger; nor shall any person be subject for the same offense to be twice put in jeopardy of life or limb; nor shall be compelled in any criminal case to be a witness against himself, nor be deprived of life, liberty, or property, without due process of law; nor shall private property be taken for public use, without just compensation.

Amendment 6. *Right to a Jury Trial in Criminal Cases (1791)*

In all criminal prosecutions, the accused shall enjoy the right to a speedy and public trial, by an impartial jury of the state and district wherein the crime shall have been committed, which district shall have been previously ascertained by law, and to be informed of the nature and cause of the accusation; to be confronted with the witnesses against him; to have compulsory process for obtaining witnesses in his favor, and to have the assistance of counsel for his defense.

Amendment 7. *Right to a Jury Trial in Civil Cases (1791)*

In suits at common law, where the value in controversy shall exceed twenty dollars, the right of trial by jury shall be preserved, and no fact tried by a jury shall be otherwise reexamined in any court of the United States than according to the rules of the common law.

Amendment 8. *Protection from Unfair Fines and Punishment (1791)*

Excessive bail shall not be required, nor excessive fines imposed, nor cruel and unusual punishments inflicted.

Amendment 9. *Other Rights of the People (1791)*

The enumeration in the Constitution, of certain rights, shall not be construed to deny or disparage others retained by the people.

The rights of the people are not limited to those stated in the Constitution.

Amendment 10. *Powers of the States and the People (1791)*

The powers not delegated to the United States by the Constitution, nor prohibited by it to the states, are reserved to the states respectively, or to the people.

Powers not granted to the United States government and not forbidden to the states are left to the states or to the people.

Amendment 11. *Limiting Law Cases Against States (1798)*

The judicial power of the United States shall not be construed to extend to any suit in law or equity, commenced or prosecuted against one of the United States, by citizens of another state, or by citizens or subjects of any foreign state.

A state government cannot be sued in a federal court by people of another state or by people from a foreign country.

Amendment 12. *Election of President and Vice President (1804)*

The electors shall meet in their respective states, and vote by ballot for President and Vice President, one of whom, at least, shall not be an inhabitant of the same state with themselves; they shall name in their ballots the person voted for as President, and in distinct ballots the person voted for as Vice President, and they shall make distinct lists of all persons voted for as President, and of all persons voted for as Vice President, and of the number of votes for each, which lists they shall sign and certify, and transmit, sealed, to the seat of government of the United States, directed to the President of the Senate; the President of the Senate shall, in the presence of the Senate and House of Representatives, open all the certificates and the votes shall then be counted; the person having the greatest number of votes for President shall be the President, if such number be a majority of the whole number of electors appointed; and if no person have such majority, then from the persons having the highest numbers not exceeding three on the list of those voted for as President, the House of Representatives shall choose immediately, by ballot, the President. But in choosing the President, the votes shall be taken by states, the representation from each state having one vote; a quorum for this purpose shall consist of a member or members from two-thirds of the states, and a majority of all the states shall be neces-

person accused of a crime. People convicted of crimes cannot be fined an unfairly high amount. Nor can they be punished in a cruel or unusual way.

This amendment changed the method of choosing a President and Vice President. This method is called the Electoral College. The main change caused by this amendment is that candidates for President and Vice President now run for office together, and each elector casts only one vote. Before, candidates for President and Vice President ran for office separately, and each elector cast two votes. Under the Electoral College, people called electors meet in their home states and vote for President and Vice President. Electors choose one person for President and a different person for Vice President. (One of the people voted for must be from a different state than the elector.) These electoral votes are then sent to the United States Senate where all the electoral votes for President are counted. The person who receives more than half the electoral votes for President is elected President. The person who receives more than half the electoral votes for Vice President is elected Vice President. If no person receives more than half the electoral votes for President, the House of Representatives chooses the President. A list of the top three vote-getters is sent to the House of Representatives. From this list, the Representatives vote for President with each state entitled to one vote. The person who receives more than half the votes of the states in the House of Representatives is elected President. If no person receives more than half the vote, the Representatives vote again. If the Representatives fail to elect a President by March 4 (later changed to January 20), the Vice President serves as President. If no person receives at least half the electoral votes for Vice President, no one becomes Vice President and a list of the top two vote-getters is sent to the Senate. From this list, the Senators then vote for Vice President, with each Senator entitled to one vote. The person who receives more than half the votes in the Senate becomes Vice President. Qualifications for the office of Vice President are the same as those of President.

Slavery is outlawed in the United States.

Congress can pass any laws necessary to carry out this amendment.

All people born in or made citizens by the United States are citizens of both the United States and the state in which they live. No state can deny any citizen the basic rights outlined in the 5th Amendment. All states must treat people equally under the law. This amendment made formerly enslaved people citizens of both the United States and the states in which they lived.

The number of a state's Representatives in Congress can be lowered if the state prevents qualified citizens

sary to a choice. ~~And if the House of Representatives shall not choose a President whenever the right of choice shall devolve upon them, before the fourth day of March next following, then the Vice President shall act as President, as in the case of the death or other constitutional disability of the President.~~ The person having the greatest number of votes as Vice President, shall be the Vice President, if such number be a majority of the whole number of electors appointed, and if no person have a majority, then from the two highest numbers on the list, the Senate shall choose the Vice President; a quorum for the purpose shall consist of two-thirds of the whole number of Senators, and a majority of the whole number shall be necessary to a choice. But no person constitutionally ineligible to the office of President shall be eligible to that of Vice President of the United States.

Amendment 13. *Slavery Outlawed (1865)*

Section 1. *Abolition of Slavery*

Neither slavery nor involuntary servitude, except as a punishment for crime whereof the party shall have been duly convicted, shall exist within the United States, or any place subject to their jurisdiction.

Section 2. *Enforcement*

Congress shall have power to enforce this article by appropriate legislation.

Amendment 14. *Rights of Citizens (1868)*

Section 1. *Citizenship*

All persons born or naturalized in the United States and subject to the jurisdiction thereof, are citizens of the United States and of the state wherein they reside. No state shall make or enforce any law which shall abridge the privileges or immunities of citizens of the United States; nor shall any state deprive any person of life, liberty, or property, without due process of law; nor deny to any person within its jurisdiction the equal protection of the laws.

Section 2. *Representation in Congress*

Representatives shall be apportioned among the several states according to their respective numbers, counting the whole number of persons in each state, ~~excluding Indians not taxed~~. But when the right to vote at any election for the choice of electors for President and Vice President of the United States, Representatives in Congress, the executive and judicial officers of a state, or the members of the legislature thereof, is denied to any of the ~~male~~ inhabitants of such state, being ~~twenty one years of age and~~ citizens of the United States, or in any way abridged, except for participation in rebellion, or other crime, the basis of representation therein shall be reduced in the proportion which the number of such ~~male~~ citizens shall bear to the whole number of ~~male~~ citizens ~~twenty one years of age~~ in such state.

from voting. This section aimed to force states in the South to allow African Americans to vote.

Section 3. Penalties for Confederate Leaders

No person shall be a Senator or Representative in Congress, or elector of President and Vice President, or hold any office, civil or military, under the United States, or under any state, who, having previously taken an oath, as a member of Congress, or as an officer of the United States, or as a member of any state legislature, or as an executive or judicial officer of any state, to support the Constitution of the United States, shall have engaged in insurrection or rebellion against the same, or given aid or comfort to the enemies thereof. But Congress may, by vote of two-thirds of each house, remove such disability.

Any official of the federal or state governments who took part in the Civil War against the United States cannot again hold any federal or state office. But Congress can remove this restriction by a two-thirds vote.

Section 4. Responsibility for Public Debt

The validity of the public debt of the United States, authorized by law, including debts incurred for payment of pensions and bounties for services in suppressing insurrection or rebellion, shall not be questioned. But neither the United States nor any state shall assume or pay any debt or obligation incurred in aid of insurrection or rebellion against the United States ~~or any claim for the loss or emancipation of any slave~~; but all such debts, obligations, and claims shall be held illegal and void.

All money borrowed by the United States government to fight the Civil War is to be paid back. No debts owed to the Confederate states or to the Confederate government to pay for the Civil War are to be paid back by the federal or state governments. No money would be paid to anyone for the loss of people they once held in slavery.

Section 5. Enforcement

The Congress shall have power to enforce, by appropriate legislation, the provisions of this article.

Congress can pass any laws necessary to carry out this amendment.

Amendment 15. *Voting Rights (1870)*

Section 1. Black Suffrage

The right of citizens of the United States to vote shall not be denied or abridged by the United States or any state on account of race, color, or previous condition of servitude.

No federal or state government can prevent people from voting because of their race, color, or because they were once enslaved. This amendment aimed to give black men the right to vote.

Congress can pass any laws necessary to carry out this amendment.

Section 2. Enforcement

The Congress shall have power to enforce this article by appropriate legislation.

Amendment 16. *Income Tax (1913)*

Congress has the power to collect an income tax regardless of the population of any state.

The Congress shall have the power to lay and collect taxes on incomes, from whatever source derived, without apportionment among the several states, and without regard to any census or enumeration.

Amendment 17. *Direct Election of Senators (1913)*

Section 1. *Method of Election*

Senators are to be elected by the voters of each state. This amendment changed the method by which state legislatures elected Senators as outlined in Article 1, Section 3, Clause 1 of the Constitution.

The Senate of the United States shall be composed of two Senators from each state, elected by the people thereof, for six years; and each Senator shall have one vote. The electors in each state shall have the qualifications requisite for electors of the most numerous branch of the state legislatures.

Section 2. *Vacancies*

Special elections can be held to fill empty seats in the Senate. State legislatures may permit the governor to name a person to fill an empty seat for a short time until the next election.

When vacancies happen in the representation of any state in the Senate, the executive authority of such state shall issue writs of election to fill such vacancies: *provided* that the legislature of any state may empower the executive thereof to make temporary appointments until the people fill the vacancies by election as the legislature may direct.

Section 3. *Those Elected under Previous Rules*

This amendment does not affect the election or term of office of any Senator in office before the amendment becomes part of the Constitution.

This amendment shall not be so construed as to affect the election or term of any Senator chosen before it becomes valid as part of the Constitution.

Amendment 18. *Prohibition of Alcoholic Drinks (1919)*

Section 1. *Prohibition*

Making, selling, or transporting alcoholic, or intoxicating, drinks in the United States is illegal. This amendment was called the Prohibition Amendment because it prohibited, or banned, the use of alcohol.

After one year from the ratification of this article the manufacture, sale, or transportation of intoxicating liquors within, the importation thereof into, or the exportation thereof from, the United States and all territory subject to the jurisdiction thereof for beverage purposes is hereby prohibited.

Section 2. *Enforcement*

Both Congress and the states can pass any laws necessary to carry out this amendment.

The Congress and the several states shall have concurrent power to enforce this article by appropriate legislation.

Section 3. Time Limit on Ratification

~~The article shall be inoperative unless it shall have been ratified as an amendment to the Constitution by the legislatures of the several states, as provided in the Constitution, within seven years from the date of the submission hereof to the states by the Congress.~~

This amendment is to become part of the Constitution only if it is approved within seven years. It was repealed, or canceled, by the 21st Amendment.

Amendment 19. *Women's Right to Vote (1920)*

Section 1. Women Made Voters

The right of citizens of the United States to vote shall not be denied or abridged by the United States or by any state on account of sex.

No federal or state government can prevent people from voting because of their sex. This amendment grants women the right to vote.

Section 2. Enforcement

Congress shall have power to enforce this article by appropriate legislation.

Congress can pass any laws necessary to carry out this amendment.

Amendment 20. *Terms of Office (1933)*

Section 1. Start of Terms of Office

The terms of the President and Vice President shall end at noon on the 20th day of January, and the terms of Senators and Representatives at noon on the 3rd day of January, of the years in which such terms would have ended if this article had not been ratified; and the terms of their successors shall then begin.

The terms of office for the President and Vice President begin on January 20. This date is called Inauguration Day. The terms of office for members of Congress begin on January 3. Originally their terms began on March 4.

Section 2. Meeting Time of Congress

The Congress shall assemble at least once in every year, and such meeting shall begin at noon on the 3rd day of January, unless they shall by law appoint a different day.

Congress must meet at least once a year beginning at noon on January 3. However, Congress may pick a different day to first meet.

Section 3. Providing for a Successor of the President-Elect

If at the time fixed for the beginning of the term of the President, the President-elect shall have died, the Vice President-elect shall become President. If a President shall not have been chosen before the time fixed for the beginning of his term, or if the President-elect shall have failed to qualify, then the Vice President-elect shall act as President until a President shall have qualified; and the Congress may by law provide for the case wherein neither a President-elect nor a Vice President-elect shall have qualified, declaring who shall then act as President, or the manner in which one who is to act shall be selected, and such person shall act accordingly until a President or Vice President shall have qualified.

If the person elected President dies before taking office, the Vice President becomes President. If no person is elected President before the term of office begins, or if the person elected President is not qualified to serve, then the Vice President acts as President until a qualified President is chosen. If both the person elected President and the person elected Vice President are disqualified from holding office, Congress selects the President.

If, during the time Congress is selecting the President and Vice President, one of these two people dies, Congress may pass a law determining how to choose the President and Vice President.

Section 4. Elections Decided by Congress

The Congress may by law provide for the case of the death of any of the persons from whom the House of Representatives may choose a President whenever the right of choice shall have devolved upon them, and for the case of the death of any of the persons from whom the Senate may choose a Vice President whenever the right of choice shall have devolved upon them.

Sections 1 and 2 of this amendment take effect on the 15th day of October after this amendment becomes part of the Constitution.

Section 5. Effective Date

Sections 1 and 2 shall take effect on the 15th day of October following the ratification of this article.

This amendment is to become part of the Constitution only if it is approved by three-fourths of the state legislatures within seven years.

Section 6. Time Limit on Ratification

This article shall be inoperative unless it shall have been ratified as an amendment to the Constitution by the legislatures of three-fourths of the several states within seven years from the date of its submission.

Amendment 21. Repeal of Prohibition (1933)

Section 1. Prohibition Ends

The 18th Amendment is repealed, or no longer in effect.

The Eighteenth article of amendment to the Constitution of the United States is hereby repealed.

Section 2. Protection of State and Local Prohibition Laws

Any state or territory of the United States may pass prohibition laws.

The transportation or importation into any state, territory, or possession of the United States for delivery or use therein of intoxicating liquors, in violation of the laws thereof, is hereby prohibited.

Section 3. Time Limit on Ratification

This amendment is to become part of the Constitution only if state conventions approve it within seven years.

This article shall be inoperative unless it shall have been ratified as an amendment to the Constitution by conventions in the several states, as provided in the Constitution, within seven years from the date of the submission hereof to the states by the Congress.

Amendment 22. President Limited to Two Terms (1951)

Section 1. Limit on Number of Terms

No person can be elected more than two times to the office of President. No person can be elected more than once to the office of President who has served more than two years of another President's term. This amend-

No person shall be elected to the office of the President more than twice, and no person who has held the office of President, or acted as President, for more than two years of a term to which some other person was elected President shall be elected to the office of the President more than once. ~~But this Article shall not apply to any person holding the office of President when this Article was proposed by the Congress, and shall not prevent any person who may be holding the office of President, or acting as President, during the term within which this Article becomes operative from holding the office of President or acting as President during the remainder of such term.~~

ment does not affect any President who is in office when this amendment becomes part of the Constitution.

Section 2. Time Limit on Ratification

~~This Article shall be inoperative unless it shall have been ratified as an amendment to the Constitution by the legislatures of three-fourths of the several states within seven years from the date of its submission to the states by the Congress.~~

This amendment is to become part of the Constitution only if three-fourths of the state legislatures approve it within seven years.

Amendment 23. *Presidential Elections for the District of Columbia (1961)*

Section 1. Presidential Electors in the District of Columbia

The District constituting the seat of Government of the United States shall appoint in such manner as the Congress may direct: A number of electors of President and Vice President equal to the whole number of Senators and Representatives in Congress to which the District would be entitled if it were a State, but in no event more than the least populous State; they shall be in addition to those appointed by the States, but they shall be considered, for the purposes of the election of President and Vice President, to be electors appointed by a State; and they shall meet in the District and perform such duties as provided by the twelfth article of amendment.

People living in Washington, D.C. (the District of Columbia), have the right to vote in Presidential elections. The number of electoral votes of Washington, D.C., can never be more than the number of electoral votes of the state with the fewest number of people.

Section 2. Enforcement

The Congress shall have power to enforce this article by appropriate legislation.

Congress can pass any laws necessary to carry out this amendment.

Amendment 24. *Poll Tax Ended (1964)*

Section 1. Poll Taxes Not Allowed in Federal Elections

The right of citizens of the United States to vote in any primary or other election for President or Vice President, for electors for President or Vice President, or for Senator or Representative in Congress, shall not be denied or abridged by the United States or any state by reason of failure to pay any poll tax or other tax.

No person can be prevented from voting in a federal election for failing to pay a poll tax or any other kind of tax.

Congress can pass any laws necessary to carry out this amendment.

Section 2. Enforcement

The Congress shall have the power to enforce this article by appropriate legislation.

Amendment 25. *Presidential Succession (1967)*

Section 1. Filling the Vacant Office of President

If the President dies, resigns, or is removed from office, the Vice President becomes President.

In case of the removal of the President from office or of his death or resignation, the Vice President shall become President.

Section 2. Filling the Vacant Office of Vice President

If the office of Vice President becomes empty, the President names a new Vice President, with the approval of both houses of Congress.

Whenever there is a vacancy in the office of the Vice President, the President shall nominate a Vice President who shall take the office upon confirmation by a majority vote of both houses of Congress.

Section 3. Disability of the President

If the President is unable to carry out the powers and duties of office, the President may inform the leaders of Congress. The Vice President then serves as Acting President. The President may return to office only when he or she informs the leaders of Congress that he or she can again carry out the powers and duties of office.

Whenever the President transmits to the President pro tempore of the Senate and the Speaker of the House of Representatives his written declaration that he is unable to discharge the powers and duties of his office, and until he transmits to them a written declaration to the contrary, such powers and duties shall be discharged by the Vice President as Acting President.

Section 4. When Congress Designates an Acting President

If the Vice President and at least half the Cabinet, or President's top advisers (or a special committee), inform the leaders of Congress that the President cannot carry out the powers and duties of office, the Vice President immediately becomes Acting President. If the President informs the leaders of Congress that he or she is able to serve as President, he or she again becomes President. But if, within four days, the Vice President and at least half the Cabinet (or a special committee) inform the leaders of Congress that the President still cannot carry out the powers and duties of office, the President does not return to office. Instead, Congress must meet within 48 hours. In the next 21 days, Congress must decide if the President is able to carry out the powers and duties of office. If two-thirds of both houses of Congress vote that the President is unable to serve, the Presi-

Whenever the Vice President and a majority of either the principal officers of the executive departments or of such other body as Congress may by law provide, transmit to the President pro tempore of the Senate and the Speaker of the House of Representatives their written declaration that the President is unable to discharge the powers and duties of his office, the Vice President shall immediately assume the powers and duties of the office as Acting President. Thereafter, when the President transmits to the President pro tempore of the Senate and the Speaker of the House of Representatives his written declaration that no inability exists, he shall resume the powers and duties of his office unless the Vice President and a majority of either the principal officers of the executive departments or of such other body as Congress may by law provide, transmit within four days to the President pro tempore of the Senate and the Speaker of the House of Representatives their written declaration that the President is unable to discharge the powers and duties of his office. Thereupon Congress shall decide the issue, assembling within 48 hours for that purpose if not in session. If the Congress, within 21 days after receipt of the latter written declaration, or, if Congress is not in session, within 21 days after Congress is required to assemble, determines by two-thirds vote of both houses that the President is unable to discharge the powers and duties of his office, the Vice President shall continue to discharge the same as Acting President; otherwise, the President shall assume the powers and duties of his office.

dent is removed from office and the Vice President becomes Acting President. If two-thirds do not vote this way, the President stays in office.

Amendment 26. *Vote for Eighteen-Year-Olds (1971)*

Section 1. Voting Age

The right of citizens of the United States, who are 18 years of age or older, to vote shall not be denied or abridged by the United States or any state on account of age.

No federal or state government can prevent people 18 years of age or older from voting because of their age. This amendment grants people who are at least 18 years old the right to vote.

Section 2. Enforcement

The Congress shall have the power to enforce this article by appropriate legislation.

Congress can pass any laws necessary to carry out this amendment.

Amendment 27. *Limits on Salary Changes (1992)*

No law, varying the compensation for the services of the Senators and Representatives, shall take effect, until an election of Representatives shall have intervened.

No law changing the salaries of members of Congress can take effect until after the next election of the House of Representatives.

Time Line of Our PRESIDENTS

George Washington
(1732-1799)

Years in Office 1789-1797
Vice President John Adams
Home State Virginia
Occupation Planter, military leader
First Lady Martha Dandridge Washington
Religion Episcopalian

New States
Vermont 1791; Kentucky 1792; Tennessee 1796

Major Events
- 1789 Roman Catholics found Georgetown University
- 1790 First spinning mill in U.S. opened
- 1790 First U.S. census
- 1791 First recorded Cabinet meeting
- 1791 Bill of Rights added to Constitution
- 1791 (First) Bank of the U.S. established
- 1792 New York Stock Exchange founded
- 1796 Washington's Farewell Address

John Adams
(1735-1826)

Years in Office 1797-1801
Vice President Thomas Jefferson
Home State Massachusetts
Occupation Lawyer
First Lady Abigail Smith Adams
Religion Unitarian

Major Events
- 1798 Navy Department established
- 1798-1800 Undeclared war with France
- 1801 John Marshall appointed Chief Justice

Thomas Jefferson
(1743-1826)

Years in Office 1801-1809
Vice Presidents Aaron Burr 1801-1805; George Clinton 1805-1809
Home State Virginia
Occupation Lawyer
First Lady (none)
Religion No specific denomination

New States
Ohio 1803

Major Events
- 1802 West Point military academy opens
- 1803 Louisiana Purchase
- 1804-1806 Lewis and Clark expedition
- 1807 Trial run of steamboat *Clermont*
- 1808 Importing slaves into U.S. ends

James Madison
(1751-1836)

Years in Office 1809-1817
Vice Presidents George Clinton 1809-1812, died; Elbridge Gerry 1813-1814, died
Home State Virginia
Occupation Lawyer
First Lady Dolley Payne Madison
Religion Episcopalian

New States
Louisiana 1812; Indiana 1816

Major Events
- 1811 Construction of National Road begins
- 1812-1814 War of 1812
- 1814 "Star-Spangled Banner" written
- 1814 Building of new White House begins
- 1815 Battle of New Orleans
- 1816 (Second) Bank of the U.S. established

James Monroe
(1758-1831)

Years in Office 1817-1825
Vice President Daniel D. Tompkins
Home State Virginia
Occupation Lawyer, soldier
First Lady Elizabeth Kortright Monroe
Religion Episcopalian

New States
Mississippi 1817; Illinois 1818; Alabama 1819; Maine 1820; Missouri 1821

Major Events
- 1817 American Colonization Society founded
- 1817-1818 First Seminole War
- 1819 Washington Irving's "Rip Van Winkle" and "The Legend of Sleepy Hollow"
- 1819 Adams-Onís Treaty with Spain gives Florida to U.S.
- 1820 Missouri Compromise
- 1823 Monroe Doctrine

John Quincy Adams
(1767-1848)

Years in Office 1825-1829
Vice President John C. Calhoun
Home State Massachusetts
Occupation Lawyer
First Lady Louisa Johnson Adams
Religion Unitarian

Major Events
- 1825 Erie Canal completed
- 1826 First railway steam locomotive
- 1827 *Freedom's Journal,* first African American newspaper published
- 1828 Congress passes the "tariff of abominations"
- 1828 Noah Webster publishes dictionary

Andrew Jackson
(1767-1845)

Years in Office 1829-1837
Vice Presidents John C. Calhoun 1829-1832, resigned; Martin Van Buren 1833-1837
Home State Tennessee
Occupation Lawyer

First Lady (none)
Religion Presbyterian

New States
Arkansas 1836; Michigan 1837

Major Events
- 1829 First commercial railroad, the Baltimore & Ohio
- 1832 Black Hawk War
- 1832-1833 Nullification crisis
- 1835-1842 Second Seminole War
- 1836 Texas Revolution against Mexico
- 1836 Jackson issues *Species Circular*
- 1837 Panic of 1837

Martin Van Buren
(1782-1862)

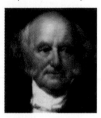

Years in Office 1837-1841
Vice President Richard M. Johnson
Home State New York
Occupation Lawyer
First Lady (none)
Religion Dutch Reformed

Major Events
- 1837 Methodists found Oberlin College, first U.S. coed college
- 1837 Horace Mann establishes U.S. Board of Education
- 1837 Samuel F.B. Morse files for telegraph patent
- 1838-1839 Trail of Tears
- 1839 Aroostock War
- 1839 Abner Doubleday lays out first baseball diamond

William Henry Harrison
(1773-1841)

Years in Office 1841-1841 (one month; died in office)
Vice President John Tyler
Home State Ohio
Occupation Military leader
First Lady Anna Symmes Harrison
Religion Episcopalian

Major Events
- 1841 10-hour work day established for federal workers
- 1841 Horace Greeley founds the New York *Tribune*
- 1841 Harrison becomes first President to die in office

John Tyler
(1790-1862)

Years in Office 1841-1845
Vice President (none)
Home State Virginia
Occupation Lawyer
First Ladies Letitia Christian Tyler, died 1842; Julia Gardiner Tyler
Religion Episcopalian

New States
Florida 1845

Major Events
- 1842 Webster-Ashburton Treaty
- 1844 Charles Goodyear, Sr., patents rubber-hardening process

Time Line of Our PRESIDENTS

James K. Polk
(1795-1849)

Years in Office 1845-1849
Vice President George M. Dallas
Home State Tennessee
Occupation Lawyer
First Lady Sarah Childress Polk
Religion Presbyterian

New States
Texas 1845; Iowa 1846; Wisconsin 1848

Major Events
- 1846 Ether used as anesthetic
- 1846 Smithsonian Institution founded
- 1846-1847 War with Mexico
- 1848 Treaty of Guadalupe Hidalgo
- 1848 Stephen Foster writes "Oh, Susanna"
- 1848 Gold discovered in California
- 1848 First women's rights convention held in Seneca Falls, NY

Zachary Taylor
(1784-1850)

Years in Office 1849-1850 (died in office)
Vice President Millard Fillmore
Home State Kentucky
Occupation Planter, military leader
First Lady Margaret Smith Taylor
Religion Episcopalian

Major Events
- 1849 California Gold Rush
- 1849 Interior Department established
- 1850 Compromise of 1850 proposed by Henry Clay

Millard Fillmore
(1800-1874)

Years in Office 1850-1853
Vice President (none)
Home State New York
Occupation Lawyer
First Lady Abigail Powers Fillmore
Religion Unitarian

New States
California 1850

Major Events
- 1850 Compromise of 1850, included the Fugitive Slave Law
- 1851 First U.S. chapter of the YMCA opens
- 1852 *Uncle Tom's Cabin* published
- 1852 Commodore Perry sent to open trade with Japan

Franklin Pierce
(1804-1869)

Years in Office 1853-1857
Vice President William R. King, died 1853
Home State New Hampshire
Occupation Lawyer
First Lady Jane Appleton Pierce
Religion Episcopalian

Major Events
- 1853 Gadsden Purchase
- 1854 Kansas-Nebraska Act
- 1854 Henry David Thoreau's *Walden*
- 1855 Walt Whitman's *Leaves of Grass*

James Buchanan
(1791-1868)

Years in Office 1857-1861
Vice President John C. Breckinridge
Home State Pennsylvania
Occupation Lawyer
First Lady (none)
Religion Presbyterian

New States
Minnesota 1858; Oregon 1859; Kansas 1861

Major Events
- 1857 First amateur baseball clubs formed
- 1857 Dred Scott Decision
- 1859 John Brown's raid at Harpers Ferry, Virginia
- 1860 South Carolina secedes
- 1861 Confederate States of America formed

Abraham Lincoln
(1809-1865)

Years in Office 1861-1865 (assassinated)
Vice Presidents Hannibal Hamlin 1861-1865; Andrew Johnson 1865
Home State Illinois
Occupation Lawyer
First Lady Mary Todd Lincoln
Religion No specific denomination

New States
West Virginia 1863; Nevada 1864

Major Events
- 1861 Civil War begins
- 1862 Homestead, Pacific Railroad, and Land-Grant acts passed

- 1862 Julia Ward Howe's "The Battle Hymn of the Republic" published
- 1863 Henry Wadsworth Longfellow publishes "Paul Revere's Ride"
- 1863 Emancipation Proclamation
- 1865 Civil War ends

Andrew Johnson
(1808-1875)

Years in Office 1865-1869
Vice President (none)
Home State Tennessee
Occupation Lawyer
First Lady Eliza McCardle Johnson
Religion No specific denomination

New States
Nebraska 1867

Major Events
- 1867 University of Illinois, one of first land-grant colleges, founded
- 1867 U.S. buys Alaska from Russia
- 1868 Johnson impeached; found not guilty
- 1869 John Wesley Powell explores Grand Canyon

Ulysses S. Grant
(1822-1885)

Years in Office 1869-1877
Vice Presidents Schuyler Colfax 1869-1873; Henry Wilson 1873-1875, died
Home State Illinois
Occupation Farmer, military leader
First Lady Julia Dent Grant
Religion Methodist

New States
Colorado 1876

Major Events
- 1869 Transcontinental railroad is completed
- 1871 Great Chicago Fire
- 1872 Yellowstone is made first national park
- 1876 Bell invents telephone
- 1876 Battle of the Little Bighorn

Rutherford B. Hayes
(1822-1893)

Years in Office 1877-1881
Vice President William A. Wheeler
Home State Ohio
Occupation Lawyer, soldier
First Lady Lucy Webb Hayes
Religion Methodist

Major Events
- 1877 Reconstruction ends
- 1877 Chief Joseph surrenders after Nez Percé War
- 1879 Edison invents light bulb
- 1879 First inter-city telephone communications
- 1880 U. S. branch of Salvation Army formed

James A. Garfield
(1831-1881)

Years in Office 1881-1881 (assassinated)
Vice President Chester A. Arthur
Home State Ohio
Occupation Teacher, soldier
First Lady Lucretia Rudolph Garfield
Religion Disciples of Christ

Major Events
- 1881 Barton founds the American Red Cross
- 1881 Shootout at the OK Corral in Tombstone, AZ

Chester A. Arthur
(1829-1886)

Years in Office 1881-1885
Vice President (none)
Home State New York
Occupation Lawyer, teacher
First Lady (none)
Religion Episcopalian

Major Events
- 1881 Tuskegee Institute established by Booker T. Washington
- 1883 Brooklyn Bridge opens
- 1884 Statue of Liberty cornerstone laid
- 1884 First skycraper built, in Chicago

Grover Cleveland
(1837-1908)

Years in Office 1885-1889, 1893-1897
Vice Presidents Thomas A. Hendricks, died 1885; Adlai E. Stevenson 1893-1897
Home State New York
Occupation Lawyer
First Lady Frances Folsom Cleveland
Religion Presbyterian

New States
Utah 1896

Major Events
- 1887 Interstate Commerce Act
- 1888 First *National Geographic* magazine published
- 1891 Sears & Roebuck Company founded
- 1894 Labor Day holiday established

Benjamin Harrison
(1833-1901)

Years in Office 1889-1893
Vice President Levi P. Morton
Home State Indiana
Occupation Lawyer
First Lady Caroline Scott Harrison
Religion Presbyterian

New States
Washington, Montana, North Dakota, South Dakota 1889; Wyoming, Idaho 1890

Major Events
- 1889 Jane Addams starts Hull House
- 1889 Johnstown, PA Flood
- 1890 Sherman Anti-Trust Act limits monopolies
- 1891 James Naismith invents basketball
- 1892 Ellis Island begins accepting immigrants
- 1893 First gasoline-powered automobile

William McKinley
(1843-1901)

Years in Office 1897-1901 (assassinated)
Vice Presidents Garret A. Hobart 1897-1899, died; Theodore Roosevelt 1901
Home State Ohio
Occupation Lawyer, teacher

First Lady Ida Saxton McKinley
Religion Methodist

Major Events
- 1898 Spanish-American War
- 1898 U.S. gains Puerto Rico, Guam, and the Philippines
- 1900 U.S. troops enter China to fight in the Boxer Rebellion

Theodore Roosevelt
(1858-1919)

Years in Office 1901-1909
Vice President Charles W. Fairbanks (1905-1909)
Home State New York
Occupation Law enforcement, military leader
First Lady Edith Carow Roosevelt
Religion Dutch Reformed

New States
Oklahoma 1907

Major Events
- 1903 First national wildlife refuge established, in Florida
- 1903 Wright brothers make first successful plane flight
- 1903 U.S. acquires Panama Canal Zone
- 1905 National Audubon Society formed
- 1906 Sinclair's *The Jungle* published
- 1906 San Francisco earthquake

William Howard Taft
(1857-1930)

Years in Office 1909-1913
Vice President James S. Sherman 1909-1912, died
Home State Ohio
Occupation Lawyer
First Lady Helen Herron Taft
Religion Unitarian

New States
New Mexico, Arizona 1912

Major Events
- 1909 Ford produces Model T
- 1909 NAACP founded
- 1909 Robert Edwin Peary's expedition reaches North Pole
- 1910 Boy Scouts founded
- 1911 First transcontinental airplane flight
- 1912 First state minimum wage law
- 1912 Girl Scouts founded
- 1912 *Titanic* sinks

Woodrow Wilson
(1856-1924)

Years in Office 1913-1921
Vice President Thomas R. Marshall
Home State New Jersey
Occupation University professor and president
First Ladies Ellen Louise Axson Wilson, died 1914; Edith Bolling Galt Wilson
Religion Presbyterian

Major Events
- 1913 Congress passes income tax law

- 1913 Federal Reserve Bank established
- 1914 Panama Canal opens
- 1915 New York and San Francisco linked by telephone
- 1915 Sinking of the *Lusitania*
- 1917-1918 U.S. in World War I
- 1919-1933 Prohibition
- 1920 Nineteenth Amendment ratified, giving women the right to vote

Warren G. Harding
(1865-1923)

Years in Office 1921-1923 (died in office)
Vice President Calvin Coolidge
Home State Ohio
Occupation Journalist, publisher
First Lady Florence King DeWolfe Harding
Religion Baptist

Major Events
- 1921 Washington Conference limits weapons
- 1921 Einstein visits New York to discuss Theory of Relativity
- 1922 Teapot Dome Scandal begins
- 1922 Lincoln Memorial dedicated

Calvin Coolidge
(1872-1933)

Years in Office 1923-1929
Vice President Charles G. Dawes (1925-1929)
Home State Massachusetts
Occupation Lawyer
First Lady Grace Goodhue Coolidge
Religion Congregationalist

Major Events
- 1924 All Native Americans made citizens

- 1924 Immigration from Europe limited
- 1926 First artifacts of prehistoric life in New Mexico found
- 1927 First talking movie shown in theaters
- 1927 Lindbergh flies solo across the Atlantic Ocean

Herbert Hoover
(1874-1964)

Years in Office 1929-1933
Vice President Charles Curtis
Home State California
Occupation Engineer, businessman
First Lady Lou Henry Hoover
Religion Quaker

Major Events
- 1929 Stock market crashes; Great Depression begins
- 1930 U.S. astronomers discover Pluto
- 1931 "Star-Spangled Banner" made national anthem
- 1932 Reconstruction Finance Corporation established
- 1932 Earhart becomes first woman pilot to cross Atlantic

Franklin D. Roosevelt
(1882-1945)

Years in Office 1933-1945 (died in office)
Vice Presidents John Nance Garner 1933-1941; Henry Wallace 1941-1945; Harry S. Truman 1945
Home State New York
Occupation Lawyer
First Lady Anna Eleanor Roosevelt
Religion Episcopalian

Major Events
- 1933 New Deal begins

- 1934 Drought creates Dust Bowl
- 1937 Golden Gate Bridge opens
- 1939 Marian Anderson sings at Lincoln Memorial
- 1939 John Steinbeck's *The Grapes of Wrath* published
- 1939 The film *Gone With the Wind* opens
- 1941 "Four Freedoms" speech
- 1941 Japanese Attack Pearl Harbor
- 1941-1945 U.S. in World War II

Harry S. Truman
(1884-1972)

Years in Office 1945-1953
Vice President Alben W. Barkley (1949-1953)
Home State Missouri
Occupation Farmer, businessman, judge
First Lady Elizabeth (Bess) Wallace Truman
Religion Baptist

Major Events
- 1945 United Nations formed
- 1945 Commercial television broadcasting begins
- 1947 Jackie Robinson begins playing for Brooklyn Dodgers
- 1950 U.S. enters Korean War
- 1952 U.S. tests hydrogen bomb
- 1952 Puerto Rico becomes U.S. commonwealth

Dwight D. Eisenhower
(1890-1969)

Years in Office 1953-1961
Vice President Richard M. Nixon
Home State New York
Occupation Military leader
First Lady Marie (Mamie) Doud Eisenhower
Religion Presbyterian

New States
Alaska, Hawaii 1959

Major Events
- 1954 Supreme Court rules against school segregation
- 1954 Jonas Salk develops polio vaccine
- 1955-1956 Montgomery bus boycott
- 1956 Building of interstate highway system begins
- 1957 First nuclear power plant opens, in Shippingport, PA

John F. Kennedy
(1917-1963)

Years in Office 1961-1963 (assassinated)
Vice President Lyndon B. Johnson
Home State Massachusetts
Occupation Legislator
First Lady Jacqueline Bouvier Kennedy
Religion Roman Catholic

Major Events
- 1961 Peace Corps established
- 1961 Alan B. Shepherd, Jr., becomes the first American in outer space
- 1962 Cuban Missile Crisis

- 1962 National Farm Workers Association founded
- 1962 Rachel Carson publishes *Silent Spring*
- 1963 March on Washington for civil rights

Lyndon Baines Johnson
(1908-1973)

Years in Office 1963-1969
Vice President Hubert H. Humphrey
Home State Texas
Occupation Teacher, legislator
First Lady Claudia (Lady Bird) Taylor Johnson
Religion Disciples of Christ

Major Events
- 1964 Johnson's War on Poverty begins
- 1964 Civil Rights Act
- 1965 Voting Rights Act
- 1968 Tet Offensive signals turning point in Vietnam War
- 1968 César Chávez protests for migrant workers' rights with his first hunger strike

Richard M. Nixon
(1913-1994)

Years in Office 1969-1974 (resigned)
Vice Presidents Spiro T. Agnew 1969-1973, resigned; Gerald R. Ford 1973-1974
Home State New York
Occupation Lawyer
First Lady Thelma (Pat) Ryan Nixon
Religion Quaker

Major Events
- 1969 U.S. lands first astronauts on the moon
- 1972 Nixon visits communist China
- 1972-1974 Watergate Scandal
- 1973 U.S. troops leave Vietnam

Gerald R. Ford
(1913-)

Years in Office 1974-1977
Vice President Nelson A. Rockefeller
Home State Michigan
Occupation Lawyer
First Lady Elizabeth (Betty) Bloomer Ford
Religion Episcopalian

Major Events
- 1974 Ford pardons Nixon for Watergate acts
- 1975 *Apollo-Soyuz* joint U.S.-USSR space mission
- 1975 *Viking* sends first close-up photographs of Mars
- 1976 U.S. celebrates Bicentennial

James Earl Carter
(1924-)

Years in Office 1977-1981
Vice President Walter F. Mondale
Home State Georgia
Occupation Farmer, businessman, navy officer
First Lady Rosalynn Smith Carter
Religion Baptist

Major Events
- 1977 U.S. signs treaty to give Panama Canal Zone to Panama in 2000

- 1979 Carter negotiates peace treaty between Egypt and Israel
- 1979-1981 American hostages held in Iran

Ronald W. Reagan
(1911-   )

Years in Office 1981-1989
Vice President George Bush
Home State California
Occupation Radio announcer, actor, labor union official
First Lady Nancy Davis Reagan
Religion Presbyterian

Major Events

- 1981 Reagan survives assassination attempt
- 1981 Sandra Day O'Connor becomes first woman Supreme Court justice
- 1981 Henry Cisneros becomes first Latino mayor of a major city, San Antonio, TX
- 1982 Vietnam War Memorial, designed by Maya Lin, unveiled
- 1983 U.S. troops invade Grenada
- 1986 Space Shuttle *Challenger* explodes
- 1986-1988 Iran-Contra affair
- 1988-1989 U.S. and USSR sign treaty to reduce nuclear weapons

George Bush
(1924-   )

Years in Office 1989-1993
Vice President J. Danforth (Dan) Quayle
Home State Texas
Occupation Businessman
First Lady Barbara Pierce Bush
Religion Episcopalian

Major Events

- 1989 U.S. troops invade Panama
- 1989 L. Douglas Wilder becomes first African American govenor
- 1991 Persian Gulf War
- 1989-1992 Cold War ends
- 1992 NAFTA treaty
- 1992-1994 U.S. troops lead U.N. sponsored peace-keeping force in Somalia

William Jefferson Clinton
(1946-   )

Years in Office 1993-
Vice President Albert Gore, Jr.
Home State Arkansas
Occupation Law professor, attorney
First Lady Hillary Rodham Clinton
Religion Baptist

Major Events

- 1994 U.S. troops restore democratically elected government in Haiti
- 1995 U.S. troops take part in peacekeeping mission in Bosnia
- 1995 A bomb explodes in a federal building in Oklahoma City, Oklahoma, killing 162 people
- 1996 Astronaut Shannon Lucid ended a 188-day stay in space — longer than any other woman
- 1997 Sojourner space craft lands on Mars
- 1998 Clinton becomes the first elected U.S. President to be impeached by the House of Representatives

Sources: *New Columbia Encyclopedia, 1975; The Complete Book of U.S. Presidents, 1993; World Almanac, 1995.*

OUR FIFTY STATES

ALABAMA
★ Montgomery

DATE OF STATEHOOD 1819

NICKNAME Heart of Dixie

POPULATION 4,273,084

AREA 52,423 sq mi;
135,776 sq km

REGION Southeast

CONNECTICUT
★ Hartford

DATE OF STATEHOOD 1788

NICKNAME Constitution State

POPULATION 3,274,238

AREA 5,544 sq mi;
14,359 sq km

REGION Northeast

ALASKA
★ Juneau

DATE OF STATEHOOD 1959

NICKNAME The Last Frontier

POPULATION 607,007

AREA 656,424 sq mi;
1,700,138 sq km

REGION West

DELAWARE
★ Dover

DATE OF STATEHOOD 1787

NICKNAME First State

POPULATION 724,842

AREA 2,489 sq mi;
6,447 sq km

REGION Northeast

DECEMBER 7, 1787

ARIZONA
★ Phoenix

DATE OF STATEHOOD 1912

NICKNAME Grand Canyon State

POPULATION 4,428,068

AREA 114,006 sq mi;
295,276 sq km

REGION Southwest

FLORIDA
★ Tallahassee

DATE OF STATEHOOD 1845

NICKNAME Sunshine State

POPULATION 14,399,985

AREA 65,758 sq mi;
170,313 sq km

REGION Southeast

ARKANSAS
★ Little Rock

DATE OF STATEHOOD 1836

NICKNAME Land of Opportunity

POPULATION 2,509,793

AREA 53,182 sq mi;
137,741 sq km

REGION Southeast

ARKANSAS

GEORGIA
★ Atlanta

DATE OF STATEHOOD 1788

NICKNAME Peach State

POPULATION 7,353,225

AREA 59,441 sq mi;
153,952 sq km

REGION Southeast

CALIFORNIA
★ Sacramento

DATE OF STATEHOOD 1850

NICKNAME Golden State

POPULATION 31,878,234

AREA 163,707 sq mi;
424,001 sq km

REGION West

CALIFORNIA REPUBLIC

HAWAII
★ Honolulu

DATE OF STATEHOOD 1959

NICKNAME The Aloha State

POPULATION 1,183,723

AREA 10,932 sq mi;
28,314 sq km

REGION West

COLORADO
Denver ★

DATE OF STATEHOOD 1876

NICKNAME Centennial State

POPULATION 3,822,676

AREA 104,100 sq mi;
269,619 sq km

REGION West

IDAHO
★ Boise

DATE OF STATEHOOD 1890

NICKNAME Gem State

POPULATION 1,189,251

AREA 83,574 sq mi;
216,457 sq km

REGION West

ILLINOIS
★
Springfield

DATE OF STATEHOOD 1818

NICKNAME **The Prairie State**

POPULATION **11,846,544**

AREA **57,918 sq mi; 150,008 sq km**

REGION **Middle West**

MAINE
Augusta
★

DATE OF STATEHOOD 1820

NICKNAME **Pine Tree State**

POPULATION **1,243,316**

AREA **35,387 sq mi; 91,652 sq km**

REGION **Northeast**

INDIANA
★
Indianapolis

DATE OF STATEHOOD 1816

NICKNAME **Hoosier State**

POPULATION **5,840,528**

AREA **36,420 sq mi; 94,328 sq km**

REGION **Middle West**

MARYLAND
Annapolis ★

DATE OF STATEHOOD 1788

NICKNAME **Free State**

POPULATION **5,071,604**

AREA **12,407 sq mi; 32,134 sq km**

REGION **Northeast**

IOWA
★
Des Moines

DATE OF STATEHOOD 1846

NICKNAME **Hawkeye State**

POPULATION **2,851,792**

AREA **56,276 sq mi; 145,755 sq km**

REGION **Middle West**

Boston ★

MASSACHUSETTS

DATE OF STATEHOOD 1788

NICKNAME **Bay State**

POPULATION **6,092,352**

AREA **10,555 sq mi; 27,337 sq km**

REGION **Northeast**

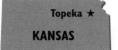

Topeka ★

KANSAS

DATE OF STATEHOOD 1861

NICKNAME **Sunflower State**

POPULATION **2,572,150**

AREA **82,282 sq mi; 213,110 sq km**

REGION **Middle West**

MICHIGAN

★
Lansing

DATE OF STATEHOOD 1837

NICKNAME **Wolverine State**

POPULATION **9,594,350**

AREA **96,810 sq mi; 250,738 sq km**

REGION **Middle West**

KENTUCKY

★
Frankfort

DATE OF STATEHOOD 1792

NICKNAME **Bluegrass State**

POPULATION **3,883,723**

AREA **40,411 sq mi; 104,664 sq km**

REGION **Southeast**

MINNESOTA

St. Paul ★

DATE OF STATEHOOD 1858

NICKNAME **North Star State**

POPULATION **4,657,758**

AREA **86,943 sq mi; 225,182 sq km**

REGION **Middle West**

LOUISIANA

Baton Rouge ★

DATE OF STATEHOOD 1812

NICKNAME **Pelican State**

POPULATION **4,350,579**

AREA **51,843 sq mi; 134,273 sq km**

REGION **Southeast**

MISSISSIPPI

★
Jackson

DATE OF STATEHOOD 1817

NICKNAME **Magnolia State**

POPULATION **2,716,115**

AREA **48,434 sq mi; 125,444 sq km**

REGION **Southeast**

OUR FIFTY STATES

MISSOURI
★ Jefferson City

DATE OF STATEHOOD 1821

NICKNAME Show Me State

POPULATION 5,358,692

AREA 69,709 sq mi;
180,546 sq km

REGION Middle West

MONTANA
★ Helena

DATE OF STATEHOOD 1889

NICKNAME Treasure State

POPULATION 879,372

AREA 147,046 sq mi;
380,849 sq km

REGION West

NEBRASKA
Lincoln ★

DATE OF STATEHOOD 1867

NICKNAME Cornhusker State

POPULATION 1,652,093

AREA 77,358 sq mi;
200,357 sq km

REGION Middle West

NEVADA
★ Carson City

DATE OF STATEHOOD 1864

NICKNAME Silver State

POPULATION 1,603,163

AREA 110,567 sq mi;
286,369 sq km

REGION West

NEW HAMPSHIRE
Concord ★

DATE OF STATEHOOD 1788

NICKNAME Granite State

POPULATION 1,162,481

AREA 9,351 sq mi;
24,219 sq km

REGION Northeast

NEW JERSEY
★ Trenton

DATE OF STATEHOOD 1787

NICKNAME Garden State

POPULATION 7,987,933

AREA 8,722 sq mi;
22,590 sq km

REGION Northeast

NEW MEXICO
★ Santa Fe

DATE OF STATEHOOD 1912

NICKNAME Land of Enchantment

POPULATION 1,713,407

AREA 121,598 sq mi;
314,939 sq km

REGION Southwest

NEW YORK
Albany ★

DATE OF STATEHOOD 1788

NICKNAME Empire State

POPULATION 18,184,774

AREA 54,475 sq mi;
141,090 sq km

REGION Northeast

NORTH CAROLINA
Raleigh ★

DATE OF STATEHOOD 1789

NICKNAME Tar Heel State

POPULATION 7,322,870

AREA 53,821 sq mi;
139,396 sq km

REGION Southeast

NORTH DAKOTA
Bismarck ★

DATE OF STATEHOOD 1889

NICKNAME Peace Garden State

POPULATION 643,539

AREA 70,704 sq mi;
183,123 sq km

REGION Middle West

OHIO
★ Columbus

DATE OF STATEHOOD 1803

NICKNAME Buckeye State

POPULATION 11,172,782

AREA 44,828 sq mi;
116,105 sq km

REGION Middle West

OKLAHOMA
★ Oklahoma City

DATE OF STATEHOOD 1907

NICKNAME Sooner State

POPULATION 3,300,902

AREA 69,903 sq mi;
181,049 sq km

REGION Southwest

OREGON
★ Salem

DATE OF STATEHOOD 1859

NICKNAME Beaver State

POPULATION 3,203,735

AREA 98,386 sq mi;
254,820 sq km

REGION West

PENNSYLVANIA

Harrisburg ★

DATE OF STATEHOOD 1787

NICKNAME Keystone State

POPULATION 12,056,112

AREA 46,058 sq mi;
119,290 sq km

REGION Northeast

VERMONT

★
Montpelier

DATE OF STATEHOOD 1791

NICKNAME Green Mountain State

POPULATION 588,654

AREA 9,615 sq mi;
24,903 sq km

REGION Northeast

RHODE ISLAND

Providence ★

DATE OF STATEHOOD 1790

NICKNAME Ocean State

POPULATION 990,226

AREA 1,545 sq mi;
4,002 sq km

REGION Northeast

VIRGINIA

Richmond ★

DATE OF STATEHOOD 1788

NICKNAME Old Dominion

POPULATION 6,675,451

AREA 42,769 sq mi;
110,772 sq km

REGION Southeast

SOUTH CAROLINA
★
Columbia

DATE OF STATEHOOD 1788

NICKNAME Palmetto State

POPULATION 3,698,746

AREA 32,007 sq mi;
82,898 sq km

REGION Southeast

★ Olympia
WASHINGTON

DATE OF STATEHOOD 1889

NICKNAME Evergreen State

POPULATION 5,532,939

AREA 71,303 sq mi;
184,675 sq km

REGION West

Pierre ★
SOUTH DAKOTA

DATE OF STATEHOOD 1889

NICKNAME Mount Rushmore State

POPULATION 732,405

AREA 77,121 sq mi;
199,743 sq km

REGION Middle West

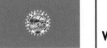

WEST VIRGINIA

★ Charleston

DATE OF STATEHOOD 1863

NICKNAME Mountain State

POPULATION 1,825,754

AREA 24,231 sq mi;
62,758 sq km

REGION Southeast

TENNESSEE

★ Nashville

DATE OF STATEHOOD 1796

NICKNAME Volunteer State

POPULATION 5,319,654

AREA 42,146 sq mi;
109,158 sq km

REGION Southeast

WISCONSIN

Madison
★

DATE OF STATEHOOD 1848

NICKNAME Badger State

POPULATION 5,159,795

AREA 65,503 sq mi;
169,653 sq km

REGION Middle West

TEXAS

Austin ★

DATE OF STATEHOOD 1845

NICKNAME Lone Star State

POPULATION 19,128,261

AREA 268,601 sq mi;
695,677 sq km

REGION Southwest

Salt Lake City ★

UTAH

DATE OF STATEHOOD 1896

NICKNAME Beehive State

POPULATION 2,000,494

AREA 84,904 sq mi;
219,901 sq km

REGION West

WYOMING

Cheyenne
★

DATE OF STATEHOOD 1890

NICKNAME Equality State

POPULATION 481,400

AREA 97,818 sq mi;
253,349 sq km

REGION West

Sources: population—U.S. Bureau of Census; area—U.S. Bureau of Census, 1991; capital—*World Almanac*, 1995.

Dictionary of GEOGRAPHIC TERMS

STRAIT (strāt) A narrow waterway that connects two larger bodies of water.

GULF (gulf) Part of an ocean that extends into the land; larger than a bay.

PLATEAU (pla tō′) An area of elevated flat land.

DAM (dam) A wall built across a river, creating a lake that stores water.

RESERVOIR (rez′ər vwär) A natural or artificial lake used to store water.

CANYON (kan′yən) A deep, narrow valley with steep sides.

MESA (mā′sə) A hill with a flat top; smaller than a plateau.

DUNE (dün) A mound, hill, or ridge of sand heaped up by the wind.

HILL (hil) A rounded, raised landform; not as high as a mountain.

BUTTE (būt) A small, flat-topped hill; smaller than a mesa or plateau.

VALLEY (val′ē) An area of low land between hills or mountains.

COAST (kōst) The land along an ocean.

DESERT (dez′ərt) A dry environment with few plants and animals.

BAY (bā) Part of an ocean or lake that extends deeply into the land.

ISTHMUS (is′məs) A narrow strip of land that connects two larger bodies of land.

ISLAND (ī′lənd) A body of land completely surrounded by water.

PENINSULA (pə nin′sə lə) A body of land nearly surrounded by water.

VOLCANO (vol kā′nō) An opening in Earth's surface through which hot rock and ash are forced out.

MOUNTAIN (moun′tən) A high landform with steep sides; higher than a hill.

PEAK (pēk) The top of a mountain.

GLACIER (glā′shər) A huge sheet of ice that moves slowly across the land.

HARBOR (här′bər) A sheltered place along a coast where boats dock safely.

CANAL (kə nal′) A channel built to carry water for irrigation or navigation.

LAKE (lāk) A body of water completely surrounded by land.

TRIBUTARY (trib′yə ter ē) A smaller river that flows into a larger river.

PORT (pôrt) A place where ships load and unload their goods.

SOURCE (sôrs) The starting point of a river.

TIMBERLINE (tim′bər lin) A line beyond which trees do not grow.

RIVER BASIN (riv′ər bā′sin) All the land that is drained by a river and its tributaries.

WATERFALL (wô′tər fôl) A flow of water falling vertically.

MOUNTAIN RANGE (moun′tən rānj) A row or chain of mountains.

PLAIN (plān) A large area of nearly flat land.

RIVER (riv′ər) A stream of water that flows across the land and empties into another body of water.

BASIN (bā′sin) A bowl-shaped landform surrounded by higher land.

DELTA (del′tə) Land made of silt left behind as a river drains into a larger body of water.

MOUNTAIN PASS (moun′tən pas) A narrow gap through a mountain range.

MOUTH (mouth) The place where a river empties into a larger body of water.

OCEAN (ō′shən) A large body of salt water; oceans cover much of Earth's surface.

R59

Gazetteer

This Gazetteer is a geographical dictionary that will help you to pronounce and locate the places discussed in this book. Latitude and longitude are given for cities and some other places. The page numbers tell you where each place appears on a map or in the text.

A

Abilene (ab'ə lēn) A city in central Kansas; in the 1860s, Abilene was the northern end of the Chisholm Trail; 39°N, 97°W. (m. 521, t. 520)

Africa (af'ri kə) One of Earth's seven continents. (m. 121, t. 120)

Alamo, The (al'ə mō) A mission in San Antonio, Texas, where Mexican troops defeated Texan defenders in 1836; 30°N, 98°W. (t. 419)

Alaska Range (ə las'kə rānj) A mountain range in southern Alaska. (m. R10)

Albany (ôl'bə nē) Capital of New York State; 43°N, 74°W. (m. 34)

Alberta (al bûr'tə) A province of Canada, in the southwestern part of the country. (m. 653)

Allegheny Mountains (al i gā'nē moun'tənz) A mountain range in Pennsylvania, Virginia, and West Virginia, part of the Appalachians. (m. R11)

Amazon River (am'ə zon riv'ər) The longest river in South America, flowing from the Andes Mountains to the Atlantic Ocean. (m. 665, t. 665)

Anchorage (ang'kər ij) A city in southern Alaska, the largest city in the state and an important port; 61°N, 150°W. (m. R10, t. 83)

Andes Mountains (an'dēz moun'tənz) A mountain range along the west coast of South America, the world's longest chain of mountains. (m. 665, t. 664)

Angel Island (ān'jəl i'lənd) An island in San Francisco Bay, California, which served as the west coast entry point for immigrants from the 1880s to the early 1920s; 38°N, 122°W. (t. 546)

Annapolis (ə nap'ə lis) Capital of Maryland and site of the U.S. Naval Academy; 39°N, 76°W. (m. 34)

Antarctic Circle (ant ärk'tik sûr'kəl) A line of latitiude at 66°33'S. (m. R14)

Antarctica (ant ärk'ti kə) One of Earth's seven continents. (m. G5, t. G4)

Antietam (an tē'təm) A creek near the town of Sharpsburg, Maryland, site of a major Civil War battle in 1862; 39°N, 78°W. (m. 491, t. 478)

Appalachian Mountains (ap ə lā'chē ən moun'tənz) Chain of mountains stretching from Canada to Alabama. (m. R11, t. 214)

Appomattox Court House (ap ə mat'əks kôrt hous) A town in central Virginia, where Confederate General Lee surrendered to Union General Grant in 1865, ending the Civil War; 37°N, 79°W. (m. 491, t. 492)

Arctic Circle (ärk'tik sûr'kəl) A line of latitude at 66°30'N. (m. R14)

Arctic Ocean (ärk'tik ō'shən) The smallest of Earth's four oceans. (m. G5, t. G4)

Argentina (är jən tē'nə) A country in southern South America. (m. 665, t. 664)

Asia (ā'zhə) The largest of Earth's seven continents. (m. R15, t. 114)

Atlanta (at lan'tə) Capital and largest city in the state of Georgia; 34°N, 84°W. (m. 33, t. 489)

Atlantic Ocean (at lan'tik ō'shən) One of Earth's four oceans. (m. R14, t. G4)

Augusta (ô gus'tə) Capital of Maine; 44°N, 70°W. (m. 34)

Austin (ôs'tin) Capital of Texas; 30°N, 98°W. (m. 31)

Australia (ôs trāl'yə) The smallest of Earth's seven continents. (m. G5, t. G4)

B

Bahama Islands (bə hä'mə i'ləndz) A chain of islands in the West Indies, southeast of Florida. (m. 139, t. 141)

Baja California (bä'hə kal ə fôr'nyə) A long, narrow peninsula that juts out from the northwest corner of Mexico. (m. 657)

Baltimore (bôl'tə môr) The largest city in Maryland and a port on Chesapeake Bay; 39°N, 77°W. (m. R9, t. 388)

Baton Rouge (bat'ən rüzh') Capital of Lousiana; 30°N, 91°W. (m. 33)

pronunciation key

a	at	ī	ice	u	up	th	thin
ā	ape	îr	pierce	ū	use	th	this
ä	far	o	hot	ü	rule	zh	measure
âr	care	ō	old	u̇	pull	ə	about, taken,
e	end	ô	fork	ûr	turn		pencil, lemon,
ē	me	oi	oil	hw	white		circus
i	it	ou	out	ng	song		

Belize (bā lēz′) A country on the northeastern coast of Central America, on the Caribbean Sea. (m. 661, t. 661)

Bering Strait (ber′ing strāt) A narrow waterway connecting the Bering Sea and the Arctic Ocean. (m. R10, t. 86)

Beringia (bə rin′jē ə) A sunken land bridge that once connected North America and Asia. The first people to come to North America may have used this route across what is now the Bering Strait; 62°N, 167°W. (t. 76)

Berlin (bər lin′) The capital of Germany, divided from 1945 to 1989; 53°N, 13°E. (m. 603, t. 603)

Berlin Wall (bər lin′ wôl) A wall that separated communist East Berlin and democratic West Berlin. It was torn down in 1989 as part of a democratic revolution. (t. 635)

Birmingham (bûr′ming ham) A city in north-central Alabama, the largest city in the state; 34°N, 87°W. (m. R9)

Bismark (biz′märk) Capital of North Dakota; 47°N, 101°W. (m. 32)

Black Hills (blak hilz) A mountain range in southwestern South Dakota and northeastern Wyoming. (m. R10, t. 98)

Boise (boi′sē) Capital and largest city of Idaho; 44°N, 116°W. (m. 30)

Bolivia (bə liv′ē ə) A country in west-central South America. (m. 665, t. 651)

Boonesborough (bünz′bər ə) A town in east-central Kentucky, now Boonesboro; site of fort founded in 1775 by Daniel Boone; 38°N, 84°W. (m. 376, t. 377)

Boston (bôs′tən) Capital and largest city of Massachusetts; 42°N, 71°W. (m. 34, t. 204)

Boswash (bôs′wôsh) Unofficial name given to the megalopolis of cities running south from Boston, Massachusetts, to Washington, D.C. (m. 34, t. 34)

Brasília (brə zēl′yə) The capital of Brazil; 16°S, 48°W. (m. 665, t. 651)

Brazil (bre zīl′) The largest country in South America, in the eastern part of the continent. (m. 665, t. 664)

British Columbia (brit′ish kə lum′bē ə) A province in southwestern Canada. (m. 653)

Brooks Range (brüks rānj) A mountain range extending across the northern part of Alaska. (m. R10)

Buenos Aires (bwā′nəs ī′rəs) The capital of Argentina; 35°S, 58°W. (m. 665, t. 651)

Bull Run (bùl run) A stream in northeastern Virginia near Washington, D.C.; site of two major Civil War battles in which the Union forces were defeated (1861 and 1862); 39°N, 77°W. (m. 491, t. 475)

C

Cahokia (kə hō′kē ə) A city founded around 1,300 years ago by moundbuilding peoples near the Mississippi River, in present-day Illinois; 38°N, 90°W. (m. 74, t. 73)

California Trail (kal ə fôr′nyə trāl) A trail through the Rocky Mountains and the Sierra Nevada mountains to the California gold fields used by "Forty-Niners" in 1849. (m. 431, t. 432)

Cambodia (kam bō′dē ə) A country in southeastern Asia. (m. 628, t. 629)

Canada (kan′ə də) A country in northern North America, bordering the United States. The second-largest country in the world, it is made up of ten provinces and two territories. (m. 6, t. 264)

Canadian Shield (kə nā′dē ən shēld) A low-lying plateau of ancient rocks that covers more than half of Canada. (m. 653, t. 653)

Cape Canaveral (kāp kə nav′ə rəl) The site of the Kennedy Space Center; main United States launching and testing center for missiles and spacecraft, on the Atlantic coast of Florida; 28°N, 81°W. (t. 639)

Cape Cod (kāp kod) A peninsula in southeastern Massachusetts, enclosing Cape Cod Bay. (m. 188, t. 187)

Cape Horn (kāp hôrn) The southernmost tip of South America. (m. 665)

Cape of Good Hope (kāp əv gùd hōp) The southernmost tip of Africa; 34°S, 18°E. (m. 126, t. 127)

Caribbean Sea (kar ə bē′ən sē) A part of the Atlantic Ocean, due east of Central America. (m. 661, t. 660)

Carson City (kär′sən sit′ē) Capital of Nevada; 39°N, 120°W. (m. 30)

Cascade Range (kas kād′ rānj) A mountain range extending from northern California through Oregon and Washington. (m. R10)

Catskill Mountains (kats′kil moun′tənz) A mountain range in New York State, part of the Appalachian Range. (m. 214)

Central America (sen′trəl ə mer′i kə) A region between the Pacific Ocean and the Caribbean Sea, occupying the southern part of the North American continent south of Mexico. (m. 661, t. 660)

Central Valley (sen′trəl val′ē) A valley lying between the Coast Ranges and the Sierra Nevada mountains in California. (m. R10)

Chapultepec (chə pul′tə pek) A rocky hill in Mexico City, Mexico, site of a fortress captured by United States forces in 1847 in the Mexican War; 19°N, 99°W. (t. 424)

Charleston (chärlz′tən) Capital and largest city in West Virginia; 38°N, 82°W (m. 33) and a coastal city in southeastern South Carolina, originally Charles Town; 33°N, 80°W. (m. 332, t. 243)

Charlestown (chärlz'taun) A town in Massachusetts across the Charles River from Boston; the Battle of Bunker Hill was fought near there in 1775; 42°N, 71°W. (m. 301, t. 304)

Chesapeake Bay (ches'ə pēk bā) A long arm of the Atlantic Ocean surrounded by Maryland and Virginia. (m. 179, t. 178)

Cheyenne (shī en') Capital of Wyoming; 41°N, 105°W. (m. 30)

Chicago (shi kä'gō) A city in northeastern Illinois, the largest city in the state, a transportation and manufacturing center; 42°N, 88°W. (m. R9, t. 267)

Chile (chil'ē) A country in southwestern South America. (m. 665, t. 665)

China (chī'nə) A country in eastern Asia, the most populous in the world. (m. 116, t. 114)

Chisholm Trail (chiz'əm trāl) A cattle trail from San Antonio, Texas, to Abilene, Kansas, in use from 1867 to 1886. (m. 521, t. 520)

Coast Ranges (kōst rānj'əz) The mountain ranges along the Pacific Coast of North America. (m. R10)

Colorado River (kol ə rad'ō riv'ər) A river in the southwestern United States, flowing from Colorado to the Gulf of California. (m. R10)

Columbia (kə lum'bē ə) Capital and largest city in South Carolina; 34°N, 81°W. (m. 33)

Columbia River (kə lum'bē ə riv'ər) A river in northwestern North America which begins in Canada and flows between Oregon and Washington into the Pacific Ocean. (m. G10, t. 382)

Columbus (kə lum'bəs) Capital of Ohio; 40°N, 83°W. (m. 32)

Concord (kon'kōrd) Capital of New Hampshire; 43°N, 72°W. (m. 34)

Concord (kong'kərd) A town in eastern Massachusetts, site of one of the first battles of the American Revolution; 42°N, 71°W. (m. 301, t. 301)

Continental Divide (kon'tə nen'təl di vīd') An elevation of land that runs along the tops of the Rocky Mountains. Rivers to the west drain into the Pacific Ocean and rivers to the east drain into the Atlantic Ocean or Gulf of Mexico. (m. 30, t. 30)

Corn Belt (kôrn belt) An area of the Middle West well-suited to growing corn. (m. 32, t. 32)

Costa Rica (kos'tə rē'kə) A country in southern Central America. (m. 661, t. 650)

Cuba (kū'bə) An island country in the Caribbean Sea, the largest and westernmost of the West Indies. (m. 661, t. 556)

Cumberland Gap (kum'bər lənd gap) A natural pass through the Cumberland Mountains, of Kentucky. 37°N, 84°W. (m. 376, t. 377)

D

Dallas (dal'əs) A city in northeastern Texas; 33°N, 97°W. (m. R9, t. 625)

Death Valley (deth val'ē) The lowest point in the Western Hemisphere, part of the Mojave Desert in California; 37°N, 117°W. (m. R10)

Denver (den'vər) Capital and largest city in Colorado; 40°N, 105°W. (m. 30)

Des Moines (də moin') Capital and largest city in Iowa. 42°N, 84°W; (m. 32)

Detroit (di troit') A city in southeastern Michigan, the largest city in the state, an important manufacturing center; 42°N, 83°W. (m. R9, t. 267)

District of Columbia (dis'trikt uv kə lum'bē ə) Area encompassing the capital of the United States; 39°N, 77°W. (m. R9, t. 378)

Dodge City (däj sit'ē) A city in southwestern Kansas. In the 1870s and 1880s, Dodge City was a railhead at the end of a major cattle trail; 38°N, 100°W. (m. 521, t. 520)

Dominican Republic (də min'i kən ri pub'lik) A country in the West Indies, occupying the eastern part of the island of Hispaniola. (m. 661, t. 650)

Dover (dō'vər) Capital of Delaware; 39°N, 76°W. (m. 34)

Dust Bowl (dust bōl) A 150,000-square-mile area of the Great Plains that suffered years of drought and dust storms in the 1930s. (m. 593, t. 593)

E

Eastern Hemisphere (ēs'tərn hem'is fêr) The half of Earth that lies east of the Prime Meridian (0° longitude) and west of 180° longitude. (m. G5, t. G4)

Ecuador (ek'wə dôr) A country on the northwestern coast of South America. (m. 665, t. 651)

El Camino Real (el cä mē'nō rā äl) A number of routes that connected Spain's colonies in the American Southwest to Mexico from the late 1500s to the middle 1800s. (m. 260, t. 257)

El Salvador (el sal'və dôr) A country in western Central America. (m. 661, t. 660)

Ellis Island (el'is ī'lənd) A small island in upper New York Bay which served as the chief United States point of arrival for immigrants from 1892 to 1943; 41°N, 74°W. (m. 539, t. 546)

England (ing'glənd) A part of the United Kingdom of Great Britain and Northern Ireland. England occupies the southern part of the island of Great Britain. (m. R15, t. 125)

equator (i kwā'tər) An imaginary line encircling Earth halfway between the North Pole and the South Pole, designated as 0° latitude. (m. G5, t. G4)

Erie Canal (ir'ē kə nal') A human-made waterway across New York State, connecting the Hudson River with Lake Erie. (m. 413, t. 412)

Europe (yu̇r′əp) One of Earth's seven continents, between Asia and the Atlantic Ocean. (m. G5, t. 18)

F

Florida Keys (flôr′i də kēz) A chain of small islands off the southern coast of Florida. (m. R11)

Fort Duquesne (fôrt dü kān′) A fort built by the French in 1754 where Pittsburgh stands today. (t. 273)

Fort McHenry (fôrt mək hen′rə) A fort protecting the harbor of Baltimore, Maryland. (t. 388)

Fort Necessity (fôrt nə ses′i tē) A temporary fort built 60 miles south of Fort Duquesne in 1754 by troops under George Washington's command; 40°N, 80°W; (t. 273)

Fort Sumter (fôrt səm′tər) A fort guarding the entrance to Charleston Harbor, South Carolina; site of the first battle of the Civil War; 33°N, 80°W. (m. 491, t. 472)

Fort Ticonderoga (fôrt tī kon də rō′gə) A fort on Lake Champlain, New York; site of important battles in the American Revolution; 44°N, 74°W. (m. 332, t. 304)

Fort Vincennes (fôrt vin senz′) A fort on the site of present-day Vincennes, Indiana, on the Wabash River; 39°N, 88°W. (m. 332, t. 329)

Fort Wagner (fôrt wag′nər) A fort on Morris Island in Charleston Harbor, South Carolina; 33°N, 80°W. (t. 480)

Four Corners (fôr kôr′nərz) The place at which the states of Arizona, New Mexico, Utah, and Colorado meet; 37°N, 109°W. (m. 74, t. 74)

France (frans) A country in western Europe. (m. 603, t. 125)

Frankfort (frangk′fərt) Capital of Kentucky; 38°N, 85°W. (m. 33)

French Guiana (french gē an′ə) An overseas department of France on the Atlantic coast of South America. (m. 665, t. 651)

G

Gao (gou) In the 1400s, the capital of the African kingdom of Songhai; 16°N, 0°W. (m. 121, t. 122)

Gettysburg (get′iz bûrg) A town in south-central Pennsylvania, site of a major Union victory during the Civil War; 40°N, 77°W. (m. 491, t. 484)

Goliad (gō′lē ad) A city in Texas where Texan defenders were defeated by Mexican troops in 1836; 29°N, 97°W. (t. 419)

Grand Canyon (grand kan′yən) A vast and richly colored canyon on the Colorado River in northwestern Arizona. (m. 31, t. 31)

Great Lakes (grāt lāks) A group of five fresh-water lakes in North America along the border between Canada and the United States. The Great Lakes are Lake Superior, Lake Michigan, Lake Huron, Lake Erie, and Lake Ontario. (m. R11, t. 264)

Great Salt Lake (grāt sôlt lāk) A lake in northwestern Utah, the largest salt lake in North America; 41°N, 113°W. (m. R10, t. 429)

Great Wall (grāt wôl) A fortified barrier of stone and earth that winds continuously over 1,500 miles in northern China. (m. 116, t. 115)

Greensboro (grēnz′bûr ō) A city in north-central North Carolina; 36°N, 80°W. (t. 620)

Grenada (gri nā′də) An island country in the West Indies. (m. 661, t. 650)

Guadalajara (gwä də lə här′ə) The second largest city in Mexico, located northwest of Mexico City; 21°N, 103°W. (m. 657, t. 659)

Guam (gwäm) An island in the western Pacific Ocean; 14°N, 143°E. (m. 556, t. 557)

Guatemala (gwä tə mä′lə) A country in the northern part of Central America. (m. 661, t. 661)

Gulf of Mexico (gulf əv mek′si kō) An arm of the Atlantic Ocean, between the United States and Mexico. (m. 657, t. 267)

Guyana (gī an′ə) A country on the northeastern coast of South America. (m. 665, t. 651)

H

Haiti (hā′tē) A country in the West Indies, occupying the western part of the island of Hispaniola. (m. 661, t. 660)

Harlem (här′ləm) A district of New York City, on Manhattan Island. (t. 585)

Harpers Ferry (här′pərz fer′ē) A town in northeastern West Virginia; 39°N, 78°W. (m. 443, t. 463)

Harrisburg (har′is bûrg) Capital of Pennsylvania; 40°N, 77°W. (m. 34)

Hartford (härt′fərd) Capital of Connecticut; 42°N, 73°W. (m. 34)

---

pronunciation key

a **at**; ā **ape**; ä **far**; âr **care**; e **end**; ē **me**; i **it**; ī **ice**; îr **pierce**; o **hot**; ō **old**; ô **fork**; oi **oil**; ou **out**; u **up**; ū **use**; ü **rule**; u̇ **pull**; ûr **turn**; hw **white**; ng **song**; th **thin**; <u>th</u> **this**; zh **measure**; ə **about, taken, pencil, lemon, circus**

Helena (hel′ə nə) Capital of Montana; 47°N, 112°W. (m. 30)

Hiroshima (hîr ə shē′mə) A port in southwestern Japan on the island of Honshu; the first city where an atomic bomb was dropped; 34°N, 132°E. (m. 602, t. 605)

Hispaniola (his pən yō′la) An island in the Greater Antilles, in the Caribbean. (m. 139, t. 142)

Hodenosaunee Trail (hō den ō sä′nē trāl) A 250-mile path connecting the homelands of five Iroquois peoples in the 1500s. (m. 104, t. 104)

Honduras (hon dür′əs) A country in northern Central America. (m. 661, t. 661)

Honolulu (hon ə lü′lü) Capital and largest city of Hawaii; 21°N, 158°E. (m. 30, t. 555)

Hoover Dam (hü′vər dam) A dam built in 1936 on the Colorado River at the Nevada-Arizona border by the Works Project Admistration (WPA); it forms Lake Mead; 36°N, 115°W. (t. 596)

Houston (hüs′tən) The largest city in Texas and a major port; 30°N, 95°W. (m. R9, t. 420)

Hudson Bay (hud′sən bā) A large inland sea in northeastern Canada. (m. 653)

Hudson River (hud′sən riv′ər) A tidal river in eastern New York that empties into the Atlantic Ocean. (m. 34, t. 175)

I

India (in′dē ə) A large peninsular country in southern Asia. (m. 116, t. 116)

Indian Ocean (in′dē ən ō′shən) One of Earth's four largest bodies of water, south of Asia, between Africa and Australia. (m. G5, t. G4)

Indian Territory (in′dē ən ter′i tôr ē) Land set aside by the Indian Removal Act of 1830 as a place for Native Americans forced from their homelands. (m. 398, t. 397)

Indianapolis (in dē ə nap′ə lis) Capital and largest city in Indiana; 40°N, 86°W. (m. 32)

Iraq (i rak′) A country in southwestern Asia. (m. R15, t. 636)

Isthmus of Panama (pan′ə mä) A narrow strip of land connecting North America and South America. (m. 661, t. 562)

Italy (it′ə lē) A country in southern Europe. (m. 603, t. 125)

J

Jackson (jak′sən) Capital and largest city in Mississippi; 32°N, 90°W. (m. 33)

Jamaica (jə mā′kə) An island country in the West Indies, south of Cuba. (m. 661, t. 661)

Jamestown (jāmz′toun) A town in southeastern Virginia; the first permanent English settlement in North America, founded in 1607; 37°N, 77°W. (m. 176, t. 180)

Jefferson City (jef′ər sən sit′ē) Capital of Missouri; 39°N, 92°W. (m. 32)

Jenne (je nā′) A city located on the Niger River in present-day Mali, in Africa; 14°N, 5°W. (m. 121, t. 121)

Juneau (jü′nō) Capital of Alaska; 58°N, 135°W. (m. 30, t. 555)

K

Kansas City (kan′zəs sit′ē) A city in western Missouri, the largest city in the state; 39°N, 95°W. (m. R9)

Kitty Hawk (kit′ē hôk) A village on the Outer Banks off the coast of North Carolina. Wilbur and Orville Wright made the first successful airplane flight there in 1903; 36°N, 76°W. (m. 539, t. 563)

Kuwait (kü wāt′) A country in southwestern Asia. (m. R15, t. 636)

L

Lake Erie (lāk îr′ē) The southernmost of the Great Lakes, bordering Canada and the United States. (m. R11, t. 412)

Lake Huron (lāk hyür′ən) Second largest of the Great Lakes, bordering Canada and the United States. (m. R11)

Lake Michigan (lāk mish′i gən) Third largest of the Great Lakes, between Michigan and Wisconsin. (m. R11)

Lake Ontario (lāk on târ′ē ō) The smallest and easternmost of the Great Lakes, bordering Canada and the United States. (m. R11)

Lake Superior (lāk sə pîr′ē ər) The largest and northernmost of the Great Lakes, bordering Canada and the United States. (m. R11)

Lansing (lan′sing) Capital of Michigan; 43°N, 85°W. (m. 32)

Latin America (lat′in ə mer′i kə) The part of the Western Hemisphere south of the United States—including Mexico, Central America, South America, and the West Indies. (m. R6, t. 390)

Lexington (lek′sing tən) A town in eastern Massachusetts, site of one of the first battles of the American Revolution; 42°N, 71°W. (m. 301, t. 302)

Lincoln (ling′kən) Capital of Nebraska; 41°N, 97°W. (m. 32)

Little Bighorn River (lit′əl big′hôrn riv′ər) A river in northern Wyoming and southern Montana. (t. 532)

Little Rock (lit′əl rok) Capital and largest city of Arkansas; 41°N, 97°W. (m. 33)

Los Angeles (lōs an′jə ləs) A city in southwestern California, the chief port and largest city in the state, the second largest city in the United States; 34°N, 118°W. (m. R8 t. 626)

Lowell (lō′əl) A city in northeastern Massachusetts; 42°N, 71°W. (t. 406)

M

Madison (mad′ə sən) Capital of Wisconsin; 43°N, 89°W. (m. 32)

Manitoba (man i tō′bə) A province of Canada, in the southern part of the country. (m. 653)

Menlo Park (men′lō pärk) A town in central New Jersey, site of Thomas Edison's laboratory; 41°N, 74°W. (t. 541)

Mesa Verde (mā′sə vərd′ē) The name given an Anasazi village built around A.D. 900 into the side of a steep cliff, located in present-day Colorado; 57°N, 108°W. (m. 74, t. 75)

Mexico (mek′si kō) A North American country on the southern border of the United States. (m. 657, t. 656)

Mexico City (mek′si kō sit′ē) Capital and largest city in Mexico, the second largest city in the world; 19°N, 99°W. (m. 161, t. 156)

Miami (mī am′ē) A port city in southeastern Florida; 26°N, 80°W. (m. R9)

Middle Colonies (mid′əl kol′ə nēz) The name given to the English colonies of Delaware, New Jersey, New York, and Pennsylvania before the American Revolution. (m. 212, t. 212)

Mississippi River (mis ə sip′ē riv′ər) A river in the central United States, flowing from Minnesota to the Gulf of Mexico; the longest river in the United States. (m. R11, t. 33)

Missouri River (mi zŭr′ē riv′ər) A large tributary of the Mississippi, flowing from Montana to the Mississippi River north of St. Louis. (m. R10, t. 382)

Mojave Desert (mō hä′vē dez′ərt) A desert in southeastern California; 35°N, 117°W. (m. R10)

Montgomery (mont gum′ə rē) Capital of Alabama; 32°N, 86°W. (m. 33, t. 618)

Monticello (mänt ə sel′ō) The home designed by Thomas Jefferson, southeast of Charlottesville, Virginia; 38°N, 78°W. (t. 314)

Montpelier (mont pēl′yər) Capital of Vermont; 44°N, 73°W. (m. 34)

Montreal (mon trē ôl′) A port city in southern Quebec; Canada's largest city; 46°N, 74°W. (m. 653)

Mormon Trail (môr′mən trāl) A route west named for the 20,000 Mormons who migrated from Nauvoo, Illinois, between 1837 and 1847. (m. 431, t. 429)

Mount McKinley (mount mə kin′lē) The highest mountain in North America, elevation 20,320 feet (6,194 m), located in the Alaska Range in south-central Alaska; also known as Denali, or "Great One"; 64°N, 153°W. (m. R10)

Mount Vernon (mount vûr′nən) The Virginia home and burial place of George Washington, on the Potomac River; 39°N, 77°W. (t. 322)

Mount Whitney (mount hwit′nē) The highest mountain in the continental United States, elevation 14,494 (4,418 m), located in southeast California; 37°N, 118°W. (m. R10)

N

Nagasaki (nä gə sä′kē) A city in Japan on the western coast of the island of Kyushu. It was the second city struck by an atomic bomb; 33°N, 130°E. (m. 602, t. 605)

Nashville (nash′vil) Capital of Tennessee; 36°N, 87°W. (m. 33)

National Road (nash′ə nəl rōd) A road built in the first half of the 1800s. It ran from Maryland to the Mississippi River, opening the way for pioneers moving west. (m. 413, t. 410)

New Amsterdam (nü am′stər dam) An early Dutch settlement in New Netherland, on the site of present-day New York City; 41°N, 74°W. (m. 176, t. 210)

New Brunswick (nü brunz′wik) A province of Canada, in the southeastern part of the country. (m. 653)

New England (nü ing′glənd) Northeastern region of the United States, containing the states of Maine, Vermont, New Hampshire, Massachusetts, Connecticut, and Rhode Island. (m. 188, t. 187)

New France (nü frans) French possessions in North America during colonial times. It included large parts of what are now Canada and the United States. (m. 266, t. 264)

New Netherland (nü neth′ər lənd) A Dutch colony in North America from 1609 to 1664 that included parts of present-day New York, New Jersey, and Connecticut. (t. 210)

New Orleans (nü ôr′lē ənz) A city in southern Louisiana, largest in the state and a major port; 30°N, 90°W. (m. R9, t. 275)

pronunciation key

a at; ā ape; ä far; âr care; e end; ē me; i it; ī ice; îr pierce; o hot; ō old; ô fork; oi oil; ou out; u up; ū use; ü rule, u̇ pull; ûr turn; hw white; ng song; th thin; <u>th</u> this; zh measure; ə about, taken, pencil, lemon, circus

New Spain (nü spān) Colonial lands held by Spain, mainly in North America. New Spain included parts of what are now the United States, Mexico, Central America, and islands in the West Indies. (m. 157, t. 151)

New Sweden (nü swē'dən) A Swedish colony along the Delaware River in North America from 1638 to 1664 in what are now New Jersey, Pennsylvania, and Delaware. (m. 176)

New York City (nü yōrk sit'ē) The largest city in the United States, located in southeastern New York State; 41°N, 74°W. (m. R9, t. 210)

Newfoundland (nü'fənd lənd) The easternmost province of Canada, including Labrador and the island of Newfoundland. (m. 653)

Nicaragua (nik ə rä'gwə) The largest country in Central America, located in the middle part of the region. (m. 661, t. 660)

Nicodemus (nik ə de'məs) A town in Kansas formed by freed African Americans from Kentucky following the Civil War; 39°N, 100°W. (t. 528)

North America (nôrth ə mer'i kə) The third largest of Earth's seven continents. It includes Canada, Mexico, the West Indies, and the continental United States. (m. G5, t. G4)

North Korea (nôrth kə rē'ə) A country occupying the northern part of the Korean peninsula. (m. R15, t. 610)

North Pole (nôrth pōl) The northernmost point on Earth; the northern end of Earth's axis; 90°N. (m. G5, t. G4)

North Vietnam (nôrth vī et näm') From 1954 to 1975 a country in southeast Asia, now part of Vietnam. (m. 628, t. 628)

Northern Hemisphere (nôr'thərn hem'i sfîr) The half of Earth north of the equator. (m. G5, t. G4)

Northwest Territories (nôrth west' ter'i tôr ēz) An administrative division of Canada, in the northern part of the country. (m. 653)

Northwest Territory (nôrth west' ter'i tôr ē) The land claimed by the United States after the Revolutionary War and organized as a territory in 1787, including what became the states of Indiana, Wisconsin, Ohio, Michigan, and Illinois. (m. 344, t. 344)

Nova Scotia (nō'və skō'shə) A province of Canada, in the southeastern part of the country. (m. 653, t. 655)

Nunavut (nun'ə vut) A vast section of Canada's Northwest Territories and homeland of the Inuit. (m. 653, t. 653)

Ohio River (ō hī'ō riv'ər) A river in the east-central United States, flowing from Pittsburgh, Pennsylvania, southwest into the Mississippi River. (m. R11, t. 273)

Ohio River valley (ō hī'ō riv'ər val'ē) The region along the banks of the Ohio River, known for its industry and farming. (m. R11, t. 273)

Oklahoma City (ō klə hō'mə sit'ē) Capital and largest city of Oklahoma; 35°N, 98°W. (m. 31)

Old Oraibi (ōld ō rä ē'bē) A pueblo in Arizona inhabited by the Hopi for about 800 years, one of the oldest continuously populated settlements in the United States; 36°N, 111°W. (t. 91)

Olympia (ō lim'pē ə) Capital of Washington State; 47°N, 123°W. (m. 30)

Omaha (ō'mə hä) A city in east-central Nebraska, the largest city in the state; 41°N, 96°W. (m. G9, t. 511)

Ontario (on târ'ē ō) A province of Canada, in the southeastern part of the country. (m. 653)

Oregon Territory (or'i gən ter'i tōr ē) The area of the Western region of the United States during the middle 1800s. It comprised all or parts of what are now the states of Oregon, Washington, Idaho, Wyoming, and Montana. (m. 402, t. 428)

Oregon Trail (ôr'i gən trāl) A route west used by pioneers in the 1840s that stretched from Independence, Missouri, to northwestern Oregon. (m. 431, t. 428)

Ottawa (ot'ə wə) The capital of Canada, in the province of Ontario; 45°N, 76°W. (m. 653, t. 650)

P

Pacific Ocean (pə sif'ik ō'shən) The largest of Earth's four oceans. (m. G5, t. G4)

Panama (pan'ə mä) The southernmost country in Central America. (m. 562, t. 562)

Panama Canal (pan'ə mä kə nal') A human-made waterway across the Isthmus of Panama that connects the Atlantic and Pacific Oceans. (m. 562, t. 562)

Paraguay (par'ə gwā) A country in south-central South America. (m. 665, t. 651)

Pearl Harbor (pûrl här'bər) A major United States naval base near Honolulu, Hawaii, on the island of Oahu. Japan bombed Pearl Harbor on December 7, 1941, bringing the United States into World War II; 21°N, 158°W. (m. 602, t. 599)

Persia (pûr'zhə) An ancient empire in southwest Asia centered in what is now the country of Iran. (m. 116, t. 115)

Peru (pə rü') A country in northwestern South America. (m. 665, t. 651)

Petersburg (pēt'erz bûrg) A city in southeastern Virginia; 37°N, 77°W. (t. 492)

Philadelphia (fil ə del'fē ə) A city in southeastern Pennsylvania; the largest city in the state. From 1790 to 1800 it was the capital of the United States; 40°N, 75°W. (m. R9, t. 211)

Philippines (fil´ə pēnz) A group of islands off the coast of southeast Asia making up the country of the Philippines. (m. 556, t. 556)

Phoenix (fē´niks) Capital and largest city of Arizona; 34°N, 112°W. (m. 31, t. 94)

Pierre (pîr) Capital of South Dakota; 44°N, 100°W. (m. 32)

Pikes Peak (pīks pēk) A mountain in the Rocky Mountains, in east-central Colorado, elevation 14,110 (4,301 m); 39°N, 105°W. (m. R10)

Pittsburgh (pits´bûrg) A city in southwestern Pennsylvania, a leading center of iron-making and steel-making; 40°N, 80°W. (m. R9, t. 542)

Platte River (plat riv´ər) A river flowing from central Nebraska into the Missouri River. (m. R9)

Plymouth (plim´əth) A town in southeastern Massachusetts, founded by the Pilgrims in 1620; 42°N, 71°W. (m. 188, t. 186)

Portsmouth (pôrts´məth) A town in southeastern Rhode Island founded in 1637 by Anne Hutchinson; 43°N, 71°W. (m. 205, t. 208)

Portugal (pôr´chə gəl) A country in southwestern Europe. (m. 126, t. 124)

Prime Meridian (prīm mə rid´ē ən) The meridian, or line of longitude, that passes through Greenwich, England, and from which longitudes east and west are measured; 0° longitude. (m. G5, t. 40)

Prince Edward Island (prins ed´wərd ī´lənd) The smallest province of Canada, located in the Gulf of St. Lawrence; the island that makes up this province. (m. 653)

Promontory Point (präm´ən tōr ē point) The place in northwestern Utah where the Union Pacific and the Central Pacific railroads met in 1869, completing the first transcontinental railroad in the United States; 41°N, 113°W. (m. 515, t. 514)

Providence (prov´i dəns) Capital and largest city of Rhode Island; 42°N, 71°W. (m. 34, t. 208)

Pueblo Bonito (pweb´lō bə nē´tō) An Anasazi village that flourished from about A.D. 950 to 1300, now in ruins, located in what is now northwestern New Mexico; 36°N, 108°W. (m. 74, t. 75)

Puerto Rico (pwer´tō rē´kō) An island in the West Indies, a commonwealth of the United States. (m. 556, t. 556)

Puget Sound (pū´jit sound) An arm of the Pacific Ocean, extending into the northwestern part of Washington state. (m. R10)

Q

Quebec (kwi bek´) The largest province of Canada in the eastern part of the country; also the capital city of this province; 47°N, 71°W. (m. 653, t. 265)

R

Raleigh (rô´lē) Capital of North Carolina; 36°N, 79°W. (m. 33)

Richmond (rich´mənd) Capital of Virginia; Confederate capital from 1861 to 1865; 38°N, 78°W. (m. 33, t. 474)

Rio Grande (rē´ō grand´) A river in southwestern North America, flowing from Colorado into the Gulf of Mexico. It forms part of the border between the United States and Mexico. (m. R10, t. 422)

Roanoke Island (rō´ə nōk ī´lənd) An island off the coast of North Carolina, the site of the "Lost Colony" founded by Sir Walter Raleigh in 1587; 36°N, 76°W. (m. 169, t. 169)

Rocky Mountains (rok´ē moun´tənz) A high, rugged mountain chain in western North America stretching from Alaska into Mexico. (m. R10, t. 30)

S

Sacramento (sak rə men´tō) Capital of California; 39°N, 122°W. (m. 30, t. 511)

Sahara (sə har´ə) The largest desert in the world, stretching across most of North Africa. (m. 121, t. 120)

Salem (sā´ləm) Capital of Oregon; 45°N, 123°W. (m. 30)

Salt Lake City (sôlt lāk sit´ē) Capital and largest city of Utah; 41°N, 112°W. (m. 30, t. 429)

San Antonio (san an tō´nē ō) A city in south-central Texas; 29°N, 99°W. (m. 260, t. 260)

San Diego (san dē ā´gō) A port city in southern California; 33°N, 117°W. (m. R8, t. 261)

San Francisco (san frən sis´kō) A city in west-central California; 38°N, 122°W. (m. R8, t. 261)

San Jacinto River (san jə sint´ō riv´ər) A river in southeastern Texas that flows into Galveston Bay. (t. 419)

San Jose (san hō zā´) A city in western California; 37°N, 122°W. (m. R8)

San Salvador (san sal´və dôr) Capital and largest city of El Salvador; 14°N, 89°W (m. 661, t. 650) Also one of the Bahama Islands, also known as Watling Island. It is believed to be the site of Columbus's first landing in North America, in 1492; 24°N, 75°W. (m. 142, t. 141)

pronunciation key

a **at**; ā **ape**; ä **far**; âr **care**; e **end**; ē **me**; i **it**; ī **ice**; îr **pierce**; o **hot**; ō **old**; ô **fork**; oi **oil**; ou **out**; u **up**; ū **use**; ü **rule**; u̇ **pull**; ûr **turn**; hw **white**; ng **song**; th **thin**; th **this**; zh measure; ə **about**, tak**e**n, penc**i**l, lem**o**n, circ**u**s

Santa Fe (san'tə fā') Capital of New Mexico; 35°N, 106°W. (m. 31, t. 257)

São Paulo (sou pou'lō) The largest city in Brazil; 24°N, 47°W. (m. 665, t. 667)

Saratoga (sar ə tō'gə) Site in northeastern New York of an important Patriot victory in the Revolutionary War; 43°N, 75°W. (m. 332, t. 324)

Saskatchewan (sas kach'ə won) A province of Canada, in the south-central part of the country (m. 653)

Savannah (sə van'ə) A port city in southeastern Georgia, site of important battles in the American Revolution and the Civil War; 32°N, 81°W. (m. R9, t. 218)

Seattle (sē at'əl) A city in northwestern Washington, the largest in the state and a major port; 48°N, 122°W. (m. R8)

Seneca Falls (sen'i kə fôlz) A village in west-central New York, site of the first women's rights convention in the United States, in 1848; 43°N, 77°W. (m. 443, t. 456)

Shenandoah Valley (shen ən dō'ə val'ē) A rich agricultural valley in Virginia. (m. 248, t. 249)

Shiloh (shī'lō) The site of a bloody Union victory in southwestern Tennessee in 1862; 35°N, 88°W. (m. 491, t. 483)

Sierra Madres (sē er'ə mä'drā) A mountain system in Mexico. (m. 657)

Sierra Nevada (sē er'ə nə vad'ə) A mountain range in eastern California. (m. R10, t. 511)

Silk Road (silk rōd) An ancient network of overland trade routes that stretched from China to what is now Iran. (m. 116, t. 115)

Sitka (sit'kə) A city on Baranof Island, Alaska, in the Alexander chain of islands; 57°N, 135°W. (t. 82)

Snake River (snāk riv'ər) A river in the northwestern United States that flows into the Columbia River. (m. R10, t. 382)

Songhai (sông'hī) A powerful and wealthy kingdom that ruled a large part of West Africa in the 1400s. (m. 121, t. 120)

South America (south ə mer'i kə) One of Earth's seven continents; located in the Western Hemisphere. (m. 665, t. 664)

South Bend (south bend) A city in northern Indiana, a manufacturing center; 42°N, 86°W. (t. 526)

South Korea (south kə rē'ə) A country occupying the southern part of the Korean peninsula. (m. R15, t. 610)

South Pole (south pōl) The southernmost point on Earth; the southern end of Earth's axis; 90°S. (m. G5, t. G4)

South Vietnam (south vī et näm') From 1954 to 1975 a country in southeast Asia, now part of Vietnam. (m. 628, t. 628)

Southern Colonies (suth'ərn kol'ə nēz) The name given to the English colonies of Georgia, Maryland, North Carolina, South Carolina, and Virginia before the American Revolution. (m. 218, t. 216)

Southern Hemisphere (suth'ərn hem'i sfîr) The half of Earth that lies south of the equator. (m. G5, t. G4)

Spain (spān) A country in southwestern Europe. (m. 126, t. 124)

Springfield (spring'fēld) Capital of Illinois; 40°N, 90°W. (m. 32)

St. Augustine (sānt ô'gə stēn) A port city in northeast Florida; the oldest city in the United States, founded by the Spanish in 1565; 30°N, 81°W. (m. 176, t. 256)

St. Lawrence River (sānt lôr'əns riv'ər) A river in eastern North America between the United States and Canada, flowing from Lake Ontario into the Atlantic Ocean. (m. R11, t. 264)

St. Louis (sānt lü'is) A city in western Missouri located near the joining of the Missouri and the Mississippi rivers; 39°N, 90°W. (m. R9, t. 267)

St. Paul (sānt pôl) Capital of Minnesota; 45°N, 93°W. (m. 32)

Strait of Magellan (strāt əv mə jel'ən) The narrow waterway between the southern tip of South America and Tierra del Fuego that links the Atlantic Ocean to the Pacific Ocean. (m. 154)

Suriname (sùr'ə näm) A country on the northeastern coast of South America. (m. 665, t. 651)

Sutter's Mill (su'tərz mil) The sawmill on the American River where gold was discovered in California in 1848, starting the California gold rush; 39°N, 121°W. (m. 431, t. 432)

T

Tallahassee (tal ə has'ē) Capital of Florida; 30°N, 84°W. (m. 33)

Tenochtitlán (te nōch tē tlän') The capital of the ancient Aztec empire, on the site of present-day Mexico City; 19°N, 99°W. (m. 65, t. 65)

Tikal (ti käl') An ancient Maya city in northern Guatemala; 17°N, 90°W. (m. 61, t. 61)

Timbuktu (tim buk tü') A West African city in the present-day country of Mali; 17°N, 03°W. (m. 121, t. 121)

Topeka (tə pē'kə) Capital of Kansas; 39°N, 96°W. (m. 32, t. 617)

Toronto (tə ron'tō) Capital and largest city of the Canadian province of Ontario; 44°N, 79°W. (m. 653, t. 655)

Trenton (tren'tən) Capital of New Jersey, site of an important battle in the American Revolution; 40°N, 75°W. (m. 34, t. 323)

Tsenacomacoh (sen ə käm′ə kō) The name the Powhatan peoples of eastern Virginia had given to their homeland. (m. 179, t. 178)

U

Umbler (um′blər) A community of free African Americans in central Virginia that began during the 1700s. (t. 449)

Uruguay (yür′ə gwā) A country on the southeastern coast of South America. (m. 665, t. 651)

V

Valley Forge (val′ē fōrj) A village in southeastern Pennsylvania where George Washington and his army camped during the harsh winter of 1777–1778; 40°N, 75°W. (m. 332, t. 325)

Valley of Mexico (val′ē əv mek′si kō) An area of lower-lying land in central Mexico where the Aztec established their capital, Tenochtitlán. (t. 65)

Vancouver (van kü′vər) A port city in southwestern British Columbia, Canada; 49°N, 123°W. Also an island of British Columbia, Canada. (m. 653, t. 654)

Venezuela (ven ə zwā′lə) A country in northwestern South America, on the Caribbean Sea. (m. 665, t. 664)

Versailles (vār sī′) A city southwest of Paris, France, and site of such international peace conferences as the one that ended World War I; 49°N, 2°W. (t. 581)

Vicksburg (viks′bûrg) A city in west-central Mississippi on the Mississippi River, site of a major battle during the Civil War; 32°N, 91°W. (m. 491, t. 483)

Virgin Islands (vûr′jin ī′ləndz) A group of islands in the Caribbean Sea east of Puerto Rico that are divided politically between the United States and Great Britain. (m. 661, t. 579)

W

Wallowa River (wä laü′ə riv′ər) A river in northeastern Oregon. (t. 533)

Washington, D.C. (wô′shing tən) Capital of the United States; 39°N, 77°W. (m. R9, t. 12)

Watts (wäts) An area in the city of Los Angeles, California, the scene of severe rioting in 1965; 34°N, 118°W. (t. 626)

Weeksville (wēks′vil) A community in Brooklyn, New York. (t. 449)

West Indies (west in′dēz) The islands stretching from Florida in North America to Venezuela in South America. (m. 231, t. 229)

Wilderness Road (wil′dər nis rōd) An early road across the Appalachians, between western Virginia and eastern Kentucky. (m. 376, t. 377)

Williamsburg (wil′yəmz bûrg) Colonial capital of Virginia from 1699 to 1779, where the House of Burgesses met; 37°N, 77°W. (m. 248, t. 288)

Y

Yorktown (yôrk′toun) A town in southeastern Virginia, site of the last major battle of the American Revolution; 37°N, 77°W. (m. 337, t. 334)

Yosemite National Park (yō sem′i tē) A national park in east-central California noted for its valley, waterfalls, and sequoia trees; 38°N, 120°W. (t. 564)

Yucatán peninsula (ū kə tan′ pə nin′sə lə) A peninsula in southeastern Mexico. (m. 61, t. 657)

Yukon Territory (ū′kon ter′i tōr ēz) A province in the northwestern corner of Canada. (m. 653)

pronunciation key

a **a**t; ā **a**pe; ä f**a**r; âr c**a**re; e **e**nd; ē m**e**; i **i**t; ī **i**ce; îr p**i**erce; o h**o**t; ō **o**ld; ô f**o**rk; oi **oi**l; ou **ou**t; u **u**p; ū **u**se; ü r**u**le; u̇ p**u**ll; ûr t**u**rn; hw **wh**ite; ng so**ng**; th **th**in; <u>th</u> **th**is; zh mea**s**ure; ə **a**bout, tak**e**n, penc**i**l, lem**o**n, circ**u**s

Biographical Dictionary

This Biographical Dictionary tells you about the people you have learned about in this book. The Pronunciation Key tells you how to say their names. The page numbers tell you where each person first appears in the text.

A

Adams, Abigail (ad′əmz), 1744–1818 First Lady to President John Adams. She wrote many letters about the role of women in the new country. (p. 296)

Adams, Henry (ad′əmz), 1843–1884? Former slave who led thousands of African American exodusters to Kansas in 1879. (p. 528)

Adams, John (ad′əmz), 1735–1826 Second President of the United States from 1797 to 1801. He was a member of the Continental Congress and the Constitutional Convention. (p. 289)

Adams, John Quincy (ad′əmz), 1767–1848 Sixth President of the United States from 1825 to 1829. (p. 394)

Adams, Samuel (ad′əmz), 1722–1803 Patriot and leader in the American Revolution. He was a member of the Sons of Liberty and a cousin of John Adams. (p. 293)

Addams, Jane (ad′əmz), 1860–1935 Reformer who founded Hull House in Chicago in 1889, the first settlement house in the United States. (p. 550)

Allen, Ethan (al′ən), 1738–1789 Leader of the "Green Mountain Boys," the Vermont militiamen who captured Fort Ticonderoga in the American Revolution. (p. 304)

Allen, Richard (al′ən), 1760–1831 Abolitionist and founder of the Free African Society in 1787. He helped found the first African Methodist Episcopal Church in 1816 with Absalom Jones. (p. 342)

Anthony, Susan B. (an′thə nē), 1820–1906 A leader in the movement for women's suffrage. (p. 588)

Armistead, James (är′mə sted), 1760–1832 Patriot spy who helped defeat the British general Charles Cornwallis at Yorktown in 1781. (p. 334)

Armstrong, Neil (ärm′strông), 1930– United States astronaut who became the first person to set foot on the moon in 1969. (p. 639)

Arnold, Benedict (är′nəld), 1741–1801 Colonial general in the Continental Army who later became a traitor to the American Revolution. (p. 330)

Attucks, Crispus (at′əks), 1723?–1770 Patriot and former slave who was the first person killed in the Boston Massacre in 1770. (p. 294)

Austin, Stephen F. (ôs′tən), 1793–1836 Pioneer who led about 300 American families to Texas in 1822. (p. 417)

B

Balboa, Vasco Núñez de (bäl bō′ä, väs′kō nü′nyes de), 1475–1519 Explorer who led the first European expedition across the Isthmus of Panama to the Pacific Ocean in 1513. (p. 152)

Banneker, Benjamin (ban′i kər), 1731–1806 Scientist, writer, and planner of the District of Columbia. He was probably the first African American to be hired by the federal government. (p. 378)

Barton, Clara (bär′tən), 1821–1912 Nurse for the Union forces during the Civil War known as the "Angel of the Battlefield." She later founded the American Red Cross. (p. 482)

Bell, Alexander Graham (bel), 1847–1922 Inventor who built the first working telephone in 1876. (p. 541)

Bolívar, Simón (bō lē′vär, sē mōn′), 1783–1830 Venezuelan military and revolutionary leader who helped free much of northern South America in the early 1800s; known as "The Liberator." (p. 664)

Bonaparte, Napoleon (nə pō′lē ən bō′nə pärt), 1769–1821 Emperor of France who sold the Louisiana Territory to the United States in 1803. (p. 379)

Boone, Daniel (bün), 1734–1820 Virginia pioneer and trailblazer, nicknamed "the Pathfinder." He guided settlers through the Cumberland Gap into Kentucky. (p. 374)

Bowie, Jim (bō′ē), 1796–1836 Soldier who died defending The Alamo in 1836. (p. 418)

Braddock, Edward (brad′ək), 1695–1755 British general in the French and Indian War who died at the Battle of Fort Duquesne. (p. 273)

Bradford, William (brad′fərd), 1590–1657 Governor of the Plymouth Colony beginning in 1621. (p. 189)

pronunciation key

a	at	ī	ice	u	up	th	thin
ā	ape	îr	pierce	ū	use	th	this
ä	far	o	hot	ü	rule	zh	measure
âr	care	ō	old	u̇	pull	ə	about, taken,
e	end	ô	fork	ûr	turn		pencil, lemon,
ē	me	oi	oil	hw	white		circus
i	it	ou	out	ng	song		

Brant, Joseph (brant), 1742–1807 Mohawk leader who sided with the British in the American Revolution. (p. 335)

Brown, Emma (broun), 1844–? Kansas homesteader in 1870s whose letters describe pioneer life on the Great Plains. (p. 526)

Brown, John (broun), 1800–1859 Abolitionist who led a raid on Harpers Ferry, Virginia, in 1859. (p. 463)

Bruce, Blanche K. (brüs), 1841–1898 The first African American to serve a full term in the United States Senate from 1875 to 1881. (p. 497)

Burgoyne, John (bər goin'), 1722–1792 British general whose defeat at the Battle of Saratoga in 1777 marked a turning point in the American Revolution. (p. 324)

Bush, George (bush), 1924– The 41st President of the United States from 1989 to 1993. (p. 636)

C

Cabeza de Vaca, Álvar Núñez (kä be'sä de vä'kä, äl'vär nün' yes), 1490?–1560? Spanish explorer who was the first to reach Texas. (p. 152)

Cabot, John (kab'ət), 1450?–1498? Italian sea captain in the service of England who was the first European to explore North America in search of a Northwest Passage. (p. 176)

Calhoun, John C. (kal hün'), 1782–1850 United States Senator from South Carolina and Vice President under John Quincy Adams and Andrew Jackson. He supported slavery and states' rights. (p. 386)

Carnegie, Andrew (kär'ni gē), 1835–1919 Business leader who developed the steel industry and philanthropist who established many charities. (p. 542)

Carter, James E. (kär'tər), 1924– The 39th President of the United States from 1977 to 1981. He negotiated the first peace treaty between Israel and Egypt. (p. 634)

Carter, Robert, III (kär'tər), 1728–1804 Virginia planter and slave-owner who freed the 500 people enslaved on his plantation, beginning in 1791. (p. 241)

Cartier, Jacques (kär tyä' zhäk), 1491–1557 French explorer who became the first European to navigate the St. Lawrence River in 1535. (p. 176)

Castro, Fidel (käs'trō), 1926– Communist dictator of Cuba since 1959. (p. 625)

Catt, Carrie Chapman (kat), 1859–1947 Women's rights leader who helped bring about the passage of the Nineteenth Amendment in 1920. (p. 588)

Champlain, Samuel de (sham plän'), 1567–1635 Explorer and founder of Quebec, the first permanent French settlement in North America, in 1608. He is known as the "Father of New France." (p. 176)

Charles I (chärlz), 1600–1649 King of England who gave the Puritans a charter to form the Massachusetts Bay Colony in 1629. (p. 204)

Charles II (chärlz), 1630–1685 King of England when England made the Dutch colony of New Netherland a part of the Middle Colonies. (p. 210)

Chávez, César (chä'ves, se'sär), 1927–1993 A founder of the United Farm Workers labor union. (p. 627)

Chisholm, Shirley (chiz'əm), 1924– United States Representative from New York from 1969 to 1983. She was the first African American woman to be elected to Congress. (p. 632)

Clark, George Rogers (klärk), 1752–1818 Revolutionary War general and frontier leader who defeated the British at Fort Vincennes in 1779. (p. 329)

Clark, William (klärk), 1770–1838 Explorer of the Louisiana Purchase with Meriweather Lewis. He was the brother of George Rogers Clark. (p. 381)

Clay, Henry (klā), 1777–1852 United States Senator who helped work out the Missouri Compromise in 1820 and the Compromise of 1850. (p. 386)

Clinton, William J. (klin'tən), 1946– The 42nd President of the United States, elected in 1992. (p. 636)

Clinton, DeWitt (klin'tən), 1769–1828 New York governor who supported the building of the Erie Canal. (p. 412)

Coffin, Catherine (ko'fin), 1803–1881 Quaker conductor on the Underground Railroad in Indiana. (p. 455)

Coffin, Levi (ko'fin), 1798–1877 Quaker conductor on the Underground Railroad in Indiana. (p. 455)

Columbus, Christopher (kə lum'bəs), 1451?–1506 Italian sea captain and explorer. Sailing under the flag of Spain, he reached the Americas in 1492 in search of a sea route to Asia. (p. 133)

Cook, James (kuk), 1728–1779 British sea captain and explorer who reached Hawaiian Islands in 1778. (p. 555)

Cooper, Peter (kü'pər), 1791–1883 New York merchant and inventor of a steam-driven train, the *Tom Thumb*. (p. 414)

Cornwallis, Charles (kôrn wol'is), 1738–1805 British general who surrendered at Yorktown, the last major battle of the American Revolution, in 1781. (p. 331)

Coronado, Francisco de (kô rō nä'dō, frän sēs' kō de), 1510–1554 Spanish explorer of the American Southwest from 1540 to 1542. (p. 152)

Cortés, Hernando (kôr tes', er nän'dō), 1485–1547 Spanish conquistador who defeated the Aztec in 1521. He founded Mexico City. (p. 148)

Crazy Horse (krā′zē hôrs), 1849?–1877 Lakota chief who, with Sitting Bull, defeated Colonel Custer at the Battle of the Little Bighorn in 1876. (p. 531)

Crocker, Charles (krok′ər), 1822–1888 Business leader who directed the building of the Central Pacific Railroad. (p. 511)

Crockett, David (krok′it), 1786–1836 United States Representative and frontier scout who died defending The Alamo. (p. 418)

Cuauhtémoc (kwä tā′mok), 1495?–1525 Aztec ruler following the death of Moctezuma II who led the Aztec in the final battle for Tenochtitlán. (p. 151)

Custer, George (kus′tər), 1839–1876 United States Army colonel defeated by the Lakota, Cheyenne, and Arapaho at the Battle of the Little Bighorn in 1876. (p. 532)

D

Da Gama, Vasco (də gam′ə, väs′kō), 1460–1524 Portuguese navigator who was the first European to sail from Europe to Asia in 1498. (p. 127)

Davis, Jefferson (dā′vis), 1808–1889 United States Senator who was President of the Confederate States of America from 1861 to 1865. (p. 465)

Dawes, William (dôz′), 1745–1799 Patriot who rode with Paul Revere on April 18, 1775, to warn colonists that British troops were coming. (p. 301)

De Soto, Hernando (de sō′tō, er nän′dō), 1500?–1542 Spanish explorer of the Southeast from 1539 to 1542. He was the first European to see the Mississippi River. (p. 153)

Deere, John (dîr), 1804–1886 Illinois blacksmith who invented the steel plow in 1837. (p. 408)

Deganawida (dā gän ə wē′ də), 1500s A founder of the Iroquois Confederacy in 1570. (p. 106)

Dewey, George (dü′ē), 1837–1917 United States admiral who defeated the Spanish in the Philippines during the Spanish-American War in 1898. (p. 556)

Dias, Bartholomeu (dē′əsh, bâr tù lù mā′ù), 1450?–1500 Portuguese ship captain who reached the Cape of Good Hope in 1487, opening a sea route from Europe to Asia. (p. 127)

Dickenson, Suzanna (dik′ən sən), 1820–1883 Alamo survivor who carried word of the Texans' defeat to Sam Houston, leader of the Texas forces. (p. 419)

Dodge, Grenville (doj), 1831–1916 Former Union general in charge of building the Union Pacific Railroad. (p. 511)

Douglass, Frederick (dug′ləs), 1817–1895 Abolitionist and writer who led the attack on slavery in the middle 1800s by describing his own enslavement. (p. 446)

Du Bois, W.E.B. (dü bois′), 1868–1963 A founder of the National Association for the Advancement of Colored People (NAACP) in 1909. (p. 582)

Du Sable, Jean Baptiste Point (dü sä′blə, zhän′ bap tēst′ pwän′), 1745–1818 Haitian fur trader who established a trading post that later became the city of Chicago. (p. 267)

E

Earhart, Amelia (ar′härt), 1898–1937 Airplane pilot who was the first woman passenger to fly across the Atlantic in 1928. (p. 587)

Edison, Thomas Alva (ed′ə sən), 1847–1931 Inventor of the light bulb in 1879, the phonograph, and over 1,000 other inventions. (p. 541)

Einstein, Albert (in′stīn), 1879–1955 Scientist from Germany whose theories led to the development of nuclear power. (p. 605)

Eisenhower, Dwight D. (i′zən hou ər), 1890–1969 The 34th President of the United States from 1953 to 1961. He was Supreme Allied Commander in World War II and directed the Allied invasion of Europe from 1944 to 1945. (p. 602)

Elizabeth I (i liz′ə bəth), 1533–1603 Queen of England during the founding of the Roanoke colony and the defeat of the Spanish Armada. (p. 168)

Ellington, Duke (el′ing tən), 1889–1974 Composer; African American musician who brought jazz to a wide audience in the 1920s. (p. 585)

Equiano, Olaudah (i kwē ä′nō, ōl′ə dä), 1750–1797 African who wrote of being kidnapped, enslaved, and transported to North America. (p. 227)

Ericson, Leif (er′ik sən, lēf), 980?–1025? Viking leader who was probably the first European to explore North America, around A.D. 1000. (p. 138)

Estevanico (es te vä nē′kō), 1500s African scout whose story of the "Seven Cities of Gold" convinced Francisco de Coronado to explore the American Southwest in 1540. (p. 157)

F

Ferdinand (fûr′də nand), 1452–1516 King of Spain who, with his wife Queen Isabella, paid for Columbus's voyages to the Americas. (p. 140)

Findley, John (find′lē), 1722–1772? Frontier trader who blazed trails with Daniel Boone over the Cumberland Gap to Kentucky. (p. 376)

Fitzgerald, F. Scott (fits jer′əld), 1896–1940 Writer whose early work captured the feeling of the Roaring Twenties. (p. 585)

Ford, Gerald (fôrd), 1913– The 38th President of the United States from 1974 to 1977, following the resignation of President Nixon in 1974. (p. 631)

Ford, Henry (fôrd), 1863–1947 Automaker who introduced assembly line mass production to the auto industry. (p. 563)

Forten, Charlotte (fôr′tən), 1837–1914 African American writer who taught freed African Americans in South Carolina during the Civil War. (p. 479)

Franklin, Benjamin (frang′klin), 1706–1790 Writer, scientist, delegate to the Continental Congress, signer of the Declaration of Independence, and delegate to the Constitutional Convention. (p. 244)

Fray Marcos de Niza (frī mär′kōs de nē′sä), 1500s Roman Catholic priest from Spain who accompanied Coronado on his search for the "Seven Cities of Gold." (p. 157)

Fulton, Robert (fůl′tən), 1765–1815 Builder of the first successful steamboat, the *Clermont*, in 1807. (p. 411)

G

Gálvez, Bernardo de (gäl′ves), 1746–1786 Spanish Governor of Louisiana who was an ally of the Patriots during the American Revolution. (p. 331)

Garrison, William Lloyd (gar′ə sən), 1805–1879 Abolitionist and founder of the newspaper *The Liberator* in 1831. (p. 453)

George II (jôrj), 1683–1760 King of England during the French and Indian War. (p. 217)

George III (jôrj), 1738–1820 King of England during the American Revolution. (p. 275)

Glenn, John (glen), 1921– United States Senator, astronaut, and the first American to orbit Earth in 1962. (p. 639)

Glidden, Joseph F. (glid′ən), 1813–1906 Inventor of barbed wire in 1873. (p. 527)

Gompers, Samuel (gom′pərz), 1850–1924 Labor union leader who founded the American Federation of Labor in 1886. (p. 545)

Gorbachev, Mikhail (gôr′bə chəf, mi kīl′), 1931– Last leader of the Soviet Union from 1984 to 1991. (p. 635)

Gorgas, William (gôr′gəs), 1854–1920 United States Army doctor who helped control the spread of malaria during the building of the Panama Canal from 1904 to 1914. (p. 562)

Grant, Ulysses S. (grant), 1822–1885 The 18th President of the United States from 1869 to 1877. He was Commander of the Union Army from 1864 to 1865. (p. 483)

Greene, Nathanael (grēn), 1742–1786 Patriot general during the American Revolution who forced the British out of Georgia and the Carolinas. (p. 331)

Greenhow, Rose (grēn′haů), 1815?–1864 Confederate spy during the Civil War. (p. 477)

Grimké, Angelina Emily (grim′kē), 1805–1879 Southern abolitionist who, with her sister Sarah, spoke out against slavery. (p. 453)

Grimké, Sarah Moore (grim′kē), 1792–1873, Southern abolitionist who, with her sister Angelina, spoke out against slavery. (p. 453)

Gutenberg, Johannes (gü′tən bûrg, yō hän′əs), 1400?–1468 German printer whose invention of movable type in 1436 helped spread learning. (p. 125)

H

Hale, Nathan (hāl), 1755–1776 Patriot hanged by the British as a spy in the American Revolution. (p. 320)

Hamilton, Alexander (ham′əl tən), 1757–1804 Colonial assembly member, delegate to the Constitutional Convention, and first Secretary of the Treasury from 1789 to 1795. (p. 346)

Hancock, John (han′kok), 1737–1793 Patriot and president of the Continental Congress from 1775 to 1777; known for his boldly written signature on the Declaration of Independence. (p. 301)

Hays, Mary Ludwig (hāz), 1752–1832 American Patriot; known as "Molly Pitcher." (p. 330)

Henry, Patrick (hen′rē), 1736–1799 Virginia Burgess who encouraged the colonists to fight for their independence from Great Britain. (p. 293)

Henry, Prince (hen′rē), 1394–1460 Prince of Portugal who established a school for sailors; known as "the Navigator." (p. 126)

Hiawatha (hī ə wä′thə), 1500s A founder of the Iroquois Confederacy in 1570. (p. 106)

Hidalgo, Miguel (ē däl′gō, mē gel′), 1753–1811 Roman Catholic priest and Mexican leader of the Indian and mestizo revolt that started Mexico's war for independence from Spain in 1810. (p. 656)

pronunciation key

a **at**; ā **ape**; ä **far**; âr **care**; e **end**; ē **me**; i **it**; ī **ice**; îr **pierce**; o **hot**; ō **old**; ô **fork**; oi **oil**; ou **out**; u **up**; ū **use**; ü **rule**; ů **pull**; ûr **turn**; hw **white**; ng **song**; th **thin**; <u>th</u> **this**; zh measure; ə **about**, **taken**, **pencil**, **lemon**, **circus**

Hitler, Adolf (hit′lər), 1889–1945 Nazi dictator of Germany from 1933 to 1945 whose actions led to the start of World War II and the destruction of Jews that became known as the Holocaust. (p. 598)

Hooker, Thomas (hŭk′ər), 1586–1647 Puritan minister who founded the colony of Connecticut in 1639. (p. 208)

Hoover, Herbert (hü′vər), 1874–1964 The 31st President of the United States from 1929 to 1933 who served during the beginning of the Great Depression. (p. 594)

Hoskens, Jane (häs′kənz), 1694–? Indentured servant whose autobiography described life in colonial Pennsylvania. (p. 226)

Houston, Sam (hūs′tən), 1793–1863 Leader of the Texas army during the Texas Revolution and first president of the Republic of Texas in 1836. (p. 419)

Howe, William (hou), 1729–1867 Commander of British forces in the American colonies from 1775 to 1778. (p. 311)

Hudson, Henry (hud′sən), ?–1611 English explorer who searched for a Northwest Passage through North America beginning in 1609. (p. 175)

Huerta, Dolores (wer′tä), 1929– A founder of the United Farm Workers labor union. (p. 627)

Hughes, Langston (hūz), 1902–1967 Major African American writer of the Harlem Renaissance. (p. 585)

Hutchinson, Anne (huch′ən sən), 1591–1643 Puritan founder of the Portsmouth, Rhode Island in 1636. (p. 208)

I

Isabella (iz ə bel′ə), 1451–1504 Queen of Spain who, with her husband King Ferdinand, paid for Columbus's voyages to the Americas. (p. 140)

J

Jackson, Andrew (jak′sən), 1767–1845 Seventh President of the United States from 1829 to 1837. He defeated the British at the Battle of New Orleans during the War of 1812 and was known as "Old Hickory." (p. 388)

Jackson, Helen Hunt (jak′sən), 1830–1885 Massachusetts writer who criticized treatment of Native Americans in the late 1800s. (p. 534)

Jackson, Thomas "Stonewall" (jak′sən), 1824–1863 Confederate general who played an important role in the Confederate victories at both Battles of Bull Run. (p. 475)

Jefferson, Thomas (jef′ər sən), 1743–1826 Third President of the United States from 1801 to 1809. He was also a political philosopher and the author of the Declaration of Independence who later bought the Louisiana Purchase from France. (p. 288)

Johnson, Andrew (jon′sən), 1808–1875 The 17th President of the United States from 1865 to 1869. He took office after President Lincoln's assassination. (p. 495)

Johnson, Lyndon Baines (jon′sən), 1908–1973 The 36th President of the United States from 1963 to 1969. He took office after President Kennedy's assassination. (p. 620)

Jolliet, Louis (jō′lē et), 1645–1700 French explorer who sailed with Jacques Marquette through the Great Lakes and down the Mississippi to the mouth of the Arkansas River in 1673. (p. 266)

Jones, Absalom (jōnz), 1746–1818 Abolitionist who, with Richard Allen, helped found the first African Methodist Episcopal Church in 1816. (p. 391)

Jones, John Paul (jōnz), 1747–1792 American sea captain who commanded the *Bonhomme Richard* and defeated the British ship *Serapis* in 1779. (p. 329)

Jones, Mary Harris (jōnz), 1830–1930 American labor union leader. She fought against child labor and was known as "Mother Jones." (p. 544)

Joseph, Chief (jō′zəf), 1840–1904 Leader of the Nez Percé whose people were captured and forced onto a reservation. (p. 533)

Juárez, Benito (hwä′res, be nē′tō), 1806–1872 Zapotec Indian who, as Mexico's president in the middle 1800s, tried to make conditions fairer for all. (p. 658)

K

Kennedy, John F. (ken′i dē), 1917–1963 The 35th President of the United States from 1961 to 1963 who was the youngest person elected President. (p. 620)

Key, Francis Scott (kē), 1779–1843 Writer of "The Star–Spangled Banner" during the War of 1812. This poem later became the national anthem. (p. 388)

King, Martin Luther, Jr. (king), 1929–1968 Baptist minister and major civil rights leader during the 1950s and 1960s. (p. 618)

Knox, Henry (noks), 1750–1806 Revolutionary War officer who helped drive the British from Boston in 1776. (p. 311)

Kosciuszko, Thaddeus (kos ē us′kō), 1746–1817 Patriot from Poland who served in the Continental Army from 1776 to 1784. (p. 324)

L

La Salle, Robert (lə sal'), 1643–1687 French explorer who reached the mouth of the Mississippi River in 1682 and claimed the Mississippi River valley for France. (p. 267)

Lafayette, Marquis de (laf ē et', mär kē' də), 1757–1834 French general who joined the Continental Army during the American Revolution. (p. 324)

Las Casas, Bartolomé de (läs kä'säs, bär tō lō me' de), 1474–1566 Roman Catholic missionary from Spain who opposed the mistreatment of Indians in New Spain. (p. 158)

Latimer, Lewis (lat'ə mər), 1848–1928 African American inventor who assisted in the invention of Bell's telephone and Edison's lightbulb. (p. 541)

Lee, Richard Henry (lē), 1732–1794 Virginia planter, patriot, and signer of the Declaration of Independence. (p. 288)

Lee, Robert E. (lē), 1807–1870 United States Army officer who commanded the Confederate Army during the Civil War. (p. 475)

L'Enfant, Pierre (län fän', pē yâr'), 1754–1825 French engineer and architect who designed the plan of the District of Columbia. (p. 378)

Leo Africanus (lē'ō af ri kā'nəs), 1485–1554 Arab historian from Spain who wrote one of the earliest descriptions of the Songhai kingdom. (p. 120)

Lewis, Meriwether (lü'is), 1774–1809 United States Army officer and scout who explored the Louisiana Territory with William Clark from 1803 to 1806. (p. 381)

Liliuokalani (lē lē ü wō kä lä'nē), 1838–1917 Last queen of Hawaii from 1891 to 1893, who was overthrown by American planters. (p. 555)

Lincoln, Abraham (ling'kən), 1809–1865 The 16th President of the United States from 1861 to 1865 who led the country during the Civil War. He wrote the Gettysburg Address and was known as the "Great Emancipator." (p. 377)

Lindbergh, Charles (lind'bûrg), 1902–1974 Airplane pilot who was the first person to fly solo nonstop across the Atlantic Ocean in 1927. (p. 587)

Locke, John (lok), 1632–1704 English philosopher whose thinking influenced Thomas Jefferson in the writing of the Declaration of Independence. (p. 314)

Love, Nat (luv), 1854–1921 American cowboy and writer who had been enslaved. (p. 519)

Lowell, Francis Cabot (lō'əl), 1775–1817 Cloth factory owner who built the first power loom in the United States in 1813. (p. 406)

M

Madison, Dolley (mad'ə sən), 1768–1849 First Lady to President James Madison who saved George Washington's portrait from British forces invading Washington, D.C., during the War of 1812. (p. 388)

Madison, James (mad'ə sən), 1751–1836 Fourth President of the United States from 1809 to 1817 and author of *The Federalist Papers*. He was known as the "Father of the Constitution" because of his influence at the Constitutional Convention. (p. 346)

Magellan, Ferdinand (mə jel'ən, fûr'də nand), 1480?–1521 Portuguese explorer sailing for Spain who led the first known voyage around the world. (p. 153)

Malcolm X (mal'kəm eks), 1925–1965 African American civil rights leader in the early 1960s. (p. 627)

Marina, Doña (mä rē'nä, dōn'yä), 1501?–1550 Aztec princess also called Malinche (mä lēn' chä) who aided Hernando Cortés in his conquest of Tenochtitlán in 1521. (p. 150)

Marion, Francis (mâr'ē ən), 1732–1795 Revolutionary War commander who fought the British army throughout the Carolinas; known as the "Swamp Fox." (p. 330)

Marquette, Jacques (mär ket', zhäk), 1637–1675 Roman Catholic priest from France who sailed with Louis Jolliet through the Great Lakes and down the Mississippi to the mouth of the Arkansas River in 1673. (p. 266)

Marshall, Thurgood (mär'shəl), 1907–1993 Civil rights lawyer who helped end segregation in public schools in 1954. He was also the first African American Supreme Court justice from 1967 to 1991. (p. 617)

Mason, George (mā'sən), 1725–1792 Delegate to the Constitutional Convention who called for a bill of rights. (p. 347)

Massasoit (mas'ə soit), 1580?–1661 Main Wampanoag sachem who made a peace agreement with the Pilgrims at Plymouth. (p. 188)

McCarthy, Joseph (mə kär'thē), 1908–1957 United States Senator who led an anticommunist campaign from 1950 to 1954 that unjustly accused many government and military officials. (p. 610)

---

pronunciation key

a **at**; ā **ape**; ä **far**; âr **care**; e **end**; ē **me**; i **it**; ī **ice**; îr **pierce**; o **hot**; ō **old**; ô **fork**; oi **oil**; ou **out**; u **up**; ū **use**; ü **rule**; ù **pull**; ûr **turn**; hw **white**; ng **song**; th **thin**; <u>th</u> **this**; zh measure; ə **about, taken, pencil, lemon, circus**

Biographical Dictionary

McCormick, Cyrus (mə kôr′mək), 1809–1884 Inventor of the reaper in 1831. (p. 408)

McCoy, Elijah (mə kôi′), 1843–1929 Inventor of the oil cup called the "real McCoy" in 1872. (p. 542)

McCoy, Joseph (mə kôi′), 1837–1915 Business leader who made Abilene, Kansas, a center of the cattle industry in 1866. (p. 520)

McKinley, William (mə kin′lē), 1843–1901 The 25th President of the United States from 1897 to 1901. (p. 556)

Meade, George (mēd), 1815–1872 General who commanded the Union forces at the Battle of Gettysburg in 1863. (p. 484)

Menchú, Rigoberta (men chü′), 1959– Guatemalan human rights leader whose campaign for equal treatment for Guatemalan Indians won her the Nobel Prize for Peace in 1992. (p. 662)

Metacomet (met ə käm′ət), 1639?–1676 Wampanoag sachem known to the English colonists as King Philip. He led one of the last Native American battles against the colonists in New England in 1676. (p. 209)

Moctezuma II (mäk tə zü′mə), 1480?–1520 Aztec emperor defeated by the Spanish conquistador Hernando Cortés in 1520. (p. 148)

Monroe, James (mən rō′), 1758–1831 Fifth President of the United States from 1817 to 1825. He proclaimed the Monroe Doctrine, which opposed European interference in the Western Hemisphere. (p. 380)

Mott, Lucretia (mot), 1793–1880 Abolitionist and women's rights leader who, with Elizabeth Cady Stanton, helped organize the Seneca Falls Convention in 1848. (p. 456)

Muir, John (myür), 1838–1914 Conservationist who worked to establish Yosemite National Park in 1890. (p. 564)

Mussolini, Benito (mü sə lē′nē), 1883–1945 Italian dictator who joined the Axis in World War II. (p. 598)

N

Nampeyo (näm pä′ō), 1859?–1942 Hopi potter who renewed interest in traditional Hopi pottery. (p. 93)

Nixon, Richard (nik′sən), 1913–1994 The 37th President of the United States from 1969 to 1974 who resigned from office. (p. 628)

O

O'Connor, Sandra Day (ō kon′ər), 1930– Arizona judge who became the first woman to serve on the United States Supreme Court in 1981. (p. 632)

Oglethorpe, James (ō′gəl thôrp), 1696–1785 British military officer who founded the colony of Georgia in 1732. (p. 217)

Oliver, James (äl′iv ər), 1823–1908 Inventor of a new type of "sodbusting" steel plow in 1877. (p. 526)

Oñate, Don Juan de (ō nyä′te, dōn hwän′ de), 1549?–1628? Conquistador from Mexico who founded Santa Fe, New Mexico, about 1609. (p. 257)

Openchancanough (ō pən chän′kən awf), 1545?–1644 Powhatan chief who led one of the last major Native American battles against the English in Virginia in 1622. (p. 184)

Osceola (ä sē ō′lə), 1800–1838 Seminole chief who resisted his people's removal from Florida. (p. 399)

Otermín, Antonio de (ō ter mēn′), late 1600s Spanish governor of New Mexico in 1680. (p. 259)

P

Paine, Thomas (pān), 1737–1809 American Patriot who wrote *Common Sense* in 1776. (p. 311)

Parker, John (pär′kər), 1729–1775 Patriot captain at the Battle of Lexington on April 19, 1775, where the first shots in the American Revolution were fired. (p. 302)

Parks, Rosa (pärks), 1913– Civil rights leader who fought segregation on city buses in Montgomery, Alabama, in 1955. She is known as the "Mother of the Civil Rights Movement." (p. 618)

Penn, William (pen), 1644–1718 Quaker leader who founded the colony of Pennsylvania in 1681. (p. 210)

Perry, Oliver Hazard (per′ē), 1785–1819 United States Navy captain who defeated the British in the Battle of Lake Erie during the War of 1812. (p. 387)

Philip II (fil′ip), 1527–1598 King of Spain during the English defeat of the Spanish Armada in 1588. (p. 170)

Pickett, George (pik′ət), 1848–1918 Confederate general who led "Pickett's Charge" at the Battle of Gettysburg in 1863. (p. 484)

Pinckney, Elizabeth Lucas (pink′nē), 1722?–1793 South Carolina planter who made indigo a major cash crop for the Southern Colonies. (p. 229)

Pizarro, Francisco (pē sär′rō), 1471?–1541 Spanish conquistador who defeated the Inca in 1533. (p. 152)

Pocahontas (pō kə hon′təs), 1595?–1617 Daughter of Chief Powhatan whose marriage to John Rolfe led to the "Peace of Pocahontas" from 1614 to 1617. (p. 181)

Polk, James K. (pōk), 1795–1849 Eleventh President of the United States from 1845 to 1849, during the Mexican War. (p. 421)

Polo, Marco (pō′lō), 1254?–1324? Italian merchant whose book about his travels through China from 1274 to 1292 stirred European interest in Asia. (p. 124)

Ponce de León, Juan (pōn′ se de le ōn′), 1460?–1521 Spanish explorer who reached Florida in 1513. (p. 153)

Pontiac (pon′tē ak), 1720–1769 Ottawa chief who led attacks against the British after losing the French and Indian War in 1763. (p. 275)

Popé (pō pā′), ?–1688 Pueblo leader who drove the Spanish out of New Mexico for 12 years, beginning in 1680. (p. 259)

Powhatan, Chief (pou ə tan′), 1550?–1618 Chief of the Powhatan who helped the English settlement at Jamestown. (p. 179)

Putnam, Israel (pət′nəm), 1718–1790 Patriot general at the Battle of Bunker Hill. (p. 305)

R

Raleigh, Sir Walter (rô′lē), 1552?–1618 English explorer, historian, and soldier who started two unsuccessful colonies at Roanoke Island, in 1584 and 1587. (p. 169)

Reagan, Ronald (rā′gən), 1911– The 40th President of the United States from 1981 to 1989. (p. 634)

Revels, Hiram R. (rev′əlz), 1822–1901 First African American Senator, who finished the term of Jefferson Davis from 1870 to 1871. (p. 497)

Revere, Paul (rə vîr′), 1735–1818 Boston Patriot and silversmith who, on the night of April 18, 1775, rode to warn the people of Lexington that British troops were coming. (p. 235)

Robinson, Jo Ann (rob′in sən), 1912– Teacher, civil rights worker, and organizer of the Montgomery bus boycott of 1956. (p. 618)

Rockefeller, John D. (rok′ə fel ər), 1839–1937 Business leader who started the Standard Oil Company, one of the largest monopolies in the United States. (p. 543)

Rolfe, John (rälf), 1585–1622 Jamestown leader whose method of curing tobacco made it a successful cash crop; married Pocahantas. (p. 182)

Roosevelt, Eleanor (rō′zə velt), 1884–1962 Writer and First Lady to the 32nd President Franklin D. Roosevelt; she traveled widely across the United States during the Depression. (p. 594)

Roosevelt, Franklin D. (rō′zə velt), 1882–1945 The 32nd President of the United States from 1933 to 1945. He created New Deal programs to fight the Great Depression and led the country during World War II. (p. 594)

Roosevelt, Theodore (rō′zə velt), 1858–1919 The 26th President of the United States from 1901 to 1909. He led the Rough Riders during the Spanish-American War in 1898. (p. 556)

Ross, John (rôs), 1790–1866 Cherokee chief from 1828 to 1866 whose people were forced to march to the Indian Territory in 1838. (p. 398)

S

Sacajawea (sak ə jə wē′ə), 1787?–1812 Shoshone guide and translator for the Lewis and Clark expedition from 1805 to 1806. (p. 382)

Salem, Peter (sā′ləm), 1750?–1816 Patriot and former slave whose shot killed British Colonel Pitcairn at the Battle of Bunker Hill. (p. 305)

Salomon, Haym (sal′ə mən), 1740–1785 Business leader who raised money for the Continental Army during the American Revolution. (p. 331)

Samoset (sam′ə set), 1590?–1655 Wamponoag sachem who was among those who first met the Pilgrims at Plymouth in 1620. (p. 188)

San Martín, José de (sän mär tēn′), 1778–1850 Argentinian military leader who freed Argentina and Chile from Spanish rule in the early 1800s. (p 664)

Santa Anna, Antonio López de (sän′tä än′ä), 1795–1876 Mexican general who defeated the Texans defending The Alamo in 1836. (p. 418)

Scott, Winfield (skot), 1786–1866 United States general during the Civil War who proposed the Anaconda Plan. (p. 424)

Seguín, Juan (se gēn′), 1806–1889 Tejano leader who organized volunteers to fight the Mexican army in the Texas Revolution. (p. 418)

Sequoyah (si kwoi′ə), 1766?–1843 Cherokee leader who invented an alphabet for his people's language. (p. 396)

Serra, Junípero (ser′rä, hü nē′pe rō), 1713–1784 Roman Catholic missionary who built missions in California in the 1700s. (p. 261)

Shaw, Robert Gould (shô), 1837–1863 Union commander of the first African American volunteer regiment in 1863. (p. 480)

pronunciation key

a **at**; ā **ape**; ä **far**; âr **care**; e **end**; ē **me**; i **it**; ī **ice**; îr **pierce**; o **hot**; ō **old**; ô **fork**; oi **oil**; ou **out**; u **up**; ū **use**; ü **rule**, ù **pull**; ûr **turn**; hw **white**; ng **song**; th **thin**; <u>th</u> **this**; zh measure; ə **about**, tak**e**n, penc**i**l, lem**o**n, circ**u**s

Biographical Dictionary

Shays, Daniel (shāz), 1747?–1825 American Revolutionary officer who led a rebellion of Massachusetts farmers against state courts in 1786. (p. 343)

Sherman, Roger (shûr′mən), 1721–1793 Patriot who proposed the Great Compromise at the Constitutional Convention in 1787 that established the two houses of Congress. (p. 350)

Sherman, William Tecumseh (shûr′mən, wil′yəm tə kum′sə), 1820–1891 Union general whose destructive march through Georgia in 1864 helped defeat the Confederacy. (p. 489)

Sinclair, Upton (sin klār′), 1878–1968 Writer whose novel *The Jungle* in 1906 exposed unsafe practices in the meat-packing industry. (p. 561)

Sitting Bull (sit′ing bul′), 1834–1890 Lakota chief who, with Crazy Horse, defeated Colonel Custer at the Battle of the Little Bighorn in 1876. (p. 532)

Slater, Samuel (slā′tər), 1768–1835 English engineer who built the first water-powered spinning mill in the United States in 1789. (p. 404)

Smith, John (smith), 1579?–1631 English army captain whose strict discipline helped the Jamestown settlement to survive. (p. 180)

Squanto (skwon′tō) 1585?–1622 Pawtuxet Native American who helped the Pilgrims at Plymouth to survive. (p. 188)

Stalin, Josef (stä′lin), 1879–1953 Dictator of the Soviet Union from 1923 to 1953. (p. 600)

Standish, Miles (stan′dish), 1584?–1656 English army captain at Plymouth who helped defend the Pilgrim colony. (p. 190)

Stanton, Elizabeth Cady (stant′ən), 1815–1902 Abolitionist and women's rights leader who helped write the "Declaration of Rights and Sentiments" at the Seneca Falls Convention in 1848. (p. 456)

Steuben, Frederich von (stü′bən), 1730–1794 Patriot officer from Germany who helped train the Continental Army at Valley Forge during the American Revolution. (p. 325)

Stowe, Harriet Beecher (stō), 1811–1896 Abolitionist and writer of *Uncle Tom's Cabin* in 1851. (p. 462)

Sunni Ali (su′nē ä′lē), ?–1492 King of Songhai in West Africa in the late 1400s. (p. 121)

T

Tarbell, Ida (tär′bəl), 1857–1944 Muckraker and writer whose articles described the unfair business practices of the Standard Oil Company in 1903. (p. 561)

Taylor, Zachary (tā′lər), 1784–1850 The 12th President of the United States from 1849 to 1850. He led United States forces during the War with Mexico. (p. 423)

Tecumseh (tə kum′sə), 1768–1813 Shawnee chief who attempted to unite Native American peoples against new settlers in the Northwest Territory. (p. 388)

Tomochichi (tō mä chē′chē), 1650?–1739 Chief of the Yamacraw who gave James Oglethorpe land for the Savannah settlement. (p. 217)

Tompkins, Sally (täm′kənz), 1833–1916 Confederate nurse who ran a hospital in Richmond, Virginia, during the Civil War. (p. 482)

Toussaint L'Ouverture (tü san′ lü vûr tyür), 1743?–1803 Haitian military leader and former slave who fought for the independence of Haiti and end of slavery. (p. 660)

Travis, William (trav′əs), 1809–1836 Commander of the Texas army at The Alamo in 1836. (p. 418)

Truman, Harry S. (trü′mən), 1884–1972 The 33rd President of the United States from 1945 to 1953. He led the country at the end of World War II. (p. 604)

Truth, Sojourner (trüth), 1797?–1883 Abolitionist who escaped from slavery in 1827 and spoke out for women's rights. (p. 457)

Tubman, Harriet (tub′mən), 1820?–1913 Abolitionist, Underground Railroad conductor, and spy for the Union Army during the Civil War. She helped hundreds of enslaved African Americans escape to freedom. (p. 455)

Turner, Nat (tûr′nər), 1800–1831 Leader of a slave revolt in Virginia in 1831. (p. 446)

V

Vargas, Diego de (vär′gäs, dē e′gō de), 1643–1704 Commander of the Spanish army that recaptured New Mexico from the Pueblo people in 1692. (p. 260)

Verrazano, Giovanni da (vâr ə zä′nō, jō vän′ nē də), 1485?–1528? Italian sea captain in the service of France who searched for a Northwest Passage in 1524. (p. 176)

W

Warren, Mercy Otis (wôr′ən), 1728–1814 Patriot, poet, and playwright who urged women to give up tea and other taxable goods from Great Britain in the 1760s. (p. 294)

Washington, Booker T. (wô′shing tən), 1856–1915 Educator and founder of the Tuskegee Institute, an African American college, in 1881. (p. 582)

Washington, George (wô′shing tən), 1732–1799 First President of the United States from 1789 to 1797. He fought in the French and Indian War and led the Continental Army during the American Revolution. (p. 272)

Washington, George (wô′shing tən), 1790?–? Homesteader who founded the African American town of Centralia, Washington, in 1875. (p. 529)

Washington, Martha (wô′shing tən), 1731–1802 First Lady to President George Washington. She assisted the Continental Army during the American Revolution. (p. 322)

Wells–Barnett, Ida (welz′ bär′nət), 1862–1931 A founder of the National Association for the Advancement of Colored People (NAACP) in 1909. (p. 583)

Wheatley, Phillis (hwēt′lē), 1753?–1784 Enslaved American poet whose poems called for fair treatment for all people. (p. 291)

White, John (hwīt), 1500s Leader of the English colony of Roanoke in 1587. (p. 169)

Whitman, Narcissa (hwit′mən), 1808–1847 American missionary who traveled to the Oregon Territory in 1836. (p. 429)

Whitney, Eli (hwit′nē), 1765–1825 Inventor of the cotton gin in 1793. (p. 405)

Williams, Roger (wil′yəmz), 1603–1684 Puritan minister who founded the colony of Rhode Island in 1636. (p. 208)

Wilson, Woodrow (wil′sən), 1856–1924 The 28th President of the United States from 1913 to 1921. He led the United States during World War I and helped found the League of Nations. (p. 578)

Winthrop, John (win′thrəp), 1588–1649 First governor of the Massachusetts Bay Colony in 1630. (p. 204)

Woolman, John (wül′mən), 1720–1772 Quaker who spoke out against slavery in the colonies. (p. 241)

Wright, Orville (rīt), 1871–1948 Inventor who, with his brother Wilbur, made the world's first successful airplane flight in 1903. (p. 562)

Wright, Wilbur (rīt), 1867–1912 Inventor who, with his brother Orville, made the world's first successful airplane flight in 1903. (p. 562)

Y

Yanga (yang′gə), 1500s–1600s Leader of a slave revolt in New Spain in 1609. (p. 159)

York (yôrk), 1770–1832? William Clark's slave and a member of the Lewis and Clark expedition from 1804 to 1806. (p. 382)

Young, Brigham (yung), 1801–1877 Leader of the Mormons who brought the Mormons from Illinois to Utah, where they founded Salt Lake City. (p. 429)

Z

Zavala, Lorenzo de (zä vä′lä), 1788–1836 The first vice president of the Texas Republic in 1836. (p. 420)

Zenger, John Peter (zeng′ər), 1697–1746 Newspaper printer whose trial in 1734 helped to establish the idea of freedom of the press. (p. 290)

Zheng He (jäng hə), 1371?–1433? Chinese sea captain whose voyages opened Chinese exploration and trade in the early 1400s. (p. 116)

Zhu Di (zhü dē), 1360–1424 Emperor of China who encouraged exploration and trade in the early 1400s. (p. 115)

pronunciation key

a **at**; ā **ape**; ä **far**; âr **care**; e **end**; ē **me**; i **it**; ī **ice**; îr **pierce**; o **hot**; ō **old**; ô **fork**; oi **oil**; ou **out**; u **up**; ū **use**; ü **rule**; ù **pull**; ûr **turn**; hw **white**; ng **song**; th **thin**; th **this**; zh **measure**; ə **about, taken, pencil, lemon, circus**

Glossary

Glossary

This Glossary will help you to pronounce and understand the meanings of the vocabulary in this book. The page number at the end of the definition tells you where the word first appears.

A

A.D. (ā dē) "Anno Domini," Latin for "in the year of the Lord." Used before a numeral to indicate a year occurring since the birth of Jesus Christ. (p. 71)

abolitionist (ab ə lish′ə nist) A person who wanted to end slavery in the United States. (p. 452)

acid rain (asid rān) Precipitation containing harmful chemical pollution that can destroy trees and wildlife and poison water. See **precipitation**. (p. 45)

adobe (ə dō′bē) A type of clay traditionally used as a building material by Native Americans and later Spanish colonists in the Southwest. (p. 92)

agriculture (ag′ri kul chər) The business of farming. (p. 229)

Allied Powers (al′lid pou′ərz) The name given to the forces led by Great Britain, France, and Russia during World War I. The United States joined the Allied Powers in 1917. See **Central Powers**. (p. 578)

Allies (al′līz) The name given to the countries allied against the Axis Powers in World War II, including the United States, Britain, France, the Soviet Union, and China. See **Axis**. (p. 599)

almanac (ôl′mə nak) A reference book containing facts and figures. (p. 245)

alternative (ôl tûr′nə tiv) Another way of doing something. (p. 16)

amendment (ə mend′mənt) An addition to the Constitution. See **Constitution** (p. 354)

American Revolution (ə mer′i kən rev ə lü′shən) The war between Great Britain and its thirteen American colonies from 1775 to 1783 that led to the founding of the United States of America. (p. 300)

Anaconda Plan (an ə kon′də plan) The Union's three-part plan for defeating the Confederacy in the Civil War. (p. 474)

ancestor (an′ses tər) A relative who lived before you. (p. 9)

Antifederalist (an′tē fed′ər ə list) An opponent of a strong central government in the late 1700s. See **Federalist**. (p. 359)

archaeologist (är kē ol′ə jist) A scientist who looks for and studies artifacts. See **artifact**. (p. 61)

arid (ar′id) Dry. (p. 37)

armada (är mä′də) A large fleet of ships, especially warships. (p. 170)

arms race (ärmz rās) A race to build the most powerful weapons. (p. 610)

Articles of Confederation (är′ti kəlz uv kən fed ə rā′shən) The first plan of government of the United States. In effect from 1781 to 1789, it gave more power to the states than the central government. See **Constitution**. (p. 343)

artifact (är′tə fakt) An object left behind by people who lived long ago. See **archaeologist**. (p. 74)

assembly (ə sem′blē) A lawmaking body. (p. 286)

assembly line (ə sem′blē līn) A method of mass production in which the product is carried on a moving belt past workers who remain in place. (p. 563)

atlas (at′ləs) A book of maps. See **reference source**. (p. 427)

atomic bomb (ə tom′ik bom) A bomb which produces massive amounts of energy by splitting atoms. (p. 604)

autobiography (ô tə bī og′rə fē) The story of a person's own life written by himself or herself. (p. 226)

Axis (ak′sis) The name given to the countries that fought the Allies in World War II, including Germany, Italy, and Japan. See **Allies**. (p. 598)

pronunciation key

a	at	ī	ice	u	up	th	thin
ā	ape	îr	pierce	ū	use	th	this
ä	far	o	hot	ü	rule	zh	measure
âr	care	ō	old	ù	pull	ə	about, taken,
e	end	ô	fork	ûr	turn		pencil, lemon,
ē	me	oi	oil	hw	white		circus
i	it	ou	out	ng	song		

B

B.C. (bē sē) "Before Christ." Used after a numeral to indicate a year occurring before the birth of Jesus Christ. (p. 71)

backcountry (bak'kən trē) In colonial times, the name given to the eastern foothills of the Appalachian Mountains. (p. 248)

Battle of Buena Vista (ba'təl uv bwe'nä vēs'tä) The battle during the Mexican War in which heavily outnumbered United States forces led by General Zachary Taylor defeated Santa Anna's army in 1847. *See* **Mexican War.** (p. 423)

Battle of Bunker Hill (ba'təl uv bung'kər hil) Costly British "victory" in 1775 over Colonial forces at a site near Charlestown, Massachusetts. (p. 305)

Battle of Gettysburg (ba'təl uv get'iz bûrg) The Civil War battle fought in southeastern Pennsylvania in July 1863. Confederate forces under General Robert E. Lee were defeated. (p. 484)

Battle of New Orleans (bat'əl uv nü ôr'lē ənz) A United States victory over British forces in the last battle of the War of 1812. *See* **War of 1812.** (p. 390)

bilingual (bī ling'gwəl) Two languages. The ability to speak two languages equally well. (p. 652)

Bill of Rights (bil uv rīts) The first ten amendments to the Constitution, ratified in 1791. *See* **amendment** *and* **Constitution.** (p. 361)

black codes (blak kōdz) Laws passed by the Southern states after the Civil War that severely limited the rights of the newly freed African Americans. (p. 495)

blockade (blo kād') The closing of an area, especially during wartime, to keep people or supplies from moving in or out. (p. 474)

Boston Tea Party (bōs'tən tē pär'tē) A 1773 protest against British taxes in which Boston colonists disguised as Mohawks dumped valuable tea into Boston Harbor. (p. 296)

boycott (boi'kot) To refuse to do business or have contact with a person, group, country, or product. (p. 294)

C

Cabinet (kab'ə nit) The officials appointed by the President to be advisers and to head each department in the executive branch. *See* **executive branch** *and* **secretary.** (p. 362)

call number (kôl num'bər) A series of letters and numbers giving the exact location of a book on a library shelf. *See* **card catalog.** (p. 427)

canal (kə nal') A human-built waterway. *See* **lock.** (p. 412)

caravan (kar'ə van) A group of people traveling together for safety, especially through desert areas. (p. 120)

caravel (kar'ə vel) A fast sailing ship that could be steered easily and hold large amounts of cargo. (p. 126)

card catalog (kärd kat'ə lôg) A listing by call number of all the books a library contains. The catalog is arranged alphabetically by author, title, and subject. *See* **call number.** (p. 427)

cardinal direction (kär'də nəl di rek'shən) One of the four main points of the compass; north, south, east, and west. *See* **compass rose.** (p. G6)

cash crop (kash krop) A crop that is grown to be sold for profit. *See* **profit.** (p. 182)

cattle drive (kat'əl drīv) A long journey in which cowboys brought cattle from the ranch to the railroad, from about the 1860s to the 1880s. *See* **rail head.** (p. 518)

cause (kôz) Something that makes something else happen. *See* **effect.** (p. 108)

CD-ROM (sē dē räm') A type of reference source similar to a compact disc that is "read" by a computer. It combines text, sound, and even short films. *See* **reference source.** (p. 427)

census (sen'səs) An official count of all the people living in a country or region. (p. 10)

Central Powers (sen'trəl pou'ərz) The forces led by Germany, Austria-Hungary, and Turkey in World War I. *See* **Allied Powers.** (p. 578)

century (sen'chə rē) A period of 100 years. (p. 71)

charter (chär'tər) An official document giving a person permission to do something, such as settle in an area. (p. 169)

checks and balances (cheks and bal'ən səz) The system in which the power of each branch of government is balanced by the powers of other branches. (p. 356)

circle graph (sûr'kəl graf) A kind of graph that shows how something can be divided into parts. (p. 119)

citizen (sit'ə zən) A person born in a country or who chooses to become a member of that country by law. (p. 13)

civil rights (siv'əl rīts) The individual rights of all citizens to be treated equally under the law. (p. 14)

Civil War (sivəl wôr) In the United States, the war between the Union and the Confederacy from 1861 to 1865. (p. 472)

civilization (siv ə lə zā'shən) A culture that has developed complex systems of government, education, and religion. Civilizations usually have large populations with many people living in cities. (p. 60)

clan (klan) A group of families who share the same ancestor. (p. 105)

climate (klī′mit) The weather of an area over a number of years. (p. 36)

climograph (clī′mə graf) A graph that shows information about the temperature and precipitation of a place over time. (p. 242)

Cold War (kōld wôr) The conflict from 1945 to 1991 between the United States and the Soviet Union, involving ideas, words, money, and weapons. (p. 608)

colony (kol′ə nē) A settlement far away from the country that rules it. (p. 142)

Columbian exchange (kə lum′bē ən eks chānj′) The movement of people, plants, animals, and germs in either direction across the Atlantic Ocean following the voyages of Columbus. (p. 143)

Committees of Correspondence (kə mit′ēz uv kōr ə spon′dəns) Groups organized in the 1770s to keep colonists informed of important events. (p. 295)

communism (kom′yə nizm) A system in which the government owns all property and makes nearly all decisions for its citizens. (p. 600)

compass rose (kum′pəs) A drawing that indicates directions on a map, especially cardinal and intermediate directions. *See* **cardinal direction** *and* **intermediate direction**. (p. G6)

compromise (kom′prə mīz) The settling of a dispute by each side agreeing to give up part of its demands. (p. 107)

Compromise of 1850 (kom′prə mīz uv āt′tēn′ fif′tē) A law passed by Congress admitting California to the Union, allowing people in the territories to decide slavery for themselves, and obtaining the North's agreement to obey the Fugitive Slave Law. *See* **Fugitive Slave Law of 1850**. (p. 461)

concentration camp (kon sen trā′shən kamp) A type of prison in which the Nazis enslaved and murdered millions of people during World War II. *See* **Holocaust**. (p. 604)

conclusion (kən klü′zhən) A statement reached by considering all the information about something. (p. 270)

Conestoga (kon ə stō′gə) A sturdy wagon used by colonists and pioneers to carry people and goods. (p. 212)

Confederate States of America (kən fed′ər it stāts uv ə mer′i kə) The name adopted by the 11 Southern states that seceded from the Union during the Civil War. (p. 465)

conquistador (kōn kēs tä dôr′) A name for the Spanish conquerors who first came to the Americas in the 1500s. (p. 148)

conservation (kon sər vā′shən) The protection and careful use of natural resources. (p. 46)

Constitution (kon sti tü′shən) A plan of government. In the United States it is the supreme law and plan of the national government, adopted in 1789. (p. 12)

Constitutional Convention (kon sti tü′shə nəl kən ven′shən) The meeting of twelve states' delegates in Philadelphia, Pennsylvania, that replaced the Articles of Confederation with a new Constitution. *See* **Articles of Confederation** *and* **Constitution**. (p. 346)

continent (kon′tə nənt) One of Earth's seven large bodies of land, including Africa, Antarctica, Asia, Australia, Europe, North America, and South America. (p. G4)

Continental Army (kon′tə nen′təl är′mē) The army created by the Second Continental Congress in May 1775 with George Washington as commander-in-chief. *See* **Second Continental Congress**. (p. 312)

corporation (kôr pə rā′shən) A business that is owned by individuals who invest in that company. *See* **shareholders**. (p. 543)

cotton gin (kot′ən jin) A machine that separates cotton from its seeds, invented by Eli Whitney in 1793. (p. 405)

coup stick (kü stik) A special weapon used by a Lakota Sioux soldier to show his bravery by touching, but not killing, his enemy. (p. 98)

coureur de bois (kü rər′ də bwä′) In New France, a person who trapped furs without permission from the French government. (p. 268)

covenant (kuv′ə nənt) A special agreement. In colonial New England, a contract signed by each free man that bound his family to live by Puritan rules. (p. 206)

credibility (cred ə bil′i tē) Accuracy or believability. (p. 606)

Cuban Missile Crisis (kyü′bən mis′əl krīs′is) A confrontation in 1962 between the United States and the Soviet Union over nuclear missiles in Cuba. (p. 625)

culture (kul′chər) The entire way of life of a people, including their customs, beliefs, and language. (p. 8)

D

dateline (dāt′līn) A line at the beginning of a newspaper article that tells when and where the story was written. (p. 459)

debtor (det′ər) A person who owes money. (p. 217)

decade (dek′ād) A period of ten years. (p. 71)

decision (dis izh′ən) A choice made from a number of alternatives. *See* **alternative**. (p. 16)

Declaration of Independence (dek lə rā′shən əv in di pen′dəns) The official document issued by the Second Continental Congress on July 4, 1776, explaining why the American colonies were breaking away from Great Britain. (p. 313)

degree (di grē′) A unit of measurement. It can be used for calculating latitude and longitude. (p. 40)

delegate (del′i git) A member of an elected assembly. *See* **assembly**. (p. 289)

democracy (di mok′rə sē) A form of government in which the people make the laws and run the government. (p. 12)

dictator (dik′tā tər) A leader with complete authority over the government. (p. 598)

discrimination (di skrim′ə nā shən) An unfair difference in the treatment of people. (p. 582)

diversity (di vûr′si tē) Variety; differences. (p. 8)

Dred Scott Decision (dred skät di sizh′ən) An 1857 Supreme Court decision that said slaves were private property. (p. 462)

drought (drout) A long period with very little rain. (p. 75)

E

economy (i kon′ə mē) The way a country's people use natural resources, money, and knowledge to produce goods and services. (p. 44)

editor (ed′i tər) A person who helps to run a publication, such as a newspaper or a magazine. (p. 459)

editorial (ed i tôr′ē əl) A newspaper article in which the editors give their opinions on important issues. (p. 459)

effect (i fekt′) Something that happens as a result of a cause. *See* **cause**. (p. 108)

elevation (el ə vā′shən) The height of an area above sea level. *See* **elevation map**. (p. 214)

elevation map (el ə vā′shən map) A physical map that uses colors to show the elevation, or height, of land above sea level. *See* **physical map**. (p. G10)

Emancipation Proclamation (ē man si pā′shən prōk lə mā′shən) An official announcement issued by President Abraham Lincoln in 1862 that led to the end of slavery in the United States. (p. 478)

empire (em′pīr) A large area in which different groups of people are controlled by one ruler or government. (p. 64)

encomienda (en kō mē en′dä) A very large piece of land in New Spain given by the Spanish government to certain Spanish colonists during the 1500s. (p. 156)

encyclopedia (en sī klə pē′dē ə) A book or set of books that gives information about people, places, things, and past events. (p. 426)

environment (en vī′rən mənt) All the surroundings in which people, plants, and animals live. (p. 44)

equator (i kwā′tər) An imaginary line encircling Earth halfway between the North Pole and the South Pole, designated as 0° latitude. *See* **latitude**. (p. G4)

Era of Good Feelings (îr′ə uv gu̇d fē′lingz) The name given to the period of peace and prosperity that followed the War of 1812. (p. 390)

ethnic group (eth′nik grüp) People with the same customs and language, often having a common history. (p. 9)

evaluate (i val′ ū āt) To determine the value or meaning of something. (p. 16)

executive branch (eg zek′yə tiv branch) The part of government, headed by the President, that carries out the laws. (p. 349)

exoduster (ek′sō dus tər) The term describing one of the many African Americans from the South who went to Kansas in the 1860s. (p. 528)

expedition (ek spi dish′ən) A journey made for a special purpose. (p. 140)

export (ek′spôrt) To send goods to other countries for sale or use. *See* **import**. (p. 228)

F

fact (fakt) A statement that can be checked and proved true. *See* **opinion**. (p. 172)

fall line (fôl lin) The boundary between an upland area and a lowland area. (p. 215)

favela (fä vā′lä) The name for any slum near São Paulo, Brazil. *See* **slum**. (p. 667)

feature article (fē′chər är′ti kəl) A newspaper article that is a detailed report on a person, an issue, or an event. (p. 459)

federal (fed′ər əl) The word describing the central, or national, government. (p. 12)

federal system (fed′ər əl sis′təm) A system of government in which power is shared between the central government and the state governments. The United States has a federal system of government. *See* **states' rights**. (p. 355)

---

pronunciation key

a **at**; ā **ape**; ä **far**; âr **care**; e **end**; ē **me**; i **it**; ī **ice**; îr **pierce**; o **hot**; ō **old**; ô **fork**; oi **oil**; ou **out**; u **up**; ū **use**; ü **rule**; u̇ **pull**; ûr **turn**; hw **white**; ng **song**; th **thin**; <u>th</u> **this**; zh **measure**; ə **about**, tak**e**n, penc**i**l, lem**o**n, circ**u**s

Federalist (fed'ər ə list) A supporter of a strong federal system of government in the late 1700s. *See* **Antifederalist**. (p. 359)

Fifteenth Amendment (fif'tēnth' ə mend'mənt) An amendment to the Constitution, ratified in 1870, that made it illegal to withhold voting rights "on account of race or color." *See* **amendment** *and* **ratify**. (p. 497)

First Battle of Bull Run (fûrst ba'təl uv bùl run) The first major battle of the Civil War, in July 1861. (p. 475)

First Continental Congress (fûrst kon'tə nen'təl kong'gris) The assembly of colonial delegates from every colony except Georgia that met in 1774 in Philadelphia to oppose the Intolerable Acts. *See* **Intolerable Acts** *and* **Second Continental Congress**. (p. 300)

Forty-Niners (fôr'tē ni'nərz) People who came to California in 1849 in search of gold. (p. 432)

fossil fuel (fos'əl fū'əl) A fuel, such as oil, natural gas, and coal, that is formed from the remains of plants and animals that lived millions of years ago. (p. 43)

Fourteenth Amendment (fôr'tēnth' ə mend'mənt) An amendment to the Constitution, ratified in 1868, that officially established blacks as citizens with the same legal rights as whites. *See* **amendment** *and* **ratify**. (p. 496)

free enterprise (frē en'tər prīz) An economic system in which people can own property and businesses and are free to decide what to make, how much to produce, and what price to charge. (p. 229)

Freedmen's Bureau (frēd'mənz byùr'ō) A government agency created in 1865 that provided food, schools, and medical care for freed slaves and others in the South. (p. 496)

French and Indian War (french ənd in'dē ən wôr) A conflict between Great Britain and France in North America from 1756 to 1763. British colonists used this name to describe those they were fighting—the French and their Native American allies. (p. 272)

frontier (frun tîr') A word used by colonists and pioneers to describe land on the edge of their settlements. (p. 244)

Fugitive Slave Law of 1850 (fū'ji tiv slāv lô) A law passed by Congress that required police in free states to help capture escaping slaves. *See* **Compromise of 1850**. (p. 461)

G

generalization (jen ər ə lə zā'shən) A broad statement that ties together a number of separate facts, ideas, or examples. (p. 486)

geography (jē og'rə fē) The study of Earth and the way people live on it and use it. (p. 28)

Gettysburg Address (get'iz bûrg ə dres') The speech made by President Lincoln at the site of the Battle of Gettysburg in 1863, explaining the purpose of the Civil War. (p. 484)

gold rush (gōld rush) The sudden rush of people to an area where gold has been discovered, as in California in 1849. (p. 432)

graph (graf) A diagram that presents information in a way that makes it easy to detect patterns, trends, or changes over time. (p. 118)

Great Chicago Fire (grāt shi kä'gō fīr) A fire in 1871 that destroyed a third of the city in 24 hours. (p. 547)

Great Compromise (grāt kom' prə mīz) The plan drawn up by Roger Sherman at the Constitutional Convention in 1787. It proposed the establishment of two houses of Congress. (p. 350)

Great Depression (grāt di presh'ən) The period of widespread economic hardship in the 1930s. (p. 592)

Great Migration (grāt mī grā'shən) The journey of hundreds of thousands of African Americans from the South to such northern manufacturing cities as Chicago that peaked in the early 1900s. (p. 582)

grid (grid) A set of squares formed by criss-crossing lines that can help you to determine locations, such as on a map or globe. (p. 41)

H

headline (hed'lin) A sentence or phrase printed in large type across the top of a news article to get the reader's attention. (p. 459)

hemisphere (hem'i sfîr) One half of a sphere or globe. Earth can be divided into four hemispheres. The equator divides Earth into the Northern and Southern hemispheres. The prime meridian divides it into the Eastern and Western hemispheres. *See* **equator** *and* **prime meridian**. (p. G4)

historian (hi stōr'ē ən) A person who studies the past. (p. 19)

historical atlas (hi stôr'i kəl at'ləs) A book that includes maps of important events from the past. *See* **reference source** (p. 427)

historical map (hi stôr'i kəl map) A map that shows information about the past or where past events took place. (p. G11)

history (his'tə rē) The study or record of what happened in the past. (p. 18)

Holocaust (hol'ə kôst) The murder of 6 million Jews by Nazi Germany during World War II. (p. 604)

Homestead Act (hōm'sted act) A law that gave free farmland to any adult male or widow who agreed to work it for five years. (p. 525)

homesteader (hōm'sted ər) A person who claimed land on the Great Plains under the Homestead Act of 1862. (p. 525)

House of Burgesses (hous uv bûr'jis əz) The law-making body of colonial Virginia, established in Jamestown in 1619. (p. 184)

House of Representatives (hous uv rep ri zen'tə tivz) The house of Congress in which each state's number of representatives is determined according to its population. *See* **legislative branch** *and* **Senate**. (p. 350)

humid (hū'mid) Wet; moist. (p. 37)

hurricane (hûr'i kān) A storm with violent winds above 75 miles per hour revolving around a calm center. It is accompanied by heavy rains, high tides, and flooding in coastal regions. (p. 661)

hydroelectricity (hī drō i lek tris'i tē) Electricity generated by the force of running water. (p. 596)

I

immigrant (im'i grənt) A person who leaves one country to live in another. (p. 9)

impeach (im pēch') To charge a government official with wrongdoing. (p. 497)

import (im'pōrt') To bring goods from another country for sale or use. *See* **export**. (p. 228)

indentured servant (in den'chərd sûr'vənt) A person who agreed to work for someone in colonial America for a fixed amount of time in order to pay for the ocean voyage. (p. 183)

Indian Removal Act (in'dē ən ri mü'vəl akt) A law passed by Congress in 1830 forcing Native Americans of the Southeast to move to what is now Oklahoma. (p. 397)

indigo (in'di gō) A plant that is used to produce a blue dye. *See* **cash crop**. (p. 218)

Industrial Revolution (in dus'trē əl rev ə lü'shən) The dramatic change from making goods by hand at home to making them by machine in factories. (p. 404)

industry (in'də strē) All the businesses that make one kind of product or provide one kind of service. (p. 230)

interchangeable parts (in tər chān'jə bəl pärts) Parts of a product built to a standard size so that they can be easily replaced. (p. 408)

interdependent (in tər di pen'dənt) Depending on each other to meet needs and wants. (p. 35)

intermediate direction (in tər mē'dē it di rek'shən) A direction halfway between two cardinal directions; northeast, northwest, southwest, southeast. (p. G6)

Internet (in'tər net) A computer network that connects various sources of information such as libraries to a person's home or office computer. (p. 643)

Intolerable Acts (in tä'lər ə bəl akts) The laws passed by the British Parliament in 1774 that closed Boston Harbor, dissolved the Massachusetts assembly, and forced Boston colonists to house British soldiers. *See* **Boston Tea Party**. (p. 297)

investor (in vest'ər) A person who uses money to buy or make something in order to produce a profit. *See* **profit**. (p. 412)

Iron Curtain (ī'ərn kûr'tin) The imaginary borders dividing Europe into communist and noncommunist countries from 1948 to 1991. (p. 609)

Iroquois Confederacy (ir'i kwä kən fed'ər ə sē) The union of the five major Iroquois peoples beginning about 1570. (p. 106)

irrigation (ir i gā'shən) A method of supplying dry land with water through a series of ditches or pipes. (p. 75)

J

jazz (jaz) The form of popular music that grew out of African American culture in the 1920s. (p. 585)

jerky (jûr'kē) Thin strips of sun-dried meat. (p. 99)

Jim Crow laws (jim krō lôz) Laws passed by Southern states after Reconstruction that established segregation, or separation of the races. (p. 498)

judicial branch (jü dish'əl branch) The part of government that decides the meaning of the laws. *See* **Supreme Court**. (p. 349)

K

kachina (kə chē'nə) In Pueblo religion, the living spirit of an ancestor who helps bring rains and makes crops grow. (p. 92)

Kansas-Nebraska Act (kan'zəs nə bras'kə akt) An 1854 law passed by Congress that allowed the Kansas and Nebraska territories to decide whether to become free states or slave states. (p. 462)

pronunciation key

a **at**; ā **ape**; ä **far**; âr **care**; e **end**; ē **me**; i **it**; ī **ice**; îr **pierce**; o **hot**; ō **old**; ô **fork**; oi **oil**; ou **out**; u **up**; ū **use**; ü **rule**, ù **pull**; ûr **turn**; hw **white**; ng **song**; th **thin**; th **this**; zh **measure**; ə **about, taken, pencil, lemon, circus**

Korean War (kə rē'ən wôr) A war between communist North Korea, supported by China, and South Korea, supported by the United States and other United Nations members. It lasted from 1950 to 1953. (p. 610)

Ku Klux Klan (kü' kluks klan') A secret society formed by white Southerners to terrorize blacks following the Civil War. (p. 498)

L

labor union (lā'bər ün'yən) A group of workers united to gain better wages and working conditions. (p. 544)

landform (land'fôrm) A shape on Earth's surface, such as a mountain or hill. (p. 30)

large-scale map (lärj skāl map) A map that shows a smaller area in greater detail. *See* **small-scale map**. (p. 336)

latitude (lat'i tüd) An imaginary line, or parallel, measuring distance north or south of the equator. *See* **equator** and **parallel**. (p. 40)

League of Nations (lēg uv nā'shənz) An international organization set up after World War I to prevent future wars. (p. 581)

League of Women Voters (lēg uv wim'ən vōt'ərz) A volunteer organization founded in 1920 to inform people about politics. (p. 588)

legacy (leg'ə sē) A part of our past that we value in our lives today. (p. 22)

legislative branch (lej'is lā tiv branch) The law-making part of government, with the power to raise the money needed to run the government. *See* **House of Representatives** and **Senate**. (p. 349)

liberty (lib'ər tē) Freedom. (p. 292)

line graph (līn graf) A kind of graph that shows changes over time. *See* **graph**. (p. 118)

locator (lō kā'tər) A small map inset in the corner of a larger map that helps you understand where the subject area of the larger map is located on Earth. (p. G8)

lock (lok) A kind of water elevator that moves boats within a canal to higher or lower levels. *See* **canal**. (p. 413)

lodge (loj) A type of home made of logs, grasses, sticks, and soil which the Native Americans of the Plains used when living in their villages. *See* **teepee**. (p. 96)

longhouse (lông'hous) A home shared by several related Iroquois families. (p. 104)

longitude (lon'ji tüd) An imaginary line, or meridian, measuring distance eaŝt or west of the prime meridian. *See* **meridian** and **prime meridian**. (p. 40)

Louisiana Purchase (lü ē zē an'ə pûr'chəs) The territory purchased by the United States from France in 1803, reaching from the Mississippi River to the Rocky Mountains and from the Gulf of Mexico to Canada. (p. 381)

Loyalist (loi'ə list) A colonist who supported Great Britain in the American Revolution. (p. 321)

M

magnetic compass (mag net'ik kum'pəs) An instrument invented by the Chinese about A.D. 100 to help sailors find north and south. (p. 116)

malaria (mə lâr'ē ə) A disease caused by the bite of a certain mosquito. (p. 123)

map key (map kē) A guide telling you what each symbol on a map stands for. *See* **symbol**. (p. G8)

map scale (map skāl) A line like a measuring stick drawn on a map which uses a unit of measurement, such as an inch, to represent a real distance on Earth. (p. 336)

Mayflower Compact (mā'flou ər kom'pakt) An agreement the Pilgrims made before landing in New England to make and obey "just and equal laws." (p. 187)

media (mē'dē ə) A word used to describe the methods of communication that reach a large number of people, including radio, newspapers, television, magazines, and computer networks. (p. 587)

megalopolis (meg ə lop'ə lis) A group of cities that have grown so close together that they seem to form one city. (p. 34)

mercenary (mûr'sə ner ē) A soldier paid to fight for another country. (p. 320)

meridian (mə rid'ē ən) Any line of longitude east or west of Earth's prime meridian. *See* **longitude** and **prime meridian**. (p. 40)

mestizo (me stē'zō) A person who has both Indian and Spanish ancestors. (p. 658)

Mexican War (mek'si kən wôr) A war between the United States and Mexico from 1846 to 1848. *See* **Treaty of Guadalupe Hidalgo**. (p. 423)

Middle Passage (mid'əl pas'ij) The middle leg of the triangular trade route in colonial times in which captive Africans were shipped to the West Indies to be sold into slavery. *See* **slave trade** and **triangular trade**. (p. 231)

militia (mi lish'ə) A group of volunteers who fought in times of emergency during the colonial period and the American Revolution. *See* **minutemen**. (p. 289)

mineral (min'ər əl) A substance found in the earth that is neither plant nor animal. (p. 43)

minutemen (min′it men) Well-trained volunteer soldiers who defended the American colonies against the British at a minute's notice. (p. 300)

mission (mish′ən) A settlement where missionaries lived and worked. (p. 257)

missionary (mish′ə ner ē) A person who teaches his or her religion to others who have different beliefs. (p. 158)

Missouri Compromise (mi zùr′ē kom′prə mīz) A law passed by Congress in 1820 that divided the Louisiana Territory into areas allowing slavery and areas outlawing slavery. (p. 460)

Model T (mod′əl tē) Henry Ford's famous automobile of the early 1900s, the first to be built using assembly-line mass production. See **assembly line** and **interchangeable parts**. (p. 563)

monopoly (mə nop′ə lē) A company that controls an entire industry. (p. 543)

Monroe Doctrine (mən rō dok′trin) A declaration of United States foreign policy made by President James Monroe in 1823 that opposed European colonization or interference in the Western Hemisphere. (p. 390)

N

national anthem (nash′ə nəl an′thəm) A country's official song, such as "The Star-Spangled Banner." (p. 388)

National Association for the Advancement of Colored People (NAACP) (nash′ə nəl ə sō sē ā′shən for <u>the</u> ad vans′mənt uv kul′ərd pe′pəl) An organization, founded in 1909 by both blacks and whites, whose goal is to fight prejudice and discrimination. (p. 582)

national park (nash′ə nəl pärk) An area set aside by the national government for the public to enjoy. (p. 564)

natural resource (nach′ər əl rē′sôrs) A material found in nature that people use to meet their needs and wants. (p. 42)

navigation (nav i gā′shən) The science of determining a ship's location and direction. (p. 126)

neutral (nū′trəl) Not taking sides. (p. 386)

New Deal (nū dēl) Government programs started by President Franklin D. Roosevelt in the 1930s to aid businesses, farms, and the unemployed to recover from the Great Depression. (p. 595)

New Jersey Plan (nū jûr′zē plan) The plan offered by the small states at the Constitutional Convention of 1787 that would have given all states an equal number of representatives in Congress. See **Virginia Plan**. (p. 349)

news article (nüz är′ti kəl) A newspaper story that factually describes an important recent event. (p. 458)

Nineteenth Amendment (nīn′tēnth′ ə mend′mənt) An amendment to the Constitution, ratified in 1920, that gave women the right to vote. See **amendment** and **ratify**. (p. 588)

nonrenewable resource (non ri nü′ə bəl rē′sôrs) A material found in nature that cannot be replaced, such as coal, oil, and natural gas. (p. 42)

North American Free Trade Agreement (nôrth ə mer′i kən frē trād ə grē′mənt) A treaty signed by Canada, Mexico, and the United States in 1992 that makes all of North America one trading area. (p. 655)

Northwest Ordinance (nôrth′west′ ôr′də nəns) A law passed by Congress in 1787 organizing the Northwest Territory for settlement and eventual statehood. (p. 344)

Northwest Passage (nôrth′west′ pas′ij) A water route believed to flow through North America to Asia that European explorers searched for from the 1500s to the 1700s. (p. 174)

O

ocean (ō′shən) One of Earth's four large bodies of water. They are the Arctic, Atlantic, Indian, and Pacific oceans. (p. G4)

opinion (ə pin′ yən) A personal view or belief. (p. 172)

oral history (ôr′əl his′tə rē) Spoken records, including stories, that have been passed from one generation to the next. (p. 19)

outline (out′līn) A plan for organizing written information about a subject. (p. 622)

overseer (ō′vər sē ər) A person hired to be the boss of a plantation. (p. 238)

P

Pacific Railroad Act (pə sif′ik rāl′rōd akt) A law passed by Congress in 1862 offering government loans and free land to the two companies building the transcontinental railroad. See **transcontinental railroad**. (p. 511)

pronunciation key

a **at**; ā **ape**; ä **far**; âr **care**; e **end**; ē **me**; i **it**; ī **ice**; îr **pierce**; o **hot**; ō **old**; ô **fork**; oi **oil**; ou **out**; u **up**; ū **use**; ü **rule**; ù **pull**; ûr **turn**; hw **white**; ng **song**; th **thin**; <u>th</u> **this**; zh **measure**; ə **about, taken, pencil, lemon, circus**

parallel (par′ə lel) A line of latitude. *See* **latitude**. (p. G4)

Patriot (pā′trē ət) An American colonist who supported the fight for independence. (p. 321)

Persian Gulf War (pûr′zhən gulf wôr) A war in 1991 in which international armed forces led by the United States drove Iraqi forces from Kuwait. (p. 636)

perspective (pər spek′tiv) Point of view. *See* **point of view**. (p. 19)

petition (pətish′ən) A written request signed by many people. (p. 300)

physical map (fiz′i kəl map) A map that highlights Earth's natural features. (p. G10)

pioneer (pī ə nîr′) A person who leads the way, usually to make a new home and become a settler there. (p. 374)

plantation (plan tā′shən) A large farm that often grows one crop. (p. 236)

point of view (point uv vū) The position from which a person looks at an issue or situtation. (p. 352)

political cartoon (pə lit′i kəl kär tün′) A drawing that shows a cartoonist's opinion about a political person, event, or issue. (p. 298)

political map (pə lit′i kəl map) A map that shows the boundaries of states and countries. (p. G9)

political party (pə lit′i kəl pär′tē) A group of people who share similar ideas about government. (p. 363)

pollution (pə lü′shən) Anything that dirties the air, soil, or water. (p. 45)

population (pop yə lā′shən) The total number of people living in a particular area or place. (p. 10)

portage (pôr′tij) A land route from one body of water to another. (p. 267)

potlatch (pot′lach) A special feast given by Native Americans of the Northwest Coast, in which the guests receive gifts. (p. 84)

prairie (prâr′ē) Flat or gently rolling land covered mostly with grasses and wildflowers. (p. 97)

Preamble (prē′am bəl) The introduction to the Constitution. (p. 355)

precipitation (pri sip i tā′shən) The moisture that falls to Earth as rain or snow. (p. 36)

prejudice (prej′ə dis) A negative opinion formed without proof. (p. 11)

primary source (prī mer′ē sôrs) A firsthand account of an event or an artifact created during the period of history that is being studied. *See* **artifact** *and* **secondary source**. (p. 19)

prime meridian (prīm mə rid′ē ən) The line of longitude labeled 0° longitude. Any place east of the prime meridian is labeled E, any place west of it is labeled W. *See* **longitude**. (p. G4)

Proclamation of 1763 (prok lə mā′shən) An official announcement by King George III of Great Britain outlawing colonial settlement west of the Appalachian Mountains. (p. 275)

profit (prof′it) The money remaining after the costs of a business have been paid. (p. 175)

property rights (prop′ər tē rīts) The rights to own or use something. (p. 531)

proprietor (prə prī′i tər) A person who owns a property or a business. (p. 216)

province (prov′ins) A political division of a country, as in Canada. (p. 653)

pueblo (pweb′lō) A Spanish word meaning "village" used to refer to the apartment-style homes of the Native Americans of the Southwest. (p. 91)

R

railhead (rāl′hed) Any town where a railroad begins or ends, especially on the Great Plains in the late 1800s. *See* **cattle drive**. (p. 520)

rain forest (rān fôr′ist) A dense, usually tropical forest that has lots of rain year round. (p. 657)

ratify (rat′ə fī) To give official approval, for example, to the Constitution or amendments to it. (p. 358)

reaper (rē′pər) A machine that uses sharp blades to harvest grain. (p. 408)

rebel (ri bel′) To oppose those in charge, even to the point of fighting them with weapons, because of different ideas about what is right. (p. 292)

Reconstruction (rē kən struk′shən) The period following the Civil War in which Congress passed laws designed to rebuild the country and bring the Southern states back into the Union. (p. 494)

recycle (rē sī′kəl) To save discarded items, like cans or bottles, so that they can be used again. (p. 48)

reference source (ref′ər ens sôrs) A book or other source that contains facts about many different subjects. (p. 426)

reform (ri fôrm′) A change to make government or business work better. (p. 560)

region (rē′jən) A large area with common features that set it apart from other areas. (p. 29)

relief (ri lēf′) The difference in height between land areas. See **relief map**. (p. 215)

relief map (ri lēf′ map) A physical map that uses shading to show the difference in height between areas of land. See **relief** and **physical map**. (p. G10)

relocation camp (rē lō kā′shən kamp) Prison camps in which Japanese Americans were held in the western United States during World War II. (p. 601)

Renaissance (ren′ ə säns) A period of cultural and artistic growth in Europe that began in Italy in the 1300s. (p. 125)

renewable resource (ri nü′ə bəl rē′sôrs) A material found in nature that can be replaced, such as forests. (p. 42)

repeal (ri pēl′) To withdraw or cancel. (p. 293)

republic (ri pub′lik) A form of government in which the people elect representatives to run the country. (p. 12)

reservation (rez ər vā′shən) An area set aside for Native Americans. (p. 531)

road map (rōd map) A map that indicates cities, highways, and points of interest and shows you how to get from one place to another. (p. G11)

Roaring Twenties (rôr′ing twen′tēz) The decade of the 1920s, which got this nickname because of the time's prosperity and excitement. (p. 584)

s

sachem (sā′chəm) The leader or chief of any group of Native Americans in the Eastern Woodland and Great Lakes regions. (p. 188)

satellite (sat′ə līt) An object that circles a larger object, such as the moon around Earth. (p. 639)

scale (skāl) A guide that explains the relationship between real distances on Earth and distances on a map. (p. G7)

secede (si sēd′) To break away from a group, such as the Southern states seceding from the Union in 1861. (p. 464)

Second Continental Congress (sek′ənd kon′tə nen′təl kong′gris) A meeting in Philadelphia in 1775 of delegates from all 13 colonies which established a colonial army and declared American independence. See **Continental Army** and **Declaration of Independence**. (p. 312)

secondary source (sek′ən der ē sôrs) An account of the past based on information from primary sources and written by someone who was not an eyewitness to those events. See **primary source**. (p. 19)

secretary (sek′rə ter ē) The head of each department in the executive branch of government. As a group the secretaries are called the President's Cabinet. See **Cabinet**. (p. 362)

segregation (seg ri gā′shən) The separation of people, usually based on race or religion. (p. 498)

Senate (sen′it) The house of Congress in which each state has an equal number of representatives, or Senators, regardless of population. See **legislative branch** and **House of Representatives**. (p. 350)

Seneca Falls Convention (sen′i kə fôlz kən ven′shən) The country's first women's rights meeting, held in Seneca Falls, New York, in 1848. (p. 456)

settlement house (set′əl mənt hous) In the late 1800s and early 1900s, a community center for the poor, immigrants, and others in need of child care, education, and so on. (p. 550)

sharecropping (shâr′krop ing) A system common in the South in the late 1800s and early 1900s in which farmers rented land from a landowner by promising to pay the owner with a share of their crop. (p. 496)

shareholder (shâr′hōl dər) A person who buys stock, or shares, in a corporation. See **corporation** and **stock**. (p. 543)

Shays's Rebellion (shāz ri bel′yən) A revolt in 1786 of Massachusetts farmers, led by Daniel Shays, who opposed tax decisions of the state courts. (p. 343)

slave codes (slāv cōdz) Rules made by colonial planters that controlled the lives of enslaved Africans. (p. 237)

slave trade (slāv trād) The business of buying and selling people for profit. See **triangular trade**. (p. 227)

slavery (slā′və rē) The practice of people owning other people and forcing them to work. (p. 68)

slum (slum) A poor, crowded section of a city with rundown and often unsafe housing. See **favela**. (p. 547)

small-scale map (smôl skāl map) A map that shows a large area but not much detail. See **large-scale map**. (p. 336)

sodbuster (sod′bus tər) A settler on the Great Plains in the late 1800s who had to "bust" through the thick sod to plant crops. (p. 526)

pronunciation key

a **at**; ā **ape**; ä **far**; âr **care**; e **end**; ē **me**; i **it**; ī **ice**; îr **pierce**; o **hot**; ō **old**; ô **fork**; oi **oil**; ou **out**; u **up**; ū **use**; ü **rule**, u̇ **pull**; ûr **turn**; hw **white**; ng **song**; th **thin**; <u>th</u> **this**; zh mea**s**ure; ə **about**, t**a**ken, penc**i**l, lem**o**n, circ**u**s

Sons of Liberty (sunz uv lib′ər tē) Groups of colonists who organized themselves to protest against the British government. (p. 293)

space race (spās rās) The competition between the United States and the Soviet Union during the Cold War to explore outer space. (p. 638)

Spanish-American War (span′ish ə mer′i kən wôr) The war between the United States and Spain in 1898 in which the United States gained control of Puerto Rico, Guam, and the Philippines. (p. 556)

specialize (spesh′ə līz) To spend most of one's time doing one kind of job. (p. 60)

stagecoach (stāj′kōch) A large, horse-drawn carriage in the 1800s that transported passengers, baggage, and mail on a regular schedule. (p. 410)

Stamp Act (stamp akt) A law passed by the British Parliament in 1765 requiring colonists to pay a tax on newspapers, pamphlets, legal documents, and even playing cards. (p. 293)

statehood (stāt′hůd) Becoming a state in the United States. (p. 344)

states' rights (stāts rīts) The belief that each state should be allowed to make its own decisions about issues affecting it. (p. 464)

steam engine (stēm en′jin) An engine powered by the energy produced from steam. (p. 410)

stock (stok) Shares of ownership in a company. *See* **shareholder**. (p. 180)

stock exchange (stok eks chānj′) A special market where shares of stocks are bought and sold. (p. 592)

strike (strīk) A refusal of all the workers in a business to work until the owners meet their demands. (p. 544)

suffrage (suf′rij) The right to vote. (p. 588)

Supreme Court (sə prēm′ kôrt) The head of the judicial branch of the federal government. It is the highest court in the country. *See* **judicial branch**. (p. 349)

surplus (sûr′plus) An amount greater than what is needed. (p. 60)

sweatshop (swet′shop) A small, crowded factory where people work in unsafe conditions. (p. 543)

symbol (sim′bəl) Something that stands for something else. *See* **political cartoons**. (p. G8)

T

technology (tek nol′ə jē) The design and use of tools, ideas, and methods to solve problems. (p. 84)

teepee (tē′pē) A cone-shaped tent made of animal skins used by Native Americans of the Plains. (p. 97)

temperature (tem′per ə chər) The measurement of heat and cold. (p. 36)

tenement (ten′ə mənt) An apartment building divided into many small, cramped apartments. (p. 547)

territory (ter′i tôr ē) An area of land that belongs to a government. (p. 344)

Thirteenth Amendment (thûr′tēnth′ ə mend′mənt) An amendment to the Constitution, ratified in 1865, that abolished slavery. *See* **amendment** *and* **ratify**. (p. 495)

time line (tīm′ līn) A diagram showing the order in which events took place. (p. 70)

time zone (tīm zōn) One of the 24 areas into which Earth is divided for measuring time. (p. 522)

tolerate (tol′ə rāt) To allow people to have different beliefs from your own. (p. 208)

total war (tō′təl wôr) An all-out war to destroy people's ability and will to fight. (p. 489)

totem pole (tō′təm pōl) A tall carved log used by Native Americans of the Northwest Coast to honor an important person or to mark a special event. (p. 84)

town meeting (toun mē′ting) Gathering of a town's citizens to discuss and solve local problems. (p. 287)

Townshend Acts (taůn′zend akts) Taxes passed by Parliament in 1767 for goods brought into the colonies. (p. 294)

Trail of Tears (trāl uv tîrz) The name given to the 800-mile forced march of 15,000 Cherokee in 1838 from their homes in Georgia to the Indian Territory. (p. 398)

traitor (trā′tər) Someone who turns against his or her country. *See* **treason**. (p. 313)

transcontinental railroad (trans kon ti nen′təl rāl′rōd) A railroad that crosses an entire continent. *See* **Pacific Railroad Act**. (p. 510)

travois (trə voi′) A sled-like device constructed by Native Americans of the Plains. (p. 97)

treason (trē′zən) The betrayal of one's country by giving help to an enemy. *See* **traitor**. (p. 293)

Treaty of Guadalupe Hidalgo (trē′tē uv gwä dä lü′ pe ē däl′gō) The treaty signed in 1848 that ended the Mexican War. *See* **Mexican War**. (p. 424)

Treaty of Paris of 1763 (trē′tē uv par′is) An agreement signed by Great Britain and France that brought an end to the French and Indian War. (p. 275)

Treaty of Paris of 1783 (trē′tē uv par′is) The peace treaty in which Great Britain recognized the United States as an independent country. (p. 334)

Treaty of Versailles (trē′tē uv vâr sī′) The peace treaty that the Allied Powers forced Germany to sign in 1919, officially ending World War I. (p. 581)

triangular trade (trī ang′gyə lər trād) The three-sided trade route between Africa, the West Indies, and colonial New England which involved the slave trade as well as the trading of goods. See **Middle Passage**. (p. 230)

tribute (trib′ūt) Forced payment, usually made in the form of valuable goods. (p. 66)

Underground Railroad (un′dər ground rāl′rōd) A system of secret routes used by escaping slaves to reach freedom in the North or in Canada. (p. 454)

unemployment (un em plōi′mənt) The number of workers without jobs. (p. 596)

United Nations (ū nīt′əd nā′shenz) An international organization, founded in 1945 following World War II, which works to preserve world peace. (p. 610)

unity (ū′ni tē) Being as one or in agreement. (p. 8)

values (val′ūz) The beliefs or ideals that guide the way people live. (p. 9)

veto (vē′tō) To refuse to approve. (p. 357)

Vietnam War (vī et näm′ wôr) A war between South Vietnam and North Vietnam that lasted from 1954 to 1975, when North Vietnam defeated South Vietnam and reunited the two Vietnams. (p. 628)

Virginia Plan (vər jin′yə plan) The plan, drawn up by James Madison and adopted by the Constitutional Convention in 1787, that established three branches of the federal government. See **New Jersey Plan**. (p. 349)

voyageur (vwä yä zhûr′) A trader who transported furs by canoe in New France. (p. 268)

W

wampum (wom′pəm) Polished beads used in gift-giving and trading by the Iroquois and other Native Americans. (p. 104)

War Hawks (wôr hôks) Members of Congress from the South and the West in the early 1800s who wanted the United States to go to war against Great Britain. See **War of 1812**. (p. 386)

War of 1812 (wôr uv ā′tēn′twelv) War between Great Britain and the United States from 1812 to 1815. See **Battle of New Orleans** and **War Hawks**. (p. 387)

Watergate Scandal (wô′tər gāt skan′dəl) Political scandal in which people working for President Nixon were arrested for spying on his political opponents. (p. 631)

World War I (wûrld wôr wun) A war that began in Europe in 1914 between the Central Powers and the Allied Powers, who were joined by the United States in 1917. See **Allied Powers** and **Central Powers**. (p. 578)

World War II (wûrld wôr tü) War between the Axis and the Allies that involved most of the countries of the world. It was fought from 1939 to 1945. The United States joined the Allies on Dec. 8, 1941. See **Allies, Axis,** and **Cold War**. (p. 599)

pronunciation key

a **at**; ā **ape**; ä **far**; âr **care**; e **end**; ē **me**; i **it**; ī **ice**; îr **pierce**; o **hot**; ō **old**; ô **fork**; oi **oil**; ou **out**; u **up**; ū **use**; ü **rule**; ù **pull**; ûr **turn**; hw **white**; ng **song**; th **thin**; <u>th</u> **this**; zh **measure**; ə **about, taken, pencil, lemon, circus**

index

This Index lists many topics that appear in the book, along with the pages on which they are found. Page numbers after an m refer you to a map. Page numbers after a p indicate photographs, artwork, or charts.

CREDITS

Cover: Superstock

Maps: Geosystems

Charts and Graphs: Eliot Bergman: pp. 242, 243; Dale Glasgow & Associates: pp. 38, 44-45; Hima Pamoedjo: pp. 100, 118, 119, 144, 287, 348, 405, 445, 473, 497, 595, 621, 632

Chapter Opener Globes: Greg Wakabayashi

Illustrations: Hal Brooks: pp. 140, 145, 433, 465, 543, 611, 633; Margaret Cusack: pp. 389; Drew-Brook-Cormack Associates: pp. 99, 105; John Edens: pp. 308-309; Peter Fiore: pp. 76-77; Joseph Forte: pp. 222-223, 508-509; George Gaadt: pp. 136-137, 254-255, 284-285; Michael Hampshire: pp. 207; Adam Hook: pp. 67, 442-443; David McCall Johnston: pp. 166-167, 538-539; Dave Joly: pp. 13, 39, 63, 101, 123, 171, 191, 219, 233, 269, 291, 335, 345, 391, 477; Rosanne Kakos-Main: pp. 47; Robert Korta: pp. 402-403; Dennis Lyall: pp. 430-431; Ron Mahoney: pp. 372-373; Angus McBride: pp. 112-113; Jim McMahon: pp. 232; Ed Parker: pp. 332-333; Hima Pamoedjo: pp. 100, 327, 347; Rudica Prado: pp. 176-177; Victor Stabin: pp. 258; Robert Van Nutt: pp. 202-203, 239, 340-341, 412, 470-471, 480, 616-617

Photography Credits: All photographs are by the McGraw-Hill School Division (MMSD) except as noted below.

Cover: Superstock; i: Superstock. iii: t. Bettmann Archive; m. Nawrocki Stock Photo, Inc.; b. The Image Bank. iv: t. Lawrence Migdale/Photo Researchers, Inc.; m. Bridgeman Art Library; b. National Museum, Mexico City. v: t.l. Adam Woolfit/Robert Harding Picture Library; m.l. The Metropolitan Museum of Art; b.l., b. The Granger Collection. vi: t. Guilford Courthouse National Military Park, Greensboro, NC; b.l. The Granger Collection; b.r. Colonial Williamsburg Foundation. vii: t. The Granger Collection; m. Nawrocki Stock Photo, Inc.; b. Steve Elmore/The Stock Market. viii: t. Superstock; m. The Granger Collection; b. Gill C. Kenny/The Image Bank. ix: t. Stephen Marks/The Image Bank; m. I.M. House/Tony Stone Images; b. The Granger Collection. G2: t. David R. Stoecklein; b. Cradoc Bagshaw. G3: t. Bob Krist; m. Patricia Lanza; b. Bob Clemenz. **Chapter 1** 2: t.l. Nawrocki Stock Photo, Inc; t.r. Courtesy of Yoshihiko Ito; m. The Image Bank; b.r. Ray Hendley/ProFiles West. 3: m. Flip Chalfant/The Image Bank; b.l. Nawrocki Stock Photo, Inc; b.r. Bettmann. 4-5: Harold Sund. 4: t. Phil Schermeister; b. Galen Rowell. 7: Jimmy Rudnick/The Stock Market. 8: t.l. Joe Sohm/The Stock Market. 9: b.r. David Young-Wolff/PhotoEdit. 10: b. Comstock; m. Dianne Arandt/Superstock. 11: t.r. Davi Conklin/The Picture Cube. 12: t.l. The Stock Market. 13: b.r. © 1993 Judy Griesdick/Black Star. 14: t. © 1992 Dennis Brack/Black Star. 15: t. Marc Muench/Tony Stone Images. 16: t. Bob Daemmrich/Stock Boston. 16-17: b. Francis Westfield for MMSD. 18: t.l. Miro Vintoniv/Stock Boston. 19: t. National Museum of American Art, Smithsonian Institution/Art Resource; b. Jerry Jacka. 20: b.c. Courtesy of Yoshihiko Ito; b.l. UPI/Bettmann; b.r. Brown Brothers. 21: b. Photo Researchers, Inc. 22-23: White House Collection. 23: t. Addison Thompson; b. Chip Coleman. **Chapter 2** 27: t. Jeri Gleiter/FPG International; t.m. Bill Ross/Tony Stone Images; m. Mark A. Leman/Tony Stone Images; 27: b.m. Mitchel Osborne Photography; b. Terry Qing/FPG International. 28: t.l. Paul Steel/The Stock Market. 29: t. Grant Heilman/ProFiles West; m. Henryk T. Kaiser/The Picture Cube. 30: t. Jeff Gnass/West Stock, Inc.; b. Anne Griffiths/Woodfin Camp. 31: b. Jim Richardson/Westlight; t. Larry Ulrich/Tony Stone Worldwide. 32: Peter Beck/The Stock Market; b. David Noble/FPG International. 33: t. David R. Frazier/Photo Researchers, Inc.; b. Stock Boston. 34: t.l. David Forbert/Superstock. 34-35: National Snow & Ice Data Center/Photo Researchers. 36: t. Reuters/Bettmann. 38: t. Daryl Benson/Masterfile; b. Farrell Grehan/FPG International. 42: t. Jack Stein Grove/ProFiles West. 45: t.l. Andre Jenny/Unicorn Stock Photos; t.r. John Elk III/Stock Boston. 46: b.l. Paul S. Howell/Gamma Liaison; b.r. Steve Chenn/Westlight. 47: t. Larry Lefever/Grant Heilman Photography, Inc.; b. Darrell Gulin/Tony Stone Images. 48: Bruce Hands/The Image Works. 49: Courtesy of Kathy Lam. 53: b. Monica Stevenson for MMSD. 54: t.l. The Image Collection/Nat'l Geographic Society; t.r. National Anthropological Museum, Mexico City; b. Lawrence Migdale/Photo Researchers, Inc. 55: m. Scala/Art Resource, Inc.; b.l., b.r. The Bridgeman Art Library. 56-57: Michael A. Hampshire. 56: t. Richard Alexander Cooke III. 57: t. David Brill; b. Richard Alexander Cooke III. **Chapter 3** 60: David L. Brown/Tom Stack & Associates. 61: D. Donne Bryant/DDB Stock Photography. 62: t. The Granger Collection; b. D. Donne Bryant. 63: b. David Hiser/Photographers Aspen. 64: National Geographic Society. 65: Jerry Jacka Photography. 66: Michael Fogden/DRK Photo. 68: l. Mireille Vautier/Woodfin Camp; r. National Museum of Anthropology & History, Mexico City. 69: J. Messerschmidt/Bruce Coleman, Inc. 72: D. Donne Bryant. 73: Superstock; i. Jerry Jacka Photography. 74: Jerry Jacka/Courtesy Arizona State Museum. 74-75: b. Tom Bean/The Stock Market. 75: r. Craig Aurness/Woodfin Camp & Assoc. **Chapter 4** 82: Jeff Greenberg/PhotoEdit. 83: Natalie B. Fobes. 84: l. Alan Hicks/Tony Stone Images; r. Mark Newman/Tom Stack & Associates. 85: t. Reader's Digest Association; b. Art Wolfe/Tony Stone Images. 86: l. The Granger Collection; r. Steve McCutcheon. 87: Jeff Greenberg/Unicorn Stock Photo. 88, 89: t. Jerry Jacka Photography. 89: b.l. John Running; b.r. Barry L Runk/Grant Heilman Photography. 90: Tom Bean/The Stock Market. 91: l. Adam Woolfitt/Woodfin Camp & Assoc.; r. Stephen Trimble. 92: l. The Heard Museum/Jerry Jacka Photography; r. National Museum of the American Indian, Smithsonian Institution; b. Cradoc Bagshaw/Westlight; t. David R. Stoecklein. 93: l. Southwest Museum; r. Stephen Trimble. 94: The Heard Museum/Jerry Jacka Photography. 95: Michael McDermott for MMSD. 96: Robert Frerck/Odyssey. 97: b. R.P. Kingston/The Picture Cube; Buffalo Bill Historical Center. 98: Superstock. 100: National Museum of the American Indian, Smithsonian Institution. 102, 103: Rochester Museum. 106: The Granger Collection. 107: Kevin King. 108: Rochester Museum. 109: M. Greenlar/The Image Works. **Chapter 5** 114: Jeff Foott/Bruce Coleman. 115: b. Lawrence Migdale/Photo Researchers; i. Georg Gerster/Comstock. 117: Art Resource. 120: t. Boltin Picture Library. 120-121: b. Superstock. 122: t.l. Superstock; t.r. The British Museum/Superstock; r. Betty Press/Woodfin Camp & Assoc. 124: t.l. The Granger Collection. 124-125: Pierpont Morgan Library. 125: r. Giraudon/Alinari. 126: The Granger Collection. 127: Robert Frerck/Odyssey. 131: b. Monica Stevenson for MMSD. 132: t.l. The British Museum; m.l. The British Museum/Superstock; b.l. Smithsonian Institution; t.r. Lotos Film; b.r. The Ashmolean Museum, Oxford. 133: t. National Museum, Mexico City; b. Adam Woodfitt/Robert Harding Picture Library. 134-135: Bob Sacha. 134: b. Bob Sacha. 135: t. Naval Museum, Madrid; b. Bob Sacha. **Chapter 6** 138: t.l. North Wind Picture Archive. 139: t. The Granger Collection. 140: t. Museo Navale, Genoa-Pegli/ Superstock. 141: t. The Granger Collection; b. © Florida Museum of Natural History, 1994. 143: t.l. The Granger Collection; t.r. Dag Sundberg/The Image Bank; m. John E. Swedberg/Bruce Coleman, Inc; b.l. North Carolina Collection, U.N.C. Library Photographic Service; b.l. The Granger Collection. 146: Architect of the Capitol, Washington, D.C. 147: t. m. The Granger Collection; b. El Escorial/Arxiu Mas. 148: t.l. Felipe Davalos/National Geographic Society. 149: t.l. Adam Woolfitt/Woodfin Camp & Associates; t.r. © Jonathan Blair/Woodfin Camp & Associates; b. Lotos Film. 150: r. Galleria degli Uffizi/Art Resource; l. Eric Lessing/Art Resource. 151: b. Biblioteca Nacional, Madrid/Arxiu Mas. 154: t.r. North Wind Picture Archives. 156: t.l. Museo de America, Madrid/Carousel. 158: t. Biblioteca Colombina, Sevilla/Arxiu Mas. 159: t. The Granger Collection; b. The Detroit Institute of Art. 160: b. Robert Frerck/Odyssey. 162: b. Carousel. 163: t.l. Boltin Picture Library; t.r. M.N.A.H., Biblioteca/Carousel; b.l. Codex Mendoza, M.N.A.H., Biblioteca/Carousel. **Chapter 7** 168: Frederica Georgia/Photo Researchers. 169: t. & 170: b.r. The Granger Collection. 172: b.l. Boltin Picture Library; b.r. The Granger Collection. 173: b.l. The Granger Collection; b.r. Boltin Picture Library. 174: t.l. The Granger Collection. 175: Superstock. 178: t.l. Sidney E. King/U.S. Department of the Interior. 179: b.r. Ashmolean Museum, Oxford. 180: t.r. The Granger Collection. 181: b.l. North Wind Picture Archives; b.r. The Granger Collection. 182: t.l. Greig Cranna/Stock Boston; b.l. National Portrait Gallery, Smithsonian Institution/Art Resource. 182-183: t.r. & 184: b.l. The Granger Collection; b.r. Fil Hunter for MMSD. 186: t.l. Bonnie McGrath/The Picture Cube. 187: t. Wayne McLoughlin/National Geographic Society. 188: b.r. Walter Edwards/National Geographic Society. 189: t. The Granger Collection. 190: The Bettmann Archive; t. Superstock. 192: The Norman Rockwell Museum, Stockbridge. 193: t.l. Bob Daemmrich/The Image Works; r. Painting by Sidney King/Courtesy of the Berkeley Plantation and Bicast Publishing Co., Williamsburg; b.l. Gene Peach/ The Picture Cube, Inc. 197: b. Monica Stevenson for MMSD. 198: t. Boltin Picture Library; m. Colonial Williamsburg Foundation. 198-199: b. The Granger Collection. 199: t.l. The Granger Collection; t.r. National Portrait Gallery, London/Superstock; b.r. The Metropolitan Museum of Art. 200-201: David Alan Harvey. 200: b. Colonial Williamsburg Foundation. 201: t. Colonial Williamsburg Foundation; b. Colonial Williamsburg Foundation. **Chapter 8** 204: Superstock. 205: Steven Hanson/Stock Boston. 206 & 208: l. The Granger Collection. 208: r. Kindra Clineff/The Picture Cube. 209: Shelburne Museum. 210: Colonial Williamsburg Foundation. 211: t. Superstock; b. The Granger Collection. 213: l. Ralph Krubner/H. Armstrong Roberts; r. Brown Brothers. 216: The Metropolitan Museum of Art, gift of Mr. and Mrs. Samuel Schwartz, 1979. 217: t. The Granger Collection; b. Courtesy, Winterthur Museum. 218: Laura Sikes/Stock South. **Chapter 9** 224-226: The Granger Collection. 228-229: b. New York State Historical Association, Cooperstown. 228: t.l. Superstock. 229: i. Charleston Library Society. 230: t.l. Superstock; t.r. © Gene Peach/The Picture Cube, Inc.; t.m. © Jeff Greenberg/Archive Photos; l. The Granger Collection. 231: r. Bettmann Archive. 234: t. Gift of Joseph W., William B., and Edward H.R. Revere; Courtesy, Museum of Fine Arts, Boston. 235: t. Colonial Williamsburg Foundation; m.l. The Minneapolis Institute of the Arts; m.r. Museum of the City of New York. 237: b.r. The Granger Collection. 240: b.l. Superstock; b.r. Smithsonian Institution. 241: Haverford College. 242: The Granger Collection. 244: t.l. CIGNA Museum & Art Collection. 245: The Granger Collection. 246-247: The Library Company of Philadelphia. 247: r. American Philisophical Society. 248-249: Woodfin Camp and Associates. 250: Gilcrease Museum. 251: Francis Westfield. **Chapter 10** 256: t. © Michael J. Howell/ProFiles West. 257: l. © John Lewis Stage/The Image Bank; r. Richard Elliot/Tony Stone Images. 259, 260: t.r. The Granger Collection. 260-261: © Branson Reynolds/ProFiles West. 262: t.l. The Granger Collection. 262-263: Superstock. 263: t.l. © David Stoecklein/The Stock Market; t.r. © John Eastcott & Yva Momatiuk/The Image Works; b. © David Carriere/Tony Stone Images. 264: Stock Montage, Inc. 265: t. National Archives of Canada; b. National Museum of the American Indian. 267: t.l. The Granger Collection; b.l. Stamp Design © 1986 United States Postal Service. All Rights Reserved; b.r. © David Noble, 1992/FPG International. 268: t. Buffalo Bill Historical Center, Cody, WY; Gift of Mrs. Karl Frank; b. The Granger Collection. 270: The Granger Collection. 271: Bettmann Archive. 272: © H. Mark Weidman. 273: Archive Photos. 275: Superstock. **Chapter 11** 280: t.r. Guilford Courthouse National Military Park, Greensboro, NC; m.r. Colonial Williamsburg Foundation. 281: t. The Museum of Fine Arts, Boston & The National Portrait Gallery; b. Colonial Williamsburg Foundation. 282-283: John Lewis Stage. 282: t. Valley Forge Historical Society. 283: t. Robert Llewellyn; b. Robert Llewellyn. 286: Bettmann Archive. 287: The Chrysler Museum. 288: t. Colonial Williamsburg Foundation. 288, 289 t.: Bettmann Archive. 289: b. Archive Photos. 290: t. Bettmann Archive; b.l. Brown Brothers. 292: North Wind Picture Archives. 293: The Granger Collection. 294: The Museum of Fine Arts, Boston. 295: t.r. Bettmann Archive; b. The Granger Collection. 296: t., b.l. The Granger Collection. 296-297: The Winterthur Museum. 298: The Granger Collection. 299: Kirk Anderson. 300: John Coletti/Stock Boston. 302: Bettmann Archive. 303: The Granger Collection. 304: t. H. Mark Weidman; b. Yale University Art Gallery. 304-305: The Granger Collection. **Chapter 12** 310: t. Kenneth Garrett/Woodfin Camp & Assoc. 311: l. National Geographic Society Image Collection; r. Ticonderoga Museum. 312: l. H. Mark Weidman; r. Andre Jenny/Stock South. 313: t. Stock Boston; b. Museum of Fine Arts, Boston. 314: l. Andre Jenny/Stock South; r. National Geographic Society Image Collection. 314-315: l. The Granger Collection. 315: r. Superstock. 316-317: Yale University Art Gallery. 318: m. George Chan/Photo Researchers. 319: t., m. Superstock; b. Catherine Karnow/Woodfin Camp and Assoc. 320: t. H. Mark Weidman. 321: t. Rhode Island Historical Society; b. Nawrocki Stock Photo, Inc. 322: Superstock. 323: Henley & Savage/Tony Stone Worldwide, Ltd. 324: l. Stock Montage. 324-325: Superstock. 326 & 327: t. Superstock. 327: m. Private Collection/Frick Library. 328: Superstock. 329: Nawrocki Stock Photo, Inc. 330: t.r. Nawrocki Stock Photo, Inc.; t.l., b. The Granger Collection. 331: Valentine Museum, Richmond. 333: t. Nawrocki Stock Photo, Inc.; b.l. Murray Alcosser/The Image Bank; b.r. Ted Spiegel. 335: Yale University Art Gallery. 336: m. Nawrocki Stock Photo. **Chapter 13** 342: North Wind Pictures. 343: l. Bettmann Archive; r. Nawrocki Stock Photo. 344: Bettmann Archive. 346: The Granger Collection. 347: Superstock. 348: The Library of Congress. 349: The Pennsylvania Academy of The Fine Arts. 350: The Granger Collection. 351: Michael Bryant/Woodfin Camp. 352: The Granger Collection. 353: North Wind Picture Archives. 354: Independence National Historical Park. 357: FPG International. 358: Superstock. 359: t. Bettmann Archive; b. The Shelburne Museum; m. The Granger Collection. 362: t. Superstock; b. Glenn Kulbako/The Picture Cube. 363: Colonial Williamsburg Foundation. 368: t.l. Bettmann Archive; m. Steve Elmore/The Stock Market; b. Don Mason/The Stock Market. 369: t. Nawrocki Stock Photo, Inc.; b. Brown Brothers. 370-371: Phil Schermeister. 370: t. Karen Keeney; b. Phil Schermeister. 371: b. Haynes Foundation Collection, Montana Historical Society. **Chapter 14** 374: Andre Jenny/Unicorn Stock Photos. 375: Diane Padys/FPG International. 376: l. The Granger Collection; r. Superstock. 377: University of Michigan Museum of Art, Bequest of Henry C. Lewis. 378: UPI/Bettmann. 379: t. Superstock; b.l. The Granger Collection; b.r. Culver Pictures. 380: t. Chuck Fishman/Woodfin Camp & Associates, Inc.; b. Chicago Historical Society. 381: Missouri Historical Society. 382: Montana Historical Society. 383: Larry Ulrich/Tony Stone Worldwide. 384: The New York Historical Society. 385: t.l. The Smithsonian Institution; t.r. North Wind Picture Archives; b. Renee Lynn/Davis Lynn Photography. 386: The Granger

Collection. 387:l. The Granger Collection; r. Bettmann Archive. 388: l. The Granger Collection; r. The New York Historical Society. 390: t.r. The National Portrait Gallery; Smithsonian Institution/Art Resource; t.l. The National Portrait Gallery/Smithsonian Institution; b. The Historic New Orleans Collection. 393: Archive Photos. 394: Nawrocki Stock Photo, Inc. 395: l. Bettmann Archive; r. The New York Historical Society. 396: l. Bettmann Archive; r. New Echota State Historical Site. 397: l: Nawrocki Stock Photo, Inc. 399: The Granger Collection. **Chapter 15** 404: m. Bettmann Archive. 405: t. Grant Heilman Photography; b. Bettmann Archives. 407: m. National Geographic Society. 409: t. Brown Brothers; b. Lester Sloan/Woodfin Camp and Associates. 410: Archive Photos. 411: b.l. Bettmann Archive; b.r. Nawrocki Stock Photo. 412: R. Calvert/Tony Stone Images, Inc. 414: Bettmann Archive. 415: Courtesy of Charles F. Childress III. 416: Willard Clay/Tony Stone Worldwide. 417: t. Institute of Texan Cultures, San Antonio, Texas; b. Michael Salas/The Image Bank. 418: t. Superstock; m. Texas State Library, Archives Division; b. New York Public Library. 419: Bettmann Archive. 420: t. James Randklev/Tony Stone Images; m., b. San Jacinto Museum of History. 421: b., t. Institute of Texan Cultures, San Antonio, Texas. 422: Nawrocki Stock Photo. 423: Library of Congress. 424-425: Bettmann Archive. 426: Henley & Savage/The Stock Market. 428: David Muench/Tony Stone Images. 429: t. Bettmann Archive; b. Superstock. 430: t. National Archives, U.S. Army Signal Corps Collection, photo 111-SC-88-169; b. Nebraska Game & Parks Division. 431: Nawrocki Stock Photo, Inc. 432: l. Bettmann Archive; r. Brown Brothers. 438: t.l. National Portrait Gallery/Photo Researchers, Inc.; t.r. Larry Sherer/Time Life Books, Inc.; b.l. Crandall/The Image Works.; b.r. The Granger Collection. 439: t. Superstock; b. The Granger Collection. 440-441: Farrell Grehan. 440: t. Bates Littlehales; b. Sam Abell. 441: Declan Haun. **Chapter 16** 444: USDA Photo/Courtesy Library of Congress. 446: The Granger Collection. 447: t. Superstock; b. The Granger Collection. 448: Society for the Preservation of Weeksville & Bedford Stuyvesant History. 449: Brooklyn Public Library-Brooklyn Collection. 450: t. Lyle LeDuc/Liaison International. 450-451: St. John Fisher College. 451: t.l. Library Company of Philadelphia; m.l. National Postal Museum, Smithsonian Institution. 452: The Granger Collection. 453: r. The Granger Collection; l. Bettmann Archive. 455: The Granger Collection. 456-457: The Granger Collection. 457: t. Bettmann Archive. 460: The Granger Collection. 462: l. Brown Brothers; r. Temple University. 463: The Granger Collection. 464: t.l. Myron H. Davis/Nawrocki Stock Photo Inc.; b.r. The Granger Collection 466: l. U.S. Department of the Interior, National Park Service; r. Katherine Wetzel/The Museum of the Confederacy. 467: t. National Portrait Gallery; b. Superstock. **Chapter 17** 472: The Granger Collection. 474: Superstock. 475: l. Brown Brothers; r. North Wind Picture Archives. 476: l. Bettmann Archive; r. Superstock. 478: Ronn Palm. 479, 480: The Granger Collection. 482: Nawrocki Stock Photo, Inc. 483: l. The Granger Collection; r. Brown Brothers. 484-485: The Granger Collection. 485: Bettmann Archive. 486: Larry Sherer/High Impact Photography. 488: Superstock. 489: The Granger Collection. 490: t.l., t.m., b.m. Larry Sherer/Time Life Books, Inc.; b.r. The Granger Collection. 492: b.l. Nawrocki Stock Photo, Inc. 492-493: The Granger Collection. 494: t.l. Bettmann Archive; b. UPI/Bettmann. 495: Brown Brothers. 496: l. The Granger Collection; r. Penn School Collection. 497: Nawrocki Stock Photos, Inc. 499: Courtesy, Linda Scher. 506-507: George F. Mobley. 506: t. Robert E. Hynes; b. Collection of Roderick Craib. 507: t. Union Pacific Museum Collection. **Chapter 18** 510: m. Paul Chesley/Photographers Aspen. 511: l. Dennis Flaherty/The Stock Broker; i. UPI/Bettmann; r. Archive Photos. 512: Bettmann Archive. 513: Brown Brothers. 514: b. Superstock; t. Stanford University Museum of Art, gift of David Hewes. 516: Jack Vartoogian; 517: t.l. Chermayeff and Geismar, Inc.; m. Jack Vartoogian; b.l. Paul Simcock/The Image Bank. 518: The Bettmann Archive. 519: Brown Brothers. 520: l. The Bettmann Archive; r. Brown Brothers. 522: m. The Bettmann Archive. 524: University of Oklahoma Library, Manuscript Division. 525: t. The Bettmann Archive; b. Joseph H. Bailey/National Geographic Society. 526: m. Floyd County Historical Society. 527: t. Stock Montage, Inc.; b. Stock Options. 528: t. The Granger Collection; b University of Kansas Libraries, Kansas Collection. 529: Larry Lefever/Grant Heilman Photography. 530-531: Nawrocki Stock Photo Inc. 532: t. Superstock; b. Ed Vebell/The Image Bank. 533, 534 l.: The Bettmann Archive. 534: r. Allen Russell/ProFiles West. 535: m. Alvis Upitis/The Image Bank. **Chapter 19** 540: Brown Brothers. 541: l. Nawrocki Stock Photo Inc.; r. The Granger Collection. 542: b. Bettmann Archive; t. Superstock. 544, 545: Bettmann Archive. 546: UPI/Bettmann. 547: Brown Brothers. 548: t., b. Karen Yamauchi for Chermayeff & Geismer, Inc./Metaform, Inc. 548-549: Bettmann Archive. 549: b.r. Bettmann Archives. 550: r. Bettmann Archive; l. The Granger Collection. 551: Evan Agostini/Gamma Liaison. 552-553: National Baseball Library/National Baseball Hall of Fame & Museum Inc. 554: John W. Warren/Superstock. 555: l. Susan Drinker/The Stock Market; i. The Granger Collection. 557: t. The Bettmann Archive; b. Archive Photos. 558: Remington Art Museum. 560, 561 l. : Brown Brothers. 561: r. Sepp Seitz/Woodfin Camp and Associates. 563: t. Bettmann Archive; b. The Granger Collection. 564: Yosemite National Park. 565: Bill Ross/Westlight. 566: J.B. Diederich/The Stock Market. 567: t. Courtesy of Kristin Hayes; m. Courtesy of Steve Mealey; b. Courtesy of Felice Pace. 572: l. Tony Stone Images; b. I. M. House/Tony Stone Images. 573: l. Sygma; r. Superstock; b. Bob Adelman/Magnum Photos, Inc. 574-575: Mark Segal/Tony Stone Images. 574: b. Joseph H. Bailey, Nelson Brown, Tom M. Pope. 575: t. Seny Norasingh; b. William Weems/Woodfin Camp & Associates; l. Sygma. **Chapter 20** 578: t. Nawrocki Stock Photo, Inc.; b. The Bettmann Archive. 579: t. The Granger Collection; b. Nawrocki Stock Photo, Inc. 580: t. FPG International, Inc.; b.l. UPI/Bettmann.; b.r. The Granger Collection. 581: Archive Photos. 582: b. Bettmann Archive; t. The Philipps Collection. 584: The Granger Collection. 585-586: Brown Brothers. 587: b. Culver Pictures, Inc.; t. Nawrocki Stock Photo, Inc. 588: l. Nawrocki Stock Photo, Inc.; r. The Granger Collection. 590: t. The Girl Scouts of The USA; b. Sobel/Klonsky/The Image Bank. 591: t. Nawrocki Stock Photo, Inc.; b.l., b.r. Brown Brothers. 592: Brown Brothers. 593: Culver Pictures. 594: Archive Photos. 595: Culver Pictures, Inc. 596: The Granger Collection. 597: Nawrocki Stock Photo, Inc. 598: The Granger Collection. 599: l. Superstock; r. The Granger Collection. 600: l. Superstock; r. The Granger Collection. 601: l. Bettmann Archive; r. Nawrocki Stock Photo, Inc. 602: Archive Photos. 603: UPI/Bettmann. 604: Archive Photos. 605: Brown Brothers. 606: The Granger Collection. 607: Douglas Peebles/Westlight. 608: Ron Sachs/Archive Photos. 609: Bettmann Archive. 610: t. UPI/Bettmann; b.l. Archive Photos/Blank Archives; b.r. Archive Photos. **Chapter 21** 616: AP/Wide World Photos. 617: l. Elliot Erwitt/Magnum Photos; t.r. Carl Iwasaki/Time Life; b.r. AP/Wide World Photos. 618: t. AP/Wide World Photos; b. Charles Moore/Black Star. 619: Fred Ward/Black Star. 620: UPI/Bettmann. 622: AP/Wide World Photos. 623 & 624: m. UPI/Bettmann. 625: Archive Photos. 626: l. Rhoda Galyn/Photo Researchers ; r. Yoichi R. Okamoto/LBJ Library. 627: UPI/Bettmann. 628: James Pickerell/Black Star. 629 & 630: UPI/Bettmann. 631: AP/Wide World Photos. 633: Black Star. 634: l. William Karel/Sygma; r. Brad Markel/Gamma Liaison. 635: b.l. Tom Stoddart/Woodfin Camp and Associates. 635 t.r. & 636: Reuters/Bettmann. 637: Courtesy of Sharaye LaMothe and Laura Stinson. 638: UPI/Bettmann. 639: m. Archive Photos. 640: Joseph Drivas/The Image Bank. 641: The Image Bank. 641: t. Photo Researchers. 642: m. NASA/Peter Arnold 643: Glen Allison/Tony Stone Worldwide. 649: t. Paul Lally/Stock Boston; t.m., b.m., m. Buddy Mays/Travel Stock. 652: t. Leo De Wys, Inc.; b. Canadian Heritage. 654: l. Robert Frerck/Odyssey Productions; t.r. Masterfile; b.r. H.Sutton/H.Armstrong Roberts. 654-655: George Hunter/H.Armstrong Roberts. 656: Robert Frerck/Odyssey Productions. 658: l. Buddy Mays/Travel Stock; t.r. G.Covian/The Image Bank; b.r. Martin VanderWall/Leo De Wys, Inc. 659: Robert Frerck/Odyssey Productions. 660: P.Royer/H.Armstrong Roberts. 662: l. Rochelle Lee/Leo De Wys, Inc.; t.r. Buddy Mays/Travel Stock; b.r. Ernesto Bazan/SABA. 663: Daniel Morel/Sygma. 664: Martha Cooper/Peter Arnold, Inc. 665: Tom Stack & Associates. 666: l. David Brownell/The Image Bank; m. Focus on Sports; r. Leo De Wys, Inc. 667: Michael J. Balick/Peter Arnold, Inc. R40-R46: National Geographic Society/White House Historical Association. R47: t.l. Michael Evans/Sygma; b.l. Robert Sherbow/Uniphoto. Endpapers: Bridgeman Art Library.

(continued from page ii)

Acknowledgments

From **Farm to Factory: Women's Letters, 1830-1860,** edited by Thomas Dublin. Copyright © 1981 by Columbia University Press. Reprinted with permission of the publisher.
Excerpt from **Frederick Douglass** by Sharman Apt Russell. Copyright © 1988. Chelsea House Publishers.
From **When China Ruled The Seas** by Louise Levathes. Copyright © 1994. Simon & Schuster, p. 174.
From **Civil War** by Geoffrey C. Ward with Ric Burns and Ken Burns. "1990 by American Documentaries". Copyright © 1990. Alfred A. Knopf/Random House.
From **The American West** by Dee Brown. Copyright © 1994 by Dee Brown and the Estate of Martin F. Scmitt. Reprinted with the permission of Simon & Schuster.
Brief quote as submitted from **A People's History of the United States** by Howard Zinn. Copyright © 1980 by Howard Zinn. Reprinted by permission of HarperCollins Publishers, Inc.
From **The Chinese Cinderella Story** from the Oryx Multicultural Folktale Series by Judy Sierra. Copyright © 1992. The Oryx Press. By kind permission of the Folklore Society, University College London, Grower Street, London WC 1E 6BT.
Excerpt from **Harlem Night Song** from Collected Poems by Langston Hughes Copyright © 1994 by the Estate of Langston Hughes. Reprinted by permission of Alfred A. Knopf Inc. Reprinted by permission of Harold Ober Associates, Inc. Copyright © 1951 by Langston Hughes. Copyright © renewed 1982 by George Houston Bass.
From **Before the Mayflower: A History of the Negro in America** by Lerone Bennett, Jr. Copyright © 1962. Johnson Publishing Company, Inc. Reprinted by permission of Lerone Bennett, Jr.
Excerpts from **The Boys' War** by Jim Murphy. Copyright © 1990. Reprinted by permission of Clarion Books/Houghton Mifflin Co. All rights reserved.
From **Get On Board: The Story of the Underground Railroad** by Jim Haskins. Copyright © 1993 by James Haskins. Reprinted by permission of Scholastic, Inc.
From **The New Nation,** Vol. 4 of A History of the U.S. by Joy Hakim. Copyright © 1994 by Joy Hakim. Reprinted by permission of Oxford University Press.
From **Kingdom of the Saints** by Ray B. West, Jr. Copyright © 1957. Reprinted by permission of Curtis Brown, Ltd.
From **The March on Washington Address** by Martin Luther King, Jr. Copyright © 1963 by Martin Luther King, Jr. Copyright © renewed 1991 by Coretta Scott King. Reprinted by arrangement with the heirs to the estate of Martin Luther King, Jr., c/o Writers House, Inc. as agent for the proprietor.
From **Parting the Waters** by Taylor Branch. Copyright © 1988 by Taylor Branch. Reprinted with the permission of Simon & Schuster.
From **The Royal Kingdoms of Ghana, Mali and Songhay** by Patricia and Frederick McKissack. Copyright © 1994 by Patricia and Frederick McKissack. Reprinted by permission of Henry Holt and Co., Inc.
From **Herstory: A Woman's View of American History** by June Sochen. Copyright © 1974. Alred Publishing Co., Inc. Permission granted by June Sochen.
From Eleanor Roosevelt's Speech at the United Nations. 1958.
From **To Conquer a Peace: The War Between the United States and Mexico** by John Edward Weems. Copyright © 1974. Permission granted by Texas A & M University Press.
From **Bill Helps 250,000 in Oregon** by Marion Davis, an article published July 27, 1990 in The Oregonian. Copyright © 1990. The Oregonian Publishing Co.
From **Lane's Report of Virginia, 1585** by Richard Hakluyt from The First Colonists, Hakluyt's Voyages to North America edited by A.L. Rowse. Copyright © 1986. The Folio Society.
From **Nixon: Volume II The Triumph of a Politician 1962–1972** by Stephen E. Ambrose. Reprinted with the permission of Simon & Schuster from Copyright © 1989 by Ambrose-Tubbs, Inc.
From **On The Road to Berlin** by Robert D. Marcus and David Burner. Copyright © 1989 from America Firsthand, Vol. II by Marcus & Burner. Reprinted with permission of St. Martin's Press, Inc.
From **Cowboys of the Wild West** by Russell Freedman. The Kansas Line collected, adapted and arranged by John A. Lomax and Alan Lomax. Tro- Copyright © 1938 (Renewed). Ludlow Music, Inc., New York, NY. Used by permission.
Quote from **Thomas Edison** from an article by A.W. Churchill in Scientific American. April 1, 1905. Copyright © 1905.
From **Founder of the Gray Panthers Dies At Age 89** by wire and staff reports, an article published April 23, 1995 in The Oregonian. Copyright © 1995. The Oregonian Publishing Co.
From **Life in Colonial Texas** from Documents of Texas History edited by E. Wallace, D. Vigness, G. Ward. Copyright © 1994. State House Press.
From **Make the Kaiser Dance** by Henry T. Berry. Copyright © 1978. Bantam Doubleday Dell.
From **Across the Continent: A Summer's Journey to the Rocky Mountains, the Mormons, and the Pacific States, with Speaker Colfax** by Samuel Bowles. Copyright © 1866. Readex Microprint Corporation.
From **"Brother, Can You Spare a Dime?"** printed in The American Reader by E.Y. Harburg and Jay Gorney, book edited by Diane Ravitch. Copyright © 1955 by Harms, Inc. Reprinted by permission of Harms, Inc. HarperCollins Publishers, N.Y.
From **Pueblos, Gods and Spaniards** by John Upton Terrell. Copyright © 1973. Dial Press.
From **Samuel Gompers: A Biography** by Louis Filler. Copyright © 1963. The Antioch Press.
From the **Statement of Purpose** by the National Organization for Women. Copyright © 1966. "This is an historical document 1966 and does not reflect the current language or priorities of the organization." Reprinted by permission of the National Organization for Women.
Quote from **Magellan's Voyage** by Antonio Pigafetta from Magellan: A Voyage Into the Unknown Changed Man's Understanding of his World by Alan Villiers printed in National Geographic Magazine. June 1976. Copyright © 1976. National Geographic Society.
From **The Story of New England** by Monroe Stearns. Copyright © 1967. Random House.
Excerpt from **They Have Yarns** by Carl Sandburg from The People, Yes by Carl Sandburg. Copyright © 1936. Harcourt Brace & Co. Renewed 1964 by Carl Sandburg. Reprinted by permission of the publisher.
From **Where I Stand** by Barry Goldwater. Copyright © 1964. The McGraw-Hill Companies.
From **The World Must Know: A History of the Holocaust as Told in the United States Holocaust Memorial Museum** by Michael Berenbaum. Copyright © 1993. Little, Brown and Co.

The Princeton Review
Handbook of
Test-Taking Strategies

STANDARDIZED TEST SUPPORT

DEDUCTION AND OUTSIDE KNOWLEDGE

Many questions on standardized multiple-choice tests ask you to look at a map, a chart, a graph, or a drawing. Then you must choose the correct answer based on what you see. On these questions, the information you need to answer the question will be on the map, chart, graph, or drawing. The process of looking, finding the answer to the question, and choosing the correct answer from among the answer choices is called DEDUCTION. You've been doing this ever since you learned how to read a map or a chart, or any other visual information.

Sometimes, however, multiple-choice tests will ask you to remember a fact that you learned in social studies class. You won't be able to find the correct answer on a map, chart, graph, or drawing; the correct answer will be in your memory. We call these OUTSIDE KNOWLEDGE questions.

Use the map below to answer question 1. Question 2 asks you to use outside knowledge.

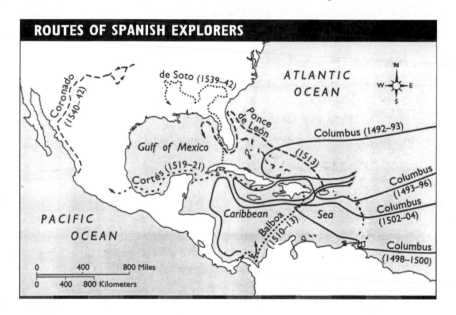

1 Which Spanish explorer traveled farthest west in the Americas?

   A   Hernando Cortés
   B   Francisco Vásquez de Coronado
   C   Ponce de León
   D   Christopher Columbus

2 What was the main goal of the Spanish explorers in the Americas?

   F   To find gold and other riches and bring them back to Spain
   G   To make friends with Native Americans
   H   To settle in a land where they could practice their religion in freedom
   J   To preserve the rain forests

Remember: Do not write in your textbook.

PROCESS OF ELIMINATION

When you take a multiple-choice test, you have an advantage that you don't have on other tests. On most tests, you must come up with the answers to the questions all on your own. For example, a test might ask "Who was the first President of the United States?" You would then have to write the name "George Washington" on your answer sheet.

On a multiple-choice test, however, the correct answer is already written down for you; it is among the answer choices! All you have to do is figure out which of the answer choices is the correct one.

This is good news for you! It means that you can still answer a question correctly *even if you can't come up with the correct answer on your own*. That's because you can ELIMINATE choices that you know are *incorrect*. Eliminating answers this way will be especially helpful on OUTSIDE KNOWLEDGE questions. Sometimes you will be able to eliminate all of the choices except one. When that happens, it means that you have found the best answer by the PROCESS OF ELIMINATION.

Try using the process of elimination to answer this question:

1 In 1899, the President of the United States was

    A Richard Nixon
    B William McKinley
    C Thomas Jefferson
    D George Bush

Were you able to eliminate any *incorrect* answers? How many?

Now try using the process of elimination to answer this question:

2 In the early 1800s, which of these inventions enabled the South to increase agricultural production?

    F Telephone
    G Airplane
    H Cotton Gin
    J Gas Lighting

Remember: Do not write in your textbook.

TABLES

On many multiple-choice tests, you are provided with the information you need to answer the question. The information will come in many different forms. It might appear in a time line, a flow chart, a map, or a graph. Sometimes, the information will be included in a table.

The table below compares the climate in two United States cities. Study the table. Then answer questions 1 and 2.

Climate in Two Cities					Rainfall Average (in.)	Annual (days)	Snowfall Average Annual (in.)
Average Monthly Temperature (°F)							
City	Jan.	Apr.	July	Oct.			
Albany, NY	21	47	71	51	36	134	66
El Paso, TX	44	64	83	64	8	47	5

Source: *Information Please Almanac, 1995*

1 On an average July day in Albany, NY, what is the temperature?

    A   21°F
    B   51°F
    C   64°F
    D   71°F

2 Based on the information in the table, which of these statements is most likely true?

    F   It snows more in the northern United States than in the southern United States.

    G   It rains more in the southern United States than in the northern United States.

    H   It is colder in the southern United States than in the northern United States.

    J   The southern United States has more days of precipitation than the northern United States has.

Remember: Do not write in your textbook.

FLOW CHARTS

A flow chart shows the sequence of steps used to complete an activity. It shows the steps in the order they happen. A flow chart usually uses arrows to show which step happens next.

The first thing to do when you look at a flow chart is to see if it has a title. The title will tell you what the flow chart is about. The next thing you should do is find the arrows. The arrows tell you the order in which you should read the chart.

Read flow charts carefully. Don't just look at the illustrations; make sure to read any text beneath the illustrations. Careless errors are the most common mistakes made when answering flow chart questions. If you take a little extra time, you can eliminate these errors.

Use the flow chart below to answer questions 1 and 2.

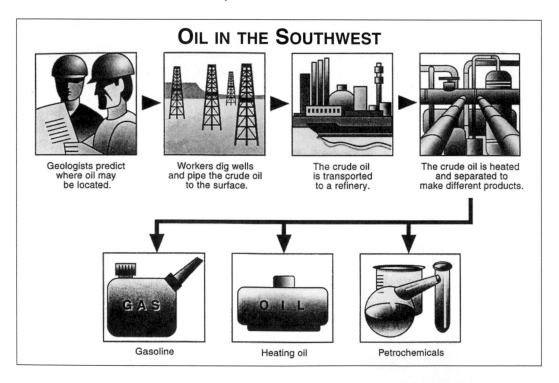

OIL IN THE SOUTHWEST

Geologists predict where oil may be located.

Workers dig wells and pipe the crude oil to the surface.

The crude oil is transported to a refinery.

The crude oil is heated and separated to make different products.

GAS — Gasoline

OIL — Heating oil

Petrochemicals

1 Who is responsible for predicting where oil is located?

A Geologists
B Workers
C Refiners
D Heating Oil Salespersons

2 What does the flow chart show about the oil industry?

F Which states produce the most crude oil
G How much money it costs to refine oil
H How crude oil is turned into useful products
J How petrochemicals are turned into plastic

Remember: Do not write in your textbook.

DIFFERENT TYPES OF GRAPHS

Different types of graphs are used to present numerical information. A **line graph** shows how something changes over time. A line graph might be used to show how the population of the United States has grown over the years. A **bar graph** compares amounts. A bar graph might show the populations of different United States cities. A **circle graph** shows how a whole is divided into smaller parts. For example, a circle graph might show how the government divides its funds to pay for roads, defense, education, and other services.

Sometimes you will see a set of questions accompanied by more than one graph. Each question will contain clues to tell you which graph you should read to find the answer. Take the extra time to make sure you are looking at the correct graph.

Use the graphs below to answer questions 1 and 2.

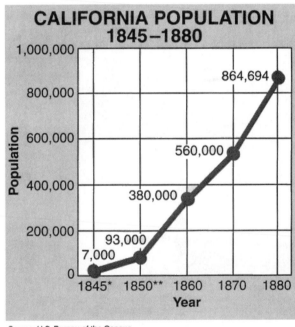

Source: U.S. Bureau of the Census

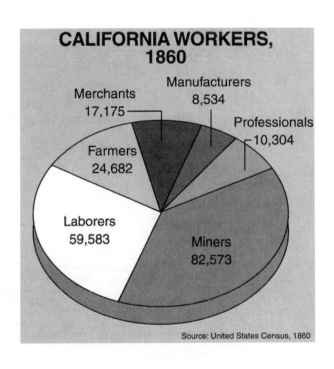

Source: United States Census, 1860

1 What was the population of California in 1870?

A 59,583
B 82,573
C 380,000
D 560,000

2 In 1860, the greatest number of workers in California were

F professionals
G miners
H merchants
J farmers

Remember: Do not write in your textbook.

MAPS

The ability to read and understand maps is an important skill in social studies. Many of the multiple-choice tests you take will require you to read a map.

Look carefully at all the parts of a map. Maps contain a lot of information. Whenever you see a map, you should ask yourself questions like these:

- What does the title of the map tell you?
- Where is the map key?
- What symbols are on the map key? What do they stand for?
- Where is the compass rose?
- What does the compass rose tell you?
- Is there a map scale?

Look at the map of the Southwest. Use the map to answer questions 1 and 2.

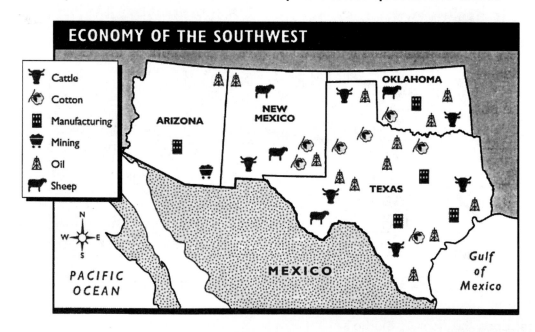

ECONOMY OF THE SOUTHWEST

1 Mining is a part of the economy of which state?

A Arizona

B New Mexico

C Oklahoma

D Texas

2 According to the map, what is a major industry in the southernmost part of Texas?

F Manufacturing

G Radio

H Oil

J Mining

Remember: Do not write in your textbook.

POLITICAL CARTOONS

Some tests will ask you to look at and interpret a political cartoon. A political cartoon is an illustration or drawing that expresses a political point of view.

When you look at a political cartoon, ask yourself the following questions:

- What do the images in the cartoon represent? Are they **symbols** for something else? Uncle Sam is an example of a symbol. When he appears in a cartoon, he is being used as a **symbol** of the United States.
- What is the cartoonist's point of view? Is the cartoonist for, or against, the political issue that is the subject of the drawing? Look carefully at the details of the drawing. Do they provide hints about the artist's point of view?

Now look at the cartoon below. It was drawn during the American Revolution. Use the cartoon to answer questions 1 and 2.

The Horse America, Throwing His Master

1 What does the rider of the horse symbolize?

   A France

   B The American colonies

   C England

   D George Washington

2 What detail shows that the master has been very cruel to the horse?

   F The type of saddle the master is using

   G The type of riding crop the master is holding

   H The type of uniform the master is wearing

   J The look of surprise on the master's face

Remember: Do not write in your textbook.

TIME LINES

Historical information is sometimes presented in the form of a time line. A time line shows events in the order in which they occurred. It is usually read from left to right, like a sentence. If the time line is drawn vertically, it is usually read from top to bottom.

Some questions may ask you to find information on a time line. They may also ask you to remember outside knowledge about the subject of the time line.

Study the time line below. Then do questions 1 and 2.

Maya History, A.D. 200–A.D. 1000

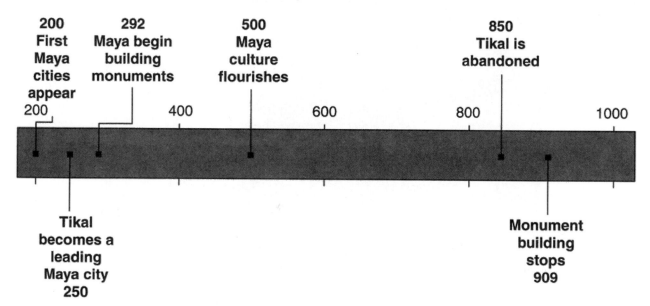

1 In what year did the Maya abandon the city of Tikal?

A   250

B   292

C   850

D   909

2 The area in which the ancient Maya lived includes present-day

F   Central America

G   Africa

H   Canada

J   Asia

Remember: Do not write in your textbook.